GREAT BRITAIN & IRELAND

TOURIST and MOT… …ER et TOURISTIQUE / STRASSEN- und REISEATLAS
TOERISTISCHE WEGENAT… …TURISTICO / ATLAS DE CARRETERAS y TURÍSTICO

Contents

Sommaire / Inhaltsübersicht / Inhoud / Sommario / Sumario

Channel Tunnel
Tunnel sous la Manche

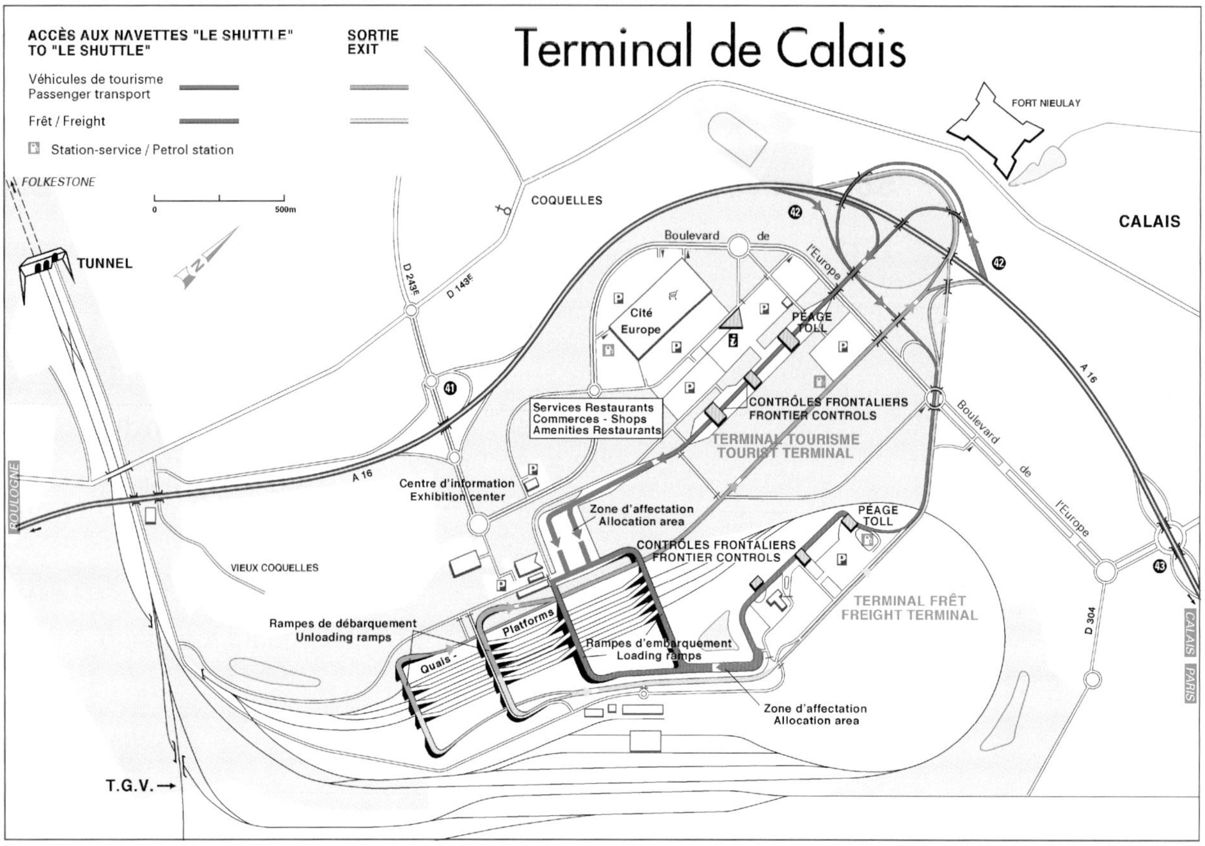
Terminal de Calais
ACCÈS AUX NAVETTES "LE SHUTTLE"
TO "LE SHUTTLE"
SORTIE
EXIT
Véhicules de tourisme
Passenger transport
Frêt / Freight
Station-service / Petrol station
FOLKESTONE
500m
TUNNEL
COQUELLES
FORT NIEULAY
CALAIS
Boulevard de l'Europe
Cité Europe
PÉAGE TOLL
CONTRÔLES FRONTALIERS
FRONTIER CONTROLS
Services Restaurants
Commerces - Shops
Amenities Restaurants
TERMINAL TOURISME
TOURIST TERMINAL
Centre d'information
Exhibition center
Zone d'affectation
Allocation area
TERMINAL FRÊT
FREIGHT TERMINAL
VIEUX COQUELLES
Rampes de débarquement
Unloading ramps
Platforms
Quais
Rampes d'embarquement
Loading ramps
T.G.V.
BOULOGNE
CALAIS
PARIS
A 16
D 243E
D 143E
D 304

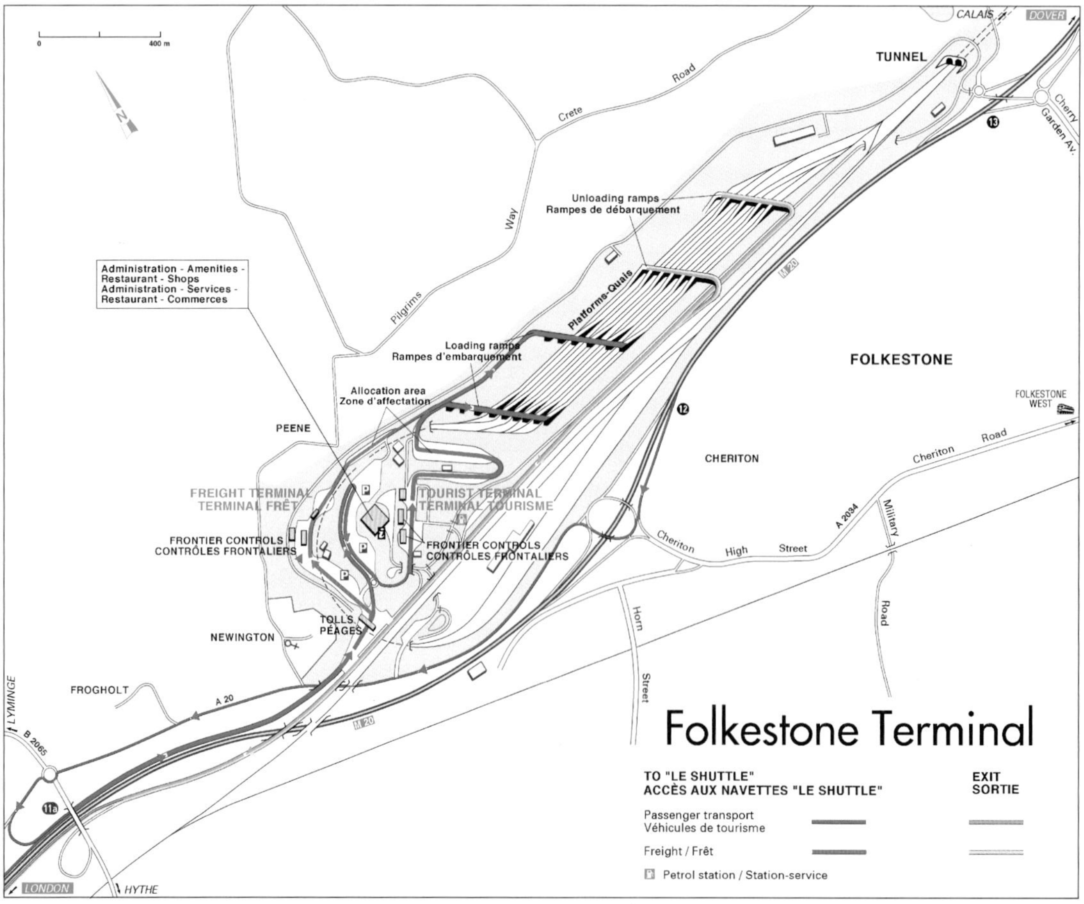
Folkestone Terminal
TO "LE SHUTTLE"
ACCÈS AUX NAVETTES "LE SHUTTLE"
EXIT
SORTIE
Passenger transport
Véhicules de tourisme
Freight / Frêt
Petrol station / Station-service
400 m
CALAIS
DOVER
TUNNEL
Crete Road
Cherry Garden Av.
Unloading ramps
Rampes de débarquement
Pilgrims Way
Administration - Amenities -
Restaurant - Shops
Administration - Services -
Restaurant - Commerces
Platforms-Quais
Loading ramps
Rampes d'embarquement
Allocation area
Zone d'affectation
FOLKESTONE
FOLKESTONE WEST
PEENE
CHERITON
Cheriton Road
FREIGHT TERMINAL
TERMINAL FRÊT
TOURIST TERMINAL
TERMINAL TOURISME
FRONTIER CONTROLS
CONTRÔLES FRONTALIERS
Cheriton High Street
A 2034
Military Road
TOLLS
PÉAGES
NEWINGTON
Horn Street
FROGHOLT
A 20
M 20
LYMINGE
B 2065
LONDON
HYTHE

SHIPPING SERVICES
LIAISONS MARITIMES

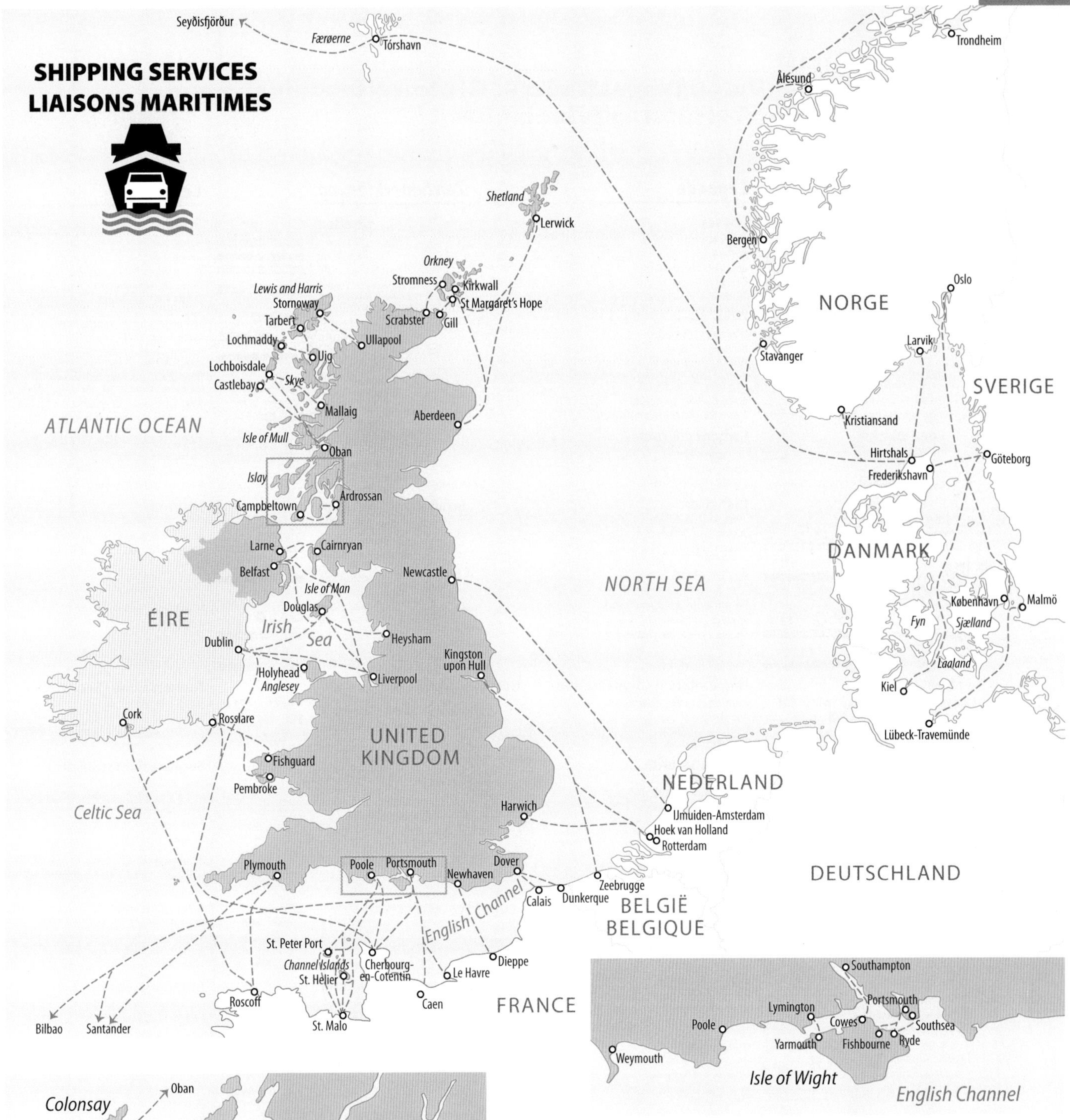

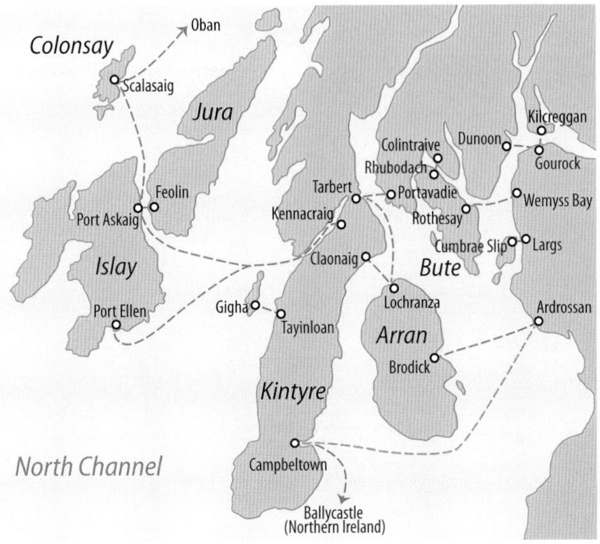

Shipping services / *Liaisons maritimes*

Car ferries		Transport des automobiles
All the year round	- - - - - -	Permanentes
Seasonal	- - - - - -	Saisonnières

Schiffsverbindungen / *Scheepvaartverbindingen*

Autotransport		Vervoeren van auto's
Ganzjährig	- - - - - -	Permanente diensten
Während der Saison	- - - - - -	Diensten in het zomerseizoen

Líneas Marítimas / *Collegamenti marittimi*

Transporte de coches		Trasporto di automobili
Todo el año	- - - - - -	Fissi
De temporada	- - - - - -	Stagionali

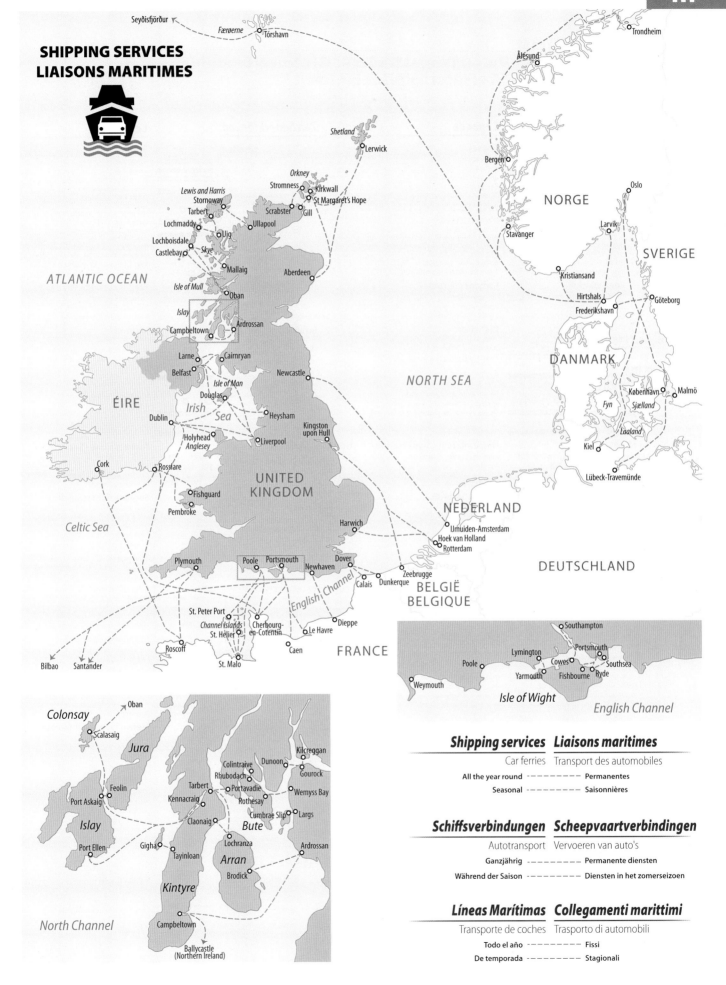

Main road map
Grands axes routiers / Durchgangsstraßen / Grote verbindingswegen
Grandi arterie stradali / Carreteras principales

Key	Légende	Zeichenerklärung	Legenda
Roads	**Routes**	**Straßen**	**Strade**
Motorway	Autoroute	Autobahn	Autostrada
Motorway: single carriageway	Route-auto	Autostraße	Strada-auto
Motorway (unclassified)	Autoroute et assimilée	Autobahn oder Schnellstraße	Autostrada, strada di tipo autostradale
Dual carriageway with motorway characteristics	Double chaussée de type autoroutier	Schnellstraße mit getrennten Fahrbahnen	Doppia carreggiata di tipo autostradale
Interchanges: complete, limited, not specified	Échangeurs : complet, partiels, sans précision	Anschlussstellen: Voll - bzw. Teilanschluss, ohne Angabe	Svincoli: completo, parziale, imprecisato
Interchange numbers	Numéros d'échangeurs	Anschlussstellennummern	Svincoli numerati
Recommended MICHELIN main itinerary	Itinéraire principal recommandé par MICHELIN	Von MICHELIN empfohlene Hauptverkehrsstraße	Itinerario principale raccomandato da MICHELIN
Recommended MICHELIN regional itinerary	Itinéraire régional ou de dégagement recommandé par MICHELIN	Von MICHELIN empfohlene Regionalstraße	Itinerario regionale raccomandato da MICHELIN
Road surfaced - unsurfaced	Route revêtue - non revêtue	Straße mit Belag - ohne Belag	Strada rivestita - non rivestita
Motorway/Road under construction	Autoroute - Route en construction	Autobahn/Straße im Bau	Autostrada - Strada in costruzione
Road widths	**Largeur des routes**	**Straßenbreiten**	**Larghezza delle strade**
Dual carriageway	Chaussées séparées	Getrennte Fahrbahnen	Carreggiate separate
2 wide lanes	2 voies larges	2 breite Fahrspuren	2 corsie larghe
2 lanes - 2 narrow lanes	2 voies - 2 voies étroites	2 Fahrspuren - 2 schmale Fahrspuren	2 corsie - 2 corsie strette
Distances (total and intermediate)	**Distances** (totalisées et partielles)	**Straßenentfernungen** (Gesamt- und Teilentfernungen)	**Distanze** (totali e parziali)
On motorway in kilometers	Sur autoroute en kilomètres	Auf der Autobahn in Kilometern	Su autostrada in chilometri
Toll roads - Toll-free section	Section à péage - Section libre	Mautstrecke - Mautfreie Strecke	Tratto a pedaggio - Tratto esente da pedaggio
On road in kilometers	Sur route en kilomètres	Auf der Straße in Kilometern	Su strada in chilometri
On motorway (Great Britain) in miles - in kilometers	Sur autoroute (Grande Bretagne) en miles - en kilomètres	Auf der Autobahn (Großbritannien) in Meilen - in Kilometern	Su autostrada (Gran Bretagna) in miglia - in chilometri
Toll roads - Toll-free section	Section à péage - Section libre	Mautstrecke - Mautfreie Strecke	Tratto a pedaggio - Tratto esente da pedaggio
On road in miles	Sur route en miles	Auf der Straße in Meilen	Su strada in miglia
Numbering - Signs	**Numérotation - Signalisation**	**Nummerierung - Wegweisung**	**Numerazione - Segnaletica**
European route - Motorway	Route européenne - Autoroute	Europastraße - Autobahn	Strada europea - Autostrada
Other roads	Autres routes	Sonstige Straßen	Altre strade
Destination on primary route network	Localités jalonnant les itinéraires principaux	Richtungshinweis auf der empfohlenen Fernverkehrsstraße	Località delimitante gli itinerari principali
Safety Warnings	**Alertes Sécurité**	**Sicherheitsalerts**	**Segnalazioni stradali**
Snowbound, impassable road during the period shown	Enneigement : période probable de fermeture	Eingeschneite Straße: voraussichtl. Wintersperre	Innevamento: probabile periodo di chiusura
Pass and its height above sea level	Col et sa cote d'altitude	Pass mit Höhenangabe	Passo ed altitudine
Steep hill - Toll barrier	Forte déclivité - Barrière de péage	Starke Steigung - Mautstelle	Forte pendenza - Casello
Ford	Gué	Furt	Guado
Transportation	**Transports**	**Verkehrsmittel**	**Trasporti**
Airport	Aéroport	Flughafen	Aeroporto
Transportation of vehicles:	Transport des autos :	Autotransport:	Trasporto auto:
year-round - seasonal	permanent - saisonnier	ganzjährig - saisonbedingte Verbindung	tutto l'anno - stagionale
by boat	par bateau	per Schiff	su traghetto
by ferry	par bac	per Fähre	su chiatta
Ferry (passengers and cycles only)	Bac pour piétons et cycles	Fähre für Personen und Fahrräder	Traghetto per pedoni e biciclette
Motorail	Auto/Train	Autoreisezug	Auto/treno
Administration	**Administration**	**Verwaltung**	**Amministrazione**
Administrative district seat	Capitale de division administrative	Verwaltungshauptstadt	Capoluogo amministrativo
Parador / Pousada	Parador / Pousada	Parador / Pousada	Parador / Pousada
Administrative boundaries	Limites administratives	Verwaltungsgrenzen	Confini amministrativi
National boundary	Frontière	Staatsgrenze	Frontiera
Principal customs post	Douane principale	Hauptzollamt	Dogana principale
Secondary customs post	Douane avec restriction	Zollstation mit Einschränkungen	Dogana con limitazioni
Restricted area for foreigners / Military property	Zone interdite aux étrangers / Zone militaire	Sperrgebiet für Ausländer / Militärgebiet	Zona vietata agli stranieri / Zona militare
Sights	**Lieux touristiques**	**Sehenswürdigkeiten**	**Mete e luoghi d'interesse**
2- and 3-star MICHELIN Green Guide sites	Sites classés 2 et 3 étoiles par le Guide Vert MICHELIN	Sehenswürdigkeiten mit 2 und 3 Sternen im Grünen Reiseführer MICHELIN	Siti segnalati con 2 e 3 stelle dalla Guida Verde MICHELIN
Religious building	Édifice religieux	Sakral-Bau	Edificio religioso
Historic house, castle	Château	Schloss, Burg	Castello
Monastery	Monastère	Kloster	Monastero
Stave church	Église en bois debout	Stabkirche	Chiesa in legno di testa
Wooden church	Église en bois	Holzkirche	Chiesa in legno
Open air museum	Musée de plein air	Freilichtmuseum	Museo all'aperto
Antiquities	Site antique	Antike Fundstätte	Sito antico
Rock carving	Gravure rupestre	Felsbilder	Incisione rupestre
Prehistoric monument	Monument mégalithique	Vorgeschichtliches Steindenkmal	Monumento megalitico
Rune stone - Ruins	Pierre runique - Ruines	Runenstein - Ruine	Pietra runica - Rovine
Cave - Windmill	Grotte - Moulin à vent	Höhle - Windmühle	Grotta - Mulino a vento
Other places of interest	Autres curiosités	Sonstige Sehenswürdigkeit	Altri luoghi d'interesse
Scenic route	Parcours pittoresque	Landschaftlich schöne Strecke	Percorso pittoresco
Other signs	**Signes divers**	**Sonstige Zeichen**	**Simboli vari**
Recreation ground	Parc de loisirs	Erholungspark	Parco divertimenti
Dam - Waterfall	Barrage - Cascade	Staudamm - Wasserfall	Diga - Cascata
National park - Nature park	Parc national - Parc naturel	Nationalpark - Naturpark	Parco nazionale - Parco naturale

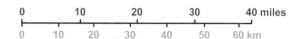

0	10	20	30	40 miles

0	10	20	30	40	50	60 km

Signos Convencionales / Verklaring van de tekens

Signos Convencionales		Verklaring van de tekens
Carreteras		**Wegen**
Autopista		Autosnelweg
Carretera		Autoweg
Autopista, Autovía		Autosnelweg of gelijksoortige weg
Autovía (otra vía similar a las autopistas)		Gescheiden rijbanen van het type autosnelweg
Accesos: completo, parcial, sin precisar		Aansluitingen: volledig, gedeeltelijk, zonder aanduiding
Números de los accesos	14 15	Afritnummers
Itinerario principal recomendado por MICHELIN		Michelin Hoofdweg
Itinerario regional recomendado por MICHELIN		Michelin Regionale weg
Carretera asfaltada - sin asfaltar		Verharde weg - onverharde weg
Autopista - Carretera en construcción		Autosnelweg - Weg in aanleg
Ancho de las carreteras		**Breedte van de wegen**
Calzadas separadas		Gescheiden rijbanen
Dos carriles anchos		2 brede rijstroken
Dos carriles - Dos carriles estrechos		2 rijstroken - 2 smalle rijstroken
Distancias (totales y parciales)		**Afstanden** (totaal en gedeeltelijk)
En autopista en kilómetros	12 12	Op autosnelwegen in kilometers
Tramo de peaje - Tramo libre		Gedeelte met tol - Tolvrij gedeelte
En carretera en kilómetros	12 5 7	Op andere wegen in kilometers
En autopista (Gran Bretaña) en millas - en kilómetros	12 12 12 12	Op autosnelwegen (Groot Brittannië) in mijlen - in kilometers
Tramo de peaje - Tramo libre		Gedeelte met tol - Tolvrij gedeelte
En carretera en millas	12 5 7	Op andere wegen in mijlen
Numeración - Señalización		**Wegnummers - Bewegwijzering**
Carretera europea - Autopista	E 50 A3	Europaweg - Autosnelweg
Otras carreteras	25 28 103	Andere wegen
Localidades situadas en los principales itinerarios	Lancaster	Plaatsen langs een hoofdweg met bewegwijzering
Alertas Seguridad		**Veiligheidswaarschuwingen**
Nevada: Período probable de cierre	11-4	Sneeuw: vermoedelijke sluitingsperiode
Puerto y su altitud	650	Bergpas en hoogte boven de zeespiegel
Pendiente Pronunciada - Barrera de peaje		Steile helling - Tol
Vado		Wad
Transportes		**Vervoer**
Aeropuerto		Luchthaven
Transporte de coches:		Vervoer van auto's:
todo el año - de temporada		het hele jaar - tijdens het seizoen
por barco		per boot
por barcaza	B B	per veerpont
Barcaza para el paso de peatones y vehículos dos ruedas		Veerpont voor voetgangers en fietsers
Auto-tren		Autotrein
Administración		**Administratie**
Capital de división administrativa	1 P R	Hoofdplaats van administratief gebied
Parador / Pousada	P	Parador / Pousada
Límites administrativos		Administratieve grenzen
Frontera		Staatsgrens
Aduana principal		Hoofddouanekantoor
Aduana con restricciones		Douanekantoor met beperkte bevoegdheden
Zona prohibida a los extranjeros / Propiedad militar		Terrein verboden voor buitenlanders / Militair gebied
Curiosidades		**Bezienswaardigheden**
Lugares clasificados con 2 y 3 estrellas por la Guía Verde MICHELIN	STRASBOURG	Locaties met 2 en 3 sterren volgens de Groene Gids van MICHELIN
Edificio religioso		Kerkelijk gebouw
Castillo		Kasteel
Monasterio		Klooster
Iglesia de madera		Stavkirke (houten kerk)
Iglesia de madera		Houten kerk
Museo al aire libre		Openluchtmuseum
Zona de vestigios antiguos		Overblijfsel uit de Oudheid
Grabado rupestre		Rotstekening
Monumento megalítico		Megaliet
Piedra rúnica - Ruinas		Runensteen - Ruïne
Cueva - Molino de viento		Grot - Molen
Otras curiosidades		Andere bezienswaardigheden
Recorrido pintoresco		Schilderachtig traject
Signos diversos		**Diverse tekens**
Zona recreativa		Recreatiepark
Presa - Cascada		Stuwdam - Waterval
Parque nacional - Parque natural		Nationaal park - Natuurpark

Republic of Ireland: All distances and speed limits are signed in kilometres.

République d'Irlande: Les distances et les limitations de vitesse sont exprimées en kilomètres.

Irland: Alle Entfernungsangaben und Geschwindigkeitsbegrenzungen in km.

Ierland: Alle afstanden en maximumsnelheden zijn uitsluitend in kilometers aangegeven.

Repubblica d'Irlanda: Distanze e limiti di velocità sono espressi soltanto in chilometri.

República de Irlanda: Distancias y límites de velocidad están expresados sólo en kilómetros.

Key to 1:1 000 000 map pages

Légende des cartes au 1/1 000 000

Zeichenerklärung der Karten 1:1 000 000

Verklaring van de tekens voor kaarten met schaal 1:1 000 000

Legenda carte scala 1:1 000 000

Signos convencionales de los mapas a escala 1:1 000 000

ENGLAND

UNITARY AUTHORITIES

1 Bath and North East Somerset
2 Bedford
3 Blackburn with Darwen
4 Blackpool
5 Bournemouth, Christchurch and Poole
6 Bracknell Forest
7 Brighton and Hove
8 Buckinghamshire
9 Cambridgeshire
10 Central Bedfordshire
11 Cheshire East
12 Cheshire West and Chester
13 City of Bristol
14 City of Leicester
15 Cornwall
16 Cumbria
17 Derby
18 Derbyshire
19 Devon
20 Dorset
21 Durham
22 East Riding of Yorkshire
23 East Sussex
24 Essex
25 Gloucestershire
26 Greater London
27 Greater Manchester
28 Halton
29 Hampshire
30 Hartlepool
31 Herefordshire
32 Hertfordshire
33 Kent
34 Kingston-upon-Hull
35 Lancashire
36 Leicestershire
37 Lincolnshire
38 Luton
39 Medway
40 Merseyside
41 Middlesbrough
42 Milton Keynes
43 Norfolk
44 North East Lincolnshire
45 North Lincolnshire
46 North Northamptonshire
47 North Somerset
48 North Yorkshire
49 Northumberland
50 Nottingham
51 Nottinghamshire
52 Oxfordshire
53 Peterborough
54 Plymouth
55 Portsmouth
56 Reading
57 Redcar and Cleveland
58 Rutland
59 Shropshire
60 Somerset
61 South Gloucestershire
62 South Yorkshire
63 Southend-on-Sea
64 Staffordshire
65 Stockton-on-Tees
66 Stoke-on-Trent
67 Suffolk
68 Surrey
69 Swindon
70 Telford and Wrekin
71 Thurrock
72 Torbay
73 Tyne and Wear
74 Warrington
75 Warwickshire
76 West Berkshire
77 West Midlands
78 West Northamptonshire
79 West Sussex
80 West Yorkshire
81 Wiltshire
82 Windsor and Maidenhead
83 Wokingham
84 Worcestershire
85 York

[32]
32 = UNITARY AUTHORITIES

SCOTLAND

UNITARY AUTHORITIES

[1] 1 Aberdeen City
[2] 2 Aberdeenshire
[3] 3 Angus
[4] 4 Argyll and Bute
[5] 5 Clackmannanshire
[6] 6 City of Edinburgh
[7] 7 City of Glasgow
[8] 8 Dumfries and Galloway
[9] 9 Dundee City
[10] 10 East Ayrshire
[11] 11 East Dunbartonshire
[12] 12 East Lothian
[13] 13 East Renfrewshire
[14] 14 Falkirk
[15] 15 Fife
[16] 16 Highland
[17] 17 Inverclyde
[18] 18 Midlothian
[19] 19 Moray
[20] 20 North Ayrshire
[21] 21 North Lanarkshire
[22] 22 Orkney Islands
[23] 23 Perthshire and Kinross
[24] 24 Renfrewshire
[25] 25 Scottish Borders
[26] 26 Shetland Islands
[27] 27 South Ayrshire
[28] 28 South Lanarkshire
[29] 29 Stirling
[30] 30 West Dunbartonshire
[31] 31 West Lothian
[32] 32 Western Isles

NORTHERN IRELAND

DISTRICT COUNCILS

[1] 1 Antrim and Newtownabbey
[2] 2 Ards and North Down
[3] 3 Armagh City, Banbridge & Craigavon
[4] 4 Belfast
[5] 5 Causeway Coast and Glens
[6] 6 Derry City and Strabane
[7] 7 Fermanagh and Omagh
[8] 8 Lisburn and Castlereagh
[9] 9 Mid and East Antrim
[10] 10 Mid Ulster
[11] 11 Newry, Mourne and Down

WALES

UNITARY AUTHORITIES

[1] 1 Anglesey/Sir Fôn
[2] 2 Blaenau Gwent
[3] 3 Bridgend/Pen-y-bont ar Ogwr
[4] 4 Caerphilly/Caerffili
[5] 5 Cardiff/Caerdydd
[6] 6 Carmarthenshire/Sir Gaerfyrddin
[7] 7 Ceredigion
[8] 8 Conwy
[9] 9 Denbighshire/Sir Ddinbych
[10] 10 Flintshire/Sir y Fflint
[11] 11 Gwynedd
[12] 12 Merthyr Tydfil/Merthyr Tudful
[13] 13 Monmouthshire/Sir Fynwy
[14] 14 Neath Port Talbot/Castell-nedd Phort Talbot
[15] 15 Newport/Casnewydd
[16] 16 Pembrokeshire/Sir Benfro
[17] 17 Powys
[18] 18 Rhondda Cynon Taff/Rhondda Cynon Taf
[19] 19 Swansea/Abertawe
[20] 20 Torfaen/Tor-faen
[21] 21 Vale of Glamorgan/Bro Morgannwg
[22] 22 Wrexham/Wrecsam

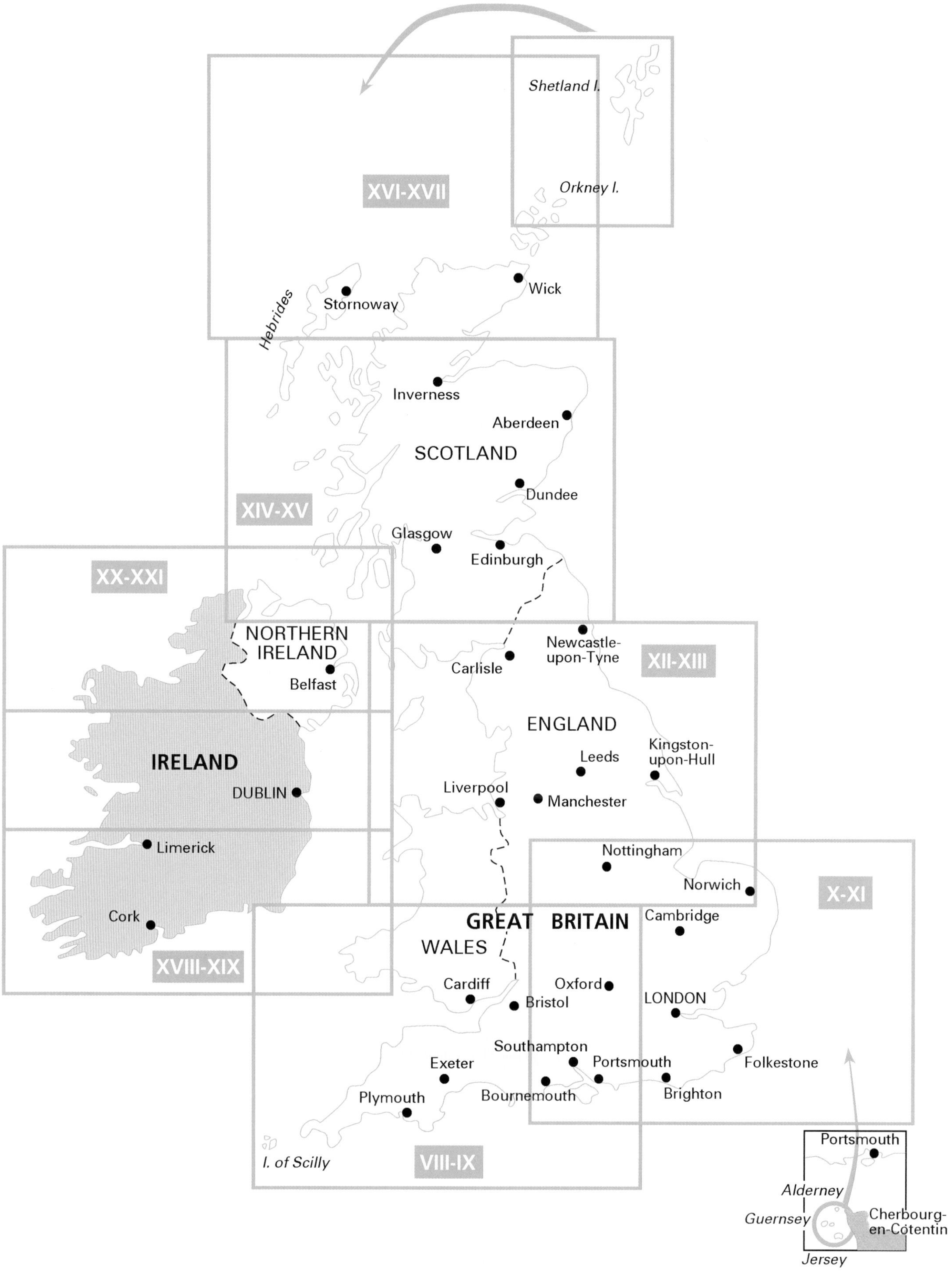

XVI-XVII
Shetland I.
Orkney I.
Wick
Stornoway
Hebrides
XIV-XV
Inverness
Aberdeen
SCOTLAND
Dundee
Glasgow
Edinburgh
XX-XXI
NORTHERN IRELAND
Belfast
Newcastle-upon-Tyne
Carlisle
XII-XIII
ENGLAND
IRELAND
Kingston-upon-Hull
Leeds
DUBLIN
Liverpool
Manchester
Limerick
Nottingham
Norwich
X-XI
Cork
GREAT BRITAIN
Cambridge
WALES
XVIII-XIX
Cardiff
Oxford
Bristol
LONDON
Southampton
Folkestone
Exeter
Portsmouth
Bournemouth
Brighton
Plymouth
I. of Scilly
VIII-IX
Portsmouth
Alderney
Guernsey
Cherbourg-en-Cotentin
Jersey

St. George's Channel
Bristol Channel
Pembrokeshire Coast National Park
Strumble Head
St. David's Head
St. David's
Fishguard/Abergwaun
Newport
Pentre Ifan
Cardigan
Aberporth
Synod Inn
New Quay
Aberaeron
Llanrhystud
Devil's Bridge
Elan Valley
Tregaron
Lampeter
Llanwrtyd Wells
Newcastle Emlyn
Llandysul
National Wool Museum
Crymmych
Llandovery
Llangadog
Sennybridge
Brecon Beacons National Park
Black Mountain
Llandeilo
Carmarthen/Caerfyrddin
St. Clears
Narberth
Whitland
Haverfordwest/Hwlffordd
St. Bride's Bay
Milford Haven/Aberdaugleddau
Neyland
Pembroke Dock
Pembroke
Saundersfoot
Tenby/Dinbych-y-pysgod
Carmarthen Bay
St. Govan's Head
Pendine
Kidwelly
Cross Hands
Ammanford
Pontarddulais
Pontardawe
Burry Port
Llanelli
Swansea/Abertawe
Neath/Castell-Nedd
Merthyr
Hirwaun
Aberdare/Aberdar
Maesteg
Port Talbot
The Mumbles
Rhossili
Worms Head
Gower Peninsula
Port-Eynon
Porthcawl
Bridgend/Pen-y-bont
Lundy
Ilfracombe
Combe Martin
Lynton
Lynmouth
Porlock
Mortehoe
Croyde
Braunton
Simonsbath
Tarr Steps
Barnstaple
Northam
Hartland Point
Clovelly
Bideford
South Molton
Dulverton
Great Torrington
Cliffs of Morwenstow
Kilkhampton
Stratton
Bude
Holsworthy
Hatherleigh
Winkleigh
Tiverton
Crediton
Poundstock
Okehampton
Exeter
Boscastle
Tintagel
Launceston
Lydford Gorge
High Willhays
Drogo
Moretonhampstead
Dartmoor National Park
Brent Tor
Port Isaac
Camelford
Padstow
Wadebridge
Tavistock
Callington
Princetown
Ashburton
Bovey Tracey
Newton Abbot
Bodmin
Liskeard
Buckland
Buckfastleigh
Newquay
Lanhydrock
Saltash
Plympton
Totnes
Fraddon
Lostwithiel
Trewithen
St. Austell
Fowey
Polperro
West Looe
Torpoint
St Germans
Plymstock
Saltram
Modbury
Newton Ferrers
Plymouth
Dartmouth
Kingsbridge
Salcombe
Start Point
Truro
Tregony
Mevagissey
Camborne
Redruth
Trelissick
Penryn
St. Mawes
Falmouth
St. Ives
Hayle
St. Just
Penzance
St. Michael's Mount
Mount's Bay
Helston
Glendurgan
St. Keverne
Coverack
Sennen
Land's End
Lizard
Lizard Point
Subtropical Gardens
Tresco
St. Martin's
Isles of Scilly
St. Mary's

Redditch
Royal Leamington Spa
Warwick
Daventry
Stourport
Bromsgrove
Droitwich
Worcester
Leominster
Presteigne
Berrington Hall
Llandrindod Wells
Builth Wells
Kington
Bromyard
Pershore
Great Malvern
Evesham
Stratford-upon-Avon
Ettington
Hidcote Manor
Shipston-on-Stour
Banbury
Brackley
Towcester
Newport Pagnell
Wolverton
MILTON KEYNES
Bletchley
Woburn
Leighton Buzzard
Buckingham
Hay-on-Wye
Hereford
Hay Bluff
Talgarth
Ledbury
Upton
Tewkesbury
Broadway
Chipping Campden
Moreton
Chastleton
Winchcombe
Stow-on-the-Wold
Chipping Norton
Bicester
Waddesdon
Dunstable
Kilpeck
Pontrilas
Ross-on-Wye
Black Mountains
Llanthony Priory
GLOUCESTER
Cheltenham
Woodstock
Blenheim Palace
Kidlington
Aylesbury
Tring
Berkhamsted
Hemel Hempstead
Beacons
Brecon
Crickhowell
Abergavenny
Monmouth/Trefynwy
Northleach
Burford
Witney
Ebbw Vale/Glyn Ebwy
Blaenavon
Coleford
Newnham
Painswick
Cotswolds
Bibury
Fairford
OXFORD
Thame
Tydfil
Tredegar
Abertillery
Raglan
Lydney
Stroud
Lechlade
Abingdon
High Wycombe
Amersham
Beaconsfield
Pontypool
Usk
Bargoed
Tintern Abbey
Berkeley
Nailsworth
Cirencester
Dursley
Cricklade
Faringdon
Cwmbrân
Chepstow
SEVERN BRIDGE
Tetbury
Wallingford
Marlow
Maidenhead
Slough
Rhondda
Bedwas
Risca
Malmesbury
SWINDON
Wantage
Henley-on-Thames
Chipping Sodbury
Streatley
Pontypridd
Caerphilly/Caerffili
Newport/Casnewydd
Pangbourne
Windsor
Avonmouth
Wroughton
Chippenham
Calne
Marlborough
READING
Bracknell
CARDIFF/CAERDYDD
Portishead
Clifton Bridge
BRISTOL
Avebury
Hungerford
Newbury
Wokingham
Cowbridge
Penarth
Clevedon
Keynsham
Corsham
Melksham
Camberley
Woking
Barry/Barri
Congresbury
Bath
Bradford-on-Avon
Devizes
Pewsey
Basingstoke
Farnborough
Weston-Super-Mare
Trowbridge
Upavon
Aldershot
Guildford
Cheddar Gorge
Radstock
Beckington
Westbury
Warminster
Farnham
Godalming
Minehead
Burnham-on-Sea
Wells
Frome
Weyhill
Andover
Alton
Dunster
Watchet
Shepton Mallet
Longleat
Stonehenge
Shrewton
Amesbury
Milford
Glastonbury
Stourhead
Stockbridge
Hindhead
Haslemere
Williton
Exmoor National Park
Bridgwater
Street
Bruton
Mere
Wilton
Lopcombe Corner
New Alresford
Othery
Wincanton
Salisbury
Winchester
Petworth House
Petersfield
Harold Hillier Gardens
South Downs
Midhurst
Langport
Gillingham
Shaftesbury
Romsey
Eastleigh
Bampton
Taunton
Wellington
Ilchester
Montacute
Sherborne
Henstridge
Fordingbridge
Botley
National Park
Ilminster
Yeovil
Sturminster Newton
Cranborne
SOUTHAMPTON
Havant
Chichester
Cullompton
Crewkerne
Chard
Ringwood
Lyndhurst
Fawley
Fareham
Cosham
Blandford Forum
Wimborne Minster
New Forest N.P.
Beaulieu
Gosport
PORTSMOUTH
Honiton
Beaminster
Cerne Abbas
Lymington
Cowes
Osborne
Southsea
Bognor Regis
Axminster
Bridport
Dorchester
Bere Regis
Poole
Christchurch
Yarmouth
Newport
Fishbourne
Ryde
Selsey
Selsey Bill
Foreland
Ottery St Mary
Lyme Regis
Seaton
Maiden
BOURNEMOUTH
The Solent
Carisbrooke
Brading
Sandown
Sidmouth
Branscombe
Abbotsbury
Wareham
Corfe Castle
The Needles
Old Harry Rocks
Freshwater
Shanklin
Niton
Budleigh Salterton
Lyme Bay
Weymouth
Lulworth Cove
Swanage
ISLE OF WIGHT
Ventnor
St. Catherine's Point
Exmouth
Dawlish
Isle of Portland
Fortuneswell
St. Alban's Head
Teignmouth
Bill of Portland
Torquay/Torbay
Paignton
Brixham
Kingswear
E N G L I S H C H A N N E L
Alderney
Cap de la Hague
Cap Lévi
Pointe de Barfleur

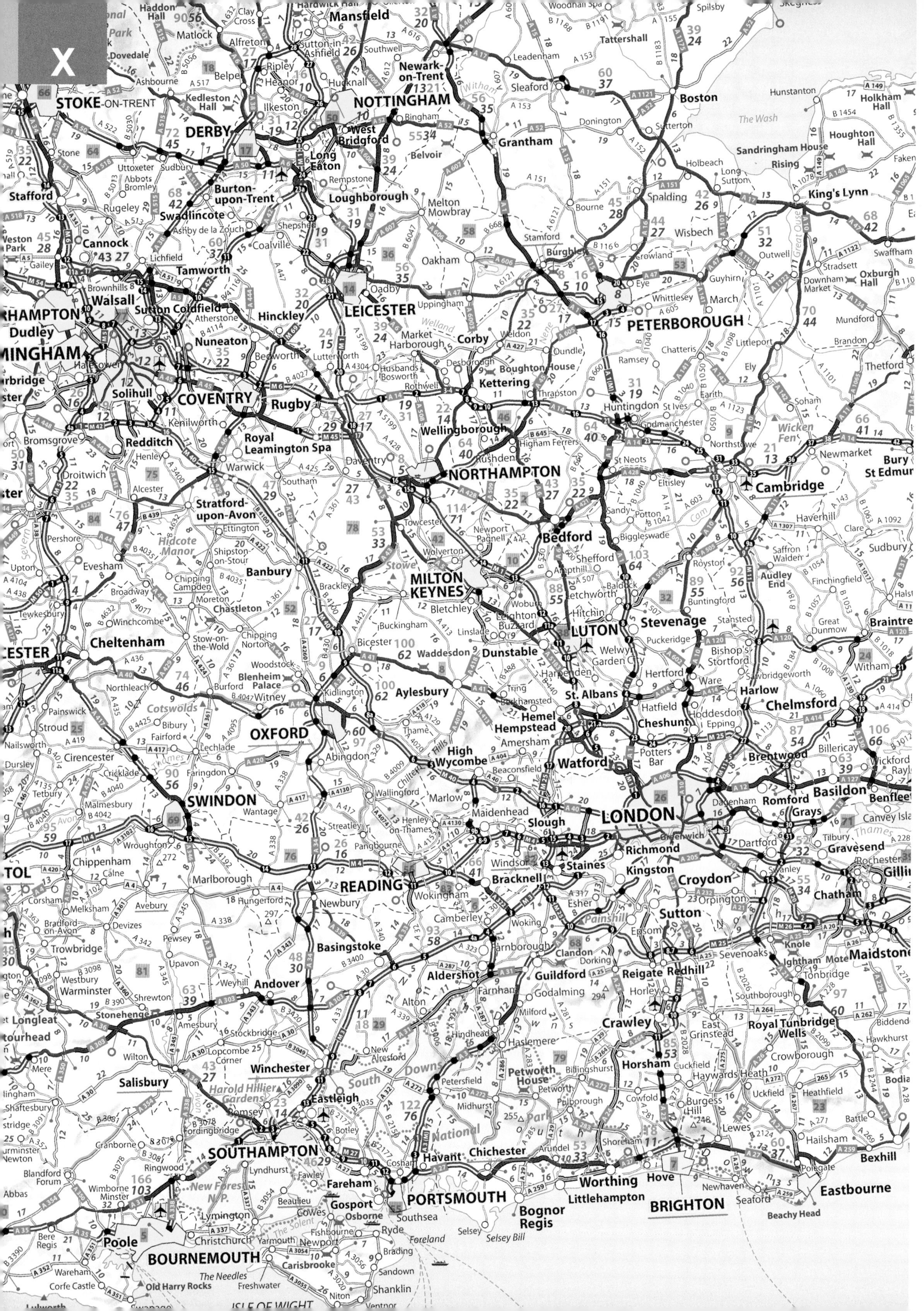

X
Mansfield
NOTTINGHAM
Newark-on-Trent
STOKE-ON-TRENT
DERBY
Matlock
Alfreton
Ripley
Belper
Ilkeston
Hucknall
West Bridgford
Long Eaton
Sleaford
Boston
Tattershall
Spilsby
Grantham
Hunstanton
Holkham Hall
Sandringham House
Houghton Hall
King's Lynn
Spalding
Stafford
Uttoxeter
Burton-upon-Trent
Swadlincote
Loughborough
Melton Mowbray
Belvoir
Rugeley
Cannock
Lichfield
Tamworth
Coalville
Oakham
Stamford
Burghley
Bourne
Wisbech
Swaffham
Walsall
Sutton Coldfield
LEICESTER
Oadby
Uppingham
PETERBOROUGH
Downham Market
Oxburgh Hall
March
Dudley
Nuneaton
Hinckley
Market Harborough
Corby
Oundle
Thetford
Brandon
Ely
Solihull
COVENTRY
Rugby
Kettering
Boughton House
Thrapston
Huntingdon
St Ives
Bromsgrove
Redditch
Royal Leamington Spa
Warwick
Wellingborough
NORTHAMPTON
Daventry
Rushden
Higham Ferrers
St Neots
Newmarket
Cambridge
Bury St Edmunds
Droitwich
Stratford-upon-Avon
Alcester
Evesham
Hidcote Manor
Banbury
Towcester
Bedford
Sandy
Biggleswade
Haverhill
Saffron Walden
Audley End
Sudbury
MILTON KEYNES
Stowe
Chipping Campden
Moreton
Chastleton
Bletchley
Buckingham
Luton
Stevenage
Hitchin
Letchworth
Royston
Tewkesbury
Cheltenham
Stow-on-the-Wold
Chipping Norton
Bicester
Waddesdon
Dunstable
Welwyn Garden City
Bishop's Stortford
Braintree
Great Dunmow
Witham
Woodstock
Blenheim Palace
Witney
Burford
Aylesbury
Tring
Berkhamsted
St. Albans
Harpenden
Hertford
Ware
Harlow
Chelmsford
Cotswolds
Stroud
Cirencester
OXFORD
Kidlington
Thame
Abingdon
Hemel Hempstead
Amersham
Watford
Hatfield
Cheshunt
Epping
Brentwood
Billericay
Wickford
High Wycombe
Beaconsfield
Tetbury
Malmesbury
SWINDON
Wantage
Wallingford
Marlow
Maidenhead
Slough
LONDON
Romford
Basildon
Grays
Benfleet
Canvey Island
Henley-on-Thames
Chippenham
Calne
Marlborough
Avebury
Newbury
Hungerford
READING
Wokingham
Bracknell
Windsor
Staines
Richmond
Kingston
Croydon
Greenwich
Dartford
Gravesend
Rochester
Chatham
Melksham
Devizes
Trowbridge
Camberley
Esher
Epsom
Sutton
Orpington
Sevenoaks
Maidstone
Westbury
Warminster
Andover
Basingstoke
Aldershot
Farnham
Farnborough
Guildford
Woking
Dorking
Reigate
Redhill
Tonbridge
Royal Tunbridge Wells
Longleat
Stourhead
Stonehenge
Amesbury
Alton
Godalming
Haslemere
Crawley
East Grinstead
Salisbury
Winchester
New Alresford
Petworth House
Horsham
Haywards Heath
Crowborough
Heathfield
Shaftesbury
Romsey
Eastleigh
Petersfield
Midhurst
Burgess Hill
Lewes
Hailsham
Battle
Bexhill
SOUTHAMPTON
Fareham
Havant
Chichester
Arundel
Worthing
Hove
BRIGHTON
Eastbourne
Seaford
Beachy Head
Ringwood
Lyndhurst
New Forest N.P.
Gosport
PORTSMOUTH
Southsea
Bognor Regis
Littlehampton
Selsey
Poole
BOURNEMOUTH
Christchurch
Lymington
Cowes
Osborne
Newport
Ryde
Carisbrooke
Sandown
Shanklin
The Needles
Old Harry Rocks
Wareham
Corfe Castle
Wimborne Minster
Blandford Forum
ISLE OF WIGHT

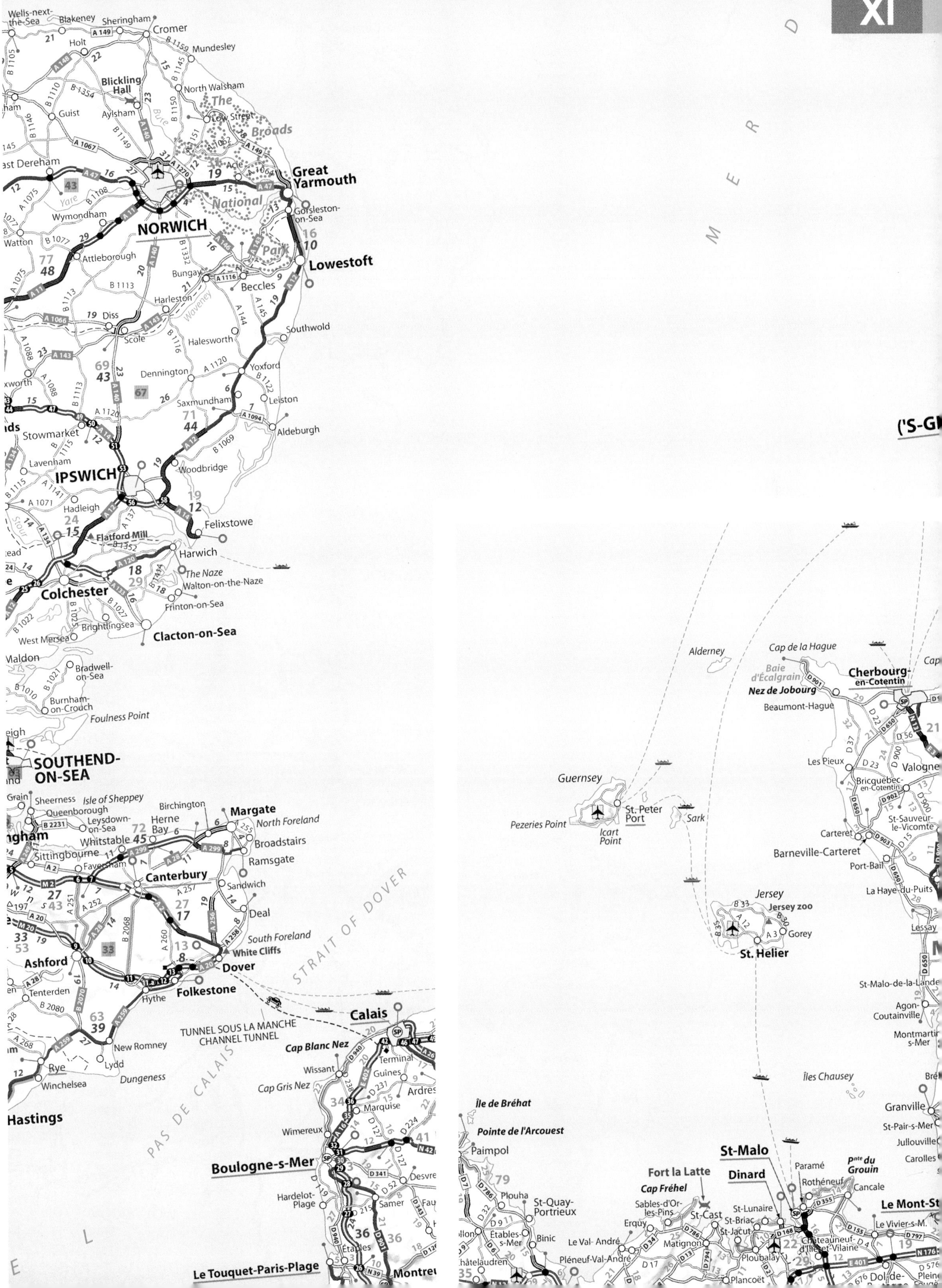

Wells-next-the-Sea
Blakeney
Sheringham
Cromer
Holt
Mundesley
Blickling Hall
North Walsham
The Broads National Park
Guist
Aylsham
Low Street
East Dereham
Acle
Great Yarmouth
NORWICH
Wymondham
Gorleston-on-Sea
Watton
Attleborough
Lowestoft
Bungay
Beccles
Harleston
Diss
Scole
Southwold
Halesworth
Yoxford
Dennington
Saxmundham
Leiston
Aldeburgh
Stowmarket
Lavenham
IPSWICH
Woodbridge
Hadleigh
Felixstowe
Flatford Mill
Harwich
The Naze
Walton-on-the-Naze
Colchester
Frinton-on-Sea
Brightlingsea
Clacton-on-Sea
West Mersea
Maldon
Bradwell-on-Sea
Burnham-on-Crouch
Foulness Point
SOUTHEND-ON-SEA
Sheerness
Isle of Sheppey
Queenborough
Leysdown-on-Sea
Birchington
Margate
North Foreland
Herne Bay
Whitstable
Broadstairs
Ramsgate
Sittingbourne
Faversham
Canterbury
Sandwich
Deal
South Foreland
White Cliffs
Ashford
Dover
Folkestone
Hythe
Tenterden
STRAIT OF DOVER
Calais
TUNNEL SOUS LA MANCHE
CHANNEL TUNNEL
Cap Blanc Nez
Terminal
Wissant
Guînes
Ardres
New Romney
Lydd
Rye
Winchelsea
Dungeness
Cap Gris Nez
Marquise
Hastings
PAS DE CALAIS
Wimereux
Boulogne-s-Mer
Desvres
Hardelot-Plage
Samer
Étaples
Le Touquet-Paris-Plage
Montreuil
MER DU
('S-G
Alderney
Cap de la Hague
Baie d'Écalgrain
Nez de Jobourg
Cherbourg-en-Cotentin
Beaumont-Hague
Les Pieux
Valognes
Bricquebec-en-Cotentin
Guernsey
St. Peter Port
Sark
Pezeries Point
Icart Point
Carteret
St-Sauveur-le-Vicomte
Barneville-Carteret
Port-Bail
La Haye-du-Puits
Jersey
Jersey zoo
Gorey
St. Helier
Lessay
St-Malo-de-la-Lande
Agon-Coutainville
Montmartin-s-Mer
Îles Chausey
Granville
St-Pair-s-Mer
Jullouville
Carolles
Île de Bréhat
Pointe de l'Arcouest
Paimpol
St-Malo
Paramé
Pointe du Grouin
Fort la Latte
Dinard
Rothéneuf
Cancale
Cap Fréhel
Plouha
St-Quay-Portrieux
Sables-d'Or-les-Pins
St-Cast
St-Lunaire
St-Briac
Le Mont-St
Erquy
St-Jacut
Étables-s-Mer
Binic
Le Val-André
Matignon
Ploubalay
Châteauneuf-d'Ille-et-Vilaine
Le Vivier-s-M.
Châtelaudren
Pléneuf-Val-André
Plancoët
Dol-de-

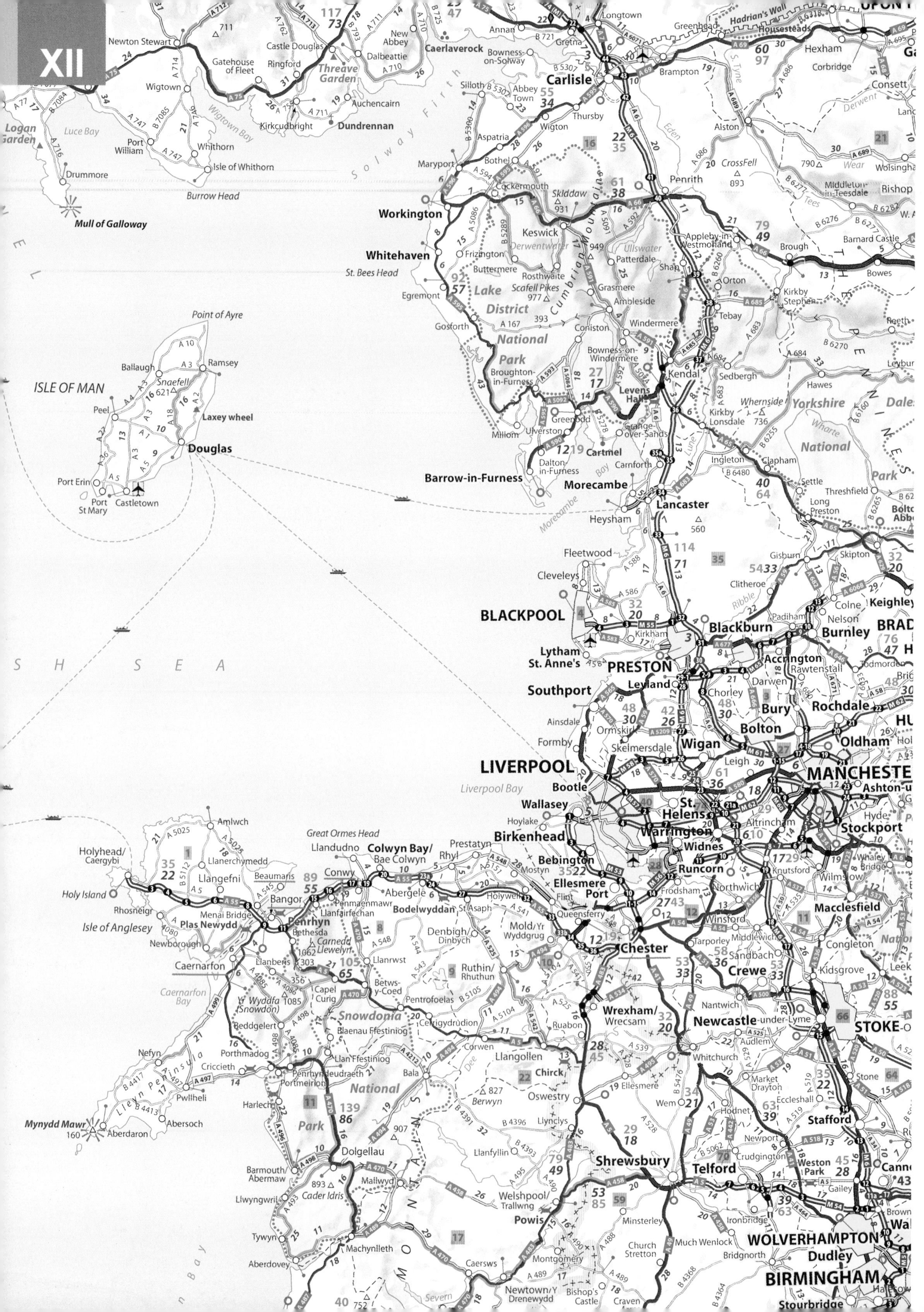
Newton Stewart
Gatehouse of Fleet
Castle Douglas
Ringford
Threave Garden
Dalbeattie
New Abbey
Caerlaverock
Annan
Gretna
Longtown
Hadrian's Wall
Housesteads
Greenhead
Hexham
Corbridge
Consett
Bowness-on-Solway
Carlisle
Brampton
Silloth
Abbey Town
Wigtown
Kirkcudbright
Auchencairn
Dundrennan
Wigtown Bay
Solway Firth
Logan Garden
Luce Bay
Port William
Whithorn
Isle of Whithorn
Drummore
Burrow Head
Mull of Galloway
Thursby
Wigton
Aspatria
Alston
Cross Fell
Maryport
Bothel
Cockermouth
Workington
Skiddaw
Penrith
Middleton-in-Teesdale
Bishop
Keswick
Derwentwater
Ullswater
Appleby-in-Westmorland
Brough
Barnard Castle
Bowes
Whitehaven
Frizington
St. Bees Head
Buttermere
Patterdale
Shap
Orton
Kirkby Stephen
Egremont
Lake District National Park
Rosthwaite
Scafell Pikes
Grasmere
Ambleside
Tebay
Gosforth
Coniston
Windermere
Cumbrian Mountains
Point of Ayre
Bowness-on-Windermere
Kendal
Sedbergh
Hawes
Ballaugh
Ramsey
Snaefell
ISLE OF MAN
Broughton-in-Furness
Levens Hall
Peel
Laxey wheel
Greenodd
Whernside
Yorkshire Dales National Park
Kirkby Lonsdale
Millom
Ulverston
Grange-over-Sands
Douglas
Cartmel
Ingleton
Clapham
Dalton-in-Furness
Carnforth
Port Erin
Castletown
Port St Mary
Barrow-in-Furness
Settle
Morecambe
Threshfield
Long Preston
Lancaster
Morecambe Bay
Heysham
Pennines
Fleetwood
Gisburn
Skipton
Cleveleys
Clitheroe
Ribble
Colne
Keighley
Nelson
BLACKPOOL
Padiham
Blackburn
Burnley
Kirkham
Lytham St. Anne's
PRESTON
Accrington
Rawtenstall
Todmorden
Leyland
Darwen
Southport
Chorley
Bury
Rochdale
Ainsdale
Ormskirk
Bolton
Oldham
Formby
Skelmersdale
Wigan
LIVERPOOL
Leigh
MANCHESTER
Bootle
Liverpool Bay
Ashton-under-Lyne
Wallasey
St. Helens
Hyde
Hoylake
Altrincham
Stockport
Birkenhead
Warrington
Widnes
Great Ormes Head
Llandudno
Colwyn Bay/Bae Colwyn
Prestatyn
Rhyl
Bebington
Mostyn
Amlwch
Holyhead/Caergybi
Llanerchymedd
Runcorn
Knutsford
Whaley Bridge
Wilmslow
Holy Island
Llangefni
Beaumaris
Conwy
Abergele
Bodelwyddan
St Asaph
Holywell
Ellesmere Port
Flint
Northwich
Macclesfield
Frodsham
Rhosneigr
Bangor
Penmaenmawr
Llanfairfechan
Isle of Anglesey
Menai Bridge
Plas Newydd
Penrhyn
Bethesda
Carnedd Llewelyn
Denbigh/Dinbych
Mold/Yr Wyddgrug
Queensferry
Winsford
Middlewich
Congleton
Newborough
Llanrwst
Chester
Tarporley
Sandbach
Caernarfon
Llanberis
Ruthin/Rhuthun
Crewe
Kidsgrove
Leek
Capel Curig
Betws-y-Coed
Caernarfon Bay
Yr Wyddfa (Snowdon)
Pentrefoelas
Wrexham/Wrecsam
Nantwich
Snowdonia
Cerrigydrudion
Newcastle-under-Lyme
STOKE
Beddgelert
Blaenau Ffestiniog
Ruabon
Audlem
Nefyn
Porthmadog
Llan Ffestiniog
Corwen
Llangollen
Whitchurch
Criccieth
Penrhyndeudraeth
Portmeirion
Bala
Chirk
Market Drayton
Stone
Lleyn Peninsula
Pwllheli
National Park
Berwyn
Ellesmere
Oswestry
Eccleshall
Harlech
Wem
Hodnet
Mynydd Mawr
Aberdaron
Abersoch
Llynclys
Stafford
Newport
Dolgellau
Llanfyllin
Barmouth/Abermaw
Shrewsbury
Crudgington
Telford
Weston Park
Cannock
Mallwyd
Cader Idris
Gailey
Llwyngwril
Welshpool/Trallwng
Powis
Brownhills
Walsall
Tywyn
Minsterley
Ironbridge
WOLVERHAMPTON
Machynlleth
Church Stretton
Much Wenlock
Dudley
Aberdovey
Montgomery
Bridgnorth
BIRMINGHAM
Caersws
Newtown/Y Drenewydd
Bishop's Castle
Craven
Halesowen
Stourbridge
Severn
Cambrian Mountains
IRISH SEA

Tynemouth
Jarrow
South Shields
SUNDERLAND
Gateshead
Beamish Hall
Washington
Seaham
Stanley
Chester-le-Street
Houghton-le-Spring
Durham
Horden
Crook
Spennymoor
Peterlee
Hartlepool
Sedgefield
Auckland
Redcar
Marske-by-the-Sea
Newton Aycliffe
Billingham
Saltburn-by-the-Sea
Brotton
Stockton-on-Tees
Loftus
Guisborough
Darlington
MIDDLESBROUGH
Whitby
Eaglescliffe
Richmond
Cleveland Hills
North York Moors National Park
Northallerton
Scalby
Scarborough
Hutton-le-Hole
Rievaulx Abbey
Bedale
Thirsk
Helmsley
Pickering
Filey
Swale
Derwent
Malton
Flamborough Head
Fountains Abbey
Ripon
Burton Agnes Hall
Easingwold
Howard
Norton
Bridlington
Pateley Bridge
Boroughbridge
Ure
Driffield
Beeford
Knaresborough
YORK
Wetwang
Harrogate
Wetherby
Hornsea
Tadcaster
Market Weighton
Leven
Ilkley
Otley
Harewood
Bingley
Burton Constable Hall
Beverley
BRADFORD
LEEDS
Selby
Barlby
KINGSTON UPON HULL
Garforth
Hedon
Withernsea
Halifax
Castleford
Howden
Goole
River Humber
Patrington
Snaith
Barton-upon-Humber
Kilnsea
Dewsbury
Wakefield
Pontefract
Immingham Dock
Immingham
Spurn Head
HUDDERSFIELD
Thorne
Crowle
Scunthorpe
Grimsby
Cleethorpes
Barnsley
Brigg
Caistor
Doncaster
Bentley
Conisbrough
Epworth
Ashton-under-Lyne
Glossop
Stocksbridge
Rotherham
Bawtry
Market Rasen
SHEFFIELD
Maltby
Gainsborough
Louth
High Peak
Castleton
Mablethorpe
Sutton-on-Sea
Chapel-en-le-Frith
Dronfield
Worksop
Retford
Wragby
Peak District
Staveley
Alford
Buxton
Lincoln
Baslow
Chesterfield
Horncastle
Partney
Skegness
Bakewell
Chatsworth
Tuxford
Spilsby
Haddon Hall
Hardwick Hall
Ollerton
Woodhall Spa
Mansfield
Clay Cross
Matlock
Tattershall
Peak District National Park
Alfreton
Sutton-in-Ashfield
Southwell
Newark-on-Trent
Leadenham
Dovedale
Ripley
Heanor
Hucknall
Belper
Sleaford
Ashbourne
Kedleston Hall
NOTTINGHAM
Ilkeston
Witham
Boston
Wells-next-the-Sea
Blakeney
Sheringham
Hunstanton
Holkham Hall
Holt
STOKE-ON-TRENT
Bingham
Donington
The Wash
DERBY
West Bridgford
Grantham
Sutterton
Houghton Hall
Long Eaton
Belvoir
Sandringham House
Fakenham
Uttoxeter
Sudbury
Holbeach
Rising
Guist
Abbots Bromley
Rempstone
Long Sutton
Burton-upon-Trent
Loughborough
Spalding
King's Lynn
Melton Mowbray
Bourne
East Dereham
Swadlincote
Ashby de la Zouch
Shepshed
Coalville
Wisbech
Lichfield
Oakham
Stamford
Outwell
Swaffham
Wymondham
Tamworth
Burghley
Crowland
Stradsett
Great Ouse
Yare
Oadby
Guyhirn
Downham Market
Oxburgh Hall
Watton
Attleborough
Walsall
Sutton Coldfield
LEICESTER
Uppingham
Eye
March
Atherstone
Hinckley
Whittlesey
Nuneaton
Welland
Market Harborough
Corby
Weldon
PETERBOROUGH
Mundford
Bedworth
Lutterworth
Nene
Oundle
Littleport
Brandon
Husbands Bosworth
Desborough
Boughton House
Ramsey
Chatteris
Ely
Thetford
Diss
Rothwell
Kettering

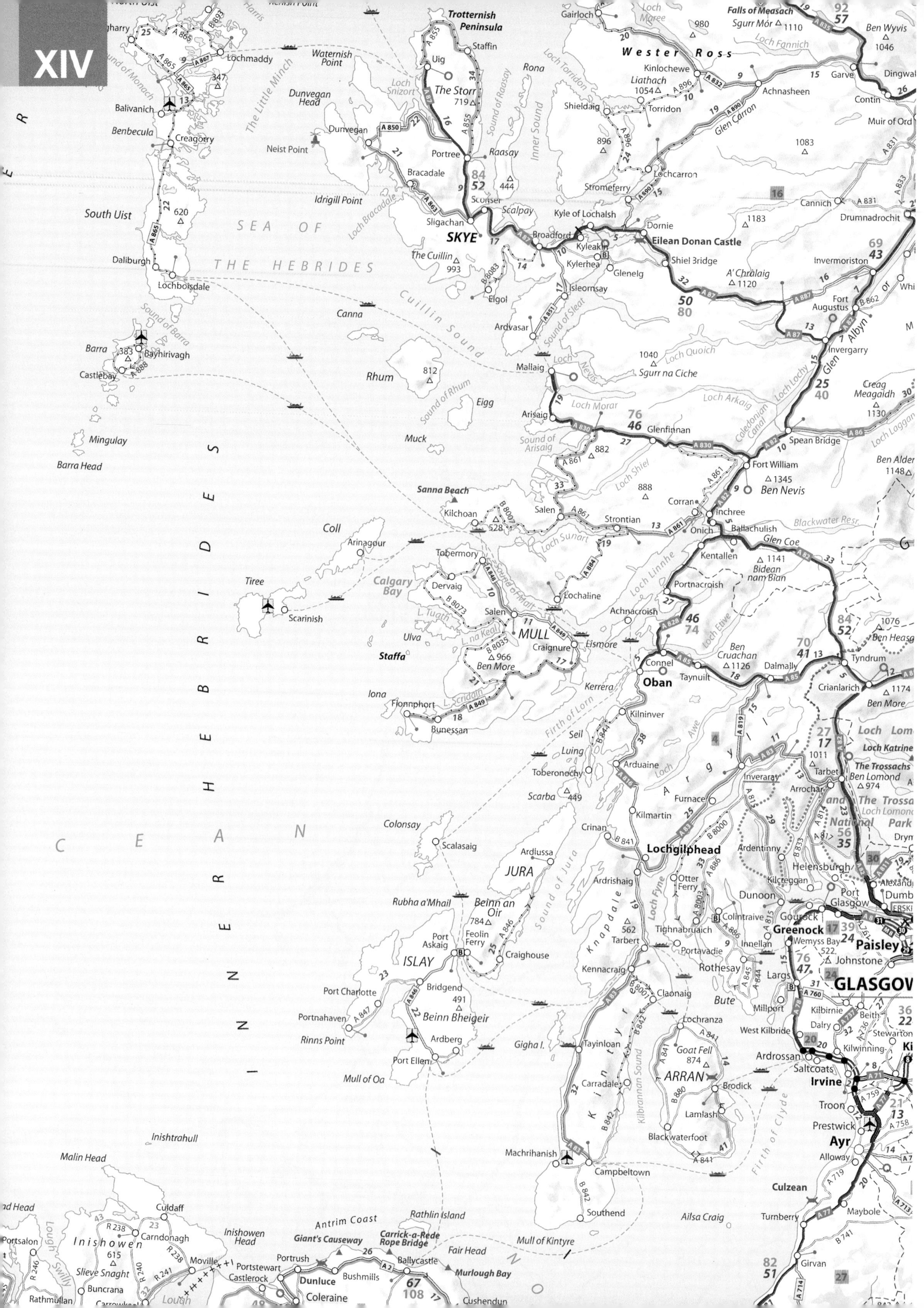
Trotternish Peninsula
Staffin
Uig
The Storr
Waternish Point
Lochmaddy
Balivanich
Benbecula
Creagorry
Dunvegan Head
Dunvegan
Neist Point
Portree
Raasay
Bracadale
Idrigill Point
South Uist
SEA OF THE HEBRIDES
Sligachan
SKYE
The Cuillin
Broadford
Kyleakin
Kyle of Lochalsh
Eilean Donan Castle
Dornie
Shiel Bridge
Glenelg
Kylerhea
Isleornsay
Elgol
Daliburgh
Lochboisdale
Canna
Barra
Bayhirivagh
Castlebay
Rhum
Eigg
Muck
Mallaig
Arisaig
Glenfinnan
Mingulay
Barra Head
Gairloch
Wester Ross
Kinlochewe
Liathach
Torridon
Shieldaig
Lochcarron
Stromeferry
Achnasheen
Garve
Dingwall
Contin
Muir of Ord
Falls of Measach
Sgurr Mór
Ben Wyvis
Glen Carron
Cannich
Drumnadrochit
Invermoriston
A'Chralaig
Fort Augustus
Invergarry
Sgurr na Ciche
Loch Quoich
Loch Arkaig
Caledonian Canal
Creag Meagaidh
Spean Bridge
Fort William
Ben Nevis
Ben Alder
Corran
Inchree
Onich
Ballachulish
Glen Coe
Blackwater Resr.
Kentallen
Bidean nam Bian
Portnacroish
Sanna Beach
Kilchoan
Salen
Strontian
Loch Sunart
Coll
Arinagour
Tiree
Scarinish
Tobermory
Calgary Bay
Dervaig
Lochaline
Achnacroish
MULL
Craignure
Lismore
Ulva
Staffa
Ben More
Iona
Fionnphort
Bunessan
Loch Linnhe
Loch Etive
Ben Cruachan
Connel
Oban
Taynuilt
Dalmally
Tyndrum
Crianlarich
Kerrera
Firth of Lorn
Kilninver
Seil
Luing
Arduaine
Toberonochy
Scarba
Colonsay
Scalasaig
Argyll
Inveraray
Arrochar
Tarbet
Ben Lomond
Loch Lomond
Loch Katrine
The Trossachs
Furnace
Kilmartin
Crinan
Lochgilphead
Ardrishaig
Ardlussa
JURA
Sound of Jura
Rubha a'Mhail
Beinn an Oir
Port Askaig
Feolin Ferry
Craighouse
ISLAY
Bridgend
Port Charlotte
Portnahaven
Rinns Point
Beinn Bheigeir
Ardbeg
Port Ellen
Mull of Oa
Ardentinny
Helensburgh
Kilcreggan
Dunoon
Port Glasgow
Greenock
Gourock
Paisley
Johnstone
GLASGOW
Otter Ferry
Colintraive
Tighnabruaich
Tarbert
Knapdale
Loch Fyne
Portavadie
Innellan
Wemyss Bay
Rothesay
Bute
Largs
Kennacraig
Claonaig
Millport
Kilbirnie
Dalry
Beith
West Kilbride
Kilwinning
Stewarton
Ardrossan
Saltcoats
Irvine
Gigha I.
Tayinloan
Lochranza
Goat Fell
ARRAN
Brodick
Lamlash
Kintyre
Kilbrannan Sound
Carradale
Blackwaterfoot
Firth of Clyde
Troon
Prestwick
Ayr
Alloway
Machrihanish
Campbeltown
Southend
Culzean
Turnberry
Maybole
Ailsa Craig
Mull of Kintyre
Girvan
Inishtrahull
Malin Head
Culdaff
Carndonagh
Inishowen
Inishowen Head
Moville
Portsalon
Slieve Snaght
Buncrana
Rathmullan
Lough Swilly
Antrim Coast
Rathlin Island
Giant's Causeway
Carrick-a-Rede Rope Bridge
Fair Head
Murlough Bay
Ballycastle
Bushmills
Portrush
Portstewart
Castlerock
Dunluce
Coleraine
Cushendun

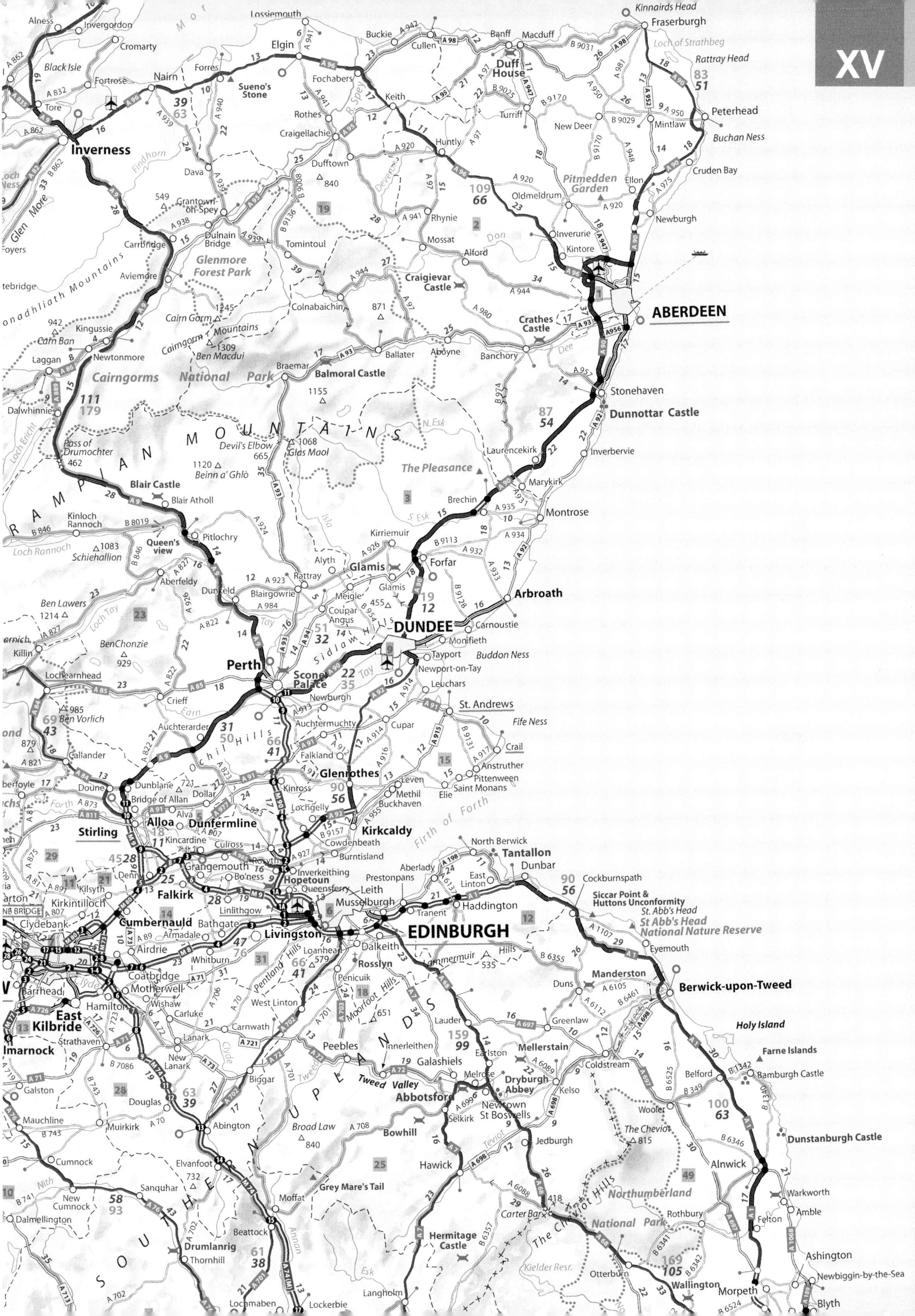

Kinnairds Head
Fraserburgh
Loch of Strathbeg
Rattray Head
Peterhead
Buchan Ness
Cruden Bay
Lossiemouth
Alness
Invergordon
Cromarty
Black Isle
Fortrose
Nairn
Forres
Elgin
Buckie
Cullen
Banff
Macduff
Duff House
Sueno's Stone
Fochabers
Keith
Turriff
New Deer
Mintlaw
Tore
Inverness
Rothes
Craigellachie
Huntly
Dufftown
Dava
Pitmedden Garden
Ellon
Newburgh
Oldmeldrum
Grantown-on-Spey
Rhynie
Glen More
Foyers
Carrbridge
Dulnain Bridge
Tomintoul
Mossat
Alford
Inverurie
Kintore
Glenmore Forest Park
Aviemore
Craigievar Castle
ABERDEEN
Colnabaichin
Cairn Gorm
Cairngorm Mountains
Ben Macdui
Kingussie
Newtonmore
Laggan
Crathes Castle
Banchory
Ballater
Aboyne
Braemar
Balmoral Castle
Cairngorms National Park
Dalwhinnie
Stonehaven
Dunnottar Castle
Pass of Drumochter
GRAMPIAN MOUNTAINS
Devil's Elbow
Glas Maol
Beinn a' Ghlò
Laurencekirk
Inverbervie
The Pleasance
Blair Castle
Blair Atholl
Marykirk
Brechin
Montrose
Kinloch Rannoch
Pitlochry
Loch Rannoch
Schiehallion
Queen's view
Kirriemuir
Forfar
Alyth
Glamis
Aberfeldy
Dunkeld
Blairgowrie
Rattray
Arbroath
Ben Lawers
Meigle
Coupar Angus
DUNDEE
Carnoustie
Monifieth
Killin
Sidlaw Hills
Tayport
Buddon Ness
Lochearnhead
Perth
Scone Palace
Newport-on-Tay
Leuchars
Crieff
Newburgh
St. Andrews
Fife Ness
Ben Vorlich
Auchterarder
Auchtermuchty
Cupar
Callander
Ochil Hills
Falkland
Crail
Anstruther
Glenrothes
Pittenweem
Dunblane
Doune
Kinross
Leven
Methil
Elie
Saint Monans
Bridge of Allan
Dollar
Buckhaven
Stirling
Alloa
Dunfermline
Lochgelly
Kirkcaldy
Firth of Forth
Kincardine
Culross
Rosyth
Cowdenbeath
Burntisland
North Berwick
Tantallon
Dunbar
Grangemouth
Bo'ness
Hopetoun
Inverkeithing
Aberlady
Prestonpans
East Linton
Cockburnspath
Denny
Kilsyth
Falkirk
S. Queensferry
Leith
Musselburgh
Tranent
Haddington
Siccar Point & Huttons Unconformity
St. Abb's Head
St Abb's Head National Nature Reserve
Kirkintilloch
Linlithgow
Clydebank
Cumbernauld
Bathgate
Livingston
EDINBURGH
Armadale
Dalkeith
Airdrie
Whitburn
Loanhead
Rosslyn
Lammermuir Hills
Eyemouth
Coatbridge
Penicuik
Pentland Hills
Manderston
Duns
Berwick-upon-Tweed
Motherwell
Barrhead
Wishaw
Hamilton
East Kilbride
West Linton
Moorfoot Hills
Carluke
Lauder
Greenlaw
Holy Island
Carnwath
Strathaven
Lanark
Peebles
Innerleithen
Earlston
Mellerstain
Coldstream
Farne Islands
Kilmarnock
New Lanark
Galashiels
Melrose
Belford
Bamburgh Castle
Galston
Biggar
Tweed Valley
Abbotsford
Dryburgh Abbey
Kelso
Douglas
Newtown St Boswells
Selkirk
Wooler
Mauchline
Muirkirk
Abington
Broad Law
Bowhill
The Cheviot
Dunstanburgh Castle
Jedburgh
Cumnock
Elvanfoot
Hawick
Alnwick
Sanquhar
Grey Mare's Tail
Northumberland National Park
Warkworth
New Cumnock
Moffat
Carter Bar
The Cheviot Hills
Amble
Rothbury
Felton
Dalmellington
Beattock
Hermitage Castle
Drumlanrig
Thornhill
Kielder Resr.
Otterburn
Ashington
Newbiggin-by-the-Sea
Wallington
Morpeth
Langholm
Lochmaben
Lockerbie
Blyth
SOUTHERN UPLANDS

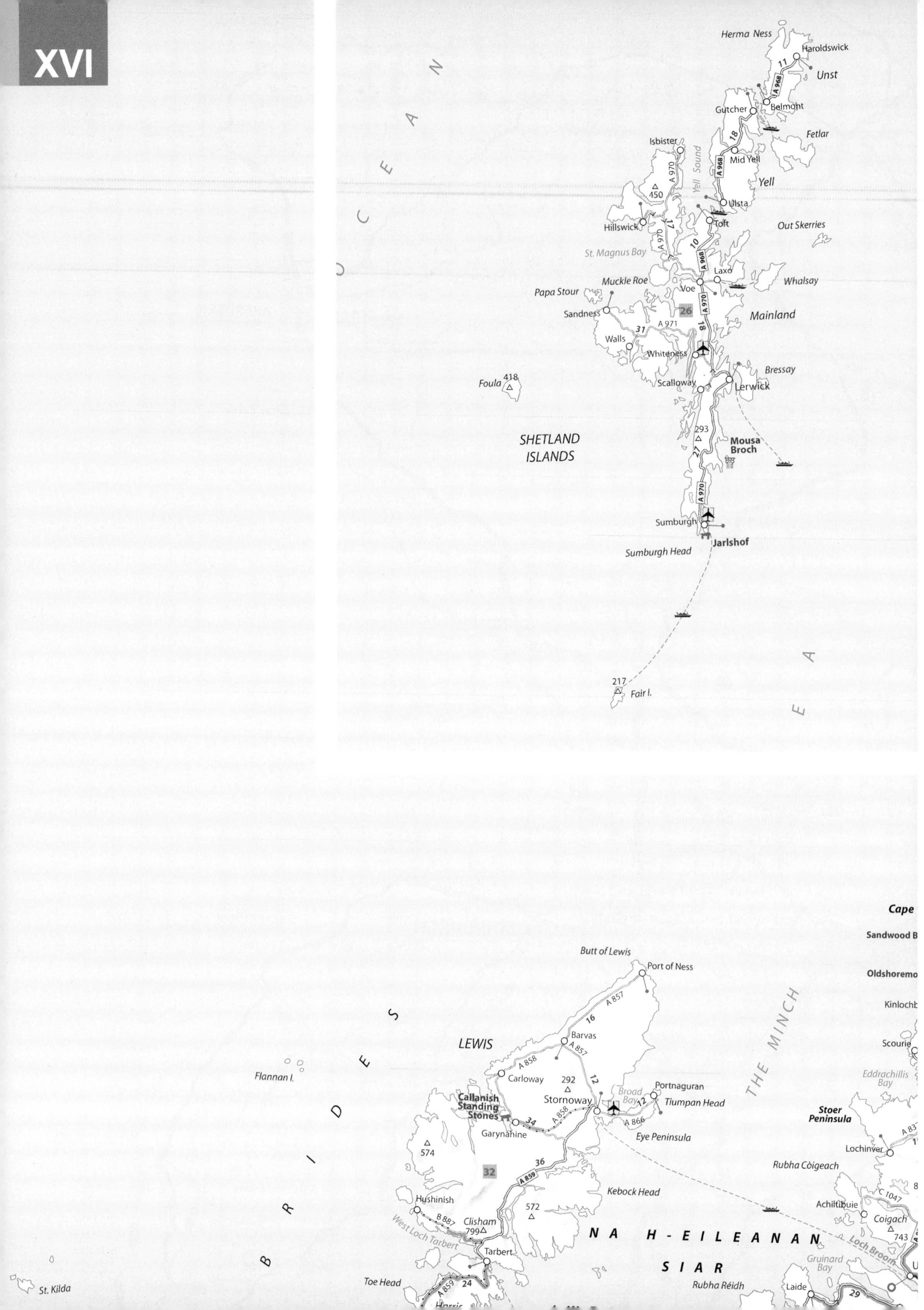

Herma Ness
Haroldswick
11
A 968
Unst
Gutcher
Belmont
Fetlar
18
Isbister
Yell Sound
A 970
450
A 968
Mid Yell
Yell
Ulsta
17
Toft
Hillswick
Out Skerries
A 970
10
St. Magnus Bay
A 968
Laxo
Muckle Roe
Whalsay
Papa Stour
Voe
26
A 970
Sandness
Mainland
A 971
31
18
Walls
Whiteness
Bressay
418
Foula
Scalloway
Lerwick
293
SHETLAND
ISLANDS
Mousa
Broch
27
A 970
Sumburgh
Jarlshof
Sumburgh Head
217
Fair I.
O
C
E
A
N
S
E
A
Cape
Sandwood B
Oldshoremo
Kinlochb
Butt of Lewis
Port of Ness
A 857
16
Barvas
A 857
LEWIS
THE MINCH
Scourie
Flannan I.
A 858
Carloway
292
12
Eddrachillis
Bay
Portnaguran
Callanish
Standing
Stones
Stornoway
Broad
Bay
12
Tiumpan Head
34
A 858
A 866
Stoer
Peninsula
Garynahine
Eye Peninsula
574
Lochinver
36
Rubha Còigeach
32
A 859
Kebock Head
Hushinish
572
Achiltibuie
C 1047
B 887
Clisham
799
Coigach
743
West Loch Tarbert
NA H-EILEANAN
Loch Broom
Tarbert
SIAR
Gruinard
Bay
Toe Head
A 859
24
Rubha Réidh
Laide
29
St. Kilda
H
E
B
R
I
D
E
S

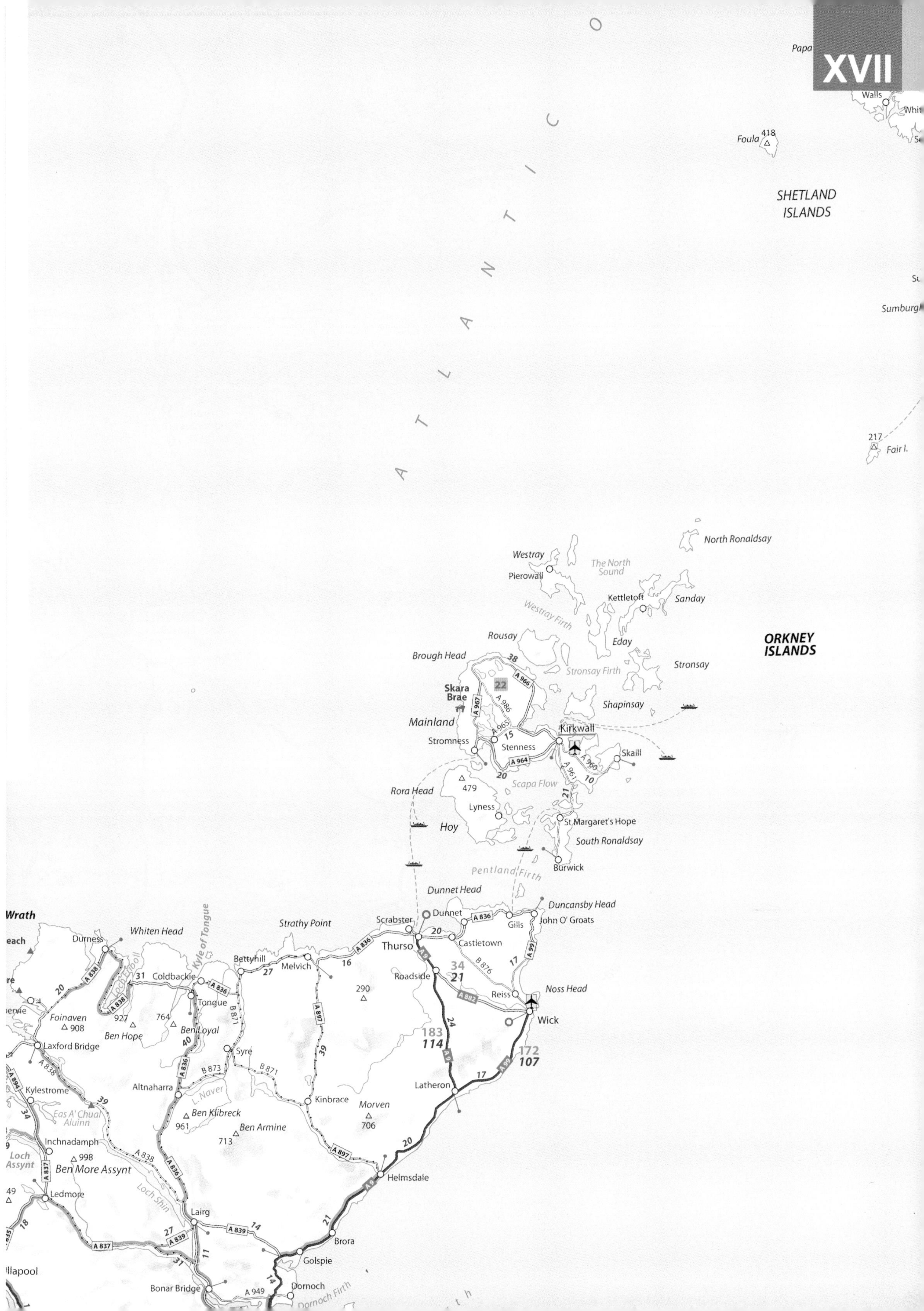
A T L A N T I C O
Papa
Walls
Foula
418
SHETLAND
ISLANDS
Sumburgh
217
Fair I.
North Ronaldsay
Westray
Pierowall
The North
Sound
Kettletoft
Sanday
Westray Firth
Rousay
Eday
ORKNEY
ISLANDS
Brough Head
38
A 966
Stronsay Firth
Stronsay
22
Skara
Brae
A 967
A 986
Shapinsay
Mainland
A 965
15
Kirkwall
Stromness
Stenness
Skaill
A 964
A 960
A 961
10
20
Scapa Flow
479
21
Rora Head
Lyness
Hoy
St Margaret's Hope
South Ronaldsay
Burwick
Pentland Firth
Dunnet Head
Duncansby Head
Wrath
Scrabster
Dunnet
A 836
Gills
John O' Groats
Whiten Head
Strathy Point
Durness
Kyle of Tongue
Loch Eriboll
20
Thurso
Castletown
A 836
Bettyhill
Melvich
16
A 838
31
Coldbackie
27
A 836
A 9
34
21
B 876
17
A 99
Roadside
Tongue
290
A 897
B 871
A 882
Reiss
Noss Head
Foinaven
908
927
764
Wick
Ben Hope
Ben Loyal
24
183
114
Laxford Bridge
40
Syre
39
172
107
A 838
B 873
B 871
A 836
A 99
17
A 894
Kylestrome
Altnaharra
Latheron
39
L. Naver
Kinbrace
34
Eas A' Chual
Aluinn
Ben Klibreck
Morven
961
Ben Armine
706
713
Inchnadamph
A 838
20
Loch
Assynt
998
A 897
A 837
Ben More Assynt
A 836
A 9
Helmsdale
Ledmore
Loch Shin
18
21
Lairg
A 839
14
27
A 839
A 837
Brora
31
11
Golspie
Ullapool
14
Bonar Bridge
A 949
Dornoch
Dornoch Firth

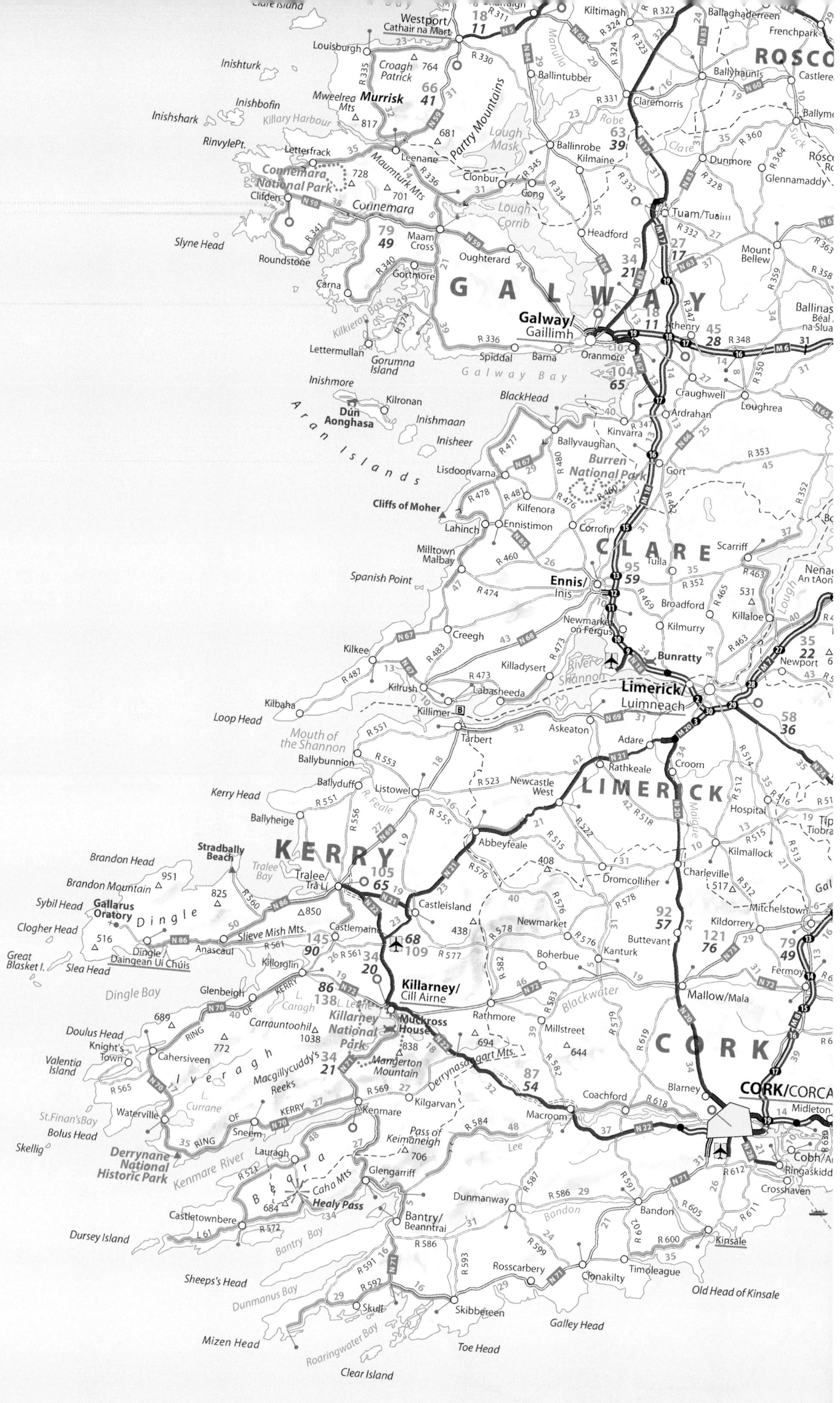

Westport/
Cathair na Mart
Kiltimagh
Ballaghaderreen
Frenchpark
ROSCO
Louisburgh
Inishturk
Croagh Patrick
Ballintubber
Ballyhaunis
Castlerea
Inishbofin
Mweelrea Mts
Murrisk
Partry Mountains
Claremorris
Inishshark
Killary Harbour
Lough Mask
RinvylePt.
Letterfrack
Leenane
Maumturk Mts
Ballinrobe
Kilmaine
Dunmore
Glennamaddy
Connemara National Park
Clonbur
Cong
Clifden
Connemara
Lough Corrib
Tuam/Tuaim
Headford
Slyne Head
Roundstone
Maam Cross
Oughterard
Mount Bellew
Carna
Gorthmore
GALWAY
Ballinasloe
Kilkieran Bay
Galway/
Gaillimh
Athenry
Lettermullan
Gorumna Island
Spiddal
Barna
Oranmore
Galway Bay
Inishmore
Dún Aonghasa
Kilronan
Black Head
Craughwell
Loughrea
Ardrahan
Inishmaan
Kinvarra
Inisheer
Ballyvaughan
Aran Islands
Burren National Park
Lisdoonvarna
Gort
Cliffs of Moher
Kilfenora
Lahinch
Ennistimon
Corrofin
CLARE
Scarriff
Milltown Malbay
Tulla
Spanish Point
Ennis/
Inis
Broadford
Killaloe
Lough Derg
Newmarket on Fergus
Kilmurry
Creegh
Kilkee
Bunratty
Newport
Killadysert
River Shannon
Kilrush
Labasheeda
Limerick/
Luimneach
Kilbaha
Killimer
Loop Head
Mouth of the Shannon
Tarbert
Askeaton
Adare
Ballybunnion
Rathkeale
Croom
Ballyduff
Listowel
Newcastle West
LIMERICK
Kerry Head
R. Feale
Hospital
Tipperary
Ballyheige
Abbeyfeale
Kilmallock
Stradbally Beach
Brandon Head
KERRY
Dromcolliher
Charleville
Brandon Mountain
Tralee Bay
Tralee/
Trá Lí
Mitchelstown
Sybil Head
Gallarus Oratory
Dingle
Castleisland
Kildorrery
Clogher Head
Slieve Mish Mts.
Castlemaine
Newmarket
Buttevant
Anascaul
Dingle
Daingean Uí Chúis
Kanturk
Great Blasket I.
Slea Head
Killorglin
Boherbue
Fermoy
Dingle Bay
Glenbeigh
Killarney/
Cill Airne
Blackwater
Mallow/Mala
L. Caragh
Rathmore
Carrauntoohil
Killarney National Park
Muckross House
Millstreet
Doulus Head
CORK
Knight's Town
Cahersiveen
Mangerton Mountain
Derrynasaggart Mts.
Valentia Island
Iveragh
Macgillycuddy's Reeks
L. Currane
Kilgarvan
Coachford
Blarney
CORK/CORCAIGH
St.Finan's Bay
Waterville
Kenmare
Macroom
Midleton
Bolus Head
Sneem
Pass of Keimaneigh
Skellig
Derrynane National Historic Park
Lauragh
Kenmare River
Lee
Cobh
Beara
Caha Mts.
Glengarriff
Ringaskiddy
Crosshaven
Healy Pass
Dunmanway
Bandon
Castletownbere
Bantry/
Beanntraí
Kinsale
Dursey Island
Bantry Bay
Rosscarbery
Clonakilty
Timoleague
Sheeps's Head
Dunmanus Bay
Skull
Skibbereen
Old Head of Kinsale
Galley Head
Mizen Head
Roaringwater Bay
Toe Head
Clear Island

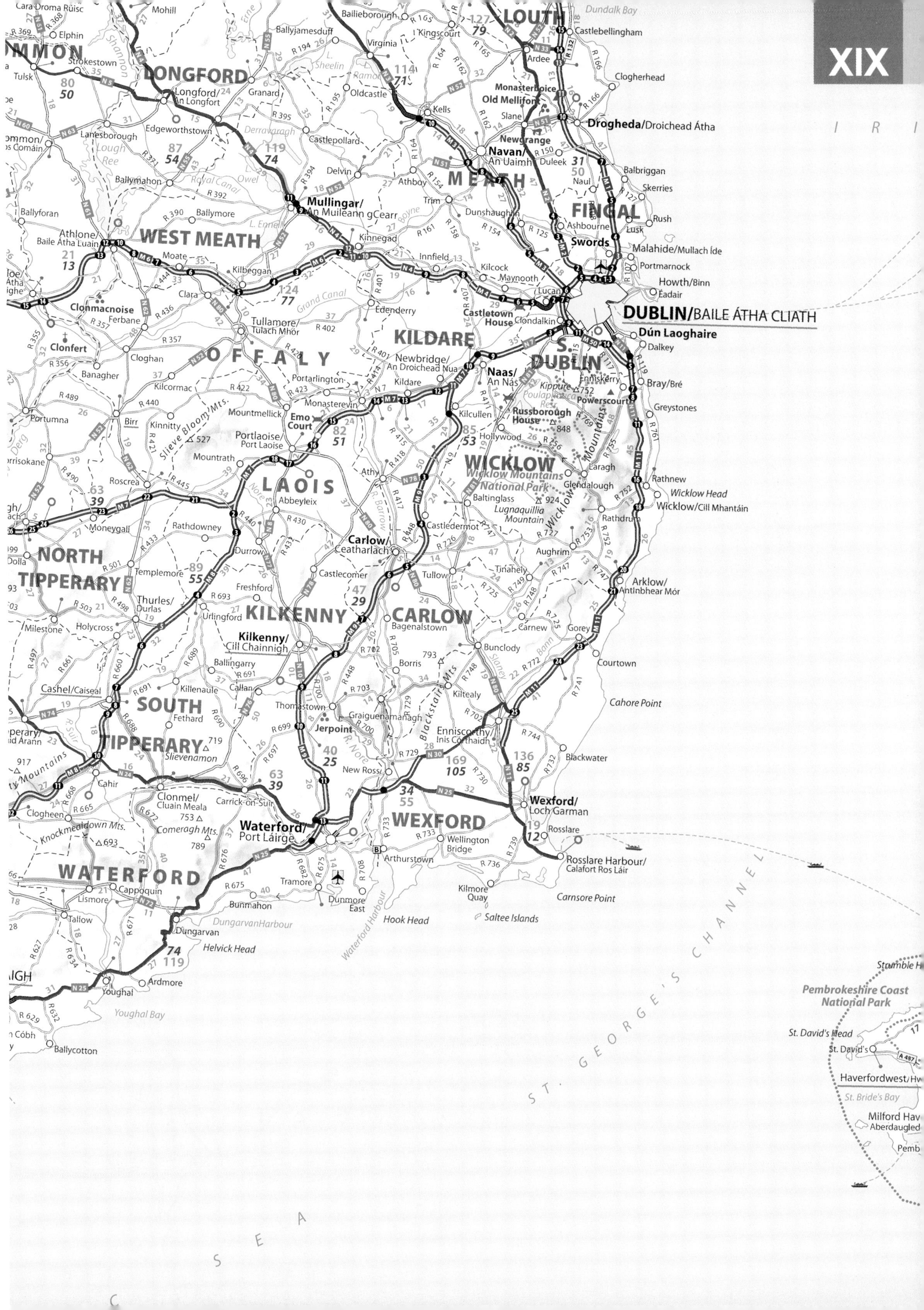
LONGFORD
Longford/An Longfort
WEST MEATH
Mullingar/An Muileann gCearr
Athlone/Baile Átha Luain
MEATH
Navan/An Uaimh
LOUTH
Dundalk Bay
Drogheda/Droichead Átha
FINGAL
Swords
Malahide/Mullach Íde
Howth/Binn Éadair
DUBLIN/BAILE ÁTHA CLIATH
Dún Laoghaire
S. DUBLIN
KILDARE
Naas/An Nás
Newbridge/An Droichead Nua
OFFALY
Tullamore/Tulach Mhór
LAOIS
Portlaoise/Port Laoise
WICKLOW
Wicklow Mountains National Park
Wicklow/Cill Mhantáin
Arklow/An tInbhear Mór
CARLOW
Carlow/Ceatharlach
KILKENNY
Kilkenny/Cill Chainnigh
NORTH TIPPERARY
SOUTH TIPPERARY
Clonmel/Cluain Meala
WATERFORD
Waterford/Port Láirge
Dungarvan
Youghal
WEXFORD
Wexford/Loch Garman
Enniscorthy/Inis Córthaidh
Rosslare Harbour/Calafort Ros Láir
Carnsore Point
Hook Head
Saltee Islands
ST. GEORGE'S CHANNEL
CELTIC SEA
Pembrokeshire Coast National Park
St. David's Head
St. David's
Haverfordwest
St. Bride's Bay
Milford Haven/Aberdaugleddau

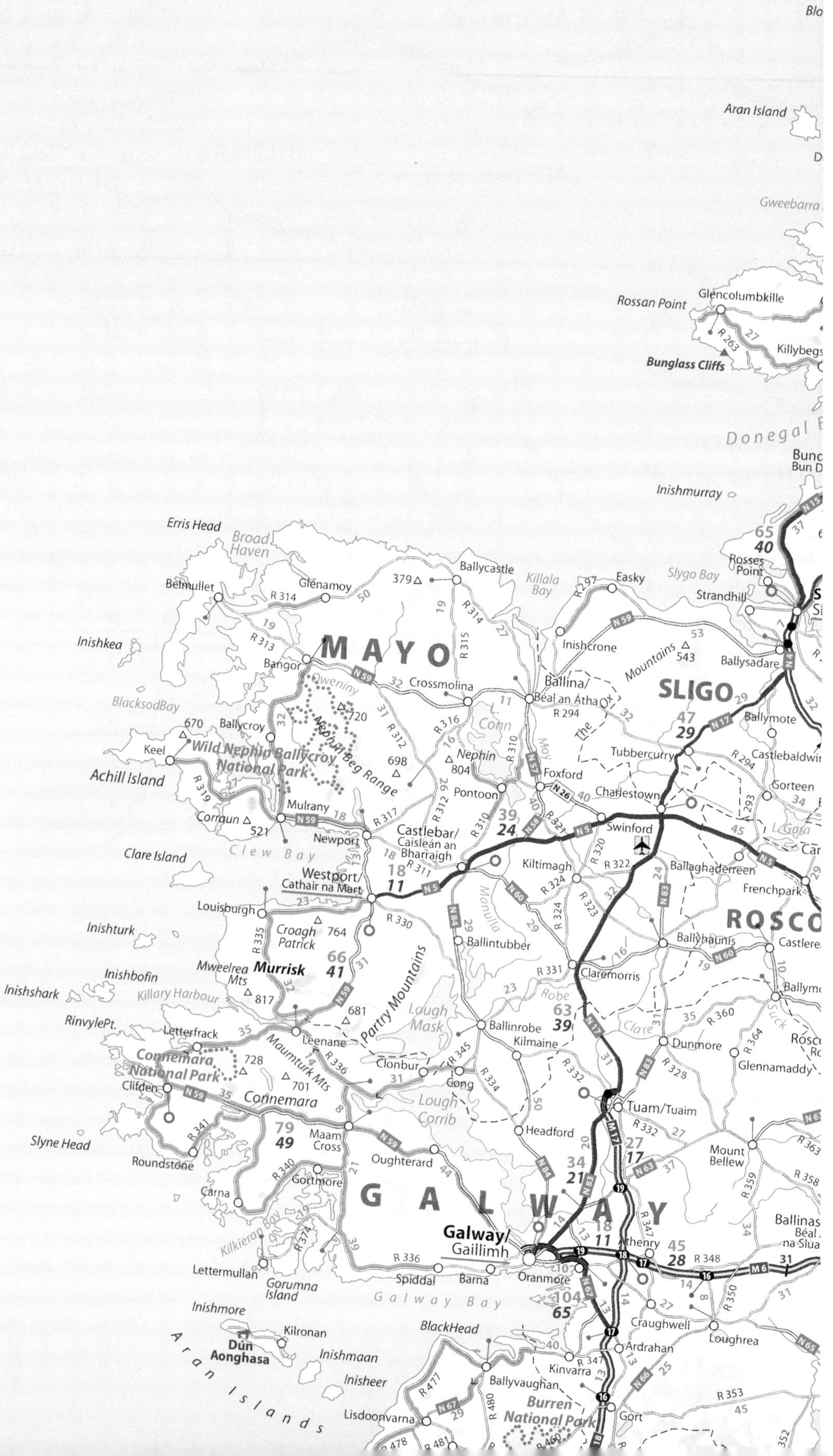
Aran Island
Rossan Point
Glencolumbkille
Killybegs
Bunglass Cliffs
Inishmurray
Erris Head
Broad Haven
Belmullet
Glenamoy
Ballycastle
Killala Bay
Easky
Slygo Bay
Rosses Point
Strandhill
Inishkea
MAYO
Bangor
Crossmolina
Inishcrone
Ballina/
Béal an Átha
SLIGO
Ballysadare
Mountains
Blacksod Bay
Ballycroy
Nephin Beg Range
Wild Nephin Ballycroy National Park
Keel
Achill Island
Nephin
Pontoon
Foxford
Tubbercurry
Ballymote
Castlebaldwin
Gorteen
Charlestown
Mulrany
Corraun
Clew Bay
Newport
Castlebar/
Caisleán an Bharraigh
Swinford
Clare Island
Westport/
Cathair na Mart
Kiltimagh
Ballaghaderreen
Frenchpark
Louisburgh
Croagh Patrick
Inishturk
Ballintubber
Ballyhaunis
Mweelrea Mts
Murrisk
Partry Mountains
Claremorris
Inishbofin
Inishshark
Killary Harbour
Lough Mask
Ballinrobe
Kilmaine
Dunmore
Glennamaddy
RinvylePt.
Letterfrack
Leenane
Connemara National Park
Maumturk Mts
Clonbur
Cong
Lough Corrib
Clifden
Connemara
Tuam/Tuaim
Headford
Maam Cross
Slyne Head
Roundstone
Oughterard
Mount Bellew
Gortmore
Carna
GALWAY
Galway/
Gaillimh
Kilkieran Bay
Athenry
Lettermullan
Gorumna Island
Spiddal
Barna
Oranmore
Galway Bay
Inishmore
Kilronan
Dún Aonghasa
Aran Islands
Inishmaan
Inisheer
BlackHead
Craughwell
Loughrea
Ardrahan
Kinvarra
Ballyvaughan
Burren National Park
Lisdoonvarna
Gort
Donegal Bay
Gweebarra

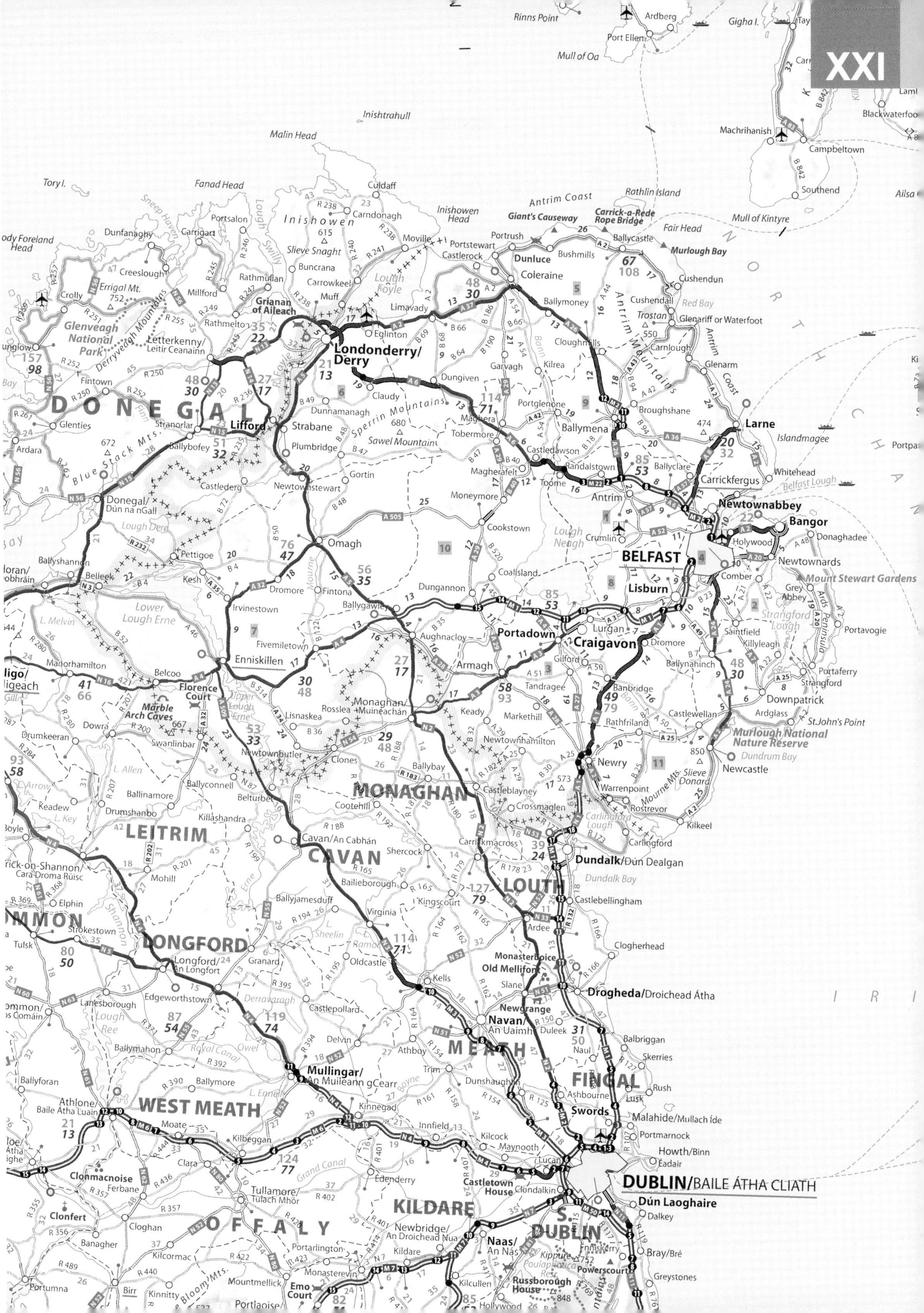
Rinns Point
Ardberg
Gigha I.
Port Ellen
Mull of Oa
Blackwaterfoot
Machrihanish
Campbeltown
Southend
Ailsa
Inishtrahull
Malin Head
Tory I.
Fanad Head
Culdaff
Inishowen
Inishowen Head
Antrim Coast
Rathlin Island
Giant's Causeway
Carrick-a-Rede Rope Bridge
Fair Head
Murlough Bay
Mull of Kintyre
Bloody Foreland Head
Dunfanaghy
Carrigart
Portsalon
Lough Swilly
Slieve Snaght
Moville
Portstewart
Castlerock
Portrush
Dunluce
Bushmills
Ballycastle
Creeslough
Errigal Mt. 752
Crolly
Buncrana
Rathmullan
Carrowkeel
Lough Foyle
Coleraine
Cushendun
Glenveagh National Park
Derryveagh Mountains
Millford
Rathmelton
Grianan of Aileach
Muff
Limavady
Ballymoney
Cushendall
Red Bay
Trostan 550
Glenariff or Waterfoot
Antrim Mountains
Letterkenny/ Leitir Ceanainn
Londonderry/ Derry
Eglinton
Cloughmills
Carnlough
Glenarm
Antrim Coast
Dunglow
Fintown
Dungiven
Garvagh
Kilrea
DONEGAL
Glenties
Ardara
Stranorlar
Ballybofey
Lifford
Strabane
Dunnamanagh
Claudy
Sperrin Mountains
Sawel Mountain 680
Portglenone
Broughshane
Ballymena
Larne
Islandmagee
Blue Stack Mts. 672
Plumbridge
Maghera
Tobermore
Castledawson
Randalstown
Ballyclare
Whitehead
Gortin
Magherafelt
Carrickfergus
Belfast Lough
Donegal/ Dún na nGall
Castlederg
Newtownstewart
Toome
Moneymore
Antrim
Newtownabbey
Bangor
Lough Derg
Omagh
Cookstown
Lough Neagh
Crumlin
Holywood
Donaghadee
Ballyshannon
Pettigoe
BELFAST
Newtownards
Belleek
Kesh
Dromore
Fintona
Coalisland
Comber
Mount Stewart Gardens
Lower Lough Erne
Irvinestown
Dungannon
Lisburn
Grey Abbey
Ards Peninsula
L. Melvin
Ballygawley
Portadown
Lurgan
Craigavon
Strangford Lough
Portavogie
Fivemiletown
Aughnacloy
Dromore
Saintfield
Killyleagh
Manorhamilton
Enniskillen
Armagh
Gilford
Ballynahinch
Portaferry
Sligo/ Sligeach
Belcoo
Florence Court
Marble Arch Caves
Upper Lough Erne
Monaghan/ Muineachán
Tandragee
Banbridge
Strangford
Downpatrick
Dowra
Rosslea
Lisnaskea
Keady
Markethill
Ardglass
St.John's Point
Drumkeeran
Swanlinbar
Castlewellan
Rathfriland
Murlough National Nature Reserve
Newtownbutler
Clones
Newtownhamilton
Dundrum Bay
Newcastle
Slieve Donard 850
L. Allen
Ballybay
Newry
Ballyconnell
MONAGHAN
Castleblayney
Warrenpoint
Mourne Mts.
Rostrevor
Lough Arrow
Ballinamore
Belturbet
Keadew
Drumshanbo
Killashandra
Cootehill
Crossmaglen
Carlingford Lough
Kilkeel
Boyle
LEITRIM
Cavan/An Cabhán
Carrickmacross
Carlingford
Carrick-on-Shannon/ Cara Droma Rúisc
CAVAN
Shercock
Dundalk/Dún Dealgan
Mohill
Bailieborough
LOUTH
Dundalk Bay
Elphin
Kingscourt
Castlebellingham
ROSCOMMON
Ballyjamesduff
Strokestown
Virginia
Lough Sheelin
Ardee
Tulsk
LONGFORD
Clogherhead
Granard
Longford/ An Longfort
Oldcastle
Monasterboice
Old Mellifont
Kells
Slane
Drogheda/Droichead Átha
Lanesborough
Edgeworthstown
Derravaragh
Castlepollard
Newgrange
Navan/ An Uaimh
Duleek
Roscommon/ Ros Comáin
Lough Ree
Naul
Balbriggan
Ballymahon
Royal Canal
Delvin
Athboy
MEATH
Skerries
Ballyforan
Ballymore
Mullingar/ An Muileann gCearr
Trim
Dunshaughlin
FINGAL
Rush
Athlone/ Baile Átha Luain
WEST MEATH
Lough Ennell
Kinnegad
Ashbourne
Lusk
Swords
Malahide/Mullach Íde
Moate
Kilbeggan
Innfield
Kilcock
Portmarnock
Maynooth
Howth/Binn Éadair
Clara
Lucan
Clonmacnoise
Ferbane
Tullamore/ Tulach Mhór
Grand Canal
Edenderry
Castletown House
Clondalkin
DUBLIN/BAILE ÁTHA CLIATH
Dún Laoghaire
Dalkey
Clonfert
Cloghan
OFFALY
KILDARE
S. DUBLIN
Newbridge/ An Droichead Nua
Naas/ An Nás
Banagher
Portarlington
Kildare
Kippure 752
Enniskerry
Bray/Bré
Kilcormac
Powerscourt
Portumna
Birr
Kinnitty
Slieve Bloom Mts.
Mountmellick
Monasterevin
Emo Court
Kilcullen
Russborough House
Greystones
Portlaoise
Hollywood

Key

Roads
Motorway - Service areas
Dual carriageway with motorway characteristics
Interchanges: complete, limited
Interchange numbers
International and national road network
Interregional and less congested road
Road surfaced - unsurfaced
Footpath - Waymarked footpath / Bridle path
Motorway / Road under construction (when available: with scheduled opening date)

Road widths
Dual carriageway
4 lanes - 2 wide lanes
2 lanes - 2 narrow lanes

Distances (total and intermediate)
Toll roads on motorway
Toll-free section on motorway
in miles - in kilometers
on road

Numbering - Signs
Motorway - GB: Primary route
IRL : National primary and secondary route
Other roads
Destination on primary route network

Obstacles
Roundabout - Pass and its height above sea level (meters)
Steep hill (ascent in direction of the arrow)
IRL: Difficult or dangerous section of road
In Scotland: narrow road with passing places
Level crossing: railway passing, under road, over road
Prohibited road - Road subject to restrictions
Toll barrier - One way road
Height limit under 15'6" IRL, 16'6" GB
Load limit (under 16 t.)

Transportation
Railway - Passenger station
Airport - Airfield
Transportation of vehicles: (seasonal services in red)
by boat
by ferry (load limit in tons)
Ferry (passengers and cycles only)

Accommodation - Administration
Administrative boundaries
Scottish and Welsh borders
National boundary - Customs post

Sport & Recreation Facilities
Golf course - Horse racetrack
Racing circuit - Pleasure boat harbour
Caravan and camping sites
Waymarked footpath - Country park
Safari park, zoo - Bird sanctuary, refuge
IRL: Fishing - Greyhound track
Tourist train
Funicular, cable car, chairlift

Sights
Principal sights: see THE GREEN GUIDE
Towns or places of interest, Places to stay
Religious building - Historic house, castle
Ruins - Prehistoric monument - Cave
Garden, park - Other places of interest
IRL: Fort - Celtic cross - Round Tower
Panoramic view - Viewpoint
Scenic route

Other signs
Industrial cable way
Telecommunications tower or mast - Lighthouse
Power station - Quarry
Mine - Industrial activity
Refinery - Cliff
National forest park - National park

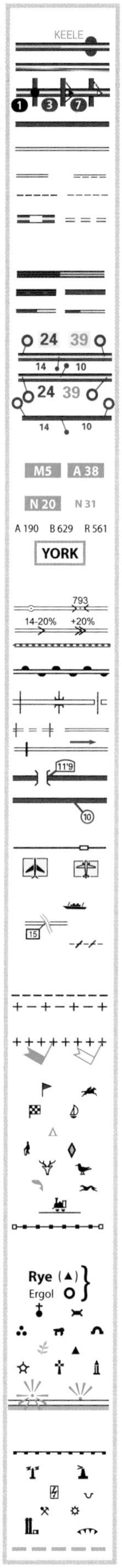

Légende

Routes
Autoroute - Aires de service
Double chaussée de type autoroutier
Échangeurs : complet, partiels
Numéros d'échangeurs
Route de liaison internationale ou nationale
Route de liaison interrégionale ou de dégagement
Route revêtue - non revêtue
Sentier - Sentier balisé/Allée cavalière
Autoroute - Route en construction (le cas échéant : date de mise en service prévue)

Largeur des routes
Chaussées séparées
4 voies - 2 voies larges
2 voies - 2 voies étroites

Distances (totalisées et partielles)
Section à péage sur autoroute
Section libre sur autoroute
en miles - en kilomètres
sur route

Numérotation - Signalisation
Autoroute - GB : itinéraire principal (Primary route)
IRL : itinéraire principal (National primary et secondary route)
Autres routes
Localités jalonnant les itinéraires principaux

Obstacles
Rond-point - Col et sa cote d'altitude (en mètres)
Forte déclivité (flèches dans le sens de la montée)
IRL : Parcours difficile ou dangereux
En Écosse : route très étroite avec emplacements pour croisement
Passages de la route : à niveau, supérieur, inférieur
Route interdite - Route réglementée
Barrière de péage - Route à sens unique
Hauteur limitée au dessous de 15'6" IRL, 16'6"GB
Limites de charge (au-dessous de 16 t.)

Transports
Voie ferrée - Gare
Aéroport - Aérodrome
Transport des autos: (liaison saisonnière en rouge)
par bateau
par bac (charge maximum en tonnes)
Bac pour piétons et cycles

Hébergement - Administration
Limites administratives
Limite de l'Écosse et du Pays de Galles
Frontière - Douane

Sports - Loisirs
Golf - Hippodrome
Circuit automobile - Port de plaisance
Camping, caravaning
Sentier balisé - Base ou parc de loisirs
Parc animalier, zoo - Réserve d'oiseaux
IRL : Pêche - Cynodrome
Train touristique
Funiculaire, téléphérique, télésiège

Curiosités
Principales curiosités : voir LE GUIDE VERT
Localités ou sites intéressants, lieux de séjour
Édifice religieux - Château
Ruines - Monument mégalithique - Grotte
Jardin, parc - Autres curiosités
IRL : Fort - Croix celte - Tour ronde
Panorama - Point de vue
Parcours pittoresque

Signes divers
Transporteur industriel aérien
Tour ou pylône de télécommunications - Phare
Centrale électrique - Carrière
Mine - Industries
Raffinerie - Falaise
Parc forestier national - Parc national

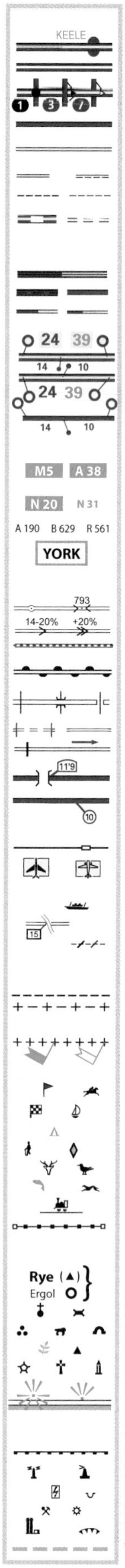

Zeichenerklärung

Straßen
Autobahn - Tankstelle mit Raststätte
Schnellstraße mit getrennten Fahrbahnen
Anschlussstellen: Voll - bzw. Teilanschlussstellen
Anschlussstellennummern
Internationale bzw.nationale Hauptverkehrsstraße
Überregionale Verbindungsstraße oder Umleitungsstrecke
Straße mit Belag - ohne Belag
Pfad - Ausgeschilderter Weg / Reitpfad
Autobahn - Straße im Bau (ggf. voraussichtliches Datum der Verkehrsfreigabe)

Straßenbreiten
Getrennte Fahrbahnen
4 Fahrspuren - 2 breite Fahrspuren
2 Fahrspuren - 1 Fahrspur

Entfernungen (Gesamt- und Teilentfernungen)
Mautstrecke auf der Autobahn
Mautfreie Strecke auf der Autobahn
in Meilen - in Kilometern
Auf der Straße

Nummerierung - Wegweisung
Autobahn - GB: Empfohlene Fernverkehrsstraße (Primary route)
IRL: Empfohlene Fernverkehrsstraße (National primary und secondary route)
Sonstige Straßen
Richtungshinweis auf der empfohlenen Fernverkehrsstraße

Verkehrshindernisse
Verkehrsinsel - Pass mit Höhenangabe (in Meter)
Starke Steigung (Steigung in Pfeilrichtung)
IRL: Schwierige oder gefährliche Strecke
In Schottland: sehr schmale Straße mit Ausweichstellen (passing places)
Bahnübergänge: schienengleich, Unterführung, Überführung
Gesperrte Straße - Straße mit Verkehrsbeschränkungen
Mautstelle - Einbahnstraße
Beschränkung der Durchfahrtshöhe bis 15'6" IRL, 16'6' GB
Höchstbelastung (angegeben, wenn unter 16 t)

Verkehrsmittel
Bahnlinie - Bahnhof
Flughafen - Flugplatz
Autotransport: (rotes Zeichen: saisonbedingte Verbindung)
per Schiff
per Fähre (Höchstbelastung in t)
Fähre für Personen und Fahrräder

Unterkunft - Verwaltung
Verwaltungshauptstadt
Grenze von Schottland und Wales
Staatsgrenze - Zoll

Sport - Freizeit
Golfplatz - Pferderennbahn
Rennstrecke - Yachthafen
Campingplatz
Ausgeschilderter Weg - Freizeitanlage
Tierpark, Zoo - Vogelschutzgebiet
IRL: Angeln - Windhundrennen
Museumseisenbahn
Standseilbahn, Seilbahn, Sessellift

Sehenswürdigkeiten
Hauptsehenswürdigkeiten: siehe GRÜNER REISEFÜHRER
Sehenswerte Orte, Ferienorte
Sakral-Bau - Schloss, Burg
Ruine - Vorgeschichtliches Steindenkmal - Höhle
Garten, Park - Sonstige Sehenswürdigkeit
IRL: Fort, Festung - Keltisches Kreuz - Rundturm
Rundblick - Aussichtspunkt
Landschaftlich schöne Strecke

Sonstige Zeichen
Industrieschwebebahn
Funk-, Sendeturm - Leuchtturm
Kraftwerk - Steinbruch
Bergwerk - Industrieanlagen
Raffinerie - Klippen
Waldschutzgebiet - Nationalpark

Verklaring van de tekens

Wegen
Autosnelweg - Serviceplaatsen
Gescheiden rijbanen van het type autosnelweg
Aansluitingen: volledig, gedeeltelijk
Afritnummers
Internationale of nationale verbindingsweg
Interregionale verbindingsweg

Verharde weg - Onverharde weg
Pad - Bewegwijzerd wandelpad / Ruiterpad
Autosnelweg in aanleg - weg in aanleg (indien bekend: datum openstelling)

Breedte van de wegen
Gescheiden rijbanen
4 rijstroken - 2 brede rijstroken
2 rijstroken - 2 smalle rijstroken

Afstanden (totaal en gedeeltelijk)
Gedeelte met tol op autosnelwegen
Tolvrij gedeelte op autosnelwegen
in mijlen - in kilometers
op andere wegen

Wegnummers - Bewegwijzering
Autosnelweg - GB: Hoofdweg (Primary route)
IRL: Hoofdweg (National primary en secondary route)
Andere wegen
Plaatsen langs een autosnelweg of Primary route met bewegwijzering

Hindernissen
Rotonde - Bergpas en hoogte boven de zeespiegel (in meters)
Steile helling (pijlen in de richting van de helling)
IRL: Moeilijk of gevaarlijk traject
In Schotland: smalle weg met uitwijkplaatsen

Wegovergangen: gelijkvloers, overheen, onderdoor
Verboden weg - Beperkt opengestelde weg
Tol - Weg met eenrichtingsverkeer
Vrije hoogte indien lager dan 15'6" IRL, 16'6" GB
Maximum draagvermogen (indien minder dan 16 t)

Vervoer
Spoorweg - Reizigersstation
Luchthaven - Vliegveld
Vervoer van auto's: (tijdens het seizoen: rood teken)
per boot
per veerpont (maximum draagvermogen in t.)
Veerpont voor voetgangers en fietsers

Verblijf - Administratie
Administratieve grenzen
Grens van Schotland en Wales

Staatsgrens - Douanekantoor

Sport - Recreatie
Golfterrein - Renbaan
Autocircuit - Jachthaven
Kampeerterrein (tent, caravan)
Sentiero segnalato - Recreatiepark
Safaripark, dierentuin - Vogelreservaat
IRL: Vissen - Hondenrenbaan
Toeristentreintje
Kabelspoor, kabelbaan, stoeltjeslift

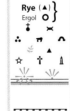

Bezienswaardigheden
Belangrijkste bezienswaardigheden: zie DE GROENE GIDS
Interessante steden of plaatsen, vakantieoorden
Kerkelijk gebouw - Kasteel
Ruïne - Megaliet - Grot
Tuin, park - Andere bezienswaardigheden
IRL: Fort - Keltisch kruis - Ronde toren
Panorama - Uitzichtpunt
Schilderachtig traject

Diverse tekens
Kabelvrachtvervoer
Telecommunicatietoren of -mast - Vuurtoren
Elektriciteitscentrale - Steengroeve
Mijn - Industrie
Raffinaderij - Klif
Staatsbos - Nationaal park

Legenda

Strade
Autostrada - Aree di servizio
Doppia carreggiata di tipo autostradale
Svincoli: completo, parziale
Svincoli numerati
Strada di collegamento internazionale o nazionale
Strada di collegamento interregionale o di disimpegno

Strada rivestita - non rivestita
Sentiero - Sentiero segnalato / Pista per cavalli
Autostrada, strada in costruzione (data di apertura prevista)

Larghezza delle strade
Carreggiate separate
4 corsie - 2 corsie larghe
2 corsie - 2 corsie strette

Distanze (totali e parziali)
Tratto a pedaggio su autostrada
Tratto esente da pedaggio su autostrada
in migla - in chilometri
su strada

Numerazione - Segnaletica
Autostrada - GB: itinerario principale (Strada «Primary»)
IRL: itinerario principale (Strada «National primary» e «Secondary»)
Altre Strade
Località delimitante gli itinerari principali

Ostacoli
Rotonda - Passo ed altitudine (in metri)
Forte pendenza (salita nel senso della freccia)
IRL: Percorso difficile o pericoloso
In Scozia: Strada molto stretta con incrocio

Passaggi della strada: a livello, cavalcavia, sottopassaggio
Strada vietata - Strada a circolazione regolamentata
Casello - Strada a senso unico
Limite di altezza inferiore a 15'6" IRL, 16'6"GB
Limite di portata (inferiore a 16 t.)

Trasporti
Ferrovia - Stazione viaggiatori
Aeroporto - Aerodromo
Trasporto auto: (stagionale in rosso)
su traghetto
su chiatta (carico massimo in t.)
Traghetto per pedoni e biciclette

Risorse alberghiere - Amministrazione
Confini amministrativi
Confine di Scozia e Galles

Frontiera - Dogana

Sport - Divertimento
Golf - Ippodromo
Circuito Automobilistico - Porto turistico
Campeggi, caravaning
Sentiero segnalato - Area o parco per attività ricreative
Parco con animali, zoo - Riserva ornitologica
IRL: Pesca - Cinodromo
Trenino turistico
Funicolare, funivia, seggiovia

Mete e luoghi d'interesse
Principali luoghi d'interesse, vedere LA GUIDA VERDE
Località o siti interessanti, luoghi di soggiorno
Edificio religioso - Castello
Rovine - Monumento megalitico - Grotta
Giardino, parco - Altri luoghi d'interesse
IRL: Forte - Croce celtica - Torre rotonda
Panorama - Vista
Percorso pittoresco

Simboli vari
Teleferica industriale
Torre o pilone per telecomunicazioni - Faro
Centrale elettrica - Cava
Miniera - Industrie
Raffineria - Falesia
Parco forestale nazionale - Parco nazionale

Signos convencionales

Carreteras
Autopista - Áreas de servicio
Autovía
Enlaces: completo, parciales
Números de los accesos
Carretera de comunicación internacional o nacional
Carretera de comunicación interregional o alternativo

Carretera asfaltada - sin asfaltar
Sendero - Sendero señalizado / Camino de caballos
Autopista, carretera en construcción (en su caso: fecha prevista de entrada en servicio)

Ancho de las carreteras
Calzadas separadas
Cuatro carriles - Dos carriles anchos
Dos carriles - Dos carriles estrechos

Distancias (totales y parciales)
Tramo de peaje en autopista
Tramo libre en autopista
en millas - en kilómetros
en carretera

Numeración - Señalización
Autopista - GB: Vía principal (Primary route)
IRL: Vía principal (National primary et secondary route)
Otras carreteras
Localidad en itinerario principal

Obstáculos
Rotonda - Puerto y su altitud (en métros)
Pendiente Pronunciada (las flechas indican el sentido del ascenso)
IRL: Recorrido difícil o peligroso
En escocia: carretera muy estrecha con ensanchamientos para poder cruzarse

Pasos de la carretera: a nivel, superior, inferior
Tramo prohibido - Carretera restringida
Barrera de peaje - Carretera de sentido único
Altura limitada (15'6" IRL, 16'6"GB)
Limite de carga (inferior a 16 t)

Transportes
Línea férrea - Estación de viajeros
Aeropuerto - Aeródromo
Transporte de coches: (Enlace de temporada: signo rojo)
por barco
por barcaza (carga máxima en toneladas)
Barcaza para el paso de peatones y vehículos dos ruedas

Alojamiento - Administración
Limites administrativos
Limites de Escocia y del País de Gales

Frontera - Puesto de aduanas

Deportes - Ocio
Golf - Hipódromo
Circuito de velocidad - Puerto deportivo
Camping, caravaning
Sendero señalizado - Parque de ocio
Reserva de animales, zoo - Reserva de pájaros
IRL: Pêche - Cynodrome
Tren turístico
Funicular, Teleférico, telesilla

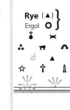

Curiosidades
Principales curiosidades: ver LA GUÍA VERDE
Localidad o lugar interesante, lugar para quedarse
Edificio religioso - Castillo
Ruinas - Monumento megalítico - Cueva
Jardín, parque - Curiosidades diversas
IRL: Fortaleza - Cruz celta - Torre redonda
Vista panorámica - Vista parcial
Recorrido pintoresco

Signos diversos
Transportador industrial aéreo
Emisor de Radiodifusión - Faro
Central eléctrica - Cantera
Mina - Industrias
Refinería - Acantilado
Parque forestal nacional - Parque nacional

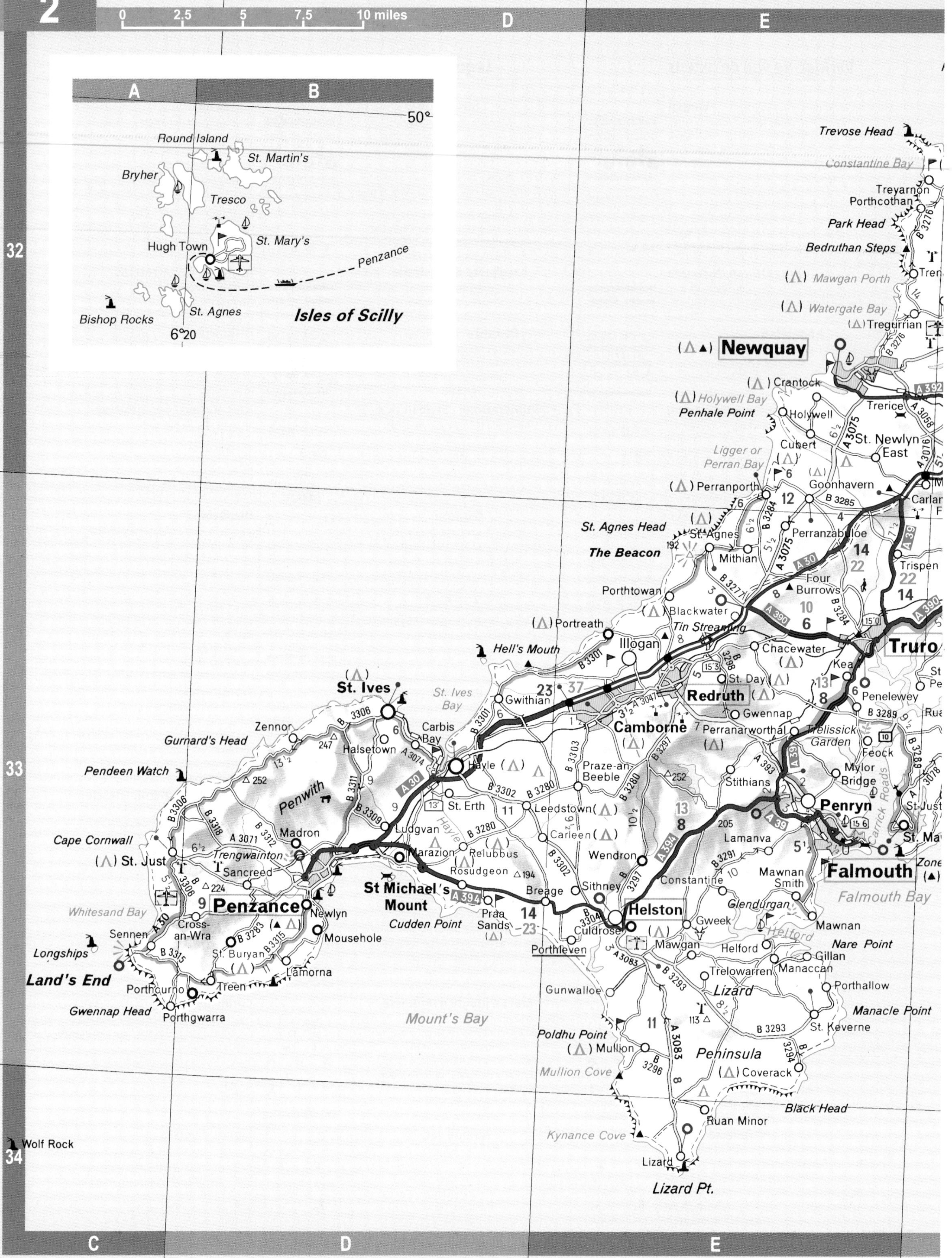
0 2.5 5 7.5 10 miles
D
E
Isles of Scilly
50°
6°20
A
B
Round Island
St. Martin's
Bryher
Tresco
Hugh Town
St. Mary's
Penzance
St. Agnes
Bishop Rocks
32
33
34
Trevose Head
Constantine Bay
Treyarnon
Porthcothan
Park Head
Bedruthan Steps
Mawgan Porth
Watergate Bay
Tregurrian
Newquay
Crantock
Holywell Bay
Penhale Point
Holywell
Trerice
Cubert
St. Newlyn East
Ligger or Perran Bay
Perranporth
Goonhavern
St. Agnes Head
The Beacon
St. Agnes
Mithian
Perranzabuloe
Trispen
Porthtowan
Four Burrows
Blackwater
Tin Streaming
Portreath
Hell's Mouth
Illogan
Chacewater
Kea
Truro
St. Ives
St. Ives Bay
Gwithian
Redruth
St. Day
Penelewey
Camborne
Gwennap
Zennor
Carbis Bay
Halsetown
Perranarworthal
Trelissick Garden
Feock
Gurnard's Head
Pendeen Watch
Penwith
Hayle
Praze-an-Beeble
Stithians
Mylor Bridge
Carrick Roads
St. Erth
Leedstown
Penryn
St. Just
Cape Cornwall
Madron
Ludgvan
Carleen
Lamanva
Falmouth
Trengwainton
Marazion
Relubbus
Wendron
Sancreed
Rosudgeon
Constantine
Mawnan Smith
St Michael's Mount
Breage
Sithney
Falmouth Bay
Whitesand Bay
Penzance
Newlyn
Praa Sands
Helston
Glendurgan
Cross-an-Wra
Cudden Point
Culdrose
Gweek
Mawnan
Sennen
Mousehole
Porthleven
Helford
Nare Point
Longships
St. Buryan
Mawgan
Gillan
Land's End
Lamorna
Trelowarren
Manaccan
Porthcurno
Treen
Lizard
Porthallow
Gunwalloe
Gwennap Head
Porthgwarra
Manacle Point
Mount's Bay
St. Keverne
Poldhu Point
Mullion
Peninsula
Mullion Cove
Coverack
Black Head
Ruan Minor
Wolf Rock
Kynance Cove
Lizard
Lizard Pt.
C
D
E

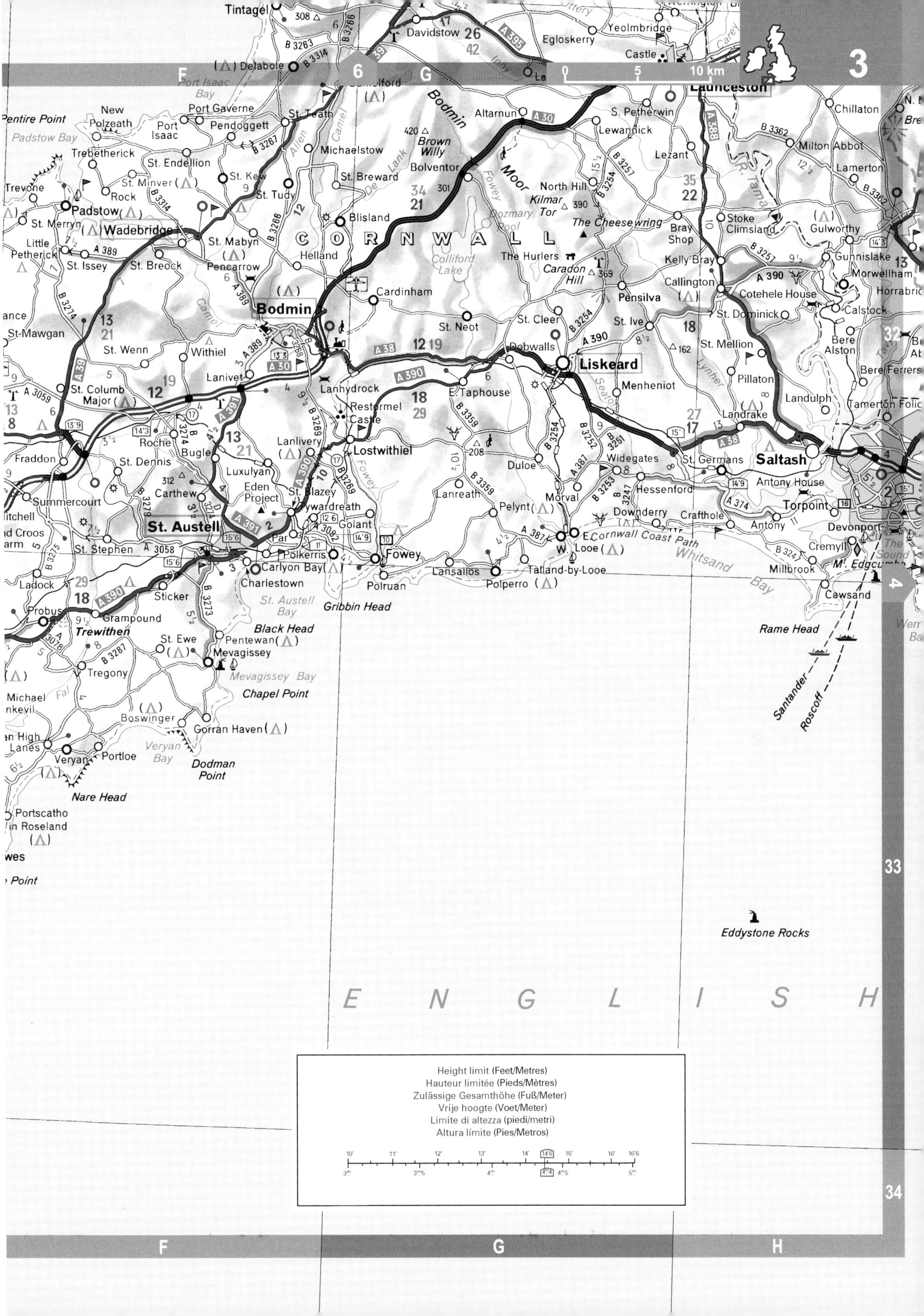
Tintagel
Davidstow
Yeolmbridge
Egloskerry
Castle
Delabole
Camelford
Launceston
Port Isaac Bay
Pentire Point
New Polzeath
Port Gaverne
Port Isaac
Pendoggett
St. Teath
Padstow Bay
Trebetherick
St. Endellion
Michaelstow
Brown Willy
Bodmin Moor
Altarnun
S. Petherwin
Lewannick
Chillaton
Milton Abbot
Lezant
Lamerton
Trevone
St. Minver
Rock
St. Kew
St. Tudy
St. Breward
Bolventor
North Hill
Kilmar Tor
Padstow
St. Merryn
Wadebridge
Little Petherick
St. Issey
St. Breock
St. Mabyn
Blisland
CORNWALL
Dozmary Pool
The Cheesewring
Bray Shop
Stoke Climsland
Gulworthy
Gunnislake
Morwellham
Pencarrow
Helland
Colliford Lake
The Hurlers
Caradon Hill
Kelly Bray
Callington
Cotehele House
Calstock
Horrabridge
Cardinham
Pensilva
St. Dominick
Bodmin
St. Neot
St. Cleer
St. Ive
Bere Alston
St-Mawgan
St. Wenn
Withiel
Dobwalls
Liskeard
St. Mellion
Bere Ferrers
Lanivet
Lanhydrock
Menheniot
Pillaton
St. Columb Major
Restormel Castle
E. Taphouse
Landulph
Tamerton Foliot
Landrake
Fraddon
Roche
Bugle
Lanlivery
Lostwithiel
St. Dennis
Luxulyan
Duloe
Widegates
St. Germans
Saltash
Eden Project
St. Blazey
Hessenford
Antony House
Carthew
Lanreath
Morval
Summercourt
Tywardreath
Pelynt
Downderry
Crafthole
Torpoint
Golant
Antony
Devonport
St. Austell
St. Stephen
Par
Polkerris
Fowey
E. Looe
W. Looe
Cornwall Coast Path
Whitsand Bay
Cremyll
The Sound
Ladock
Carlyon Bay
Lansallos
Polperro
Talland-by-Looe
Millbrook
Mt. Edgcumbe
Charlestown
Polruan
Cawsand
St. Austell Bay
Gribbin Head
Probus
Grampound
Sticker
Trewithen
Black Head
Pentewan
Rame Head
St. Ewe
Mevagissey
Tregony
Mevagissey Bay
Chapel Point
Santander
Roscoff
Boswinger
Gorran Haven
Veryan
Portloe
Veryan Bay
Dodman Point
Nare Head
Portscatho
Eddystone Rocks
E N G L I S H
Height limit (Feet/Metres)
Hauteur limitée (Pieds/Mètres)
Zulässige Gesamthöhe (Fuß/Meter)
Vrije hoogte (Voet/Meter)
Limite di altezza (piedi/metri)
Altura límite (Pies/Metros)
F
G
H
0 5 10 km

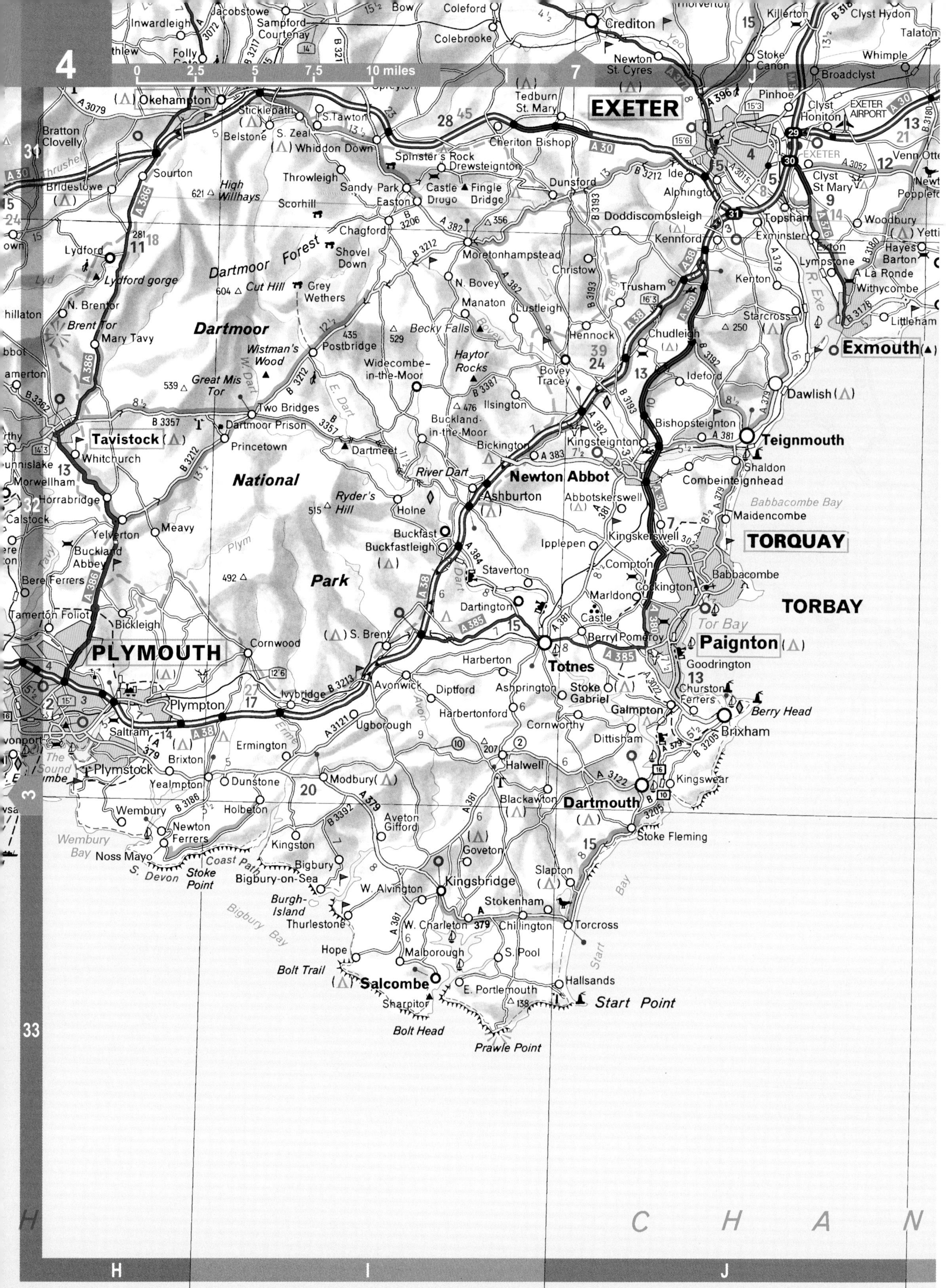

4
0
2,5
5
7,5
10 miles
7
Okehampton
EXETER
Crediton
Jacobstowe
Inwardleigh
Sampford Courtenay
Bow
Coleford
Colebrooke
Newton St. Cyres
Killerton
Clyst Hydon
Talaton
Whimple
Stoke Canon
Broadclyst
Pinhoe
Clyst Honiton
EXETER AIRPORT
Tedburn St. Mary
Sticklepath
S. Tawton
Belstone
S. Zeal
Whiddon Down
Cheriton Bishop
Bratton Clovelly
Sourton
Bridestowe
Spinster's Rock
Drewsteignton
Throwleigh
Sandy Park
Castle Drogo
Fingle Bridge
Dunsford
Ide
Alphington
Clyst St Mary
Venn Ottery
High Willhays
Scorhill
Easton
Chagford
Doddiscombsleigh
Topsham
Woodbury
Exminster
Exton
Kennford
Lydford
Lydford gorge
Dartmoor Forest
Shovel Down
Moretonhampstead
Christow
Lympstone
Hayes Barton
A La Ronde
Withycombe
Cut Hill
Grey Wethers
N. Bovey
Trusham
Kenton
N. Brentor
Brent Tor
Mary Tavy
Dartmoor
Manaton
Lustleigh
Starcross
Littleham
Exmouth
Becky Falls
Hennock
Chudleigh
Postbridge
Wistman's Wood
Widecombe-in-the-Moor
Haytor Rocks
Bovey Tracey
Ideford
Dawlish
Great Mis Tor
Two Bridges
Ilsington
Bishopsteignton
Tavistock
Dartmoor Prison
Buckland-in-the-Moor
Kingsteignton
Teignmouth
Whitchurch
Princetown
Dartmeet
Bickington
Shaldon
Morwellham
National
River Dart
Newton Abbot
Combeinteignhead
Horrabridge
Ryder's Hill
Ashburton
Abbotskerswell
Babbacombe Bay
Calstock
Holne
Maidencombe
Meavy
Yelverton
Buckfast
Kingskerswell
TORQUAY
Buckland Abbey
Buckfastleigh
Ipplepen
Compton
Bere Ferrers
Park
Staverton
Babbacombe
Cockington
Dartington
Marldon
TORBAY
Tamerton Foliot
Bickleigh
Castle
Tor Bay
S. Brent
Berry Pomeroy
Paignton
PLYMOUTH
Cornwood
Totnes
Harberton
Goodrington
Avonwick
Diptford
Ashprington
Stoke Gabriel
Churston Ferrers
Ivybridge
Plympton
Galmpton
Berry Head
Saltram
Ugborough
Harbertonford
Cornworthy
Brixham
Ermington
Dittisham
The Sound
Brixton
Plymstock
Halwell
Kingswear
Yealmpton
Dunstone
Modbury
Dartmouth
Wembury
Holbeton
Blackawton
Newton Ferrers
Aveton Gifford
Wembury Bay
Noss Mayo
Kingston
Goveton
Stoke Fleming
Coast Path
S. Devon
Stoke Point
Bigbury
Bigbury-on-Sea
Slapton
Burgh-Island
W. Alvington
Kingsbridge
Stokenham
Bigbury Bay
Thurlestone
W. Charleton
Chillington
Torcross
Hope
Malborough
S. Pool
Bolt Trail
Salcombe
Hallsands
E. Portlemouth
Sharpitor
Start Point
Bolt Head
Prawle Point
H
I
J
C H A N

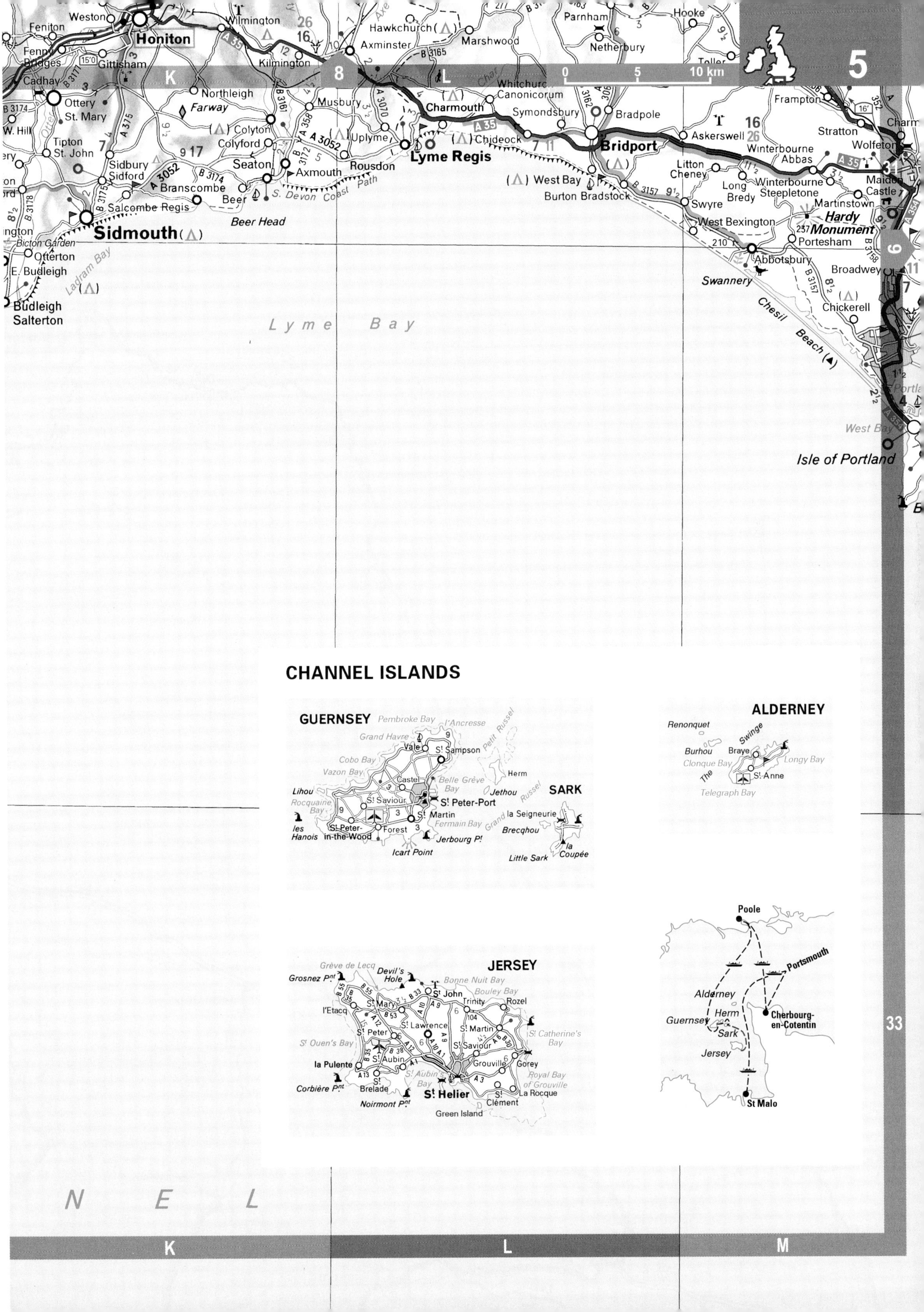
Weston
Feniton
Fenny Bridges
Honiton
Gittisham
Wilmington
Hawkchurch
Axminster
Marshwood
Kilmington
Parnham
Netherbury
Hooke
Toller
Cadhay
Ottery St. Mary
Northleigh
Farway
W. Hill
Tipton St. John
Colyton
Colyford
Musbury
Uplyme
Charmouth
Whitchurch Canonicorum
Symondsbury
Bradpole
Chideock
Lyme Regis
Bridport
Askerswell
Frampton
Stratton
Wolfeton
Winterbourne Abbas
Sidbury
Sidford
Seaton
Axmouth
Rousdon
Branscombe
Beer
Salcombe Regis
Beer Head
S. Devon Coast Path
West Bay
Burton Bradstock
Litton Cheney
Long Bredy
Winterbourne Steepletone
Maiden Castle
Martinstown
Swyre
West Bexington
Hardy Monument
Portesham
Abbotsbury
Swannery
Broadwey
Chickerell
Chesil Beach
Sidmouth
Bicton Garden
Otterton
E. Budleigh
Ladram Bay
Budleigh Salterton
Lyme Bay
West Bay
Isle of Portland
0 5 10 km
K
L
M
N E L
CHANNEL ISLANDS
GUERNSEY
Pembroke Bay
l'Ancresse
Grand Havre
Vale
St Sampson
Cobo Bay
Vazon Bay
Castel
Belle Grève Bay
Herm
Lihou
St Saviour
St Peter-Port
Jethou
SARK
Rocquaine Bay
St Martin
Fermain Bay
la Seigneurie
les Hanois
St Peter-in-the-Wood
Forest
Jerbourg Pt
Brecqhou
Icart Point
Little Sark
la Coupée
Grand Russel
Petit Russel
ALDERNEY
Renonquet
The Swinge
Burhou
Braye
Longy Bay
Clonque Bay
St Anne
Telegraph Bay
JERSEY
Grève de Lecq
Grosnez Pnt
Devil's Hole
Bonne Nuit Bay
Bouley Bay
St John
Trinity
Rozel
St Mary
l'Etacq
St Lawrence
St Martin
St Catherine's Bay
St Ouen's Bay
St Peter
St Saviour
St Aubin
Grouville
Gorey
la Pulente
Royal Bay of Grouville
Corbière Pnt
Brelade
St Aubin's Bay
St Helier
La Rocque
Noirmont Pnt
St Clément
Green Island
Poole
Portsmouth
Alderney
Herm
Cherbourg-en-Cotentin
Guernsey
Sark
Jersey
St Malo

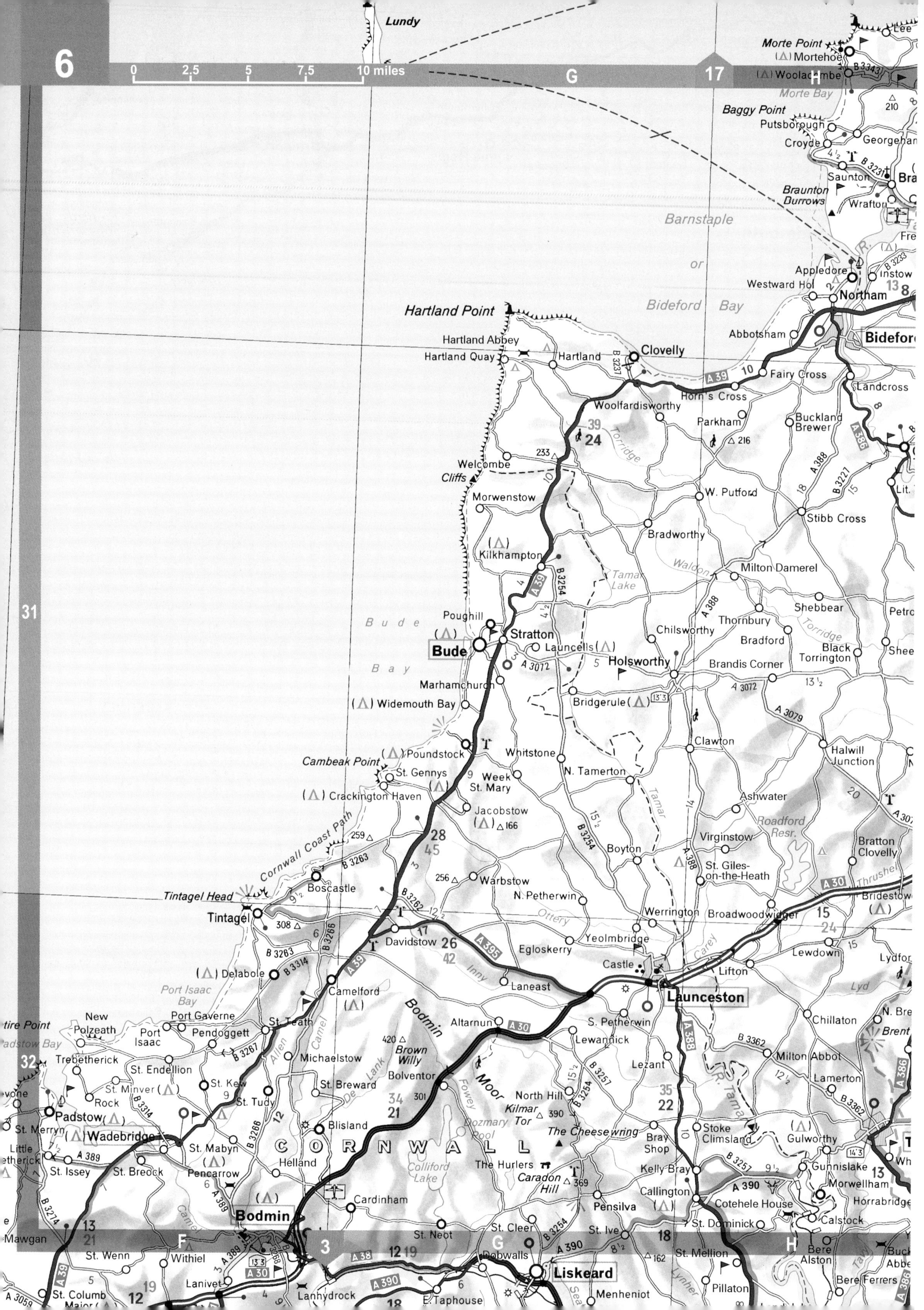
Lundy
0 2.5 5 7.5 10 miles
G
17
H
31
32
Morte Point
Mortehoe
Woolacombe
Lee
Morte Bay
Baggy Point
Putsborough
Croyde
Georgeham
Saunton
Braunton Burrows
Wrafton
Barnstaple
or
Bideford Bay
Appledore
Instow
Westward Ho!
Northam
Abbotsham
Bideford
Hartland Point
Hartland Abbey
Hartland Quay
Hartland
Clovelly
Fairy Cross
Horn's Cross
Landcross
Woolfardisworthy
Parkham
Buckland Brewer
Welcombe
Cliffs
Morwenstow
W. Putford
Stibb Cross
Bradworthy
Kilkhampton
Tamar Lake
Waldon
Milton Damerel
Shebbear
Torridge
Poughill
Bude
Bay
Stratton
Launcells
Holsworthy
Chilsworthy
Thornbury
Bradford
Black Torrington
Brandis Corner
Marhamchurch
Widemouth Bay
Bridgerule
Clawton
Halwill Junction
Poundstock
Cambeak Point
Whitstone
St. Gennys
Crackington Haven
Week St. Mary
N. Tamerton
Ashwater
Jacobstow
Tamar
Roadford Resr.
Cornwall Coast Path
Virginstow
Bratton Clovelly
Boscastle
Boyton
St. Giles-on-the-Heath
Warbstow
N. Petherwin
Tintagel Head
Tintagel
Davidstow
Ottery
Werrington
Broadwoodwidger
Bridestow
Yeolmbridge
Egloskerry
Lewdown
Lydford
Delabole
Castle
Lifton
Camelford
Laneast
Launceston
Port Isaac Bay
Inny
Bodmin
Lyd
New Polzeath
Port Gaverne
Port Isaac
Pendoggett
St. Teath
Altarnun
S. Petherwin
Chillaton
Brent Tor
Padstow Bay
Trebetherick
St. Endellion
Allen
Camel
Michaelstow
Brown Willy
Lewannick
Milton Abbot
Lezant
St. Minver
Rock
St. Kew
St. Tudy
De Lank
St. Breward
Bolventor
Moor
Fowey
Lamerton
North Hill
Kilmar Tor
Padstow
St. Merryn
Little Petherick
Wadebridge
St. Mabyn
Blisland
Dozmary Pool
The Cheesewring
Bray Shop
Stoke Climsland
Gulworthy
CORNWALL
St. Issey
St. Breock
Pencarrow
Helland
Colliford Lake
The Hurlers
Caradon Hill
Kelly Bray
Gunnislake
Morwellham
Callington
Cotehele House
Horrabridge
Bodmin
Cardinham
Pensilva
St. Dominick
Calstock
St. Cleer
St. Neot
St. Ive
St. Mellion
Bere Alston
Mawgan
St. Wenn
Withiel
Lanivet
Lanhydrock
Dobwalls
Liskeard
Lynher
Pillaton
Bere Ferrers
St. Columb Major
E. Taphouse
Menheniot
Sea
A 39
A 30
A 38
A 390
A 395
A 388
A 386
A 3072
A 3079
A 389
B 3254
B 3262
B 3263
B 3266
B 3267
B 3314
B 3257
B 3362
B 3237
B 3231
B 3343
B 3233
B 3227
B 3274
B 3268
Thrushel
Tamar
Carey
Torridge
R. Tamar

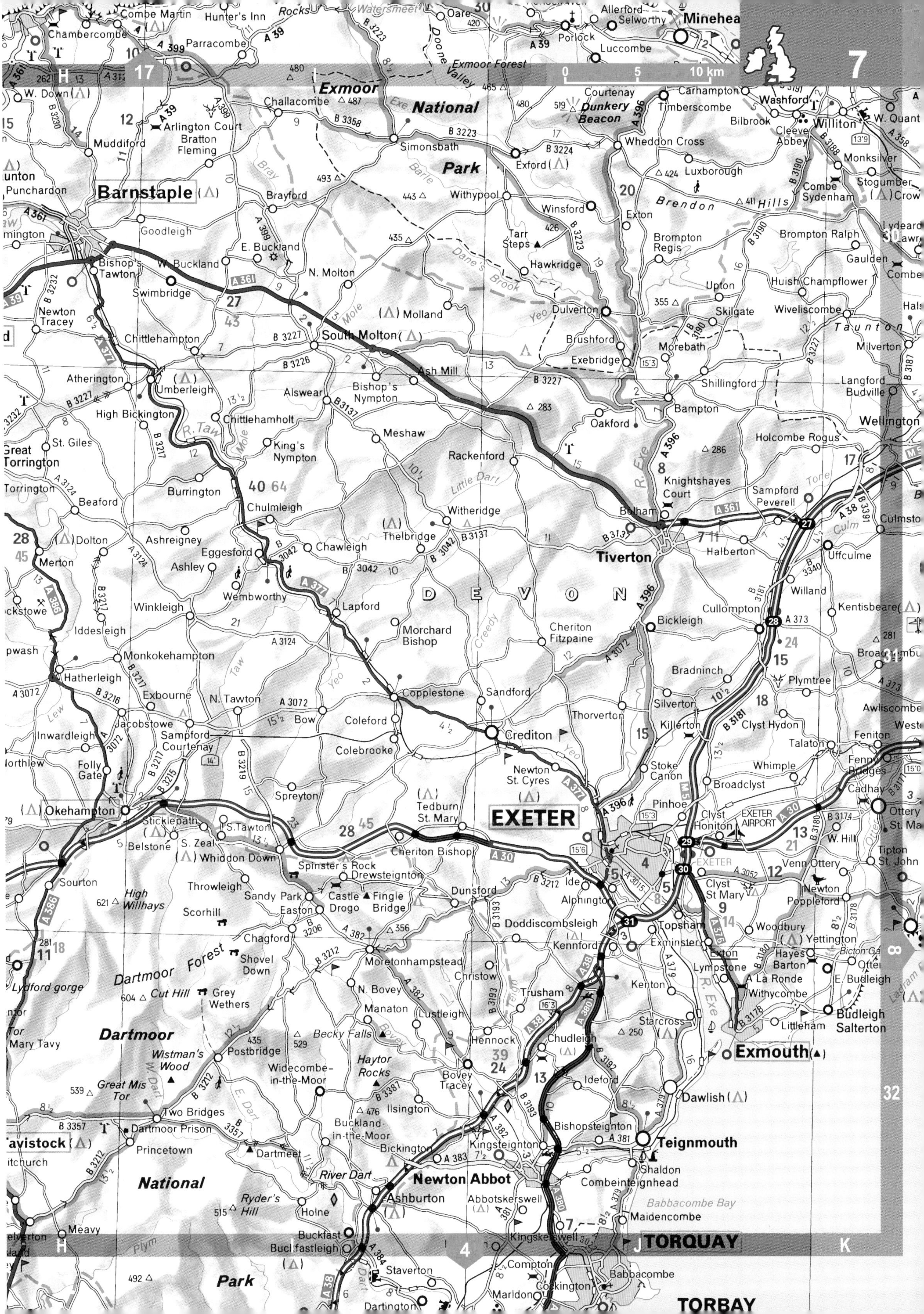
Combe Martin
Hunter's Inn
Rocks
Watersmeet
Oare
Allerford
Selworthy
Minehead
Chambercombe
Parracombe
Porlock
Luccombe
Doone Valley
Exmoor Forest
0 5 10 km
Exmoor
National
Park
Courtenay
Dunkery Beacon
Carhampton
Washford
Timberscombe
Bilbrook
Cleeve Abbey
Williton
W. Quantoxhead
W. Down
Challacombe
Arlington Court
Bratton Fleming
Muddiford
Simonsbath
Exford
Wheddon Cross
Luxborough
Monksilver
Stogumber
Combe Sydenham
Crowcombe
Barnstaple
Brayford
Withypool
Winsford
Exton
Brendon Hills
Brompton Regis
Brompton Ralph
Lydeard
Goodleigh
E. Buckland
Tarr Steps
Hawkridge
Gaulden
Combe
Bishop's Tawton
W. Buckland
Swimbridge
N. Molton
Dane's Brook
Upton
Huish Champflower
Newton Tracey
Molland
Dulverton
Skilgate
Wiveliscombe
Taunton
Chittlehampton
South Molton
Brushford
Morebath
Milverton
Exebridge
Atherington
Umberleigh
Bishop's Nympton
Ash Mill
Shillingford
Langford Budville
Alswear
Bampton
Wellington
High Bickington
Chittlehamholt
Oakford
R. Taw
Mole
Meshaw
Holcombe Rogus
Great Torrington
St. Giles
King's Nympton
Rackenford
Little Dart
Knightshayes Court
Sampford Peverell
Torrington
Beaford
Burrington
Chulmleigh
Witheridge
Bolham
Culmstock
Dolton
Ashreigney
Thelbridge
Tiverton
Halberton
Uffculme
Merton
Eggesford
Chawleigh
Culm
Ashley
Willand
Wembworthy
DEVON
Kentisbeare
Cullompton
Winkleigh
Lapford
Morchard Bishop
Cheriton Fitzpaine
Bickleigh
Iddesleigh
Monkokehampton
Creedy
Bradninch
Broadhembury
Hatherleigh
Plymtree
Copplestone
Sandford
Silverton
Exbourne
N. Tawton
Bow
Thorverton
Killerton
Clyst Hydon
Awliscombe
Jacobstowe
Coleford
Crediton
Feniton
Inwardleigh
Sampford Courtenay
Talaton
Colebrooke
Folly Gate
Newton St. Cyres
Stoke Canon
Whimple
Fenny Bridges
Broadclyst
Cadhay
Okehampton
Spreyton
Tedburn St. Mary
EXETER
Pinhoe
Clyst Honiton
EXETER AIRPORT
Ottery St. Mary
Sticklepath
S. Tawton
Belstone
S. Zeal
Whiddon Down
Cheriton Bishop
W. Hill
Tipton St. John
Sourton
Spinster's Rock
Drewsteignton
Ide
Clyst St Mary
Venn Ottery
Throwleigh
Sandy Park
Castle Drogo
Fingle Bridge
Dunsford
Alphington
Newton Poppleford
High Willhays
Scorhill
Easton
Doddiscombsleigh
Topsham
Woodbury
Chagford
Kennford
Exminster
Yettington
Exton
Shovel Down
Moretonhampstead
Lympstone
Hayes Barton
Bicton Gardens
Otterton
Dartmoor Forest
Christow
A La Ronde
E. Budleigh
Lydford gorge
Cut Hill
Grey Wethers
N. Bovey
Trusham
Kenton
Withycombe
Manaton
Lustleigh
Starcross
Littleham
Budleigh Salterton
Mary Tavy
Dartmoor
Becky Falls
Hennock
Chudleigh
Exmouth
Wistman's Wood
Postbridge
Haytor Rocks
Widecombe-in-the-Moor
Bovey Tracey
Ideford
Dawlish
Great Mis Tor
Ilsington
Two Bridges
Buckland-in-the-Moor
Bishopsteignton
Dartmoor Prison
Teignmouth
Tavistock
Princetown
Dartmeet
Bickington
Kingsteignton
Shaldon
Whitchurch
National
River Dart
Newton Abbot
Combeinteignhead
Ryder's Hill
Ashburton
Abbotskerswell
Babbacombe Bay
Holne
Maidencombe
Yelverton
Meavy
Buckfast
Buckfastleigh
Kingskerswell
TORQUAY
Plym
Staverton
Compton
Babbacombe
Park
Cockington
Marldon
Dartington
TORBAY
Ladram Bay

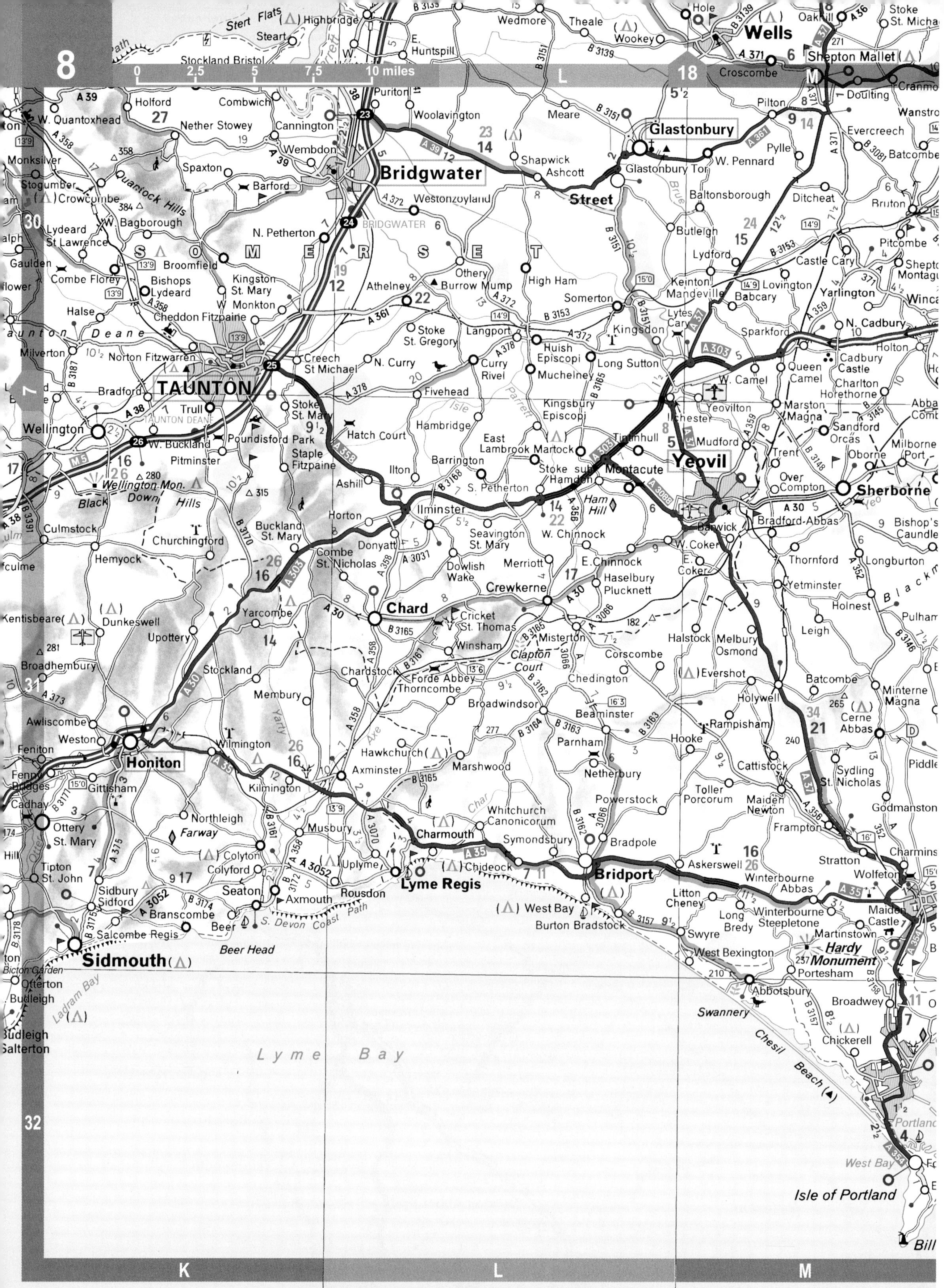
0 2,5 5 7,5 10 miles
18
Stert Flats
Highbridge
Steart
Stockland Bristol
Wedmore
Theale
Wookey
Hole
Wells
Oakhill
Stoke St. Michael
E. Huntspill
Shepton Mallet
Croscombe
Doulting
Cranmore
Puriton
Woolavington
Meare
Glastonbury
Pilton
Wanstrow
Holford
Combwich
W. Quantoxhead
Nether Stowey
Cannington
Wembdon
Shapwick
Ashcott
Glastonbury Tor
W. Pennard
Pylle
Evercreech
Batcombe
Monksilver
Stogumber
Crowcombe
Quantock Hills
Spaxton
Barford
Bridgwater
Street
Baltonsborough
Ditcheat
Bruton
Lydeard St Lawrence
W. Bagborough
Westonzoyland
BRIDGWATER
N. Petherton
Butleigh
Lydford
Pitcombe
Castle Cary
Shepton Montague
Gaulden
SOMERSET
Combe Florey
Broomfield
Bishops Lydeard
Kingston St. Mary
W. Monkton
Athelney
Othery
Burrow Mump
High Ham
Keinton Mandeville
Lovington
Babcary
Yarlington
Wincanton
Halse
Cheddon Fitzpaine
Somerton
Lytes Cary
Taunton Deane
Milverton
Norton Fitzwarren
Creech St Michael
Stoke St. Gregory
Langport
Huish Episcopi
Kingsdon
Sparkford
N. Cadbury
Holton
TAUNTON
N. Curry
Curry Rivel
Muchelney
Long Sutton
Cadbury Castle
Queen Camel
W. Camel
Charlton Horethorne
Bradford
Trull
TAUNTON DEANE
Wellington
Stoke St. Mary
Fivehead
Isle
Parrett
Kingsbury Episcopi
Ilchester
Yeovilton
Marston Magna
Sandford Orcas
Abbas Combe
Hatch Court
Hambridge
East Lambrook
Martock
Tintinhull
Mudford
Milborne Port
W. Buckland
Poundisford Park
Pitminster
Staple Fitzpaine
Barrington
Yeovil
Trent
Oborne
Ilton
Stoke sub Hamdon
Montacute
Over Compton
Sherborne
Wellington Mon.
Ashill
S. Petherton
Ham Hill
Black Down Hills
Culmstock
Churchingford
Horton
Ilminster
Seavington St. Mary
W. Chinnock
Barwick
Bradford Abbas
Bishop's Caundle
Hemyock
Buckland St. Mary
Donyatt
Combe St. Nicholas
Dowlish Wake
Merriott
E. Chinnock
W. Coker
E. Coker
Thornford
Longburton
Crewkerne
Haselbury Plucknett
Yetminster
Culme
Kentisbeare
Dunkeswell
Yarcombe
Chard
Cricket St. Thomas
Misterton
Holnest
Pulham
Upottery
Winsham
Clapton Court
Halstock
Melbury Osmond
Leigh
Broadhembury
Stockland
Chardstock
Forde Abbey
Thorncombe
Corscombe
Evershot
Batcombe
Minterne Magna
Chedington
Membury
Broadwindsor
Beaminster
Holywell
Cerne Abbas
Awliscombe
Weston
Yarty
Axe
Parnham
Rampisham
Feniton
Honiton
Wilmington
Hawkchurch
Marshwood
Netherbury
Hooke
Cattistock
Sydling St. Nicholas
Piddletrenthide
Fenny Bridges
Gittisham
Kilmington
Axminster
Toller Porcorum
Maiden Newton
Godmanstone
Cadhay
Ottery St. Mary
Northleigh
Farway
Musbury
Char
Whitchurch Canonicorum
Powerstock
Frampton
Charmouth
Symondsbury
Bradpole
Charminster
Otter
Colyton
Colyford
Uplyme
Chideock
Bridport
Askerswell
Stratton
Tipton St. John
Sidbury
Sidford
Seaton
Axmouth
Rousdon
Lyme Regis
Winterbourne Abbas
Wolfeton
Litton Cheney
Maiden Castle
Branscombe
West Bay
Long Bredy
Winterbourne Steepleton
Beer
S. Devon Coast Path
Burton Bradstock
Swyre
Martinstown
Salcombe Regis
Hardy Monument
Sidmouth
Beer Head
West Bexington
Portesham
Bicton Garden
Otterton
Abbotsbury
Broadwey
Budleigh
Ladram Bay
Swannery
Chickerell
Budleigh Salterton
Chesil Beach
Lyme Bay
Portland
West Bay
Isle of Portland
Bill
K
L
M
30
31
32

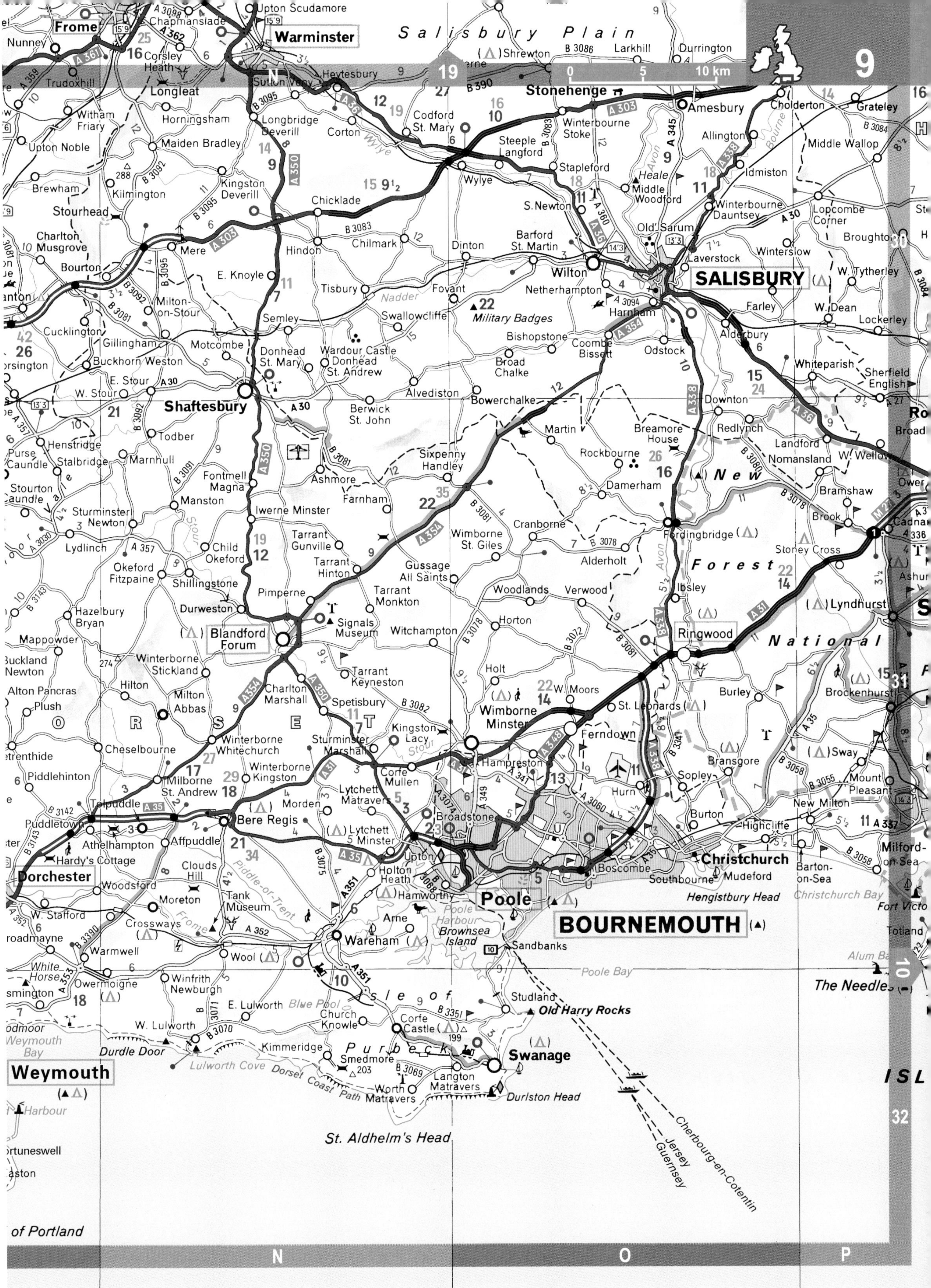
Salisbury Plain
Frome
Warminster
Upton Scudamore
Chapmanslade
Nunney
Corsley Heath
Trudoxhill
Longleat
Heytesbury
Sutton Veny
Shrewton
Larkhill
Durrington
Stonehenge
Amesbury
Cholderton
Grateley
Witham Friary
Horningsham
Longbridge Deverill
Corton
Codford St. Mary
Winterbourne Stoke
Steeple Langford
Allington
Middle Wallop
Upton Noble
Maiden Bradley
Wylye
Stapleford
Heale
Middle Woodford
Idmiston
Brewham
Kilmington
Kingston Deverill
Chicklade
S. Newton
Winterbourne Dauntsey
Lopcombe Corner
Stourhead
Old Sarum
Charlton Musgrove
Mere
Hindon
Chilmark
Dinton
Barford St. Martin
Wilton
Laverstock
Broughton
Winterslow
Bourton
E. Knoyle
Tisbury
Fovant
Netherhampton
SALISBURY
W. Tytherley
Nadder
Military Badges
Harnham
Farley
W. Dean
Lockerley
Milton-on-Stour
Semley
Swallowcliffe
Cucklington
Gillingham
Motcombe
Donhead St. Mary
Wardour Castle
Donhead St. Andrew
Bishopstone
Coombe Bissett
Odstock
Alderbury
Broad Chalke
Whiteparish
Sherfield English
Buckhorn Weston
E. Stour
W. Stour
Shaftesbury
Berwick St. John
Alvediston
Bowerchalke
Downton
Redlynch
Landford
Nomansland
W. Wellow
Todber
Martin
Breamore House
Henstridge
Purse Caundle
Stalbridge
Marnhull
Sixpenny Handley
Rockbourne
Damerham
New
Bramshaw
Fontmell Magna
Ashmore
Farnham
Stourton Caundle
Manston
Sturminster Newton
Iwerne Minster
Cranborne
Fordingbridge
Brook
Stoney Cross
Lydlinch
Child Okeford
Tarrant Gunville
Tarrant Hinton
Wimborne St. Giles
Alderholt
Forest
Okeford Fitzpaine
Shillingstone
Gussage All Saints
Ibsley
Woodlands
Verwood
Pimperne
Tarrant Monkton
Lyndhurst
Hazelbury Bryan
Durweston
Signals Museum
Witchampton
Horton
Ringwood
National
Mappowder
Blandford Forum
Buckland Newton
Winterborne Stickland
Tarrant Keyneston
Holt
W. Moors
Burley
Brockenhurst
Alton Pancras
Hilton
Milton Abbas
Charlton Marshall
Spetisbury
Wimborne Minster
St. Leonards
Plush
DORSET
Kingston Lacy
Ferndown
Sway
Cheselbourne
Winterborne Whitechurch
Sturminster Marshall
Stour
Hampreston
Bransgore
Piddletrenthide
Piddlehinton
Milborne St. Andrew
Winterborne Kingston
Corfe Mullen
Hurn
Sopley
Mount Pleasant
Tolpuddle
Lytchett Matravers
Morden
Broadstone
New Milton
Puddletown
Bere Regis
Lytchett Minster
Burton
Highcliffe
Athelhampton
Affpuddle
Upton
Christchurch
Barton-on-Sea
Milford-on-Sea
Hardy's Cottage
Dorchester
Clouds Hill
Holton Heath
Boscombe
Southbourne
Mudeford
Woodsford
Tank Museum
Hamworthy
Poole
Hengistbury Head
Christchurch Bay
Fort Victoria
W. Stafford
Moreton
Piddle or Trent
Arne
Poole Harbour
Brownsea Island
BOURNEMOUTH
Crossways
Frome
Wareham
Totland
Broadmayne
Warmwell
Wool
Sandbanks
Alum Bay
White Horse
Owermoigne
Winfrith Newburgh
Poole Bay
The Needles
Studland
Old Harry Rocks
Isle of Purbeck
E. Lulworth
Blue Pool
Church Knowle
Corfe Castle
W. Lulworth
Kimmeridge
Smedmore
Swanage
Durdle Door
Lulworth Cove
Dorset Coast Path
Langton Matravers
Worth Matravers
Durlston Head
Weymouth Bay
Weymouth
Harbour
St. Aldhelm's Head
Cherbourg-en-Cotentin
Jersey
Guernsey
Fortuneswell
Easton
Isle of Portland
ISLE
N
O
P
0 5 10 km
19
10
30
31
32

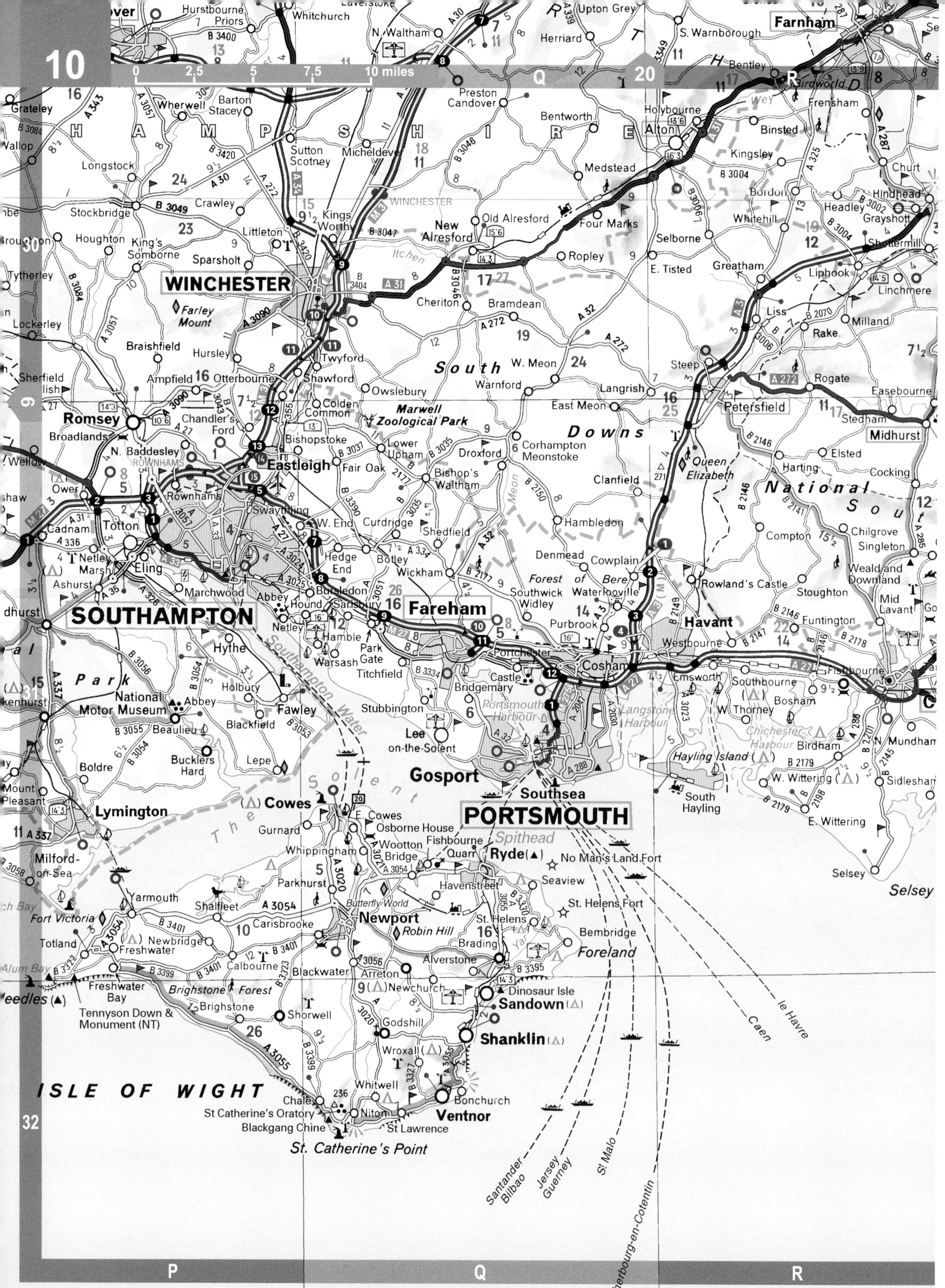
0 2.5 5 7.5 10 miles
P
Q
R
20
30
31
32
9
HAMPSHIRE
WINCHESTER
SOUTHAMPTON
PORTSMOUTH
Fareham
Gosport
Southsea
Eastleigh
Romsey
Totton
Havant
Petersfield
Midhurst
Alton
Farnham
Lymington
Cowes
Newport
Ryde
Sandown
Shanklin
Ventnor
Yarmouth
Freshwater
Totland
Hythe
Fawley
Beaulieu
Emsworth
Hayling Island
South Hayling
Selsey
East Wittering
West Wittering
Bosham
Fishbourne
Stockbridge
New Alresford
Bishop's Waltham
Wickham
Lee-on-the-Solent
Stubbington
Titchfield
Hamble
Netley
Bursledon
Botley
Hedge End
Waterlooville
Cowplain
Cosham
Portchester
Liphook
Liss
Grayshott
Hindhead
Headley
Bordon
Selborne
Four Marks
Ropley
South Downs
National Park
Marwell Zoological Park
Queen Elizabeth
National Motor Museum
Bucklers Hard
The Solent
Southampton Water
Spithead
Portsmouth Harbour
Langstone Harbour
Chichester Harbour
ISLE OF WIGHT
St. Catherine's Point
St Catherine's Oratory
Blackgang Chine
Needles
Alum Bay
Tennyson Down & Monument (NT)
Osborne House
Robin Hill
Butterfly World
Dinosaur Isle
Foreland
No Man's Land Fort
St. Helens Fort
Santander Bilbao
Jersey Guernsey
St. Malo
Cherbourg-en-Cotentin
Caen
le Havre

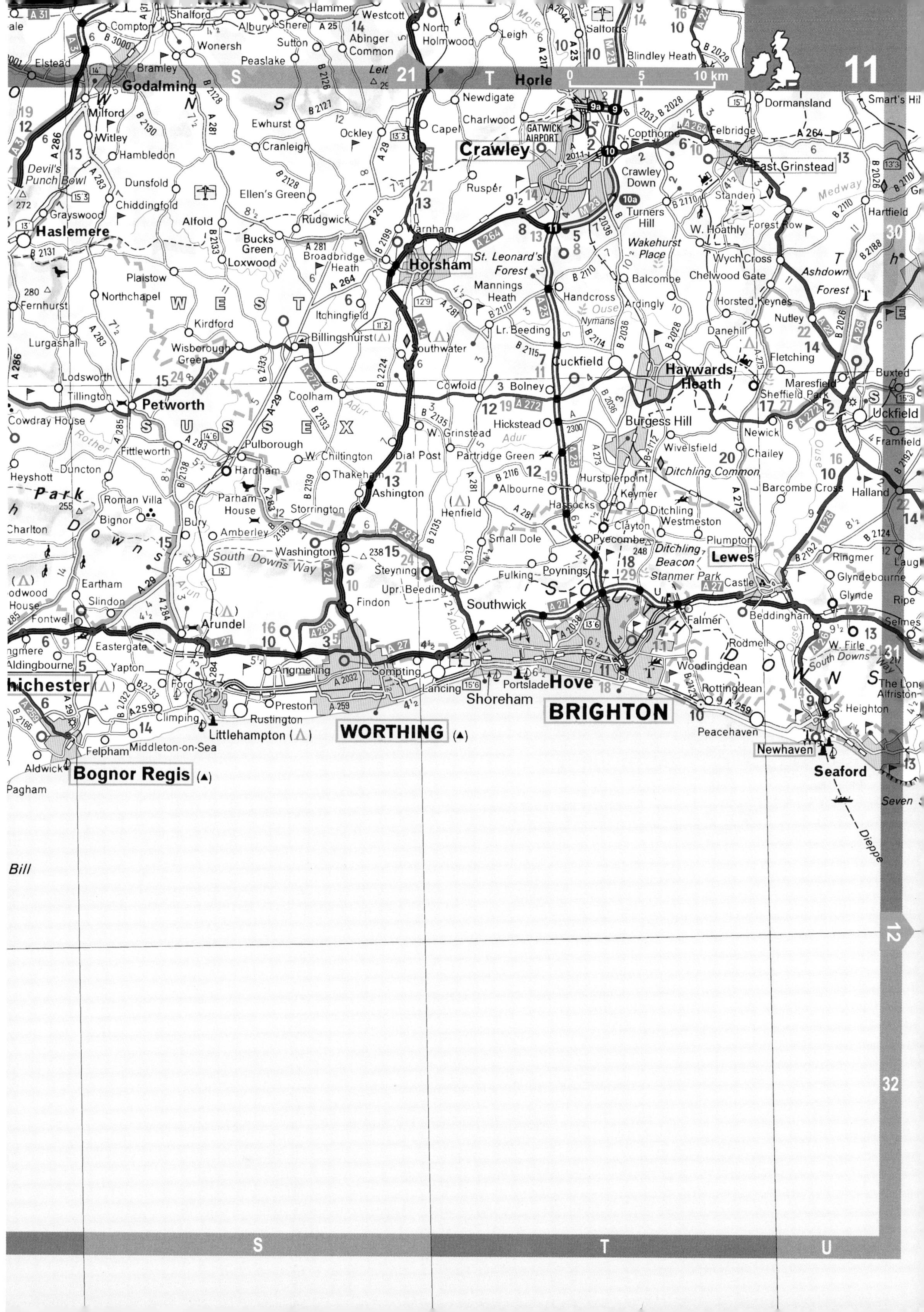

Shalford
Compton
Hammer
Westcott
North Holmwood
Leigh
Salfords
Blindley Heath
Wonersh
Albury
Shere
Abinger Common
Sutton
Peaslake
Elstead
Bramley
Godalming
Horley
0 5 10 km
Milford
Witley
Hambledon
Ewhurst
Cranleigh
Ockley
Capel
Newdigate
Charlwood
GATWICK AIRPORT
Crawley
Copthorne
Felbridge
Dormansland
Smart's Hill
East Grinstead
Devil's Punch Bowl
Dunsfold
Chiddingfold
Ellen's Green
Rusper
Crawley Down
Standen
Medway
Hartfield
Grayswood
Haslemere
Alfold
Rudgwick
Bucks Green
Loxwood
Warnham
Turners Hill
W. Hoathly
Forest Row
Wakehurst Place
Wych Cross
Ashdown Forest
Broadbridge Heath
Horsham
St. Leonard's Forest
Balcombe
Chelwood Gate
Plaistow
Northchapel
Fernhurst
Mannings Heath
Handcross
Nymans
Ardingly
Horsted Keynes
Nutley
WEST SUSSEX
Itchingfield
Lr. Beeding
Danehill
Kirdford
Billingshurst
Southwater
Cuckfield
Fletching
Lurgashall
Wisborough Green
Haywards Heath
Maresfield
Sheffield Park
Buxted
Lodsworth
Coolham
Cowfold
Bolney
Tillington
Petworth
Uckfield
Cowdray House
W. Grinstead
Hickstead
Burgess Hill
Newick
Framfield
Rother
Fittleworth
Pulborough
Adur
Wivelsfield
Chailey
Heyshott
Duncton
Hardham
W. Chiltington
Dial Post
Partridge Green
Ditchling Common
Park
Thakeham
Ashington
Albourne
Hurstpierpoint
Barcombe Cross
Halland
Roman Villa
Parham House
Keymer
Charlton
Bignor
Storrington
Henfield
Hassocks
Ditchling
Westmeston
Bury
Amberley
Clayton
Downs
Small Dole
Pyecombe
Plumpton
South Downs Way
Washington
Ditchling Beacon
Lewes
Ringmer
Steyning
Fulking
Poynings
Glyndebourne
Earthsm
Stanmer Park
Castle
Glynde
Upr. Beeding
Ripe
Slindon
Findon
Southwick
Beddingham
Selmes
Fontwell
Arundel
Falmer
Eastergate
Rodmell
W. Firle
Aldingbourne
Yapton
Angmering
Sompting
Portslade
Hove
Woodingdean
South Downs Way
Chichester
Ford
Lancing
Shoreham
Rottingdean
Alfriston
Preston
Clymping
Rustington
BRIGHTON
S. Heighton
Littlehampton
WORTHING
Peacehaven
Felpham
Middleton-on-Sea
Newhaven
Aldwick
Bognor Regis
Seaford
Pagham
Seven
Dieppe
Bill
S
T
U

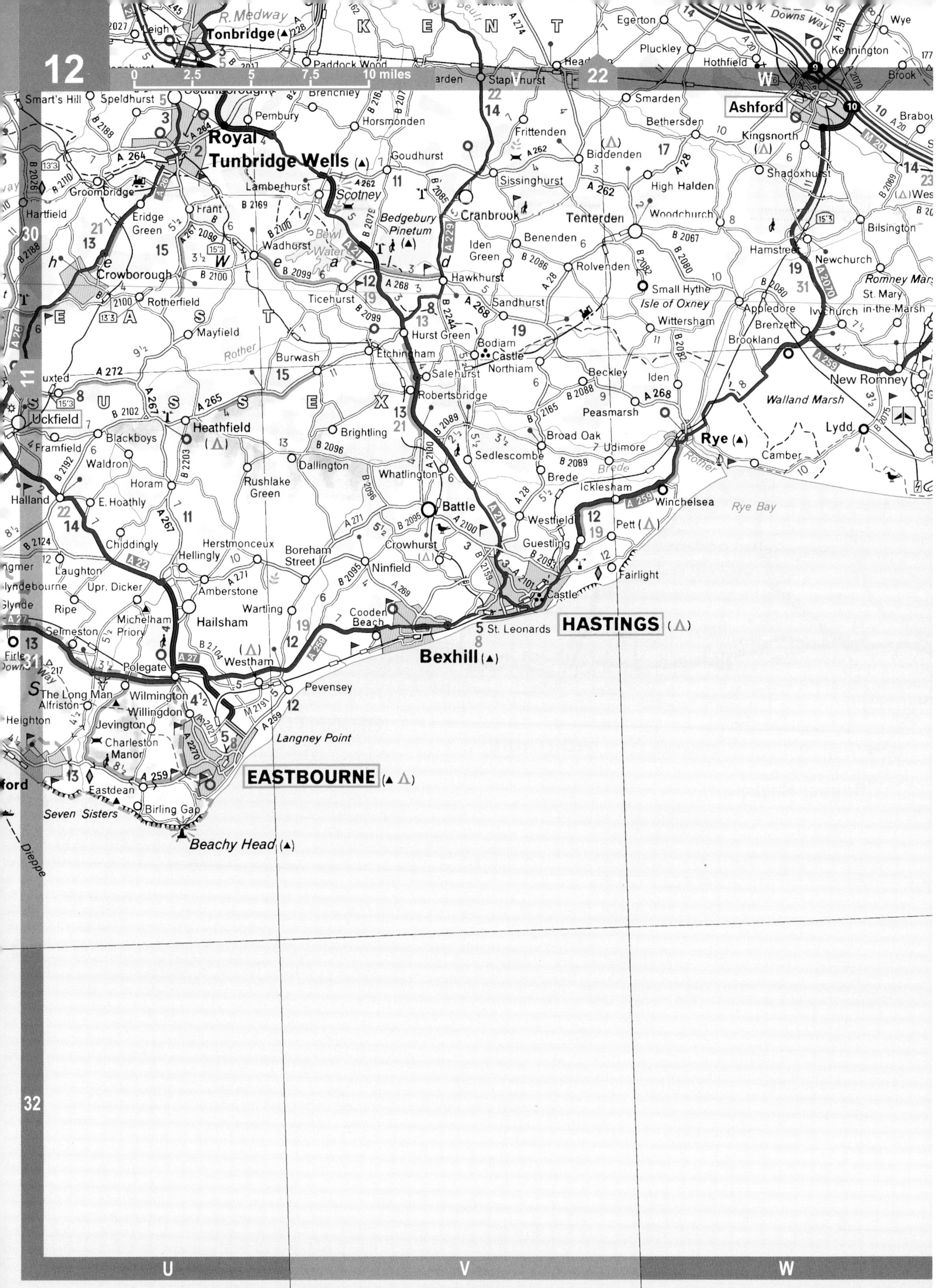
12
0 2.5 5 7.5 10 miles
K E N T
Tonbridge
R. Medway
Leigh
Paddock Wood
Staplehurst
Headcorn
Egerton
Pluckley
Hothfield
Wye
Kennington
Brook
Ashford
N. Downs Way
Smarden
Bethersden
Kingsnorth
Shadoxhurst
Smart's Hill
Speldhurst
Southborough
Brenchley
Pembury
Horsmonden
Royal Tunbridge Wells
Goudhurst
Frittenden
Biddenden
High Halden
Woodchurch
Groombridge
Lamberhurst
Scotney
Sissinghurst
Cranbrook
Tenterden
Hartfield
Eridge Green
Frant
Bedgebury Pinetum
Bewl Water
Wadhurst
Iden Green
Benenden
Rolvenden
Hamstreet
Newchurch
Bilsington
Crowborough
Rotherfield
Ticehurst
Hawkhurst
Sandhurst
Small Hythe
Isle of Oxney
Wittersham
Appledore
Brenzett
Ivychurch
St. Mary-in-the-Marsh
Romney Marsh
Brookland
E A S T
Mayfield
Burwash
Etchingham
Hurst Green
Bodiam Castle
Northiam
Salehurst
Robertsbridge
Rother
Beckley
Iden
New Romney
Walland Marsh
U S S E X
Uckfield
Framfield
Blackboys
Heathfield
Brightling
Dallington
Peasmarsh
Broad Oak
Udimore
Sedlescombe
Rye
Camber
Lydd
Waldron
Horam
Rushlake Green
Whatlington
Brede
Icklesham
Winchelsea
Halland
E. Hoathly
Battle
Westfield
Pett
Rye Bay
Chiddingly
Herstmonceux
Hellingly
Boreham Street
Crowhurst
Guestling
Laughton
Ninfield
Fairlight
Upr. Dicker
Amberstone
Ripe
Michelham Priory
Hailsham
Wartling
Cooden Beach
Castle
St. Leonards
HASTINGS
Selmeston
Westham
Bexhill
Polegate
Pevensey
The Long Man
Wilmington
Alfriston
Willingdon
Heighton
Jevington
Charleston Manor
Langney Point
EASTBOURNE
Eastdean
Birling Gap
Seven Sisters
Beachy Head
Dieppe
U
V
W
22
30
31
32
11

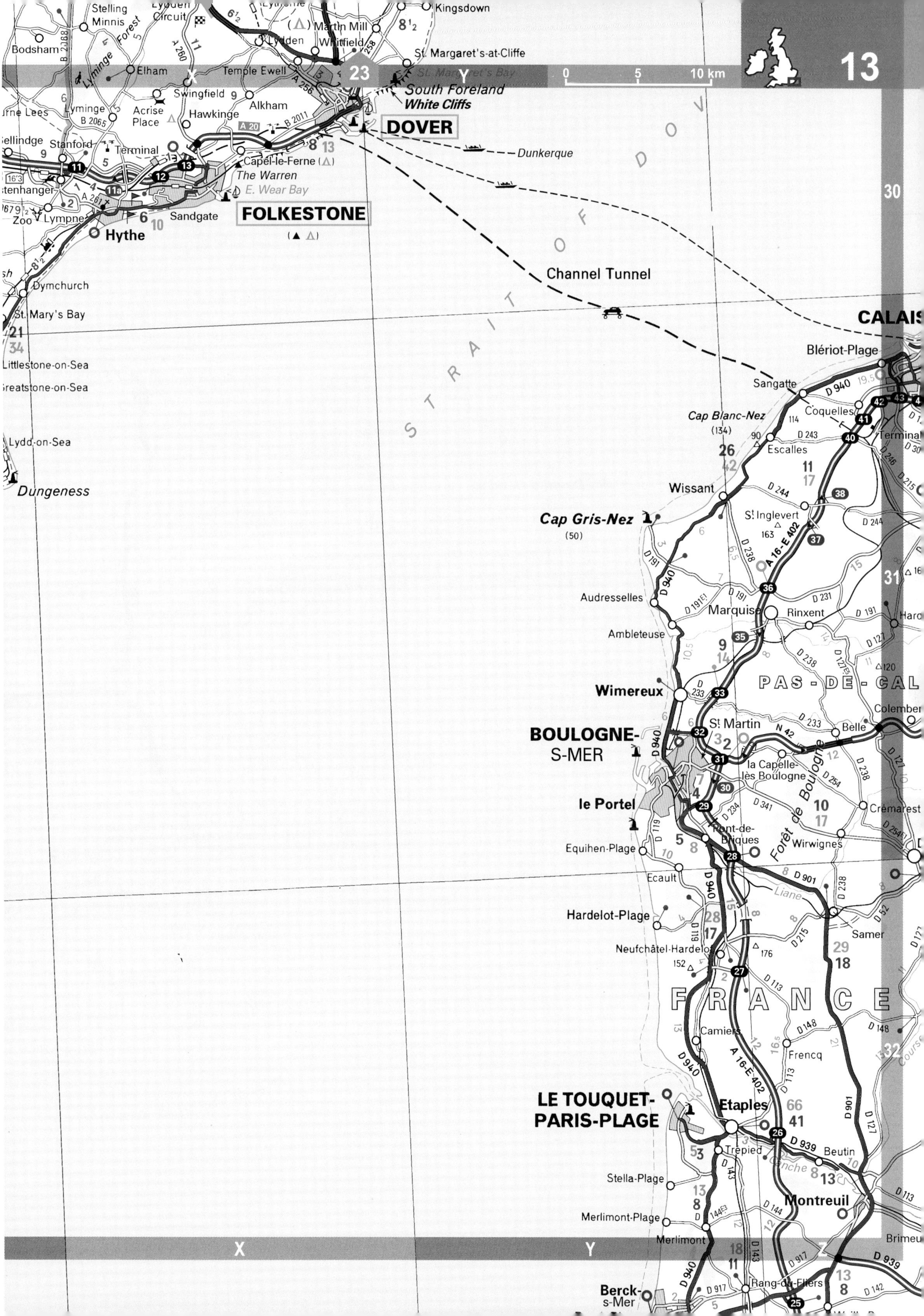
Stelling Minnis
Lydden Circuit
Kingsdown
Martin Mill
Whitfield
Lydden
Bodsham
St. Margaret's-at-Cliffe
Elham
Temple Ewell
St. Margaret's Bay
South Foreland
White Cliffs
Lyminge Forest
Swingfield
Alkham
Lyminge
Acrise Place
Hawkinge
DOVER
Stanford
Terminal
Dunkerque
Capel-le-Ferne
The Warren
E. Wear Bay
Zoo
Lympne
Sandgate
FOLKESTONE
Hythe
STRAIT OF DOVER
Channel Tunnel
Dymchurch
St. Mary's Bay
CALAIS
Littlestone-on-Sea
Greatstone-on-Sea
Blériot-Plage
Sangatte
Coquelles
Cap Blanc-Nez
(134)
Escalles
Terminal
Lydd-on-Sea
Dungeness
Wissant
St Inglevert
Cap Gris-Nez
(50)
Audresselles
Marquise
Rinxent
Ambleteuse
PAS-DE-CAL
Wimereux
Colembert
BOULOGNE-S-MER
St Martin
Belle
la Capelle-lès-Boulogne
le Portel
Forêt de Boulogne
Crémarest
Pont-de-Briques
Equihen-Plage
Wirwignes
Ecault
Liane
Hardelot-Plage
Samer
Neufchâtel-Hardelot
FRANCE
Camiers
Frencq
LE TOUQUET-PARIS-PLAGE
Etaples
Trépied
Beutin
Canche
Stella-Plage
Montreuil
Merlimont-Plage
Merlimont
Brimeux
Rang-du-Fliers
Berck-s-Mer
A 16-E 402
D 940
A 20
A 260
A 256
B 2011
B 2065
B 2068
D 901
D 939
0 5 10 km

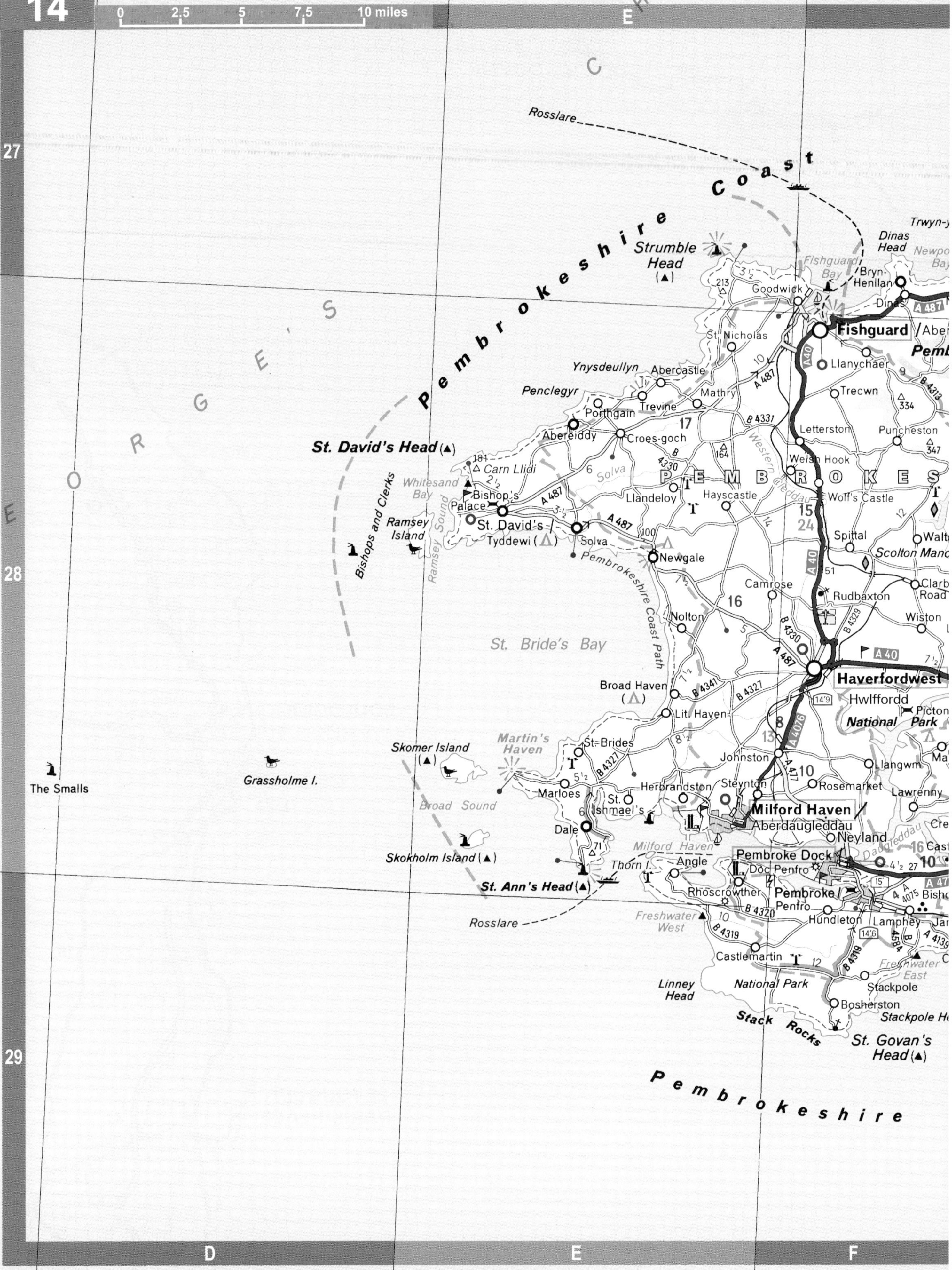
0 2.5 5 7.5 10 miles
E
D
E
F
27
28
29
S T . G E O R G E ' S C H A
Rosslare
Pembrokeshire Coast
Strumble Head (▲)
Trwyn-y
Dinas Head
Newport Bay
Fishguard Bay
Bryn-Henllan
Goodwick
Dinas
A 487
Fishguard /Aber
Pemb
St. Nicholas
Llanychaer
Ynysdeullyn
Abercastle
Penclegyr
Trecwn
334
Porthgain
Trevine
Mathry
A 487
A 40
B 4313
B 4331
17
Letterston
Puncheston
Abereiddy
Croes-goch
St. David's Head (▲)
181
Carn Llidi
B 4330
164
Western Cleddau
Welsh Hook
347
Whitesand Bay
Bishop's Palace
Solva
P E M B R O K E S
Bishops and Clerks
Ramsey Island
Ramsey Sound
St. David's / Tyddewi (Δ)
A 487
Llandeloy
Hayscastle
Wolf's Castle
15
24
Solva
100
Spittal
Walt
Scolton Manor
Newgale
Pembrokeshire Coast Path
A 40
51
Clarbeston Road
Camrose
16
Rudbaxton
Nolton
Wiston
B 4330
B 4329
St. Bride's Bay
A 40
A 487
Haverfordwest
Broad Haven (Δ)
B 4341
B 4327
Hwlffordd
Picton
Lit. Haven
National Park
Martin's Haven
St. Brides
Skomer Island (▲)
13
8
A 4076
Johnston
Llangwm
The Smalls
Grassholme I.
B 4327
Marloes
A 477
10
Herbrandston
Steynton
Rosemarket
Lawrenny
Broad Sound
St. Ishmael's
Milford Haven
Aberdaugleddau
Dale
Neyland
Cre
Daugleddau
Milford Haven
Pembroke Dock
Doc Penfro
16
Cast
Skokholm Island (▲)
Thorn I.
Angle
71
10
St. Ann's Head (▲)
A 477
Rhoscrowther
Pembroke / Penfro
A 4075
Bisho
B 4320
Rosslare
Freshwater West
Hundleton
Lamphey
B 4319
14'6
B 4584
A 4139
Castlemartin
12
Freshwater East
Linney Head
National Park
B 4319
Stackpole
Bosherston
Stack Rocks
Stackpole Head
St. Govan's Head (▲)
Pembrokeshire

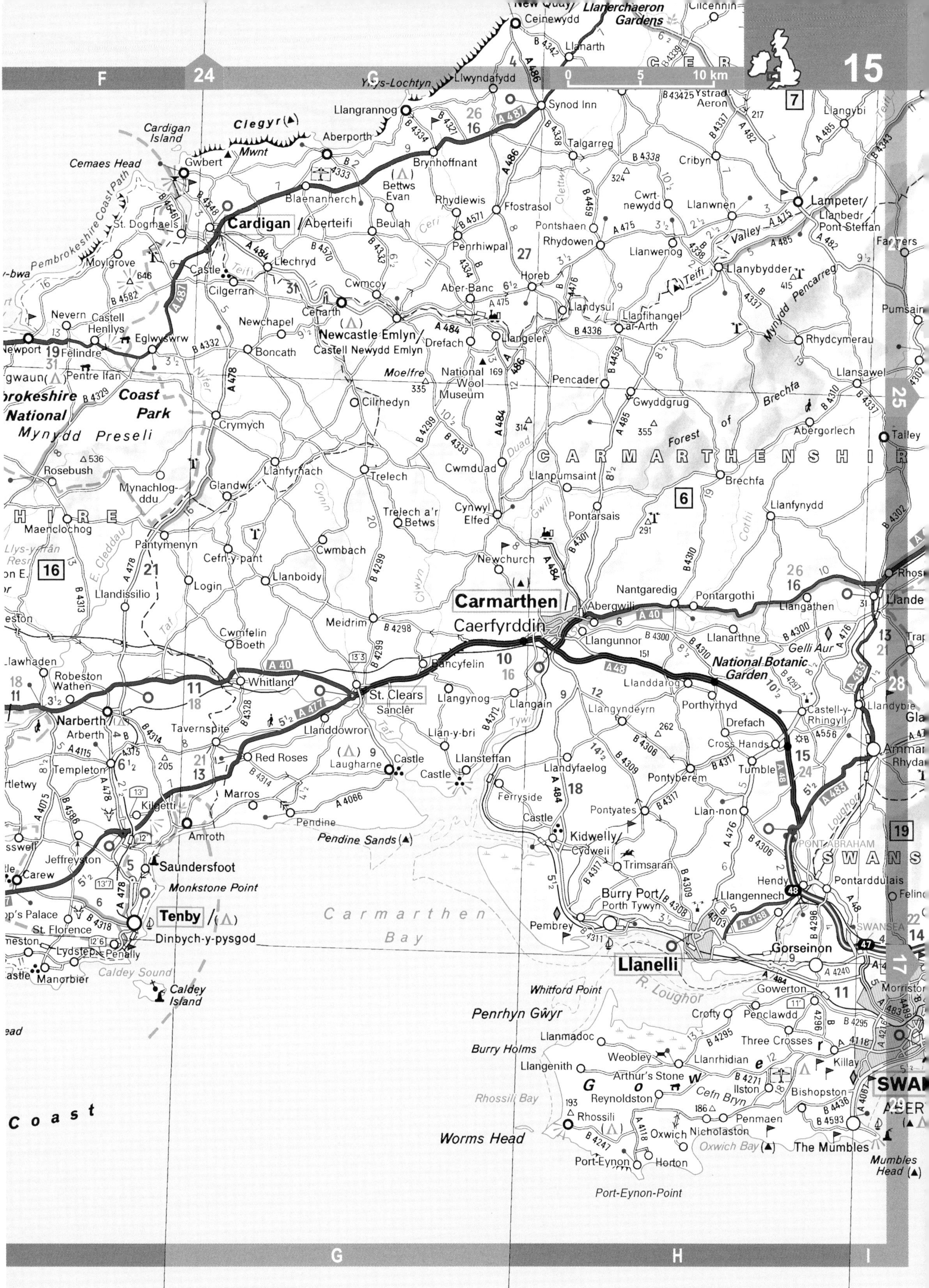

New Quay/
Llanerchaeron Gardens
Cilcennin
Ceinewydd
Llanarth
Llwyndafydd
Ynys-Lochtyn
Synod Inn
Ystrad Aeron
Llangybi
Llangrannog
Clegyr
Cardigan Island
Mwnt
Aberporth
Cemaes Head
Gwbert
Brynhoffnant
Talgarreg
Cribyn
Bettws Evan
Blaenannerch
Rhydlewis
Ffostrasol
Cwrt-newydd
Llanwnen
Lampeter/ Llanbedr Pont Steffan
Pembrokeshire Coast Path
St. Dogmaels
Cardigan
Aberteifi
Beulah
Pontshaen
Rhydowen
Penrhiwpal
Llanwenog
Llanybydder
Farmers
Moylgrove
Castle
Teifi
Llechryd
Cilgerran
Cwmcoy
Horeb
Aber-Banc
Valley
Mynydd Pencarreg
Cenarth
Llandysul
Nevern
Castell Henllys
Newchapel
Newcastle Emlyn/ Castell Newydd Emlyn
Drefach
Llangeler
Llanfihangel-ar-Arth
Pumsaint
Newport
Felindre
Eglwyswrw
Boncath
Rhydcymerau
Pentre Ifan
Moelfre
National Wool Museum
Pencader
Llansawel
Pembrokeshire Coast National Park
Mynydd Preseli
Cilrhedyn
Gwyddgrug
Forest of Brechfa
Crymych
Abergorlech
Talley
Rosebush
Llanfyrnach
Trelech
Cwmduad
CARMARTHENSHIRE
Llanpumsaint
Brechfa
Mynachlog-ddu
Glandwr
Maenclochog
Trelech a'r Betws
Cynwyl Elfed
Pontarsais
Llanfynydd
Llys-y-frân Resr.
Pantymenyn
Cwmbach
Cefn-y-pant
Newchurch
Llandissilio
Login
Llanboidy
Nantgaredig
Pontargothi
Carmarthen / Caerfyrddin
Abergwili
Llangathen
Rhos
Llandeilo
Cwmfelin Boeth
Meidrim
Llangunnor
Llanarthne
Gelli Aur
Llawhaden
Robeston Wathen
Whitland
Bancyfelin
National Botanic Garden
Narberth/ Arberth
St. Clears
Sanclêr
Llangynog
Llangain
Llanddarog
Porthyrhyd
Llandybie
Tavernspite
Llanddowror
Llangyndeyrn
Drefach
Castell-y-Rhingyll
Templeton
Red Roses
Laugharne
Castle
Llan-y-bri
Llansteffan
Cross Hands
Tumble
Ammanford
Llandyfaelog
Pontyberem
Marros
Ferryside
Kilgetty
Pendine
Pendine Sands
Pontyates
Llan-non
Amroth
Kidwelly/ Cydweli
Pont Abraham
SWANSEA
Jeffreyston
Trimsaran
Saundersfoot
Carew
Monkstone Point
Burry Port/ Porth Tywyn
Hendy
Pontarddulais
Llangennech
Tenby / Dinbych-y-pysgod
Carmarthen Bay
Pembrey
St. Florence
Penally
Lydstep
Manorbier
Llanelli
Gorseinon
Caldey Sound
Caldey Island
Whitford Point
R. Loughor
Gowerton
Morriston
Penrhyn Gŵyr
Crofty
Penclawdd
Llanmadoc
Three Crosses
Burry Holms
Weobley
Llanrhidian
Killay
Llangenith
Arthur's Stone
Gower
Reynoldston
Ilston
Cefn Bryn
Bishopston
Rhossili Bay
Rhossili
Oxwich
Nicholaston
Penmaen
Worms Head
Port-Eynon
Horton
Oxwich Bay
The Mumbles
Mumbles Head
Port-Eynon-Point
Coast
0 5 10 km
F G H I

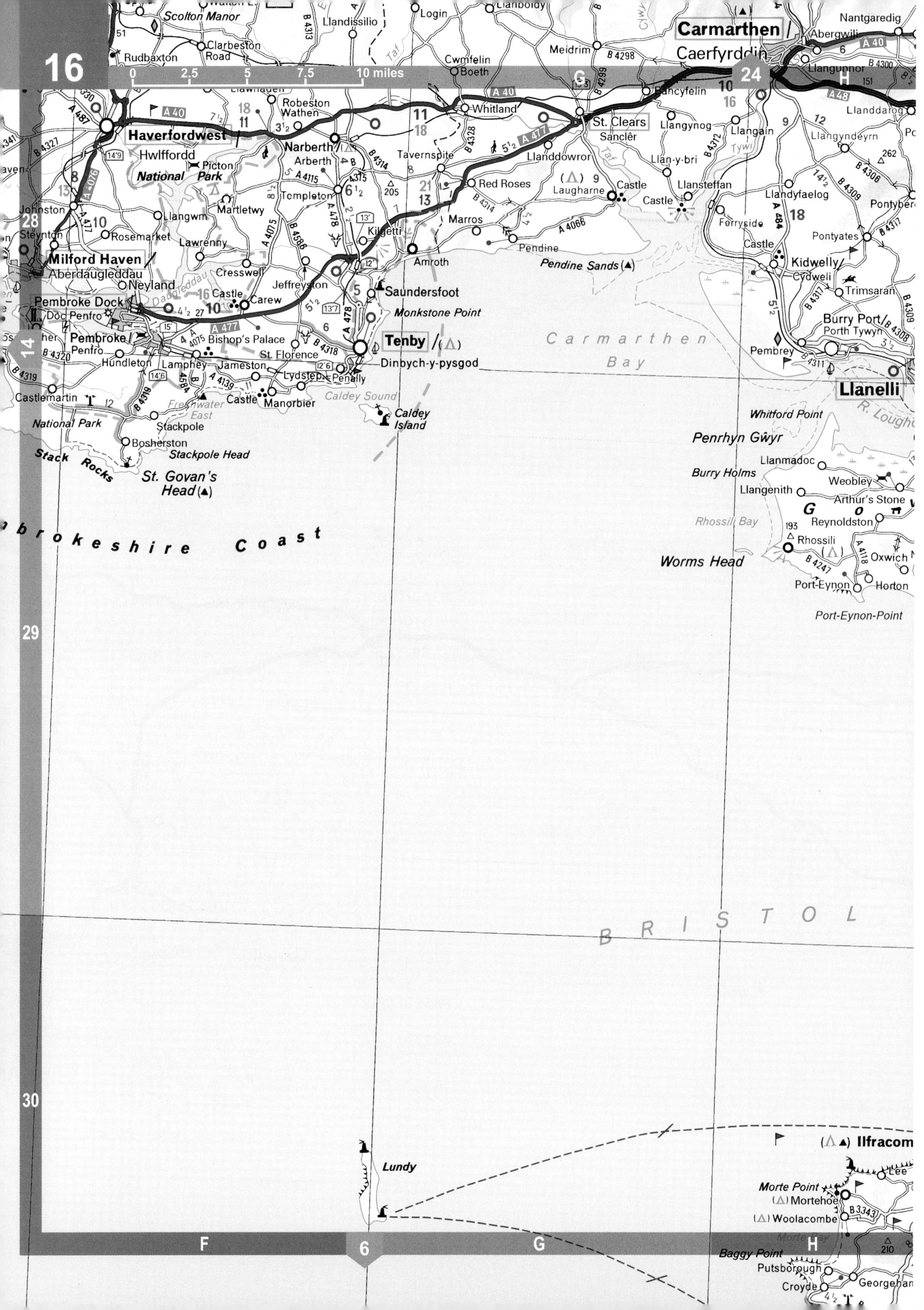

0 2.5 5 7.5 10 miles
Scolton Manor
Llandissilio
Login
Llanboidy
Carmarthen
Caerfyrddin
Nantgaredig
Abergwili
Rudbaxton
Clarbeston Road
Cwmfelin
Boeth
Meidrim
Llangunnor
Robeston Wathen
Whitland
Bancyfelin
Llanddarog
Haverfordwest
Hwlffordd
National Park
Picton
Narberth
Arberth
Tavernspite
St. Clears
Sanclêr
Llangynog
Llangain
Llangyndeyrn
Llanddowror
Llan-y-bri
Llansteffan
Laugharne
Castle
Red Roses
Templeton
Martletwy
Llangwm
Johnston
Steynton
Rosemarket
Lawrenny
Marros
Kilgetti
Llandyfaelog
Pontyberem
Ferryside
Pontyates
Kidwelly
Cydweli
Trimsaran
Milford Haven
Aberdaugleddau
Neyland
Cresswell
Jeffreyston
Amroth
Pendine
Pendine Sands
Saundersfoot
Monkstone Point
Pembroke Dock
Doc Penfro
Carew
Pembroke
Penfro
Bishop's Palace
St. Florence
Tenby
Dinbych-y-pysgod
Carmarthen Bay
Burry Port
Porth Tywyn
Pembrey
Llanelli
Hundleton
Lamphey
Jameston
Lydstep
Penally
Castlemartin
Freshwater East
Manorbier
Caldey Sound
Caldey Island
National Park
Stackpole
Bosherston
Stackpole Head
Stack Rocks
St. Govan's Head
Whitford Point
Penrhyn Gŵyr
Llanmadoc
Burry Holms
Weobley
Llangenith
Arthur's Stone
Gower
Reynoldston
Rhossili Bay
Rhossili
Oxwich
Worms Head
Port-Eynon
Horton
Port-Eynon-Point
Pembrokeshire Coast
BRISTOL
Lundy
Ilfracombe
Lee
Morte Point
Mortehoe
Woolacombe
Morte Bay
Baggy Point
Putsborough
Croyde
Georgeham
A 40
A 477
A 478
A 4075
A 4076
A 487
A 4066
A 484
A 48
B 4313
B 4298
B 4299
B 4328
B 4314
B 4315
B 4586
B 4318
B 4139
B 4584
B 4319
B 4320
B 4327
B 4312
B 4306
B 4309
B 4317
B 4308
B 4311
B 4300
B 4247
A 4118
B 3343
F
G
H
6
14
24
28
29
30

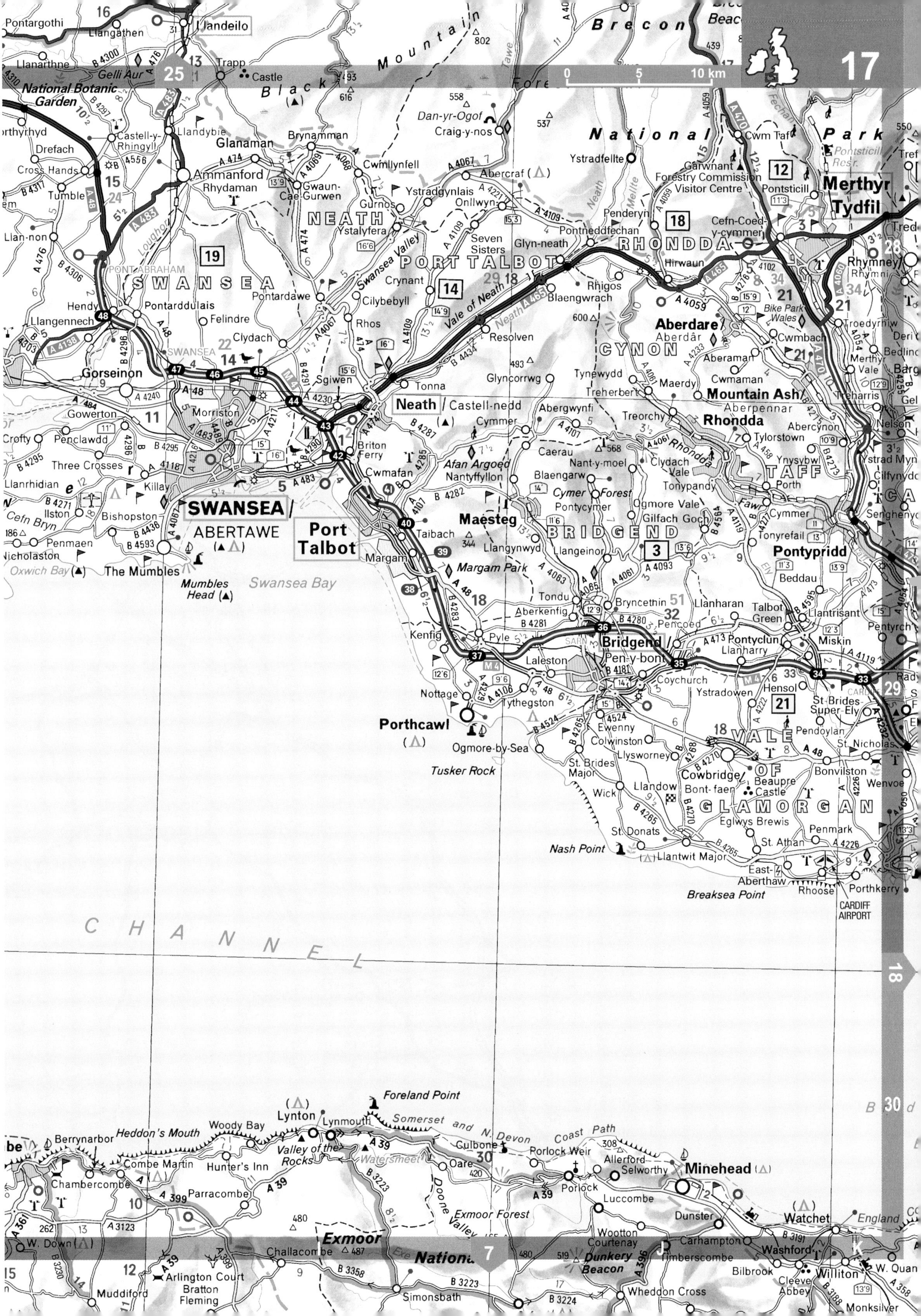
0 5 10 km
Brecon Beacons
Black Mountain
National Park
Pontargothi
Llangathen
Llandeilo
Llanarthne
National Botanic Garden
Gelli Aur
Trapp
Castle
Dan-yr-Ogof
Craig-y-nos
Glanaman
Brynamman
Cwmllynfell
Ammanford
Rhydaman
Gwaun-Cae-Gurwen
Castell-y-Rhingyll
Drefach
Cross Hands
Tumble
Llan-non
Abercraf
Ystradfellte
Cwm Taf
Garwnant Forestry Commission Visitor Centre
Pontsticill
Merthyr Tydfil
Ystradgynlais
Onllwyn
Gurnos
Ystalyfera
NEATH PORT TALBOT
Seven Sisters
Glyn-neath
Penderyn
Pontneddfechan
RHONDDA CYNON TAFF
Cefn-Coed-y-cymmer
Hirwaun
Rhigos
Blaengwrach
Aberdare
Aberdâr
Rhymney
Troedyrhiw
Merthyr Vale
Treharris
Nelson
Abercynon
Mountain Ash
Aberpennar
Cwmaman
Aberaman
Cwmbach
PONT ABRAHAM
SWANSEA
Hendy
Llangennech
Pontarddulais
Felindre
Pontardawe
Swansea Valley
Crynant
Cilybebyll
Rhos
Clydach
Vale of Neath
Resolven
Tonna
Sgiwen
Gorseinon
Gowerton
Penclawdd
Crofty
Three Crosses
Llanrhidian
Killay
Morriston
Neath / Castell-nedd
Briton Ferry
Cwmafan
Cymmer
Afan Argoed
Nantyffyllon
Glyncorrwg
Tynewydd
Treherbert
Maerdy
Abergwynfi
Treorchy
Rhondda
Caerau
Nant-y-moel
Clydach Vale
Tonypandy
Tylorstown
Ynysybwl
Porth
Cymmer
Blaengarw
Pontycymer
Ogmore Vale
Gilfach Goch
Tonyrefail
Pontypridd
Beddau
Maesteg
BRIDGEND
Cymer Forest
Llangynwyd
Llangeinor
SWANSEA
ABERTAWE
Port Talbot
Taibach
Margam
Margam Park
Bishopston
Ilston
Cefn Bryn
Penmaen
Nicholaston
Oxwich Bay
The Mumbles
Mumbles Head
Swansea Bay
Tondu
Aberkenfig
Bryncethin
Llanharan
Talbot Green
Llantrisant
Pencoed
Pontyclun
Llanharry
Miskin
Kenfig
Pyle
Laleston
Bridgend
Pen-y-bont
Coychurch
Ystradowen
Hensol
Nottage
Porthcawl
Tythegston
Ogmore-by-Sea
Ewenny
Colwinston
Llysworney
St. Brides Major
Wick
Llandow
Cowbridge
Bont-faen
Beaupre Castle
VALE OF GLAMORGAN
Pendoylan
St. Brides-Super-Ely
St. Nicholas
Bonvilston
Wenvoe
Tusker Rock
Eglwys Brewis
Penmark
St. Athan
St. Donats
Nash Point
Llantwit Major
East Aberthaw
Rhoose
Porthkerry
Breaksea Point
CARDIFF AIRPORT
CHANNEL
Foreland Point
Lynton
Lynmouth
Woody Bay
Heddon's Mouth
Berrynarbor
Somerset and N. Devon Coast Path
Valley of the Rocks
Watersmeet
Combe Martin
Hunter's Inn
Chambercombe
Parracombe
Culbone
Oare
Porlock Weir
Porlock
Allerford
Selworthy
Minehead
Luccombe
Dunster
Watchet
Doone Valley
Exmoor Forest
Exmoor National Park
Challacombe
W. Down
Wootton Courtenay
Dunkery Beacon
Carhampton
Timberscombe
Washford
Williton
Bilbrook
Cleeve Abbey
Arlington Court
Bratton Fleming
Muddiford
Simonsbath
Wheddon Cross
Monksilver

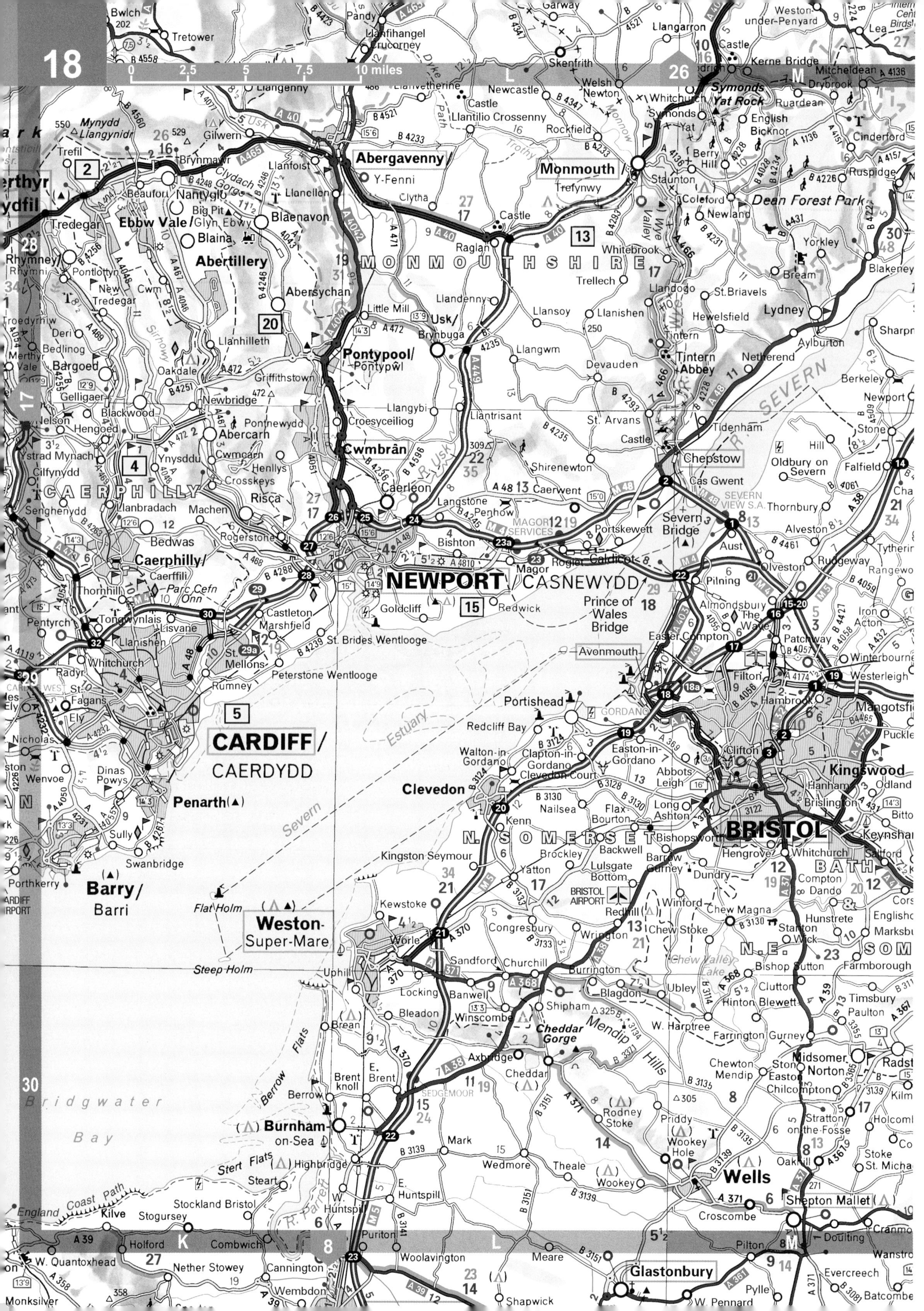
0 2,5 5 7,5 10 miles
MONMOUTHSHIRE
CAERPHILLY
N. SOMERSET
BATH
N.E. SOM
Abergavenny / Y-Fenni
Monmouth / Trefynwy
Merthyr Tydfil
Ebbw Vale / Glyn Ebwy
Abertillery
Blaenavon
Tredegar
Rhymney / Rhymni
Blaina
Nantyglo
Abersychan
Pontypool / Pontypŵl
Usk / Brynbuga
Cwmbrân
Caerleon
Raglan
Chepstow / Cas Gwent
Tintern Abbey
Lydney
Dean Forest Park
Symonds Yat Rock
Coleford
Cinderford
NEWPORT / CASNEWYDD
Caerphilly / Caerffili
Castell Coch
Parc Cefn Onn
Risca
Abercarn
CARDIFF / CAERDYDD
Penarth
Barry / Barri
Porthkerry
Cardiff Airport
Flat Holm
Steep Holm
Weston-Super-Mare
Clevedon
Portishead
Avonmouth
Prince of Wales Bridge
Severn Bridge
SEVERN VIEW S.A.
MAGOR SERVICES
R. Severn
Severn Estuary
BRISTOL
Bristol Airport
Kingswood
Keynsham
Filton
Cheddar Gorge
Cheddar
Mendip Hills
Wookey Hole
Wells
Shepton Mallet
Glastonbury
Burnham-on-Sea
Bridgwater Bay
Brean
Berrow
Highbridge
Stert Flats
Stockland Bristol
Stogursey
Kilve
England Coast Path
Nether Stowey
Holford
W. Quantoxhead
Cannington
Wembdon
Puriton
Woolavington
SEDGEMOOR
Wedmore
Axbridge
Congresbury
Yatton
Nailsea
Chew Magna
Chew Valley Lake
Midsomer Norton
Radstock
Blagdon
Burrington
Shipham
Winscombe
Banwell
Locking
Worle
Uphill
Kewstoke
Kingston Seymour
Caldicot
Magor
Redwick
Goldcliff
St. Brides Wentlooge
Peterstone Wentlooge
Marshfield
Castleton
Rumney
St. Mellons
Lisvane
Llanishen
Whitchurch
Radyr
St. Fagans
Ely
Dinas Powys
Sully
Swanbridge
Wenvoe
Pilning
Almondsbury
Thornbury
Olveston
Patchway
Winterbourne
Westerleigh
Mangotsfield
Hanham
Brislington
Whitchurch
Saltford
Long Ashton
Backwell
Flax Bourton
Barrow Gurney
Dundry
Winford
Chew Stoke
Compton Dando
Hunstrete
Stanton Wick
Bishop Sutton
Clutton
Hinton Blewett
Ubley
Timsbury
Paulton
Farrington Gurney
Chewton Mendip
Priddy
Rodney Stoke
Theale
Wookey
Croscombe
Pilton
Doulting
W. Pennard
Meare
Shapwick
Mark
E. Huntspill
W. Huntspill
R. Parrett
Combwich
Monksilver
Skenfrith
Welsh Newton
Whitchurch
Llangarron
Kerne Bridge
Mitcheldean
Drybrook
Ruardean
English Bicknor
Berry Hill
Staunton
Newland
Bream
Yorkley
Blakeney
St. Briavels
Hewelsfield
Llandogo
Whitebrook
Trellech
Llanishen
Devauden
St. Arvans
Tidenham
Aylburton
Sharpness
Berkeley
Newport
Stone
Falfield
Oldbury on Severn
Aust
Alveston
Tytherington
Rangeworthy
Iron Acton
Rudgeway
Easter Compton
The Wave
Hambrook
Clifton
Easton-in-Gordano
Abbots Leigh
Walton-in-Gordano
Clapton-in-Gordano
Clevedon Court
Redcliff Bay
Kenn
Brockley
Lulsgate Bottom
Redhill
Wrington
Churchill
Sandford
Bleadon
Brent Knoll
E. Brent
Cranmore
Evercreech
Pylle
Batcombe
Wanstrow
Oakhill
Stratton on the Fosse
Chilcompton
Emborough
Ston Easton
Holcombe
Kilmersdon
Stoke St. Michael
Farmborough
Marksbury
Englishcombe
Corston
Bitton
Odland
Pucklechurch
Caerwent
Penhow
Langstone
Bishton
Portskewett
Rogiet
Shirenewton
Llangwm
Llansoy
Llandenny
Llantrisant
Llangybi
Croesyceiliog
Little Mill
Clytha
Llanellen
Llanfoist
Gilwern
Brynmawr
Beaufort
Big Pit
Llanhilleth
Griffithstown
Pontnewydd
Newbridge
Oakdale
Blackwood
Bargoed
Gelligaer
Hengoed
Ystrad Mynach
Nelson
Cilfynydd
Senghenydd
Llanbradach
Machen
Bedwas
Rogerstone
Crosskeys
Cwmcarn
Henllys
Ynysddu
Thornhill
Tongwynlais
Pentyrch
Castell Coch
Trefil
Mynydd Llangynidr
Tretower
Bwlch
Pandy
Llanfihangel Crucorney
Llanvetherine
Llangenny
Garway
Newcastle
Llantilio Crossenny
Rockfield
Castle
Dyke Path
Llanvihangel
Goodrich
Weston-under-Penyard
Lea
Pontlottyn
New Tredegar
Deri
Bedlinog
Merthyr Vale
Troedyrhiw
Cwm
Nicholaston
Wenvoe
Holford
Combwich
Puriton
Woolavington
Burrington
Highbridge
Steart
Stockland Bristol
Berrow Flats
Severn
Estuary

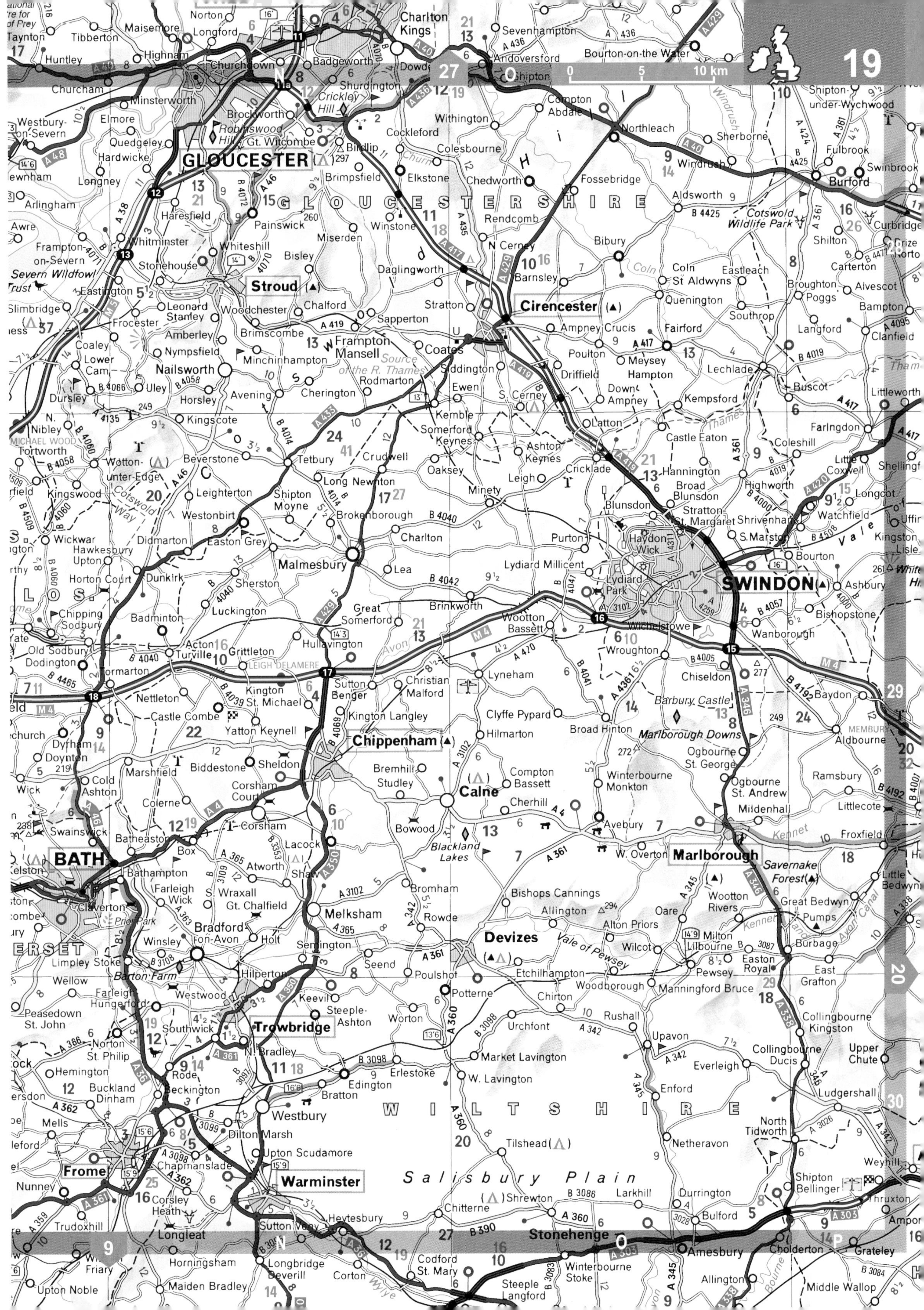
0 5 10 km
GLOUCESTER
Cheltenham
Charlton Kings
Churchdown
Maisemore
Longford
Highnam
Tibberton
Taynton
Huntley
Churcham
Minsterworth
Elmore
Westbury-on-Severn
Quedgeley
Hardwicke
Longney
Arlingham
Awre
Frampton-on-Severn
Severn Wildfowl Trust
Slimbridge
Whitminster
Haresfield
Stonehouse
Eastington
Leonard Stanley
Frocester
Coaley
Lower Cam
Dursley
Uley
Nympsfield
Nailsworth
Horsley
Kingscote
N. Nibley
Michael Wood
Tortworth
Wotton-under-Edge
Kingswood
Wickwar
Hawkesbury Upton
Horton Court
Chipping Sodbury
Yate
Old Sodbury
Dodington
Tormarton
Badminton
Acton Turville
Stroud
Painswick
Whiteshill
Woodchester
Amberley
Brimscombe
Chalford
Minchinhampton
Avening
Bisley
Miserden
Winstone
Brimpsfield
Birdlip
Cockleford
Colesbourne
Elkstone
Withington
Chedworth
Compton Abdale
Northleach
Sherborne
Windrush
Burford
Fulbrook
Swinbrook
Shipton-under-Wychwood
Bourton-on-the-Water
Sevenhampton
Andoversford
Shipton
Dowdeswell
Shurdington
Badgeworth
Crickley Hill
Brockworth
Robinswood Hill
Gt. Witcombe
Cotswold Wildlife Park
Shilton
Curbridge
Carterton
Alvescot
Broughton Poggs
Bampton
Clanfield
Langford
Southrop
Eastleach
Coln St Aldwyns
Quenington
Fairford
Bibury
Barnsley
Aldsworth
Fossebridge
Rendcomb
N Cerney
Daglingworth
Stratton
Cirencester
Ampney Crucis
Poulton
Meysey Hampton
Lechlade
Buscot
Kempsford
Down Ampney
Driffield
Siddington
S. Cerney
Ewen
Kemble
Coates
Sapperton
Frampton Mansell
Source of the R. Thames
Rodmarton
Cherington
Tetbury
Beverstone
Leighterton
Westonbirt
Didmarton
Shipton Moyne
Long Newnton
Crudwell
Oaksey
Somerford Keynes
Ashton Keynes
Minety
Leigh
Cricklade
Latton
Castle Eaton
Hannington
Highworth
Coleshill
Faringdon
Littleworth
Shellingford
Little Coxwell
Longcot
Watchfield
Shrivenham
Uffington
Kingston Lisle
Bourton
Ashbury
Bishopstone
Wanborough
Broad Blunsdon
Blunsdon
Stratton-St. Margaret
S.Marston
Haydon Wick
Lydiard Park
SWINDON
Purton
Lydiard Millicent
Wootton Bassett
Wichelstowe
Wroughton
Chiseldon
Baydon
Aldbourne
Ramsbury
Littlecote
Froxfield
Marlborough
Savernake Forest
Little Bedwyn
Great Bedwyn
Wootton Rivers
Pumps
Burbage
East Grafton
Easton Royal
Pewsey
Milton Lilbourne
Oare
Manningford Bruce
Woodborough
Wilcot
Alton Priors
Vale of Pewsey
Allington
Bishops Cannings
Devizes
Etchilhampton
Chirton
Rushall
Upavon
Urchfont
Market Lavington
W. Lavington
Enford
Everleigh
Collingbourne Kingston
Collingbourne Ducis
Ludgershall
Upper Chute
North Tidworth
Netheravon
Weyhill
Shipton Bellinger
Thruxton
Amport
Durrington
Bulford
Larkhill
Amesbury
Stonehenge
Cholderton
Grateley
Allington
Middle Wallop
Winterbourne Stoke
Steeple Langford
Shrewton
Tilshead
Salisbury Plain
Chitterne
Codford St. Mary
Heytesbury
Sutton Veny
Longbridge Deverill
Corton
Warminster
Upton Scudamore
Dilton Marsh
Westbury
Bratton
Edington
Erlestoke
Chapmanslade
Corsley Heath
Longleat
Horningsham
Maiden Bradley
Frome
Nunney
Trudoxhill
Upton Noble
Mells
Buckland Dinham
Hemington
Beckington
Rode
Norton St. Philip
Southwick
Trowbridge
N. Bradley
Hilperton
Steeple Ashton
Keevil
Worton
Potterne
Poulshot
Seend
Semington
Melksham
Rowde
Bromham
Bowood
Blackland Lakes
Calne
Cherhill
Avebury
W. Overton
Compton Bassett
Hilmarton
Bremhill
Studley
Chippenham
Lacock
Shaw
Atworth
Gt. Chalfield
S. Wraxall
Bradford-on-Avon
Holt
Winsley
Limpley Stoke
Barton Farm
Westwood
Farleigh Hungerford
Wellow
Peasedown St. John
Bathampton
Claverton
Prior Park
Farleigh Wick
Box
Batheaston
BATH
Swainswick
Cold Ashton
Marshfield
Colerne
Corsham
Corsham Court
Biddestone
Sheldon
Yatton Keynell
Castle Combe
Nettleton
Kington St. Michael
Kington Langley
Sutton Benger
Christian Malford
Lyneham
Clyffe Pypard
Broad Hinton
Winterbourne Monkton
Marlborough Downs
Barbury Castle
Ogbourne St. George
Ogbourne St. Andrew
Mildenhall
Hullavington
Grittleton
Leigh Delamere
Luckington
Sherston
Easton Grey
Malmesbury
Brokenborough
Charlton
Lea
Brinkworth
Great Somerford
Dyrham
Doynton
Wick
GLOUCESTERSHIRE
WILTSHIRE
Cotswold Way
Cotswold Hills
Windrush
Coln
Churn
Thames
Kennet
Avon
Wylye
Kennet and Avon Canal

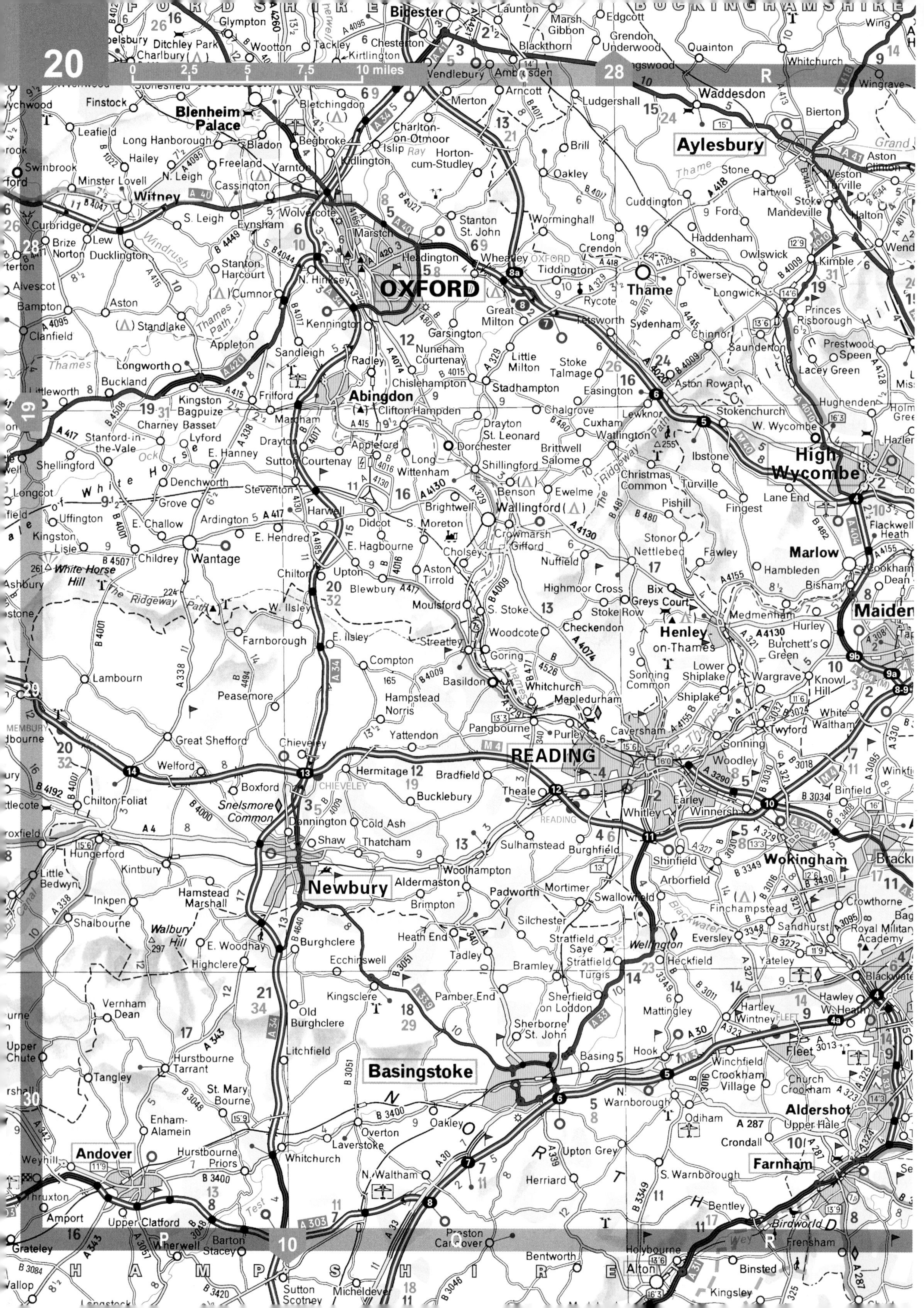
0 2.5 5 7.5 10 miles
28
19
29
30
10
OXFORD
READING
Aylesbury
Abingdon
Newbury
Basingstoke
Andover
High Wycombe
Marlow
Wokingham
Farnham
Aldershot
Witney
Thame
Wantage
Wallingford
Henley-on-Thames
Bicester
Blenheim Palace
Kidlington
Woodstock
Charlbury
Glympton
Ditchley Park
Wootton
Tackley
Chesterton
Kirtlington
Launton
Marsh Gibbon
Edgcott
Grendon Underwood
Blackthorn
Quainton
Wing
Whitchurch
Wingrave
Waddesdon
Ludgershall
Bierton
Weston Turville
Aston Clinton
Stone
Hartwell
Stoke Mandeville
Halton
Wendover
Cuddington
Ford
Haddenham
Owlswick
Kimble
Towersey
Longwick
Princes Risborough
Chinnor
Saunderton
Prestwood
Speen
Lacey Green
Hughenden
Sydenham
Aston Rowant
Stokenchurch
Lewknor
W. Wycombe
Hazlemere
Ibstone
Turville
Fingest
Lane End
Flackwell Heath
Christmas Common
Pishill
Stonor
Nettlebed
Fawley
Hambleden
Cookham
Bisham
Highmoor Cross
Bix
Greys Court
Medmenham
Hurley
Burchett's Green
Stoke Row
Checkendon
Wargrave
Knowl Hill
Lower Shiplake
Shiplake
Sonning Common
Twyford
White Waltham
Caversham
Sonning
Woodley
Earley
Winnersh
Binfield
Whitley
Shinfield
Arborfield
Finchampstead
Crowthorne
Sandhurst
Royal Military Academy
Eversley
Yateley
Blackwater
Hawley
W. Heath
Hartley Wintney
Fleet
Winchfield
Crookham Village
Church Crookham
Hook
Basing
N. Warnborough
Odiham
Upper Hale
Crondall
S. Warnborough
Bentley
Birdworld
Frensham
Holybourne
Alton
Binsted
Kingsley
Upton Grey
Herriard
Bentworth
Preston Candover
Oakley
Overton
Laverstoke
Whitchurch
N. Waltham
Micheldever
Sutton Scotney
Barton Stacey
Wherwell
Upper Clatford
Amport
Thruxton
Weyhill
Grateley
Hurstbourne Priors
Enham-Alamein
St. Mary Bourne
Hurstbourne Tarrant
Tangley
Upper Chute
Vernham Dean
Litchfield
Old Burghclere
Kingsclere
Sherborne St. John
Sherfield on Loddon
Pamber End
Bramley
Turgis
Stratfield Saye
Wellington
Heckfield
Mattingley
Tadley
Heath End
Silchester
Padworth
Mortimer
Swallowfield
Aldermaston
Brimpton
Woolhampton
Burghclere
Ecchinswell
Highclere
E. Woodhay
Walbury Hill
Inkpen
Shalbourne
Hamstead Marshall
Kintbury
Hungerford
Little Bedwyn
Froxfield
Chilton Foliat
Boxford
Snelsmore Common
Donnington
Cold Ash
Shaw
Thatcham
Bucklebury
Bradfield
Hermitage
Chieveley
Welford
Great Shefford
Lambourn
Peasemore
Hampstead Norris
Yattendon
Pangbourne
Purley
Mapledurham
Theale
Sulhamstead
Burghfield
Basildon
Whitchurch
Goring
Streatley
Woodcote
S. Stoke
Moulsford
Compton
E. Ilsley
W. Ilsley
Farnborough
Chilton
Upton
Blewbury
Aston Tirrold
Cholsey
Crowmarsh Gifford
Nuffield
Brightwell
S. Moreton
Didcot
E. Hagbourne
Harwell
E. Hendred
Ardington
Childrey
Kingston Lisle
Uffington
White Horse Hill
Ashbury
Grove
E. Challow
Denchworth
Steventon
Sutton Courtenay
Appleford
Long Wittenham
Dorchester
Shillingford
Benson
Ewelme
Brittwell Salome
Watlington
Cuxham
Chalgrove
Drayton St. Leonard
Clifton Hampden
Stadhampton
Chiselhampton
Easington
Stoke Talmage
Little Milton
Great Milton
Tetsworth
Rycote
Tiddington
Wheatley
Garsington
Nuneham Courtenay
Radley
Sandleigh
Kennington
Headington
Marston
N. Hinksey
Cumnor
Appleton
Wootton
Frilford
Marcham
Drayton
Milton
Steventon
Kingston Bagpuize
Longworth
Buckland
Littleworth
Charney Basset
Lyford
E. Hanney
Stanford-in-the-Vale
Shellingford
Longcot
Standlake
Stanton Harcourt
Aston
Bampton
Clanfield
Alvescot
Brize Norton
Ducklington
Curbridge
Minster Lovell
Swinbrook
Asthall
Leafield
Finstock
Hailey
N. Leigh
Freeland
Long Hanborough
Bladon
Begbroke
Yarnton
Cassington
Eynsham
S. Leigh
Wolvercote
Bletchingdon
Islip
Charlton-on-Otmoor
Horton-cum-Studley
Merton
Arncott
Ambrosden
Wendlebury
Brill
Oakley
Worminghall
Long Crendon
Stanton St. John
Thames
Thames Path
Windrush
The Ridgeway Path
Vale of White Horse
Chiltern Hills
Blackwater
R. Thames
Grand Union
Ray
Ock
Test
Wey
FORDSHIRE
BUCKINGHAMSHIRE
HAMPSHIRE
NORTH DOWNS
OXFORD
READING
CHIEVELEY
MEMBURY
FLEET
M4
M40
M3
A34
A40
A41
A418
A4
A33
A30
A303
A339
A329
A4074
A4130
A338
A417
A420
A415
A343

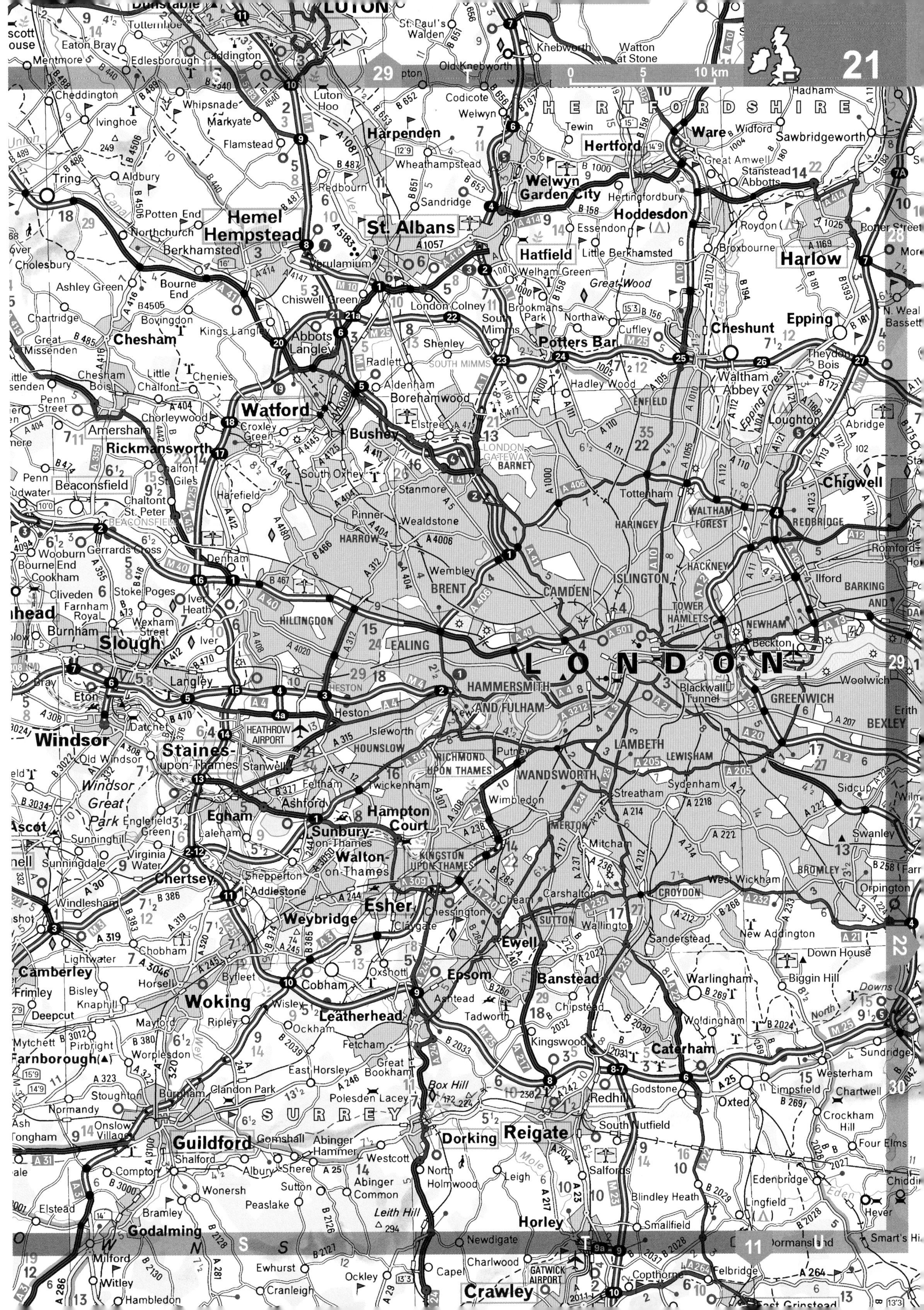
21
29
0 5 10 km
HERTFORDSHIRE
SURREY
LUTON
Dunstable
Totternhoe
Eaton Bray
Edlesborough
Caddington
Mentmore
Cheddington
Whipsnade
Markyate
Luton Hoo
Ivinghoe
Flamstead
Tring
Aldbury
Potten End
Northchurch
Berkhamsted
Hemel Hempstead
Redbourn
Harpenden
Wheathampstead
St. Paul's Walden
Knebworth
Old Knebworth
Watton at Stone
Codicote
Welwyn
Tewin
Hertford
Ware
Widford
Sawbridgeworth
Great Amwell
Stanstead Abbotts
Hertingfordbury
Welwyn Garden City
Hoddesdon
Essendon
Sandridge
St. Albans
Verulamium
Hatfield
Little Berkhamsted
Welham Green
Great Wood
Brookmans Park
Northaw
Cuffley
Roydon
Broxbourne
Harlow
Potter Street
Cholesbury
Ashley Green
Bourne End
Chartridge
Bovingdon
Kings Langley
Great Missenden
Chesham
Chiswell Green
London Colney
South Mimms
Abbots Langley
Shenley
Radlett
Potters Bar
Cheshunt
Epping
Theydon Bois
Waltham Abbey
Epping Forest
Loughton
Abridge
Chesham Bois
Little Chalfont
Chenies
Aldenham
Borehamwood
Hadley Wood
ENFIELD
Penn Street
Amersham
Chorleywood
Watford
Croxley Green
Bushey
Elstree
LONDON GATEWAY
BARNET
Rickmansworth
Chalfont St. Giles
South Oxhey
Stanmore
Tottenham
WALTHAM FOREST
Chigwell
REDBRIDGE
Penn
Beaconsfield
Chalfont St. Peter
Harefield
Pinner
Wealdstone
HARROW
HARINGEY
Romford
Gerrards Cross
Wooburn
Bourne End
Cookham
Denham
Wembley
BRENT
CAMDEN
ISLINGTON
HACKNEY
Ilford
BARKING
Cliveden
Farnham Royal
Stoke Poges
Iver Heath
HILLINGDON
TOWER HAMLETS
NEWHAM
Burnham
Wexham Street
Slough
Iver
EALING
LONDON
Beckton
Langley
HESTON
HAMMERSMITH AND FULHAM
Blackwall Tunnel
GREENWICH
Woolwich
Eton
Windsor
Datchet
Heston
Kew
HEATHROW AIRPORT
Isleworth
HOUNSLOW
LAMBETH
LEWISHAM
Erith
BEXLEY
Old Windsor
Staines-upon-Thames
Stanwell
RICHMOND UPON THAMES
Putney
WANDSWORTH
Windsor Great Park
Feltham
Twickenham
Wimbledon
Streatham
Sydenham
Sidcup
Ascot
Englefield Green
Egham
Ashford
Hampton Court
Sunbury-on-Thames
Sunninghill
Laleham
MERTON
Mitcham
Swanley
Sunningdale
Virginia Water
Walton-on-Thames
KINGSTON UPON THAMES
BROMLEY
Chertsey
Shepperton
Addlestone
Carshalton
West Wickham
CROYDON
Orpington
Windlesham
Esher
Cheam
Chessington
SUTTON
Wallington
Weybridge
Claygate
Sanderstead
New Addington
Lightwater
Chobham
Ewell
Down House
Camberley
Horsell
Byfleet
Oxshott
Epsom
Banstead
Warlingham
Biggin Hill
Frimley
Bisley
Knaphill
Cobham
Woking
Wisley
Ashtead
Tadworth
Chipstead
Deepcut
Mayford
Ripley
Leatherhead
Woldingham
Ockham
Kingswood
Caterham
Sundridge
Mytchett
Pirbright
Worplesdon
Fetcham
Farnborough
Great Bookham
East Horsley
Oxted
Westerham
Limpsfield
Chartwell
Stoughton
Burpham
Clandon Park
Box Hill
Redhill
Godstone
Normandy
Polesden Lacey
Crockham Hill
Ash
Tongham
Onslow Village
Guildford
Gomshall
Abinger Hammer
Westcott
Dorking
Reigate
South Nutfield
Four Elms
Shalford
Compton
Albury
Shere
North Holmwood
Leigh
Salfords
Edenbridge
Wonersh
Sutton
Abinger Common
Blindley Heath
Hever
Elstead
Bramley
Peaslake
Leith Hill
Horley
Lingfield
Godalming
Smallfield
Newdigate
Dormansland
Milford
Charlwood
GATWICK AIRPORT
Ewhurst
Ockley
Capel
Copthorne
Felbridge
Witley
Cranleigh
Crawley
Hambledon
East Grinstead

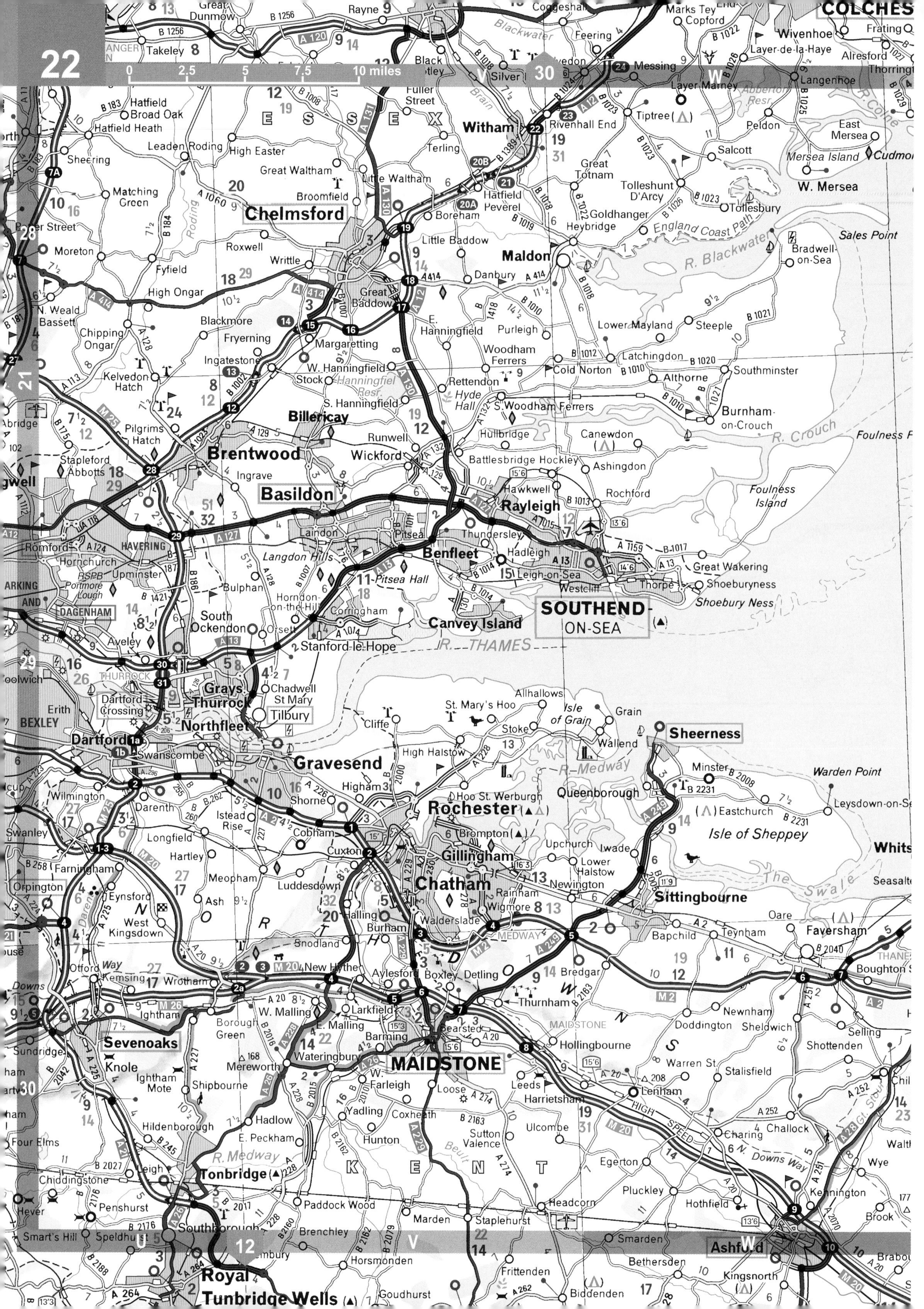
0
2.5
5
7.5
10 miles
E S S E X
K E N T
N O R T H D O W N S
Great Dunmow
Takeley
Rayne
Coggeshall
Marks Tey
Copford
COLCHESTER
Wivenhoe
Frating
Layer-de-la-Haye
Alresford
Thorrington
Feering
Kelvedon
Messing
Langenhoe
Layer Marney
Abberton Resr.
Tiptree
Peldon
East Mersea
Mersea Island
Cudmore
W. Mersea
Salcott
Black Notley
Silver End
Fuller Street
Blackwater
Brain
Witham
Rivenhall End
Hatfield Broad Oak
Hatfield Heath
Leaden Roding
High Easter
Terling
Sheering
Great Waltham
Little Waltham
Great Totham
Tolleshunt D'Arcy
Tollesbury
Matching Green
Broomfield
Hatfield Peverel
Boreham
Goldhanger
Heybridge
England Coast Path
R. Blackwater
Bradwell-on-Sea
Sales Point
Chelmsford
Roding
Roxwell
Writtle
Moreton
Fyfield
Little Baddow
Maldon
Danbury
High Ongar
Great Baddow
N. Weald Bassett
Chipping Ongar
Blackmore
Fryerning
Margaretting
E. Hanningfield
Purleigh
Lower Mayland
Steeple
Ingatestone
W. Hanningfield
Stock
Hanningfield Resr.
S. Hanningfield
Woodham Ferrers
Cold Norton
Latchingdon
Althorne
Southminster
Kelvedon Hatch
Rettendon
Hyde Hall
S. Woodham Ferrers
Burnham-on-Crouch
Pilgrims Hatch
Billericay
Runwell
Wickford
Hullbridge
Canewdon
R. Crouch
Foulness Point
Stapleford Abbotts
Brentwood
Ingrave
Battlesbridge
Hockley
Ashingdon
Rochford
Foulness Island
Hawkwell
Rayleigh
Basildon
Laindon
Pitsea
Thundersley
Romford
HAVERING
Hornchurch
Upminster
RSPB Rainham Marshes
Langdon Hills
Benfleet
Hadleigh
Leigh-on-Sea
Westcliff
Thorpe Bay
Great Wakering
Shoeburyness
Shoebury Ness
BARKING AND DAGENHAM
Bulphan
Horndon-on-the-Hill
Pitsea Hall
Corringham
Canvey Island
SOUTHEND-ON-SEA
South Ockendon
Orsett
Stanford-le-Hope
R. THAMES
Aveley
THURROCK
Woolwich
Grays Thurrock
Chadwell St Mary
Tilbury
Dartford Crossing
Erith
BEXLEY
Dartford
Swanscombe
Northfleet
Gravesend
Cliffe
St. Mary's Hoo
Allhallows
Isle of Grain
Grain
Stoke
Wallend
Sheerness
High Halstow
R. Medway
Minster
Warden Point
Wilmington
Darenth
Istead Rise
Higham
Shorne
Hoo St. Werburgh
Queenborough
Eastchurch
Leysdown-on-Sea
Isle of Sheppey
Swanley
Longfield
Cobham
Cuxton
Rochester
Brompton
Gillingham
Upchurch
Iwade
Lower Halstow
Whitstable
Hartley
Farningham
Meopham
Luddesdown
Chatham
Rainham
Newington
Sittingbourne
The Swale
Seasalter
Orpington
Eynsford
Ash
Wigmore
Halling
Burham
Walderslade
Bapchild
Teynham
Oare
Faversham
West Kingsdown
Snodland
MEDWAY
Otford
Kemsing
Wrotham
New Hythe
Aylesford
Boxley
Detling
Bredgar
Boughton Street
Ightham
Borough Green
W. Malling
Larkfield
E. Malling
Thurnham
Newnham
Doddington
Sheldwich
Selling
Sundridge
Sevenoaks
Barming
Bearsted
MAIDSTONE
Hollingbourne
Shottenden
Knole
Ightham Mote
Mereworth
Wateringbury
W. Farleigh
Loose
Leeds
Harrietsham
Warren St.
Stalisfield
Lenham
HIGH SPEED
Chilham
Shipbourne
Hildenborough
Yadling
Coxheath
Sutton Valence
Ulcombe
Charing
Challock
Four Elms
Hadlow
E. Peckham
Hunton
Beult
Egerton
N. Downs Way
Wye
Chiddingstone
Leigh
Tonbridge
Pluckley
Kennington
Hever
Penshurst
Paddock Wood
Headcorn
Hothfield
Brook
Smart's Hill
Speldhurst
Southborough
Brenchley
Marden
Staplehurst
Smarden
Ashford
Brabourne
Horsmonden
Frittenden
Bethersden
Kingsnorth
Royal Tunbridge Wells
Goudhurst
Biddenden

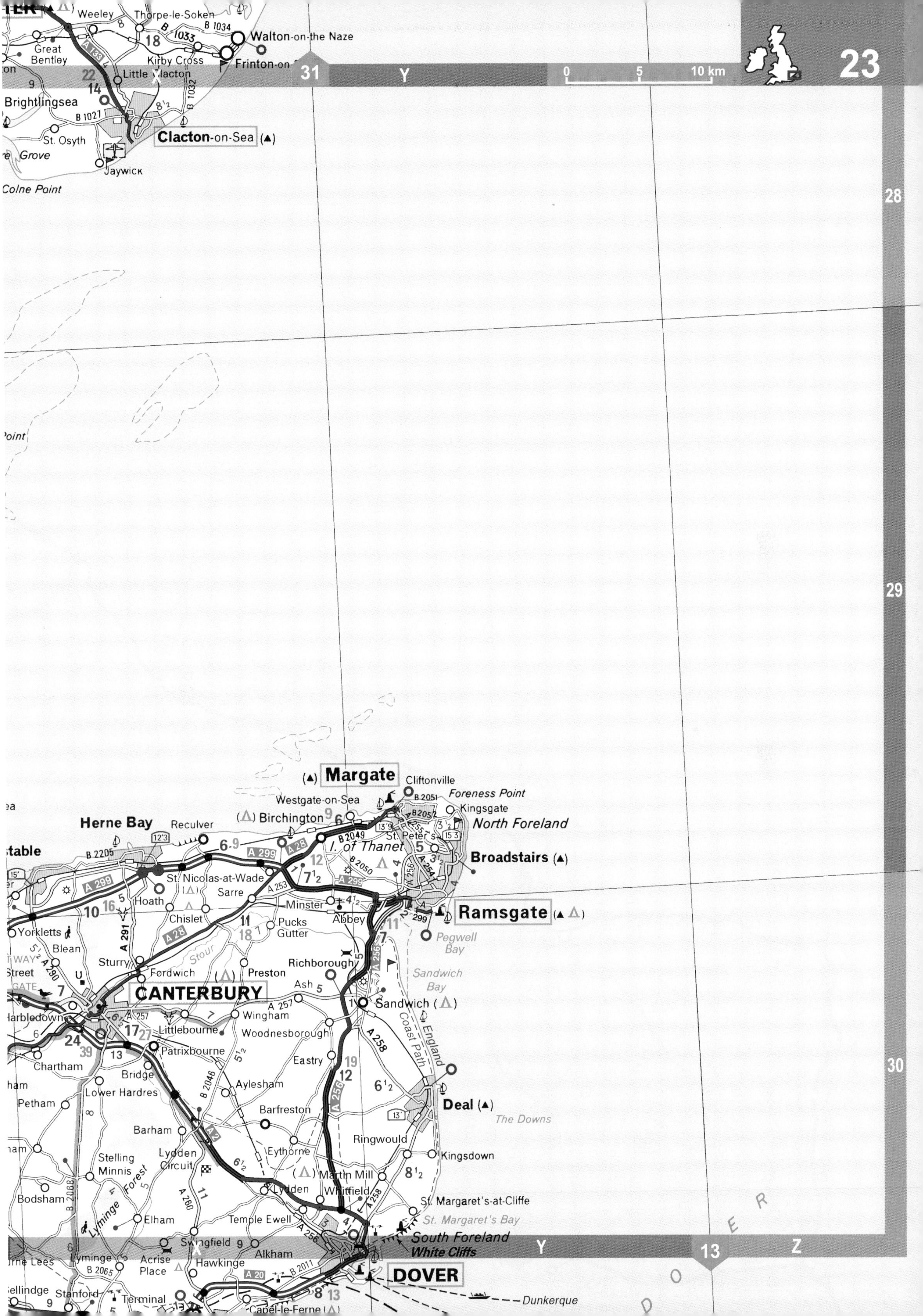
31
Y
0 5 10 km
Weeley
Thorpe-le-Soken
B 1034
B 1033
Walton-on-the Naze
Great Bentley
Kirby Cross
Frinton-on-
Little Clacton
A 133
B 1032
Brightlingsea
B 1027
St. Osyth
Clacton-on-Sea (▲)
Grove
Jaywick
Colne Point
Point
28
29
30
(▲) Margate
Cliftonville
Westgate-on-Sea
B 2051
Foreness Point
Kingsgate
(Δ) Birchington
B 2052
North Foreland
Herne Bay
Reculver
B 2049
I. of Thanet
St. Peter's
A 299
A 28
A 255
Broadstairs (▲)
B 2205
A 254
stable
B 2050
St. Nicolas-at-Wade
Sarre
A 253
Hoath
Minster
Abbey
Ramsgate (▲ Δ)
Chislet
Pucks Gutter
Pegwell Bay
Yorkletts
A 291
A 28
Blean
Stour
Sandwich Bay
A 290
Sturry
Preston
Richborough
A 256
Street
Fordwich
CANTERBURY
Ash
Sandwich (Δ)
Harbledown
A 257
Wingham
Littlebourne
Woodnesborough
Coast Path
England
Chartham
Patrixbourne
A 258
Bridge
Eastry
B 2046
Aylesham
Petham
Lower Hardres
A 256
Deal (▲)
Barfreston
The Downs
Barham
A 2
Ringwould
Stelling Minnis
Lydden Circuit
Eythorne
Kingsdown
Lyminge Forest
A 260
Martin Mill
Whitfield
A 258
Bodsham
B 2068
Lydden
St. Margaret's-at-Cliffe
Elham
Temple Ewell
St. Margaret's Bay
South Foreland
Swingfield
A 256
White Cliffs
X
Y
13
Z
Lyminge
Acrise Place
Hawkinge
Alkham
B 2065
B 2011
A 20
DOVER
Stanford
Terminal
Capel-le-Ferne (Δ)
Dunkerque
DOVER

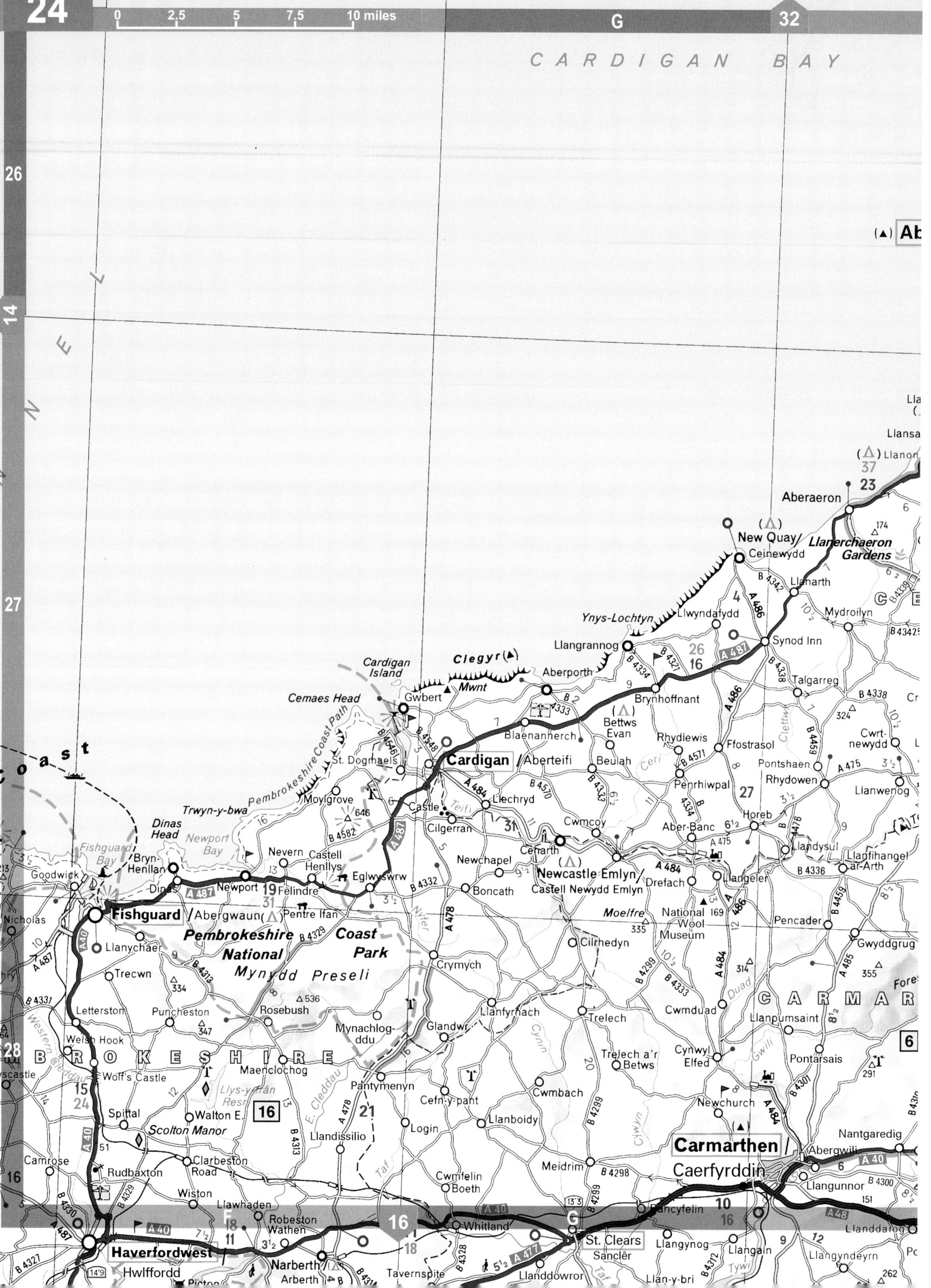
0 2,5 5 7,5 10 miles
G
32
CARDIGAN BAY
26
14
27
28
16
Aberaeron
23
New Quay/
Ceinewydd
Llanerchaeron Gardens
Llanarth
Mydroilyn
Ynys-Lochtyn
Llwyndafydd
Synod Inn
Llangrannog
Clegyr
Cardigan Island
Aberporth
Mwnt
Gwbert
Cemaes Head
Brynhoffnant
Talgarreg
Blaenannerch
Bettws Evan
Rhydlewis
Ffostrasol
Cwrt-newydd
Cardigan
/Aberteifi
St. Dogmaels
Beulah
Penrhiwpal
Pontshaen
Rhydowen
Llanwenog
Pembrokeshire Coast Path
Moylgrove
Llechryd
Castle
Cilgerran
Teifi
Trwyn-y-bwa
Dinas Head
Newport Bay
Fishguard Bay
Cwmcoy
Aber-Banc
Horeb
Llandysul
Llanfihangel ar-Arth
Cenarth
Newcastle Emlyn/
Castell Newydd Emlyn
Drefach
Llangeler
Newchapel
Boncath
Nevern
Castell Henllys
Eglwyswrw
Felindre
Bryn-Henllan
Dinas
Goodwick
Newport
Fishguard
/Abergwaun
Pentre Ifan
St. Nicholas
Llanychaer
Pembrokeshire Coast National Park
Mynydd Preseli
Moelfre
National Wool Museum
Cilrhedyn
Pencader
Gwyddgrug
Trecwn
Crymych
Letterston
Puncheston
Rosebush
Mynachlog-ddu
Llanfyrnach
Trelech
Cwmduad
Llanpumsaint
Welsh Hook
BROKESHIRE
Maenclochog
Glandwr
Trelech a'r Betws
Cynwyl Elfed
Pontarsais
Wolf's Castle
Llys-y-frân Resr
Pantymenyn
Cwmbach
Spittal
Walton E.
Scolton Manor
Cefn-y-pant
Login
Llanboidy
Newchurch
Llandissilio
Carmarthen
Caerfyrddin
Abergwili
Nantgaredig
Camrose
Rudbaxton
Clarbeston Road
Meidrim
Cwmfelin Boeth
Llangunnor
Wiston
Llawhaden
Robeston Wathen
Whitland
Pancyfelin
Llanddarog
Haverfordwest
Hwlffordd
Narberth
Arberth
Tavernspite
St. Clears
Sanclêr
Llangynog
Llangain
Llangyndeyrn
Llanddowror
Llan-y-bri
Picton
Coast
CARMAR
A 40
A 487
A 484
A 486
A 478
A 477
A 48
A 475
A 485
Abe
Llanon
Llansa
Fores
Nyfer
Gwili
Taf
Tywi
E. Cleddau
Western Cleddau
Cynin
Duad
Ceri
Clettwr

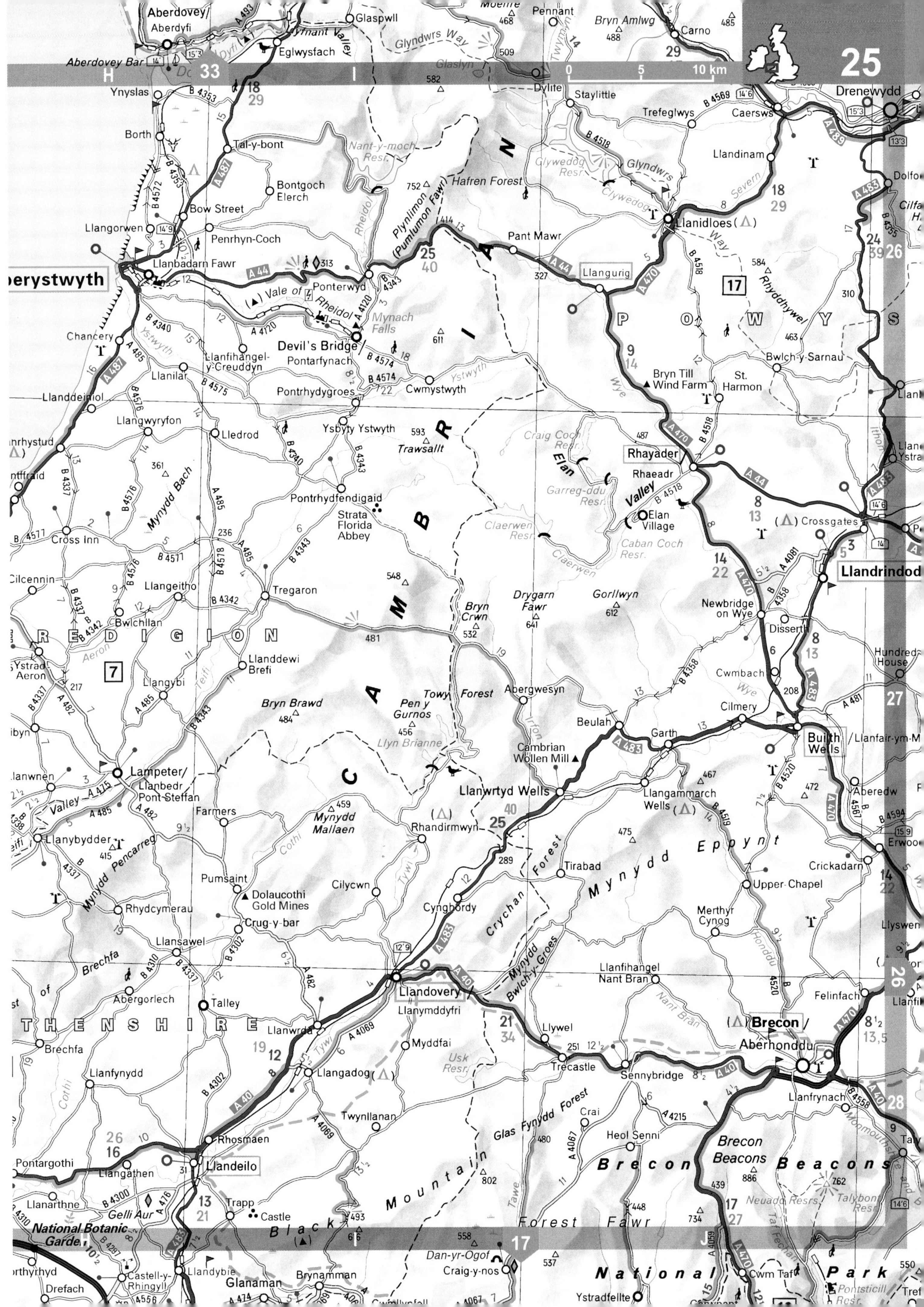
Aberdovey/
Aberdyfi
Aberdovey Bar
Eglwysfach
Glaspwll
Glyndwrs Way
Pennant
Bryn Amlwg
Carno
Glaslyn
Dylife
Staylittle
Trefeglwys
Caersws
Drenewydd
Ynyslas
Borth
Tal-y-bont
Nant-y-moch Resr.
Glywedog Resr.
Glyndwrs
Llandinam
Bontgoch
Elerch
Hafren Forest
Bow Street
Plynlimon (Pumlumon Fawr)
Llanidloes
Severn
Llangorwen
Penrhyn-Coch
Pant Mawr
Aberystwyth
Llanbadarn Fawr
Ponterwyd
Vale of Rheidol
Llangurig
Mynach Falls
Devil's Bridge
Pontarfynach
Chancery
Llanfihangel-y-Creuddyn
Llanilar
Cwmystwyth
Pontrhydygroes
POWYS
Rhyddhywel
Bwlch-y-Sarnau
Bryn Till Wind Farm
St. Harmon
Llanddeiniol
Llangwyryfon
Lledrod
Ysbyty Ystwyth
Trawsallt
Craig Coch Resr.
Rhayader
Rhaeadr
Elan
Mynydd Bach
Pontrhydfendigaid
Strata Florida Abbey
Garreg-ddu Resr.
Elan Valley
Elan Village
Cross Inn
Claerwen Resr.
Caban Coch Resr.
Crossgates
Llandrindod
CAMBRIAN
Cilcennin
Llangeitho
Tregaron
Bryn Crwn
Drygarn Fawr
Gorllwyn
Newbridge on Wye
Disserth
Bwlchllan
CEREDIGION
Ystrad Aeron
Llanddewi Brefi
Llangybi
Cwmbach
Hundred House
Bryn Brawd
Pen y Gurnos
Towy Forest
Abergwesyn
Cilmery
Beulah
Garth
Builth Wells
Llanfair-ym-M
Llyn Brianne
Cambrian Wollen Mill
Lampeter/
Llanbedr Pont Steffan
Llanwnen
Llanwrtyd Wells
Llangammarch Wells
Aberedw
Farmers
Mynydd Mallaen
Rhandirmwyn
Llanybydder
Mynydd Pencarreg
Cothi
Tirabad
Mynydd Eppynt
Erwood
Crickadarn
Pumsaint
Dolaucothi Gold Mines
Cilycwn
Upper Chapel
Rhydcymerau
Cynghordy
Crychan Forest
Merthyr Cynog
Llyswen
Crug-y-bar
Llansawel
Brechfa
Mynydd Bwlch-y-Groes
Llanfihangel Nant Bran
Abergorlech
Talley
Llandovery
Llanymddyfri
Felinfach
CARMARTHENSHIRE
Llanwrda
Llywel
Brecon/
Aberhonddu
Brechfa
Myddfai
Usk Resr.
Trecastle
Sennybridge
Llanfynydd
Llangadog
Llanfrynach
Twynllanan
Glas Fynydd Forest
Crai
Heol Senni
Brecon Beacons
Rhosmaen
Pontargothi
Llangathen
Llandeilo
Black Mountain
Brecon Beacons National Park
Llanarthne
Gelli Aur
Trapp
Castle
Neuadd Resrs
Talybont Resr.
National Botanic Garden
Forest Fawr
Dan-yr-Ogof
Craig-y-nos
Castell-y-Rhingyll
Llandybie
Glanaman
Brynamman
Drefach
Cwm Taf
Ystradfellte
Pontsticill Resr.
0 5 10 km

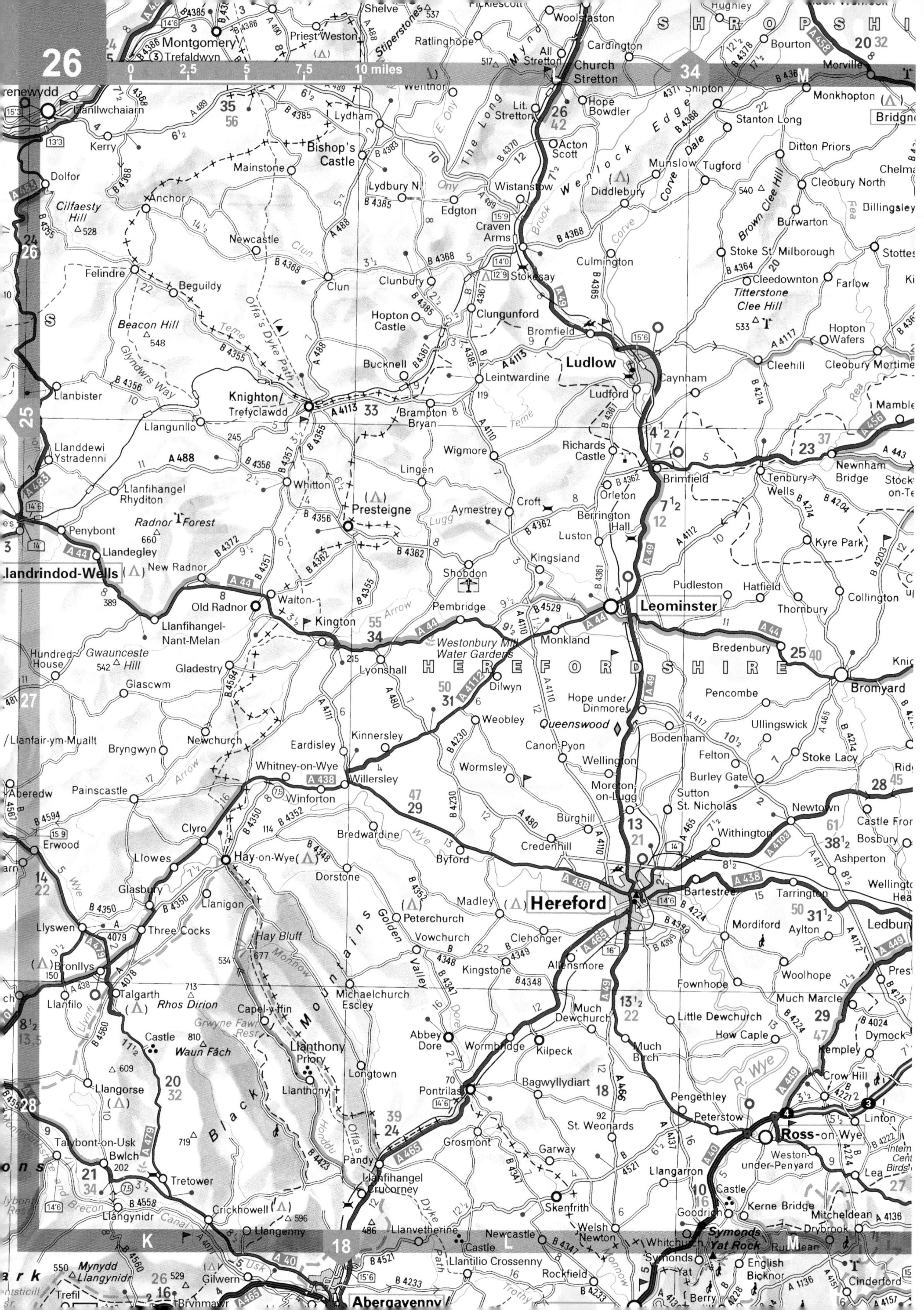
0
2,5
5
7,5
10 miles
34
25
27
28
18
SHROPSHIRE
HEREFORDSHIRE
Montgomery
Trefaldwyn
Priest Weston
Shelve
Stiperstones
Ratlinghope
Woolstaston
Cardington
Hughley
Bourton
Morville
All Stretton
Church Stretton
The Long Mynd
Wentnor
Lydham
Bishop's Castle
Llanllwchaiarn
Kerry
Dolfor
Mainstone
Anchor
Cilfaesty Hill
528
Newcastle
Clun
Felindre
Beguildy
Beacon Hill
548
Glyndwr's Way
Offa's Dyke Path
Teme
Clunbury
Hopton Castle
Clungunford
Bucknell
Knighton/
Trefyclawdd
Llanbister
Llangunllo
Brampton Bryan
Leintwardine
Lydbury N.
Edgton
Craven Arms
Wistanstow
Lit. Stretton
Hope Bowdler
Acton Scott
Shipton
Wenlock Edge
Corve Dale
Munslow
Tugford
Diddlebury
Stanton Long
Monkhopton
Ditton Priors
Brown Clee Hill
540
Cleobury North
Burwarton
Dillingsley
Chelma
Culmington
Stoke St. Milborough
Stottes
Cleedownton
Farlow
Titterstone Clee Hill
533
Hopton Wafers
Cleehill
Cleobury Mortime
Stokesay
Bromfield
Ludlow
Caynham
Ludford
Mamble
Richards Castle
Brimfield
Tenbury Wells
Newnham Bridge
Stock on-Te
Orleton
Berrington Hall
Luston
Kyre Park
Wigmore
Lingen
Llanddewi Ystradenni
Llanfihangel Rhydithon
Radnor Forest
660
Penybont
Llandegley
Llandrindod-Wells
New Radnor
Whitton
Presteigne
Aymestrey
Croft
Kingsland
Shobdon
Pembridge
Pudleston
Hatfield
Collington
Thornbury
Leominster
Old Radnor
Walton
Kington
Llanfihangel-Nant-Melan
Hundred House
Gwaunceste Hill
542
Gladestry
Glascwm
Lyonshall
Westonbury Mill Water Gardens
Dilwyn
Monkland
Bredenbury
Bromyard
Pencombe
Hope under Dinmore
Weobley
Queenswood
Ullingswick
Bodenham
Felton
Stoke Lacy
Kinnersley
Eardisley
Newchurch
Bryngwyn
Llanfair-ym-Muallt
Whitney-on-Wye
Willersley
Winforton
Painscastle
Aberedw
Erwood
Canon Pyon
Wellington
Wormsley
Moreton-on-Lugg
Burley Gate
Sutton St. Nicholas
Newtown
Castle Frome
Bosbury
Ashperton
Withington
Burghill
Credenhill
Bredwardine
Byford
Clyro
Llowes
Hay-on-Wye
Dorstone
Glasbury
Llanigon
Llyswen
Three Cocks
Peterchurch
Madley
Hereford
Bartestree
Tarrington
Wellington Heath
Ledbury
Mordiford
Aylton
Woolhope
Vowchurch
Clehonger
Kingstone
Allensmore
Fownhope
Hay Bluff
677
Bronllys
Talgarth
Llanfilo
Rhos Dirion
713
Capel-y-ffin
Grwyne Fawr Reservoir
Black Mountains
Golden Valley
Michaelchurch Escley
Much Dewchurch
Much Marcle
Little Dewchurch
How Caple
Dymock
Kempley
Castle
Waun Fâch
810
Llanthony Priory
Abbey Dore
Wormbridge
Kilpeck
Much Birch
Longtown
Llanthony
Pontrilas
Bagwyllydiart
Pengethley
Peterstow
Crow Hill
Linton
Ross-on-Wye
R. Wye
Llangorse
609
Talybont-on-Usk
Bwlch
Tretower
Pandy
Llanfihangel Crucorney
Grosmont
St. Weonards
Garway
Llangarron
Weston-under-Penyard
Lea
Castle
Goodrich
Kerne Bridge
Mitcheldean
Drybrook
Skenfrith
Llangynidr
Crickhowell
596
Llangenny
486
Llanvetherine
Newcastle
Welsh Newton
Whitchurch
Symonds Yat Rock
Ruardean
Symonds Yat
English Bicknor
Cinderford
Mynydd Llangynidr
550
Gilwern
529
Trefil
Brynmawr
Llantilio Crossenny
Rockfield
Abergavenny
Berry
Usk
Monnow
Dore
Lugg
Arrow
Honddu
Llynfi
Rea
Brecon Canal
K
L
M
A 49
A 44
A 438
A 465
A 488
A 4113
A 480
A 40
A 449

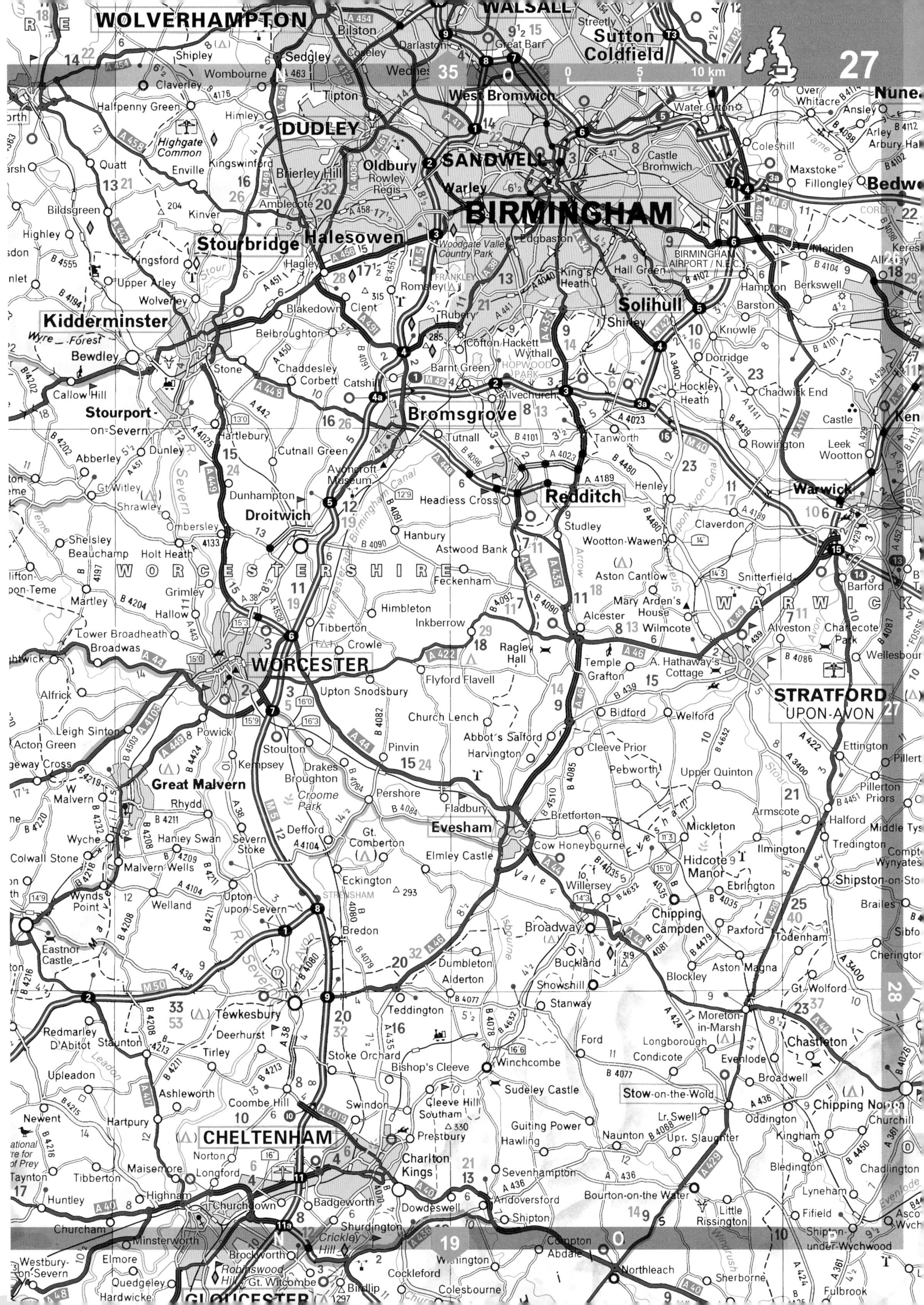
WOLVERHAMPTON
WALSALL
Sutton Coldfield
Bilston
Darlaston
Great Barr
Streetly
Sedgley
Coseley
Wombourne
Shipley
Claverley
Tipton
West Bromwich
Halfpenny Green
Himley
DUDLEY
Highgate Common
Water Orton
Over Whitacre
Ansley
Arley
Arbury Hall
Coleshill
Quatt
Enville
Kingswinford
Brierley Hill
Oldbury
Rowley Regis
SANDWELL
Castle Bromwich
Maxstoke
Fillongley
Bedworth
Warley
Amblecote
Bildsgreen
Kinver
BIRMINGHAM
Highley
Stourbridge
Halesowen
Woodgate Valley Country Park
Edgbaston
BIRMINGHAM AIRPORT / N.E.C.
Meriden
Allesley
Kingsford
Hagley
Upper Arley
Wolverley
Frankley
Romsley
King's Heath
Hall Green
Hampton
Berkswell
Barston
Kidderminster
Wyre Forest
Bewdley
Blakedown
Clent
Rubery
Solihull
Shirley
Knowle
Belbroughton
Cofton Hackett
Wythall
Hopwood Park
Dorridge
Callow Hill
Stone
Chaddesley Corbett
Catshill
Barnt Green
Alvechurch
Hockley Heath
Chadwick End
Stourport-on-Severn
Bromsgrove
Tanworth
Castle
Kenilworth
Hartlebury
Tutnall
Rowington
Leek Wootton
Abberley
Dunley
Cutnall Green
Avoncroft Museum
Headless Cross
Redditch
Henley
Warwick
Gt Witley
Shrawley
Dunhampton
Droitwich
Studley
Claverdon
Ombersley
Hanbury
Wootton Wawen
Shelsley Beauchamp
Holt Heath
Astwood Bank
WORCESTERSHIRE
Feckenham
Aston Cantlow
Snitterfield
Barford
Martley
Grimley
Himbleton
Mary Arden's House
Hallow
Inkberrow
Alcester
Wilmcote
Alveston
Charlecote Park
Lower Broadheath
Tibberton
Crowle
WARWICK
Broadwas
Ragley Hall
Temple Grafton
A. Hathaway's Cottage
Wellesbourne
WORCESTER
Flyford Flavell
Alfrick
Upton Snodsbury
STRATFORD UPON-AVON
Church Lench
Bidford
Welford
Leigh Sinton
Powick
Acton Green
Abbot's Salford
Ettington
Stoulton
Cleeve Prior
Kempsey
Drakes Broughton
Harvington
Pinvin
Pebworth
Upper Quinton
Great Malvern
Pillerton Priors
W Malvern
Rhydd
Croome Park
Pershore
Fladbury
Bretforton
Armscote
Halford
Wyche
Hanley Swan
Severn Stoke
Defford
Evesham
Mickleton
Tredington
Gt. Comberton
Cow Honeybourne
Colwall Stone
Malvern Wells
Elmley Castle
Hidcote Manor
Ilmington
Eckington
Ebrington
Shipston-on-Stour
Willersey
Strensham
Wynds Point
Welland
Upton-upon-Severn
Chipping Campden
Brailes
Bredon
Broadway
Paxford
Todenham
Eastnor Castle
Dumbleton
Buckland
Aston Magna
Cherington
Alderton
Blockley
Snowshill
Gt. Wolford
Tewkesbury
Stanway
Teddington
Moreton-in-Marsh
Redmarley D'Abitot
Deerhurst
Staunton
Chastleton
Tirley
Ford
Longborough
Stoke Orchard
Condicote
Evenlode
Upleadon
Winchcombe
Bishop's Cleeve
Broadwell
Ashleworth
Sudeley Castle
Stow-on-the-Wold
Coombe Hill
Swindon
Cleeve Hill
Chipping Norton
Southam
Oddington
Newent
Hartpury
Lr. Swell
Guiting Power
Upr. Slaughter
Churchill
Kingham
Prestbury
Hawling
Naunton
CHELTENHAM
Norton
Charlton Kings
Bledington
Chadlington
Maisemore
Longford
Sevenhampton
Taynton
Tibberton
Lyneham
Andoversford
Bourton-on-the Water
Huntley
Highnam
Churchdown
Badgeworth
Dowdeswell
Fifield
Shipton
Little Rissington
Churcham
Shurdington
Minsterworth
Crickley Hill
Compton Abdale
Shipton-under-Wychwood
Elmore
Brockworth
Withington
Westbury-on-Severn
Robinswood Hill
Gt. Witcombe
Northleach
Quedgeley
Cockleford
Hardwicke
Birdlip
Colesbourne
Sherborne
Fulbrook
GLOUCESTER
R. Severn
Stour
Teme
Arrow
Avon
Isbourne
Leadon
Windrush
Evenlode
Tame
Worcester and Birmingham Canal
Stratford upon Avon Canal
Vale of Evesham
Malvern
0 5 10 km
35
19
28

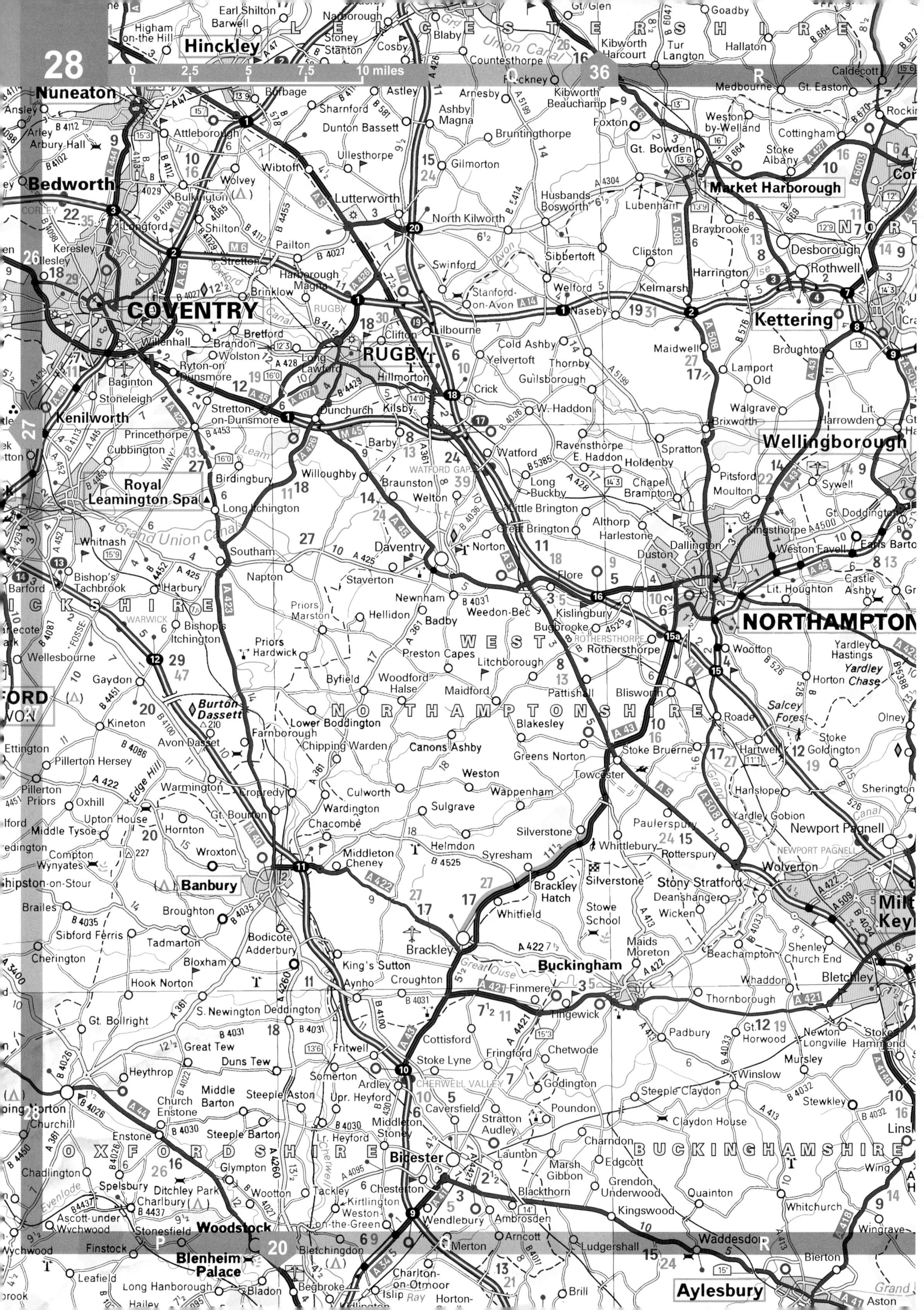

0 2.5 5 7.5 10 miles
Hinckley
Earl Shilton
Barwell
Higham on-the Hill
Narborough
Stoney Stanton
Cosby
Blaby
Countesthorpe
Grand Union Canal
LEICESTERSHIRE
Kibworth Harcourt
Tur Langton
Goadby
Hallaton
Caldecott
Medbourne
Gt. Easton
Rockingham
Peckleton
Kibworth Beauchamp
Foxton
Weston by-Welland
Cottingham
Nuneaton
Ansley
Arley
Arbury Hall
Attleborough
Burbage
Sharnford
Dunton Bassett
Astley
Arnesby
Ashby Magna
Bruntingthorpe
Gt. Bowden
Stoke Albany
Corby
Market Harborough
Bedworth
Wolvey
Bulkington
Ullesthorpe
Wibtoft
Gilmorton
Lutterworth
Husbands Bosworth
Lubenham
North Kilworth
Braybrooke
Desborough
Rothwell
Corley
Longford
Shilton
Pailton
Keresley
Allesley
Stretton
Harborough Magna
Swinford
Sibbertoft
Clipston
Harrington
Kelmarsh
Brinklow
Stanford-on-Avon
Welford
Naseby
Kettering
COVENTRY
RUGBY
Bretford
Brandon
Willenhall
Wolston
Ryton-on-Dunsmore
Clifton
Lilbourne
Long Lawford
Hillmorton
Cold Ashby
Yelvertoft
Thornby
Guilsborough
Maidwell
Lamport
Old
Broughton
Kenilworth
Baginton
Stoneleigh
Stretton-on-Dunsmore
Dunchurch
Kilsby
Crick
W. Haddon
Walgrave
Brixworth
Lit. Harrowden
Princethorpe
Cubbington
Barby
Watford
Ravensthorpe
E. Haddon
Holdenby
Spratton
Wellingborough
Royal Leamington Spa
Birdingbury
Willoughby
Braunston
WATFORD GAP
Long Buckby
Chapel Brampton
Pitsford
Moulton
Sywell
Long Itchington
Welton
Little Brington
Althorp
Great Brington
Harlestone
Kingsthorpe
Gt. Doddington
Whitnash
Southam
Daventry
Norton
Dallington
Weston Favell
Earls Barton
Barford
Bishop's Tachbrook
Harbury
Napton
Staveston
Flore
Duston
Castle Ashby
Lit. Houghton
WARWICKSHIRE
WARWICK
Priors Marston
Newnham
Hellidon
Badby
Weedon Bec
Kislingbury
NORTHAMPTON
Wellesbourne
Bishops Itchington
Priors Hardwick
WEST
Bugbrooke
ROTHERSTHORPE
Rothersthorpe
Wootton
Yardley Hastings
Yardley Chase
Gaydon
Preston Capes
Litchborough
Byfield
Woodford Halse
Maidford
Pattishall
Blisworth
Horton
Kineton
Burton Dassett
Lower Boddington
NORTHAMPTONSHIRE
Blakesley
Roade
Salcey Forest
Olney
Ettington
Avon Dassett
Farnborough
Chipping Warden
Canons Ashby
Greens Norton
Stoke Bruerne
Hartwell
Stoke Goldington
Pillerton Hersey
Pillerton Priors
Edge Hill
Warmington
Cropredy
Culworth
Weston
Wappenham
Towcester
Hanslope
Sherington
Oxhill
Upton House
Gt. Bourton
Wardington
Sulgrave
Paulerspury
Yardley Gobion
Middle Tysoe
Hornton
Chacombe
Helmdon
Silverstone
Whittlebury
Newport Pagnell
NEWPORT PAGNELL
Compton Wynyates
Wroxton
Middleton Cheney
Syresham
Potterspury
Wolverton
Shipston-on-Stour
Banbury
Brackley Hatch
Silverstone
Stony Stratford
Deanshanger
Wicken
Milton Keynes
Brailes
Broughton
Whitfield
Stowe School
Sibford Ferris
Tadmarton
Bodicote
Adderbury
Brackley
Maids Moreton
Beachampton
Shenley Church End
Cherington
Bloxham
King's Sutton
Croughton
Buckingham
Hook Norton
Aynho
Finmere
Tingewick
Whaddon
Thornborough
Bletchley
Gt. Rollright
S. Newington
Deddington
Cottisford
Padbury
Gt. Horwood
Newton Longville
Stoke Hammond
Great Tew
Duns Tew
Fritwell
Fringford
Chetwode
Mursley
Heythrop
Middle Barton
Somerton
Stoke Lyne
Ardley
CHERWELL VALLEY
Godington
Winslow
Chipping Norton
Church Enstone
Steeple Aston
Upr. Heyford
Caversfield
Poundon
Steeple Claydon
Stewkley
Churchill
Enstone
Steeple Barton
Lr. Heyford
Middleton Stoney
Stratton Audley
Claydon House
Linslade
OXFORDSHIRE
Bicester
Launton
Charndon
BUCKINGHAMSHIRE
Edgcott
Marsh Gibbon
Wing
Chadlington
Glympton
Cherwell
Chesterton
Grendon Underwood
Quainton
Spelsbury
Ditchley Park
Wootton
Tackley
Kirtlington
Weston-on-the-Green
Blackthorn
Whitchurch
Charlbury
Ascott-under-Wychwood
Evenlode
Woodstock
Wendlebury
Ambrosden
Kingswood
Wingrave
Stonesfield
Arncott
Ludgershall
Waddesdon
Wychwood
Finstock
Blenheim Palace
Bletchingdon
Merton
Bierton
Leafield
Long Hanborough
Bladon
Begbroke
Charlton-on-Otmoor
Islip
Horton-
Brill
Aylesbury
Aston
Hailey
Ray

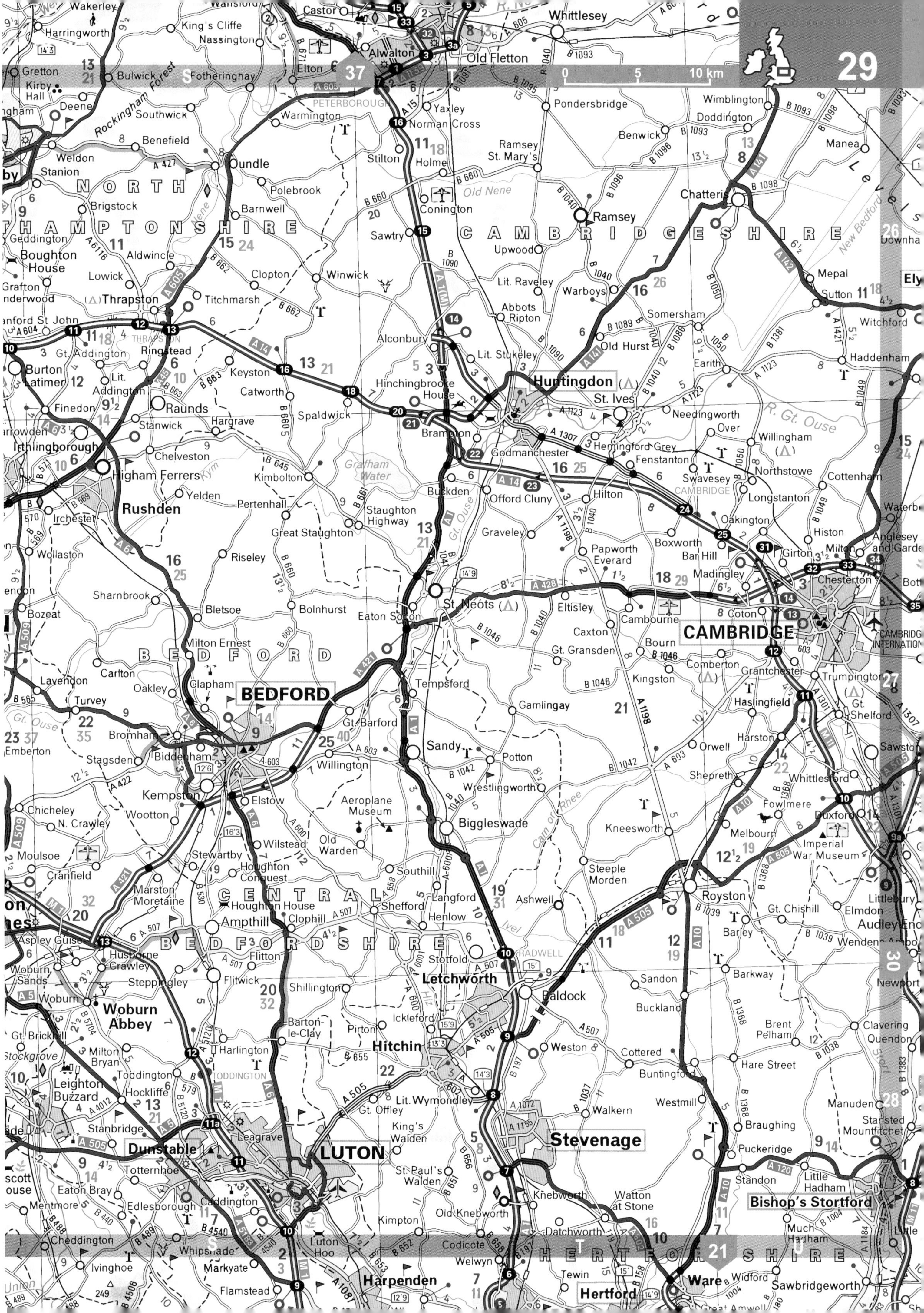

NORTHAMPTONSHIRE
CAMBRIDGESHIRE
BEDFORD
CENTRAL BEDFORDSHIRE
HERTFORDSHIRE
0 5 10 km
Wakerley
Harringworth
King's Cliffe
Nassington
Castor
Whittlesey
Alwalton
Old Fletton
Gretton
Bulwick
Fotheringhay
Elton
PETERBOROUGH
Pondersbridge
Wimblington
Doddington
Benwick
Manea
Kirby Hall
Deene
Southwick
Rockingham Forest
Warmington
Yaxley
Norman Cross
Benefield
Weldon
Stanion
Oundle
Stilton
Holme
Ramsey St. Mary's
Chatteris
Polebrook
Brigstock
Barnwell
Conington
Old Nene
Ramsey
Geddington
Aldwincle
Sawtry
Upwood
Boughton House
Lowick
Grafton Underwood
Clopton
Winwick
Lit. Raveley
Mepal
Sutton
Ely
Thrapston
Titchmarsh
Warboys
Abbots Ripton
Somersham
Witchford
Alconbury
Old Hurst
Lit. Stukeley
Earith
Haddenham
Burton Latimer
Gt. Addington
Ringstead
Keyston
Lit. Addington
Catworth
Hinchingbrooke House
Huntingdon
St. Ives
Needingworth
Over
Finedon
Raunds
Spaldwick
Brampton
Willingham
Stanwick
Hargrave
Irthlingborough
Chelveston
Godmanchester
Hemingford Grey
Fenstanton
Grafham Water
Higham Ferrers
Kimbolton
Buckden
Offord Cluny
Hilton
Swavesey
Northstowe
Cottenham
Rushden
Yelden
Pertenhall
Staughton Highway
Longstanton
Irchester
Great Staughton
Graveley
Papworth Everard
Boxworth
Bar Hill
Oakington
Histon
Girton
Milton
Wollaston
Riseley
Madingley
Chesterton
Sharnbrook
Bletsoe
Bolnhurst
Eaton Socon
St. Neots
Eltisley
Cambourne
Coton
CAMBRIDGE
Bozeat
Milton Ernest
Caxton
Gt. Gransden
Bourn
Comberton
Grantchester
Trumpington
Carlton
Lavendon
Oakley
Clapham
Tempsford
Kingston
Haslingfield
Gt. Shelford
Turvey
BEDFORD
Gamlingay
Bromham
Biddenham
Gt. Barford
Harston
Sawston
Emberton
Stagsden
Willington
Sandy
Potton
Orwell
Shepreth
Whittlesford
Kempston
Elstow
Wrestlingworth
Fowlmere
Duxford
Chicheley
N. Crawley
Wootton
Aeroplane Museum
Biggleswade
Kneesworth
Melbourn
Imperial War Museum
Wilstead
Old Warden
Moulsoe
Stewartby
Houghton Conquest
Southill
Steeple Morden
Cranfield
Marston Moretaine
Houghton House
Langford
Ashwell
Royston
Littlebury
Shefford
Gt. Chishill
Elmdon
Ampthill
Clophill
Henlow
Barley
Audley End
Aspley Guise
Husborne Crawley
Flitton
Stotfold
RADWELL
Wenden Ambo
Woburn Sands
Steppingley
Flitwick
Letchworth
Baldock
Sandon
Barkway
Newport
Woburn
Woburn Abbey
Shillington
Buckland
Gt. Brickhill
Barton-le-Clay
Pirton
Ickleford
Brent Pelham
Clavering
Quendon
Stockgrove
Milton Bryan
Harlington
Hitchin
Weston
Cottered
Hare Street
Toddington
TODDINGTON
Buntingford
Leighton Buzzard
Hockliffe
Lit. Wymondley
Gt. Offley
Westmill
Manuden
Stanbridge
Leagrave
King's Walden
Walkern
Braughing
Stansted Mountfitchet
Dunstable
LUTON
Stevenage
Puckeridge
Totternhoe
St. Paul's Walden
Standon
Little Hadham
Eaton Bray
Caddington
Knebworth
Watton at Stone
Bishop's Stortford
Mentmore
Edlesborough
Old Knebworth
Much Hadham
Kimpton
Datchworth
Cheddington
Whipsnade
Luton Hoo
Codicote
Ivinghoe
Markyate
Welwyn
Harpenden
Tewin
Ware
Widford
Sawbridgeworth
Flamstead
Hertford

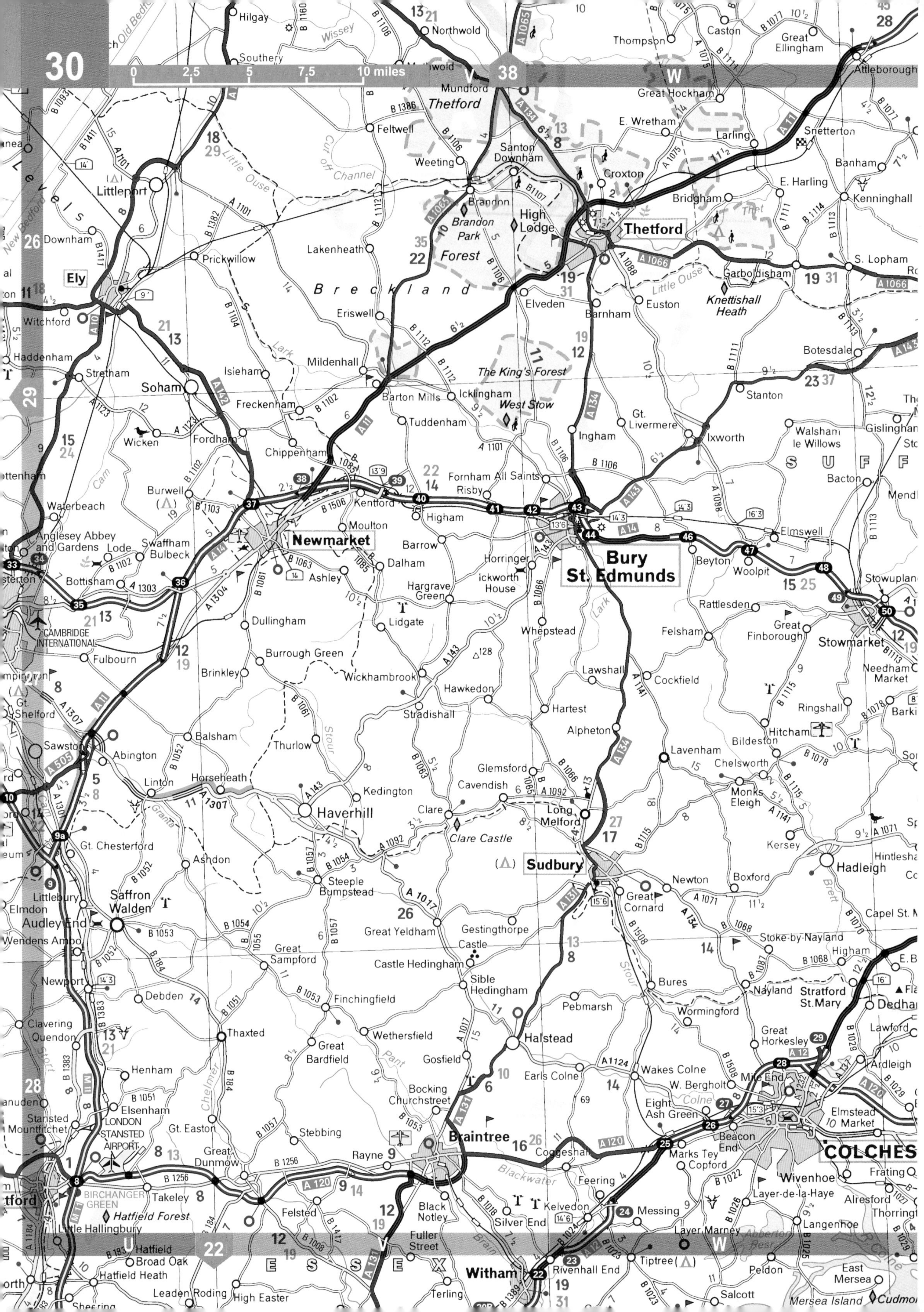
0
2.5
5
7.5
10 miles
38
Hilgay
Southery
Northwold
Thompson
Caston
Great Ellingham
Attleborough
Mundford
Thetford Forest
Great Hockham
Feltwell
E. Wretham
Larling
Snetterton
Weeting
Santon Downham
Croxton
Banham
Littleport
Little Ouse
Cut off Channel
Brandon
E. Harling
Bridgham
Kenninghall
Brandon Park Forest
High Lodge
Thetford
Downham
Lakenheath
S. Lopham
Ely
Prickwillow
Breckland
Garboldisham
Elveden
Euston
Barnham
Knettishall Heath
Witchford
Eriswell
Haddenham
Mildenhall
Botesdale
Stretham
Isleham
The King's Forest
Soham
Barton Mills
Icklingham
Stanton
Freckenham
West Stow
Tuddenham
Ingham
Gt. Livermere
Ixworth
Walsham le Willows
Wicken
Fordham
Chippenham
Gislingham
SUFF
Fornham All Saints
Risby
Bacton
Burwell
Waterbeach
Kentford
Higham
Moulton
Anglesey Abbey and Gardens
Lode
Swaffham Bulbeck
Newmarket
Barrow
Elmswell
Bury St. Edmunds
Beyton
Woolpit
Horringer
Ickworth House
Dalham
Bottisham
Ashley
Hargrave Green
Stowupland
Rattlesden
Great Finborough
Stowmarket
CAMBRIDGE INTERNATIONAL
Dullingham
Lidgate
Whepstead
Felsham
Fulbourn
Burrough Green
Brinkley
Wickhambrook
Lawshall
Cockfield
Needham Market
Hawkedon
Gt. Shelford
Stradishall
Hartest
Ringshall
Alpheton
Hitcham
Balsham
Sawston
Thurlow
Stour
Bildeston
Abington
Lavenham
Chelsworth
Glemsford
Linton
Horseheath
Kedington
Cavendish
Monks Eleigh
Haverhill
Clare
Long Melford
Clare Castle
Kersey
Gt. Chesterford
Ashdon
Sudbury
Hadleigh
Steeple Bumpstead
Newton
Boxford
Great Cornard
Littlebury
Saffron Walden
Elmdon
Audley End
Wendens Ambo
Capel St. M
Great Yeldham
Gestingthorpe
Castle
Stoke-by-Nayland
Great Sampford
Castle Hedingham
Higham
Newport
Debden
Sible Hedingham
Bures
Nayland
Stratford St. Mary
Dedham
Finchingfield
Pebmarsh
Wormingford
Clavering
Quendon
Thaxted
Wethersfield
Halstead
Great Horkesley
Lawford
Great Bardfield
Gosfield
Henham
Earls Colne
Wakes Colne
Mile End
Ardleigh
W. Bergholt
Colne
Elsenham
Bocking Churchstreet
Eight Ash Green
Stansted Mountfitchet
LONDON STANSTED AIRPORT
Gt. Easton
Stebbing
Braintree
Beacon End
Elmstead Market
Great Dunmow
Rayne
Coggeshall
Marks Tey
COLCHES
Copford
Takeley
Feering
Wivenhoe
Frating
BIRCHANGER GREEN
Felsted
Blackwater
Layer-de-la-Haye
Alresford
Hatfield Forest
Black Notley
Kelvedon
Messing
Thorrington
Little Hallingbury
Silver End
Langenhoe
Fuller Street
Layer Marney
Abberton Resr.
Hatfield Broad Oak
Witham
Tiptree
Peldon
Hatfield Heath
ESSEX
Rivenhall End
East Mersea
Leaden Roding
High Easter
Terling
Salcott
Mersea Island
Cudmo

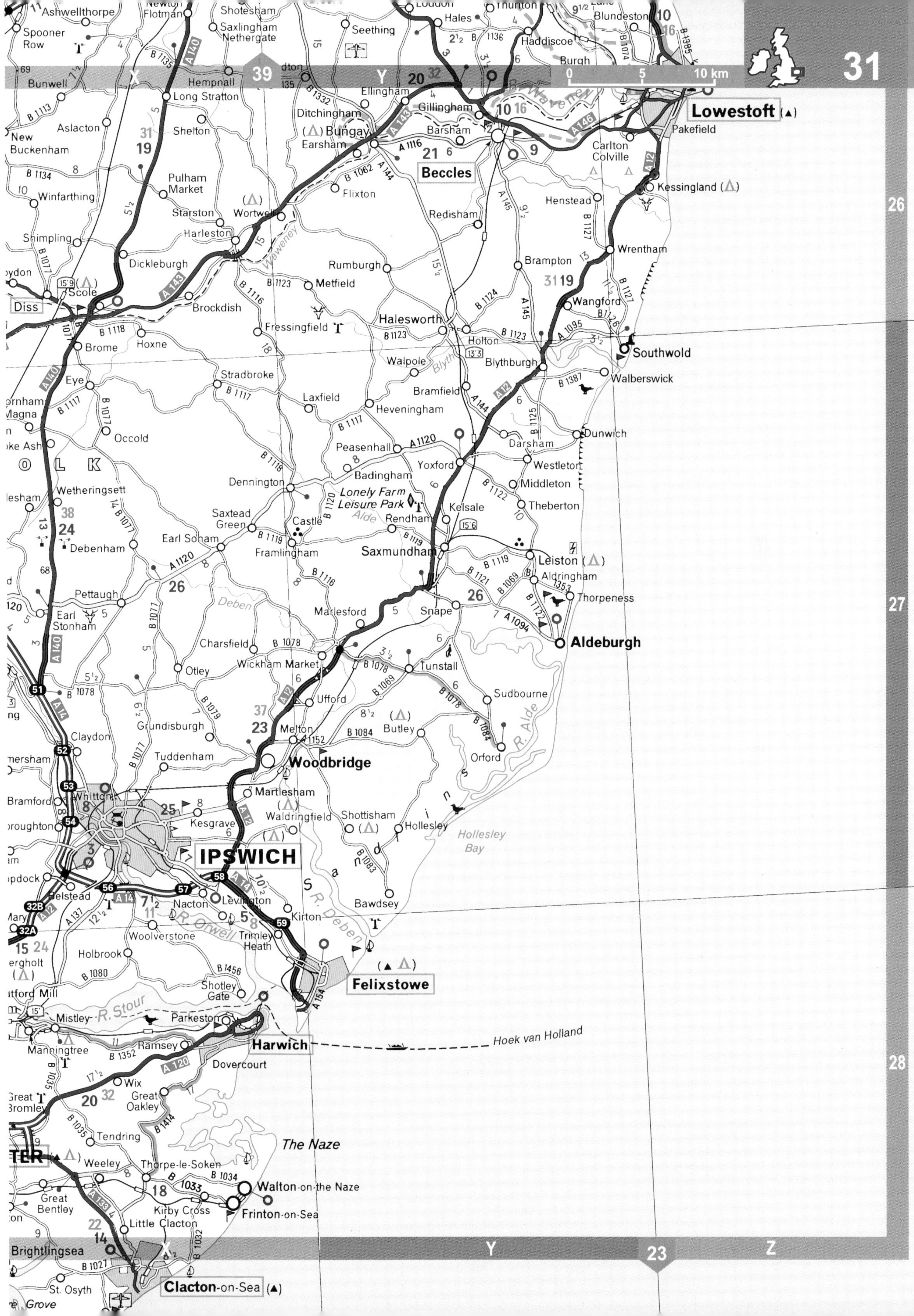
Ashwellthorpe
Spooner Row
Newton Flotman
Shotesham
Saxlingham Nethergate
Seething
Loddon
Hales
Thurlton
Haddiscoe
Burgh
Blundeston
Bunwell
Hempnall
Long Stratton
Ellingham
Gillingham
Ditchingham
Bungay
Earsham
Barsham
Beccles
Lowestoft
Pakefield
Carlton Colville
Kessingland
Henstead
New Buckenham
Aslacton
Shelton
Pulham Market
Winfarthing
Starston
Wortwell
Harleston
Flixton
Redisham
Shimpling
Dickleburgh
Rumburgh
Metfield
Brampton
Wrentham
Wangford
Diss
Scole
Brockdish
Fressingfield
Halesworth
Holton
Blythburgh
Southwold
Walberswick
Brome
Hoxne
Stradbroke
Walpole
Bramfield
Eye
Laxfield
Heveningham
Occold
Peasenhall
Yoxford
Darsham
Dunwich
Westleton
Middleton
Theberton
Badingham
Dennington
Lonely Farm Leisure Park
Wetheringsett
Debenham
Saxtead Green
Castle
Framlingham
Rendham
Kelsale
Saxmundham
Leiston
Aldringham
Thorpeness
Earl Soham
Pettaugh
Earl Stonham
Marlesford
Snape
Aldeburgh
Charsfield
Wickham Market
Tunstall
Otley
Ufford
Sudbourne
Grundisburgh
Melton
Butley
Orford
Claydon
Tuddenham
Woodbridge
Bramford
Whitton
Martlesham
Kesgrave
Waldringfield
Shottisham
Hollesley
Hollesley Bay
IPSWICH
Sproughton
Copdock
Belstead
Nacton
Levington
Kirton
Bawdsey
Woolverstone
Trimley Heath
Holbrook
Shotley Gate
Felixstowe
Mistley
Parkeston
Manningtree
Ramsey
Harwich
Hoek van Holland
Dovercourt
Wix
Great Oakley
Great Bromley
Tendring
The Naze
Weeley
Thorpe-le-Soken
Walton-on-the Naze
Frinton-on-Sea
Kirby Cross
Great Bentley
Little Clacton
Brightlingsea
St. Osyth
Clacton-on-Sea
R. Waveney
Waveney
Blyth
Alde
Deben
R. Alde
R. Deben
R. Orwell
R. Stour
Sandlings
S U F F O L K
0 5 10 km
A140
A143
A146
A12
A144
A145
A1095
A1120
A1094
A14
A137
A120
A133
A154
X
Y
Z
39
23
26
27
28

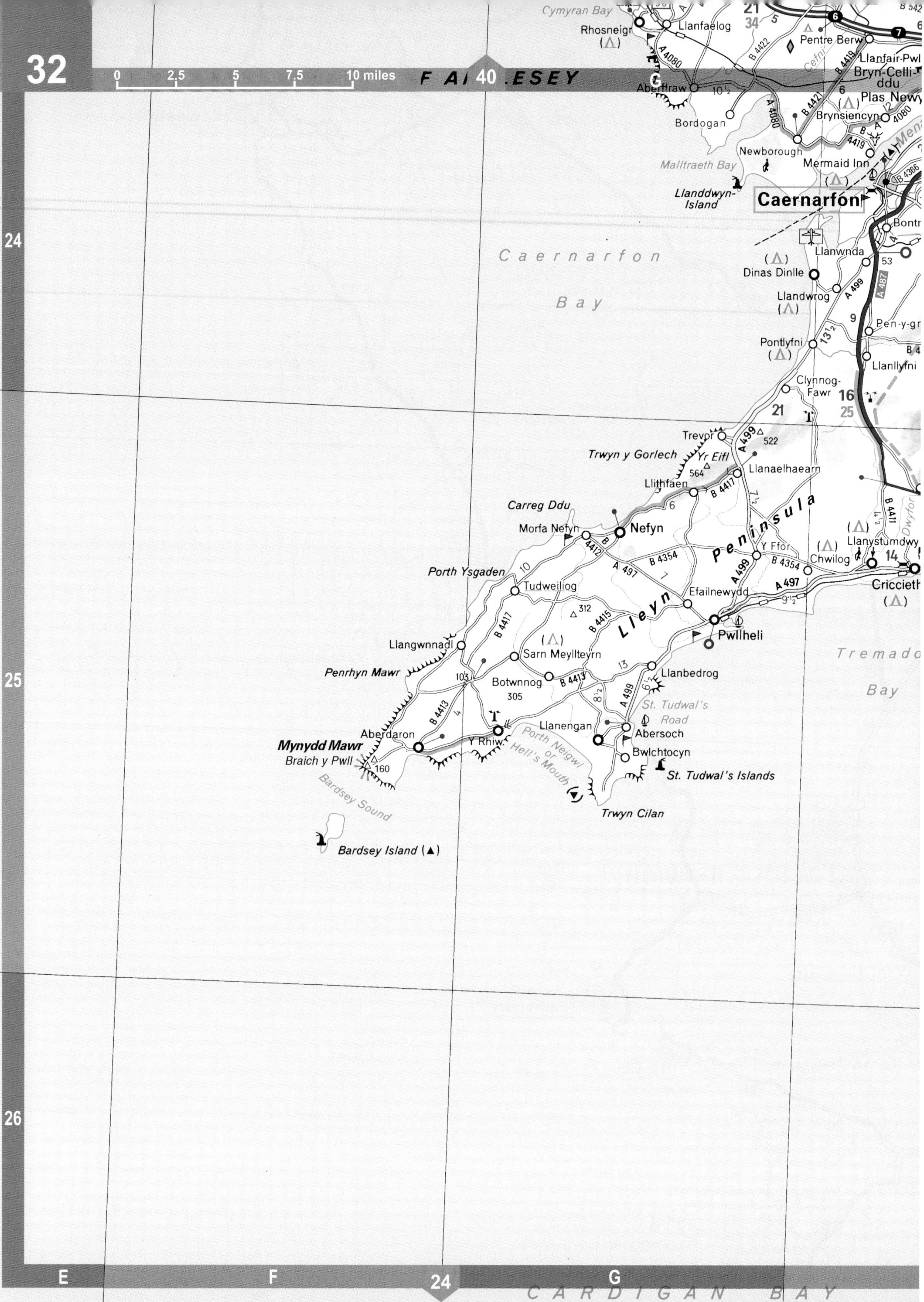
0
2.5
5
7.5
10 miles
40
Cymyran Bay
Rhosneigr
Llanfaelog
Pentre Berw
Llanfair-Pwl
Bryn-Celli-ddu
Plas Newy
Aberffraw
Bordogan
Brynsiencyn
Newborough
Mermaid Inn
Malltraeth Bay
Llanddwyn-Island
Caernarfon
Bontr
Llanwnda
Dinas Dinlle
Llandwrog
Caernarfon
Bay
Pen-y-gr
Pontlyfni
Llanllyfni
Clynnog-Fawr
Trevor
Trwyn y Gorlech
Yr Eifl
564
522
Llanaelhaearn
Llithfaen
Carreg Ddu
Nefyn
Morfa Nefyn
Peninsula
Y Ffor
Chwilog
Llanystumdwy
Criccieth
Porth Ysgaden
Tudweiliog
Efailnewydd
Lleyn
Pwllheli
Llangwnnadl
Sarn Meyllteyrn
Tremado
Bay
Penrhyn Mawr
Botwnnog
305
Llanbedrog
St. Tudwal's Road
Llanengan
Abersoch
Aberdaron
Y Rhiw
Porth Neigwl or Hell's Mouth
Bwlchtocyn
Mynydd Mawr
Braich y Pwll
160
St. Tudwal's Islands
Bardsey Sound
Trwyn Cilan
Bardsey Island
24
25
26
E
F
G
CARDIGAN BAY

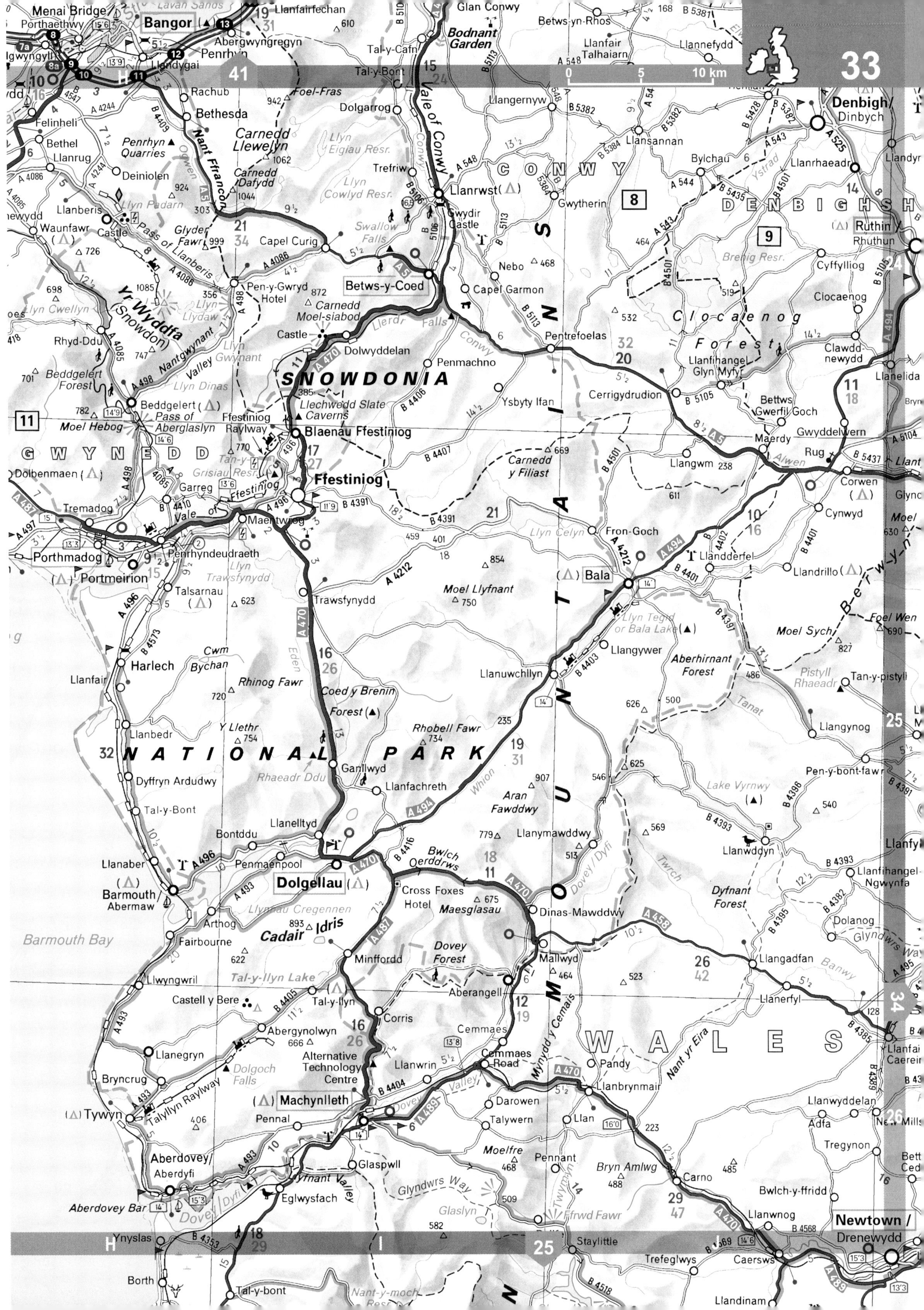

Menai Bridge
Porthaethwy
Bangor
Llanfairfechan
Abergwyngregyn
Penrhyn
Llandygai
Glan Conwy
Betws-yn-Rhos
Llanfair Talhaiarn
Llannefydd
Bodnant Garden
Tal-y-Cafn
Tal-y-Bont
0 5 10 km
Rachub
Bethesda
Felinheli
Bethel
Llanrug
Deiniolen
Penrhyn Quarries
Nant Ffrancon
Carnedd Llewelyn
Carnedd Dafydd
Foel-Fras
Dolgarrog
Llyn Eigiau Resr.
Llyn Cowlyd Resr.
Trefriw
Vale of Conwy
Llangernyw
Llansannan
Denbigh/ Dinbych
Bylchau
Llanrhaeadr
Llandyrnog
C O N W Y
Llanrwst
Gwytherin
D E N B I G H S H I R E
Ruthin Rhuthun
Llanberis
Llyn Padarn
Waunfawr
Castle
Pass of Llanberis
Glyder Fawr
Capel Curig
Swallow Falls
Gwydir Castle
Nebo
Capel Garmon
Betws-y-Coed
Brenig Resr.
Cyffylliog
Clocaenog
Clocaenog Forest
Yr Wyddfa (Snowdon)
Pen-y-Gwryd Hotel
Llyn Llydaw
Carnedd Moel-siabod
Llyn Cwellyn
Rhyd-Ddu
Castle
Dolwyddelan
Llerdr Falls
Penmachno
Pentrefoelas
Llanfihangel Glyn Myfyr
Clawdd-newydd
Llanelidan
Beddgelert Forest
Nantgwynant
Valley
Llyn Gwynant
Llyn Dinas
SNOWDONIA
Llechwedd Slate Caverns
Ysbyty Ifan
Cerrigydrudion
Bettws Gwerfil Goch
Beddgelert
Pass of Aberglaslyn
Moel Hebog
Ffestiniog Raylway
Blaenau Ffestiniog
Gwyddelwern
Maerdy
G W Y N E D D
Tan-y-Grisiau Resr.
Carnedd y Filiast
Llangwm
Rug
Corwen
Dolbenmaen
Garreg
Vale of Ffestiniog
Ffestiniog
Tremadog
Maentwrog
Fron-Goch
Llyn Celyn
Cynwyd
Moel
Porthmadog
Penrhyndeudraeth
Llandderfel
Portmeirion
Llyn Trawsfynydd
Bala
Llandrillo
Talsarnau
Trawsfynydd
Moel Llyfnant
Llyn Tegid or Bala Lake
Foel Wen
Moel Sych
Llangywer
Aberhirnant Forest
Harlech
Cwm Bychan
Llanfair
Rhinog Fawr
Coed y Brenin Forest
Llanuwchllyn
Pistyll Rhaeadr
Tan-y-pistyll
Llanbedr
Y Llethr
Rhobell Fawr
Tanat
Llangynog
NATIONAL PARK
Dyffryn Ardudwy
Rhaeadr Ddu
Ganllwyd
Llanfachreth
Aran Fawddwy
Lake Vyrnwy
Pen-y-bont-fawr
Tal-y-Bont
Llanelltyd
Bontddu
Llanymawddwy
Llanwddyn
Llanaber
Barmouth/ Abermaw
Penmaenpool
Dolgellau
Bwlch Oerddrws
Cross Foxes Hotel
Maesglasau
Dinas-Mawddwy
Dyfnant Forest
Llanfihangel-Ngwynfa
Barmouth Bay
Arthog
Llynnau Cregennen
Cadair Idris
Fairbourne
Minffordd
Dovey Forest
Mallwyd
Llangadfan
Dolanog
Llwyngwril
Tal-y-Llyn Lake
Castell y Bere
Tal-y-llyn
Aberangell
Llanerfyl
Corris
Cemmaes
Abergynolwyn
Llanegryn
Alternative Technology Centre
Llanwrin
Cemmaes Road
Mynydd y Cemais
Pandy
Nant yr Eira
W A L E S
Llanfair Caereinion
Bryncrug
Dolgoch Falls
Talyllyn Raylway
Machynlleth
Dovey Valley
Llanbrynmair
Darowen
Talywern
Llan
Llanwyddelan
Adfa
Tywyn
Pennal
New Mills
Aberdovey/ Aberdyfi
Glaspwll
Moelfre
Pennant
Bryn Amlwg
Carno
Tregynon
Aberdovey Bar
Dyfi
Eglwysfach
Cwm Rhaeadr
Glyndwrs Way
Glaslyn
Ffrwd Fawr
Bwlch-y-ffridd
Llanwnog
Newtown / Drenewydd
Ynyslas
Staylittle
Trefeglwys
Caersws
Borth
Tal-y-bont
Nant-y-moch Resr.
Llandinam

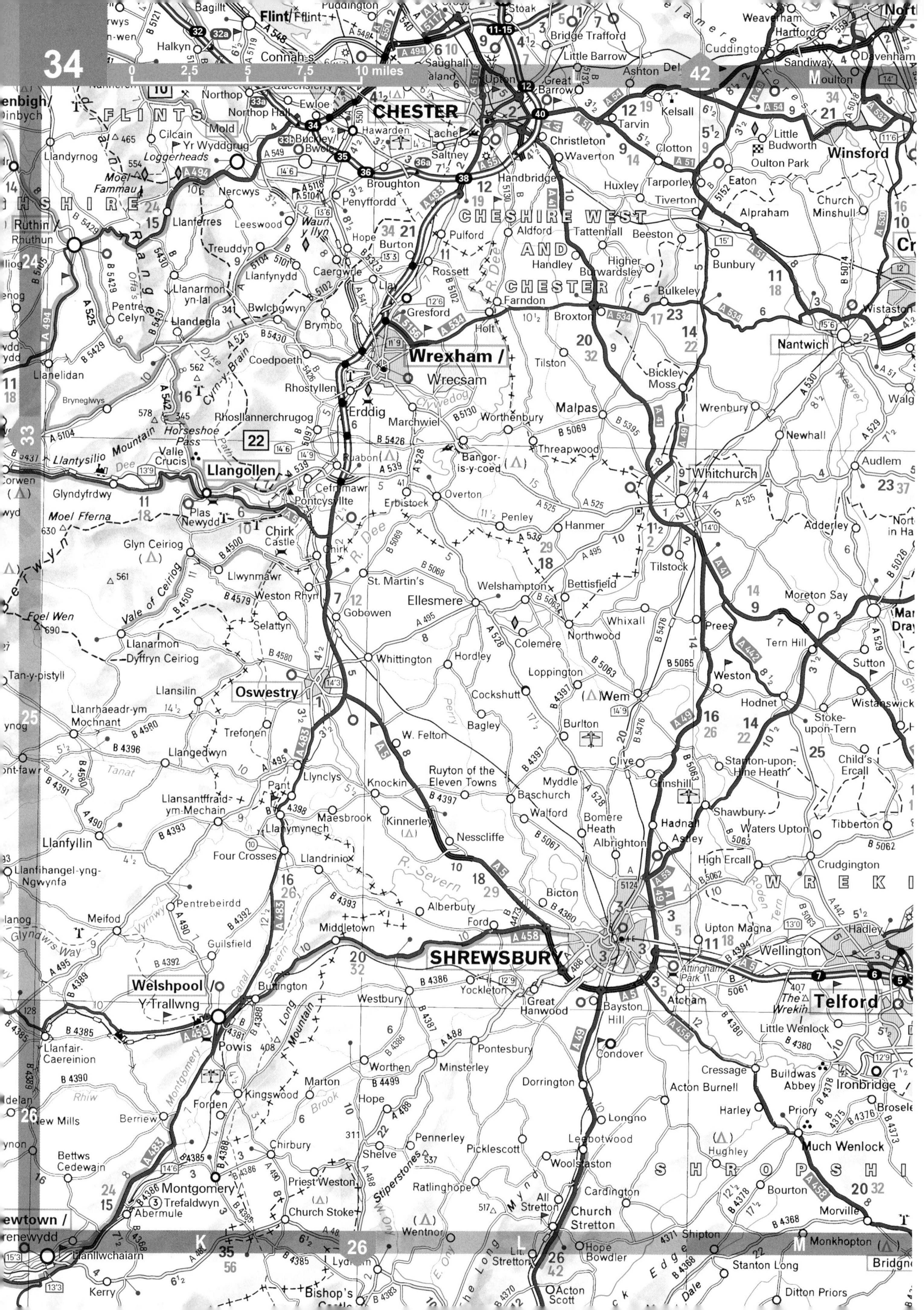
0 2.5 5 7.5 10 miles
Flint/Fflint
Connah's Quay
CHESTER
Mold
Yr Wyddgrug
FLINTS
Buckley/Bwcle
Hawarden
Saltney
Broughton
Penyffordd
Hope
Caergwrle
Ruthin
Rhuthun
Loggerheads
Moel Famau
CHESHIRE WEST AND CHESTER
Wrexham / Wrecsam
Gresford
Rossett
Pulford
Farndon
Holt
Malpas
Bangor-is-y-coed
Overton
Llangollen
Chirk Castle
Chirk
Ellesmere
Whitchurch
Nantwich
Winsford
Tarporley
Oswestry
Whittington
Wem
Shrewsbury
SHREWSBURY
Welshpool / Y Trallwng
Powis
Montgomery
Trefaldwyn
Newtown /
Wellington
Telford
The Wrekin
Ironbridge
Much Wenlock
Church Stretton
Stiperstones
Long Mountain
Vale of Ceiriog
Llanfyllin
Hodnet
Market Drayton
Llanrhaeadr-ym-Mochnant
Berwyn
Horseshoe Pass
Valle Crucis
R. Severn
R. Dee
SHROPSHIRE
WREKIN
Wenlock Edge
Long Mynd
42
26
33
K
L
M
A 5
A 483
A 49
A 41
A 458
A 494
A 534
A 55
A 51
A 525
A 528
A 495
A 490

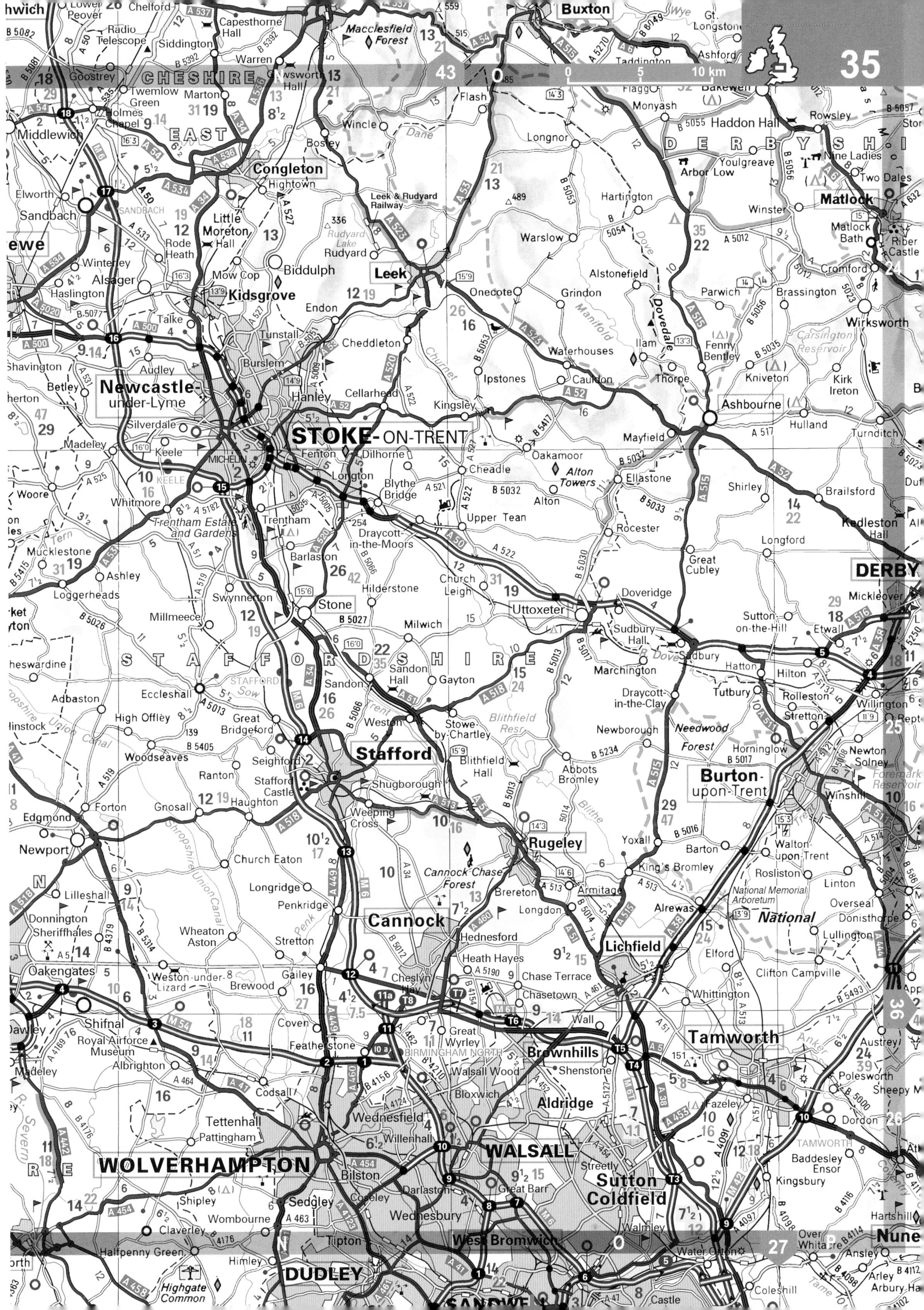
CHESHIRE EAST
DERBYSHIRE
STAFFORDSHIRE
Buxton
Macclesfield Forest
Capesthorne Hall
Siddington
Goostrey
Twemlow Green
Holmes Chapel
Middlewich
Congleton
Hightown
Leek & Rudyard Railway
Rudyard Lake
Rudyard
Biddulph
Leek
Flash
Wincle
Bosley
Longnor
Hartington
Warslow
Alstonefield
Grindon
Onecote
Bakewell
Monyash
Haddon Hall
Rowsley
Youlgreave
Arbor Low
Nine Ladies
Two Dales
Matlock
Matlock Bath
Winster
Cromford
Wirksworth
Parwich
Brassington
Carsington Reservoir
Kniveton
Kirk Ireton
Fenny Bentley
Ashbourne
Hulland
Turnditch
Dovedale
Ilam
Thorpe
Waterhouses
Cauldon
Ipstones
Kingsley
Cheddleton
Cellarhead
Endon
Elworth
Sandbach
Little Moreton Hall
Rode Heath
Alsager
Haslington
Kidsgrove
Mow Cop
Talke
Tunstall
Burslem
Hanley
Audley
Newcastle-under-Lyme
Betley
Silverdale
Madeley
Keele
STOKE-ON-TRENT
Fenton
Longton
Dilhorne
Blythe Bridge
Cheadle
Alton Towers
Alton
Oakamoor
Mayfield
Ellastone
Upper Tean
Rocester
Shirley
Brailsford
Kedleston Hall
Longford
Great Cubley
DERBY
Mickleover
Sutton-on-the-Hill
Etwall
Doveridge
Uttoxeter
Sudbury Hall
Sudbury
Marchington
Hatton
Hilton
Tutbury
Rolleston
Willington
Stretton
Draycott-in-the-Clay
Needwood Forest
Newborough
Horninglow
Burton-upon-Trent
Newton Solney
Winshill
Woore
Whitmore
Trentham Estate and Gardens
Trentham
Barlaston
Draycott-in-the-Moors
Hilderstone
Church Leigh
Mucklestone
Ashley
Loggerheads
Swynnerton
Stone
Millmeece
Milwich
Sandon
Sandon Hall
Gayton
Adbaston
Eccleshall
High Offley
Great Bridgeford
Weston
Stowe-by-Chartley
Blithfield Hall
Blithfield Resr
Abbots Bromley
Woodseaves
Seighford
Stafford
Stafford Castle
Ranton
Haughton
Shugborough
Weeping Cross
Forton
Gnosall
Edgmond
Newport
Church Eaton
Rugeley
Yoxall
Barton
Walton-upon-Trent
Rosliston
King's Bromley
Armitage
Brereton
Longdon
Cannock Chase Forest
Alrewas
National Memorial Arboretum
National
Linton
Overseal
Donisthorpe
Lullington
Longridge
Penkridge
Cannock
Hednesford
Heath Hayes
Chase Terrace
Chasetown
Lichfield
Elford
Clifton Campville
Whittington
Lilleshall
Donnington
Sheriffhales
Wheaton Aston
Stretton
Gailey
Oakengates
Weston-under-Lizard
Brewood
Cheslyn Hay
Shifnal
Royal Airforce Museum
Albrighton
Coven
Featherstone
Great Wyrley
Wall
Brownhills
Shenstone
Tamworth
Austrey
Polesworth
Sheepy
Dordon
Madeley
Codsall
Walsall Wood
Bloxwich
Aldridge
Fazeley
Wednesfield
Tettenhall
Pattingham
Willenhall
WALSALL
Baddesley Ensor
Kingsbury
WOLVERHAMPTON
Bilston
Streetly
Sutton Coldfield
Great Barr
Darlaston
Coseley
Sedgley
Shipley
Wednesbury
Wombourne
Claverley
Walmley
Tipton
West Bromwich
Halfpenny Green
Himley
DUDLEY
Highgate Common
Water Orton
Over Whitacre
Ansley
Hartshill
Arley
Coleshill
Castle
Arbury Hall
Tame
Trent
Dove
Manifold
Churnet
Penk
Sow
Blithe
Anker
R. Severn
Shropshire Union Canal
Trent and Mersey Canal
M6
M54
M6 Toll
M42
A50
A52
A34
A38
A5
A51
A515
A53
A523
0 5 10 km
Crewe
Derby
Buxton

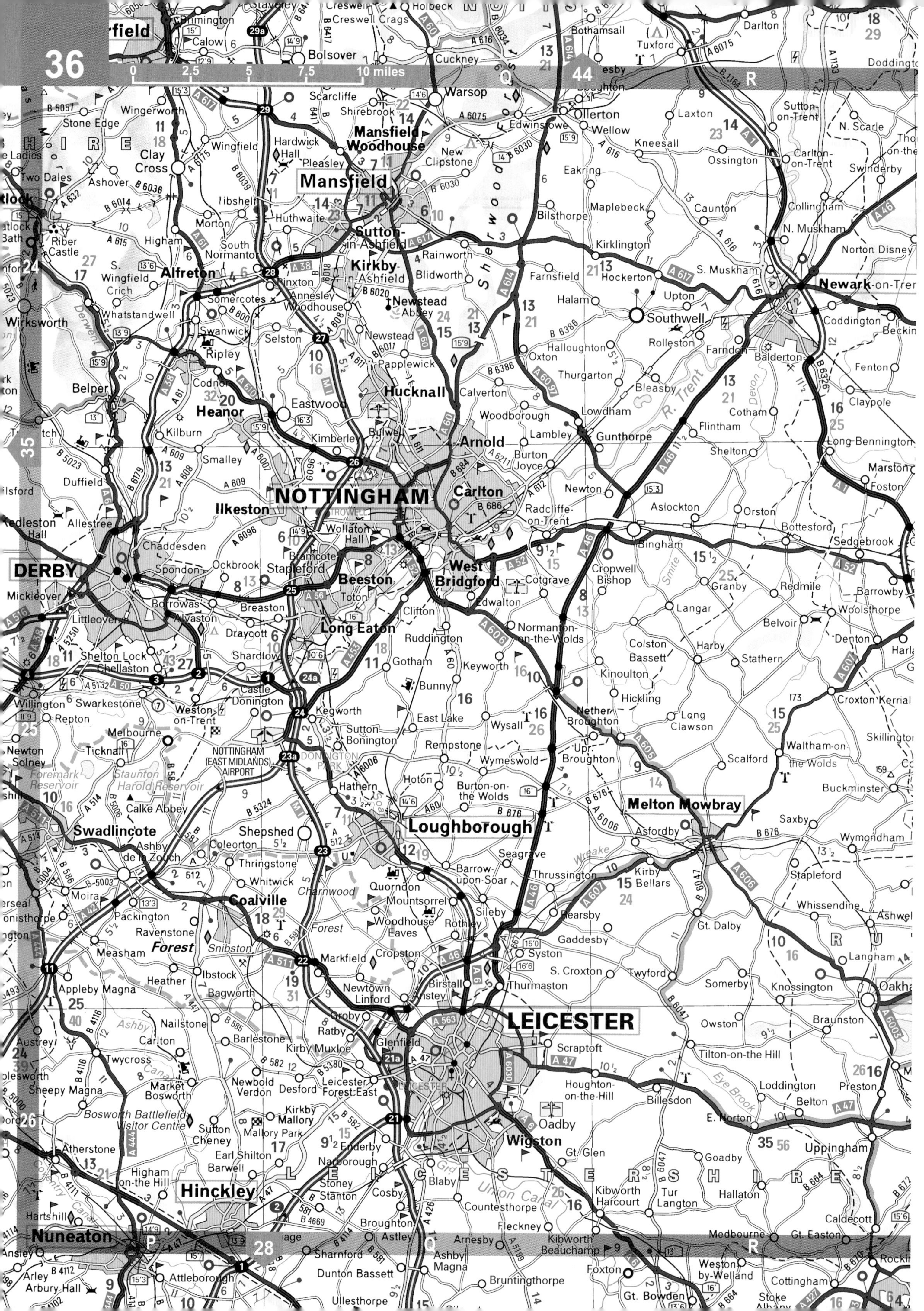
0 2.5 5 7.5 10 miles
44
35
28
Q
R
P
NOTTINGHAM
DERBY
LEICESTER
Mansfield
Mansfield Woodhouse
Sutton-in-Ashfield
Kirkby-in-Ashfield
Hucknall
Arnold
Carlton
West Bridgford
Beeston
Long Eaton
Ilkeston
Heanor
Ripley
Alfreton
Clay Cross
Belper
Matlock
Wirksworth
Eastwood
Southwell
Newark-on-Trent
Bingham
Loughborough
Melton Mowbray
Coalville
Swadlincote
Ashby de la Zouch
Hinckley
Nuneaton
Wigston
Oadby
Uppingham
Shepshed
Ollerton
Warsop
Bolsover
Tuxford
Sherwood Forest
Charnwood Forest
NOTTINGHAM (EAST MIDLANDS) AIRPORT
Bosworth Battlefield Visitor Centre
R. Trent
Kibworth Harcourt
Market Bosworth
Earl Shilton
Castle Donington
Keyworth
Radcliffe-on-Trent
Cotgrave
Syston
Birstall
Anstey
Glenfield
Enderby
Blaby
Countesthorpe
Lutterworth
M1
A1
A6
A46
A52
A60
A606
A47

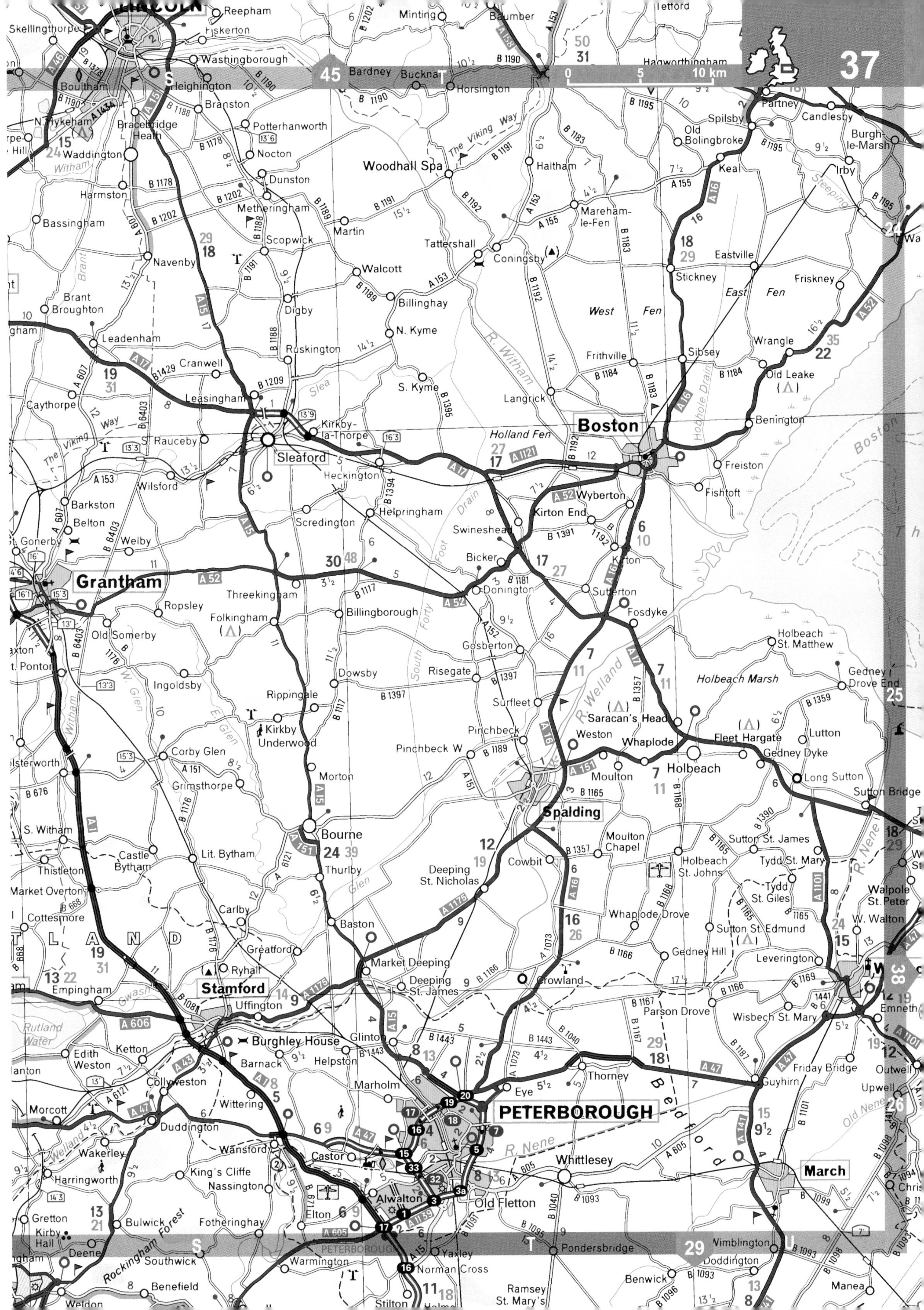

Lincoln
Reepham
Skellingthorpe
Fiskerton
Washingborough
Boultham
Heighington
Branston
N. Hykeham
Bracebridge Heath
Potterhanworth
Waddington
Nocton
Dunston
Harmston
Metheringham
Bassingham
Scopwick
Martin
Navenby
Walcott
Brant Broughton
Digby
Billinghay
Leadenham
N. Kyme
Ruskington
Cranwell
S. Kyme
Leasingham
Caythorpe
Kirkby-la-Thorpe
Rauceby
Sleaford
Heckington
Wilsford
Barkston
Belton
Helpringham
Scredington
Welby
Grantham
Threekingham
Ropsley
Folkingham
Old Somerby
Billingborough
Ingoldsby
Dowsby
Rippingale
Kirkby Underwood
Corby Glen
Grimsthorpe
Morton
Bourne
Lit. Bytham
Castle Bytham
Thurlby
Carlby
Baston
Greatford
Ryhall
Stamford
Uffington
Burghley House
Barnack
Helpston
Glinton
Market Deeping
Deeping St. James
Deeping St. Nicholas
Crowland
Marholm
Peterborough
Eye
Thorney
Whittlesey
Castor
Alwalton
Old Fletton
Yaxley
Norman Cross
Elton
Wansford
Duddington
Collyweston
Wittering
Ketton
Edith Weston
Empingham
Rutland Water
Cottesmore
Market Overton
Thistleton
S. Witham
Colsterworth
Harringworth
Wakerley
Morcott
King's Cliffe
Nassington
Fotheringhay
Bulwick
Kirby Hall
Gretton
Deene
Southwick
Warmington
Benefield
Rockingham Forest
Stilton
Ramsey St. Mary's
Pondersbridge
Benwick
Doddington
Wimblington
March
Manea
Guyhirn
Friday Bridge
Upwell
Outwell
Wisbech St. Mary
Parson Drove
Leverington
Gedney Hill
Sutton St. Edmund
Whaplode Drove
Holbeach St. Johns
Tydd St. Mary
Tydd St. Giles
Sutton St. James
Moulton Chapel
Cowbit
Spalding
Moulton
Weston
Pinchbeck
Pinchbeck W.
Surfleet
Saracen's Head
Whaplode
Holbeach
Fleet Hargate
Gedney Dyke
Lutton
Long Sutton
Sutton Bridge
Gedney Drove End
Holbeach Marsh
Holbeach St. Matthew
Fosdyke
Sutterton
Kirton
Gosberton
Risegate
Donington
Bicker
Swineshead
Kirton End
Wyberton
Fishtoft
Freiston
Boston
Benington
Old Leake
Wrangle
Sibsey
Frithville
Langrick
Holland Fen
West Fen
East Fen
Friskney
Stickney
Eastville
Coningsby
Tattershall
Mareham-le-Fen
Haltham
Woodhall Spa
Horsington
Bucknall
Bardney
Minting
Baumber
Hagworthingham
Partney
Spilsby
Old Bolingbroke
Candlesby
Burgh-le-Marsh
Irby
Keal
Walpole St. Peter
W. Walton
Emneth
Chris
Welney
0 5 10 km

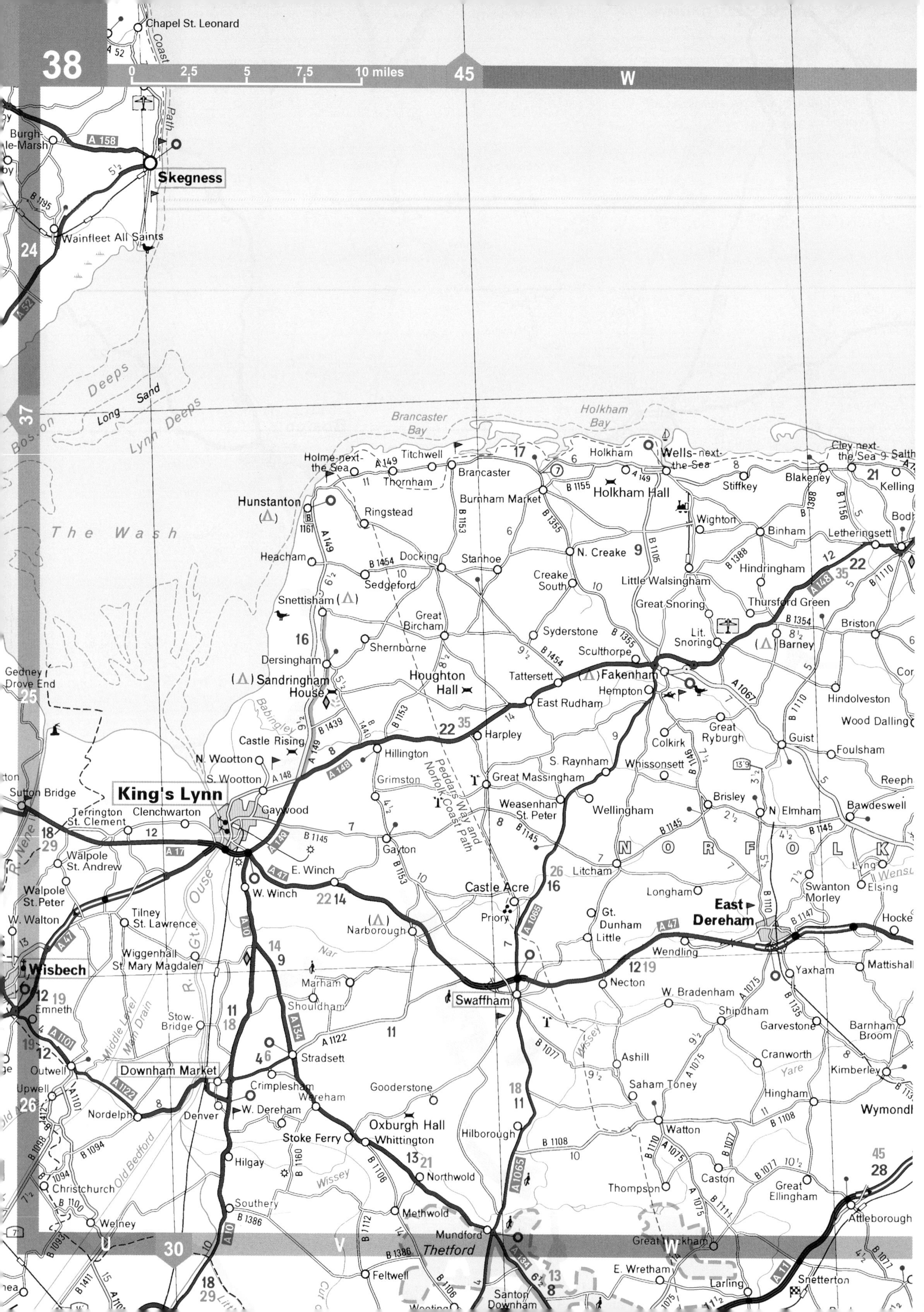
0 2.5 5 7.5 10 miles
45
W
Chapel St. Leonard
Coast
Path
A 52
Burgh-le-Marsh
A 158
Skegness
B 1195
Wainfleet All Saints
24
A 52
37
Boston Deeps
Long Sand
Lynn Deeps
Brancaster Bay
Holkham Bay
Holme-next-the Sea
A 149
Titchwell
Thornham
Brancaster
17
Holkham
Wells-next-the-Sea
Stiffkey
Blakeney
Cley-next-the Sea
21
Kelling
Hunstanton
B 1161
Ringstead
Burnham Market
B 1155
Holkham Hall
B 1153
B 1355
Wighton
Binham
Letheringsett
The Wash
Heacham
Docking
B 1454
Sedgeford
Stanhoe
N. Creake
9
B 1105
Little Walsingham
B 1388
Hindringham
12
22
35
A 148
Creake South
Thursford Green
Snettisham
Great Bircham
Syderstone
Great Snoring
B 1354
Briston
16
Shernborne
Lit. Snoring
Barney
Dersingham
Sculthorpe
Gedney Drove End
Sandringham House
Houghton Hall
Tattersett
Fakenham
Hempton
A 1067
Hindolveston
25
Babingley
B 1439
B 1440
East Rudham
Wood Dalling
Castle Rising
22 35
Harpley
Colkirk
Great Ryburgh
Guist
Foulsham
N. Wootton
A 149
Hillington
S. Raynham
Whissonsett
B 1146
Reepham
S. Wootton
A 148
Grimston
Peddars Way and Norfolk Coast Path
Great Massingham
Sutton Bridge
King's Lynn
Gaywood
Weasenham St. Peter
Wellingham
Brisley
N. Elmham
Bawdeswell
Terrington St. Clement
Clenchwarton
12
B 1145
18 29
A 17
Gayton
NORFOLK
Lyng
R. Nene
Walpole St. Andrew
E. Winch
A 47
B 1153
Litcham
Wensum
Elsing
Swanton Morley
Walpole St. Peter
W. Winch
22 14
Castle Acre
26 16
Longham
W. Walton
Tilney St. Lawrence
Ouse
Narborough
Priory
A 1065
Gt. Dunham
Little
East Dereham
B 1110
B 1147
Hockering
A 10
14 9
Wendling
Wiggenhall St. Mary Magdalen
Nar
12 19
Yaxham
Mattishall
Wisbech
Marham
Swaffham
Necton
W. Bradenham
A 1075
Emneth
Shouldham
Shipdham
B 1135
Stow Bridge
11 18
A 134
Garvestone
Barnham Broom
A 1101
Middle Level Main Drain
A 1122
11
B 1077
Wissey
Cranworth
Outwell
Stradsett
4 6
Ashill
Yare
Kimberley
Downham Market
Crimplesham
Saham Toney
Upwell
Wereham
Gooderstone
18 11
Hingham
26
A 1122
Wymondham
Nordelph
Denver
W. Dereham
B 1108
Oxburgh Hall
Stoke Ferry
Whittington
Hilborough
Watton
B 1094
Old Bedford
Hilgay
B 1160
B 1106
13 21
B 1110
A 1075
B 1077
B 1077
Northwold
10
Great Ellingham
45 28
Christchurch
Wissey
A 1065
Thompson
Caston
B 1100
Southery
B 1386
B 1112
Methwold
B 1111
Attleborough
Welney
Mundford
Great Hockham
U
30
V
B 1386
Thetford
A 134
A 11
B 1093
A 10
Feltwell
E. Wretham
Snetterton
B 1411
13 8
Larling
18 29
Santon Downham
B 1106
Wooting

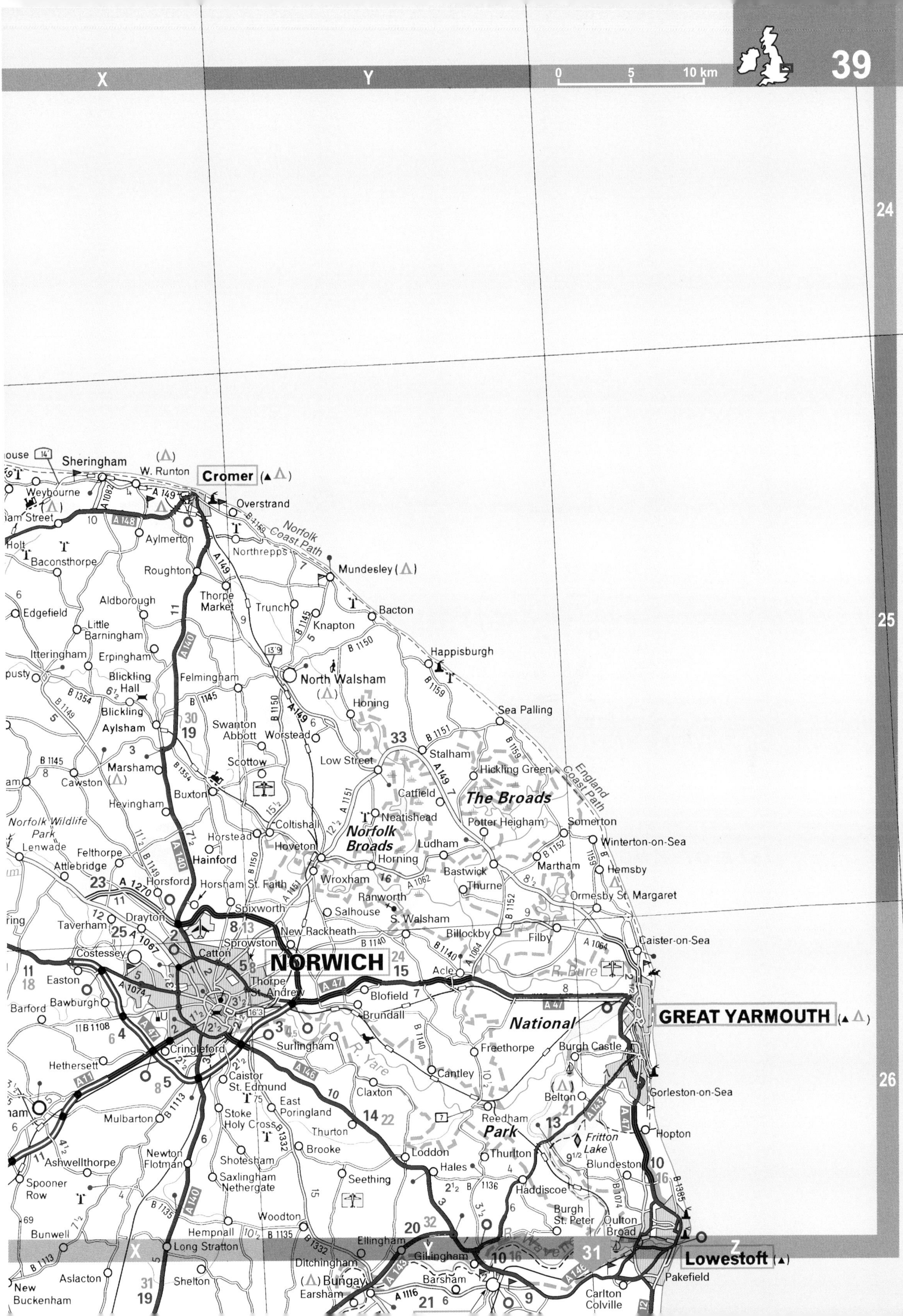
X
Y
Z
0 5 10 km
24
25
26
Sheringham
W. Runton
Cromer
Weybourne
Overstrand
Norfolk Coast Path
Aylmerton
Northrepps
Holt
Baconsthorpe
Roughton
Mundesley
Thorpe Market
Trunch
Bacton
Edgefield
Aldborough
Knapton
Little Barningham
Itteringham
Erpingham
Happisburgh
Blickling Hall
Felmingham
North Walsham
Blickling
Honing
Aylsham
Swanton Abbott
Worstead
Sea Palling
Stalham
Marsham
Scottow
Low Street
Hickling Green
Cawston
England Coast Path
Buxton
Catfield
The Broads
Hevingham
Neatishead
Norfolk Wildlife Park
Coltishall
Norfolk Broads
Potter Heigham
Somerton
Horstead
Hoveton
Ludham
Winterton-on-Sea
Lenwade
Felthorpe
Hainford
Horning
Martham
Attlebridge
Bastwick
Hemsby
Horsford
Horsham St. Faith
Wroxham
Thurne
Ranworth
Ormesby St. Margaret
Drayton
Spixworth
Salhouse
Taverham
S. Walsham
Billockby
Filby
New Rackheath
Sprowston
Caister-on-Sea
Costessey
Catton
NORWICH
Acle
R. Bure
Easton
Thorpe St. Andrew
Blofield
GREAT YARMOUTH
Barford
Bawburgh
Brundall
National
Surlingham
Freethorpe
Burgh Castle
Cringleford
R. Yare
Hethersett
Caistor St. Edmund
Cantley
Gorleston-on-Sea
Claxton
Belton
East Poringland
Mulbarton
Stoke Holy Cross
Reedham
Park
Hopton
Thurton
Fritton Lake
Newton Flotman
Brooke
Loddon
Thurlton
Blundeston
Ashwellthorpe
Shotesham
Hales
Spooner Row
Saxlingham Nethergate
Seething
Haddiscoe
Woodton
Burgh St. Peter
Oulton Broad
Bunwell
Hempnall
Long Stratton
Ellingham
Lowestoft
Ditchingham
Gillingham
R. Waveney
Aslacton
Shelton
Bungay
Barsham
Pakefield
New Buckenham
Earsham
Carlton Colville
A 149
A 148
A 140
A 1151
A 1062
A 1064
A 47
A 11
A 146
A 143
A 1067
A 1074
A 1270
A 1116
B 1159
B 1150
B 1145
B 1354
B 1149
B 1152
B 1140
B 1108
B 1113
B 1135
B 1332
B 1136
B 1074
B 1385

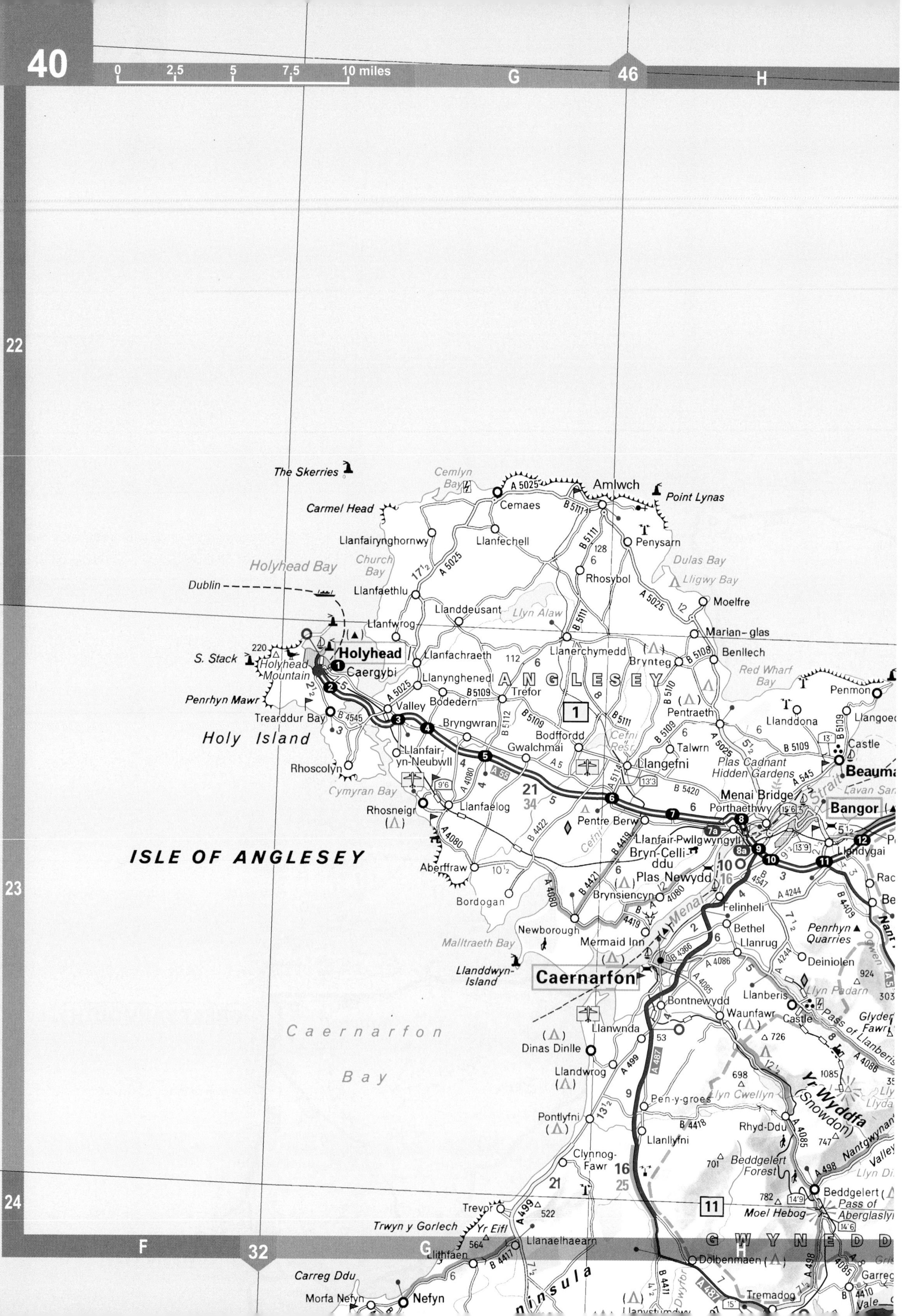
0 2,5 5 7,5 10 miles
G
46
H
22
23
24
F
32
G
H
The Skerries
Cemlyn Bay
Amlwch
Point Lynas
Cemaes
Carmel Head
Llanfairynghornwy
Llanfechell
Penysarn
Holyhead Bay
Church Bay
Dulas Bay
Rhosybol
Lligwy Bay
Dublin
Llanfaethlu
Moelfre
Llanddeusant
Llyn Alaw
Llanfwrog
Marian-glas
S. Stack
Holyhead Mountain
Holyhead
Caergybi
Llanfachraeth
Llanerchymedd
Brynteg
Benllech
Llanynghenedl
ANGLESEY
Red Wharf Bay
Penrhyn Mawr
Valley
Bodedern
Trefor
Penmon
Trearddur Bay
Pentraeth
Llanddona
Llangoed
Holy Island
Bryngwran
Bodffordd
Castle
Llanfair-yn-Neubwll
Gwalchmai
Talwrn
Beaumaris
Rhoscolyn
Llangefni
Plas Cadnant Hidden Gardens
Cymyran Bay
Menai Bridge
Porthaethwy
Bangor
Rhosneigr
Llanfaelog
Pentre Berw
Llanfair-Pwllgwyngyll
Llandygai
ISLE OF ANGLESEY
Bryn-Celli-ddu
Aberffraw
Plas Newydd
Brynsiencyn
Bordogan
Felinheli
Bethel
Llanrug
Penrhyn Quarries
Newborough
Mermaid Inn
Deiniolen
Malltraeth Bay
Llanddwyn Island
Caernarfon
Llanberis
Llyn Padarn
Bontnewydd
Waunfawr
Castle
Pass of Llanberis
Glyder Fawr
Caernarfon Bay
Llanwnda
Dinas Dinlle
Llandwrog
Yr Wyddfa (Snowdon)
Llyn Cwellyn
Pen-y-groes
Pontlyfni
Rhyd-Ddu
Llanllyfni
Clynnog-Fawr
Beddgelert Forest
Beddgelert
Pass of Aberglaslyn
Moel Hebog
Trevor
Trwyn y Gorlech
Yr Eifl
Llanaelhaearn
Llithfaen
Dolbenmaen
GWYNEDD
Carreg Ddu
Morfa Nefyn
Nefyn
Tremadog

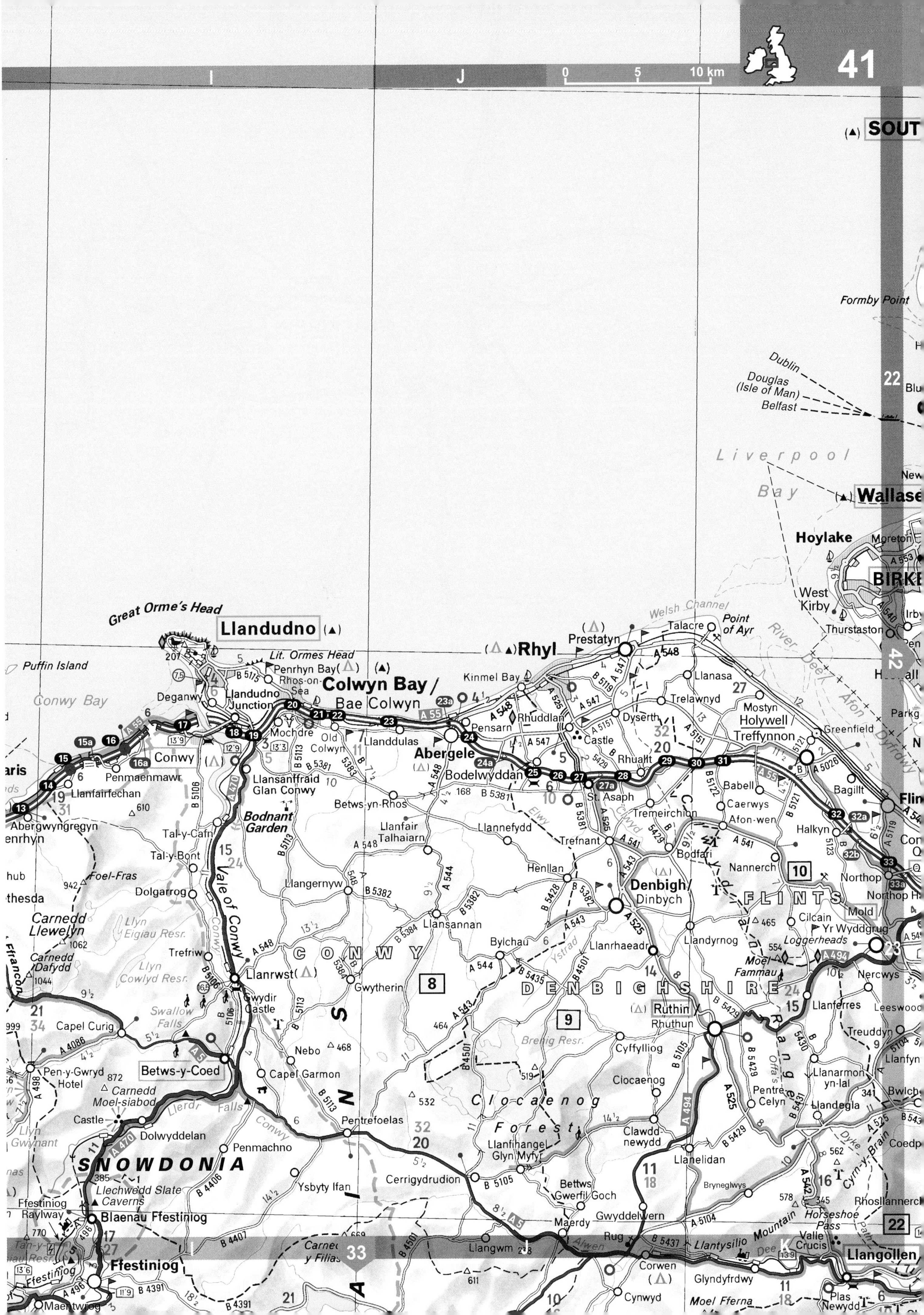

I
J
K
0 5 10 km
SOUT
Formby Point
Dublin
Douglas (Isle of Man)
Belfast
22
Liverpool Bay
Wallase
New
Hoylake
Moreton
BIRKE
West Kirby
Irby
Thurstaston
Welsh Channel
Point of Ayr
Talacre
River Dee
42
Great Orme's Head
Llandudno
Puffin Island
Lit. Ormes Head
Penrhyn Bay
Rhos-on-Sea
Colwyn Bay / Bae Colwyn
Rhyl
Prestatyn
Kinmel Bay
Conwy Bay
Deganwy
Llandudno Junction
Mochdre
Old Colwyn
Llanddulas
Abergele
Pensarn
Rhuddlan
Dyserth
Llanasa
Trelawnyd
Mostyn
Holywell / Treffynnon
Greenfield
Afon Dyfrdwy
Conwy
Penmaenmawr
Llanfairfechan
Abergwyngregyn
Llansanffraid Glan Conwy
Bodnant Garden
Betws-yn-Rhos
Bodelwyddan
St. Asaph
Castle
Rhuallt
Tremeirchion
Babell
Caerwys
Afon-wen
Bagillt
Flin
Halkyn
Llanfair Talhaiarn
Llannefydd
Trefnant
Bodfari
Nannerch
Northop
Northop H
Tal-y-Cafn
Tal-y-Bont
Foel-Fras
Dolgarrog
Carnedd Llewelyn
Llyn Eigiau Resr.
Carnedd Dafydd
Llyn Cowlyd Resr.
Trefriw
Vale of Conwy
Llangernyw
Llansannan
Henllan
Denbigh / Dinbych
FLINTS
Mold
Cilcain
Yr Wyddgrug
Loggerheads
Moel Fammau
Nercwys
Llandyrnog
Llanrhaeadr
Bylchau
CONWY
DENBIGHSHIRE
Llanrwst
Gwydir Castle
Gwytherin
Capel Curig
Swallow Falls
Betws-y-Coed
Pen-y-Gwryd Hotel
Carnedd Moel-siabod
Castle
Dolwyddelan
Lledr Falls
Capel Garmon
Nebo
Ruthin / Rhuthun
Llanferres
Leeswood
Treuddyn
Llanfyn
Cyffylliog
Brenig Resr.
Clocaenog
Clocaenog Forest
Offa's Dyke
Llanarmon-yn-Ial
Pentre Celyn
Llandegla
Bwlch
Coedp
Clawdd-newydd
Llanfihangel Glyn Myfyr
Llanelidan
Pentrefoelas
Penmachno
SNOWDONIA
Llechwedd Slate Caverns
Ffestiniog Railway
Blaenau Ffestiniog
Ysbyty Ifan
Cerrigydrudion
Bettws Gwerfil Goch
Bryneglwys
Gwyddelwern
Maerdy
Horseshoe Pass
Rhosllannerch
Valle Crucis
Llantysilio Mountain
Llangollen
Llangwm
Rug
Corwen
Alwen
Carnedd y Filiast
33
Ffestiniog
Maentwrog
Glyndyfrdwy
Moel Fferna
Cynwyd
Plas Newydd

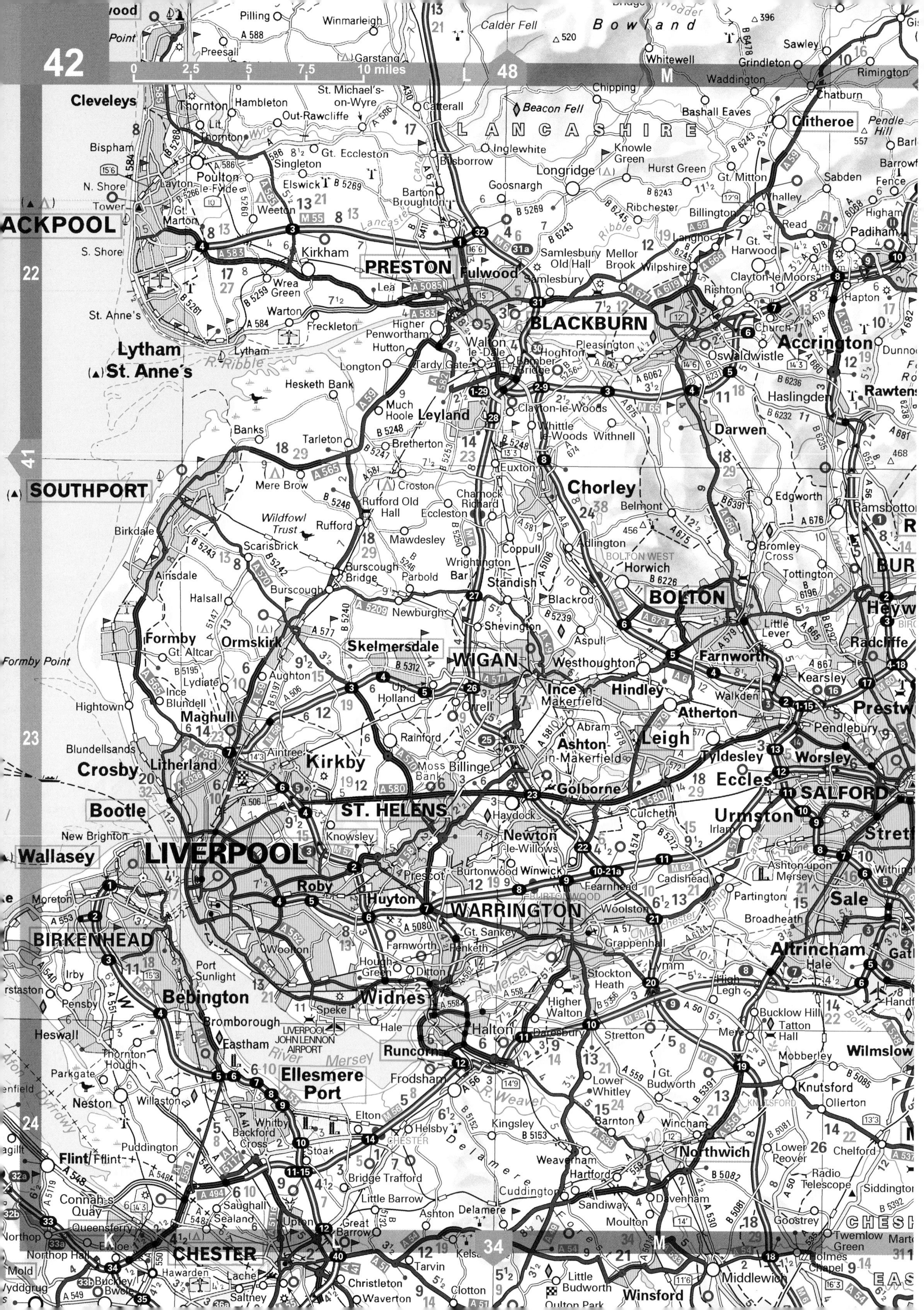

0 2,5 5 7,5 10 miles
48
34
41
22
23
24
L
M
K
Pilling
Winmarleigh
Preesall
Garstang
Calder Fell
Bowland
Whitewell
Sawley
Grindleton
Waddington
Rimington
Chatburn
Clitheroe
Pendle Hill
Cleveleys
Thornton
Hambleton
St. Michael's-on-Wyre
Out-Rawcliffe
Catterall
Chipping
Beacon Fell
Bashall Eaves
LANCASHIRE
Bispham
Poulton-le-Fylde
Gt. Eccleston
Singleton
Elswick
Bilsborrow
Inglewhite
Knowle Green
Longridge
Hurst Green
Gt. Mitton
Sabden
Barrowford
Fence
N. Shore
Layton
Tower
Weeton
Goosnargh
Barton
Broughton
Ribchester
Billington
Whalley
Higham
Padiham
ACKPOOL
Gt. Marton
Kirkham
PRESTON
Fulwood
Samlesbury Old Hall
Mellor Brook
Wilpshire
Langho
Gt. Harwood
Read
Clayton-le-Moors
S. Shore
Wrea Green
Lea
Samlesbury
Rishton
Hapton
St. Anne's
Warton
Freckleton
Higher Penwortham
BLACKBURN
Church
Accrington
Lytham St. Anne's
Lytham
R. Ribble
Hutton
Walton-le-Dale
Hoghton
Pleasington
Oswaldwistle
Longton
Tardy Gate
Bamber Bridge
Hesketh Bank
Much Hoole
Leyland
Clayton-le-Woods
Haslingden
Rawtenstall
Banks
Tarleton
Bretherton
Whittle-le-Woods
Withnell
Darwen
Euxton
Chorley
Edgworth
Mere Brow
Croston
Charnock Richard
Belmont
Ramsbottom
SOUTHPORT
Wildfowl Trust
Rufford Old Hall
Rufford
Eccleston
Birkdale
Mawdesley
Adlington
BOLTON WEST
Horwich
Bromley Cross
Scarisbrick
Coppull
Tottington
Ainsdale
Burscough Bridge
Parbold
Wrightington Bar
Standish
Blackrod
BOLTON
Burscough
Halsall
Newburgh
Shevington
Aspull
Little Lever
Heywood
Formby
Ormskirk
Skelmersdale
WIGAN
Farnworth
Radcliffe
Formby Point
Gt. Altcar
Westhoughton
Kearsley
Lydiate
Aughton
Up Holland
Ince-in-Makerfield
Hindley
Walkden
Hightown
Ince Blundell
Orrell
Atherton
Prestwich
Maghull
Abram
Pendlebury
Rainford
Ashton-in-Makerfield
Leigh
Blundellsands
Aintree
Kirkby
Tyldesley
Worsley
Crosby
Litherland
Billinge
Moss Bank
Eccles
SALFORD
Golborne
Bootle
ST. HELENS
Haydock
Culcheth
Urmston
Irlam
New Brighton
Knowsley
Newton-le-Willows
Stretford
Wallasey
LIVERPOOL
Prescot
Burtonwood
Winwick
Ashton upon Mersey
Moreton
Roby
Huyton
Fearnhead
Cadishead
Partington
Sale
BURTONWOOD
WARRINGTON
Woolston
Broadheath
BIRKENHEAD
Gt. Sankey
Woolton
Farnworth
Penketh
Grappenhall
Altrincham
Hale
Irby
Port Sunlight
Hough Green
Ditton
Stockton Heath
Lymm
High Legh
Pensby
Bebington
Widnes
Speke
Higher Walton
Bucklow Hill
Tatton Hall
Heswall
Bromborough
Hale
LIVERPOOL JOHN LENNON AIRPORT
Halton
Daresbury
Stretton
Mere
Thornton Hough
Eastham
River Mersey
Runcorn
Wilmslow
Parkgate
Mobberley
Ellesmere Port
Frodsham
Lower Whitley
Gt. Budworth
Knutsford
Neston
Willaston
R. Weaver
KNUTSFORD
Ollerton
Elton
Helsby
Barnton
Wincham
Whitby
Backford Cross
Kingsley
Puddington
Stoak
CHESTER
Delamere
Weaverham
Northwich
Lower Peover
Chelford
Flint/Fflint
Bridge Trafford
Hartford
Radio Telescope
Siddington
Connah's Quay
Saughall
Little Barrow
Cuddington
Sandiway
Davenham
Sealand
Queensferry
Upton
Ashton
Great Barrow
Delamere
Moulton
Goostrey
Twemlow Green
Northop
Ewloe
Northop Hall
CHESTER
Kelsall
Holmes Chapel
Mold
Hawarden
Lache
Tarvin
Little Budworth
Middlewich
Buckley
Bwcle
Christleton
Saltney
Waverton
Clotton
Oulton Park
Winsford

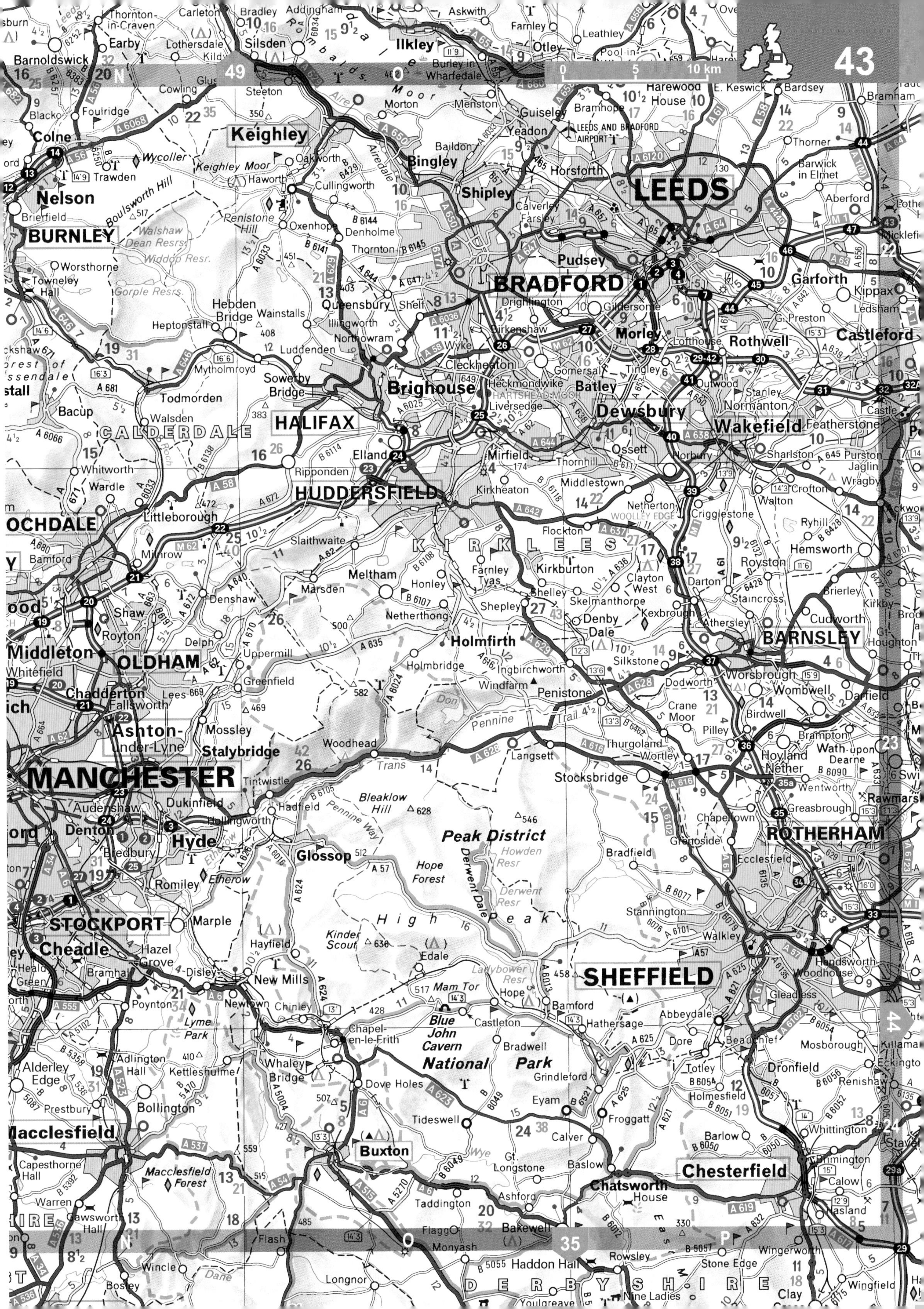
0 5 10 km
49
LEEDS
BRADFORD
HALIFAX
HUDDERSFIELD
MANCHESTER
SHEFFIELD
BARNSLEY
ROTHERHAM
OLDHAM
STOCKPORT
BURNLEY
OCHDALE
Keighley
Brighouse
Dewsbury
Wakefield
Chesterfield
Macclesfield
Buxton
Glossop
Hyde
Ashton-under-Lyne
Stalybridge
Nelson
Colne
Ilkley
Otley
Shipley
Bingley
Pudsey
Morley
Batley
Castleford
Rothwell
Garforth
Holmfirth
Penistone
Stocksbridge
Meltham
Marsden
Todmorden
Hebden Bridge
Sowerby Bridge
Elland
Mirfield
Ossett
Cheadle
Marple
Middleton
Denton
Bollington
Chatsworth House
Haddon Hall
Bakewell
Peak District
High Peak
National Park
Hope Forest
Kinder Scout
Bleaklow Hill
Mam Tor
Blue John Cavern
Castleton
Hathersage
Eyam
Tideswell
Chapel-en-le-Frith
New Mills
Whaley Bridge
Lyme Park
Macclesfield Forest
Dronfield
Wombwell
Hoyland Nether
Royston
Hemsworth
Cudworth
Kirkburton
Denby Dale
Haworth
Keighley Moor
Wycoller
CALDERDALE
KIRKLEES
DERBYSHIRE
Pennine Way
Trans Pennine Trail
LEEDS AND BRADFORD AIRPORT
HARTSHEAD MOOR
WOOLLEY EDGE
M 62
M 1
A 61
A 628
A 6
44
35

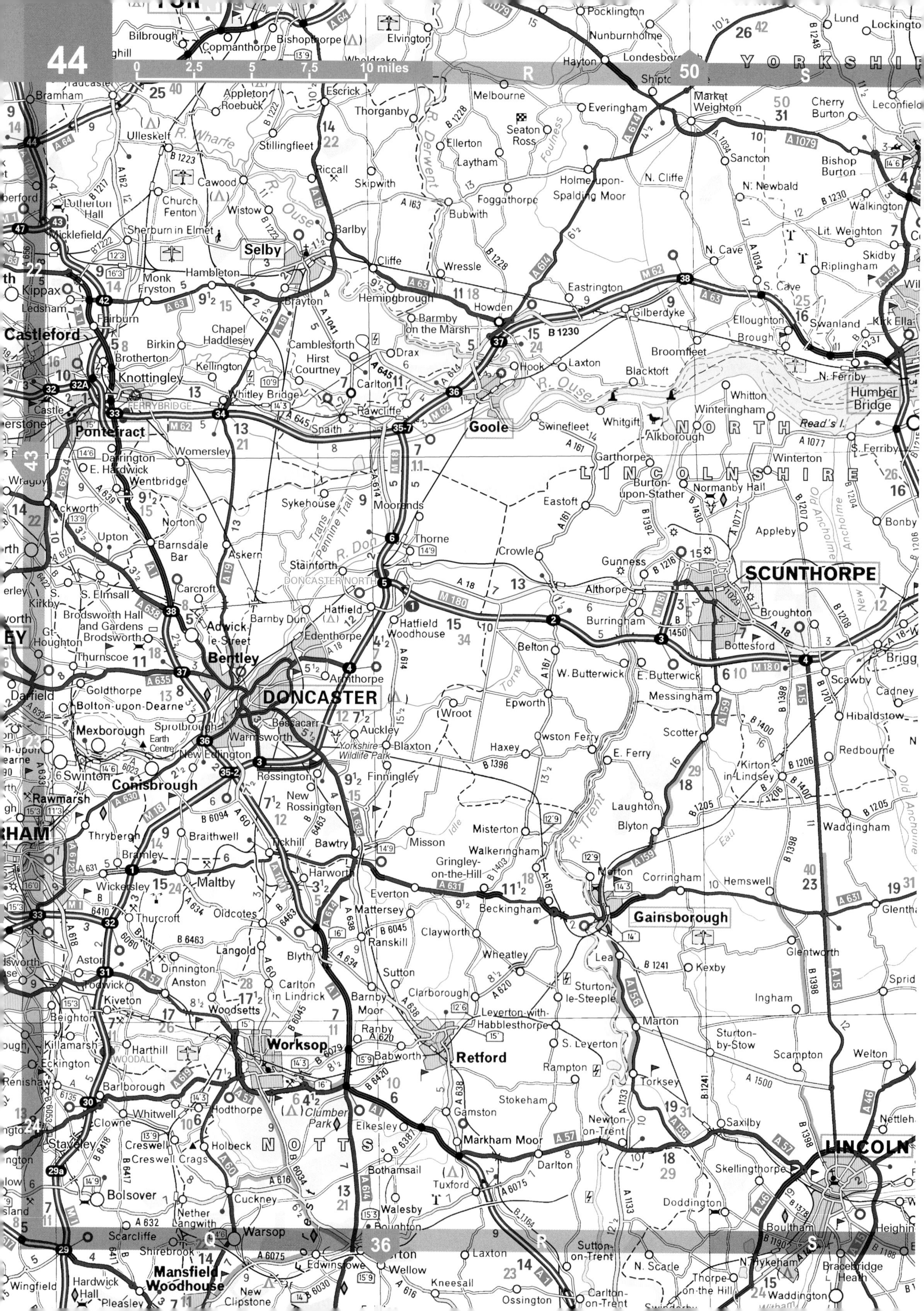

0 2.5 5 7.5 10 miles
YORKSHIRE
NORTH LINCOLNSHIRE
NOTTS
Pocklington
Nunburnholme
Lund
Lockington
Bilbrough
Copmanthorpe
Bishopthorpe
Elvington
Hayton
Londesborough
Market Weighton
Melbourne
Everingham
Cherry Burton
Leconfield
Bramham
Appleton Roebuck
Escrick
Thorganby
Seaton Ross
Ulleskelf
Stillingfleet
Ellerton
Laytham
Sancton
Bishop Burton
Riccall
Skipwith
Holme-upon-Spalding Moor
N. Cliffe
N. Newbald
Walkington
Cawood
Church Fenton
Lotherton Hall
Wistow
Foggathorpe
Bubwith
Lit. Weighton
Micklefield
Sherburn in Elmet
Barlby
Skidby
Riplingham
Selby
Hambleton
Cliffe
Wressle
N. Cave
S. Cave
Kippax
Monk Fryston
Ledsham
Brayton
Hemingbrough
Eastrington
Fairburn
Barmby on the Marsh
Howden
Gilberdyke
Elloughton
Swanland
Kirk Ella
Castleford
Chapel Haddlesey
Camblesforth
Drax
Brough
Birkin
Hirst Courtney
Brotherton
Kellington
Hook
Laxton
Broomfleet
Blacktoft
Knottingley
Carlton
N. Ferriby
Humber Bridge
Whitton
Castle
Whitley Bridge
Rawcliffe
Winteringham
Ferrybridge
Pontefract
Snaith
Goole
Swinefleet
Whitgift
Read's I.
Alkborough
Darrington
Womersley
E. Hardwick
Wentbridge
Garthorpe
Winterton
S. Ferriby
Burton-upon-Stather
Normanby Hall
Ackworth
Sykehouse
Moorends
Eastoft
Norton
Upton
Thorne
Appleby
Bonby
Barnsdale Bar
Askern
Crowle
Stainforth
Gunness
Scunthorpe
Carcroft
Doncaster North
Althorpe
S. Elmsall
Kirkby
Brodsworth Hall and Gardens
Hatfield
Burringham
Broughton
Adwick le-Street
Barnby Dun
Hatfield Woodhouse
Houghton
Brodsworth
Edenthorpe
Belton
Bottesford
Thurnscoe
Bentley
Armthorpe
W. Butterwick
E. Butterwick
Brigg
Scawby
Darfield
Goldthorpe
Doncaster
Epworth
Messingham
Cadney
Bolton-upon-Dearne
Wroot
Bessacarr
Auckley
Mexborough
Sprotbrough
Earth Centre
Warmsworth
Blaxton
Yorkshire Wildlife Park
Haxey
Owston Ferry
Scotter
Hibaldstow
Redbourne
New Edlington
E. Ferry
Kirton in Lindsey
Swinton
Conisbrough
Rossington
Finningley
Rawmarsh
New Rossington
Laughton
Blyton
Waddingham
Thrybergh
Braithwell
Tickhill
Bawtry
Misson
Misterton
Walkeringham
Bramley
Gringley-on-the-Hill
Morton
Corringham
Hemswell
Wickersley
Maltby
Harworth
Everton
Beckingham
Gainsborough
Glentham
Mattersey
Thurcroft
Oldcotes
Ranskill
Clayworth
Langold
Blyth
Wheatley
Lea
Glentworth
Kexby
Aston
Dinnington
Anston
Sutton
Todwick
Carlton in Lindrick
Clarborough
Sturton-le-Steeple
Kiveton
Barnby Moor
Ingham
Woodsetts
Leverton-with-Habblesthorpe
Marton
Beighton
Ranby
Killamarsh
Worksop
Babworth
Retford
S. Leverton
Sturton-by-Stow
Scampton
Welton
Harthill
Woodall
Eckington
Rampton
Torksey
Renishaw
Barlborough
Stokeham
Whitwell
Hodthorpe
Clumber Park
Elkesley
Gamston
Newton-on-Trent
Saxilby
Clowne
Nettleham
Staveley
Creswell
Holbeck
Creswell Crags
Markham Moor
Darlton
Lincoln
Skellingthorpe
Bothamsall
Tuxford
Bolsover
Cuckney
Doddington
Nether Langwith
Walesby
Boughton
Boultham
Scarcliffe
Warsop
Shirebrook
Laxton
Sutton-on-Trent
N. Hykeham
Edwinstowe
Ollerton
Wellow
N. Scarle
Bracebridge Heath
Mansfield Woodhouse
Hardwick Hall
Kneesall
Thorpe on the Hill
Wingfield
Pleasley
New Clipstone
Ossington
Carlton-on-Trent
Waddington
R. Wharfe
R. Ouse
R. Derwent
R. Don
R. Trent
Trans Pennine Trail

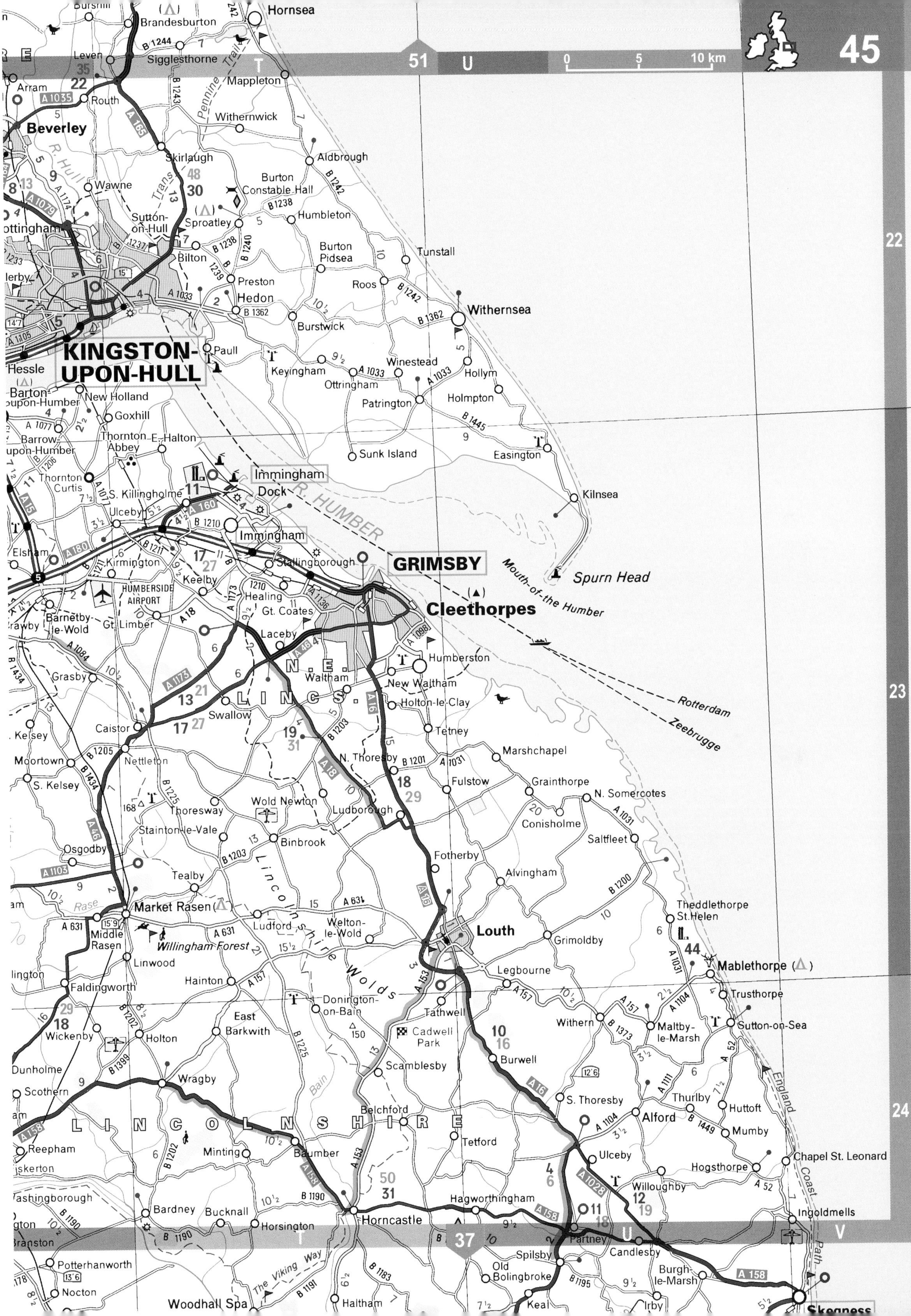
Hornsea
Brandesburton
Sigglesthorne
Leven
Mappleton
Arram
Routh
Beverley
Withernwick
Skirlaugh
Aldbrough
Burton Constable Hall
Wawne
Humbleton
Sprotley
Sutton-on-Hull
Tunstall
Bilton
Burton Pidsea
Preston
Roos
Hedon
Withernsea
Burstwick
KINGSTON-UPON-HULL
Paull
Hessle
Keyingham
Winestead
Hollym
Ottringham
Patrington
Holmpton
Barton-upon-Humber
New Holland
Goxhill
Barrow-upon-Humber
Thornton Abbey
E. Halton
Sunk Island
Easington
Thornton Curtis
Immingham Dock
R. HUMBER
Kilnsea
S. Killingholme
Ulceby
Immingham
Elsham
Kirmington
Stallingborough
GRIMSBY
Spurn Head
Mouth-of-the Humber
Keelby
HUMBERSIDE AIRPORT
Healing
Cleethorpes
Barnetby-le-Wold
Gt. Limber
Gt. Coates
Laceby
Humberston
Grasby
N. E. LINCS.
Waltham
New Waltham
Holton-le-Clay
Rotterdam
Zeebrugge
Swallow
Caistor
Tetney
Kelsey
Nettleton
N. Thoresby
Marshchapel
Moortown
S. Kelsey
Fulstow
Grainthorpe
N. Somercotes
Thoresway
Wold Newton
Ludborough
Conisholme
Stainton-le-Vale
Binbrook
Saltfleet
Osgodby
Fotherby
Tealby
Alvingham
Market Rasen
Lincolnshire Wolds
Theddlethorpe St.Helen
Middle Rasen
Ludford
Welton-le-Wold
Louth
Grimoldby
Willingham Forest
Linwood
Legbourne
Mablethorpe
Hainton
Trusthorpe
Faldingworth
Donington-on-Bain
Tathwell
Withern
Maltby-le-Marsh
Sutton-on-Sea
East Barkwith
Cadwell Park
Wickenby
Holton
Burwell
Dunholme
Scamblesby
Scothern
Wragby
S. Thoresby
Thurlby
Huttoft
Belchford
Alford
Mumby
LINCOLNSHIRE
Tetford
Reepham
Minting
Baumber
Ulceby
Chapel St. Leonard
Hogsthorpe
Willoughby
England Coast Path
Washingborough
Hagworthingham
Bardney
Bucknall
Horncastle
Ingoldmells
Horsington
Partney
Branston
Spilsby
Candlesby
Potterhanworth
Old Bolingbroke
Burgh-le-Marsh
The Viking Way
Nocton
Woodhall Spa
Haltham
Keal
Irby
Skegness
0 5 10 km
51
37
T
U
V
22
23
24

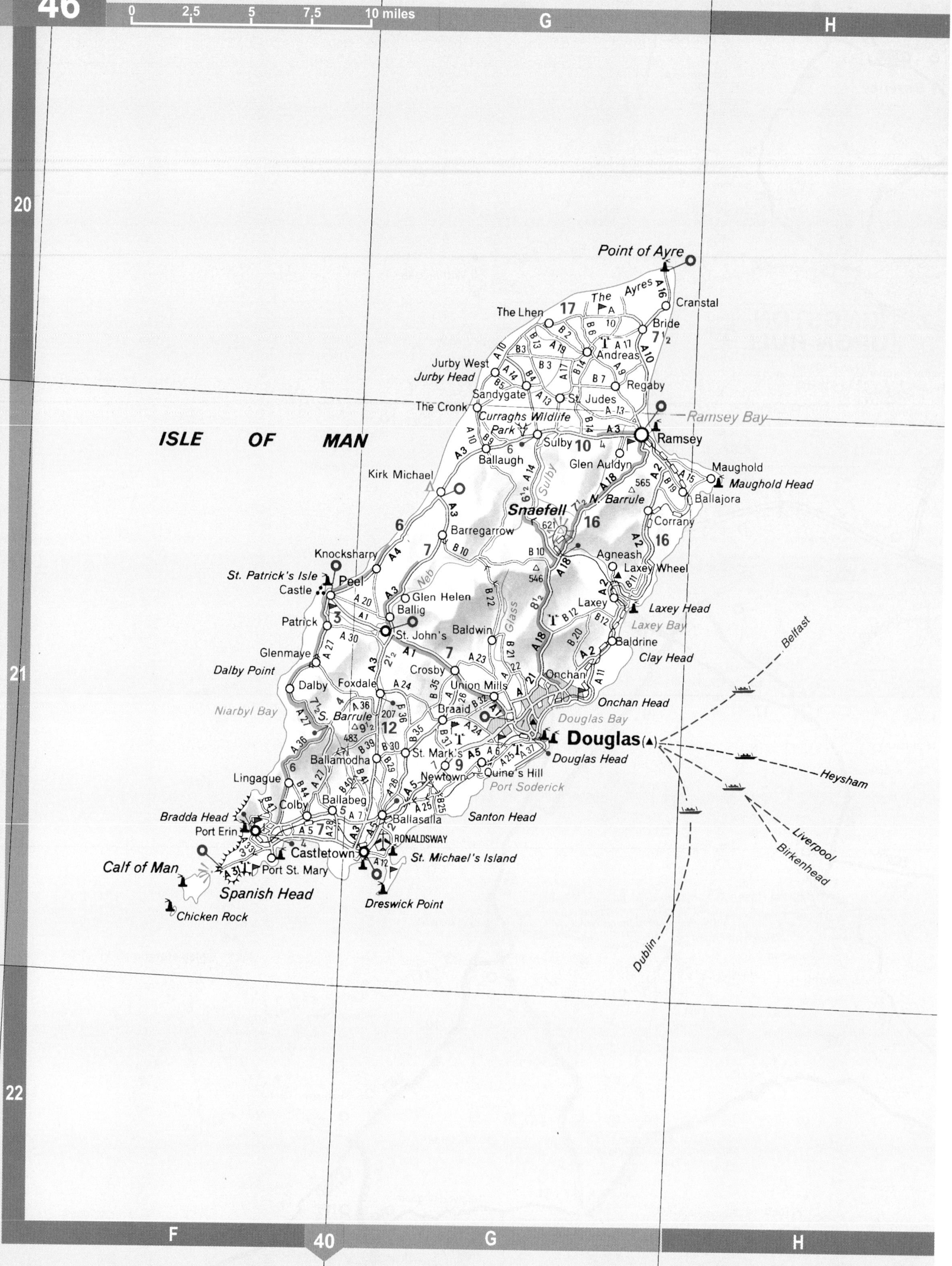
0 2.5 5 7.5 10 miles
F
G
H
20
21
22
ISLE OF MAN
Point of Ayre
The Ayres
Cranstal
The Lhen
Bride
Andreas
Jurby West
Jurby Head
Regaby
Sandygate
St. Judes
The Cronk
Curraghs Wildlife Park
Ramsey Bay
Ramsey
Sulby
Ballaugh
Glen Auldyn
Maughold
Maughold Head
Kirk Michael
Ballajora
N. Barrule
Snaefell
Corrany
Barregarrow
Agneash
Knocksharry
Laxey Wheel
St. Patrick's Isle
Peel
Castle
Glen Helen
Laxey
Ballig
Laxey Head
Patrick
Laxey Bay
St. John's
Baldwin
Baldrine
Glenmaye
Clay Head
Belfast
Crosby
Dalby Point
Dalby
Foxdale
Union Mills
Onchan
Onchan Head
Niarbyl Bay
S. Barrule
Braaid
Douglas Bay
Douglas
Douglas Head
St. Mark's
Ballamodha
Heysham
Lingague
Newtown
Quine's Hill
Port Soderick
Colby
Ballabeg
Bradda Head
Ballasalla
Santon Head
Port Erin
RONALDSWAY
Castletown
St. Michael's Island
Liverpool
Birkenhead
Calf of Man
Port St. Mary
Spanish Head
Dreswick Point
Chicken Rock
Dublin

40

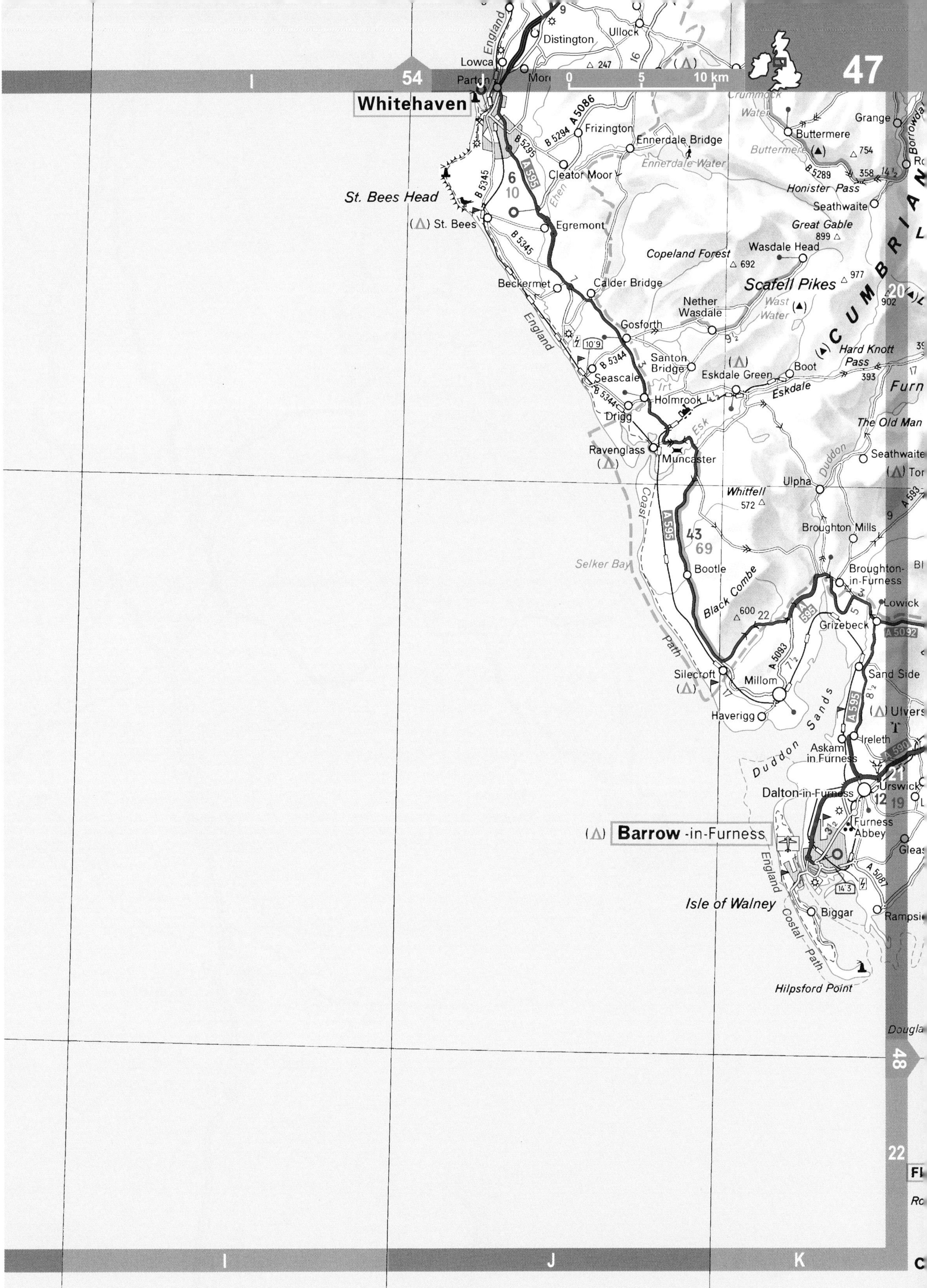

54
I
J
K
0 5 10 km
Whitehaven
Distington
Ullock
Lowca
Parton
Moresby
England
Frizington
Ennerdale Bridge
Ennerdale Water
Cleator Moor
Crummock Water
Buttermere
Grange
Honister Pass
Seathwaite
Great Gable
899
St. Bees Head
St. Bees
Egremont
Ehen
Copeland Forest
692
Wasdale Head
Scafell Pikes
977
Beckermet
Calder Bridge
Nether Wasdale
Wast Water
Gosforth
CUMBRIAN
Santon Bridge
Eskdale Green
Boot
Hard Knott Pass
393
Seascale
Irt
Holmrook
Eskdale
Drigg
Esk
Ravenglass
Muncaster
The Old Man
Seathwaite
Ulpha
Duddon
Whitfell
572
Coast
Path
Broughton Mills
Selker Bay
Bootle
Broughton-in-Furness
Black Combe
600
Lowick
Grizebeck
Silecroft
Millom
Sand Side
Haverigg
Duddon Sands
Askam in Furness
Ireleth
Dalton-in-Furness
Urswick
Furness Abbey
Barrow -in-Furness
Isle of Walney
England Costal Path
Biggar
Rampside
Hilpsford Point
Douglas
A 595
A 5086
B 5294
B 5295
B 5345
B 5344
B 5289
A 5093
A 5092
A 590
A 5087
A 593
48
22

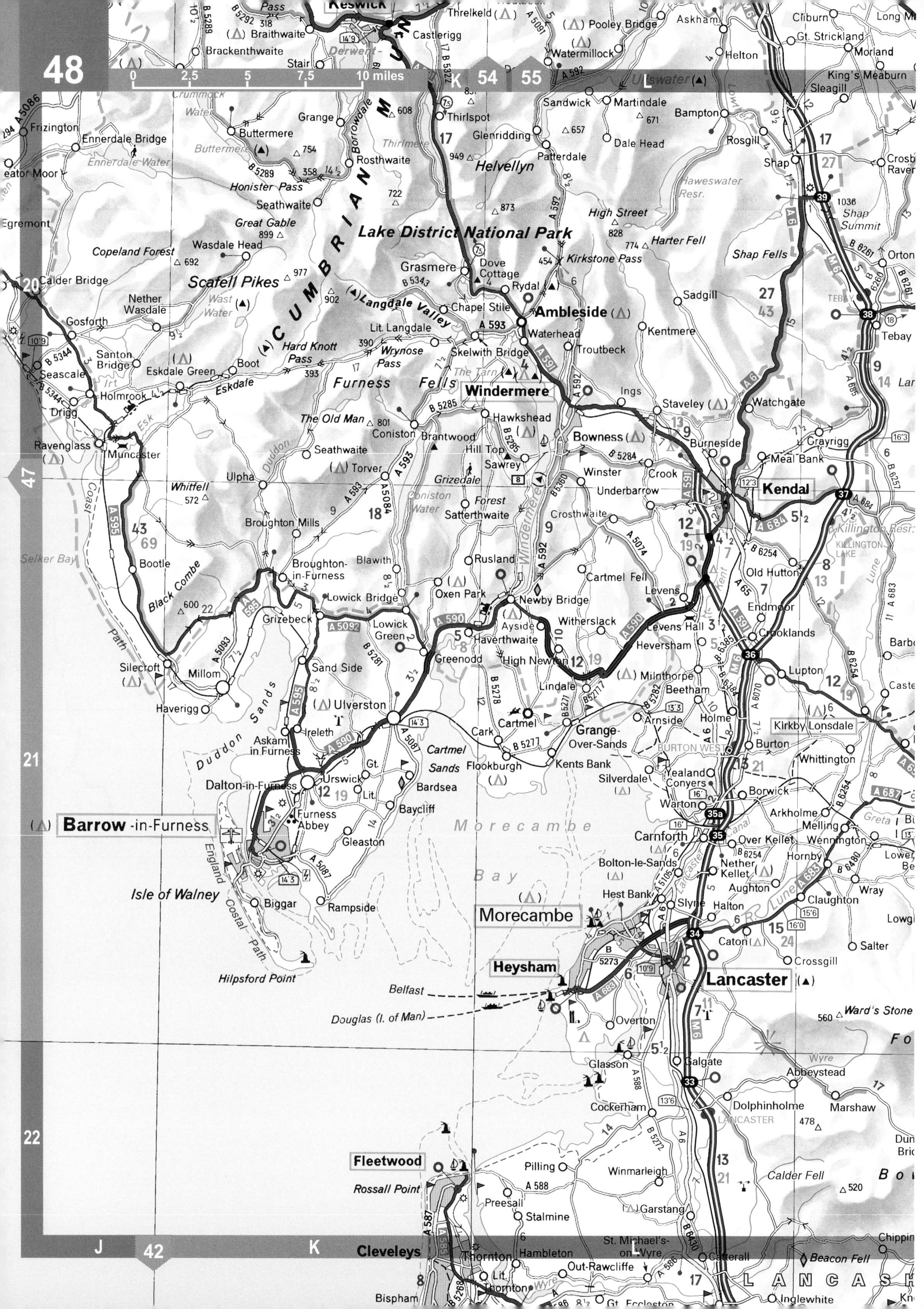
0 2.5 5 7.5 10 miles
54
55
47
42
J
K
L
20
21
22
Keswick
Threlkeld
Pooley Bridge
Askham
Cliburn
Long Marton
Braithwaite
Castlerigg
Watermillock
Helton
Gt. Strickland
Morland
Brackenthwaite
Stair
Derwent
King's Meaburn
Sleagill
Ullswater
Frizington
Ennerdale Bridge
Ennerdale Water
Cleator Moor
Crummock Water
Grange
Buttermere
Thirlspot
Sandwick
Martindale
Bampton
Thirlmere
Glenridding
Dale Head
Rosgill
Shap
Crosby Ravensworth
Rosthwaite
Honister Pass
Seathwaite
Helvellyn
Patterdale
Haweswater Resr.
CUMBRIAN MOUNTAINS
Egremont
Great Gable
High Street
Shap Summit
Lake District National Park
Harter Fell
Shap Fells
Copeland Forest
Wasdale Head
Kirkstone Pass
Orton
Calder Bridge
Scafell Pikes
Grasmere
Dove Cottage
Rydal
Ambleside
Sadgill
Tebay
Nether Wasdale
Wast Water
Langdale Valley
Chapel Stile
Gosforth
Lit. Langdale
Waterhead
Kentmere
Santon Bridge
Hard Knott Pass
Wrynose Pass
Skelwith Bridge
Troutbeck
Seascale
Eskdale Green
Boot
Eskdale
Furness Fells
The Tarn
Windermere
Ings
Staveley
Watchgate
Holmrook
Drigg
Hawkshead
The Old Man
Coniston
Brantwood
Bowness
Ravenglass
Muncaster
Seathwaite
Hill Top
Sawrey
Burneside
Grayrigg
Meal Bank
Torver
Winster
Crook
Coast Path
Grizedale
Kendal
Ulpha
Whitfell
Underbarrow
Coniston Water
Forest
Satterthwaite
Crosthwaite
Broughton Mills
Killington Resr.
Killington Lake
Selker Bay
Bootle
Rusland
Blawith
Broughton-in-Furness
Old Hutton
Cartmel Fell
Black Combe
Lowick Bridge
Oxen Park
Newby Bridge
Levens
Endmoor
Grizebeck
Lowick Green
Ayside
Witherslack
Levens Hall
Haverthwaite
Heversham
Crooklands
Silecroft
Millom
Greenodd
High Newton
Milnthorpe
Lupton
Sand Side
Lindale
Beetham
Haverigg
Duddon Sands
Ulverston
Cartmel
Arnside
Holme
Kirkby Lonsdale
Ireleth
Cark
Grange-Over-Sands
Burton
Askam in Furness
Cartmel Sands
Flookburgh
Kents Bank
Burton West
Whittington
Gt. Urswick
Silverdale
Yealand Conyers
Dalton-in-Furness
Lit.
Bardsea
Borwick
Barrow-in-Furness
Furness Abbey
Baycliff
Warton
Arkholme
Melling
Morecambe Bay
Gleaston
Carnforth
Over Kellet
Wennington
England Coastal Path
Bolton-le-Sands
Nether Kellet
Hornby
Isle of Walney
Aughton
Wray
Biggar
Rampside
Hest Bank
Slyne
Halton
Claughton
Morecambe
Caton
Lowgill
Salter
Crossgill
Heysham
Lancaster
Hilpsford Point
Belfast
Douglas (I. of Man)
Overton
Ward's Stone
Forest of Bowland
Glasson
Galgate
Wyre
Abbeystead
Cockerham
Dolphinholme
Marshaw
Lancaster
Fleetwood
Pilling
Winmarleigh
Calder Fell
Rossall Point
Preesall
Stalmine
Garstang
Cleveleys
Thornton
Hambleton
St. Michael's-on-Wyre
Catterall
Beacon Fell
Chipping
Lit. Thornton
Out-Rawcliffe
Bispham
Gt. Eccleston
Inglewhite
LANCASHIRE

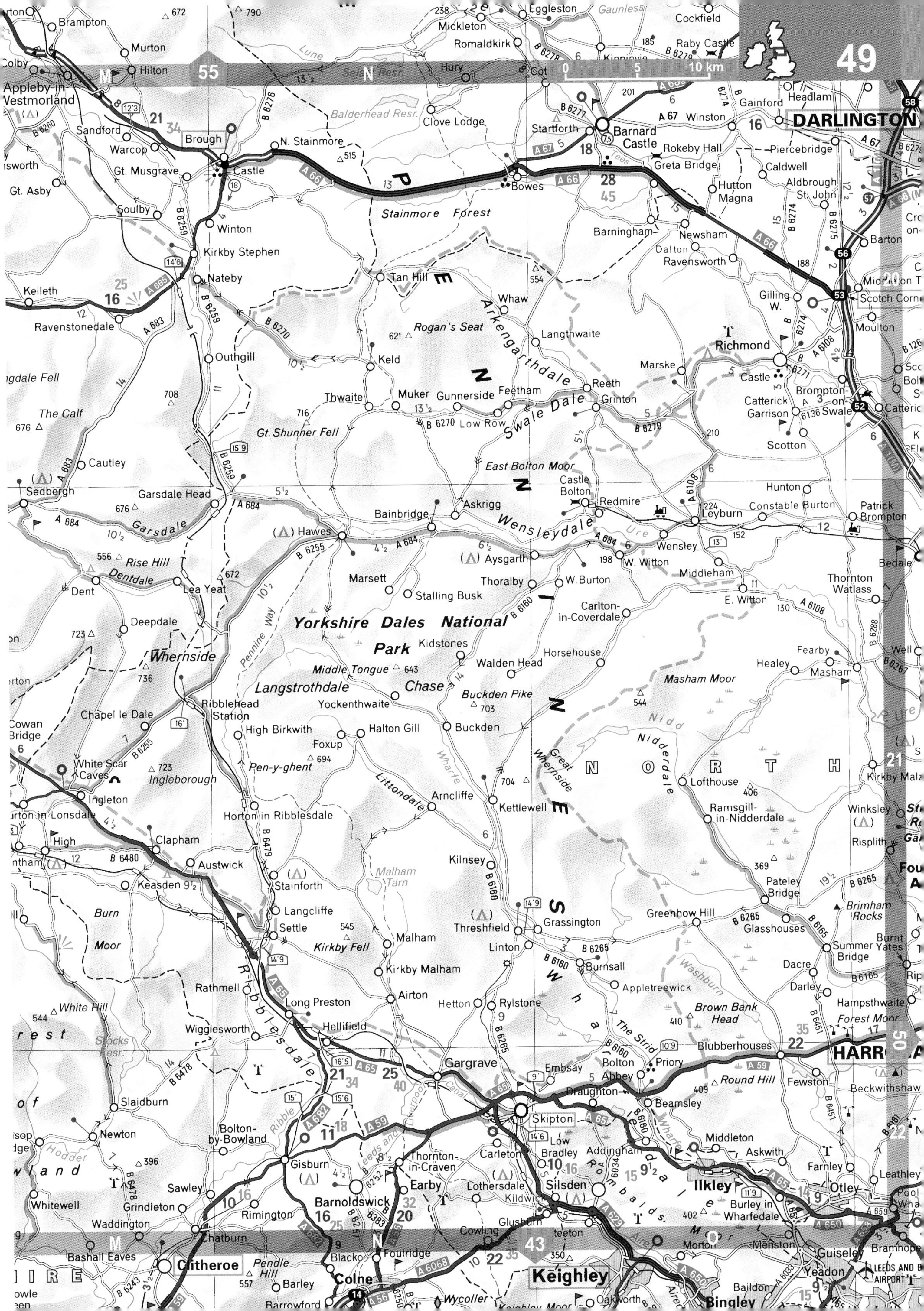

DARLINGTON
Barnard Castle
Appleby-in-Westmorland
Brough
Kirkby Stephen
Sedbergh
Hawes
Richmond
Leyburn
Bedale
Masham
Pateley Bridge
Settle
Skipton
Ilkley
Otley
Keighley
Colne
Clitheroe
Barnoldswick
Gisburn
Bingley
HARROGATE
Yorkshire Dales National Park
PENNINES
NORTH YORKSHIRE
Stainmore Forest
Swale Dale
Wensleydale
Garsdale
Dentdale
Arkengarthdale
Langstrothdale Chase
Littondale
Nidderdale
Ribblesdale
Wharfedale
Rombalds Moor
Masham Moor
Forest of Bowland
Burn Moor
East Bolton Moor
Rogan's Seat
Gt. Shunner Fell
Whernside
Ingleborough
Pen-y-ghent
Buckden Pike
Great Whernside
Kirkby Fell
Malham Tarn
Brimham Rocks
Brown Bank Head
The Strid
Round Hill
Pendle Hill
Middle Tongue
The Calf
Rise Hill
White Scar Caves
Ribblehead Station
Balderhead Resr.
Selset Resr.
Stocks Resr.
Leeds and Liverpool Canal
LEEDS AND BRADFORD AIRPORT
0 5 10 km

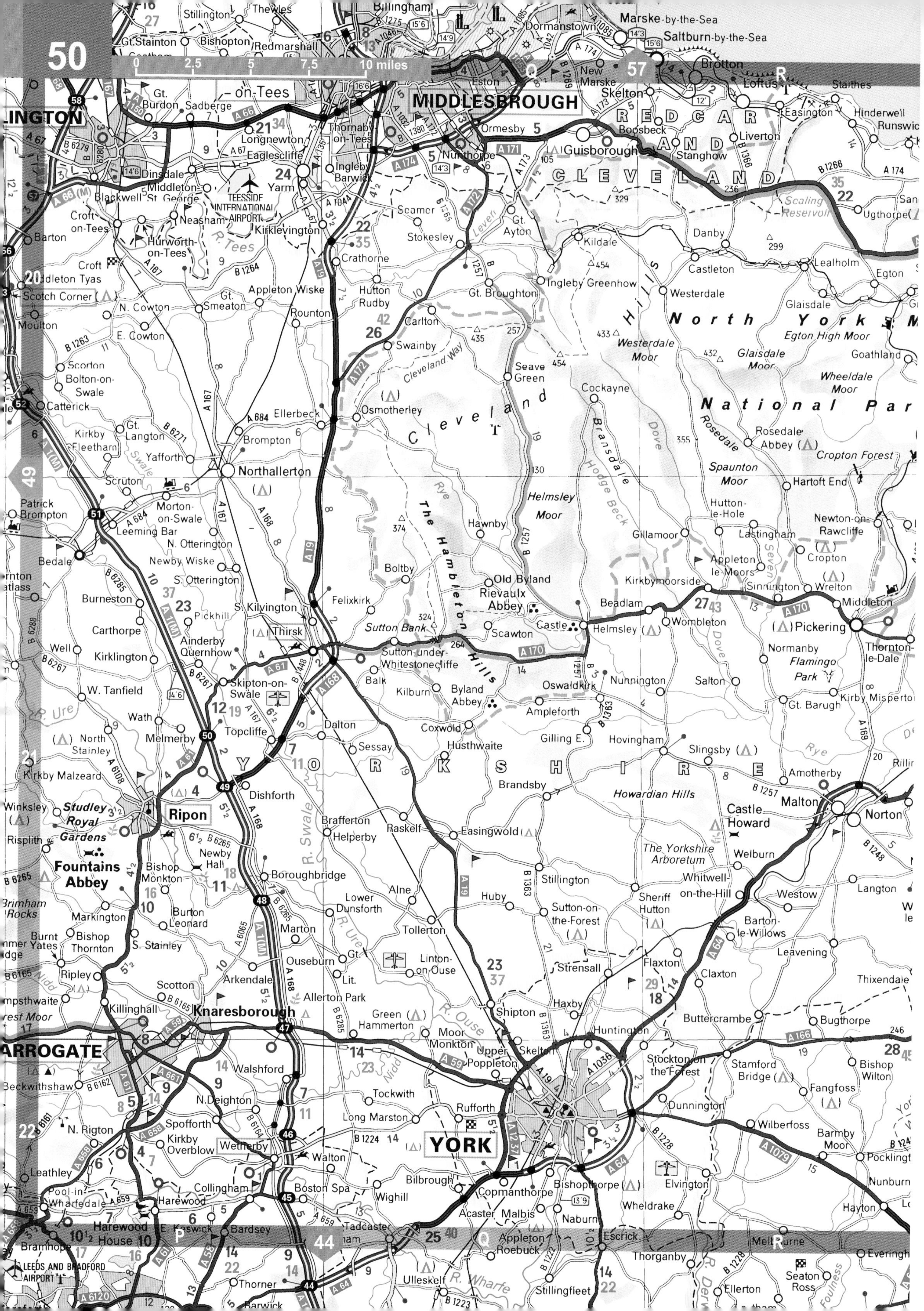

MIDDLESBROUGH
YORK
Northallerton
Thirsk
Ripon
Knaresborough
ARROGATE
LINGTON
Malton
Norton
Pickering
Helmsley
Guisborough
Stokesley
Yarm
Bedale
Easingwold
Boroughbridge
Wetherby
Tadcaster
Marske-by-the-Sea
Saltburn-by-the-Sea
Redcar
Brotton
Loftus
Skelton
Staithes
Easington
Hinderwell
Dormanstown
Eston
Ormesby
Nunthorpe
Thornaby-on-Tees
Ingleby Barwick
Eaglescliffe
Longnewton
Dinsdale
Middleton St. George
Sadberge
Gt. Burdon
Billingham
Stillington
Thewles
Gt. Stainton
Bishopton
Redmarshall
-on-Tees
Blackwell
Croft-on-Tees
Hurworth-on-Tees
Neasham
TEESSIDE INTERNATIONAL AIRPORT
Kirklevington
Scotch Corner
Middleton Tyas
Moulton
Barton
Croft
N. Cowton
E. Cowton
Gt. Smeaton
Appleton Wiske
Rounton
Hutton Rudby
Crathorne
Scorton
Bolton-on-Swale
Catterick
Kirkby Fleetham
Gt. Langton
Yafforth
Brompton
Ellerbeck
Osmotherley
Scruton
Morton-on-Swale
Leeming Bar
Patrick Brompton
N. Otterington
Newby Wiske
S. Otterington
Burneston
Carthorpe
Pickhill
Ainderby Quernhow
S. Kilvington
Felixkirk
Kirklington
Well
W. Tanfield
Wath
Skipton-on-Swale
Topcliffe
Melmerby
North Stainley
Kirkby Malzeard
Dishforth
Winksley
Studley Royal Gardens
Fountains Abbey
Risplith
Bishop Monkton
Newby Hall
Markington
Burton Leonard
Bishop Thornton
S. Stainley
Ripley
Killinghall
Scotton
Arkendale
Marton
Ouseburn
Lit. Ouseburn
Allerton Park
Green Hammerton
Lower Dunsforth
Brafferton
Helperby
Raskelf
Alne
Tollerton
Linton-on-Ouse
Shipton
Huby
Stillington
Sutton-on-the-Forest
Strensall
Haxby
Flaxton
Huntington
Skelton
Upper Poppleton
Moor Monkton
Walshford
N. Deighton
Spofforth
Kirkby Overblow
N. Rigton
Leathley
Pool-in-Wharfedale
Harewood
Collingham
Walton
Boston Spa
Bilbrough
Wighill
Tockwith
Long Marston
Rufforth
Copmanthorpe
Acaster Malbis
Naburn
Bishopthorpe
Appleton Roebuck
Escrick
Elvington
Wheldrake
Dunnington
Stamford Bridge
Stockton on the Forest
Thorganby
Stillingfleet
Ulleskelf
Bardsey
E. Keswick
Harewood House
Bramhope
LEEDS AND BRADFORD AIRPORT
Beckwithshaw
Cleveland Hills
Cleveland Way
Hambleton Hills
Hawnby
Boltby
Old Byland
Rievaulx Abbey
Scawton
Sutton Bank
Sutton-under-Whitestonecliffe
Kilburn
Byland Abbey
Balk
Coxwold
Husthwaite
Ampleforth
Oswaldkirk
Gilling E.
Dalton
Sessay
Brandsby
Hovingham
Slingsby
Nunnington
Wombleton
Beadlam
Kirkbymoorside
Gillamoor
Hutton-le-Hole
Lastingham
Appleton le-Moors
Sinnington
Wrelton
Cropton
Middleton
Newton-on-Rawcliffe
Hartoft End
Cropton Forest
Rosedale Abbey
Spaunton Moor
Helmsley Moor
Bransdale
Cockayne
Seave Green
Carlton
Swainby
Gt. Broughton
Ingleby Greenhow
Kildale
Gt. Ayton
Scamer
Danby
Castleton
Westerdale
Westerdale Moor
Glaisdale
Glaisdale Moor
Lealholm
Egton
Egton High Moor
Goathland
Wheeldale Moor
North York Moors National Park
Scaling Reservoir
Ugthorpe
Liverton
Stanghow
Boosbeck
Salton
Normanby
Flamingo Park
Thornton-le-Dale
Kirby Misperton
Gt. Barugh
Amotherby
Howardian Hills
Castle Howard
The Yorkshire Arboretum
Welburn
Whitwell-on-the-Hill
Westow
Langton
Sheriff Hutton
Barton-le-Willows
Leavening
Claxton
Thixendale
Buttercrambe
Bugthorpe
Bishop Wilton
Fangfoss
Wilberfoss
Barmby Moor
Pocklington
Nunburnholme
Hayton
Melbourne
Everingham
Seaton Ross
Ellerton
R. Tees
R. Swale
R. Ure
R. Ouse
R. Nidd
R. Wharfe
R. Derwent
Dove
Rye
Hodge Beck
Seven
0 2.5 5 7.5 10 miles

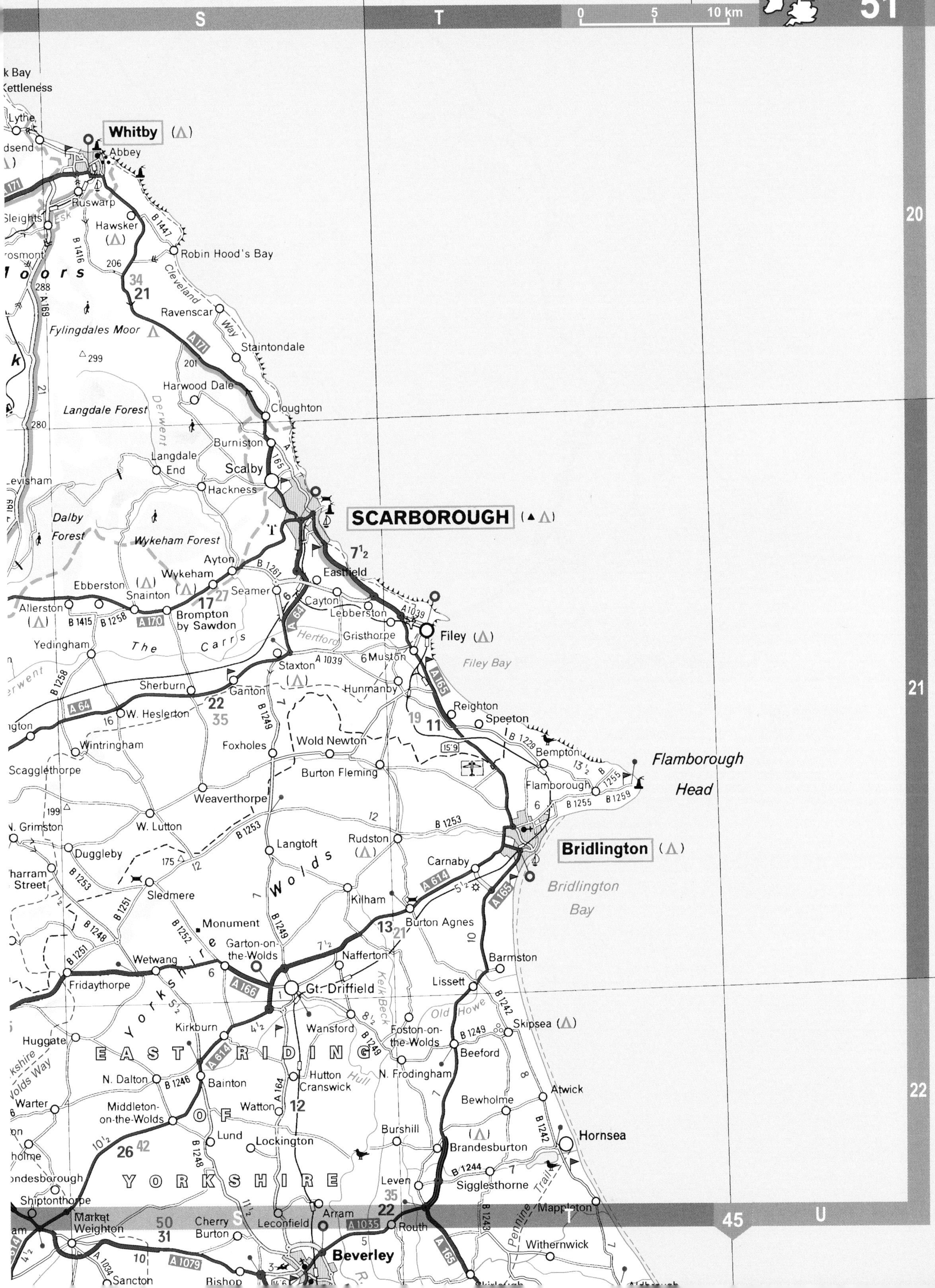
S
T
U
0 5 10 km
20
21
22
45
50
31
Whitby
Abbey
Lythe
Ruswarp
Sleights
Hawsker
Robin Hood's Bay
B 1447
B 1416
A 171
A 169
Fylingdales Moor
Ravenscar
Cleveland Way
Staintondale
Harwood Dale
Cloughton
Langdale Forest
Derwent
Burniston
Langdale End
Scalby
Hackness
Levisham
Dalby Forest
Wykeham Forest
SCARBOROUGH
Ayton
Wykeham
Ebberston
Snainton
Seamer
Eastfield
Cayton
Lebberston
A 1039
Filey
Filey Bay
Allerston
B 1415
B 1258
A 170
Brompton by Sawdon
The Carrs
A 64
Hertford
Gristhorpe
Muston
Staxton
Yedingham
Sherburn
Ganton
Hunmanby
A 165
Reighton
Speeton
B 1229
Bempton
Flamborough Head
Flamborough
B 1255
B 1259
W. Heslerton
Wintringham
Scagglethorpe
Foxholes
B 1249
Wold Newton
Burton Fleming
Weaverthorpe
W. Lutton
N. Grimston
B 1253
Langtoft
Rudston
Wolds
Bridlington
Bridlington Bay
Carnaby
A 614
Duggleby
Sledmere
B 1251
B 1252
B 1248
Kilham
Burton Agnes
Monument
Garton-on-the-Wolds
Nafferton
Barmston
Wetwang
Fridaythorpe
A 166
Gt. Driffield
Lissett
Kelk Beck
Old Howe
B 1242
Skipsea
Kirkburn
Wansford
Foston-on-the-Wolds
Beeford
Huggate
EAST RIDING OF YORKSHIRE
Hutton Cranswick
Hull
N. Frodingham
N. Dalton
B 1246
Bainton
Watton
A 164
Atwick
Bewholme
Warter
Middleton-on-the-Wolds
Lund
Lockington
Burshill
Brandesburton
Hornsea
B 1244
Sigglesthorpe
Pennine Trail
Mappleton
Leven
Arram
Market Weighton
Cherry Burton
Leconfield
A 1035
Routh
Beverley
B 1243
Withernwick
A 1034
A 1079
Sancton
Bishop
Shiptonthorpe
Yorkshire Wolds Way

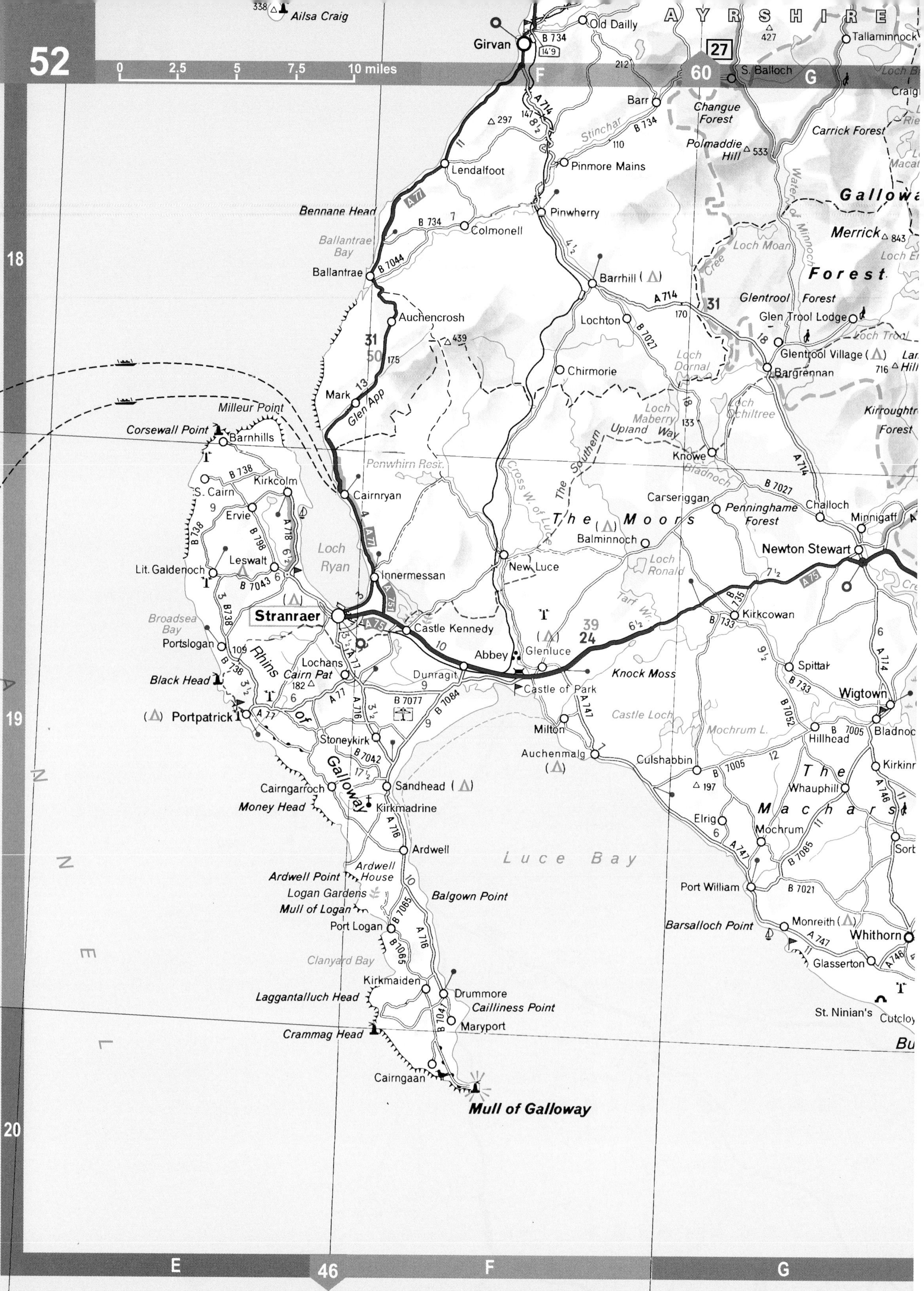
0 2.5 5 7.5 10 miles
AYRSHIRE
27
60
46
E
F
G
18
19
20
Ailsa Craig
338
Girvan
Old Dailly
B 734
14'9
Tallaminnock
427
212
S. Balloch
Barr
Changue Forest
Stinchar
B 734
110
A 714
147
8½
△ 297
Polmaddie Hill △ 533
Carrick Forest
Craigi
Lendalfoot
Pinmore Mains
A 77
Galloway
Bennane Head
Pinwherry
B 734
7
Colmonell
Merrick △ 843
Loch Moan
Water of Minnoch
Ballantrae Bay
Ballantrae
B 7044
Barrhill (△)
Forest
A 714
Cree
Glentrool
Forest
31
170
Glen Trool Lodge
Auchencrosh
Lochton
B 7027
Loch Trool
△ 439
18
Glentrool Village (△)
31
50
175
Loch Dornal
Chirmorie
Bargrennan
716 △ Hill
Mark
13
Glen App
Milleur Point
Loch Maberry
133
Loch Chiltree
Kirroughtree Forest
Corsewall Point
Barnhills
Upland Way
The Southern
Knowe
A 714
B 738
Penwhirn Resr.
Cross W. of Luce
Bladnoch
B 7027
S. Cairn
Kirkcolm
Cairnryan
Carseriggan
Penninghame Forest
Challoch
Minnigaff
9
Ervie
A 718
B 798
4
A 77
The Moors
B 738
Balminnoch
Loch Ryan
6½
Newton Stewart
Leswalt
New Luce
Loch Ronald
7½
A 75
Lit. Galdenoch
B 7043
6
Innermessan
Tarf Wa.
B 735
(△)
3
A 751
Broadsea Bay
B 738
Stranraer
Castle Kennedy
39
24
6½
Kirkcowan
B 733
6
Portslogan
109
Rhins
A 75
10
Abbey
Glenluce
9½
A 714
Lochans
A 77
Cairn Pat
182 △
Dunragit
9
Knock Moss
Spittal
Black Head
3½
6
A 77
B 7077
B 733
Castle of Park
A 747
Wigtown
(△) Portpatrick
A 77
of
A 716
3½
B 1084
9
Castle Loch
B 7052
Bladnoch
Milton
Mochrum L.
B 7005
Hillhead
Stoneykirk
B 7042
Auchenmalg (△)
7
Culshabbin
B 7005
12
Kirkinner
17½
The
Galloway
Cairngarroch
Sandhead (△)
△ 197
Whauphill
A 746
Money Head
Kirkmadrine
Machars
A 716
Elrig
6
Mochrum
11
Ardwell
A 747
B 7085
Sorbie
Luce Bay
Ardwell House
Ardwell Point
10
Port William
B 7021
Logan Gardens
Balgown Point
Mull of Logan
B 7065
Port Logan
A 716
Barsalloch Point
Monreith (△)
A 747
Whithorn
B 7065
Clanyard Bay
Glasserton
A 746
Kirkmaiden
Drummore
Laggantalluch Head
Cailliness Point
B 7041
Maryport
St. Ninian's
Cutcloy
Crammag Head
Bu
Cairngaan
Mull of Galloway
N
N
E
L

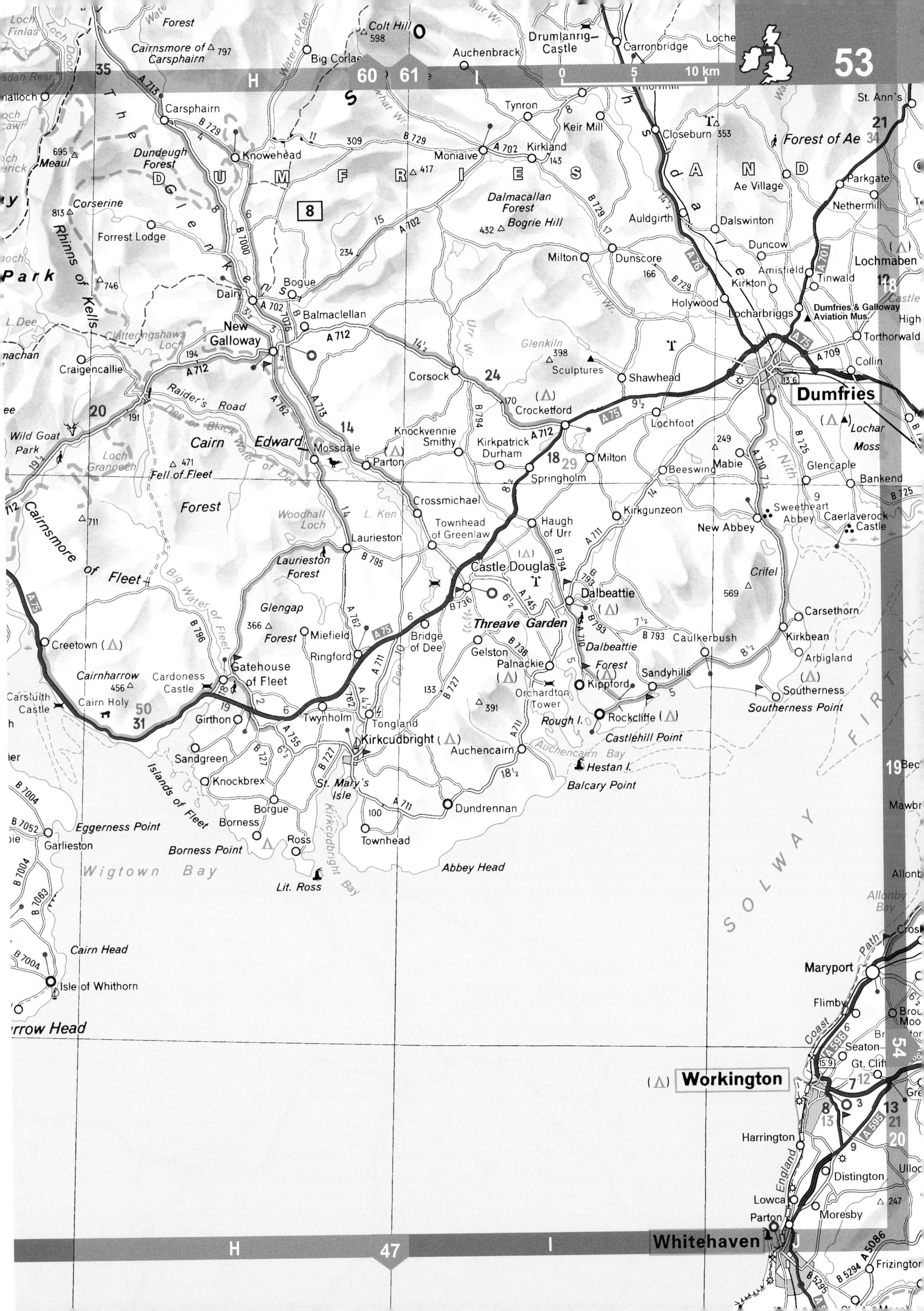
0 5 10 km
H
I
J
60
61
47
54
Dumfries
Workington
Whitehaven
Maryport
Castle Douglas
Kirkcudbright
New Galloway
Gatehouse of Fleet
Dalbeattie
Threave Garden
Carsphairn
Knowehead
Dundeugh Forest
Moniaive
Tynron
Keir Mill
Kirkland
Closeburn
Forest of Ae
Ae Village
Parkgate
Nethermill
Dalswinton
Auldgirth
Duncow
Amisfield
Tinwald
Lochmaben
Kirkton
Holywood
Locharbriggs
Dumfries & Galloway Aviation Mus.
Torthorwald
Collin
Lochar Moss
Glencaple
Bankend
Caerlaverock Castle
Sweetheart Abbey
New Abbey
Mabie
Beeswing
Lochfoot
Shawhead
Glenkiln Sculptures
Crocketford
Corsock
Kirkpatrick Durham
Springholm
Milton
Kirkgunzeon
Haugh of Urr
Crifel
Carsethorn
Kirkbean
Arbigland
Southerness
Southerness Point
Caulkerbush
Sandyhills
Kippford
Rockcliffe
Castlehill Point
Hestan I.
Balcary Point
Rough I.
Auchencairn
Auchencairn Bay
Orchardton Tower
Palnackie
Gelston
Dundrennan
Abbey Head
Townhead
Borgue
Ross
Lit. Ross
Kirkcudbright Bay
St. Mary's Isle
Tongland
Twynholm
Ringford
Bridge of Dee
Miefield
Laurieston
Laurieston Forest
Crossmichael
Townhead of Greenlaw
Parton
Mossdale
Knockvennie Smithy
Balmaclellan
Bogue
Dalry
Forrest Lodge
Corserine
Rhinns of Kells
The Glenkens
Clatteringshaws Loch
Craigencallie
Raider's Road
Cairn Edward Forest
Fell of Fleet
Woodhall Loch
L. Ken
Cairnsmore of Fleet
Glengap Forest
Creetown
Cairnharrow
Cardoness Castle
Carsluith Castle
Cairn Holy
Girthon
Sandgreen
Knockbrex
Islands of Fleet
Borness
Borness Point
Wigtown Bay
Eggerness Point
Garlieston
Cairn Head
Isle of Whithorn
Burrow Head
Wild Goat Park
Big Corlae
Colt Hill
Auchenbrack
Drumlanrig Castle
Carronbridge
Cairnsmore of Carsphairn
Dalmacallan Forest
Bogrie Hill
Dunscore
Solway Firth
Allonby Bay
Flimby
Seaton
Gt. Clifton
Harrington
Distington
Lowca
Parton
Moresby
Frizington
England Coast Path
St. Ann's
Dumfries and Galloway
Nithsdale

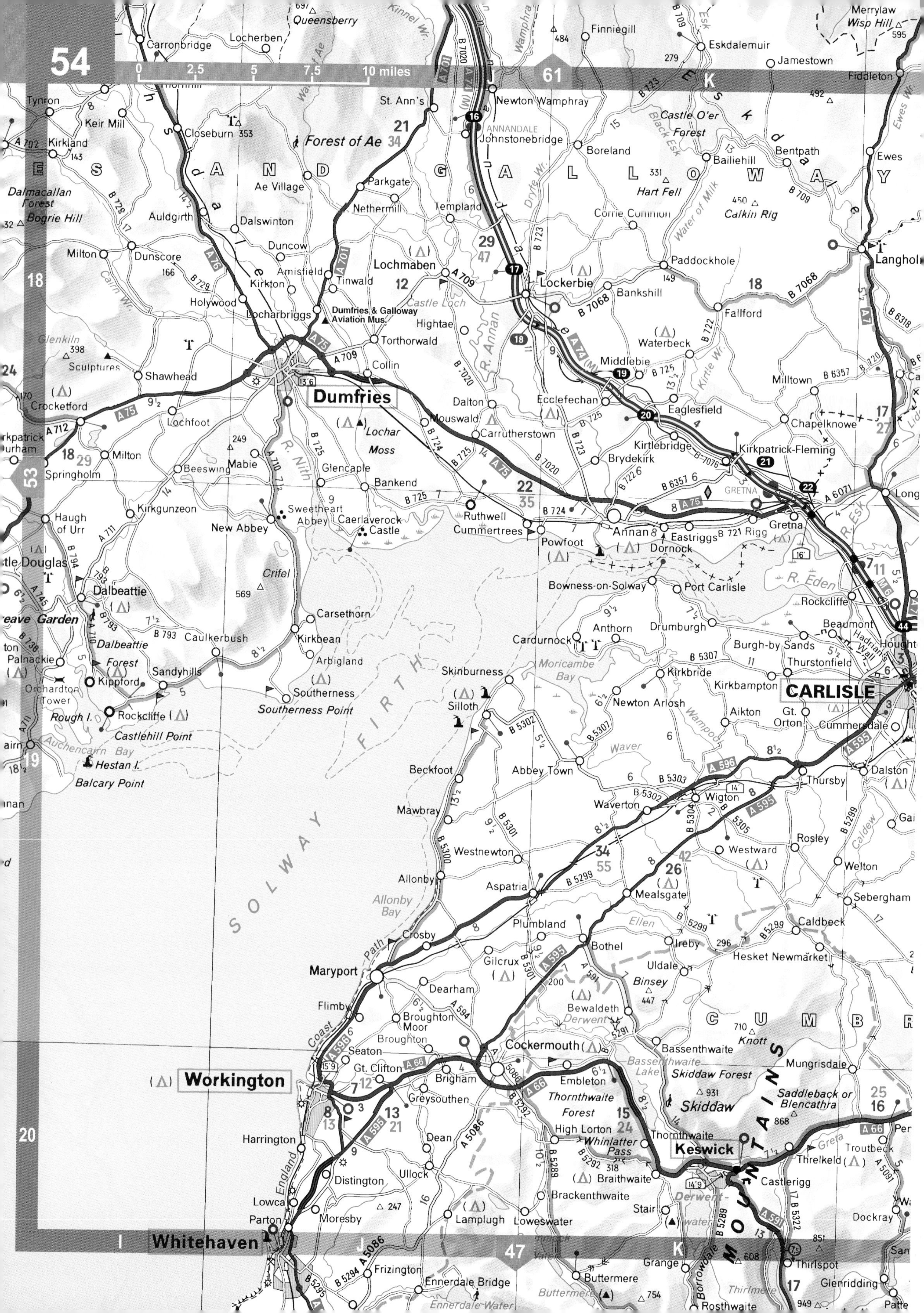
0 2.5 5 7.5 10 miles
61
Queensberry
Carronbridge
Locherben
Finniegill
Eskdalemuir
Merrylaw
Wisp Hill
Jamestown
Fiddleton
Tynron
Keir Mill
Kirkland
Closeburn
Forest of Ae
St. Ann's
Newton Wamphray
Johnstonebridge
ANNANDALE
Castle O'er Forest
Boreland
Bailiehill
Bentpath
Ewes
Dalmacallan Forest
Bogrie Hill
NITHSDALE
Ae Village
Parkgate
Nethermill
Templand
ANNANDALE
Hart Fell
ESKDALE
Calkin Rig
GALLOWAY
Auldgirth
Dalswinton
Corrie Common
Milton
Dunscore
Duncow
Amisfield
Kirkton
Lochmaben
Tinwald
Lockerbie
Paddockhole
Langholm
Holywood
Locharbriggs
Dumfries & Galloway Aviation Mus.
Castle Loch
Hightae
Bankshill
Fallford
Glenkiln
Sculptures
Torthorwald
Collin
R. Annan
Waterbeck
Middlebie
Shawhead
Dumfries
Dalton
Ecclefechan
Milltown
Crocketford
Lochfoot
Mouswald
Eaglesfield
Chapelknowe
Kirkpatrick Durham
Milton
Lochar Moss
Carrutherstown
Kirtlebridge
Kirkpatrick-Fleming
Springholm
Beeswing
Mabie
R. Nith
Glencaple
Bankend
Brydekirk
GRETNA
Longtown
Haugh of Urr
Kirkgunzeon
Sweetheart Abbey
New Abbey
Caerlaverock Castle
Ruthwell
Cummertrees
Powfoot
Annan
Eastriggs
Dornock
Rigg
Gretna
R. Esk
Castle Douglas
Criffel
Dalbeattie
Bowness-on-Solway
Port Carlisle
R. Eden
Rockcliffe
Threave Garden
Carsethorn
Anthorn
Drumburgh
Beaumont
Hadrian's Wall
Caulkerbush
Kirkbean
Cardurnock
Burgh-by-Sands
Houghton
Palnackie
Dalbeattie Forest
Arbigland
Moricambe Bay
Thurstonfield
Kippford
Sandyhills
Skinburness
Kirkbride
Orchardton Tower
Southerness
Kirkbampton
CARLISLE
Rough I.
Rockcliffe
Southerness Point
Silloth
Newton Arlosh
Aikton
Gt. Orton
Cummersdale
Castlehill Point
Auchencairn Bay
Hestan I.
Balcary Point
Waver
Wampool
SOLWAY FIRTH
Beckfoot
Abbey Town
Thursby
Dalston
Wigton
Waverton
Mawbray
Rosley
Westnewton
Westward
Welton
Allonby
Aspatria
Mealsgate
Sebergham
Allonby Bay
Plumbland
Ellen
Caldbeck
Crosby
Bothel
Ireby
Hesket Newmarket
Maryport
Gilcrux
Uldale
Dearham
Binsey
Flimby
Broughton Moor
Bewaldeth
Derwent
CUMBRIA
Knott
Coast Path
Broughton
Seaton
Cockermouth
Bassenthwaite
Bassenthwaite Lake
Mungrisdale
Workington
Gt. Clifton
Brigham
Embleton
Skiddaw Forest
Greysouthen
Thornthwaite Forest
Skiddaw
Saddleback or Blencathra
High Lorton
Whinlatter Pass
Harrington
Dean
Thornthwaite
Keswick
Troutbeck
Threlkeld
Distington
Ullock
Braithwaite
Castlerigg
Greta
Brackenthwaite
England's Coast
Lowca
Moresby
Lamplugh
Loweswater
Stair
Derwentwater
Dockray
Parton
Whitehaven
Frizington
Ennerdale Bridge
Buttermere
Grange
Borrowdale
Thirlspot
MOUNTAINS
Glenridding
Ennerdale Water
Thirlmere
Rosthwaite
Patterdale
47

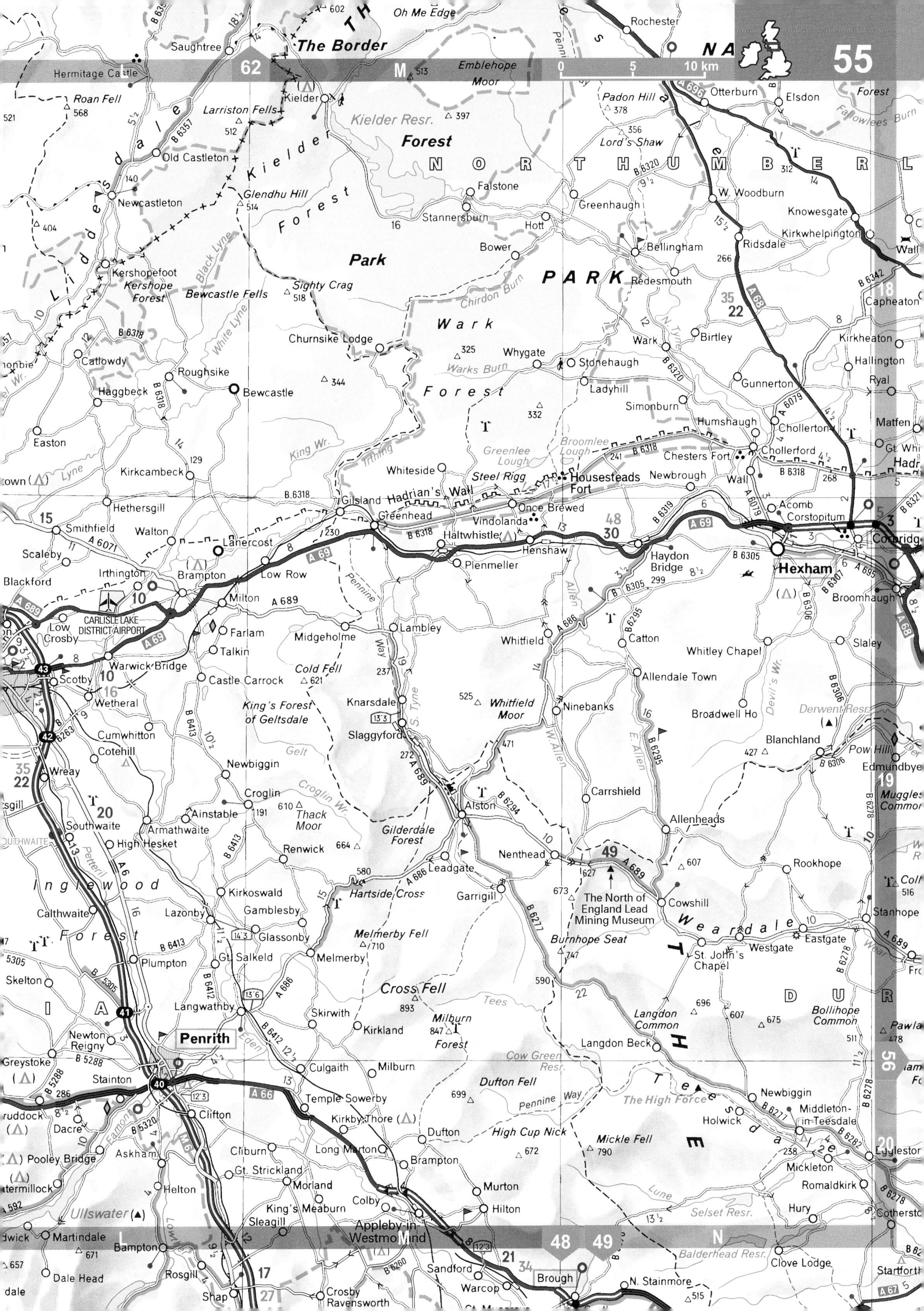
The Border
Oh Me Edge
Rochester
Saughtree
Hermitage Castle
Emblehope Moor
Kielder
Roan Fell
568
Larriston Fells
Kielder Resr.
Padon Hill
378
Otterburn
Elsdon
Forest
Fallowlees Burn
Lord's Shaw
Liddesdale
Old Castleton
Kielder Forest Park
N O R T H U M B E R L
Falstone
Greenhaugh
W. Woodburn
Newcastleton
Glendhu Hill
514
Stannersburn
Hott
Knowesgate
Kirkwhelpington
Ridsdale
Bower
Bellingham
Kershopefoot
Kershope Forest
Bewcastle Fells
Sighty Crag
518
PARK
Redesmouth
Chirdon Burn
Capheaton
Wark Forest
Churnsike Lodge
Wark
Birtley
Kirkheaton
Catlowdy
Whygate
Stonehaugh
Hallington
Roughsike
Warks Burn
Gunnerton
Ryal
Haggbeck
Bewcastle
Ladyhill
Simonburn
Humshaugh
Chollerton
Matfen
Easton
King Wr.
Greenlee Lough
Broomlee Lough
Chesters Fort
Chollerford
Kirkcambeck
Whiteside
Steel Rigg
Housesteads Fort
Newbrough
Wall
Hetherseill
Gilsland
Hadrian's Wall
Once Brewed
Acomb
Corstopitum
Smithfield
Walton
Greenhead
Vindolanda
Haltwhistle
Henshaw
Corbridge
Scaleby
Lanercost
Haydon Bridge
Hexham
Irthington
Brampton
Low Row
Plenmeller
Blackford
Milton
Broomhaugh
Low Crosby
CARLISLE LAKE DISTRICT AIRPORT
Farlam
Midgeholme
Lambley
Whitfield
Catton
Talkin
Whitley Chapel
Slaley
Warwick Bridge
Cold Fell
621
Scotby
Castle Carrock
Allendale Town
Wetheral
King's Forest of Geltsdale
Knarsdale
Whitfield Moor
Ninebanks
Broadwell Ho
Derwent Resr.
Cumwhitton
Slaggyford
Blanchland
Cotehill
Gelt
Pow Hill
Edmundbyers
Wreay
Newbiggin
Croglin
Carrshield
Muggleswick Common
Ainstable
Thack Moor
Alston
Allenheads
Southwaite
Armathwaite
Gilderdale Forest
High Hesket
Renwick
Nenthead
Rookhope
Leadgate
Inglewood Forest
Kirkoswald
Hartside Cross
Garrigill
The North of England Lead Mining Museum
Cowshill
Calthwaite
Lazonby
Gamblesby
Weardale
Glassonby
Melmerby Fell
Burnhope Seat
Westgate
Eastgate
Stanhope
Plumpton
Gt. Salkeld
Melmerby
St. John's Chapel
Skelton
Cross Fell
893
Langwathby
Skirwith
Langdon Common
Bollihope Common
Newton Reigny
Penrith
Kirkland
Milburn Forest
Langdon Beck
Greystoke
Stainton
Culgaith
Milburn
Cow Green Resr.
Dufton Fell
Temple Sowerby
The High Force
Newbiggin
Middleton-in-Teesdale
Clifton
Kirkby Thore
Holwick
Dacre
Dufton
High Cup Nick
Mickle Fell
790
Pooley Bridge
Askham
Cliburn
Long Marton
Brampton
Eggleston
Mickleton
Gt. Strickland
Morland
Murton
Romaldkirk
Helton
Colby
King's Meaburn
Hilton
Hury
Ullswater
Sleagill
Appleby-in-Westmorland
Selset Resr.
Cotherstone
Martindale
Bampton
Balderhead Resr.
Clove Lodge
Dale Head
Rosgill
Sandford
Brough
Startforth
Shap
Warcop
N. Stainmore
Crosby Ravensworth
Tees
Lune
Pennine Way
A 69
A 68
A 686
A 689
A 66
A 6
M 6
0 5 10 km

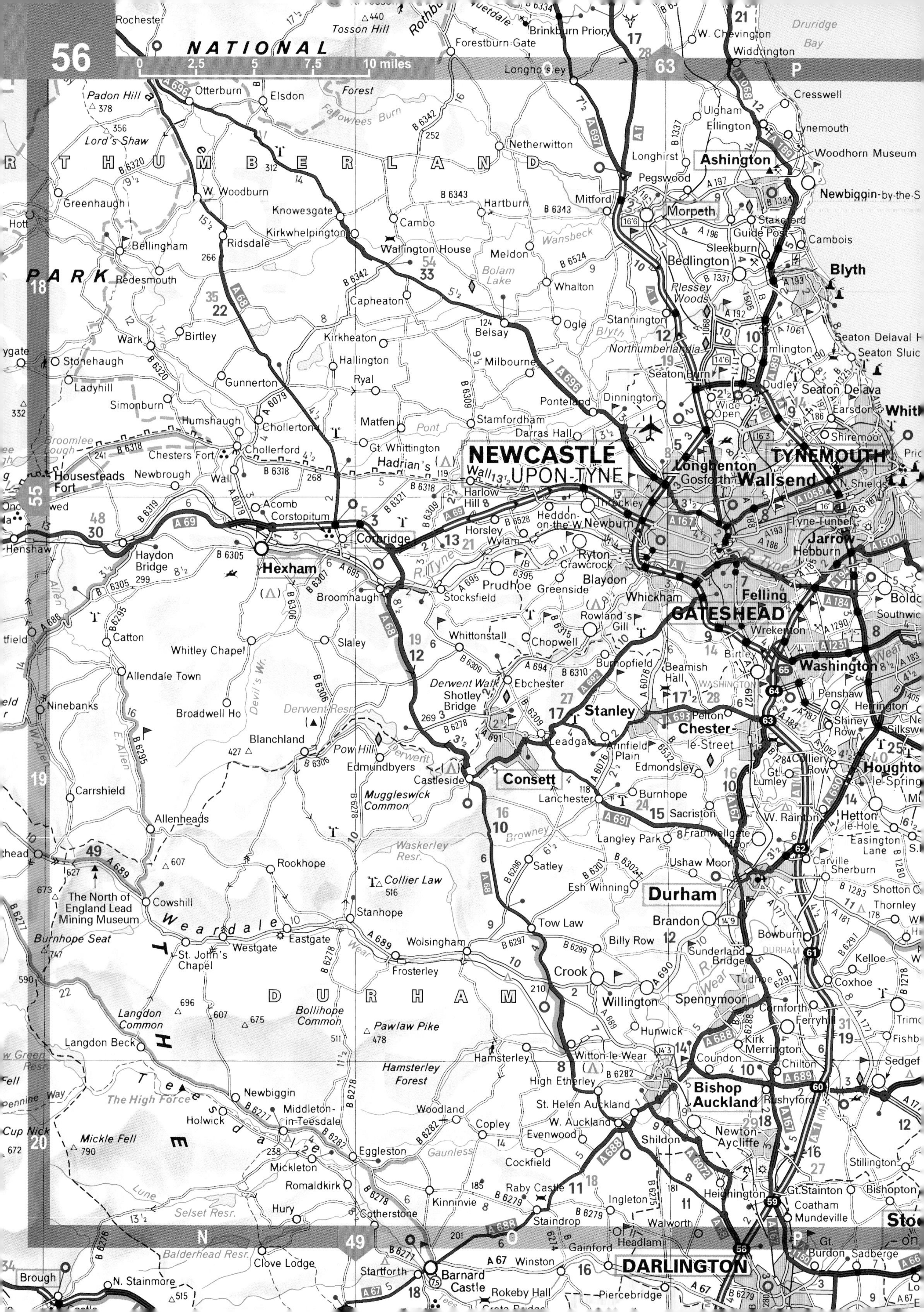
NATIONAL
0 2.5 5 7.5 10 miles
NORTHUMBERLAND
PARK
Rochester
Tosson Hill
Brinkburn Priory
Forestburn Gate
W. Chevington
Widdrington
Druridge Bay
Longhorsley
Padon Hill
Otterburn
Elsdon
Forest
Fallowlees Burn
Lord's Shaw
Cresswell
Ulgham
Ellington
Lynemouth
Netherwitton
Longhirst
Ashington
Woodhorn Museum
Pegswood
Newbiggin-by-the-Sea
Greenhaugh
W. Woodburn
Knowesgate
Hartburn
Mitford
Morpeth
Stakeford
Guide Post
Cambois
Cambo
Kirkwhelpington
Wallington House
Meldon
Wansbeck
Sleekburn
Bellingham
Ridsdale
Bolam Lake
Bedlington
Blyth
Redesmouth
Capheaton
Whalton
Plessey Woods
Ogle
Stannington
Belsay
Seaton Delaval Hall
Wark
Birtley
Kirkheaton
Blyth
Cramlington
Seaton Sluice
Stonehaugh
Hallington
Milbourne
Northumberlandia
Seaton Burn
Dudley
Seaton Delaval
Ladyhill
Gunnerton
Ryal
Ponteland
Dinnington
Wide Open
Earsdon
Simonburn
Humshaugh
Chollerton
Matfen
Stamfordham
Darras Hall
Shiremoor
Broomlee Lough
Chollerford
Chesters Fort
Gt. Whittington
Pont
Hadrian's Wall
NEWCASTLE UPON TYNE
Longbenton
TYNEMOUTH
Housesteads Fort
Newbrough
Wall
Harlow Hill
Gosforth
Wallsend
N. Shields
Acomb
Corstopitum
Throckley
Heddon-on-the-Wall
Newburn
Tyne Tunnel
Haydon Bridge
Hexham
Corbridge
Horsley
Wylam
Ryton
Crawcrook
Jarrow
Hebburn
Prudhoe
Blaydon
Greenside
Broomhaugh
Stocksfield
Whickham
Felling
GATESHEAD
Boldon
Allen
Catton
Rowland's Gill
Whittonstall
Chopwell
Wrekenton
Slaley
Whitley Chapel
Birtley
Washington
Allendale Town
Derwent Walk
Ebchester
Burnopfield
Beamish Hall
Penshaw
Ninebanks
Shotley Bridge
Stanley
Pelton
Herrington
Broadwell Ho
Derwent Resr.
Chester-le-Street
Shiney Row
Blanchland
Leadgate
Annfield Plain
Colliery Row
Houghton-le-Spring
Pow Hill
Edmundbyers
Edmondsley
Castleside
Consett
Gt. Lumley
Carrshield
Muggleswick Common
Lanchester
Burnhope
Sacriston
W. Rainton
Hetton-le-Hole
Allenheads
Waskerley Resr.
Langley Park
Framwellgate Moor
Easington Lane
Browney
Rookhope
Satley
Ushaw Moor
Carville
Sherburn
The North of England Lead Mining Museum
Collier Law
Esh Winning
Durham
Shotton
Cowshill
Stanhope
Brandon
Thornley
Weardale
Eastgate
Tow Law
Burnhope Seat
Westgate
St. John's Chapel
Wolsingham
Billy Row
Bowburn
Sunderland Bridge
Kelloe
Frosterley
Crook
Tudhoe
Coxhoe
DURHAM
Willington
Spennymoor
Cornforth
Ferryhill
Langdon Common
Bollihope Common
Pawlaw Pike
Hunwick
Kirk Merrington
Langdon Beck
Witton-le-Wear
Coundon
Chilton
Sedgefield
Hamsterley
Hamsterley Forest
High Etherley
Bishop Auckland
Rushyford
The High Force
Newbiggin
St. Helen Auckland
Holwick
Middleton-in-Teesdale
Woodland
W. Auckland
Newton Aycliffe
Cup Nick
Mickle Fell
Copley
Evenwood
Shildon
Eggleston
Gaunless
Stillington
Mickleton
Cockfield
Romaldkirk
Raby Castle
Ingleton
Heighington
Gt. Stainton
Bishopton
Lune
Hury
Kinninvie
Coatham Mundeville
Selset Resr.
Cotherstone
Staindrop
Walworth
Headlam
Gainford
Gt. Burdon
Sadberge
Balderhead Resr.
Clove Lodge
Startforth
Barnard Castle
Winston
DARLINGTON
Brough
N. Stainmore
Rokeby Hall
Piercebridge
Pennine Way
Teesdale

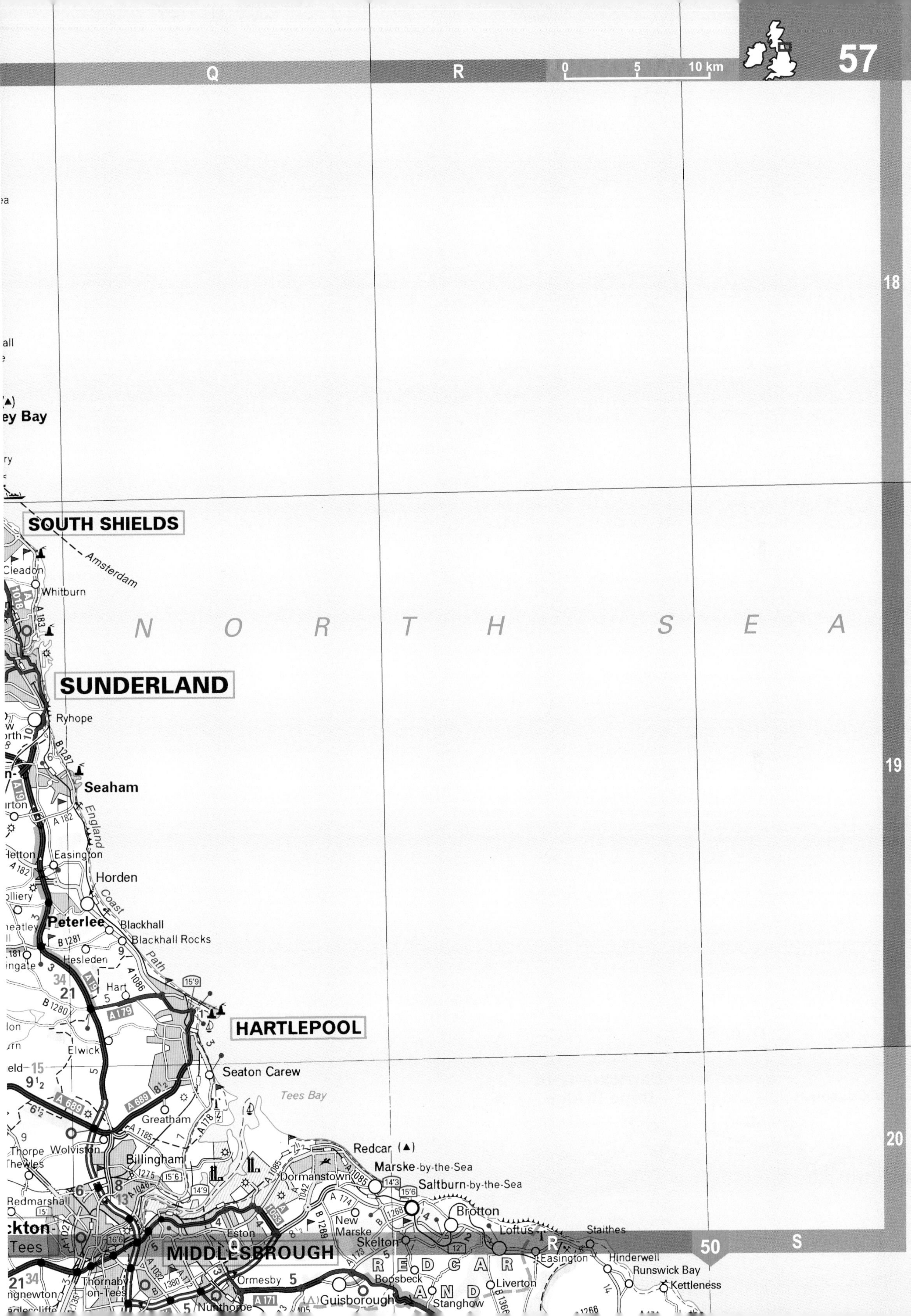
Q
R
S
0 5 10 km
18
19
20
50
N O R T H S E A
SOUTH SHIELDS
Amsterdam
Cleadon
Whitburn
SUNDERLAND
Ryhope
Seaham
England Coast Path
Easington
Horden
Peterlee
Blackhall
Blackhall Rocks
Hesleden
Hart
HARTLEPOOL
Elwick
Seaton Carew
Tees Bay
Greatham
Wolviston
Billingham
Thorpe Thewles
Redmarshall
Redcar
Marske-by-the-Sea
Saltburn-by-the-Sea
Dormanstown
New Marske
Brotton
Loftus
Staithes
Skelton
Eston
MIDDLESBROUGH
Easington
Hinderwell
Runswick Bay
Kettleness
Boosbeck
Liverton
Ormesby
Guisborough
Stanghow
Thornaby-on-Tees
Nunthorpe
REDCAR AND
Hetton
Cleveland
ey Bay

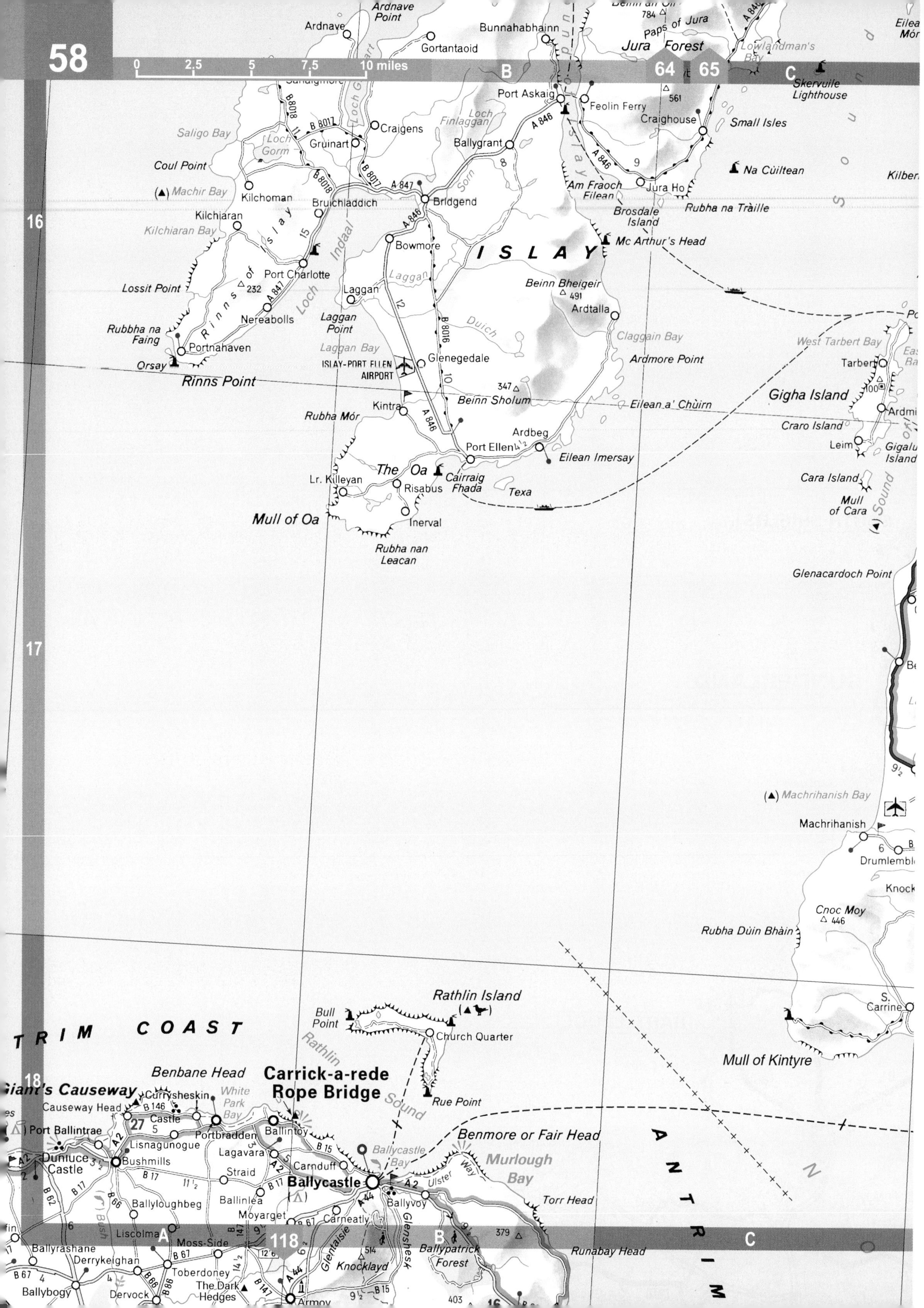
0 2.5 5 7.5 10 miles
B
C
64
65
A
118
16
17
18
Ardnave Point
Ardnave
Gortantaoid
Bunnahabhainn
Paps of Jura
784
Jura Forest
Lowlandman's Bay
Skervuile Lighthouse
Port Askaig
Feolin Ferry
561
Craighouse
Small Isles
Loch Finlaggan
Saligo Bay
Loch Gorm
B 8017
Craigens
Gruinart
Ballygrant
A 846
Coul Point
B 8018
B 8017
A 847
Machir Bay
Kilchoman
Bruichladdich
Bridgend
Na Cùiltean
Am Fraoch Eilean
Jura Ho
Rubha na Tràille
Brosdale Island
Kilchiaran
Kilchiaran Bay
Rinns of Islay
Loch Indaal
Bowmore
ISLAY
Mc Arthur's Head
Port Charlotte
Lossit Point
232
Laggan
Beinn Bheigeir
491
Ardtalla
Nereabolls
Laggan Point
B 8016
Rubbha na Faing
Portnahaven
Claggain Bay
Laggan Bay
West Tarbert Bay
Ardmore Point
Tarbert
Orsay
ISLAY-PORT ELLEN AIRPORT
Glenegedale
Rinns Point
347
Gigha Island
Beinn Sholum
Kintra
Eilean a' Chùirn
Rubha Mór
Ardminish
Craro Island
Ardbeg
Port Ellen
Leim
Eilean Imersay
Gigalum Island
The Oa
Cairraig Fhada
Lr. Killeyan
Risabus
Texa
Cara Island
Mull of Cara
Mull of Oa
Inerval
Rubha nan Leacan
Glenacardoch Point
Machrihanish Bay
Machrihanish
Drumlemble
Knock
Cnoc Moy
446
Rubha Dùin Bhàin
Rathlin Island
Bull Point
Church Quarter
S. Carrine
ANTRIM COAST
Mull of Kintyre
Rathlin Sound
Benbane Head
Carrick-a-rede Rope Bridge
Rue Point
Giant's Causeway
Currysheskin
White Park Bay
Causeway Head
B 146
Castle
Port Ballintrae
Portbradden
Ballintoy
Benmore or Fair Head
Lisnagunogue
B 15
Ballycastle Bay
Murlough Bay
Dunluce Castle
Bushmills
Lagavara
Carnduff
Straid
B 17
Ballycastle
Ulster Way
Ballinlea
Ballyvoy
Torr Head
Ballyloughbeg
Moyarget
Carneatly
Glenshesk
Liscolma
Moss-Side
379
Ballyrashane
Glentaisie
514
Ballypatrick Forest
Runabay Head
Derrykeighan
B 67
Knocklayd
Toberdoney
The Dark Hedges
Ballybogy
Dervock
B 66
B 147
A 44
B 15
Armoy
403
ANTRIM

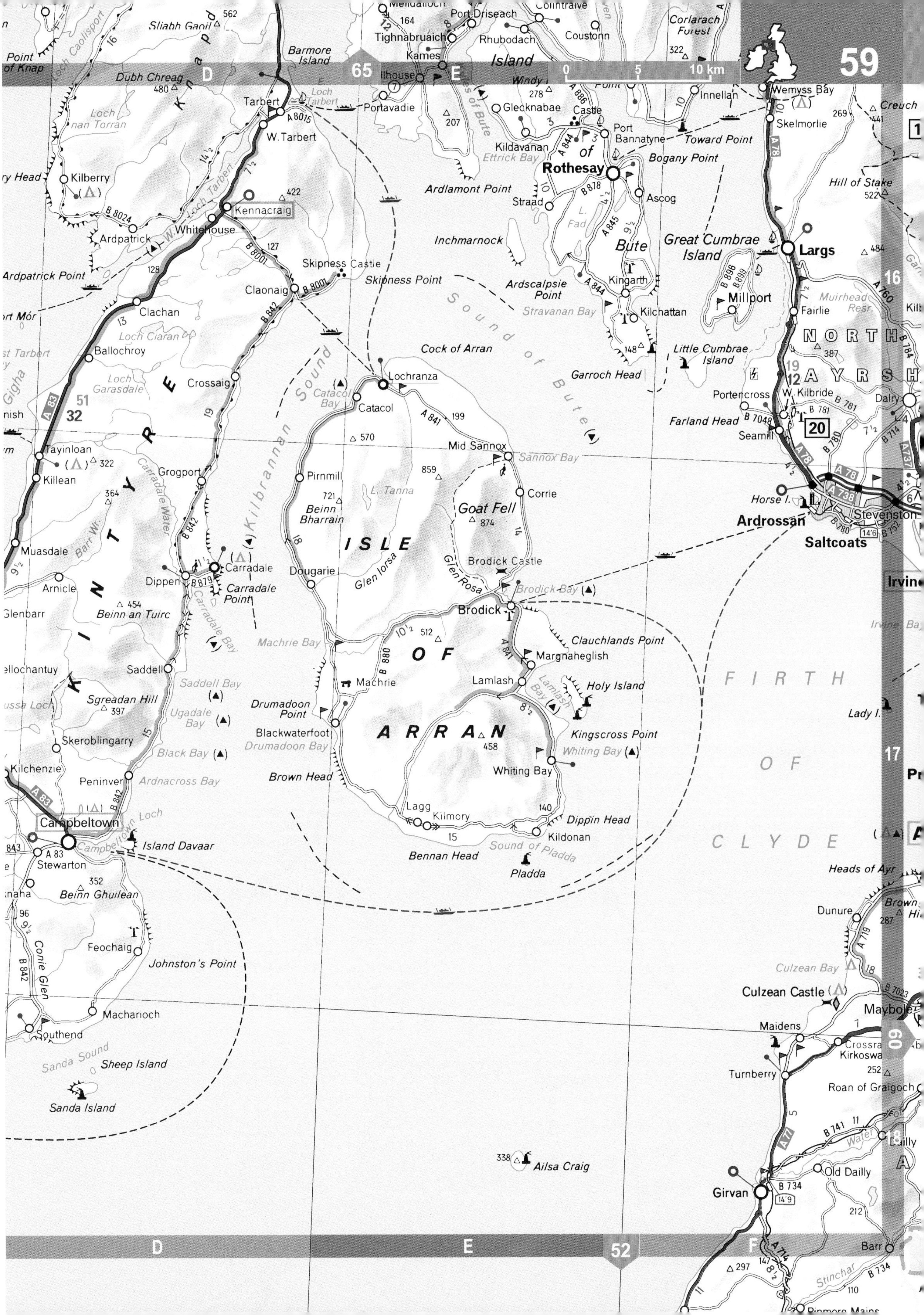

65
D
E
0 5 10 km
Tarbert
W. Tarbert
Kilberry
Kennacraig
Whitehouse
Ardpatrick
Ardpatrick Point
Claonaig
Skipness Castle
Skipness Point
Clachan
Ballochroy
Crossaig
Tayinloan
Killean
Grogport
Muasdale
Arnicle
Dippen
Carradale
Carradale Point
Glenbarr
Beinn an Tuirc
Saddell
Sgreadan Hill
Skeroblingarry
Kilchenzie
Peninver
Campbeltown
Stewarton
Beinn Ghuilean
Feochaig
Johnston's Point
Macharioch
Southend
Sheep Island
Sanda Island
Sanda Sound
KINTYRE
Kilbrannan Sound
Lochranza
Catacol
Pirnmill
Beinn Bharrain
Dougarie
Mid Sannox
Corrie
Goat Fell
Brodick Castle
Brodick
Lamlash
Margnaheglish
Holy Island
Clauchlands Point
Kingscross Point
Whiting Bay
Kildonan
Dippin Head
Lagg
Kilmory
Bennan Head
Pladda
Blackwaterfoot
Drumadoon Point
Machrie
Machrie Bay
Brown Head
ISLE OF ARRAN
Ailsa Craig
Sound of Bute
Cock of Arran
Inchmarnock
Ardlamont Point
Rothesay
Port Bannatyne
Ascog
Straad
Bute
Kingarth
Kilchattan
Ardscalpsie Point
Stravanan Bay
Garroch Head
Tighnabruaich
Kames
Portavadie
Rhubodach
Colintraive
Port Driseach
Coustonn
Innellan
Toward Point
Bogany Point
Wemyss Bay
Skelmorlie
Largs
Great Cumbrae Island
Millport
Little Cumbrae Island
Fairlie
Portencross
W. Kilbride
Farland Head
Seamill
Ardrossan
Saltcoats
Stevenston
Horse I.
Irvine
Dalry
NORTH AYRSHIRE
FIRTH OF CLYDE
Lady I.
Heads of Ayr
Dunure
Culzean Bay
Culzean Castle
Maybole
Maidens
Turnberry
Kirkoswald
Roan of Graigoch
Old Dailly
Dailly
Girvan
Barr
D
E
52
F
60
16
17
18
20

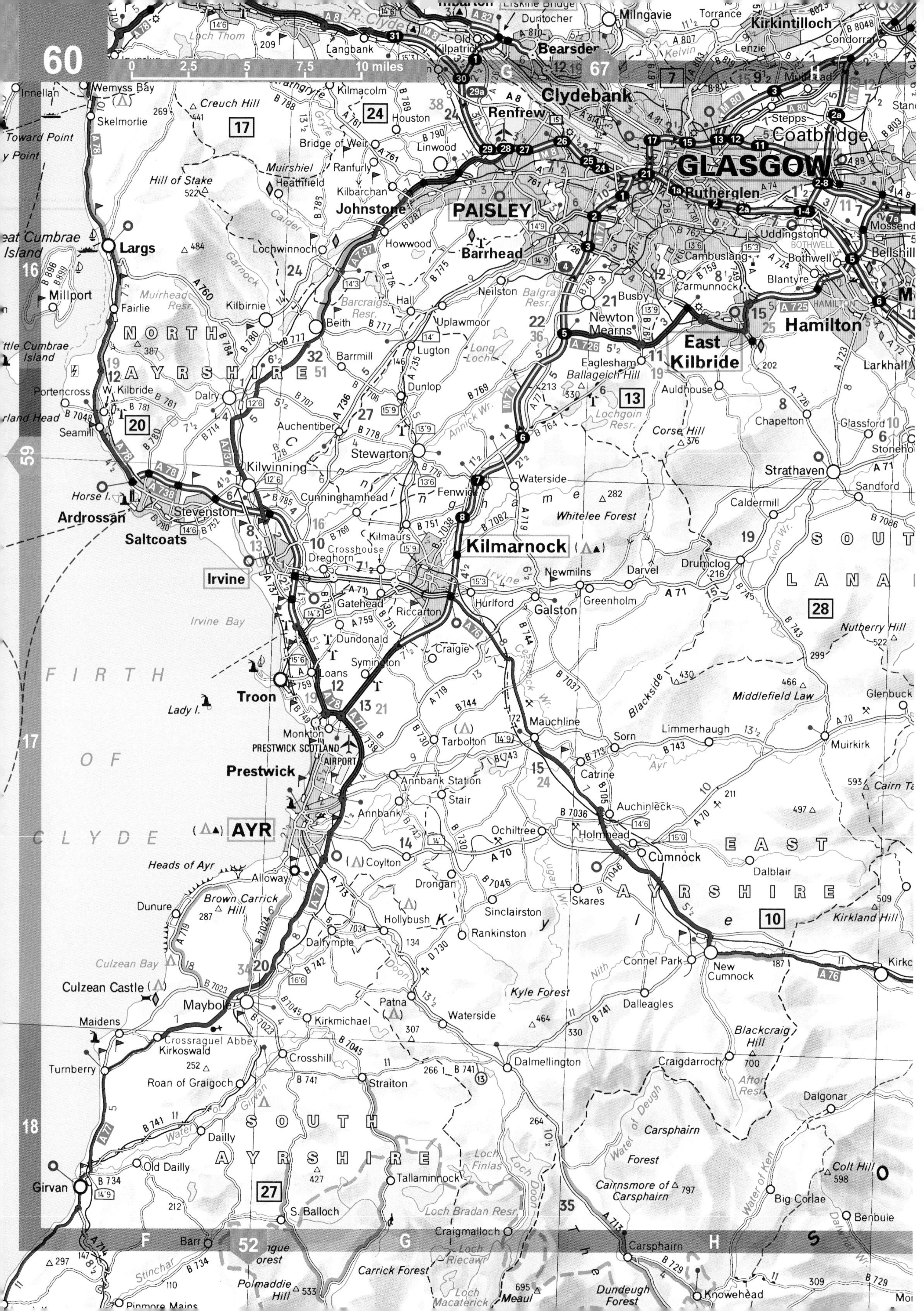
0 2.5 5 7.5 10 miles
67
59
52
GLASGOW
Clydebank
Bearsden
Milngavie
Kirkintilloch
Coatbridge
Rutherglen
Renfrew
PAISLEY
Johnstone
Barrhead
East Kilbride
Hamilton
Largs
Great Cumbrae Island
Little Cumbrae Island
Millport
Fairlie
Wemyss Bay
Skelmorlie
Innellan
Toward Point
Kilbirnie
Beith
Dalry
NORTH AYRSHIRE
Ardrossan
Saltcoats
Stevenston
Kilwinning
Irvine
Irvine Bay
Kilmarnock
Stewarton
Dunlop
Newton Mearns
Eaglesham
Strathaven
Galston
Newmilns
Darvel
Hurlford
Troon
Prestwick
PRESTWICK SCOTLAND AIRPORT
AYR
Heads of Ayr
Alloway
Dunure
Culzean Castle
Culzean Bay
Maybole
Maidens
Turnberry
Kirkoswald
Crossraguel Abbey
Girvan
Old Dailly
Dailly
Barr
Mauchline
Catrine
Sorn
Auchinleck
Cumnock
New Cumnock
Dalmellington
Patna
Drongan
Coylton
Tarbolton
Annbank
Dalrymple
Straiton
Crosshill
Kirkmichael
Carsphairn
FIRTH OF CLYDE
SOUTH AYRSHIRE
EAST AYRSHIRE
SOUTH LANARKSHIRE
Whitelee Forest
Carrick Forest
Carsphairn Forest
Kyle Forest
Loch Doon
Loch Bradan Resr.
Lady I.
Horse I.
Glenbuck
Muirkirk
Larkhall
Uddingston
Bellshill
Bothwell
Blantyre
Cambuslang
Busby
Neilston
Lochwinnoch
Bridge of Weir
Kilmacolm
Houston
Linwood
Langbank
Erskine Bridge
F
G
H

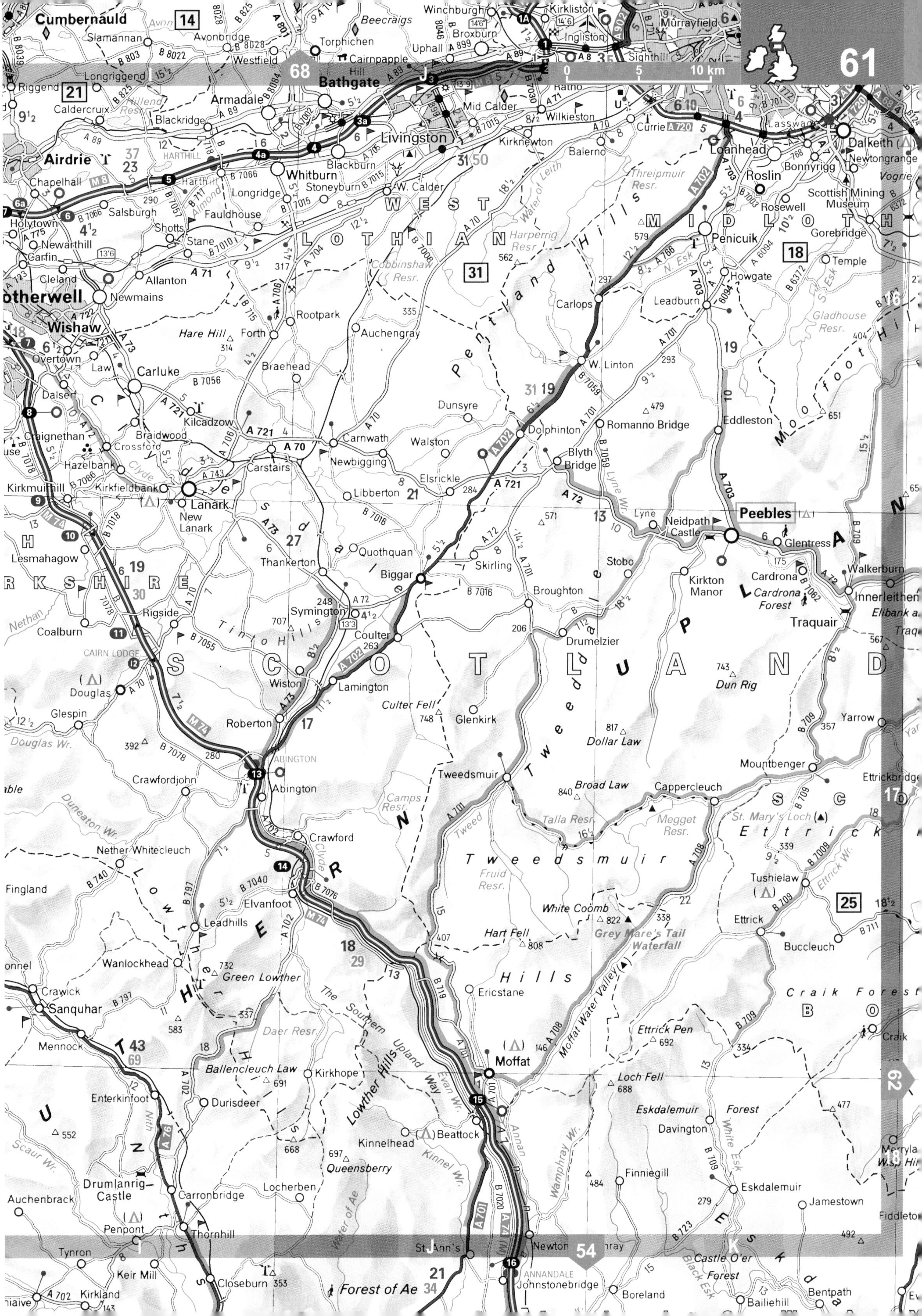
Cumbernauld
Slamannan
Avonbridge
Westfield
Torphichen
Beecraigs
Cairnpapple Hill
Winchburgh
Kirkliston
Broxburn
Uphall
Ingliston
Murrayfield
Sighthill
Longriggend
Riggend
Caldercruix
Hillend Resr.
Bathgate
Armadale
Blackridge
Mid Calder
Ratho
Wilkieston
Currie
Lasswade
Dalkeith
Airdrie
HARTHILL
Harthill
Livingston
Blackburn
Whitburn
Kirknewton
Balerno
Loanhead
Newtongrange
Bonnyrigg
Roslin
Vogrie
Chapelhall
Longridge
Stoneyburn
W. Calder
Threipmuir Resr.
Scottish Mining Museum
Rosewell
Holytown
Salsburgh
Fauldhouse
W E S T
L O T H I A N
M I D L O T H I A N
Water of Leith
Harperrig Resr.
Penicuik
Gorebridge
Newarthill
Shotts
Stane
Carfin
Cobbinshaw Resr.
Temple
Cleland
Allanton
Howgate
Motherwell
Newmains
Carlops
Leadburn
Pentland Hills
Wishaw
Rootpark
Hare Hill
Forth
Auchengray
Gladhouse Resr.
Overtown
Law
Carluke
Braehead
W. Linton
Moorfoot Hills
Dalserf
Dunsyre
Romanno Bridge
Kilcadzow
Dolphinton
Eddleston
Craignethan
Braidwood
Carnwath
Walston
Crossford
Hazelbank
Newbigging
Blyth Bridge
Carstairs
Clyde
Kirkmuirhill
Kirkfieldbank
Lanark
Elsrickle
Libberton
New Lanark
Lyne
Neidpath Castle
Peebles
Glentress
Lesmahagow
Quothquan
Thankerton
Skirling
Stobo
Cardrona
Cardrona Forest
Walkerburn
Innerleithen
Elibank
Traquair
Biggar
Kirkton Manor
Broughton
Rigside
Symington
Tinto Hills
Coulter
Drumelzier
Coalburn
Nethan
CAIRN LODGE
Douglas
Wiston
Lamington
S C O T L A N D
Dun Rig
Glespin
Culter Fell
Glenkirk
Roberton
Yarrow
Douglas Wr.
Dollar Law
Tweed
ABINGTON
Abington
Crawfordjohn
Tweedsmuir
Mountbenger
Ettrickbridge
Broad Law
Cappercleuch
Camps Resr.
Talla Resr.
Megget Resr.
St. Mary's Loch
Duneaton Wr.
Crawford
Nether Whitecleuch
Tweedsmuir
Ettrick
Fruid Resr.
Tushielaw
Fingland
Elvanfoot
Leadhills
White Coomb
Grey Mare's Tail Waterfall
Ettrick
Buccleuch
Hart Fell
Wanlockhead
Lowther Hills
Green Lowther
Hills
The Southern Upland Way
Crawick
Sanquhar
Ericstane
Craik Forest
Moffat Water Valley
Daer Resr.
Ettrick Pen
Mennock
Craik
Moffat
Ballencleuch Law
Kirkhope
Loch Fell
Enterkinfoot
Durisdeer
Eskdalemuir Forest
Davington
Beattock
Kinnelhead
Queensberry
Kinnel Wr.
Evan Wr.
Annan
Wamphray Wr.
Scaur Wr.
Drumlanrig Castle
Finniegill
Eskdalemuir
Auchenbrack
Carronbridge
Locherben
Water of Ae
Jamestown
Penpont
Thornhill
St Ann's
Newton
Tynron
Keir Mill
Closeburn
Forest of Ae
Castle O'er Forest
Black Esk
White Esk
ANNANDALE
Johnstonebridge
Boreland
Bentpath
Kirkland
Bailiehill
Fiddleton
Nith
68
54
62
0 5 10 km

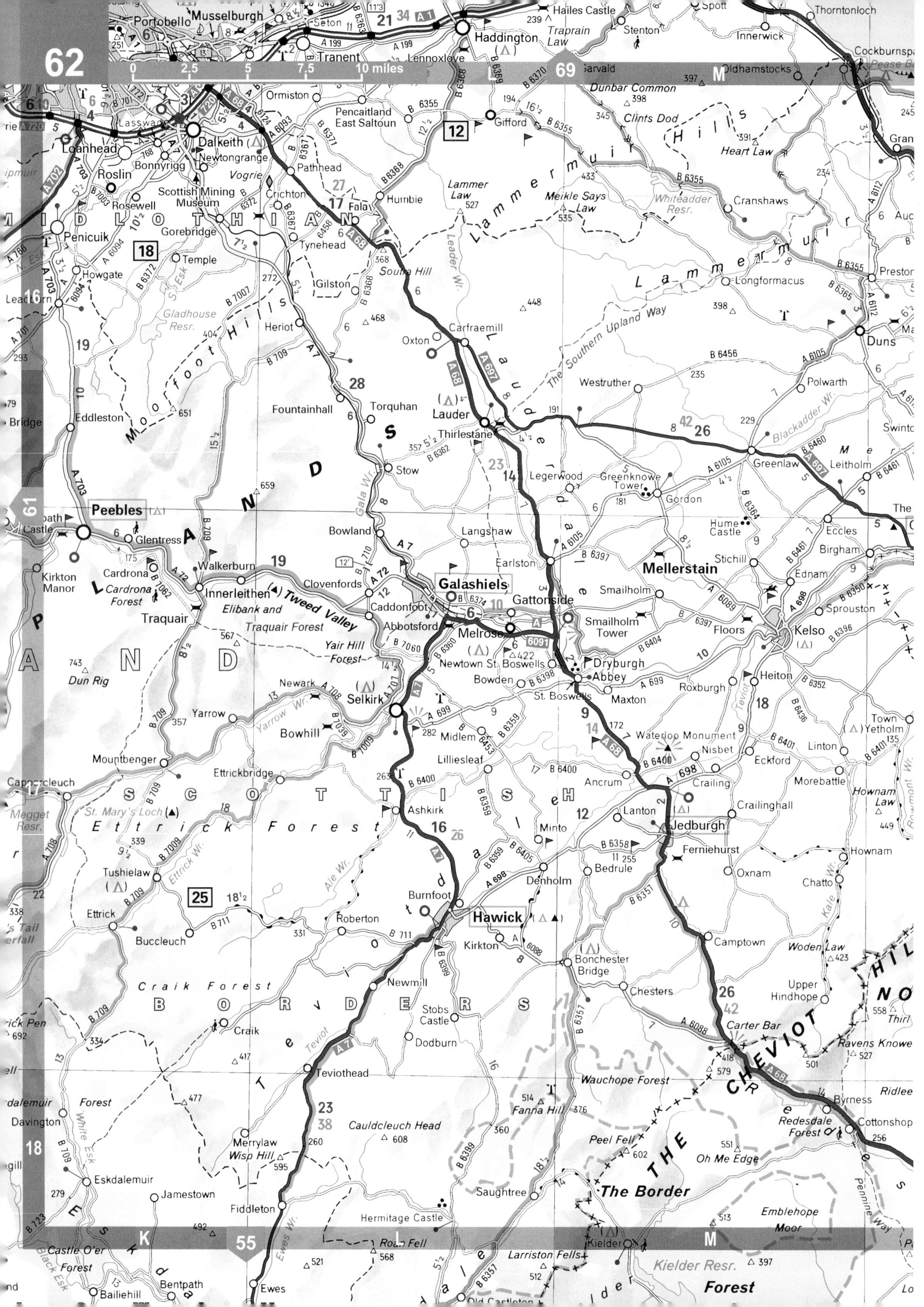

0 2.5 5 7.5 10 miles
69
61
55
Musselburgh
Portobello
Seton
Tranent
Haddington
Hailes Castle
Traprain Law
Stenton
Spott
Thorntonloch
Innerwick
Cockburnspath
Lennoxlove
Garvald
Oldhamstocks
Dunbar Common
Clints Dod
Heart Law
Ormiston
Pencaitland
East Saltoun
Gifford
Lasswade
Dalkeith
Loanhead
Newtongrange
Bonnyrigg
Roslin
Vogrie
Pathhead
Crichton
Scottish Mining Museum
Rosewell
Fala
Humbie
Lammer Law
Meikle Says Law
Whiteadder Resr.
Cranshaws
Lammermuir Hills
MIDLOTHIAN
Penicuik
Gorebridge
Tynehead
Temple
Howgate
Leadburn
Soutra Hill
Leader Wr.
Longformacus
Preston
Gilston
Gladhouse Resr.
Heriot
Moorfoot Hills
Oxton
Carfraemill
The Southern Upland Way
Duns
Westruther
Polwarth
Eddleston
Fountainhall
Torquhan
Lauder
Thirlestane
Lauderdale
Greenlaw
Blackadder Wr.
Leitholm
Merse
Stow
Gala Wr.
Legerwood
Greenknowe Tower
Gordon
Hume Castle
Eccles
Peebles
Glentress
Bowland
Langshaw
Earlston
Stichill
Birgham
Mellerstain
Ednam
Kirkton Manor
Cardrona
Cardrona Forest
Walkerburn
Innerleithen
Traquair
Clovenfords
Galashiels
Gattonside
Smailholm
Smailholm Tower
Sprouston
Kelso
Floors
Elibank and Traquair Forest
Tweed Valley
Caddonfoot
Abbotsford
Melrose
Yair Hill Forest
Newtown St. Boswells
Dryburgh Abbey
Dun Rig
Bowden
St. Boswells
Maxton
Roxburgh
Heiton
Newark
Selkirk
Town Yetholm
Yarrow
Yarrow Wr.
Bowhill
Midlem
Waterloo Monument
Nisbet
Linton
Eckford
Mountbenger
Lilliesleaf
Ancrum
Crailing
Morebattle
Cappercleuch
Ettrickbridge
Megget Resr.
St. Mary's Loch
Ettrick Forest
Ashkirk
Lanton
Crailinghall
Hownam Law
Jedburgh
Minto
Ferniehurst
Hownam
Tushielaw
Ettrick Wr.
Ale Wr.
Bedrule
Oxnam
Chatto
Denholm
Burnfoot
Hawick
Ettrick
Roberton
Kirkton
Camptown
Buccleuch
Bonchester Bridge
Woden Law
Newmill
Chesters
Upper Hindhope
Craik Forest
BORDERS
Stobs Castle
Carter Bar
Ravens Knowe
Craik
Dodburn
Teviot
Teviothead
Wauchope Forest
THE CHEVIOT
Byrness
Ridlees
Fanna Hill
Davington
Cauldcleuch Head
Redesdale Forest
Cottonshope
Merrylaw
Wisp Hill
Peel Fell
Oh Me Edge
Eskdalemuir
Jamestown
Saughtree
The Border
Pennine Way
Fiddleton
Hermitage Castle
Emblehope Moor
Ewes Wr.
Kielder
Roan Fell
Castle O'er Forest
Larriston Fells
Kielder Resr.
Black Esk
Bailiehill
Bentpath
Ewes
Forest

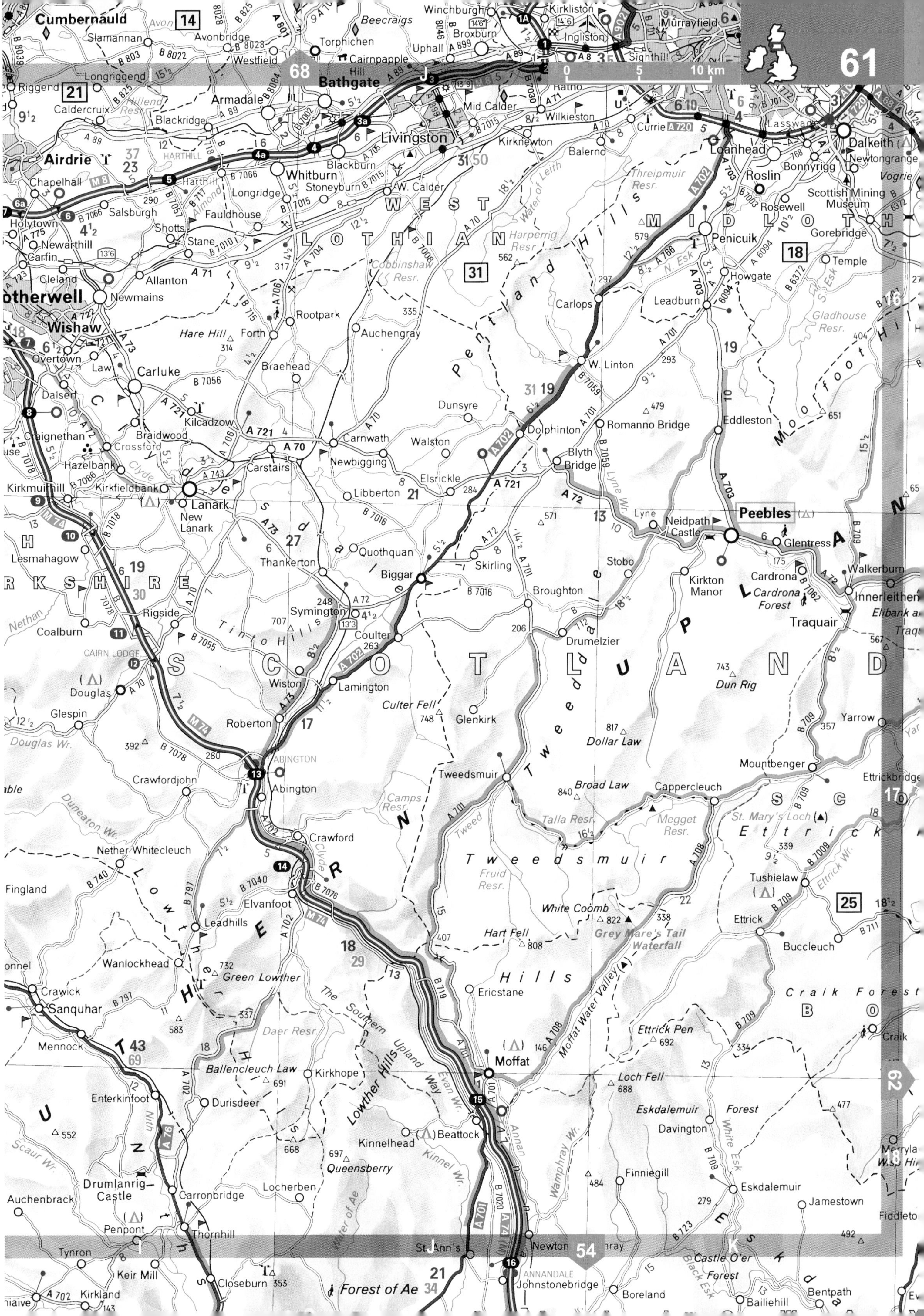

Cumbernauld
Slamannan
Avonbridge
Westfield
Torphichen
Cairnpapple Hill
Beecraigs
Winchburgh
Broxburn
Uphall
Kirkliston
Ingliston
Murrayfield
Sighthill
Ratho
Longriggend
Riggend
Caldercruix
Hillend Resr.
Armadale
Bathgate
Mid Calder
Wilkieston
Blackridge
Livingston
Kirknewton
Currie
Balerno
Loanhead
Lasswade
Dalkeith
Newtongrange
Bonnyrigg
Roslin
Vogrie
Airdrie
Harthill
Whitburn
Blackburn
Stoneyburn
W. Calder
Threipmuir Resr.
Scottish Mining Museum
Rosewell
Chapelhall
Longridge
Salsburgh
Fauldhouse
Shotts
Holytown
Newarthill
Carfin
Stane
Cleland
Allanton
Newmains
Motherwell
Wishaw
W E S T
L O T H I A N
M I D L O T H I A N
Harperrig Resr.
Cobbinshaw Resr.
Penicuik
Gorebridge
Temple
Howgate
Leadburn
Carlops
Pentland Hills
Gladhouse Resr.
Moorfoot Hills
Rootpark
Auchengray
Hare Hill
Forth
Overtown
Law
Carluke
Braehead
W. Linton
Dalserf
Craignethan
Crossford
Hazelbank
Kilcadzow
Braidwood
Dunsyre
Dolphinton
Romanno Bridge
Eddleston
Carnwath
Walston
Newbigging
Carstairs
Blyth Bridge
Kirkmuirhill
Kirkfieldbank
Lanark
New Lanark
Elsrickle
Libberton
Peebles
Lyne
Neidpath Castle
Glentress
Lesmahagow
Quothquan
Thankerton
Skirling
Stobo
Kirkton Manor
Cardrona
Cardrona Forest
Walkerburn
Innerleithen
Elibank
Traquair
Biggar
Broughton
Coalburn
Nethan
Rigside
Symington
Tinto Hills
Coulter
Drumelzier
Cairn Lodge
S C O T L A N D
Douglas
Wiston
Lamington
Dun Rig
Glespin
Culter Fell
Glenkirk
Yarrow
Douglas Wr.
Roberton
Dollar Law
Abington
Crawfordjohn
Tweedsmuir
Mountbenger
Ettrickbridge
Broad Law
Cappercleuch
Camps Resr.
Talla Resr.
Megget Resr.
St. Mary's Loch
Duneaton Wr.
Crawford
Nether Whitecleuch
Tweedsmuir
Fruid Resr.
Ettrick
Tushielaw
Fingland
Elvanfoot
White Coomb
Grey Mare's Tail Waterfall
Leadhills
Hart Fell
Buccleuch
Wanlockhead
Green Lowther
Hills
Ericstane
Craik Forest
Crawick
Sanquhar
The Southern Upland Way
Daer Resr.
Moffat Water Valley
Ettrick Pen
Mennock
Moffat
Craik
Ballencleuch Law
Kirkhope
Loch Fell
Lowther Hills
Enterkinfoot
Durisdeer
Eskdalemuir Forest
Davington
Beattock
Kinnelhead
Queensberry
Scaur Wr.
Finniegill
Drumlanrig Castle
Locherben
Eskdalemuir
Auchenbrack
Carronbridge
Jamestown
Penpont
Thornhill
Water of Ae
Tynron
St. Ann's
Newton
Castle O'er Forest
Keir Mill
Closeburn
Forest of Ae
Annandale
Johnstonebridge
Boreland
Bailiehill
Bentpath
Kirkland

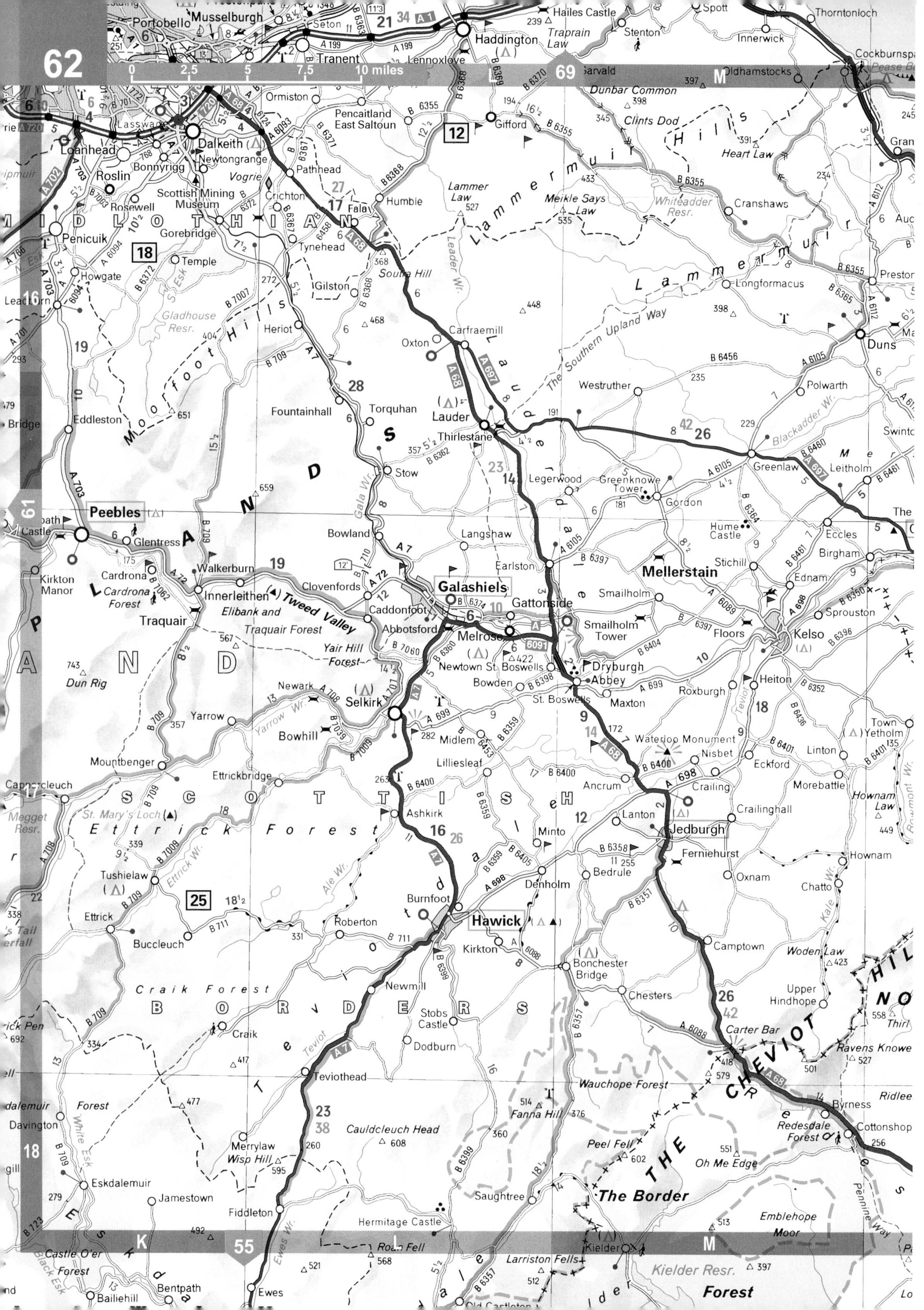
0 2,5 5 7,5 10 miles
Musselburgh
Portobello
Seton
Tranent
Hailes Castle
Haddington
Traprain Law
Lennoxlove
Stenton
Spott
Innerwick
Thorntonloch
Cockburnspath
Oldhamstocks
Dunbar Common
Clints Dod
Heart Law
Ormiston
Pencaitland
East Saltoun
Gifford
Dalkeith
Lasswade
Loanhead
Newtongrange
Bonnyrigg
Roslin
Vogrie
Pathhead
Scottish Mining Museum
Crichton
Rosewell
Fala
Humble
Lammer Law
Meikle Says Law
Whiteadder Resr.
Cranshaws
Lammermuir Hills
Penicuik
Gorebridge
MIDLOTHIAN
Tynehead
Temple
Howgate
Soutra Hill
Leader Wr.
Longformacus
Leadburn
Gladhouse Resr.
Gilston
Moorfoot Hills
Heriot
Oxton
Carfraemill
The Southern Upland Way
Duns
Westruther
Polwarth
Fountainhall
Torquhan
Lauder
Thirlestane
Lauderdale
Greenlaw
Blackadder Wr.
Leitholm
Eddleston
Stow
Legerwood
Greenknowe Tower
Gordon
Hume Castle
Peebles
Glentress
Bowland
Langshaw
Earlston
Eccles
Birgham
Kirkton Manor
Cardrona
Cardrona Forest
Walkerburn
Innerleithen
Clovenfords
Galashiels
Mellerstain
Stichill
Ednam
Traquair
Elibank and Traquair Forest
Tweed Valley
Caddonfoot
Gattonside
Smailholm
Smailholm Tower
Abbotsford
Melrose
Floors
Kelso
Sprouston
Yair Hill Forest
Newtown St. Boswells
Dryburgh Abbey
Dun Rig
Bowden
St. Boswells
Maxton
Roxburgh
Heiton
Newark
Selkirk
Yarrow
Yarrow Wr.
Bowhill
Midlem
Waterloo Monument
Nisbet
Town Yetholm
Linton
Eckford
Mountbenger
Lilliesleaf
Ancrum
Crailing
Morebattle
Cappercleuch
Ettrickbridge
Megget Resr.
St. Mary's Loch
Ashkirk
Lanton
Crailinghall
Hownam Law
Ettrick Forest
Minto
Jedburgh
Ferniehurst
Hownam
Tushielaw
Ettrick Wr.
Ale Wr.
Bedrule
Denholm
Oxnam
Chatto
Ettrick
Buccleuch
Burnfoot
Roberton
Hawick
Kirkton
Camptown
Woden Law
Bonchester Bridge
Craik Forest
Newmill
Chesters
Upper Hindhope
BORDERS
Stobs Castle
Carter Bar
Ravens Knowe
Craik
Dodburn
Teviot
THE CHEVIOT HILLS
Teviothead
Wauchope Forest
Byrness
Ridlee
Fanna Hill
Cauldcleuch Head
Redesdale Forest
Cottonshop
Eskdalemuir Forest
Davington
White Esk
Merrylaw
Wisp Hill
Peel Fell
Oh Me Edge
Eskdalemuir
Jamestown
Saughtree
The Border
Pennine Way
Fiddleton
Hermitage Castle
Emblehope Moor
Castle O'er Forest
Ewes Wr.
Roan Fell
Kielder
Larriston Fells
Kielder Resr.
Black Esk
Bailiehill
Bentpath
Ewes
Forest
Liddesdale
Kielder Forest
A 1
A 68
A 697
A 7
A 72
A 6091
A 698
A 699
A 6088
A 703
A 701
A 708
61
69
55

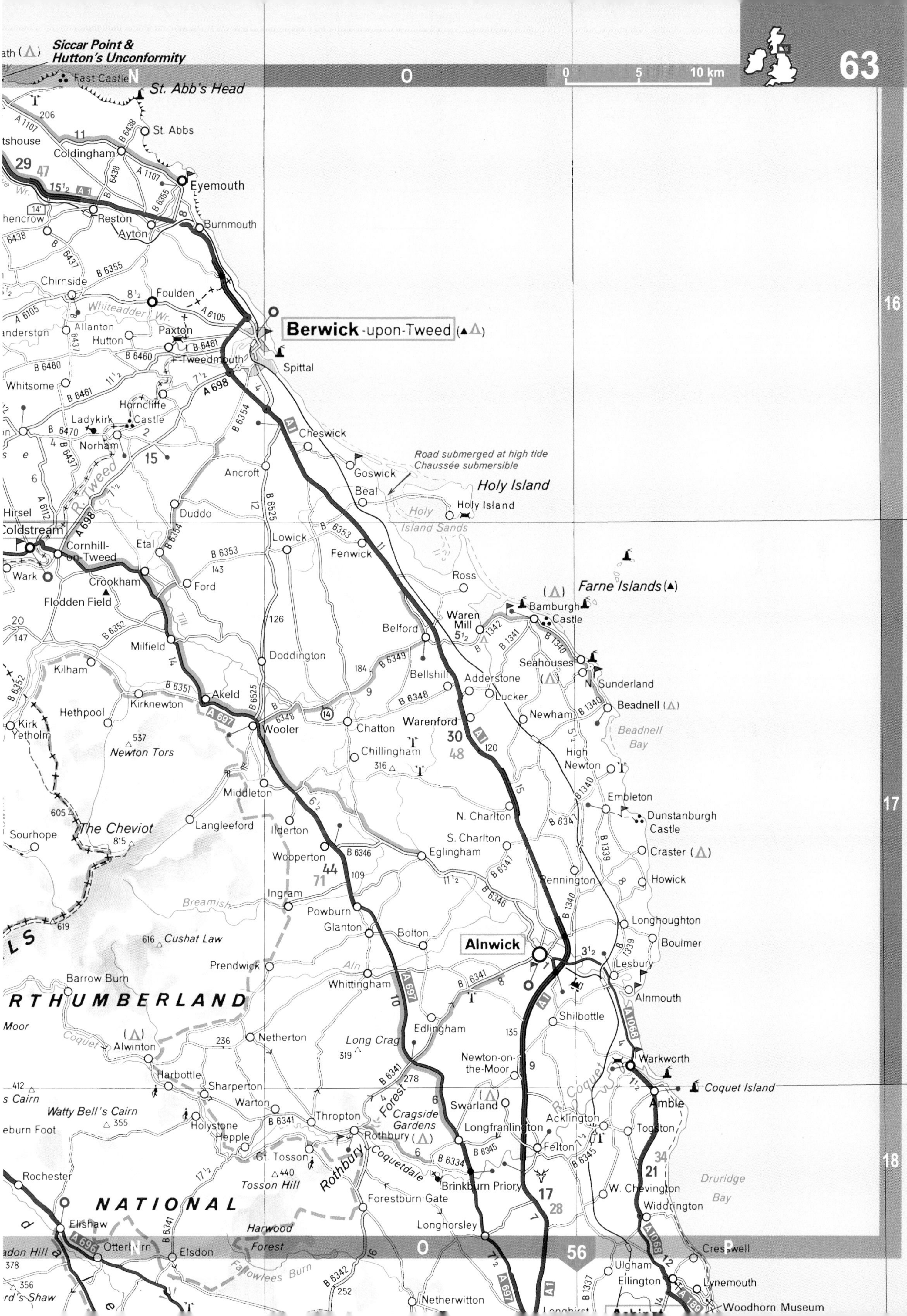
Siccar Point &
Hutton's Unconformity
Fast Castle
St. Abb's Head
N
O
P
0
5
10 km
St. Abbs
Coldingham
Eyemouth
Reston
Ayton
Burnmouth
Chirnside
Foulden
Whiteadder Wr.
Allanton
Hutton
Paxton
Berwick-upon-Tweed
Tweedmouth
Spittal
Whitsome
Horncliffe
Ladykirk
Castle
Norham
R. Tweed
Cheswick
Road submerged at high tide
Chaussée submersible
Goswick
Beal
Holy Island
Holy Island Sands
Ancroft
Duddo
Hirsel
Coldstream
Cornhill-on-Tweed
Etal
Lowick
Fenwick
Ford
Wark
Crookham
Flodden Field
Ross
Farne Islands
Bamburgh
Castle
Waren Mill
Belford
Milfield
Doddington
Bellshill
Adderstone
Lucker
Seahouses
N. Sunderland
Beadnell
Beadnell Bay
Kilham
Akeld
Kirknewton
Hethpool
Kirk Yetholm
Wooler
Chatton
Warenford
Newham
Chillingham
High Newton
Newton Tors
Middleton
Embleton
Dunstanburgh Castle
The Cheviot
Sourhope
Langleeford
Ilderton
N. Charlton
S. Charlton
Eglingham
Wooperton
Craster
Howick
Rennington
Ingram
Breamish
Powburn
Glanton
Bolton
Longhoughton
Boulmer
Alnwick
Lesbury
Alnmouth
Cushat Law
Prendwick
Whittingham
Aln
Barrow Burn
NORTHUMBERLAND
Edlingham
Shilbottle
Coquet
Alwinton
Netherton
Long Crag
Newton-on-the-Moor
Warkworth
Harbottle
Sharperton
Swarland
Amble
Coquet Island
Watty Bell's Cairn
Warton
Thropton
Cragside Gardens
Acklington
Holystone
Hepple
Rothbury
Longframlington
Togston
Rothbury Forest
Gt. Tosson
Coquetdale
Felton
Rochester
Tosson Hill
Brinkburn Priory
W. Chevington
Druridge Bay
NATIONAL
Forestburn Gate
Widdrington
Elishaw
Harwood Forest
Longhorsley
Otterburn
Elsdon
Fallowlees Burn
Cresswell
Ulgham
Ellington
Lynemouth
Netherwitton
Woodhorn Museum
56
16
17
18

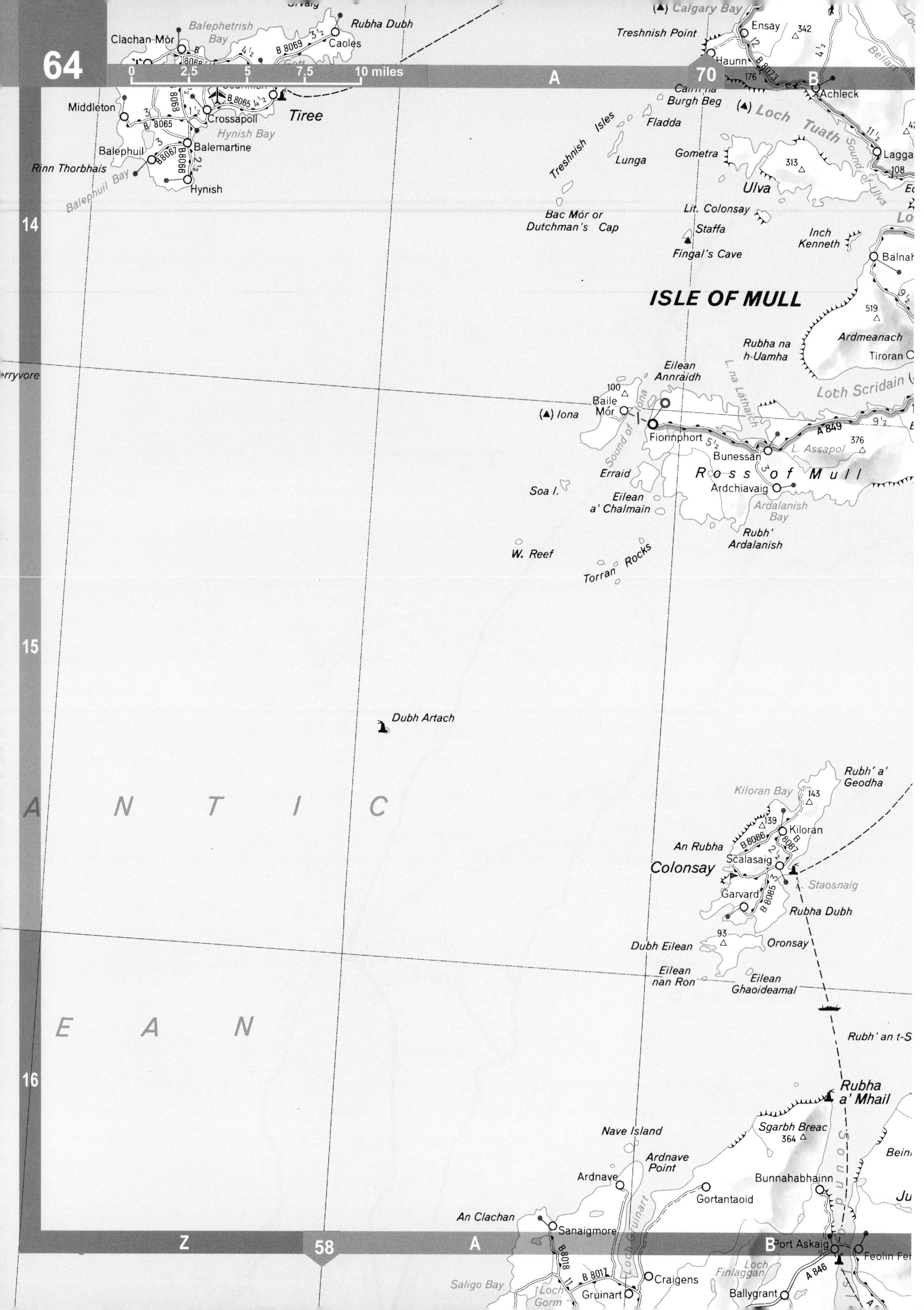
0 2.5 5 7.5 10 miles
A
70
B
14
15
16
Z
58
A
B
Calgary Bay
Treshnish Point
Ensay
342
Haunn
176
B 8073
Achleck
Rubha Dubh
Caoles
Clachan Mór
Balephetrish Bay
B 8069
Middleton
Crossapoll
Tiree
B 8065
B 8068
Hynish Bay
Balemartine
Balephuil
B 8067
B 8066
Rinn Thorbhais
Balephuil Bay
Hynish
Burgh Beg
Fladda
Loch Tuath
Treshnish Isles
Lunga
Gometra
313
Lagga
108
Ulva
Sound of Ulva
Lit. Colonsay
Staffa
Fingal's Cave
Bac Mór or Dutchman's Cap
Inch Kenneth
Balnah
ISLE OF MULL
519
Ardmeanach
Rubha na h-Uamha
Tiroran
Eilean Annraidh
L. na Làthaich
Loch Scridain
100
Baile Mór
Iona
Sound of Iona
Fionnphort
A 849
Bunessan
L. Assapol
376
Ross of Mull
Erraid
Ardchiavaig
Soa I.
Eilean a' Chalmain
Ardalanish Bay
Rubh' Ardalanish
W. Reef
Torran Rocks
rryvore
Dubh Artach
A N T I C
E A N
Rubh' a' Geodha
Kiloran Bay
143
139
Kiloran
B 8086
B 8087
An Rubha
Scalasaig
Colonsay
Staosnaig
Garvard
B 8085
Rubha Dubh
93
Dubh Eilean
Oronsay
Eilean nan Ron
Eilean Ghaoideamal
Rubh' an t-S
Rubha a' Mhail
Sgarbh Breac
364
Nave Island
Ardnave Point
Ardnave
Bunnahabhainn
Gortantaoid
An Clachan
Sanaigmore
Loch Gruinart
Port Askaig
Feolin Fe
B 8018
B 8017
Craigens
Loch Finlaggan
A 846
Saligo Bay
Loch Gorm
Gruinart
Ballygrant

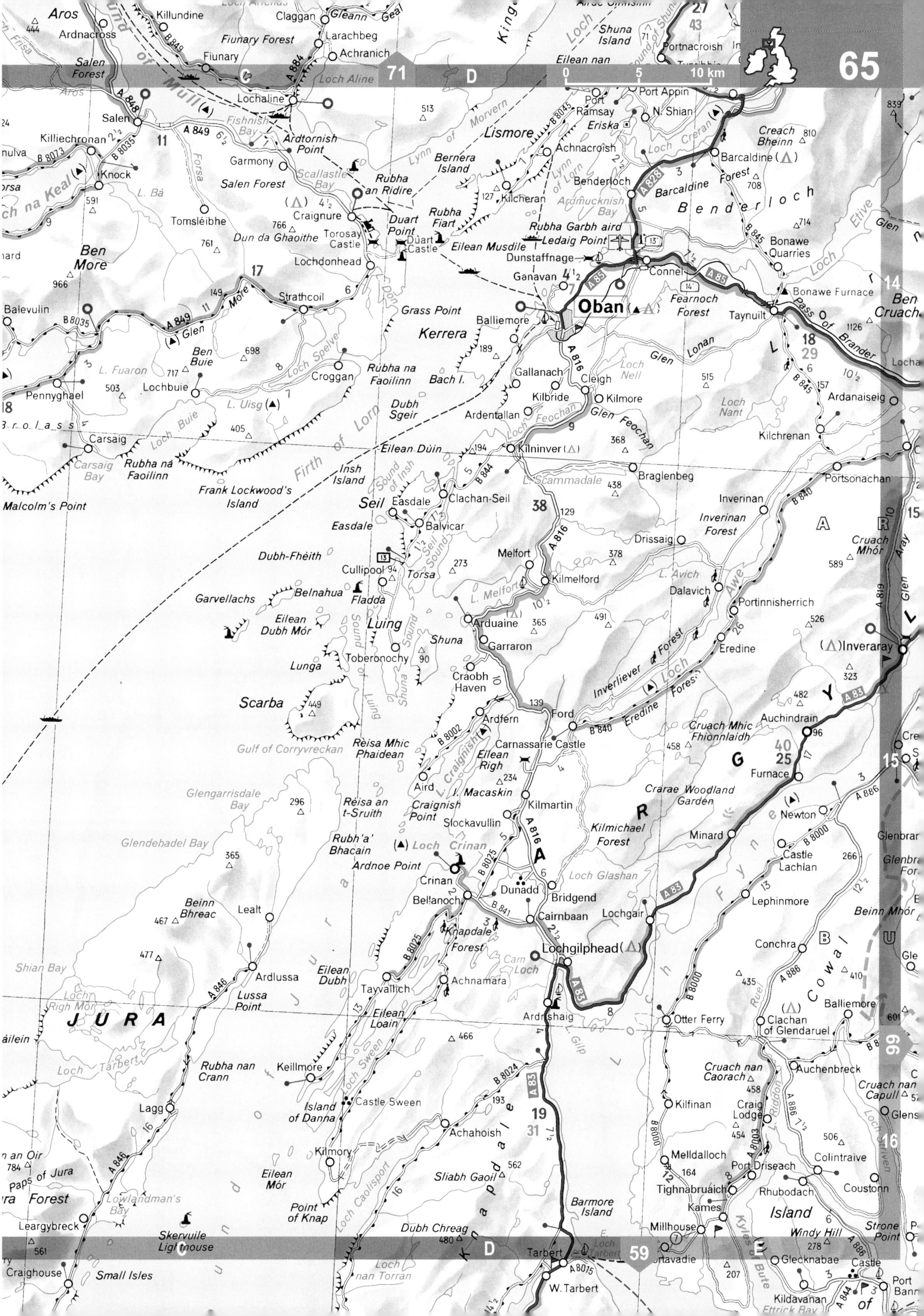

Aros
Killundine
Claggan
Gleann Geal
Ardnacross
Larachbeg
Fiunary Forest
Achranich
Fiunary
Salen Forest
Loch Aline
71
C
D
Shuna Island
Portnacroish
Eilean nan
0 5 10 km
Port Appin
Port Ramsay
Eriska
N. Shian
Lochaline
Salen
Killiechronan
Fishnish Bay
Ardtornish Point
Morvern
Lismore
Achnacroish
Loch Creran
Creach Bheinn
Barcaldine
Knock
Garmony
Scallastle Bay
Bernera Island
Lynn of Lorn
Benderloch
Barcaldine Forest
Salen Forest
Rubha an Ridire
Kilcheran
Ardmucknish Bay
Benderloch
Loch na Keal
L. Bà
Tomsléibhe
Craignure
Rubha Fiart
Rubha Garbh aird
Ledaig Point
Bonawe Quarries
Dun da Ghaoithe
Torosay Castle
Duart Point
Duart Castle
Eilean Musdile
Dunstaffnage
Connel
Loch Etive
Ben More
Lochdonhead
Ganavan
Bonawe Furnace
Strathcoil
Oban
Fearnoch Forest
Taynuilt
Ben Cruachan
Balevulin
Grass Point
Kerrera
Balliemore
Pass of Brander
Glen More
Ben Buie
Loch Spelve
Glen Lonan
L. Fuaron
Croggan
Rubha na Faoilinn
Bach I.
Gallanach
Cleigh
Loch Nell
Pennyghael
Lochbuie
Kilbride
Kilmore
Ardanaiseig
L. Uisg
Dubh Sgeir
Ardentallan
Loch Feochan
Glen Feochan
Loch Nant
Brolass
Loch Buie
Firth of Lorn
Kilchrenan
Carsaig
Carsaig Bay
Rubha na Faoilinn
Eilean Dùin
Kilninver
Insh Island
Sound of Insh
L. Scammadale
Braglenbeg
Portsonachan
Frank Lockwood's Island
Malcolm's Point
Clachan-Seil
Seil
Easdale
Inverinan
Easdale
Balvicar
Inverinan Forest
Seil Sound
Drissaig
Cruach Mhór
Dubh-Fhèith
Melfort
Cullipool
Torsa
Kilmelford
L. Avich
Dalavich
Garvellachs
Belnahua
Fladda
L. Melfort
Portinnisherrich
Luing
Eilean Dubh Mór
Arduaine
Sound of Luing
Shuna
Garraron
Eredine
Inveraray
Toberonochy
Lunga
Craobh Haven
Inverliever Forest
Loch Awe
Scarba
Ford
Eredine Forest
Auchindrain
Ardfern
Gulf of Corryvreckan
Rèisa Mhic Phaidean
Carnassarie Castle
Cruach Mhic Fhionnlaidh
Eilean Righ
Furnace
L. Craignish
Glengarrisdale Bay
Aird
Crarae Woodland Garden
I. Macaskin
Rèisa an t-Sruith
Craignish Point
Kilmartin
Newton
Slockavullin
Kilmichael Forest
Glendebadel Bay
Rubh'a' Bhacain
Loch Crinan
Minard
Castle Lachlan
Ardnoe Point
Crinan
Dunadd
Loch Glashan
Bellanoch
Bridgend
Loch Fyne
Lephinmore
Beinn Bhreac
Lealt
Cairnbaan
Lochgair
Knapdale Forest
Beinn Mhór
Lochgilphead
Conchra
Cam Loch
Shian Bay
Ardlussa
Eilean Dubh
Tayvallich
Achnamara
Cowal
Loch Righ Mór
Lussa Point
Eilean Loain
Balliemore
JURA
Ardrishaig
Otter Ferry
Clachan of Glendaruel
Loch Tarbert
Rubha nan Crann
Keillmore
Loch Sween
Cruach nan Caorach
Auchenbreck
Cruach nan Capull
Castle Sween
Kilfinan
Craig Lodge
Lagg
Island of Danna
Glens
Achahoish
Loch Riddon
Kilmory
Melldalloch
Loch Striven
Colintraive
Paps of Jura
Eilean Mór
Sliabh Gaoil
Port Driseach
Coustonn
Jura Forest
Lowlandman's Bay
Point of Knap
Loch Caolisport
Tighnabruaich
Rhubodach
Barmore Island
Kames
Knapdale
Island
Leargybreck
Skervuile Lighthouse
Dubh Chreag
Millhouse
Windy Hill
Strone Point
E. Loch Tarbert
Portavadie
Kyles of Bute
Tarbert
59
Glecknabae
Castle
Craighouse
Small Isles
Loch nan Torran
W. Tarbert
Kildavanan
Port Bannatyne
Ettrick Bay
A 848
A 849
A 884
B 849
B 8035
B 8073
B 8045
A 828
A 85
B 845
A 816
B 844
B 840
A 819
A 83
B 8002
B 8025
B 841
B 8000
A 886
A 846
B 8024
A 8015
A 844
B 8003

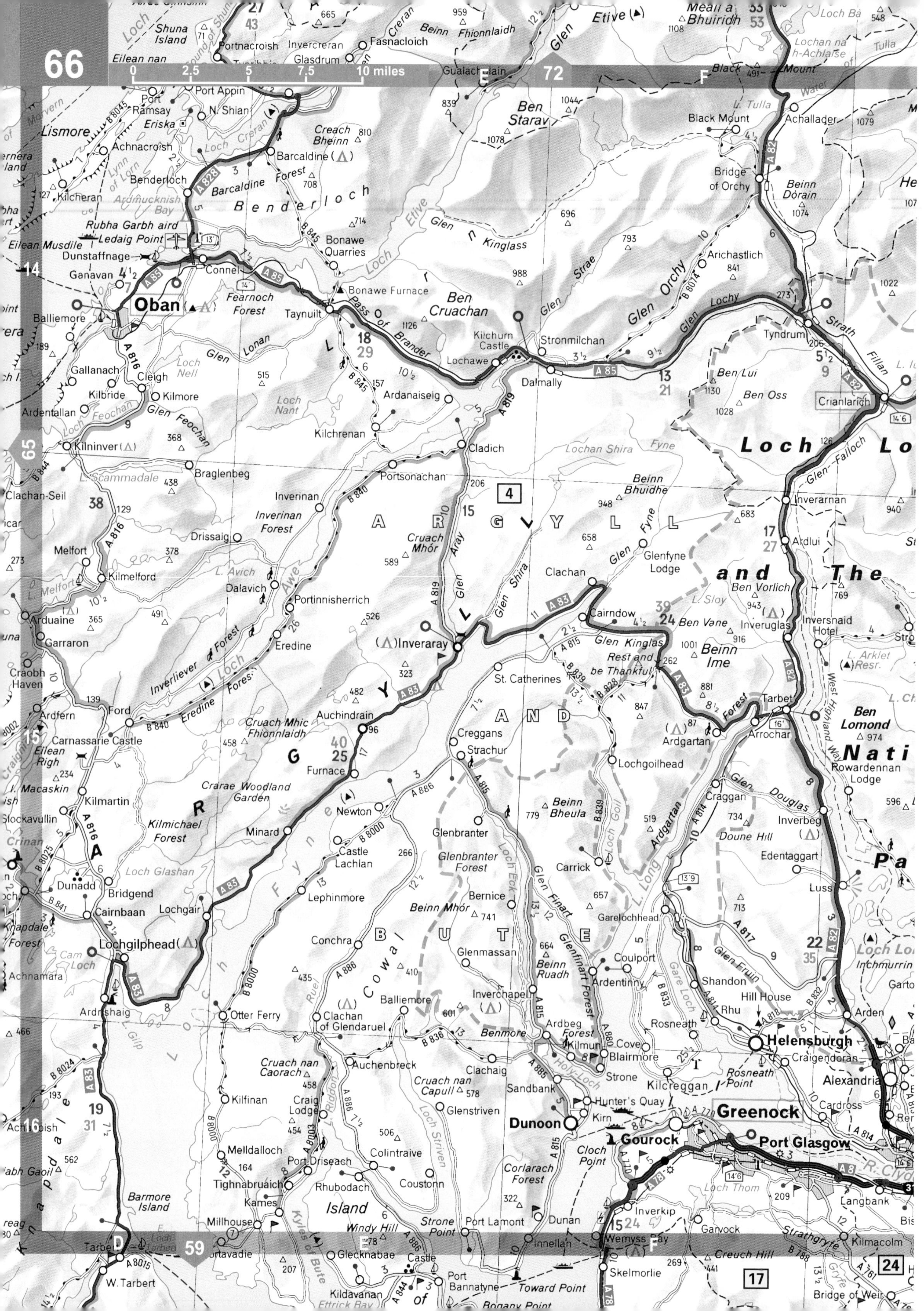
0 2.5 5 7.5 10 miles
72
65
59
Lismore
Shuna Island
Portnacroish
Invercreran
Fasnacloich
Glasdrum
Port Appin
Port Ramsay
N. Shian
Eriska
Loch Creran
Achnacroish
Creach Bheinn
Barcaldine
Barcaldine Forest
Benderloch
Kilcheran
Ardmucknish Bay
Rubha Garbh aird
Ledaig Point
Eilean Musdile
Dunstaffnage
Ganavan
Connel
Oban
Fearnoch Forest
Taynuilt
Bonawe Quarries
Bonawe Furnace
Loch Etive
Pass of Brander
Ben Cruachan
Glen Kinglass
Glen Strae
Glen Orchy
Glen Lochy
Arichastlich
Ben Starav
Glen Etive
Gualachulain
Black Mount
Achallader
Bridge of Orchy
Beinn Dòrain
Tyndrum
Strath Fillan
Crianlarich
Ben Lui
Ben Oss
Kilchurn Castle
Stronmilchan
Lochawe
Dalmally
Balliemore
Gallanach
Cleigh
Kilmore
Kilbride
Ardentallan
Loch Feochan
Glen Feochan
Glen Lonan
Loch Nell
Loch Nant
Ardanaiseig
Kilchrenan
Kilninver
Braglenbeg
L. Scammadale
Cladich
Portsonachan
Clachan-Seil
Inverinan
Inverinan Forest
Drissaig
Melfort
Kilmelford
L. Melfort
L. Avich
Dalavich
Portinnisherrich
Arduaine
Garraron
Craobh Haven
Eredine
Inverliever Forest
Eredine Forest
Loch Awe
Ford
Ardfern
Carnassarie Castle
Eilean Righ
I. Macaskin
Kilmartin
Crinan
Dunadd
Bridgend
Loch Glashan
Cairnbaan
Lochgilphead
Lochgair
Kilmichael Forest
Crarae Woodland Garden
Minard
Furnace
Auchindrain
Cruach Mhic Fhionnlaidh
Inveraray
Glen Aray
Cruach Mhòr
Glen Shira
Clachan
Cairndow
Glen Fyne
Glenfyne Lodge
Lochan Shira
Beinn Bhuidhe
Glen Kinglas
Rest and be Thankful
St. Catherines
Creggans
Strachur
Newton
Castle Lachlan
Glenbranter
Glenbranter Forest
Lephinmore
Loch Fyne
ARGYLL AND BUTE
Loch Lomond and The Trossachs National Park
Glen Falloch
Inverarnan
Ardlui
Ben Vorlich
L. Sloy
Ben Vane
Inveruglas
Beinn Ime
Inversnaid Hotel
L. Arklet Resr.
Tarbet
Arrochar
Ardgartan
Argyll Forest
Lochgoilhead
Loch Goil
Beinn Bheula
Carrick
Ben Lomond
Rowardennan Lodge
Glen Douglas
Craggan
Doune Hill
Inverbeg
Edentaggart
Luss
Loch Long
Garelochhead
Glen Fruin
Shandon
Hill House
Rhu
Arden
Inchmurrin
Loch Eck
Bernice
Beinn Mhòr
Glen Finart
Glenfinart Forest
Glenmassan
Beinn Ruadh
Coulport
Ardentinny
Inverchapel
Conchra
Cowal
Balliemore
Clachan of Glendaruel
Otter Ferry
Ardrishaig
Benmore
Ardbeg Forest
Kilmun
Cove
Blairmore
Strone
Rosneath
Helensburgh
Craigendoran
Alexandria
Cardross
Kilcreggan
Rosneath Point
Holy Loch
Sandbank
Hunter's Quay
Kirn
Dunoon
Gourock
Greenock
Port Glasgow
R. Clyde
Langbank
Cloch Point
Corlarach Forest
Loch Thom
Inverkip
Garvock
Wemyss Bay
Kilmacolm
Strathgryfe
Creuch Hill
Skelmorlie
Bridge of Weir
Innellan
Dunan
Port Lamont
Toward Point
Port Bannatyne
Strone Point
Island of Bute
Windy Hill
Kyles of Bute
Ettrick Bay
Bogany Point
Kildavanan
Glecknabae
Millhouse
Portavadie
Kames
Tighnabruaich
Rhubodach
Colintraive
Coustonn
Port Driseach
Loch Striven
Glenstriven
Cruach nan Capull
Cruach nan Caorach
Clachaig
Auchenbreck
Craig Lodge
Kilfinan
Melldalloch
Barmore Island
Knapdale
Knapdale Forest
Achnamara
Cam Loch
Tarbert
W. Tarbert
Loch Tarbert
Loch Gilp
Kilninver
A 85
A 816
A 819
A 83
A 815
A 82
A 828
A 886
A 814
A 817
A 818
A 8
A 78
A 770
A 761
A 844
A 8015
B 8045
B 845
B 840
B 8074
B 8000
B 839
B 828
B 836
B 833
B 841
B 8025
B 8024
B 8003
B 788
B 832

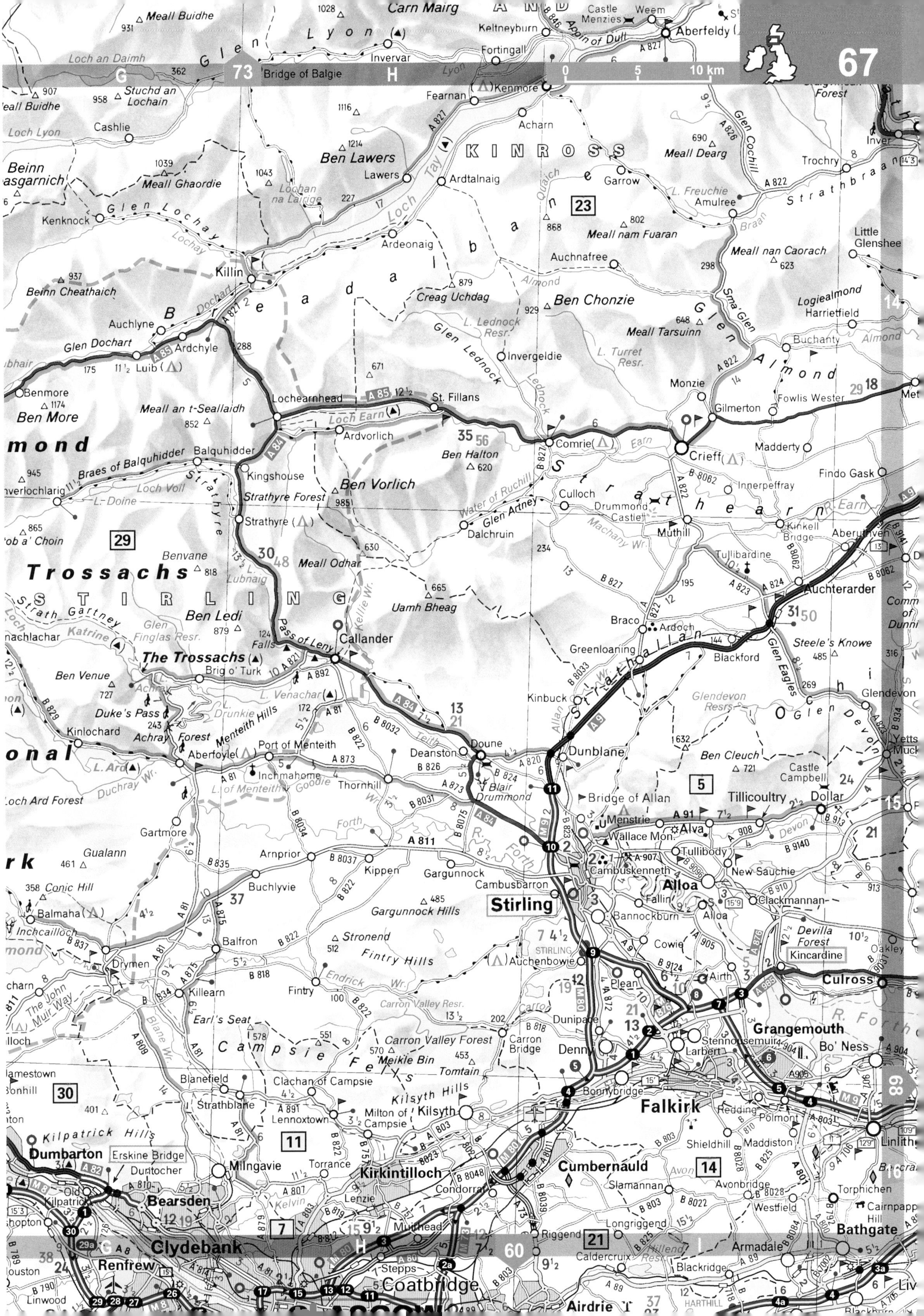
Carn Mairg
Meall Buidhe
Castle Menzies
Weem
Aberfeldy
Keltneyburn
Appin of Dull
Glen Lyon
Fortingall
Invervar
Loch an Daimh
Bridge of Balgie
73
G
H
0 5 10 km
Kenmore
Fearnan
Stuchd an Lochain
Acharn
Cashlie
Loch Lyon
Ben Lawers
KINROSS
Meall Dearg
Glen Cochill
Trochry
Inver
Beinn Heasgarnich
Meall Ghaordie
Lawers
Ardtalnaig
Garrow
Lochan na Lairige
Loch Tay
L. Freuchie
Amulree
Strathbraan
Kenknock
Glen Lochay
Ardeonaig
23
Meall nam Fuaran
Little Glenshee
Meall nan Caorach
Auchnafree
Killin
Beinn Cheathaich
Creag Uchdag
Ben Chonzie
Logiealmond
Harrietfield
Breadalbane
Dochart
Auchlyne
L. Lednock Resr.
Meall Tarsuinn
Glen Almond
Buchanty
Glen Dochart
Ardchyle
Luib
Invergeldie
L. Turret Resr.
Glen Lednock
Benmore
Ben More
Lochearnhead
St. Fillans
Monzie
Fowlis Wester
Meall an t-Seallaidh
Gilmerton
Loch Earn
Ardvorlich
Comrie
Crieff
Madderty
Balquhidder
Braes of Balquhidder
Ben Halton
Kingshouse
Loch Voil
Strathyre
Findo Gask
Innerpeffray
Inverlochlarig
L. Doine
Ben Vorlich
Strathyre Forest
Culloch
Drummond Castle
Water of Ruchill
Glen Artney
Strathearn
R. Earn
Kinkell Bridge
Aberuthven
Dalchruin
Muthill
Machany Wr.
Tullibardine
Trossachs
Benvane
Meall Odhar
Auchterarder
STIRLING
Lubnaig
Uamh Bheag
Ben Ledi
Braco
Ardoch
Strath Gartney
Glen Finglas Resr.
Loch Katrine
Callander
Pass of Leny
Kellie Wr.
Greenloaning
Blackford
Steele's Knowe
The Trossachs
Falls
Ben Venue
Brig o' Turk
Loch Venachar
Strathallan
Glen Eagles
Glendevon
Duke's Pass
Achray Forest
Menteith Hills
Kinbuck
Glendevon Resrs.
Glen Devon
Kinlochard
Aberfoyle
Port of Menteith
Deanston
Doune
Dunblane
Ben Cleuch
Castle Campbell
Loch Ard Forest
Inchmahome
L. of Menteith
Goodie
Thornhill
Blair Drummond
Bridge of Allan
Menstrie
Tillicoultry
Dollar
Duchray Wr.
Gartmore
Forth
Wallace Mon.
Alva
Devon
Gualann
Arnprior
Kippen
Gargunnock
Cambuskenneth
Tullibody
New Sauchie
Alloa
Conic Hill
Buchlyvie
Cambusbarron
Stirling
Fallin
Clackmannan
Balmaha
Gargunnock Hills
Bannockburn
Inchcailloch
Balfron
Stronend
Cowie
Devilla Forest
Kincardine
Oakley
Drymen
Fintry Hills
Auchenbowie
Plean
Airth
Culross
Killearn
Fintry
Endrick Wr.
The John Muir Way
Carron Valley Resr.
Dunipace
Grangemouth
Earl's Seat
Campsie Fells
Carron Valley Forest
Carron Bridge
Stenhousemuir
Larbert
Denny
Meikle Bin
Bo' Ness
Tomtain
Jamestown
Bonhill
Blanefield
Clachan of Campsie
Kilsyth Hills
Bonnybridge
Falkirk
Strathblane
Lennoxtown
Milton of Campsie
Kilsyth
Redding
Polmont
Linlithgow
Kilpatrick Hills
Dumbarton
Erskine Bridge
Duntocher
Milngavie
Torrance
Kirkintilloch
Cumbernauld
Shieldhill
Maddiston
Avonbridge
Torphichen
Bearsden
Lenzie
Condorrat
Slamannan
Westfield
Cairnpapple Hill
Old Kilpatrick
Kelvin
Muirhead
Riggend
Longriggend
Bathgate
Clydebank
Armadale
Renfrew
Stepps
Coatbridge
Caldercruix
Blackridge
Linwood
Airdrie
Harthill
60
89

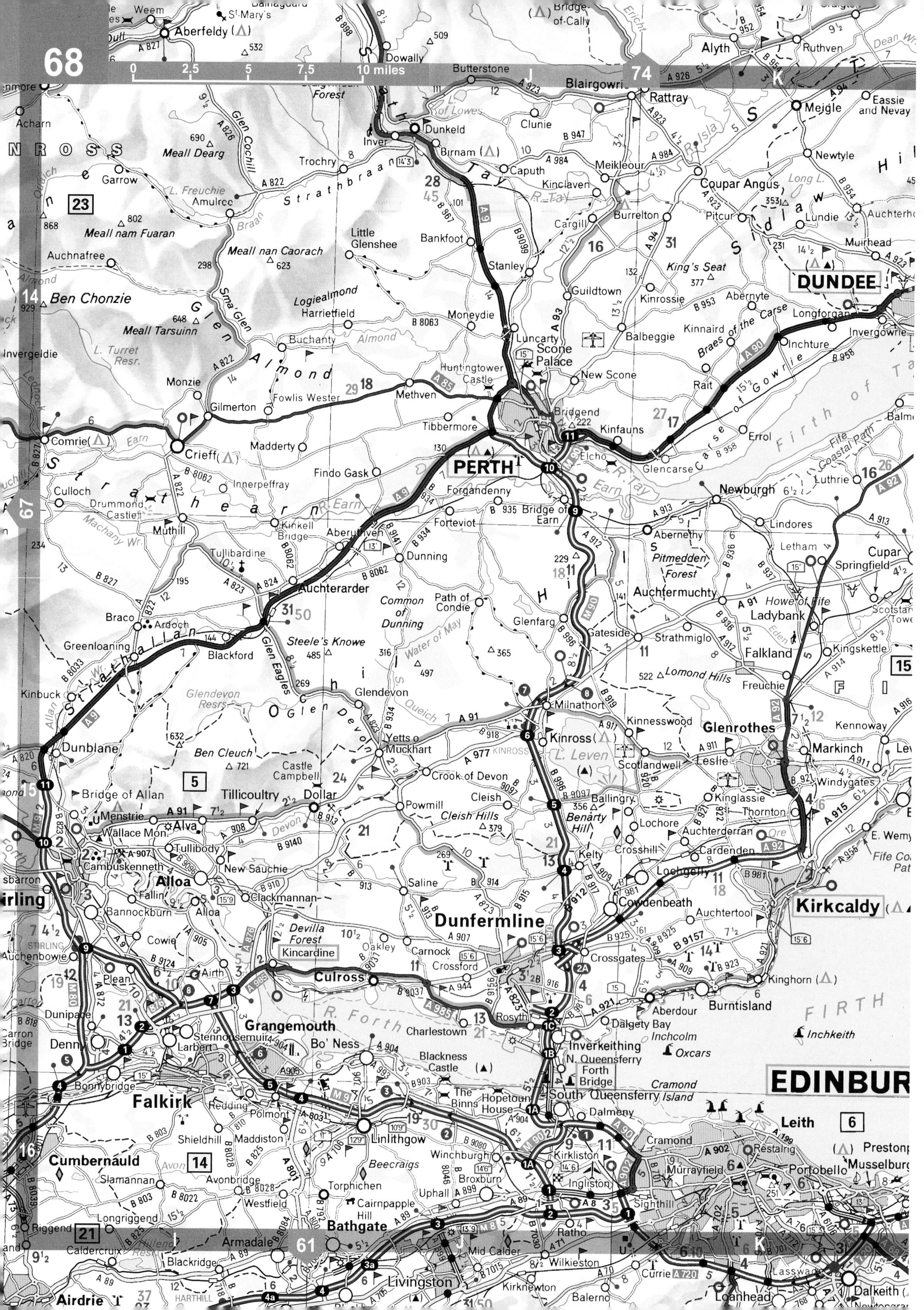
0 2,5 5 7,5 10 miles
74
61
67
Weem
St Mary's
Aberfeldy
Bridge of Cally
Alyth
Ruthven
Dowally
Butterstone
Blairgowrie
Rattray
Meigle
Eassie and Nevay
Acharn
Glen Cochill
Meall Dearg
Dunkeld
Inver
Birnam
Trochry
Clunie
Caputh
Meikleour
Newtyle
Strathbraan
Garrow
L. Freuchie
Amulree
Kinclaven
Coupar Angus
Long L.
Pitcur
Lundie
Auchterhouse
Sidlaw Hills
Meall nam Fuaran
Little Glenshee
Bankfoot
Cargill
Burrelton
Muirhead
Auchnafree
Meall nan Caorach
Stanley
King's Seat
DUNDEE
Ben Chonzie
Glen Almond
Sma' Glen
Logiealmond
Harrietfield
Guildtown
Kinrossie
Abernyte
Longforgan
Invergowrie
Meall Tarsuinn
Moneydie
Balbeggie
Kinnaird
Braes of the Carse
Inchture
L. Turret Resr.
Invergeldie
Buchanty
Almond
Luncarty
Scone Palace
Huntingtower Castle
New Scone
Rait
Monzie
Fowlis Wester
Methven
Carse of Gowrie
Firth of Tay
Gilmerton
Tibbermore
Bridgend
Kinfauns
Errol
Comrie
Earn
Crieff
Madderty
PERTH
Elcho
Glencarse
Fife Coastal Path
Luthrie
Findo Gask
Innerpeffray
Forgandenny
Newburgh
Culloch
Strathearn
Drummond Castle
Machany Wr.
R. Earn
Bridge of Earn
Forteviot
Lindores
Muthill
Kinkell Bridge
Aberuthven
Abernethy
Pitmedden Forest
Letham
Cupar
Springfield
Tullibardine
Dunning
Ochil Hills
Auchtermuchty
Auchterarder
Common of Dunning
Path of Condie
Howe of Fife
Ladybank
Scotstarvit Tower
Braco
Ardoch
Glenfarg
Gateside
Strathmiglo
Falkland
Kingskettle
Greenloaning
Blackford
Glen Eagles
Steele's Knowe
Water of May
Lomond Hills
Freuchie
Kinbuck
Strathallan
Glendevon Resrs.
Glendevon
Milnathort
Kinnesswood
Glenrothes
Kennoway
Glen Devon
Kinross
Yetts o Muckhart
Dunblane
Ben Cleuch
L. Leven
Scotlandwell
Leslie
Markinch
Castle Campbell
Crook of Devon
Windygates
Bridge of Allan
Tillicoultry
Dollar
Cleish
Ballingry
Kinglassie
Menstrie
Alva
Powmill
Cleish Hills
Benarty Hill
Thornton
Wallace Mon.
Devon
Lochore
Auchterderran
Cardenden
E. Wemyss
Tullibody
Cambuskenneth
New Sauchie
Kelty
Crosshill
Fife Coastal Path
Stirling
Alloa
Saline
Lochgelly
Fallin
Clackmannan
Cowdenbeath
Auchtertool
Kirkcaldy
Bannockburn
Devilla Forest
Dunfermline
Cowie
Oakley
Carnock
Crossford
Crossgates
Auchenbowie
Kincardine
Culross
Kinghorn
Plean
Airth
Rosyth
Aberdour
Burntisland
Firth of Forth
Dunipace
Grangemouth
R. Forth
Charlestown
Dalgety Bay
Inchcolm
Inchkeith
Carron Bridge
Stenhousemuir
Larbert
Bo' Ness
Inverkeithing
Oxcars
Denny
Blackness Castle
N. Queensferry
Forth Bridge
Bonnybridge
Falkirk
The Binns
Hopetoun House
South Queensferry
Cramond Island
EDINBURGH
Redding
Polmont
Dalmeny
Leith
Cumbernauld
Shieldhill
Maddiston
Linlithgow
Kirkliston
Cramond
Restalrig
Prestonpans
Beecraigs
Winchburgh
Murrayfield
Portobello
Musselburgh
Slamannan
Avonbridge
Broxburn
Ingliston
Torphichen
Cairnpapple Hill
Uphall
Sighthill
Longriggend
Westfield
Riggend
Bathgate
Ratho
Armadale
Caldercruix
Hillend Resr.
Blackridge
Mid Calder
Wilkieston
Currie
Lasswade
Airdrie
Livingston
Kirknewton
Balerno
Loanhead
Dalkeith

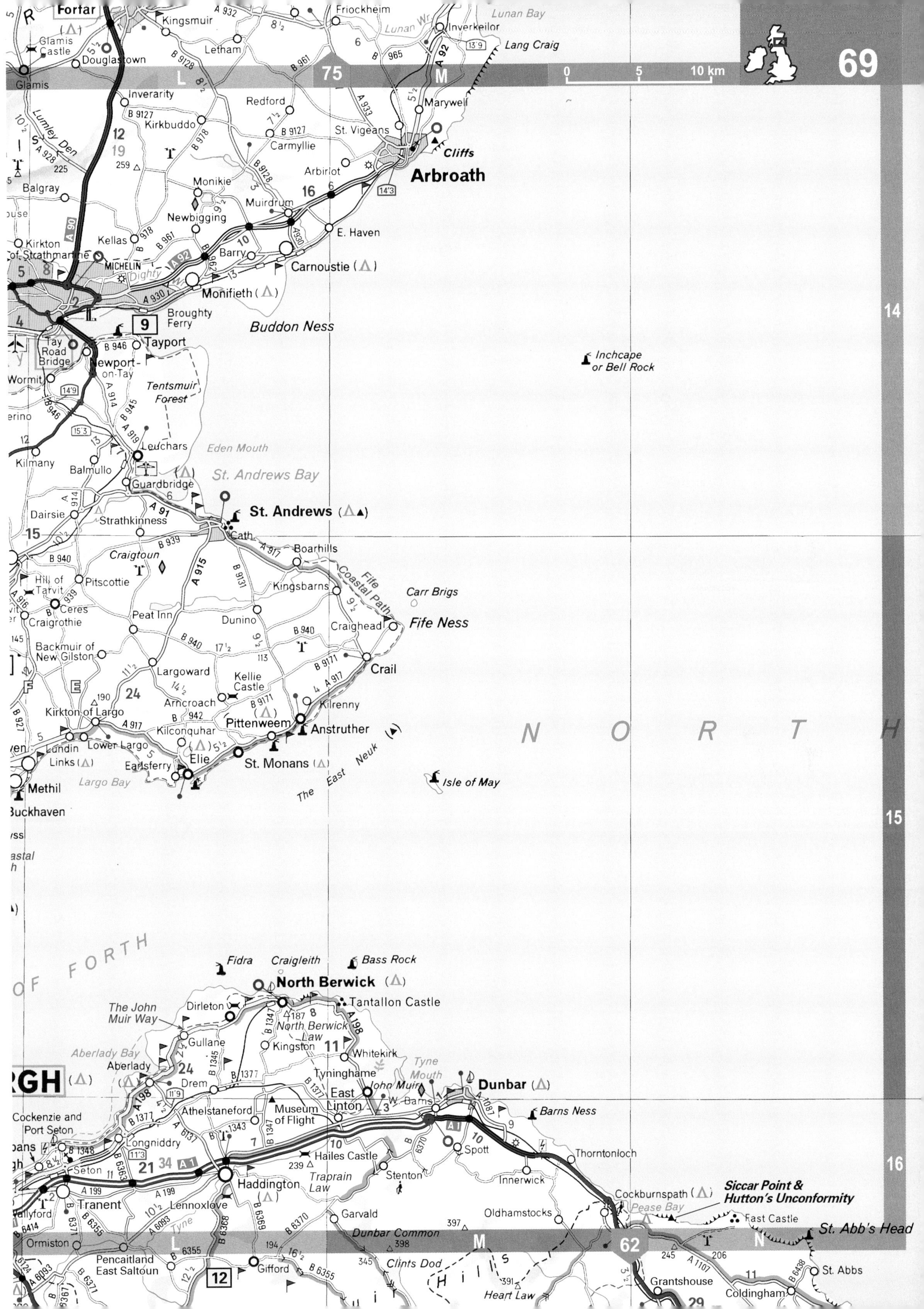

Forfar
Kingsmuir
Friockheim
Lunan Bay
Inverkeilor
Lang Craig
Glamis Castle
Douglastown
Letham
Glamis
75
0 5 10 km
Inverarity
Redford
Marywell
Kirkbuddo
Carmyllie
St. Vigeans
Cliffs
Lumley Den
Arbirlot
Arbroath
Balgray
Monikie
Muirdrum
Newbigging
E. Haven
Kellas
Barry
Kirkton of Strathmartine
MICHELIN
Carnoustie (△)
Dighty
Monifieth (△)
Broughty Ferry
Buddon Ness
9
Tayport
Tay Road Bridge
Newport-on-Tay
Wormit
Tentsmuir Forest
Inchcape or Bell Rock
14
Leuchars
Eden Mouth
Kilmany
Balmullo
St. Andrews Bay
Guardbridge
Dairsie
Strathkinness
St. Andrews (△▲)
Cath.
Boarhills
Craigtoun
Hill of Tarvit
Pitscottie
Kingsbarns
Fife Coastal Path
Carr Brigs
Ceres
Craigrothie
Peat Inn
Dunino
Craighead
Fife Ness
Backmuir of New Gilston
Largoward
Kellie Castle
Crail
Kilrenny
Arncroach
Kirkton of Largo
Pittenweem
Anstruther
NORTH
Kilconquhar
Lundin Links (△)
Lower Largo
Elie
St. Monans (△)
Earlsferry
The East Neuk
Largo Bay
Isle of May
Methil
Buckhaven
15
OF FORTH
Fidra
Craigleith
Bass Rock
North Berwick (△)
Tantallon Castle
The John Muir Way
Dirleton
North Berwick Law
Gullane
Kingston
Whitekirk
Aberlady Bay
Aberlady
Tyninghame
Tyne Mouth
Dunbar (△)
Drem
John Muir
East Linton
W. Barns
Barns Ness
Cockenzie and Port Seton
Athelstaneford
Museum of Flight
Longniddry
Spott
Thorntonloch
Hailes Castle
16
Seton
Haddington (△)
Traprain Law
Stenton
Innerwick
Cockburnspath (△)
Siccar Point & Hutton's Unconformity
Tranent
Lennoxlove
Garvald
Oldhamstocks
Pease Bay
Fast Castle
St. Abb's Head
Ormiston
Dunbar Common
62
Pencaitland
East Saltoun
Gifford
Clints Dod
Heart Law
St. Abbs
Grantshouse
Coldingham
12
29

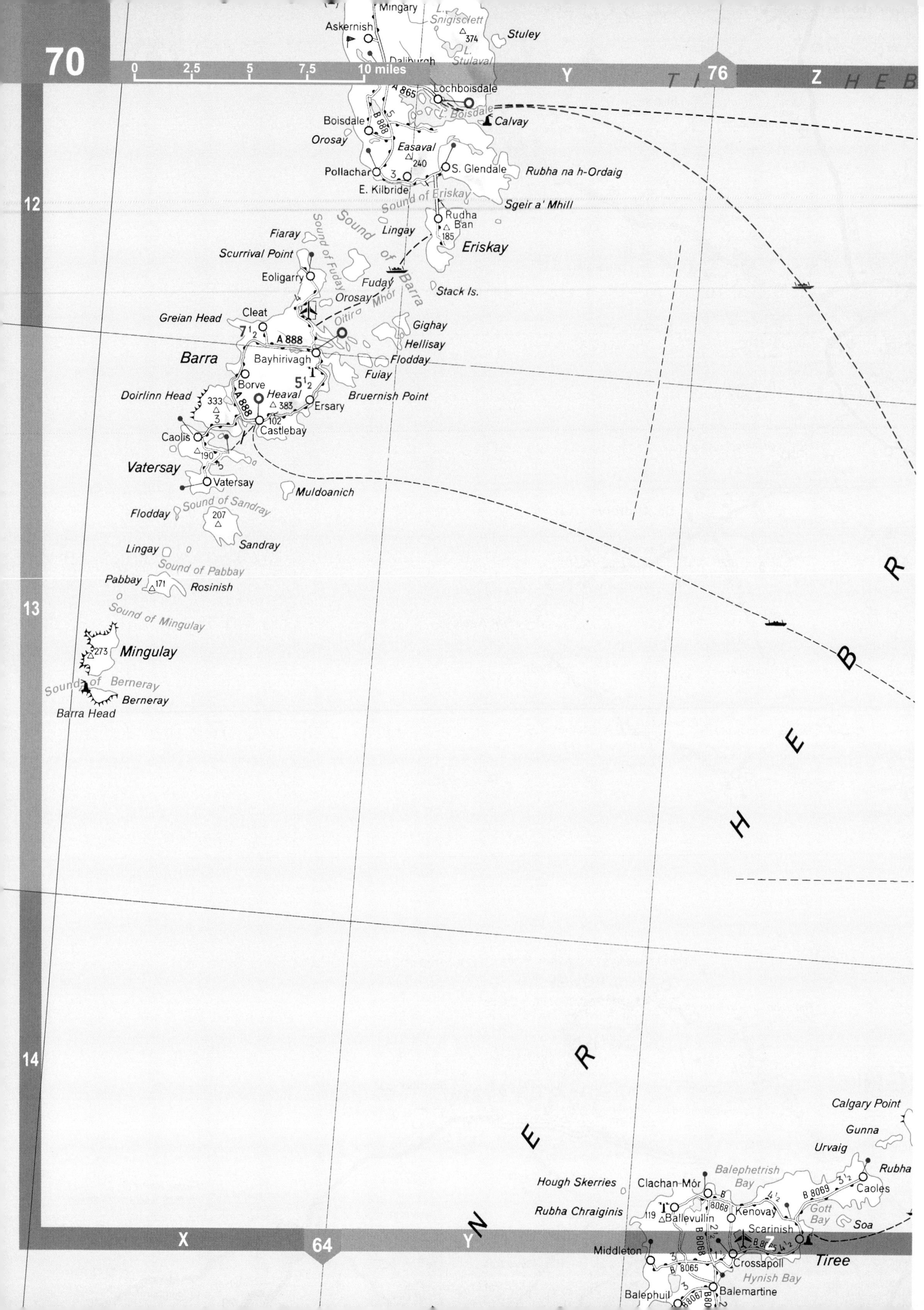
0
2.5
5
7.5
10 miles
Y
76
Z
X
64
Y
Z
12
13
14
Mingary
Askernish
L. Snigisclett
374
Stuley
Daliburgh
L. Stulaval
A 865
Lochboisdale
L. Boisdale
Calvay
Boisdale
B 888
Orosay
Easaval
240
Pollachar
3
S. Glendale
Rubha na h-Ordaig
E. Kilbride
Sound of Eriskay
Sgeir a' Mhill
Rudha Bàn
185
Eriskay
Sound of Barra
Sound of Fuday
Fiaray
Lingay
Scurrival Point
Eoligarry
Fuday
Stack Is.
Orosay
Oitir Mhòr
Greian Head
Cleat
7½
Gighay
A 888
Hellisay
Barra
Bayhirivagh
Flodday
Fuiay
5½
Borve
Bruernish Point
Doirlinn Head
333
Heaval
383
Ersary
A 888
102
Castlebay
Caolis
190
Vatersay
Vatersay
Muldoanich
Flodday
Sound of Sandray
207
Sandray
Lingay
Sound of Pabbay
Pabbay
171
Rosinish
Sound of Mingulay
273
Mingulay
Sound of Berneray
Berneray
Barra Head
T H E B R I D E S
H E B R I D E S
N E R
Calgary Point
Gunna
Urvaig
Rubha
Balephetrish Bay
Hough Skerries
Clachan Mór
B 8069
3½
Caoles
B 8068
Kenovay
Gott Bay
Soa
Rubha Chraiginis
119
Ballevullin
Scarinish
B 8068
2½
B 8065
Middleton
Crossapoll
Tiree
B 8065
Hynish Bay
Balephuil
Balemartine
B 8067

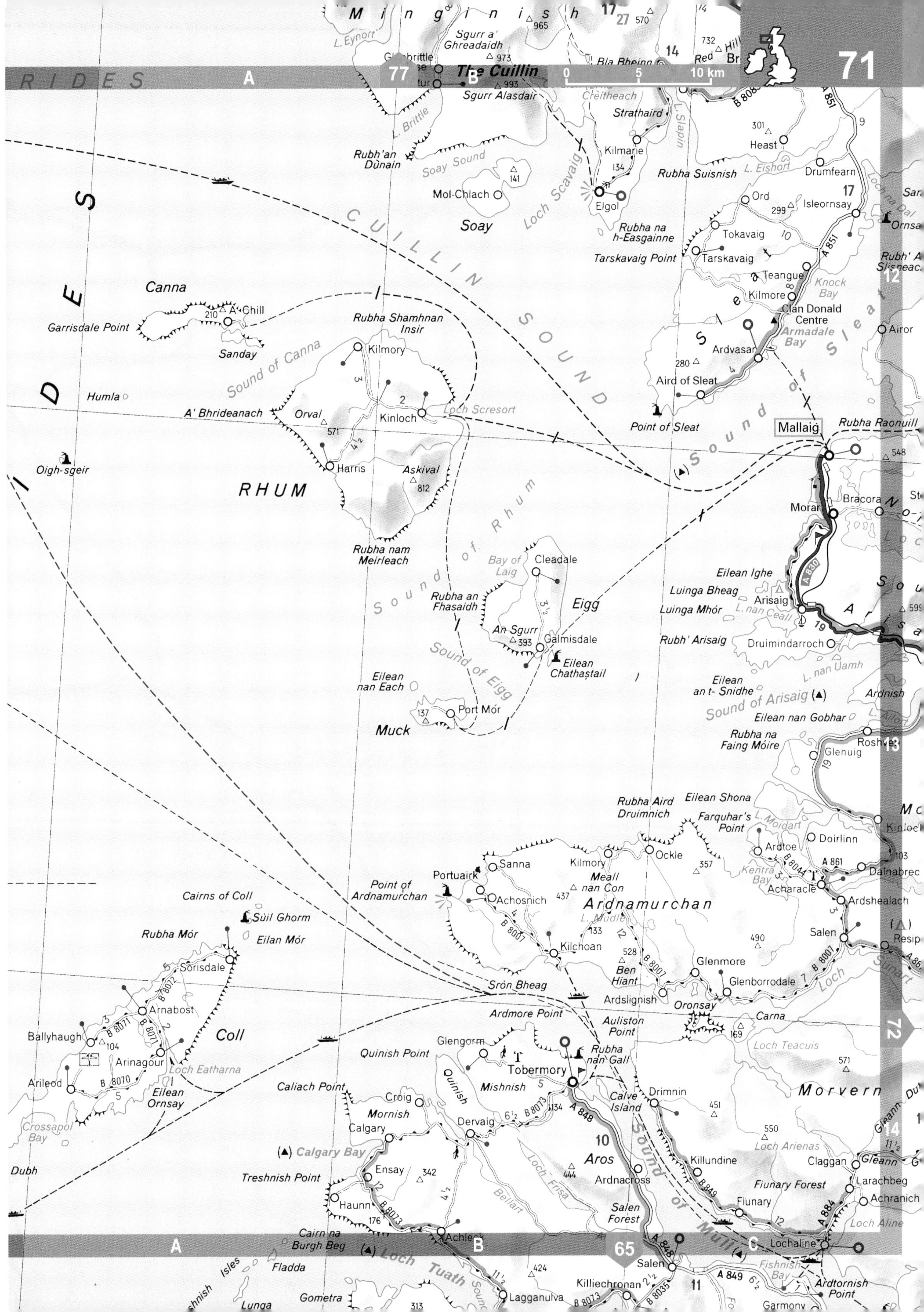
M i n g i n i s h
Sgurr a' Ghreadaidh
973
965
570
732
Red Hill
L. Eynort
Glenbrittle
The Cuillin
Sgurr Alasdair
993
Bla Bheinn
RIDES
A
B
77
0 5 10 km
Strathaird
L. Slapin
Kilmarie
134
L. Brittle
Rubh'an Dùnain
Soay Sound
141
Mol-Chlach
Soay
Loch Scavaig
Elgol
Rubha na h-Easgainne
Tarskavaig Point
Tarskavaig
Tokavaig
Ord
299
Isleornsay
Heast
301
Rubha Suisnish
L. Eishort
Drumfearn
Loch na Dal
Ornsay
Rubh' A Slisneach
Teangue
Knock Bay
Kilmore
Clan Donald Centre
Armadale Bay
Ardvasar
Airor
280
Aird of Sleat
Point of Sleat
Sound of Sleat
Mallaig
Rubha Raonuill
548
S l e a t
CUILLIN SOUND
Canna
Chill
210
Garrisdale Point
Sanday
Rubha Shamhnan Insir
Kilmory
Sound of Canna
Humla
A' Bhrideanach
Orval
571
Kinloch
Loch Scresort
Harris
Askival
812
Oigh-sgeir
RHUM
H E B R I D E S
Rubha nam Meirleach
Sound of Rhum
Bracora
Morar
Bay of Laig
Cleadale
Eigg
Rubha an Fhasaidh
An Sgurr
393
Galmisdale
Eilean Chathastail
Sound of Eigg
Eilean nan Each
137
Port Mór
Muck
Eilean Ighe
Luinga Bheag
Luinga Mhór
Arisaig
L. nan Ceall
Rubh' Arisaig
Druimindarroch
A 830
599
L. nan Uamh
Eilean an t- Snidhe
Sound of Arisaig
Ardnish
Eilean nan Gobhar
Rubha na Faing Móire
L. Ailort
Roshven
Glenuig
Rubha Aird Druimnich
Eilean Shona
Farquhar's Point
L. Moidart
Ardtoe
Dorlinn
Kinloch
103
A 861
Dalnabreck
Ockle
Kilmory
357
Sanna
Portuairk
Point of Ardnamurchan
Meall nan Con
437
Achosnich
Ardnamurchan
Kentra Bay
Acharacle
Ardshealach
L. Mudle
133
Cairns of Coll
Sùil Ghorm
Rubha Mór
Eilan Mór
B 8007
Kilchoan
528
Ben Hiant
490
Salen
Resipole
Sorisdale
Sròn Bheag
Glenmore
Glenborrodale
Loch Sunart
Ardslignish
Oronsay
Carna
Arnabost
Ardmore Point
Auliston Point
169
Ballyhaugh
104
B 8071
B 8072
Coll
Arinagour
Loch Eatharna
B 8070
Arileod
Eilean Ornsay
Crossapol Bay
Dubh
Quinish Point
Glengorm
Tobermory
Rubha nan Gall
Loch Teacuis
571
Caliach Point
Quinish
Mishnish
Drimnin
Morvern
Croig
Mornish
Calve Island
451
Dervaig
A 848
Calgary
Calgary Bay
550
Loch Arienas
Gleann Dubh
Aros
Ensay
342
444
Treshnish Point
Loch Frisa
Ardnacross
Killundine
Claggan
Larachbeg
Fiunary Forest
Achranich
Haunn
176
B 8073
Bellart
Salen Forest
Fiunary
Sound of Mull
Loch Aline
Cairn na Burgh Beg
Achleck
A
B
65
C
Lochaline
Salen
Fishnish Bay
Treshnish Isles
Fladda
Loch Tuath
424
A 849
Ardtornish Point
Gometra
Lunga
313
Lagganulva
Killiechronan
B 8035
Garmony
12
13
14
72

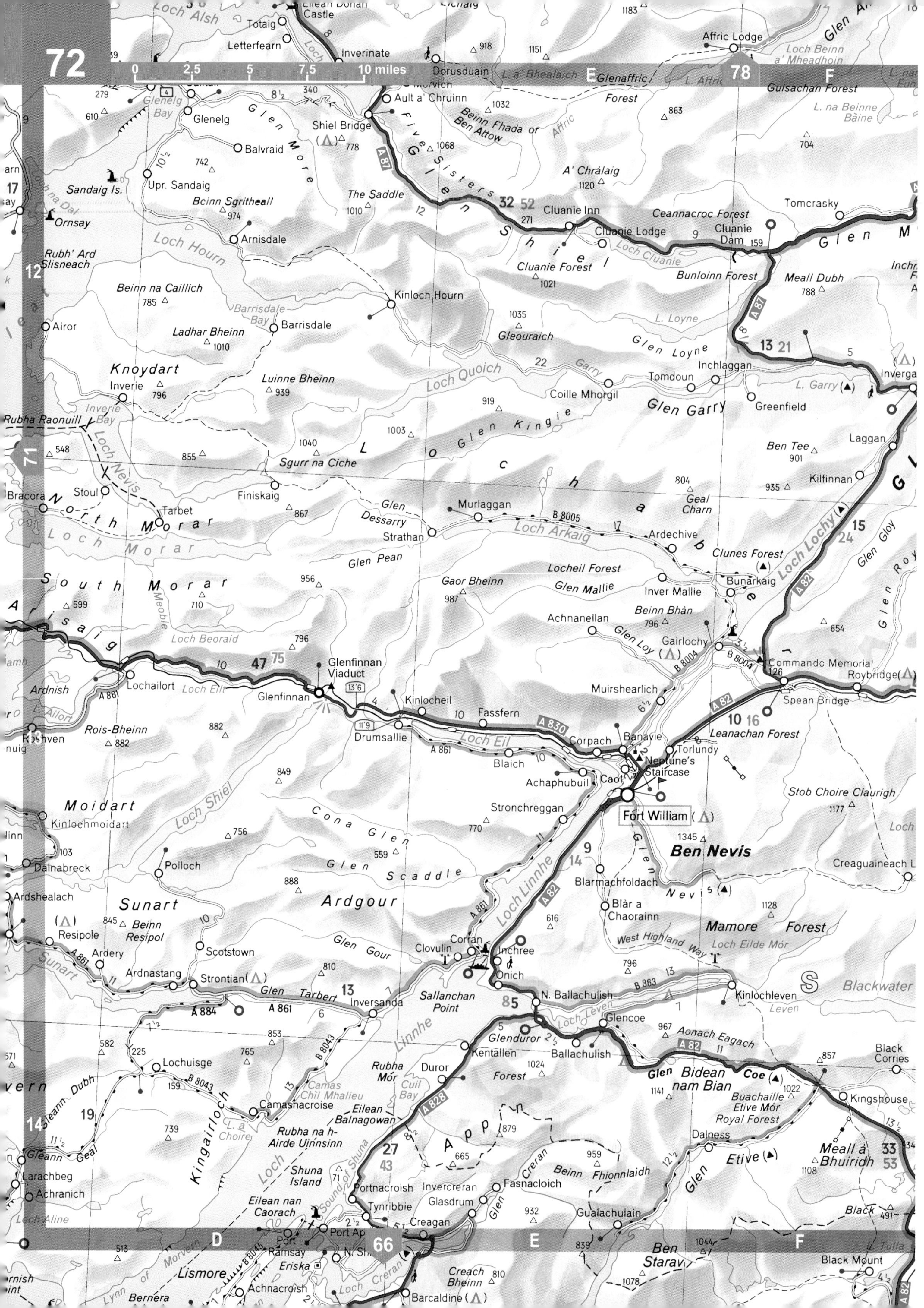
0 2.5 5 7.5 10 miles
Eilean Donan Castle
Totaig
Letterfearn
Inverinate
Dorusduain
Morvich
Ault a' Chruinn
Shiel Bridge
Glenelg
Glenelg Bay
Balvraid
Glen More
Five Sisters
Glen Shiel
Beinn Fhada or Ben Attow
Affric Lodge
Loch Beinn a' Mheadhoin
Glenaffric Forest
L. Affric
Guisachan Forest
L. na Beinne Bàine
L. a' Bhealaich
Upr. Sandaig
Sandaig Is.
Ornsay
Beinn Sgritheall
The Saddle
A' Chràlaig
Cluanie Inn
Cluanie Lodge
Loch Cluanie
Cluanie Forest
Ceannacroc Forest
Cluanie Dam
Tomcrasky
Glen Moriston
Bunloinn Forest
Meall Dubh
Arnisdale
Loch Hourn
Rubh' Ard Slisneach
Beinn na Caillich
Kinloch Hourn
Barrisdale Bay
Barrisdale
Airor
Ladhar Bheinn
Gleouraich
L. Loyne
Glen Loyne
Knoydart
Inverie
Inverie Bay
Luinne Bheinn
Loch Quoich
Garry
Tomdoun
Inchlaggan
Coille Mhorgil
Glen Garry
Greenfield
L. Garry
Invergarry
Rubha Raonuill
Loch Nevis
Loch Eil
Sgurr na Ciche
Glen Kingie
Loch Lochy
Ben Tee
Laggan
Kilfinnan
Bracora
Stoul
Tarbet
Finiskaig
North Morar
Loch Morar
Glen Dessarry
Murlaggan
Strathan
Loch Arkaig
Ardechive
Geal Charn
Clunes Forest
Glen Gloy
Glen Roy
Glen Pean
Locheil Forest
Glen Mallie
Inver Mallie
Bunarkaig
South Morar
Gaor Bheinn
Arisaig
Meoble
Loch Beoraid
Beinn Bhàn
Achnanellan
Glen Loy
Gairlochy
Commando Memorial
Roybridge
Spean Bridge
Ardnish
Lochailort
Loch Eilt
Loch Ailort
Glenfinnan
Glenfinnan Viaduct
Kinlocheil
Fassfern
Muirshearlich
Rois-Bheinn
Roshven
Drumsallie
Blaich
Corpach
Banavie
Torlundy
Leanachan Forest
Neptune's Staircase
Caol
Achaphubuil
Fort William
Stob Choire Claurigh
Moidart
Kinlochmoidart
Loch Shiel
Cona Glen
Stronchreggan
Ben Nevis
Glen Nevis
Dalnabreck
Polloch
Glen Scaddle
Blarmachfoldach
Creaguaineach Lodge
Ardshealach
Sunart
Ardgour
Blàr a Chaorainn
Beinn Resipol
Resipole
Ardery
Scotstown
Glen Gour
Clovulin
Corran
Inchree
Mamore Forest
West Highland Way
Loch Eilde Mór
Loch Sunart
Ardnastang
Strontian
Glen Tarbert
Inversanda
Sallanchan Point
Onich
N. Ballachulish
Kinlochleven
Blackwater
Loch Leven
Glencoe
Glenduror
Ballachulish
Kentallen
Aonach Eagach
Lochuisge
Loch Linnhe
Rubha Mór
Duror
Cuil Bay
Forest
Glen Coe
Bidean nam Bian
Black Corries
Kingshouse
Buachaille Etive Mór
Royal Forest
Camasnacroise
Camas Chil Mhalieu
Eilean Balnagowan
Kingairloch
Gleann Dubh
Gleann Geal
L. a' Choire
Rubha na h-Airde Uinnsinn
Appin
Dalness
Glen Etive
Meall a' Bhuiridh
Larachbeg
Achranich
Loch Aline
Shuna Island
Sound of Shuna
Portnacroish
Invercreran
Glen Creran
Fasnacloich
Beinn Fhionnlaidh
Tynribbie
Glasdrum
Eilean nan Caorach
Creagan
Gualachulain
Port Appin
Port Ramsay
Lismore
Eriska
N. Shian
Loch Creran
Ben Starav
Black Mount
L. Tulla
Lynn of Morvern
Bernera
Achnacroish
Creach Bheinn
Barcaldine
A 87
A 82
A 830
A 861
A 884
A 828
B 8005
B 8004
B 863
B 8043
B 8045

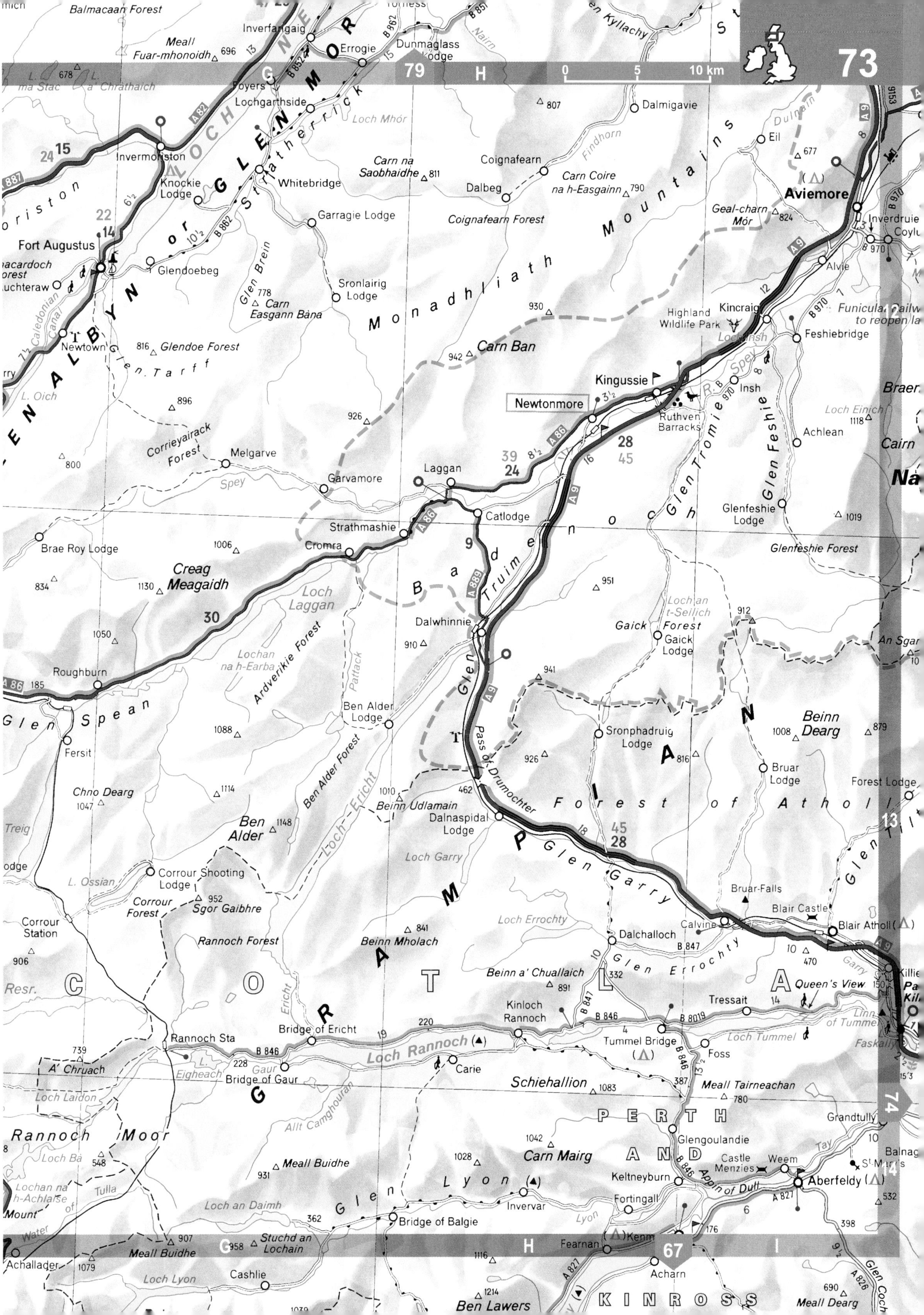
Balmacaan Forest
Inverfarigaig
Meall Fuar-mhonoidh 696
Errogie
Dunmaglass Lodge
Kyllachy
79
G
H
0 5 10 km
678
L. ma Stac
L. a' Chrathaich
Foyers
Lochgarthside
807
Dalmigavie
Loch Mhór
A 82
LOCH NESS
GLEN MOR
Stratherrick
Findhorn
Eil
Dulnain
15
24
Invermoriston
Carn na Saobhaidhe 811
Coignafearn
Carn Coire na h-Easgainn 790
677
Aviemore
A 887
Knockie Lodge
Whitebridge
Dalbeg
Monadhliath Mountains
Inverdruie
Coylum
Garragie Lodge
Coignafearn Forest
Geal-charn Mór 824
22
14
B 862
B 970
Fort Augustus
A 9
Glendoebeg
Alvie
Inchnacardoch Forest
Auchteraw
Glen Brein
Sronlairig Lodge
778 Carn Easgann Bàna
930
Highland Wildlife Park
Kincraig
Funicular Railway to reopen
Caledonian Canal
Newtown
816 Glendoe Forest
Feshiebridge
Loch Insh
942
Carn Ban
GLEN ALBYN
Glen Tarff
Kingussie
Insh
Spey
Braeriach
L. Oich
896
Newtonmore
Ruthven Barracks
Loch Einich
1118
926
Achlean
Cairn
Corrieyairack Forest
Melgarve
A 86
28
45
800
39
24
Laggan
Spey
Garvamore
Glen Tromie
Glen Feshie
Catlodge
Glenfeshie Lodge
1019
Strathmashie
Brae Roy Lodge
1006
Cromra
9
Badenoch
Glenfeshie Forest
Creag Meagaidh
834
1130
Loch Laggan
A 889
Truim
951
Loch an t-Seilich
30
Dalwhinnie
912
Gaick Forest
Gaick Lodge
1050
Ardverikie Forest
910
Lochan na h-Earba
Pattack
An Sgarsoch
Roughburn
185
941
Glen Spean
Ben Alder Lodge
Glen Garry
Beinn Dearg
1008
879
Fersit
1088
Sronphadruig Lodge
Pass of Drumochter
926
816
Bruar Lodge
Ben Alder Forest
Chno Dearg 1047
1114
1010
462
Forest Lodge
Beinn Udlamain
Dalnaspidal Lodge
Forest of Atholl
Treig
Ben Alder 1148
Loch Ericht
GRAMPIAN
Glen Tilt
Loch Garry
13
Lodge
L. Ossian
Corrour Shooting Lodge
Bruar Falls
Corrour Forest
952
Sgor Gaibhre
Blair Castle
Corrour Station
Loch Errochty
Calvine
Blair Atholl
841
Dalchalloch
Rannoch Forest
Beinn Mholach
B 847
470
906
Glen Errochty
Beinn a' Chuallaich 891
332
SCOTLAND
Queen's View
Killiecrankie
Resr.
Kinloch Rannoch
Tressait
Pitlochry
B 846
B 8019
Linn of Tummel
Loch Tummel
Rannoch Sta
Bridge of Ericht
220
Tummel Bridge
Foss
Faskally
739
Loch Rannoch
A' Chruach
L. Eigheach
228
Gaur
Bridge of Gaur
Carie
Schiehallion 1083
387
Meall Tairneachan
Loch Laidon
780
74
PERTH AND KINROSS
Allt Camghouran
Grandtully
Rannoch Moor
1042
Glengoulandie
Loch Bà
548
Meall Buidhe
1028
Carn Mairg
Castle Menzies
Weem
St Mary's
Lochan na h-Achlaise
931
Keltneyburn
Aberfeldy
Tulla
Mount
Glen Lyon
Appin of Dull
A 827
532
Loch an Daimh
Fortingall
Water
362
Invervar
Lyon
398
907
Bridge of Balgie
Stuchd an Lochain
176
Achallader
958
Meall Buidhe
1079
1116
Fearnan
Kenmore
67
Acharn
Glen Cochill
Loch Lyon
Cashlie
A 826
1214
Ben Lawers
690
Meall Dearg

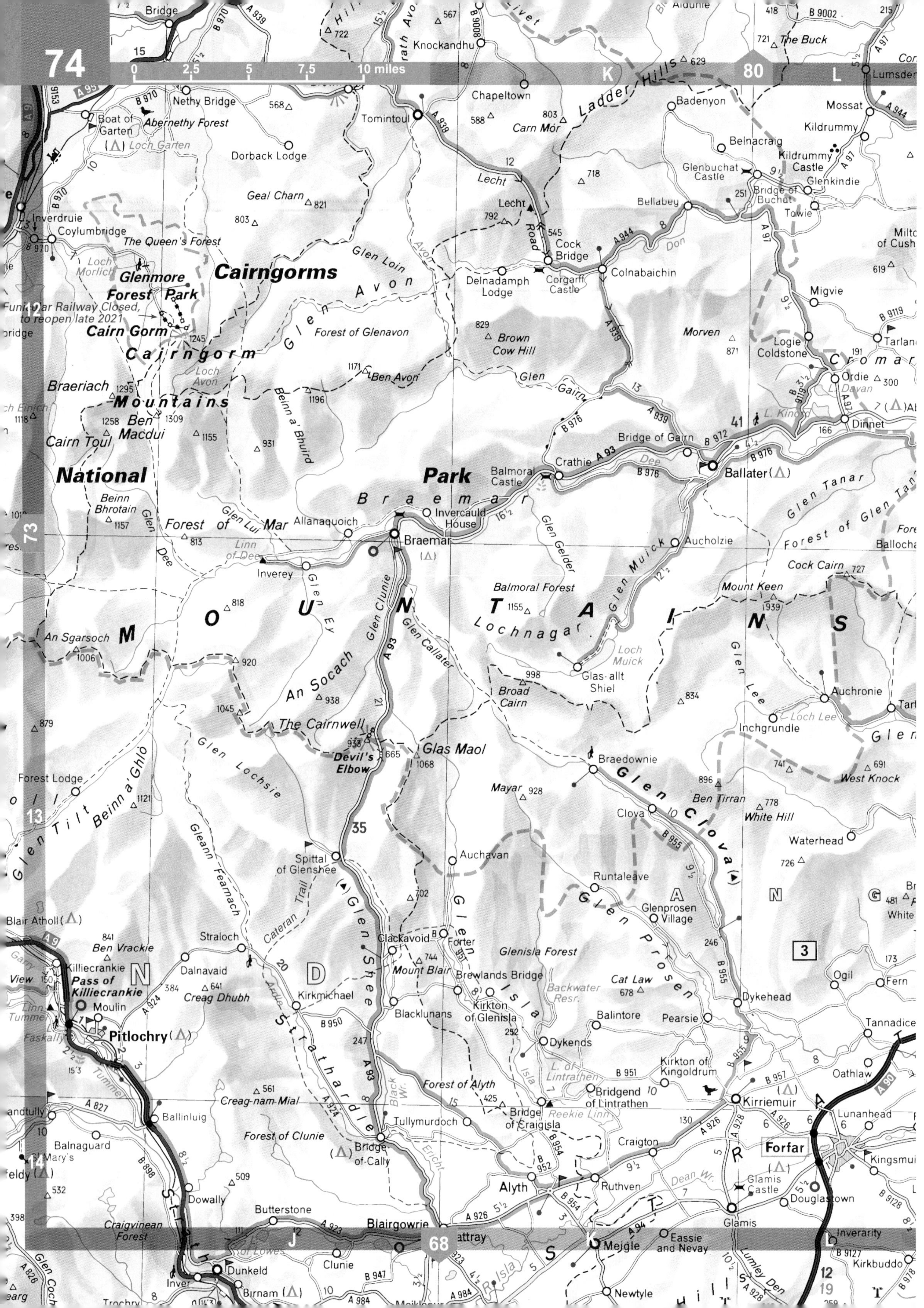

0 2,5 5 7,5 10 miles
Cairngorms National Park
Cairngorm Mountains
Glenmore Forest Park
Funicular Railway Closed, to reopen late 2021
Cairn Gorm
Braeriach
Ben Macdui
Cairn Toul
Aviemore
Boat of Garten
Nethy Bridge
Abernethy Forest
Loch Garten
Dorback Lodge
Geal Charn
Inverdruie
Coylumbridge
The Queen's Forest
Loch Morlich
Tomintoul
Knockandhu
Chapeltown
Carn Mór
Ladder Hills
Lecht
Lecht Road
Cock Bridge
Corgarff Castle
Delnadamph Lodge
Glen Loin
Glen Avon
Forest of Glenavon
Ben Avon
Beinn a' Bhuird
Loch Avon
Brown Cow Hill
Glen Gairn
Badenyon
Belnacraig
Glenbuchat Castle
Bridge of Buchat
Bellabeg
Colnabaichin
Mossat
Kildrummy
Kildrummy Castle
Glenkindie
Towie
Migvie
Morven
Logie Coldstone
Cromar
Ordie
Dinnet
L. Davan
L. Kinord
Lumsden
The Buck
Tarland
Bridge of Gairn
Ballater
Crathie
Balmoral Castle
Braemar
Invercauld House
Allanaquoich
Forest of Mar
Glen Lui
Linn of Dee
Inverey
Glen Ey
Beinn Bhrotain
Glen Dee
Glen Clunie
Glen Callater
Glen Gelder
Glen Muick
Aucholzie
Glen Tanar
Forest of Glen Tanar
Ballochan
Cock Cairn
Mount Keen
Balmoral Forest
Lochnagar
Loch Muick
Glas-allt Shiel
Broad Cairn
Glen Lee
Loch Lee
Auchronie
Inchgrundle
West Knock
An Sgarsoch
MOUNTAINS
An Socach
The Cairnwell
Devil's Elbow
Glas Maol
Braedownie
Glen Clova
Clova
Ben Tirran
White Hill
Waterhead
Mayar
Glen Lochsie
Forest Lodge
Glen Tilt
Beinn a' Ghlò
Gleann Fearnach
Spittal of Glenshee
Auchavan
Runtaleave
Glen Prosen
Glenprosen Village
Cateran Trail
Glen Shee
Glen Isla
Clackavoid
Forter
Mount Blair
Glenisla Forest
Brewlands Bridge
Kirkton of Glenisla
Backwater Resr.
Cat Law
Dykehead
Blair Atholl
Ben Vrackie
Killiecrankie
Pass of Killiecrankie
Straloch
Dalnavaid
Creag Dhubh
Kirkmichael
Strathardle
Blacklunans
Balintore
Pearsie
Dykends
Moulin
Pitlochry
Loch Tummel
Faskally
Ballinluig
Creag-nam-Mial
Forest of Alyth
Bridge of Craigisla
Reekie Linn
L. of Lintrathen
Bridgend of Lintrathen
Kirkton of Kingoldrum
Kirriemuir
Tullymurdoch
Forest of Clunie
Bridge of Cally
Alyth
Craigton
Ruthven
Glamis Castle
Glamis
Forfar
Douglastown
Kingsmuir
Lunanhead
Oathlaw
Tannadice
Ogil
Fern
Balnaguard
St Mary's
Dowally
Craigvinean Forest
Butterstone
Blairgowrie
Rattray
Clunie
Dunkeld
Birnam
Inver
Meigle
Eassie and Nevay
Newtyle
Kirkbuddo
Inverarity
Strathmore
Dean Wr.
Lumley Den
Ardle
Black Wr.
Ericht
R. Isla
Don
Dee
Avon
Garry
Tummel

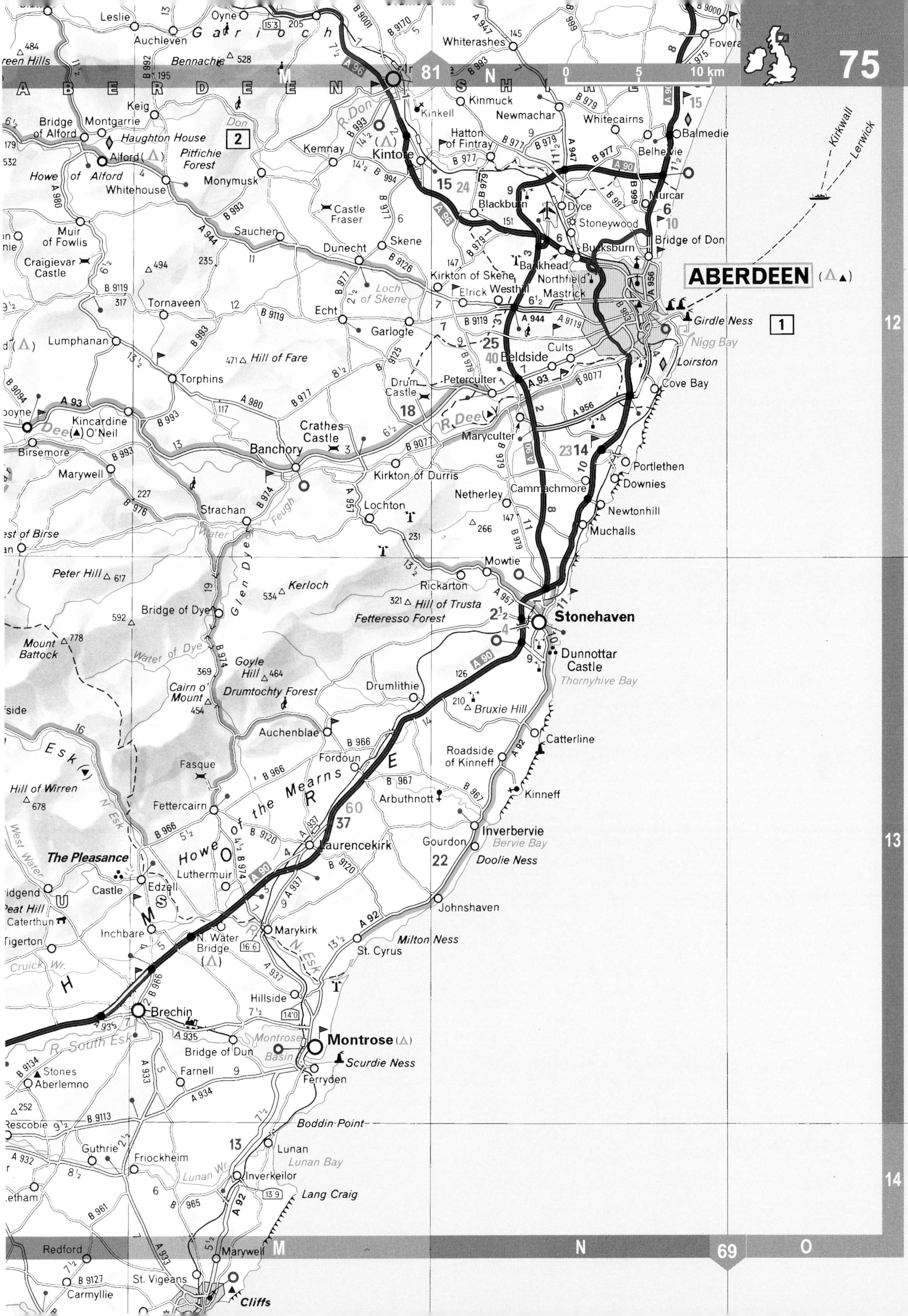

ABERDEEN
Stonehaven
Montrose
Brechin
Banchory
Laurencekirk
Kintore
Alford
Inverbervie
Johnshaven
St. Cyrus
Dunnottar Castle
Crathes Castle
Drum Castle
Castle Fraser
Craigievar Castle
Girdle Ness
Nigg Bay
Cove Bay
Portlethen
Newtonhill
Muchalls
Catterline
Kinneff
Gourdon
Milton Ness
Scurdie Ness
Ferryden
Lunan Bay
Inverkeilor
Lang Craig
Boddin Point
Cliffs
Howe of the Mearns
Fetteresso Forest
Drumtochty Forest
Hill of Fare
Bennachie
Garioch
Glen Dye
Fettercairn
Edzell
Marykirk
Westhill
Dyce
Bucksburn
Peterculter
Cults
Kirkwall
Lerwick
0 5 10 km
81
69
12
13
14

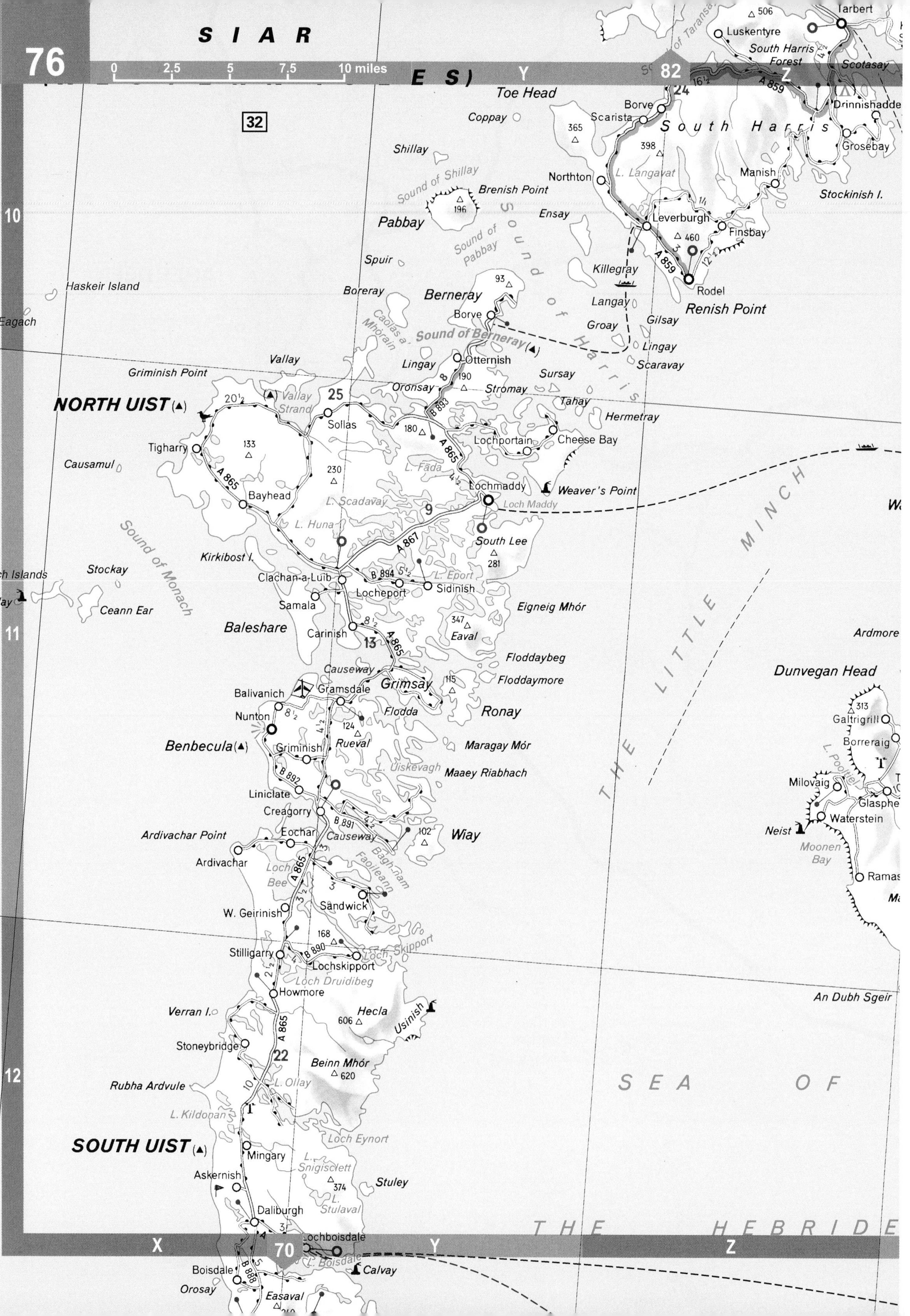
SIAR
0 2.5 5 7.5 10 miles
ES)
Y
82
Z
X
70
10
11
12
32
Tarbert
506
Luskentyre
South Harris Forest
Scotasay
Toe Head
Coppay
Borve
Scarista
365
South Harris
Drinnishadder
Grosebay
398
Shillay
Sound of Shillay
Brenish Point
196
Northton
L. Langavat
Manish
Stockinish I.
Pabbay
Ensay
Leverburgh
Finsbay
460
A 859
Sound of Pabbay
Sound of Harris
Spuir
Killegray
Rodel
Renish Point
Haskeir Island
Boreray
Berneray
93
Borve
Langay
eir Eagach
Caolas a' Mhòrain
Sound of Berneray
Groay
Gilsay
Lingay
Scaravay
Vallay
Lingay
Otternish
Sursay
190
Griminish Point
Oronsay
Stromay
Tahay
NORTH UIST
Valley Strand
25
Sollas
B 893
Hermetray
Tigharry
133
180
A 865
Lochportain
Cheese Bay
Causamul
230
L. Fada
A 865
Bayhead
Lochmaddy
Weaver's Point
L. Scadavay
9
Loch Maddy
THE LITTLE MINCH
Sound of Monach
L. Huna
South Lee
A 867
281
Kirkibost I.
Stockay
Clachan-a-Luib
B 894
L. Eport
Sidinish
nach Islands
Locheport
hillay
Ceann Ear
Samala
Eigneig Mhór
Baleshare
Carinish
347
Eaval
13
A 865
Ardmore
Floddaybeg
Causeway
Grimsay
Dunvegan Head
115
Floddaymore
Balivanich
Gramsdale
Flodda
Ronay
313
Nunton
Galtrigrill
124
Benbecula
Griminish
Rueval
Maragay Mór
Borreraig
B 892
L. Uiskevagh
Maaey Riabhach
L. Pooltiel
Liniclate
Milovaig
Creagorry
B 891
Glasphe
Waterstein
Ardivachar Point
Eochar
Causeway
102
Wiay
Neist
Ardivachar
Loch Bee
A 865
Bagh nam Faoileann
Moonen Bay
Ramas
Sandwick
W. Geirinish
168
Stilligarry
B 890
Loch Skipport
Lochskipport
Loch Druidibeg
An Dubh Sgeir
Howmore
Hecla
Verran I.
606
Usinish
A 865
Stoneybridge
22
Beinn Mhór
620
Rubha Ardvule
L. Ollay
SEA OF
L. Kildonan
SOUTH UIST
Loch Eynort
Mingary
L. Snigisclett
Stuley
Askernish
374
L. Stulaval
Daliburgh
THE HEBRIDE
Lochboisdale
L. Boisdale
Calvay
Boisdale
B 888
Orosay
Easaval

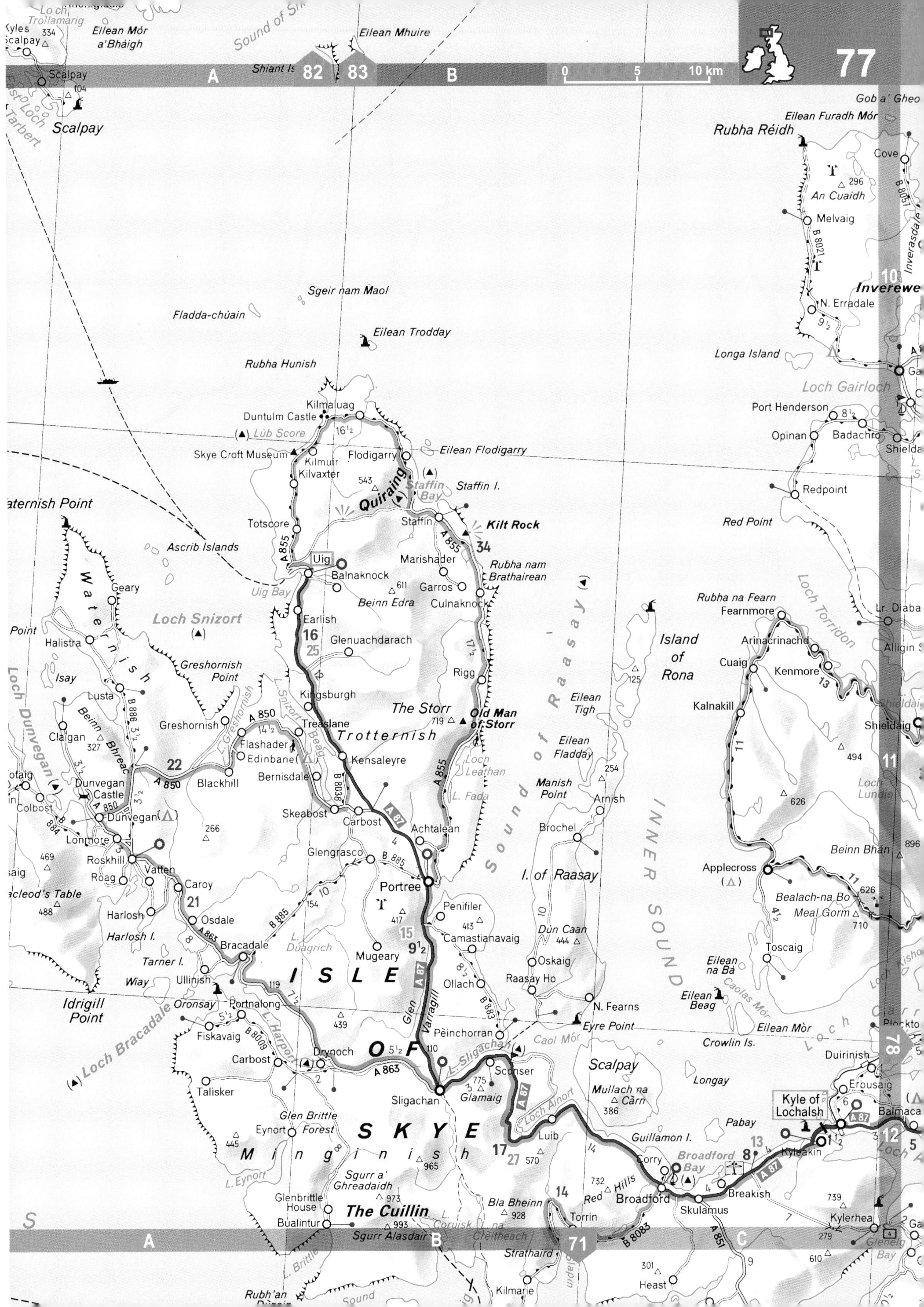
A
B
C
82
83
71
78
0
5
10 km
Scalpay
East Loch Tarbert
Shiant Is
Eilean Mhuire
Eilean Mór a'Bhàigh
Sound of Shiant
Gob a' Gheodha
Eilean Furadh Mór
Rubha Réidh
Cove
An Cuaidh
Melvaig
Inverewe
N. Erradale
Longa Island
Loch Gairloch
Port Henderson
Opinan
Badachro
Shieldaig
Redpoint
Red Point
Sgeir nam Maol
Fladda-chùain
Eilean Trodday
Rubha Hunish
Kilmaluag
Duntulm Castle
Lùb Score
Skye Croft Museum
Kilmuir
Kilvaxter
Flodigarry
Eilean Flodigarry
Quiraing
Staffin Bay
Staffin I.
Staffin
Kilt Rock
Waternish Point
Ascrib Islands
Totscore
Uig
Uig Bay
Balnaknock
Marishader
Garros
Culnaknock
Rubha nam Brathairean
Beinn Edra
Earlish
Glenuachdarach
Rigg
The Storr
Old Man of Storr
Kingsburgh
Treaslane
Trotternish
Kensaleyre
Loch Snizort
Waternish
Geary
Halistra
Greshornish Point
Isay
Lusta
Beinn Bhreac
Claigan
Greshornish
Flashader
Edinbane
Blackhill
Bernisdale
Skeabost
Carbost
Loch Dunvegan
Dunvegan Castle
Dunvegan
Colbost
Lonmore
Roskhill
Vatten
Roag
Caroy
Macleod's Table
Harlosh
Harlosh I.
Osdale
Tarner I.
Bracadale
Wiay
Ullinish
Idrigill Point
Oronsay
Portnalong
Loch Bracadale
Fiskavaig
Carbost
Talisker
Achtalean
Glengrasco
Portree
Penifiler
Camastianavaig
L. Duagrich
Mugeary
ISLE OF SKYE
Ollach
Glen Varragill
Drynoch
L. Harport
L. Sligachan
Sligachan
Sconser
Glamaig
Peinchorran
Loch Leathan
L. Fada
Sound of Raasay
Eilean Tigh
Eilean Fladday
Manish Point
Arnish
Brochel
I. of Raasay
Dùn Caan
Oskaig
Raasay Ho
N. Fearns
Eyre Point
Caol Mór
Scalpay
Mullach na Càrn
Island of Rona
INNER SOUND
Rubha na Fearn
Fearnmore
Loch Torridon
Arinacrinachd
Cuaig
Kenmore
Kalnakill
Shieldaig
Alligin
Lr. Diabaig
Loch Lundie
Applecross
Beinn Bhán
Bealach-na Bo
Meal Gorm
Toscaig
Eilean na Bà
Caolas Mór
Eilean Beag
Eilean Mòr
Crowlin Is.
Longay
Pabay
Guillamon I.
Loch Ainort
Luib
Corry
Broadford Bay
Broadford
Skulamus
Breakish
Kyle of Lochalsh
Kyleakin
Erbusaig
Duirinish
Plockton
Balmacara
Kylerhea
Glenelg Bay
Glen Brittle Forest
Eynort
Minginish
L. Eynort
Sgurr a' Ghreadaidh
Glenbrittle House
Bualintur
The Cuillin
Sgurr Alasdair
L. Coruisk
Bla Bheinn
Red Hills
Torrin
Strathaird
Kilmarie
Heast
Rubh'an Dùnain
Soay Sound
A 855
A 850
A 87
A 863
A 851
B 885
B 886
B 884
B 8036
B 883
B 8009
B 8083
B 8021
B 8056
334
104
296
543
611
719
327
469
266
488
154
417
413
444
254
125
494
626
896
626
710
119
439
110
775
386
445
965
973
993
928
732
570
739
279
610
301

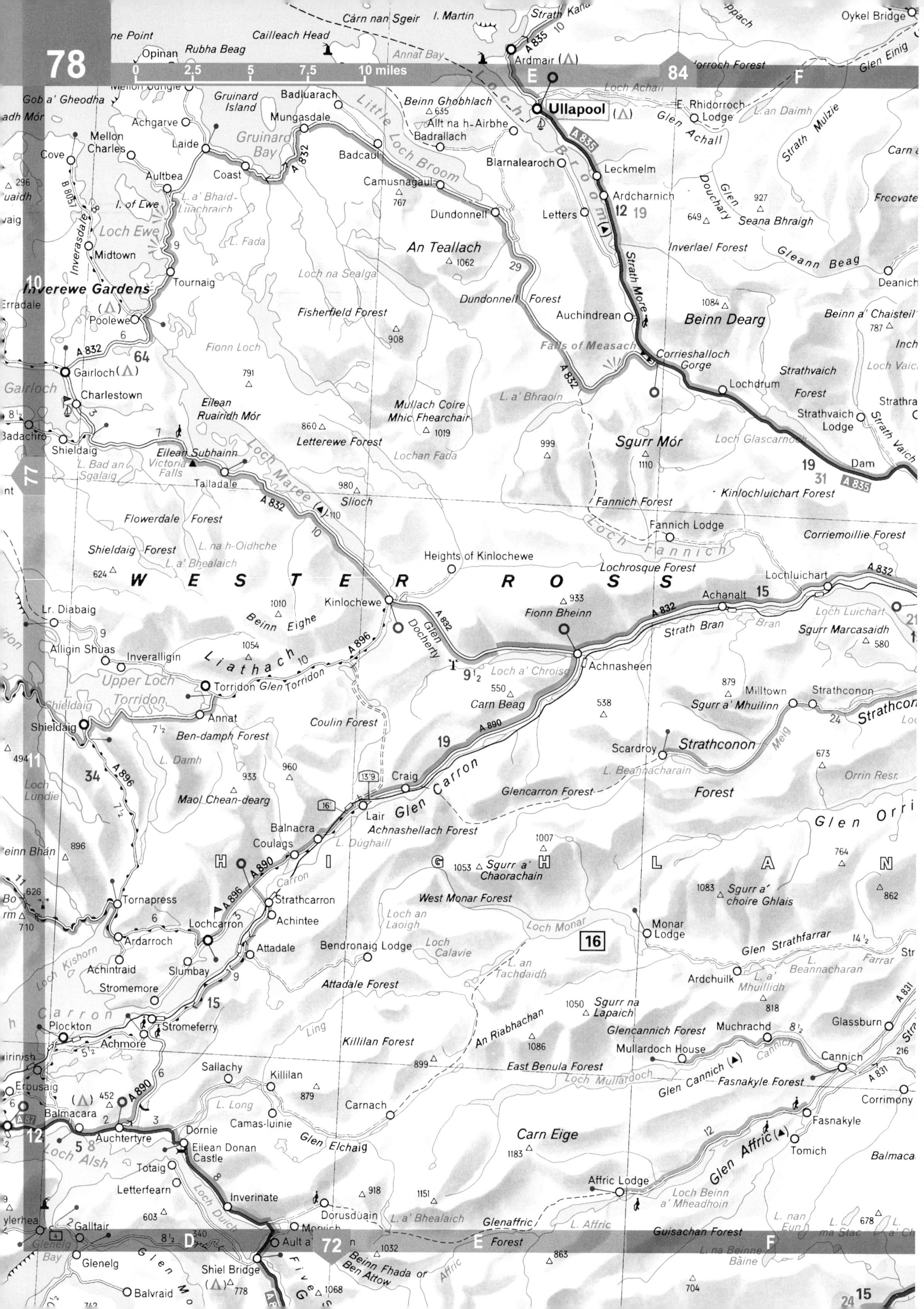

0 2.5 5 7.5 10 miles
84
77
72
E
F
D
Càrn nan Sgeir
I. Martin
Strath Kanaird
Oykel Bridge
Rubha Beag
Cailleach Head
Opinan
Annat Bay
Ardmair
Glen Einig
Corriemulzie
Rhidorroch Forest
Gob a' Gheodha
Gruinard Island
Badluarach
Mungasdale
Little Loch Broom
Beinn Ghobhlach
635
Allt na h-Airbhe
Loch Achall
Ullapool
E. Rhidorroch Lodge
Glen Achall
L. an Daimh
Strath Mulzie
Achgarve
Mellon Charles
Laide
Gruinard Bay
A 832
Badrallach
A 835
Carn a'
Cove
Aultbea
Coast
Badcaul
Blarnalearoch
Leckmelm
Strath
296
B 8057
I. of Ewe
L. a' Bhaid-Luachraich
Camusnagaul
767
Loch Broom
Ardcharnich
Glen Douchary
927
Freevater
Inverasdale
Loch Ewe
Dundonnell
Letters
12 19
649
Seana Bhraigh
Midtown
L. Fada
9
An Teallach
1062
Inverlael Forest
Gleann Beag
10
Inverewe Gardens
Tournaig
Loch na Sealga
29
Strath More
Deanich
Erradale
Dundonnell Forest
1084
Beinn a' Chaisteil
Poolewe
Fisherfield Forest
Auchindrean
Beinn Dearg
787
6
908
Inchbae
A 832
64
Fionn Loch
Falls of Measach
Corrieshalloch Gorge
Loch Vaich
Gairloch
791
A 832
Strathvaich
Lochdrum
Forest
Gairloch
Charlestown
L. a' Bhraoin
Strathrannoch
Eilean Ruairidh Mór
Mullach Coire Mhic Fhearchair
Strathvaich Lodge
8½
860
1019
Strath Vaich
Badachro
7
Letterewe Forest
999
Sgurr Mór
Loch Glascarnoch
Shieldaig
Eilean Subhainn
Loch Maree
Lochan Fada
1110
19
Dam
L. Bad an Sgalaig
Victoria Falls
31
A 835
Talladale
980
Slioch
Kinlochluichart Forest
A 832
110
Fannich Forest
Flowerdale Forest
10
Fannich Lodge
Corriemoillie Forest
L. na h-Oidhche
Loch Fannich
Shieldaig Forest
Heights of Kinlochewe
L. a' Bhealaich
Lochrosque Forest
A 832
624
W E S T E R R O S S
Lochluichart
933
Achanalt
15
Lr. Diabaig
1010
Kinlochewe
Fionn Bheinn
A 832
Loch Luichart
Beinn Eighe
Glen Docherty
Bran
Sgurr Marcasaidh
9
A 832
Strath Bran
580
Alligin Shuas
1054
A 896
Inverallgin
Liathach
10
Loch a' Chroisg
Achnasheen
Upper Loch Torridon
Torridon
Glen Torridon
9½
879
Milltown
Strathconon
550
Sgurr a' Mhuilinn
Shieldaig
Annat
Carn Beag
538
24
Strathconon
7½
Coulin Forest
A 890
Shieldaig
Ben-damph Forest
19
Scardroy
Strathconon
494
11
L. Damh
Meig
673
34
A 896
960
L. Beannacharain
Orrin Resr.
Loch Lundie
933
13'9
Craig
Glen Carron
Glencarron Forest
Forest
Maol Chean-dearg
7½
16'
Lair
Glen
Glen Orrin
Achnashellach Forest
Balnacra
Coulags
L. Dùghaill
1007
H I G H L A N
764
Beinn Bhàn
896
1053
Sgurr a' Chaorachain
A 890
Carron
1083
Sgurr a' choire Ghlais
862
626
Tornapress
A 896
Strathcarron
West Monar Forest
710
6
Achintee
Loch an Laoigh
Loch Monar
Monar Lodge
Ardarroch
Lochcarron
Loch Calavie
16
Glen Strathfarrar
14½
Loch Kishorn
Attadale
Bendronaig Lodge
Farrar
Achintraid
Slumbay
L. an Tachdaidh
L. Beannacharan
Ardchuilk
L. a' Mhuillidh
Stromemore
9
Attadale Forest
A 831
15
1050
Sgurr na Lapaich
818
Loch Carron
Stromeferry
An Riabhachan
Glassburn
Plockton
Ling
Glencannich Forest
Muchrachd
8½
Achmore
Killilan Forest
1086
Cannich
5½
Mullardoch House
216
899
East Benula Forest
Cannich
6
Sallachy
Killilan
Loch Mullardoch
Glen Cannich
Fasnakyle Forest
A 831
Erbusaig
879
452
L. Long
Corrimony
A 890
Balmacara
Carnach
Fasnakyle
A 87
2
Camas-luinie
3
Dornie
12
Glen Elchaig
Carn Eige
Glen Affric
Tomich
Auchtertyre
Eilean Donan Castle
12
5 8
1183
Loch Alsh
Balmacara
Totaig
Letterfearn
Loch Duich
918
1151
Affric Lodge
Loch Beinn a' Mheadhoin
Inverinate
603
Dorusduain
L. a' Bhealaich
Glenaffric
L. Affric
Galltair
Morvich
Guisachan Forest
L. nan Eun
678
Glenelg Bay
8½
340
Ault a' chruinn
1032
Forest
Glenelg
Shiel Bridge
Ben Fhada or Ben Attow
863
Affric
L. na Beinne Bàine
Glen More
Balvraid
778
Five Sisters
1068
704
24 15

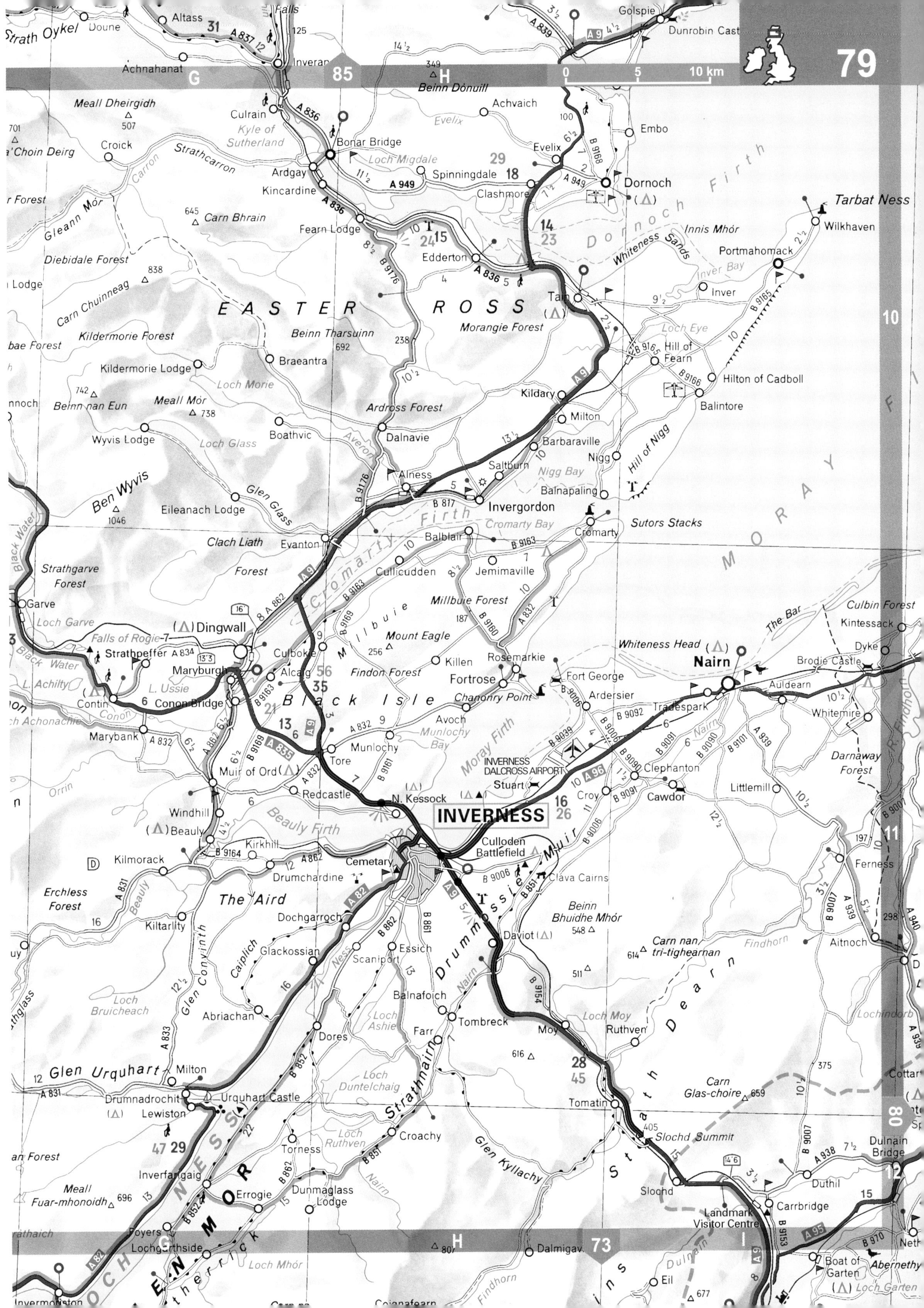
Strath Oykel
Doune
Altass
Falls
Inveran
Achnahanat
Golspie
Dunrobin Cast
0 5 10 km
Beinn Donuill
Meall Dheirgidh
Achvaich
Evelix
Culrain
Kyle of Sutherland
Croick
Bonar Bridge
Loch Migdale
Embo
Strathcarron
Carron
Ardgay
Spinningdale
Dornoch
Kincardine
Clashmore
Carn Bhrain
Fearn Lodge
Dornoch Firth
Tarbat Ness
Wilkhaven
Gleann Mór
Diebidale Forest
Edderton
Whiteness Sands
Innis Mhór
Portmahomack
Inver Bay
Inver
Carn Chuinneag
EASTER ROSS
Tain
Morangie Forest
Kildermorie Forest
Beinn Tharsuinn
Loch Eye
Hill of Fearn
Braeantra
Kildermorie Lodge
Loch Morie
Hilton of Cadboll
Beinn nan Eun
Meall Mór
Kildary
Balintore
Ardross Forest
Wyvis Lodge
Loch Glass
Boathvic
Dalnavie
Milton
Averon
Barbaraville
Nigg
Hill of Nigg
Saltburn
Nigg Bay
Alness
Balnapaling
Ben Wyvis
Glen Glass
Invergordon
Eileanach Lodge
Cromarty Bay
Sutors Stacks
Black Water
Clach Liath
Evanton
Cromarty Firth
Balblair
Cromarty
Strathgarve Forest
Forest
Cullicudden
Jemimaville
MORAY FIRTH
Garve
Millbuie Forest
Culbin Forest
Loch Garve
Dingwall
Kintessack
Falls of Rogie
Mount Eagle
The Bar
Strathpeffer
Culbokie
Millbuie
Whiteness Head
Dyke
Black Water
Maryburgh
Alcaig
Findon Forest
Killen
Rosemarkie
Nairn
Brodie Castle
L. Achilty
L. Ussie
Fortrose
Fort George
Contin
Conon Bridge
Black Isle
Chanonry Point
Ardersier
Auldearn
Conon
Avoch
Tradespark
Whitemire
Munlochy
Munlochy Bay
Darnaway Forest
Marybank
Moray Firth
Tore
INVERNESS DALCROSS AIRPORT
Clephanton
Muir of Ord
Stuart
Littlemill
Orrin
Redcastle
Croy
Cawdor
Windhill
N. Kessock
Beauly
INVERNESS
Beauly Firth
Kirkhill
Culloden Battlefield
Kilmorack
Cemetary
Drumchardine
Clava Cairns
Ferness
Erchless Forest
The Aird
Kiltarlity
Dochgarroch
Beinn Bhuidhe Mhór
Daviot
Glackossian
Essich
Scaniport
Carn nan tri-tighearnan
Findhorn
Aitnoch
Glen Convinth
Caiplich
Loch Bruicheach
Abriachan
Balnafoich
Drummossie Muir
Loch Ashie
Tombreck
Loch Moy
Lochindorb
Dores
Farr
Moy
Ruthven
Strath Dearn
Glen Urquhart
Milton
Loch Duntelchaig
Strathnairn
Carn Glas-choire
Drumnadrochit
Urquhart Castle
Lewiston
Tomatin
Loch Ness
Loch Ruthven
Croachy
Slochd Summit
Torness
Glen Kyllachy
Dulnain Bridge
Inverfarigaig
Duthil
Meall Fuar-mhonoidh
Errogie
Dunmaglass Lodge
Slochd
Carrbridge
Landmark Visitor Centre
Foyers
Lochgarthside
Dalmigav.
Nethy
Boat of Garten
Abernethy
Loch Mhór
Eil
Loch Garten
Invermoriston
Findhorn
Dulnain

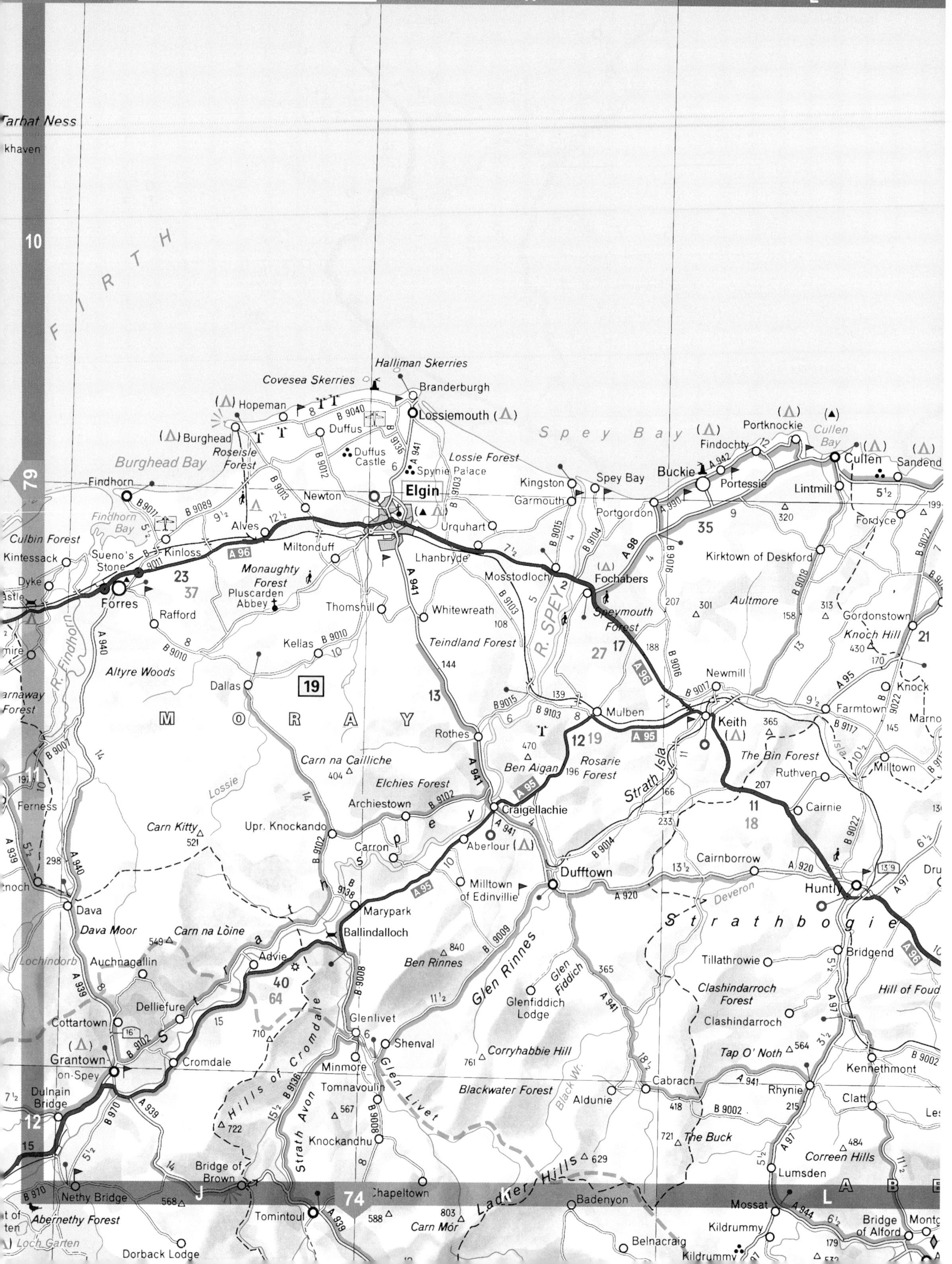
0 2,5 5 7,5 10 miles
K
L
Tarbat Ness
F I R T H
Covesea Skerries
Halliman Skerries
Branderburgh
Hopeman
Lossiemouth
Burghead
Duffus
Duffus Castle
Spynie Palace
Roseisle Forest
Burghead Bay
Findhorn
Findhorn Bay
Culbin Forest
Kintessack
Sueno's Stone
Kinloss
Alves
Newton
Elgin
Miltonduff
Lossie Forest
Spey Bay
Kingston
Garmouth
Urquhart
Lhanbryde
Mosstodloch
Portgordon
Buckie
Portessie
Findochty
Portknockie
Cullen Bay
Cullen
Sandend
Lintmill
Fordyce
Kirktown of Deskford
Fochabers
Speymouth Forest
R. Spey
Aultmore
Gordonstown
Knoch Hill
Knock
Newmill
Keith
Mulben
Farmtown
Marno
The Bin Forest
Ruthven
Milltown
Dyke
Forres
Rafford
Monaughty Forest
Pluscarden Abbey
Thomshill
Whitewreath
Teindland Forest
Kellas
Altyre Woods
Dallas
M O R A Y
Rothes
Ben Aigan
Rosarie Forest
Strath Isla
Carn na Cailliche
Elchies Forest
Archiestown
Craigellachie
Aberlour
Cairnie
Upr. Knockando
Carn Kitty
Carron
S p e y
Dufftown
Cairnborrow
Huntly
Milltown of Edinvillie
Deveron
Strathbogie
Dava
Dava Moor
Carn na Lòine
Marypark
Ballindalloch
Ben Rinnes
Glen Rinnes
Bridgend
Lochindorb
Auchnagallin
Advie
Glen Fiddich
Glenfiddich Lodge
Tillathrowie
Clashindarroch Forest
Clashindarroch
Hill of Foudland
Dulliefure
Cottartown
Grantown-on-Spey
Cromdale
Glenlivet
Shenval
Hills of Cromdale
Corryhabbie Hill
Tap O' Noth
Kennethmont
Minmore
Glen Livet
Tomnavoulin
Blackwater Forest
Black Wr.
Aldunie
Cabrach
Rhynie
Clatt
Dulnain Bridge
Strath Avon
Knockandhu
The Buck
Correen Hills
Lumsden
Bridge of Brown
Ladder Hills
Chapeltown
Nethy Bridge
Tomintoul
Carn Mòr
Badenyon
Mossat
Bridge of Alford
Abernethy Forest
Loch Garten
Dorback Lodge
Belnacraig
Kildrummy
Ferness
Darnaway Forest
R. Findhorn
Lossie
A B
J
L
74
79
10
11
12
A 96
A 95
A 941
A 98
A 920
A 939
A 940
A 97
A 944
A 990
A 942

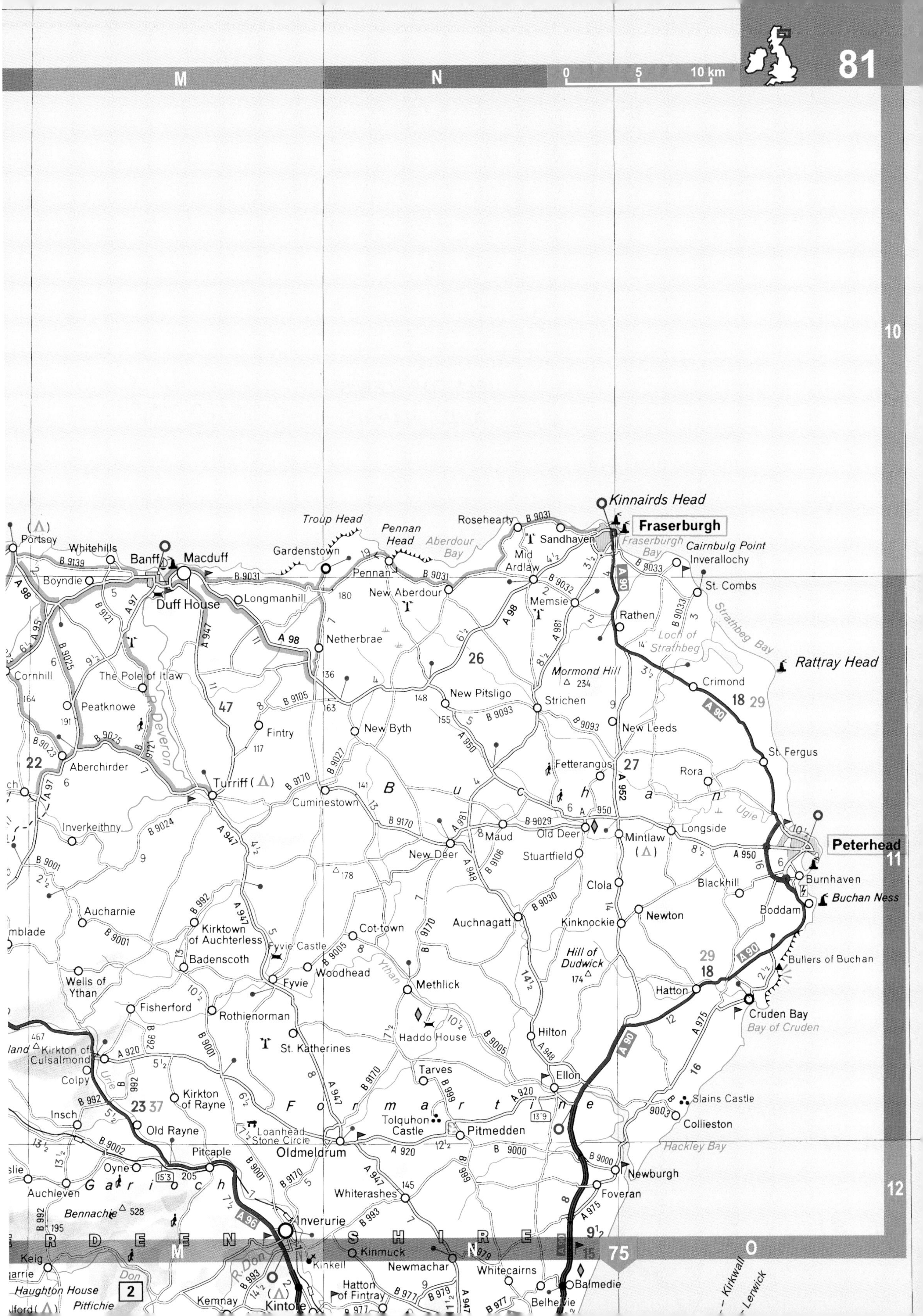
M
N
0 5 10 km
Kinnairds Head
Fraserburgh
Fraserburgh Bay
Cairnbulg Point
Inverallochy
Portsoy
Whitehills
Banff
Macduff
Troup Head
Pennan Head
Aberdour Bay
Rosehearty
Sandhaven
Gardenstown
Pennan
Mid Ardlaw
Boyndie
Duff House
Longmanhill
New Aberdeen
Memsie
St. Combs
Rathen
Loch of Strathbeg
Strathbeg Bay
Rattray Head
Netherbrae
Mormond Hill
Crimond
Cornhill
The Pole of Itlaw
New Pitsligo
Strichen
Peatknowe
Fintry
New Byth
New Leeds
St. Fergus
Aberchirder
Turriff
Fetterangus
Rora
Cuminestown
Buchan
Old Deer
Mintlaw
Longside
Peterhead
Inverkeithny
Maud
New Deer
Stuartfield
Burnhaven
Blackhill
Buchan Ness
Clola
Boddam
Aucharnie
Kirktown of Auchterless
Cot-town
Auchnagatt
Kinknockie
Newton
Fyvie Castle
Badenscoth
Woodhead
Hill of Dudwick
Bullers of Buchan
Wells of Ythan
Fyvie
Methlick
Hatton
Fisherford
Rothienorman
Cruden Bay
Bay of Cruden
Haddo House
Hilton
St. Katherines
Kirkton of Culsalmond
Colpy
Tarves
Ellon
Kirkton of Rayne
Formartine
Slains Castle
Insch
Old Rayne
Tolquhon Castle
Pitmedden
Collieston
Loanhead Stone Circle
Hackley Bay
Pitcaple
Oldmeldrum
Oyne
Newburgh
Garioch
Auchleven
Whiterashes
Foveran
Bennachie 528
Inverurie
ABERDEENSHIRE
Keig
Kinmuck
Kinkell
Newmachar
Whitecairns
Balmedie
R. Don
Haughton House
Hatton of Fintray
Kemnay
Kintore
Pitfichie
Belhelvie
Kirkwall
Lerwick
Ythan
R. Deveron
Urie
Ugie
10
11
12
75
2
O

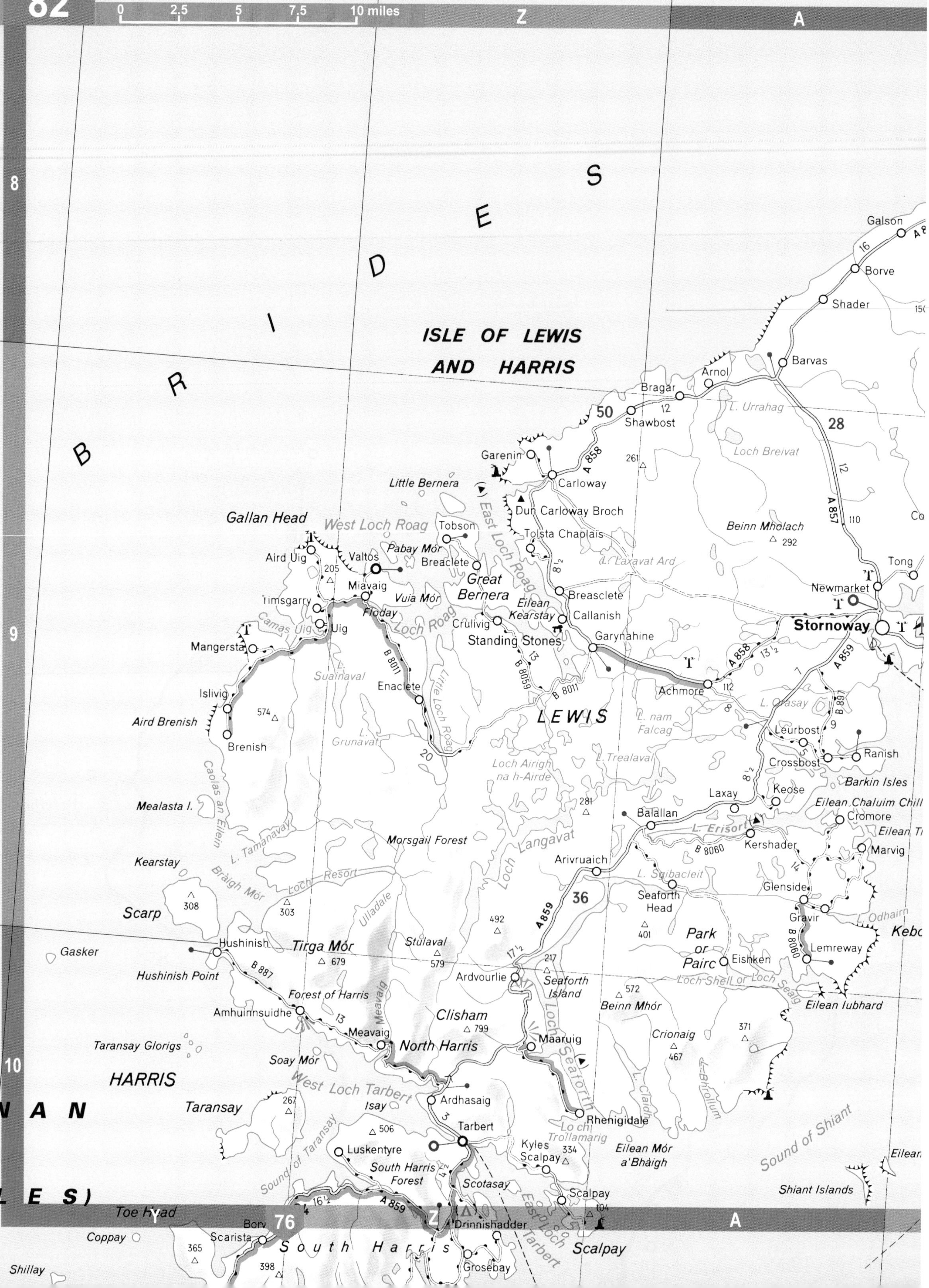
0 2,5 5 7,5 10 miles
Z
A
8
9
10
B R I D E S
ISLE OF LEWIS
AND HARRIS
Galson
Borve
Shader
Barvas
Arnol
Bragar
Shawbost
50
L. Urrahag
28
Loch Breivat
Garenin
Carloway
Little Bernera
Dun Carloway Broch
Gallan Head
West Loch Roag
Tobson
East Loch Roag
Tolsta Chaolais
Beinn Mholach
292
Tong
Newmarket
Aird Uig
Valtos
Pabay Mór
Breaclete
Great Bernera
L. Laxavat Ard
Breasclete
Miavaig
Vuia Mór
Eilean Kearstay
Callanish
Timsgarry
Camas Uig
Uig
Floday
Loch Roag
Crulivig
Standing Stones
Garynahine
Stornoway
Mangersta
L. Suainaval
B 8011
B 8059
Enaclete
Little Loch Roag
Achmore
A 858
A 859
A 857
Islivig
574
Aird Brenish
Brenish
L. Grunavat
LEWIS
L. nam Falcag
L. Orasay
Leurbost
Ranish
Crossbost
Loch Airigh na h-Airde
L. Trealaval
Barkin Isles
Caolas an Eilein
Mealasta I.
281
Laxay
Keose
Eilean Chaluim Chill
Balallan
Cromore
L. Erisort
Kershader
Marvig
L. Tamanavay
Morsgail Forest
Loch Langavat
B 8060
Kearstay
Arivruaich
L. Sgibacleit
Glenside
Bràigh Mór
Loch Resort
36
Seaforth Head
Scarp
308
303
Ulladale
492
401
Gravir
L. Odhairn
Park or Pairc
Lemreway
Gasker
Hushinish
Tirga Mór
679
Stulaval
579
217
Eishken
Hushinish Point
B 887
Ardvourlie
Seaforth Island
572
Loch Shell or Loch Seaig
Eilean Iubhard
Forest of Harris
Beinn Mhór
Amhuinnsuidhe
Meavaig
Clisham
799
Loch Seaforth
Crionaig
467
371
Taransay Glorigs
Meavaig
North Harris
Maaruig
Soay Mór
L. Bhrollum
HARRIS
L. Claidh
West Loch Tarbert
N A N
Taransay
267
Isay
Ardhasaig
Rhenigidale
506
Tarbert
Loch Trollamarig
Sound of Shiant
Luskentyre
Kyles Scalpay
334
Eilean Mór a'Bhàigh
South Harris Forest
Sound of Taransay
Scotasay
Shiant Islands
L E S)
Toe Head
Scalpay
104
Y
76
Z
A
Drinnishadder
East Loch Tarbert
Coppay
Borve
Scarista
365
South Harris
Scalpay
Shillay
398
Grosebay

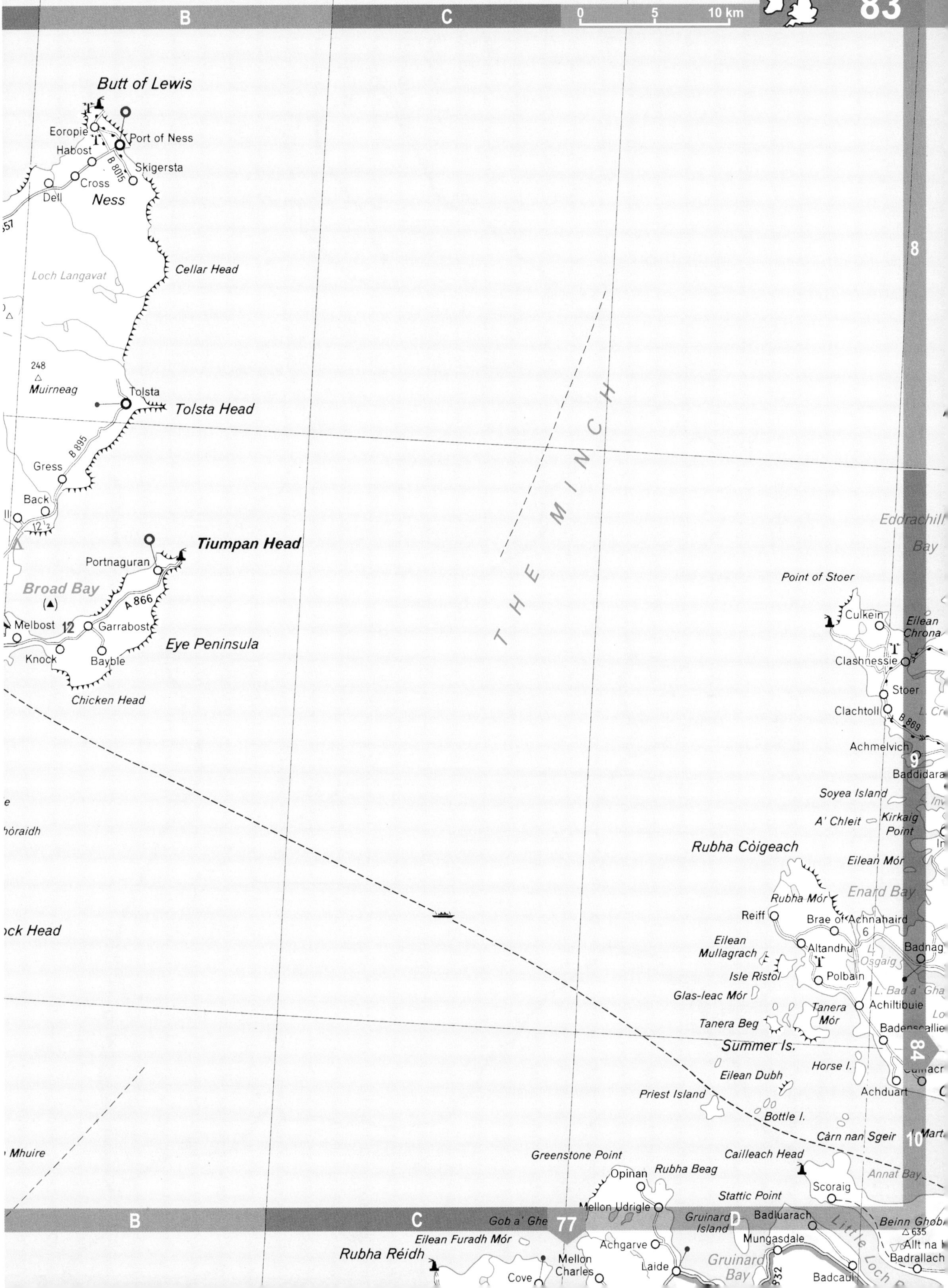
B
C
0 5 10 km
8
9
10
84
77
Butt of Lewis
Eoropie
Port of Ness
Habost
B 8015
Skigersta
Cross
Dell
Ness
Cellar Head
Loch Langavat
248
Muirneag
Tolsta
Tolsta Head
B 895
Gress
Back
Tiumpan Head
Portnaguran
Broad Bay
A 866
Melbost
12
Garrabost
Eye Peninsula
Knock
Bayble
Chicken Head
THE MINCH
Eddrachill
Bay
Point of Stoer
Culkein
Eilean Chrona
Clashnessie
Stoer
Clachtoll
B 869
Achmelvich
Baddidara
Soyea Island
A' Chleit
Kirkaig Point
Rubha Còigeach
Eilean Mór
Enard Bay
Rubha Mór
Reiff
Brae of Achnahaird
Eilean Mullagrach
Altandhu
Badnag
Osgaig
Isle Ristol
Polbain
Glas-leac Mór
L. Bad a' Gha
Tanera Mór
Achiltibuie
Tanera Beg
Badenscallie
Summer Is.
Horse I.
Eilean Dubh
Achduart
Priest Island
Bottle I.
Càrn nan Sgeir
Greenstone Point
Cailleach Head
Opinan
Rubha Beag
Annat Bay
Scoraig
Stattic Point
Mellon Udrigle
Gob a' Ghe
Gruinard Island
Badluarach
Beinn Ghobh
635
Eilean Furadh Mór
Achgarve
Mungasdale
Allt na
Rubha Réidh
Mellon Charles
Laide
Gruinard Bay
Badrallach
Cove
Badcaul
Little Loch
ock Head
Mhuire
hóraidh
D
D

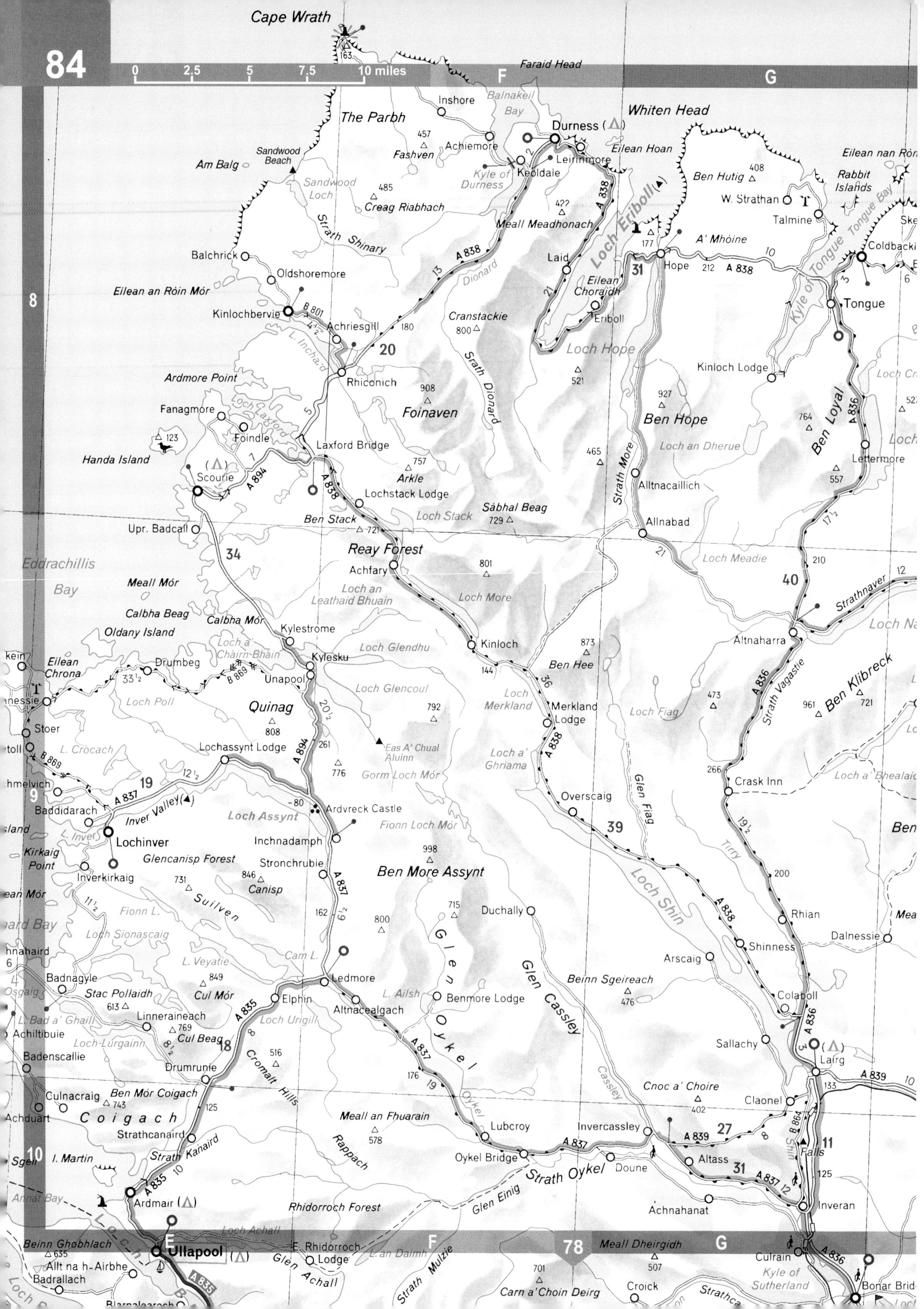
Cape Wrath
0 2.5 5 7.5 10 miles
F
G
Faraid Head
Balnakeil Bay
Inshore
The Parbh
Whiten Head
Durness
Achiemore
Fashven
Eilean Hoan
Leirinmore
Keoldale
Kyle of Durness
Sandwood Beach
Am Balg
Sandwood Loch
Creag Riabhach
Eilean nan Ròn
Rabbit Islands
Ben Hutig
W. Strathan
Talmine
Tongue Bay
Kyle of Tongue
Coldbacki
Meall Meadhonach
Loch Eriboll
A' Mhòine
Hope
A 838
Strath Shinary
Balchrick
Oldshoremore
Dionard
Laid
Eilean Choraidh
Eriboll
Eilean an Ròin Mór
Kinlochbervie
B 801
Achriesgill
Cranstackie
Loch Hope
Tongue
L. Inchard
Rhiconich
Strath Dionard
Kinloch Lodge
Ardmore Point
Loch Laxford
Foinaven
Ben Hope
Ben Loyal
Loch Cr
Fanagmore
Foindle
Handa Island
Laxford Bridge
Arkle
Loch an Dherue
Lettermore
Loch
Scourie
A 894
Strath More
Alltnacaillich
Lochstack Lodge
Sàbhal Beag
Ben Stack
Loch Stack
Allnabad
Upr. Badcall
Reay Forest
Loch Meadie
Eddrachillis Bay
Achfary
Meall Mór
Loch an Leathaid Bhuain
Loch More
Strathnaver
Loch Na
Calbha Beag
Calbha Mór
Oldany Island
Kylestrome
Altnaharra
Loch a' Chàirn Bhàin
Loch Glendhu
Kinloch
Eilean Chrona
Drumbeg
Kylesku
Ben Hee
Unapool
B 869
Loch Glencoul
Loch Merkland
Merkland Lodge
Loch Fiag
Ben Klibreck
Strath Vagastie
Loch Poll
Quinag
Stoer
L. Crocach
Lochassynt Lodge
Eas A' Chual Aluinn
Gorm Loch Mór
Loch a' Ghriama
Glen Fiag
Crask Inn
Loch a' Bhealaich
A 837
Inver Valley
Baddidarach
Loch Assynt
Ardvreck Castle
Overscaig
Lochinver
L. Inver
Inchnadamph
Fionn Loch Mór
Kirkaig Point
Glencanisp Forest
Stronchrubie
Ben More Assynt
Inverkirkaig
Canisp
Suilven
Loch Shin
Tirry
Fionn L.
Duchally
Rhian
Loch Sionascaig
Glen Oykel
Glen Cassley
Shinness
Dalnessie
Cam L.
L. Veyatie
Arscaig
Badnagyle
Stac Pollaidh
Cul Mór
Ledmore
Beinn Sgeireach
Elphin
L. Ailsh
Benmore Lodge
Colaboll
Altnacealgach
L. Bad a' Ghaill
Linneraineach
Loch Urigill
Achiltibuie
Cul Beag
Loch Lurgainn
Sallachy
Badenscallie
Cromalt Hills
Drumrunie
Lairg
A 839
Cassley
Cnoc a' Choire
Claonel
Culnacraig
Ben Mór Coigach
Achduart
Coigach
Meall an Fhuarain
Strathcanaird
Lubcroy
Invercassley
B 864
Falls
I. Martin
Strath Kanaird
Rappach
Oykel Bridge
Strath Oykel
Doune
Altass
A 835
Annat Bay
Ardmair
Glen Einig
Rhidorroch Forest
Achnahanat
Inveran
Loch Achall
Beinn Ghobhlach
E. Rhidorroch Lodge
L. an Daimh
78
Meall Dheirgidh
Culrain
Ullapool
Allt na h-Airbhe
Badrallach
Glen Achall
Strath Mulzie
Carn a' Choin Deirg
Croick
Kyle of Sutherland
Bonar Brid
Blarnalearoch

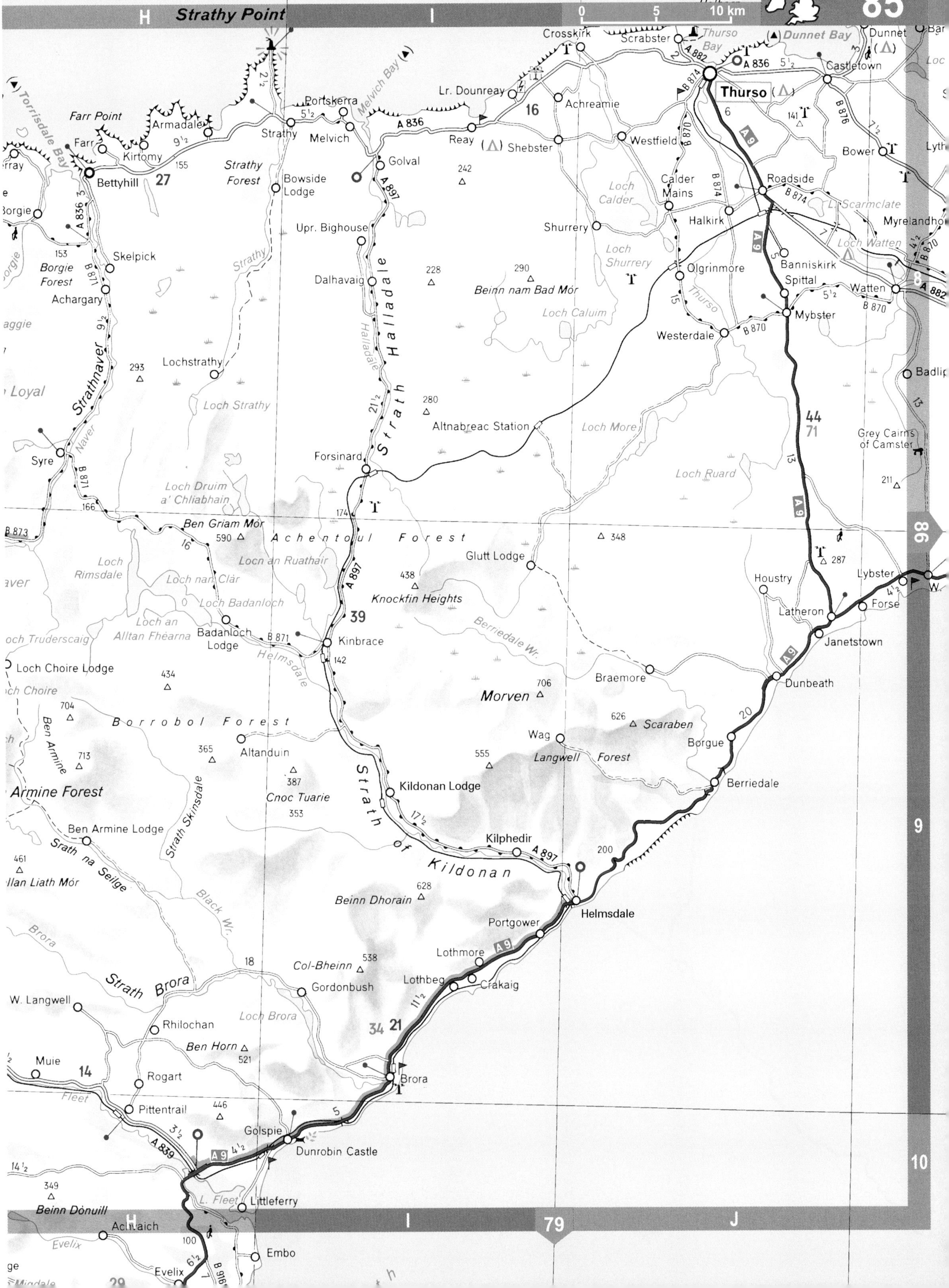
H
Strathy Point
I
0 5 10 km
Dunnet Bay
Dunnet
Crosskirk
Scrabster
Thurso Bay
A 836
Castletown
Lr. Dounreay
Achreamie
Thurso
Portskerra
Melvich Bay
Farr Point
Armadale
Strathy
Melvich
A 836
Reay
Shebster
Westfield
Bower
Torrisdale Bay
Farr
Kirtomy
Golval
Bettyhill
27
Strathy Forest
Bowside Lodge
Loch Calder
Calder Mains
Roadside
Scarmclate
Borgie
Upr. Bigehouse
Shurrery
Halkirk
Myrelandhorn
Skelpick
Loch Shurrery
Olgrinmore
Banniskirk
Loch Watten
Borgie Forest
Dalhavaig
Beinn nam Bad Mòr
Spittal
Watten
Achargary
Strath Halladale
Loch Caluim
Mybster
Westerdale
Lochstrathy
Badlipster
Loch Strathy
Strathnaver
Altnabreac Station
Loch More
Grey Cairns of Camster
Syre
Forsinard
Loch Ruard
Loch Druim a' Chliabhain
Ben Griam Mòr
Achentoul Forest
Glutt Lodge
Houstry
Lybster
Loch Rimsdale
Loch an Ruathair
Loch nan Clàr
Knockfin Heights
Latheron
Forse
Loch Badanloch
Loch an Alltan Fhèarna
Badanloch Lodge
Kinbrace
Berriedale Wr.
Janetstown
Loch Truderscaig
Helmsdale
Loch Choire Lodge
Braemore
Dunbeath
Loch Choire
Morven
Borrobol Forest
Scaraben
Ben Armine
Altanduin
Wag
Borgue
Langwell Forest
Cnoc Tuarie
Strath of Kildonan
Kildonan Lodge
Berriedale
Armine Forest
Ben Armine Lodge
Strath Skinsdale
Kilphedir
Strath na Seilge
Allan Liath Mór
Beinn Dhorain
Helmsdale
Black Wr.
Portgower
Brora
Lothmore
Strath Brora
Col-Bheinn
Lothbeg
Crakaig
Gordonbush
W. Langwell
Loch Brora
Rhilochan
Ben Horn
Muie
Rogart
Brora
Fleet
Pittentrail
Golspie
Dunrobin Castle
L. Fleet
Littleferry
Beinn Dònuill
Achuaich
Evelix
Embo
Evelix
79
J
86
8
9
10

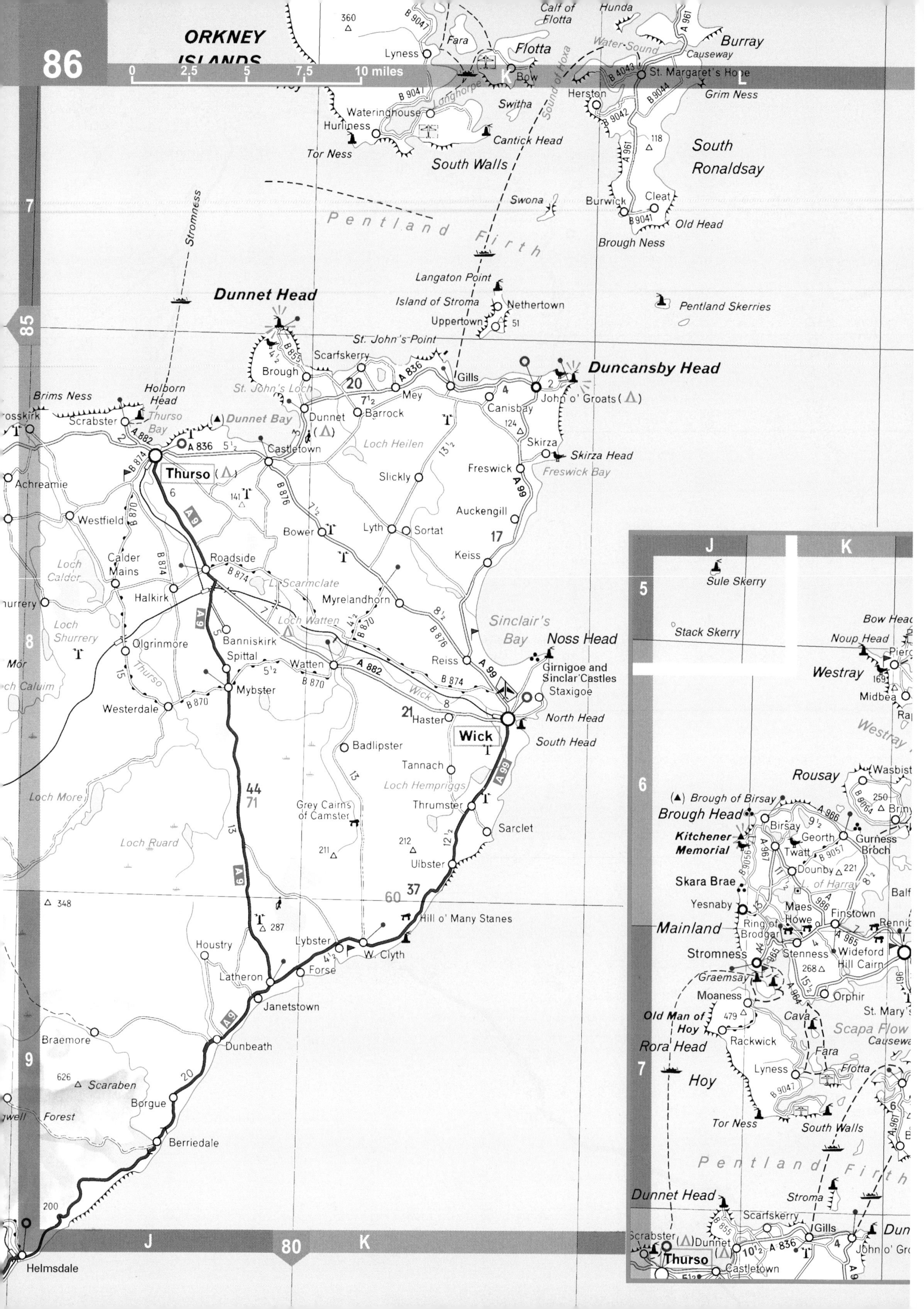
ORKNEY ISLANDS
0
2.5
5
7.5
10 miles
Calf of Flotta
Hunda
Burray
Causeway
Fara
Lyness
Flotta
Water Sound
Bow
St. Margaret's Hope
Herston
Grim Ness
Switha
Sound of Hoxa
Wateringhouse
Hurliness
Cantick Head
Tor Ness
South Walls
South Ronaldsay
Swona
Burwick
Cleat
Old Head
Brough Ness
Stromness
Pentland Firth
Langaton Point
Island of Stroma
Nethertown
Uppertown
Pentland Skerries
Dunnet Head
St. John's Point
Scarfskerry
Brough
St. John's Loch
Gills
Mey
Barrock
Duncansby Head
John o' Groats
Canisbay
Brims Ness
Holborn Head
Scrabster
Thurso Bay
Dunnet Bay
Dunnet
Castletown
Loch Heilen
Skirza
Skirza Head
Freswick
Freswick Bay
Thurso
Achreamie
Slickly
Westfield
Bower
Lyth
Sortat
Auckengill
Keiss
Loch Calder
Calder Mains
Roadside
Halkirk
Loch Scarmclate
Myrelandhorn
Shurrery
Loch Shurrery
Loch Watten
Sinclair's Bay
Noss Head
Olgrinmore
Banniskirk
Spittal
Watten
Reiss
Girnigoe and Sinclair Castles
Staxigoe
Mybster
Westerdale
Haster
North Head
Wick
South Head
Badlipster
Tannach
Loch Hempriggs
Loch More
Grey Cairns of Camster
Thrumster
Sarclet
Loch Ruard
Ulbster
Hill o' Many Stanes
Houstry
Lybster
W. Clyth
Forse
Latheron
Janetstown
Braemore
Dunbeath
Scaraben
Forest
Borgue
Berriedale
Helmsdale
J
K
L
80
85
Sule Skerry
Stack Skerry
Westray
Noup Head
Midbea
Rousay
Wasbister
Brough of Birsay
Brough Head
Kitchener Memorial
Birsay
Georth
Gurness Broch
Twatt
Dounby
Skara Brae
Yesnaby
Maes Howe
Finstown
Mainland
Ring of Brodgar
Stromness
Stenness
Wideford Hill Cairn
Graemsay
Orphir
Moaness
Old Man of Hoy
Cava
Rackwick
Scapa Flow
Rora Head
Fara
Hoy
Lyness
Flotta
Tor Ness
South Walls
Pentland Firth
Dunnet Head
Stroma
Scarfskerry
Gills
Scrabster
Dunnet
Thurso
Castletown
John o' Groats

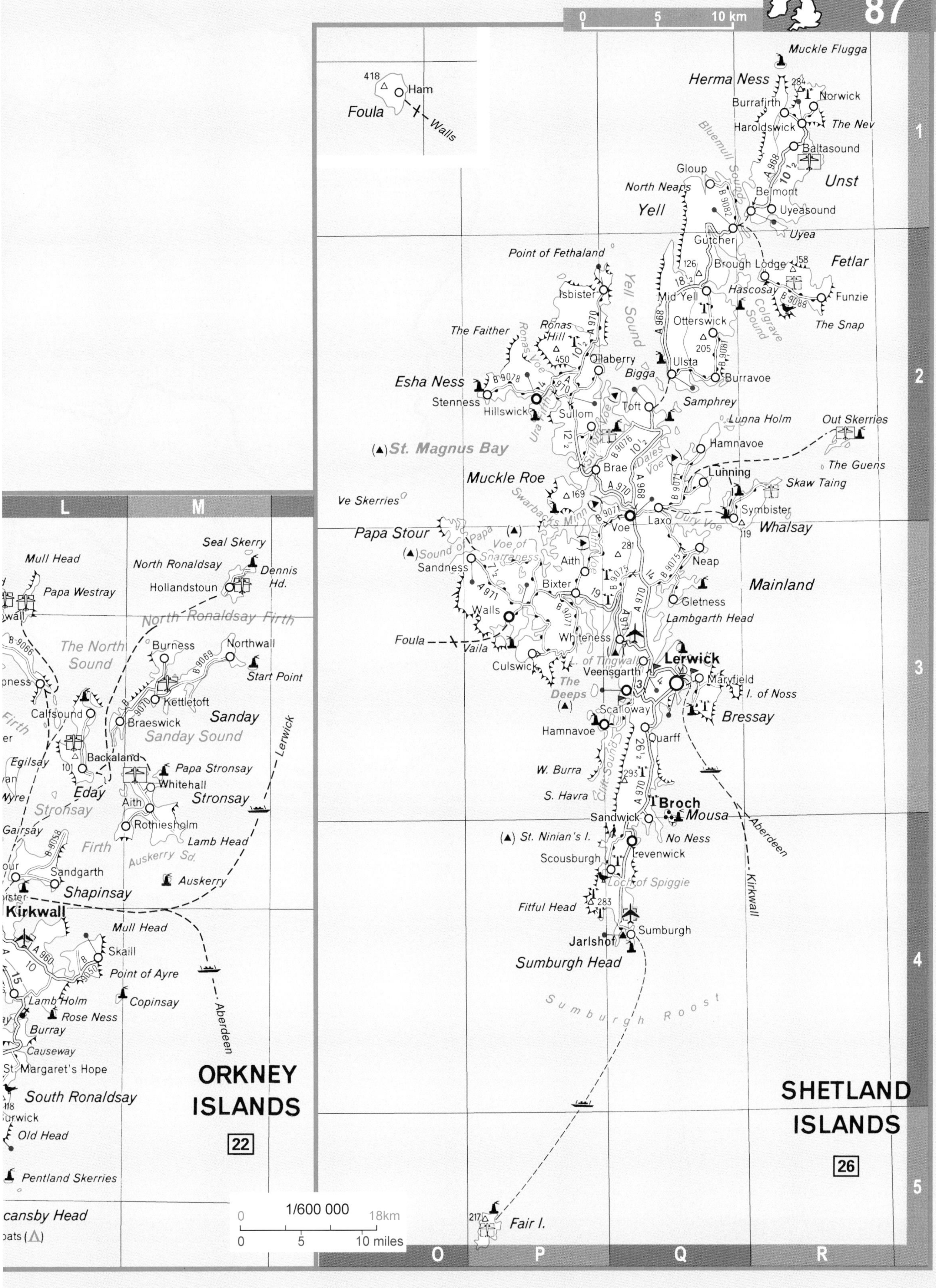
0 5 10 km
Muckle Flugga
Herma Ness
Norwick
Burrafirth
Haroldswick
The Nev
Baltasound
Bluemull Sound
Unst
Gloup
North Neaps
Belmont
Uyeasound
Yell
Uyea
Gutcher
Point of Fethaland
Brough Lodge
Fetlar
Isbister
Mid Yell
Hascosay
Funzie
Yell Sound
Colgrave Sound
The Snap
Otterswick
The Faither
Ronas Hill
Ollaberry
Ulsta
Burravoe
Esha Ness
Bigga
Stenness
Hillswick
Sullom
Toft
Samphrey
Ura Firth
Lunna Holm
Out Skerries
Hamnavoe
(▲) St. Magnus Bay
Brae
Dales Voe
The Guens
Muckle Roe
Lunning
Skaw Taing
Ve Skerries
Swarbacks Minn
Symbister
Laxo
Dury Voe
Voe
Whalsay
Papa Stour
(▲) Sound of Papa
Voe of Snarraness
Neap
Sandness
Aith
Mainland
Bixter
Gletness
Walls
Lambgarth Head
Foula
Vaila
Whiteness
Lerwick
Culswick
L. of Tingwall
Veensgarth
Maryfield
The Deeps
I. of Noss
Scalloway
Bressay
Hamnavoe
Quarff
W. Burra
S. Havra
Broch
Mousa
Sandwick
Aberdeen
(▲) St. Ninian's I.
No Ness
Levenwick
Scousburgh
Loch of Spiggie
Kirkwall
Fitful Head
Sumburgh
Jarlshof
Sumburgh Head
Sumburgh Roost
Fair I.
SHETLAND ISLANDS
26
Ham
Foula
Walls
L
M
Seal Skerry
Mull Head
North Ronaldsay
Dennis Hd.
Papa Westray
Hollandstoun
North Ronaldsay Firth
The North Sound
Burness
Northwall
Start Point
Kettletoft
Calfsound
Sanday
Braeswick
Sanday Sound
Lerwick
Egilsay
Backaland
Papa Stronsay
Eday
Whitehall
Stronsay
Stronsay
Aith
Rothiesholm
Gairsay
Lamb Head
Firth
Auskerry Sd.
Sandgarth
Auskerry
Shapinsay
Kirkwall
Mull Head
Skaill
Point of Ayre
Copinsay
Lamb Holm
Rose Ness
Burray
Causeway
Aberdeen
St. Margaret's Hope
South Ronaldsay
ORKNEY ISLANDS
Old Head
22
Pentland Skerries
1/600 000
0 18km
0 5 10 miles
O
P
Q
R
1
2
3
4
5

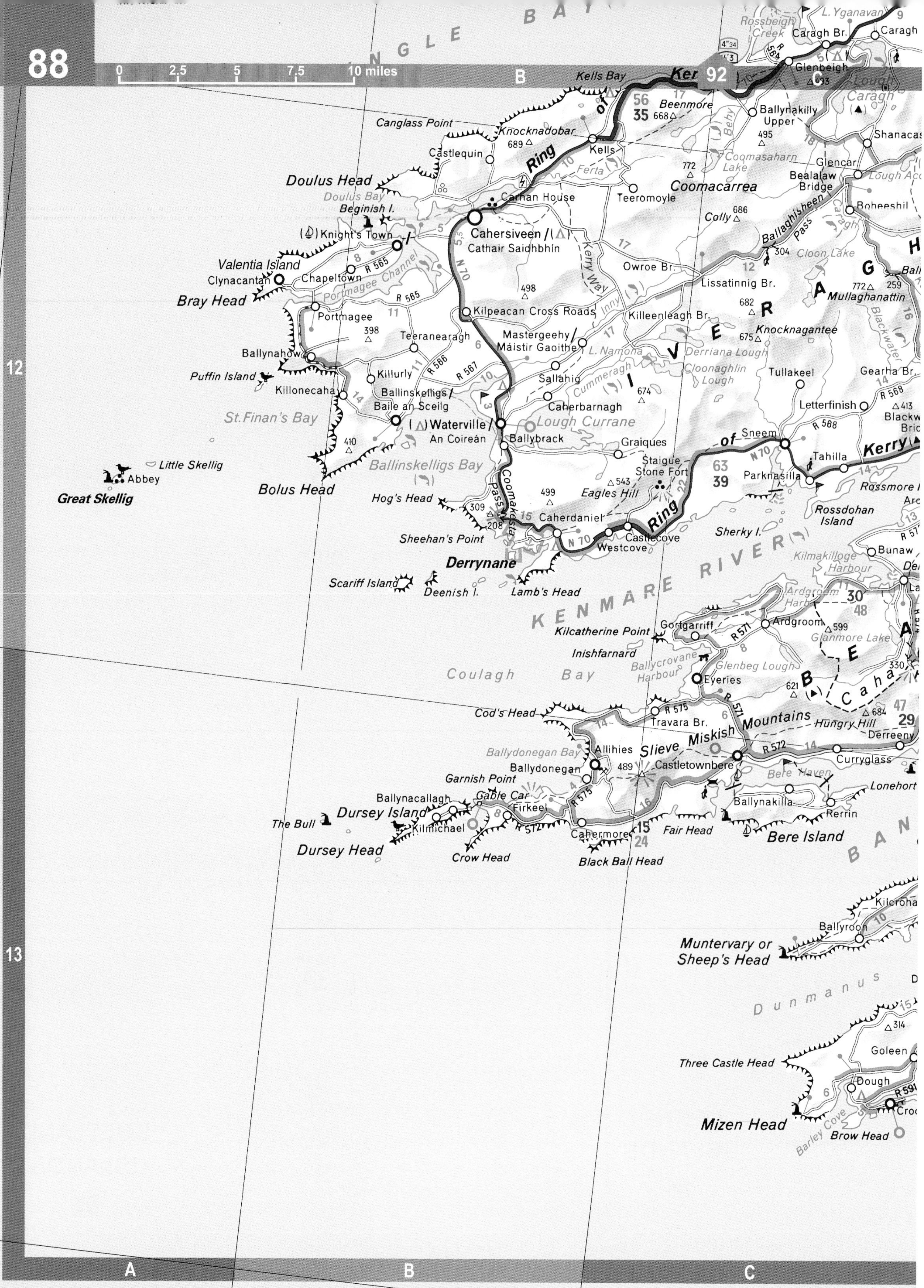
0 2,5 5 7,5 10 miles
DINGLE BAY
Kells Bay
Kerry
92
Rossbeigh Creek
L. Yganavan
Caragh Br.
Caragh
Glenbeigh
Lough Caragh
Canglass Point
Knocknadobar
689
Beenmore
668
Ballynakilly Upper
495
Shanacashel
Castlequin
Ring of Kerry
Kells
Coomasaharn Lake
Glencar
Lough Acoose
Doulus Head
Doulus Bay
Ferta
Teeromoyle
Coomacarrea
Bealalaw Bridge
Boheeshil
Beginish I.
Cahan House
Colly
686
Ballaghisheen Pass
Knight's Town
Cahersiveen
Cathair Saidhbhín
Kerry Way
Cloon Lake
Valentia Island
Clynacantan
Chapeltown
R 565
Portmagee Channel
Owroe Br.
Lissatinnig Br.
Bray Head
498
772
Mullaghanattin
Portmagee
Kilpeacan Cross Roads
Inny
Killeenleagh Br.
682
398
Teeranearagh
Mastergeehy
Máistir Gaoithe
Knocknagantee
675
Ballynahow
L. Namona
Derriana Lough
R 566
R 567
Cloonaghlin Lough
12
Puffin Island
Killurly
Sallahig
Cummeragh
674
Tullakeel
Gearha Br.
Killonecaha
Ballinskelligs
Baile an Sceilg
Caherbarnagh
IVERAGH
Letterfinish
R 568
St. Finan's Bay
Waterville
An Coireán
Lough Currane
Blackwater Bridge
Ballybrack
410
Graiques
Sneem
N 70
Little Skellig
Abbey
Great Skellig
Ballinskelligs Bay
Staigue Stone Fort
Tahilla
Kerry
Parknasilla
Bolus Head
Hog's Head
Coomakesta Pass
499
Eagles Hill
543
63
39
Rossmore I.
309
Caherdaniel
Rossdohan Island
208
Castlecove
Sherky I.
Sheehan's Point
Westcove
Derrynane
KENMARE RIVER
Kilmakilloge Harbour
Bunaw
Scariff Island
Deenish I.
Lamb's Head
Ardgroom Harbour
30
48
Kilcatherine Point
Gortgarriff
R 571
Ardgroom
599
Inishfarnard
Glanmore Lake
Ballycrovane Harbour
Glenbeg Lough
Coulagh Bay
Eyeries
621
BEARA
Caha
330
Cod's Head
R 575
Travara Br.
684
47
29
Mountains
Hungry Hill
Derreeny
Ballydonegan Bay
Allihies
Slieve Miskish
R 572
Curryglass
Ballydonegan
489
Castletownbere
Bere Haven
Garnish Point
Lonehort
Gable Car
Ballynakilla
Ballynacallagh
Dursey Island
Firkeel
Rerrin
The Bull
Kilmichael
Cahermore
15
24
Fair Head
Bere Island
Dursey Head
Crow Head
Black Ball Head
BANTRY
Kilcrohane
Ballyroon
Muntervary or Sheep's Head
13
Dunmanus
314
Goleen
Three Castle Head
Dough
R 591
Mizen Head
Barley Cove
Brow Head
Crookhaven
A
B
C

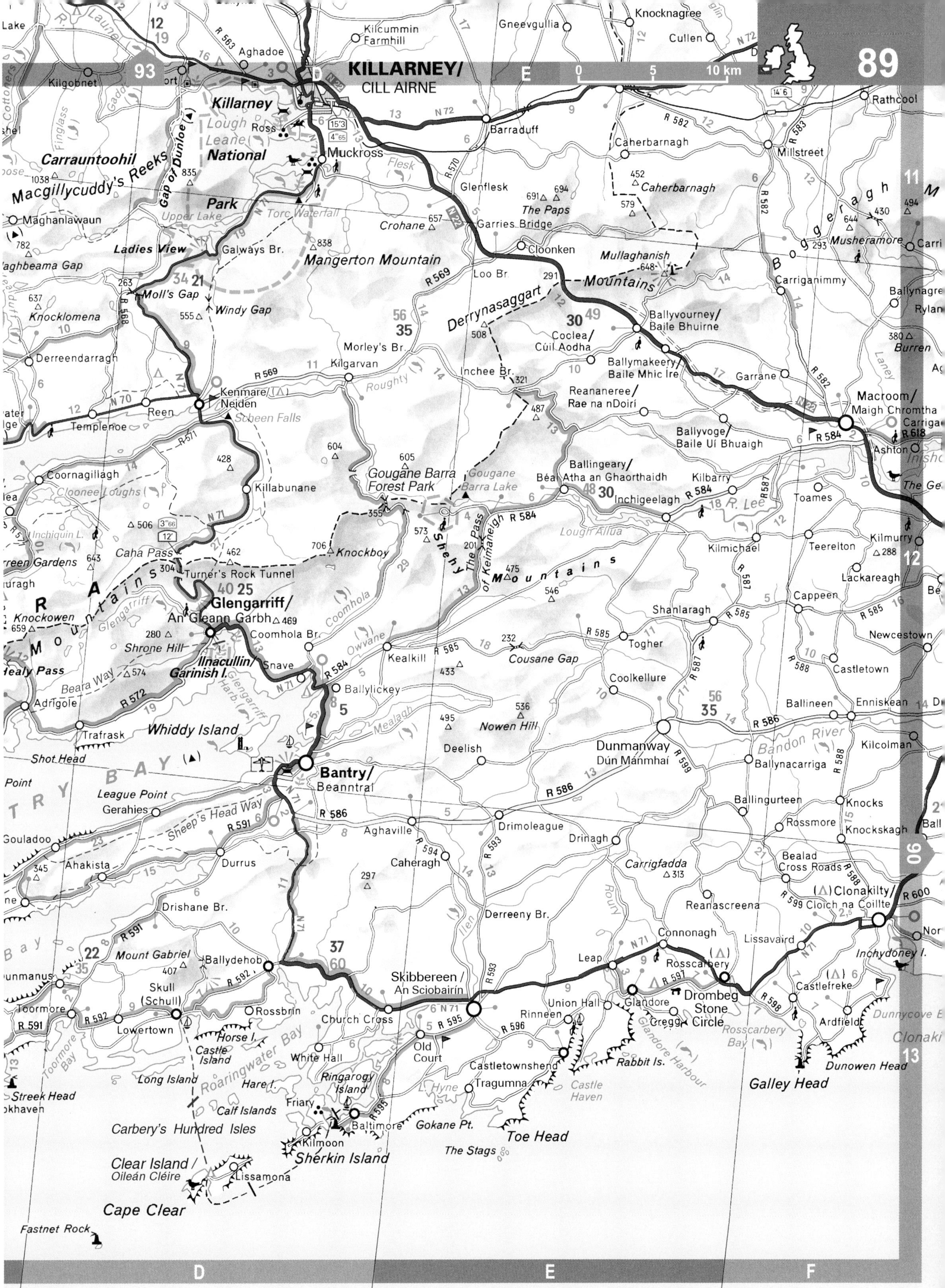

KILLARNEY/
CILL AIRNE
0 5 10 km
93
Kilgobnet
Aghadoe
Kilcummin
Farmhill
Gneevgullia
Knocknagree
Cullen
Rathcool
Killarney
Lough Leane
Ross
National
Park
Muckross
Carrauntoohil
Macgillycuddy's Reeks
Gap of Dunloe
Upper Lake
Torc Waterfall
Maghanlawaun
Ladies View
Galways Br.
Mangerton Mountain
Moll's Gap
Windy Gap
Knocklomena
Derreendarragh
Templenoe
Reen
Kenmare/
Neiden
Sheen Falls
Kilgarvan
Morley's Br.
Roughty
Barraduff
Caherbarnagh
Millstreet
Glenflesk
The Paps
Crohane
Garries Bridge
Cloonken
Mullaghanish
Mountains
Musheramore
Carriganimmy
Boggeragh
Derrynasaggart
Coolea/
Cúil Aodha
Ballyvourney/
Baile Bhuirne
Ballymakeery/
Baile Mhic Íre
Garrane
Inchee Br.
Reananeree/
Rae na nDoirí
Ballyvoge/
Baile Uí Bhuaigh
Macroom/
Maigh Chromtha
Ashton
Burren
Ballynagree
Gougane Barra
Forest Park
Gougane Barra Lake
Ballingeary/
Béal Átha an Ghaorthaidh
Inchigeelagh
Kilbarry
Toames
R. Lee
Lough Allua
Kilmichael
Teerelton
Kilmurry
Lackareagh
Shehy
The Pass of Keimaneigh
Mountains
Knockboy
Coornagillagh
Cloonee Loughs
Killabunane
Inchiquin L.
Caha Pass
Turner's Rock Tunnel
Derreen Gardens
Knockowen
Glengarriff/
An Gleann Garbh
Coomhola
Coomhola Br.
Shrone Hill
Ilnacullin/
Garinish I.
Snave
Healy Pass
Beara Way
Adrigole
Trafrask
Whiddy Island
Ballylickey
Kealkill
Cousane Gap
Togher
Shanlaragh
Cappeen
Newcestown
Castletown
Coolkellure
Enniskean
Ballineen
Owvane
Mealagh
Nowen Hill
Deelish
Dunmanway
Dún Mánmhaí
Bandon River
Kilcolman
Ballynacarriga
Shot Head
BAY
League Point
Gerahies
Bantry/
Beanntraí
Sheep's Head Way
Gouladoo
Ahakista
Durrus
Aghaville
Drimoleague
Drinagh
Ballingurteen
Knocks
Rossmore
Knockskagh
Caheragh
Carrigfadda
Bealad Cross Roads
Clonakilty/
Cloich na Coillte
Reanascreena
Drishane Br.
Derreeny Br.
Connonagh
Lissavaird
Inchydoney I.
Mount Gabriel
Ballydehob
Skull
(Schull)
Toormore
Lowertown
Rossbrin
Skibbereen/
An Sciobairín
Church Cross
Leap
Rosscarbery
Castlefreke
Glandore
Drombeg
Stone
Circle
Union Hall
Rinneen
Gregg
Ardfield
Dunnycove
Clonakilty
Horse I.
Castle Island
Roaringwater Bay
Long Island
Hare I.
White Hall
Old Court
Ringarogy Island
Castletownshend
Tragumna
Rabbit Is.
Glandore Harbour
Rosscarbery Bay
Galley Head
Dunowen Head
Streek Head
Calf Islands
Friary
Baltimore
Gokane Pt.
Castle Haven
Toe Head
The Stags
Carbery's Hundred Isles
Kilmoon
Sherkin Island
Clear Island/
Oileán Cléire
Lissamona
Cape Clear
Fastnet Rock
D
E
F

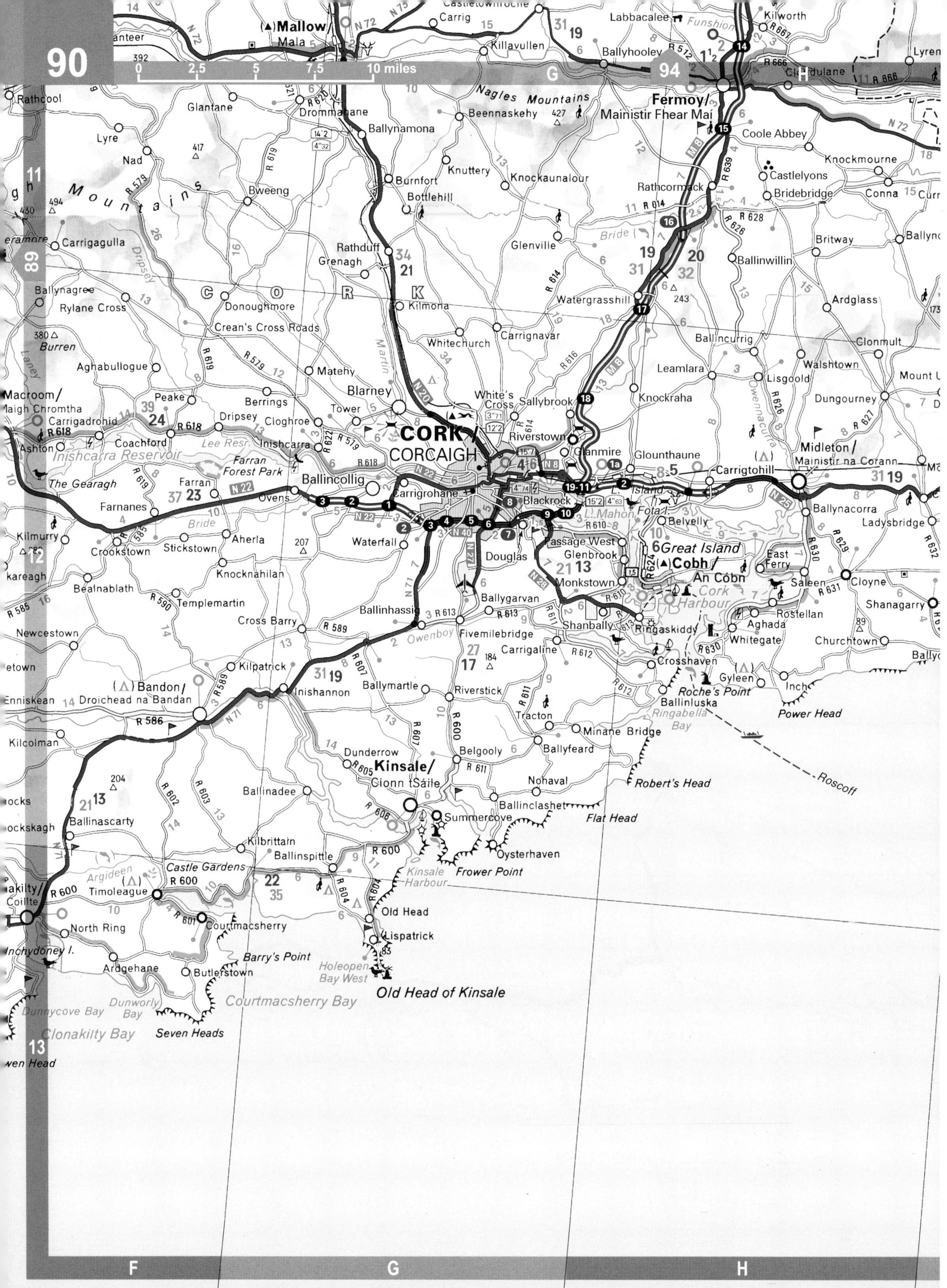

0 2.5 5 7.5 10 miles
Mallow
Mala
Carrig
Killavullen
Labbacalee
Funshion
Kilworth
Ballyhooley
Fermoy/
Mainistir Fhear Maí
Nagles Mountains
Beennaskehy
Rathcool
Glantane
Drommahane
Ballynamona
Lyre
Nad
Coole Abbey
Knockmourne
Castlelyons
Bridebridge
Conna
Mountains
Bweeng
Burnfort
Knuttery
Knockaunalour
Bottlehill
Rathcormack
Carrigagulla
Rathduff
Grenagh
Glenville
Bride
Britway
Ballinwillin
Ballynagree
Rylane Cross
CORK
Kilmona
Donoughmore
Watergrasshill
Ardglass
Crean's Cross Roads
Whitechurch
Carrignavar
Ballincurrig
Clonmult
Burren
Aghabullogue
Matehy
Martin
Leamlara
Walshtown
Lisgoold
Mount U
Macroom/
Maigh Chromtha
Carrigadrohid
Peake
Berrings
Blarney
Tower
White's Cross
Sallybrook
Knockraha
Dungourney
Dripsey
Cloghroe
Ashton
Coachford
Inishcarra Reservoir
Lee Resr.
Inishcarra
CORK/
CORCAIGH
Riverstown
Glanmire
Glounthaune
Midleton/
Mainistir na Corann
Farran Forest Park
The Gearagh
Farran
Ballincollig
Ovens
Carrigrohane
Blackrock
Carrigtohill
Island
Fota I.
L. Mahon
Belvelly
Ballynacorra
Ladysbridge
Farnanes
Bride
Kilmurry
Crookstown
Stickstown
Aherla
Waterfall
Douglas
Passage West
Glenbrook
Great Island
Cobh/
An Cóbh
East Ferry
Cork Harbour
Saleen
Cloyne
Kilmurry
Knocknahilan
Monkstown
Bealnablath
Templemartin
Ballygarvan
Shanagarry
Newcestown
Cross Barry
Ballinhassig
Shanbally
Ringaskiddy
Rostellan
Aghada
Whitegate
Churchtown
Owenboy
Fivemilebridge
Carrigaline
Crosshaven
Gyleen
Inch
Kilpatrick
Bandon/
Droichead na Bandan
Enniskean
Inishannon
Ballymartle
Riverstick
Roche's Point
Ballinluska
Ringabella Bay
Power Head
Kilcolman
Tracton
Minane Bridge
Dunderrow
Kinsale/
Cionn tSáile
Belgooly
Ballyfeard
Robert's Head
Roscoff
Nohaval
Ballinadee
Ballinclashet
Flat Head
Summercove
Ballinascarty
Oysterhaven
Kilbrittain
Ballinspittle
Frower Point
Kinsale Harbour
Castle Gardens
Argideen
Timoleague
Clonakilty/
Cloich na Coillte
Old Head
Lispatrick
North Ring
Courtmacsherry
Inchydoney I.
Barry's Point
Ardgehane
Butlerstown
Holeopen Bay West
Old Head of Kinsale
Courtmacsherry Bay
Dunnycove Bay
Dunworly Bay
Clonakilty Bay
Seven Heads
Galley Head
F
G
H

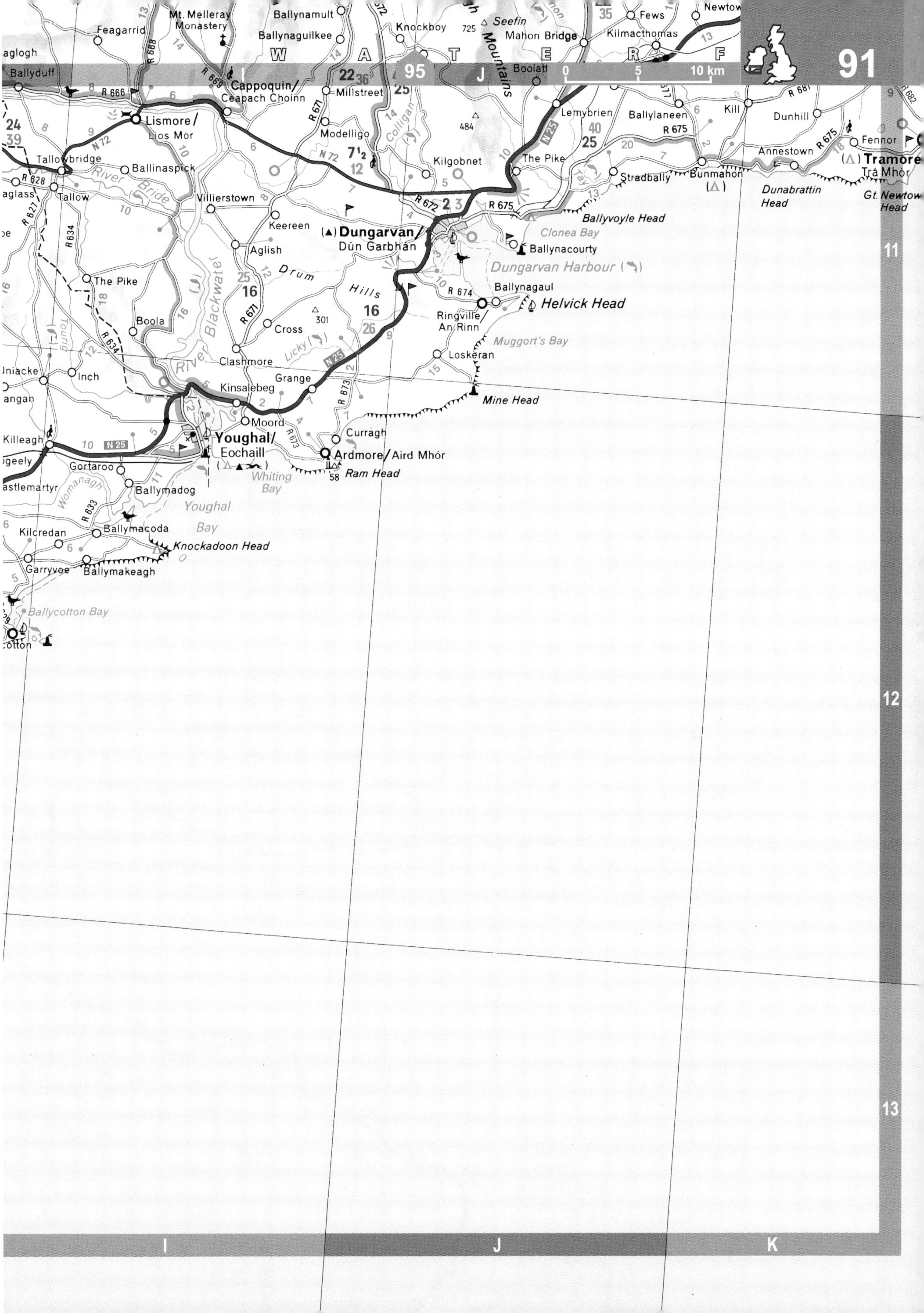

Mt. Melleray Monastery
Ballynamult
Feagarrid
Ballynaguilkee
Knockboy
Seefin
Mahon Bridge
Fews
Kilmacthomas
Newtown
WATERFORD
Mountains
Ballyduff
R 666
Cappoquin/ Ceapach Choinn
Millstreet
Boolatt
0 5 10 km
95
Lismore/ Lios Mór
Modelligo
Colligan
484
Lemybrien
Ballylaneen
R 675
Kill
Dunhill
R 681
Fennor
Tramore Trá Mhór
Annestown
Tallowbridge
Ballinaspick
River Bride
N 72
Kilgobnet
The Pike
Stradbally
Bunmahon
Dunabrattin Head
Gt. Newtown Head
Tallow
Villierstown
R 672
R 675
Ballyvoyle Head
Keereen
Dungarvan/ Dún Garbhán
Clonea Bay
Ballynacourty
Aglish
Dungarvan Harbour
Drum Hills
The Pike
R 634
River Blackwater
R 671
Ballynagaul
R 674
Helvick Head
Ringville/ An Rinn
Boola
Cross
301
Muggort's Bay
Loskeran
Licky
N 25
Clashmore
Uniacke
Inch
Grange
Kinsalebeg
R 673
Mine Head
Moord
Killeagh
Youghal/ Eochaill
Curragh
Ardmore/ Aird Mhór
Ram Head
58
Gortaroo
Whiting Bay
Castlemartyr
Ballymadog
Womanagh
Youghal Bay
R 633
Ballymacoda
Kilcredan
Knockadoon Head
Garryvoe
Ballymakeagh
Ballycotton Bay
Ballycotton
11
12
13
I
J
K

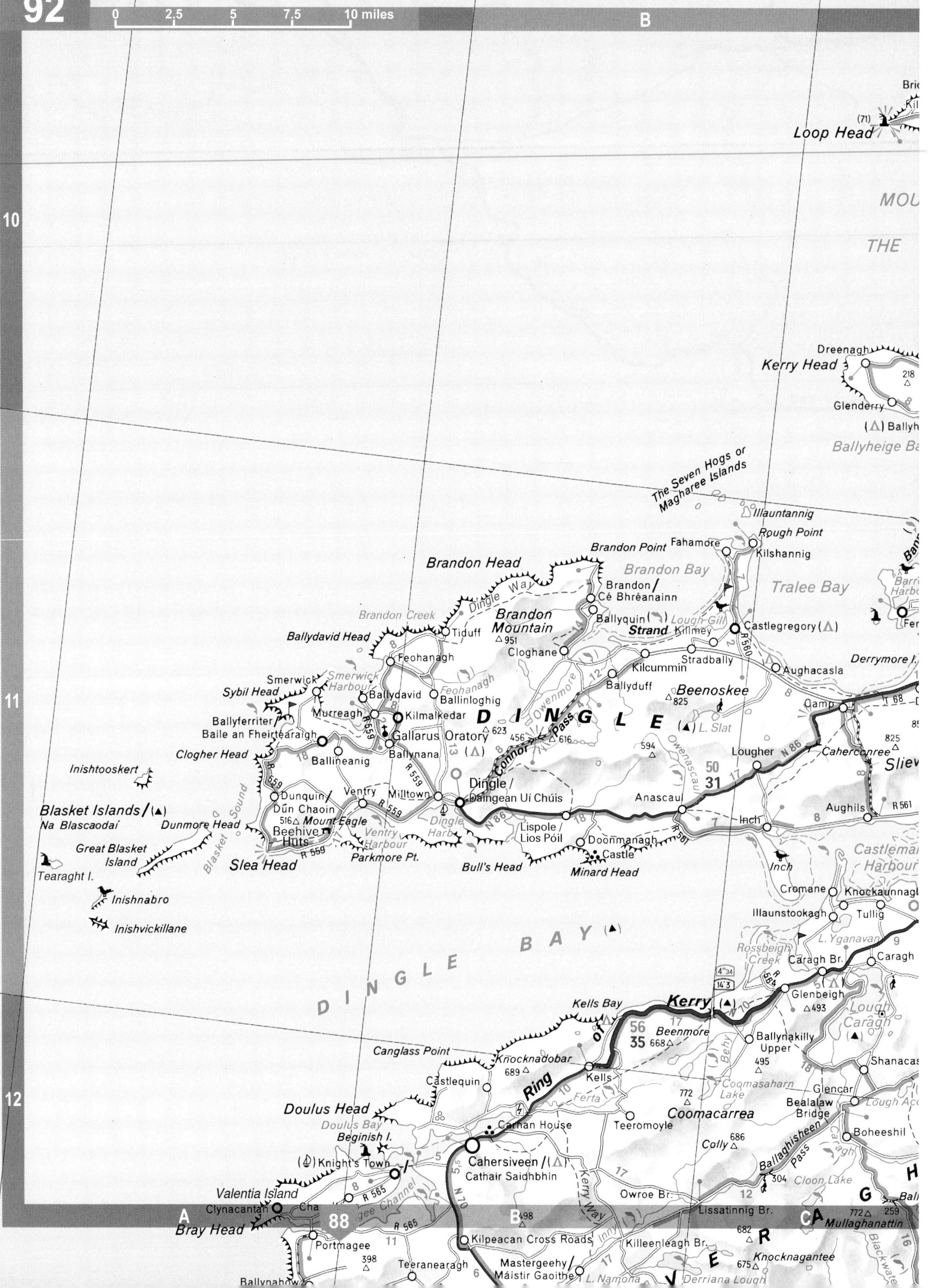
0
2.5
5
7.5
10 miles
B
10
11
12
A
88
C
Loop Head
(71)
MOU
THE
Dreenagh
Kerry Head
218
Glenderry
Ballyheige Ba
The Seven Hogs or Magharee Islands
Illauntannig
Rough Point
Fahamore
Kilshannig
Brandon Point
Brandon Bay
Tralee Bay
Brandon Head
Brandon / Cé Bhréanainn
Dingle Way
Brandon Creek
Brandon Mountain
951
Ballyquin
Lough Gill
Castlegregory
Strand
Kilmey
Ballydavid Head
Tiduff
Cloghane
Feohanagh
Kilcummin
Stradbally
Aughacasla
Derrymore I.
Smerwick
Smerwick Harbour
Ballydavid
Feohanagh
Ballinloghig
Ballyduff
Beenoskee
825
Sybil Head
Murreagh
Kilmalkedar
DINGLE
Connor Pass
Owenmore
L. Slat
Camp
Ballyferriter / Baile an Fheirtéaraigh
Gallarus Oratory
623
456
616
594
Owenascaul
Caherconree
825
Slie
Clogher Head
Ballineanig
Ballynana
Lougher
N 86
Inishtooskert
Dunquin / Dún Chaoin
Ventry
Milltown
Dingle / Daingean Uí Chúis
Anascaul
Aughils
R 561
Blasket Islands / Na Blascaodaí
Dunmore Head
Blasket Sound
516
Mount Eagle
Beehive Huts
Ventry Harbour
Dingle Harb.
Lispole / Lios Póil
Doonmanagh
Castle
Inch
Castlemai Harbour
Great Blasket Island
Slea Head
Parkmore Pt.
Bull's Head
Minard Head
Inch
Tearaght I.
Inishnabro
Inishvickillane
Cromane
Knockaunnagl
Illaunstookagh
Tullig
L. Yganavan
Rossbeigh Creek
Caragh Br.
Caragh
DINGLE BAY
Glenbeigh
493
Kells Bay
Ring of Kerry
Lough Caragh
56 35
Beenmore
668
Ballynakilly Upper
Canglass Point
Knocknadobar
689
495
Shanacas
Castlequin
Kells
Behy
Coomasaharn Lake
Glencar
Doulus Head
Ferta
772
Bealalaw Bridge
Lough Acc
Doulus Bay
Carhan House
Teeromoyle
Coomacarrea
Boheeshil
Beginish I.
Colly
686
Ballaghisheen Pass
Cahersiveen / Cathair Saidhbhín
Knight's Town
Kerry Way
Cloon Lake
Valentia Island
Owroe Br.
304
Clynacantan
Cha
Bray Head
Portmagee
Kilpeacan Cross Roads
Killeenleagh Br.
Lissatinnig Br.
Mullaghanattin
772
259
682
Knocknagantee
675
398
Teeranearagh
Mastergeehy / Máistir Gaoithe
L. Namona
Derriana Lough
Ballynahow
Blackwate

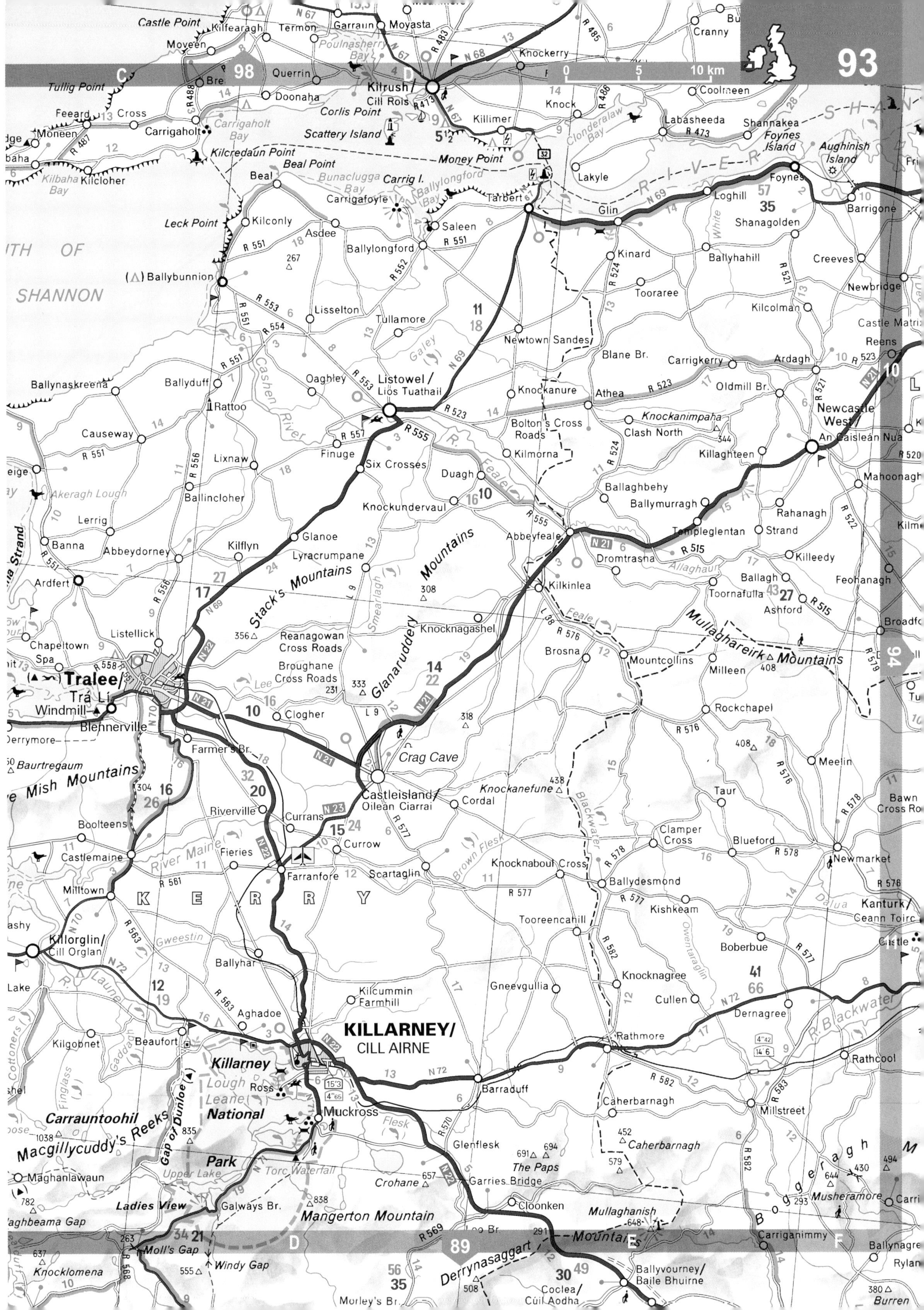

0 5 10 km
98
94
89
C
D
E
F
Castle Point
Kilfearagh
Termon
Garraun
Moyasta
Moveen
Poulnasherry Bay
Knockerry
Cranny
Querrin
Kilrush/
Cill Rois
Coolmeen
Tullig Point
Doonaha
Corlis Point
Knock
Feeard
Cross
Carrigaholt
Carrigaholt Bay
Killimer
Clonderalaw Bay
Labasheeda
Shannakea
Moneen
Scattery Island
Foynes Island
Aughinish Island
Kilbaha
Kilcredaun Point
Money Point
Beal Point
Beal
Lakyle
Foynes
Kilbaha Bay
Kilcloher
Bunaclugga Bay
Carrig I.
Ballylongford Bay
Carrigafoyle
Tarbert
Glin
Loghill
Barrigone
Shanagolden
Leck Point
Kilconly
Asdee
Saleen
Ballylongford
Kinard
Ballyhahill
Creeves
Mouth of Shannon
Ballybunnion
Tooraree
Newbridge
Lisselton
Tullamore
Kilcolman
Castle Matrix
Newtown Sandes
Reens
Blane Br.
Carrigkerry
Ardagh
Galey
Ballynaskreena
Ballyduff
Oaghley
Listowel/
Lios Tuathail
Knockanure
Athea
Oldmill Br.
Rattoo
Cashen River
Knockanimpaha
Newcastle West/
An Caisleán Nua
Causeway
Bolton's Cross Roads
Clash North
Lixnaw
Finuge
Six Crosses
Kilmorna
Killaghteen
Mahoonagh
Akeragh Lough
Duagh
Feale
Ballincloher
Ballaghbehy
Ballymurragh
Rahanagh
Knockundervaul
Lerrig
Glanoe
Abbeyfeale
Templeglentan
Strand
Banna
Abbeydorney
Kilflyn
Lyracrumpane
Stack's Mountains
Mountains
Dromtrasna
Killeedy
Allaghaun
Ardfert
Kilkinlea
Ballagh
Feohanagh
Toornafulla
Ashford
Chapeltown
Spa
Listellick
Reanagowan Cross Roads
Knocknagashel
Smearlagh
Glanaruddery Mountains
Mullaghareirk Mountains
Brosna
Mountcollins
Milleen
Broadford
Tralee/
Trá Lí
Windmill
Blennerville
Broughane Cross Roads
Lee
Clogher
Rockchapel
Derrymore
Farmer's Br.
Crag Cave
Baurtregaum
Slieve Mish Mountains
Castleisland/
Oileán Ciarraí
Cordal
Knockanefune
Meelin
Taur
Riverville
Currans
Blackwater
Bawn Cross Roads
Boolteens
Currow
Clamper Cross
Blueford
Castlemaine
River Maine
Fieries
Farranfore
Scartaglin
Brown Flesk
Knocknaboul Cross
Newmarket
Milltown
K E R R Y
Ballydesmond
Kishkeam
Dalua
Kanturk/
Ceann Toirc
Tooreencahill
Owentaraglin
Killorglin/
Cill Orglan
Gweestin
Boberbue
Castle
Ballyhar
Lake
R. Laune
Gneevgullia
Knocknagree
Cullen
Dernagree
Kilcummin
Farmhill
Aghadoe
KILLARNEY/
CILL AIRNE
Rathmore
R. Blackwater
Kilgobnet
Beaufort
Killarney
Rathcool
Lough Leane
National
Park
Ross
Barraduff
Gaddagh
Finglass
Cottoners
Gap of Dunloe
Muckross
Caherbarnagh
Millstreet
Carrauntoohil
Macgillycuddy's Reeks
Flesk
Glenflesk
The Paps
Caherbarnagh
Boggeragh Mountains
Maghanlawaun
Upper Lake
Torc Waterfall
Crohane
Garries Bridge
Musheramore
Ladies View
Galways Br.
Mangerton Mountain
Cloonken
Mullaghanish
Mountains
Caragh Gap
Moll's Gap
Windy Gap
Derrynasaggart
Carriganimmy
Ballynagree
Rylane
Knocklomena
Ballyvourney/
Baile Bhuirne
Coolea/
Cúil Aodha
Morley's Br.
Burren
N 67
N 68
N 69
N 21
N 22
N 23
N 70
N 71
N 72
R 473
R 483
R 485
R 486
R 487
R 488
R 551
R 552
R 553
R 554
R 555
R 556
R 557
R 558
R 561
R 563
R 568
R 569
R 570
R 576
R 577
R 578
R 579
R 582
R 583
R 515
R 520
R 521
R 522
R 523
R 524
L 9
L 38

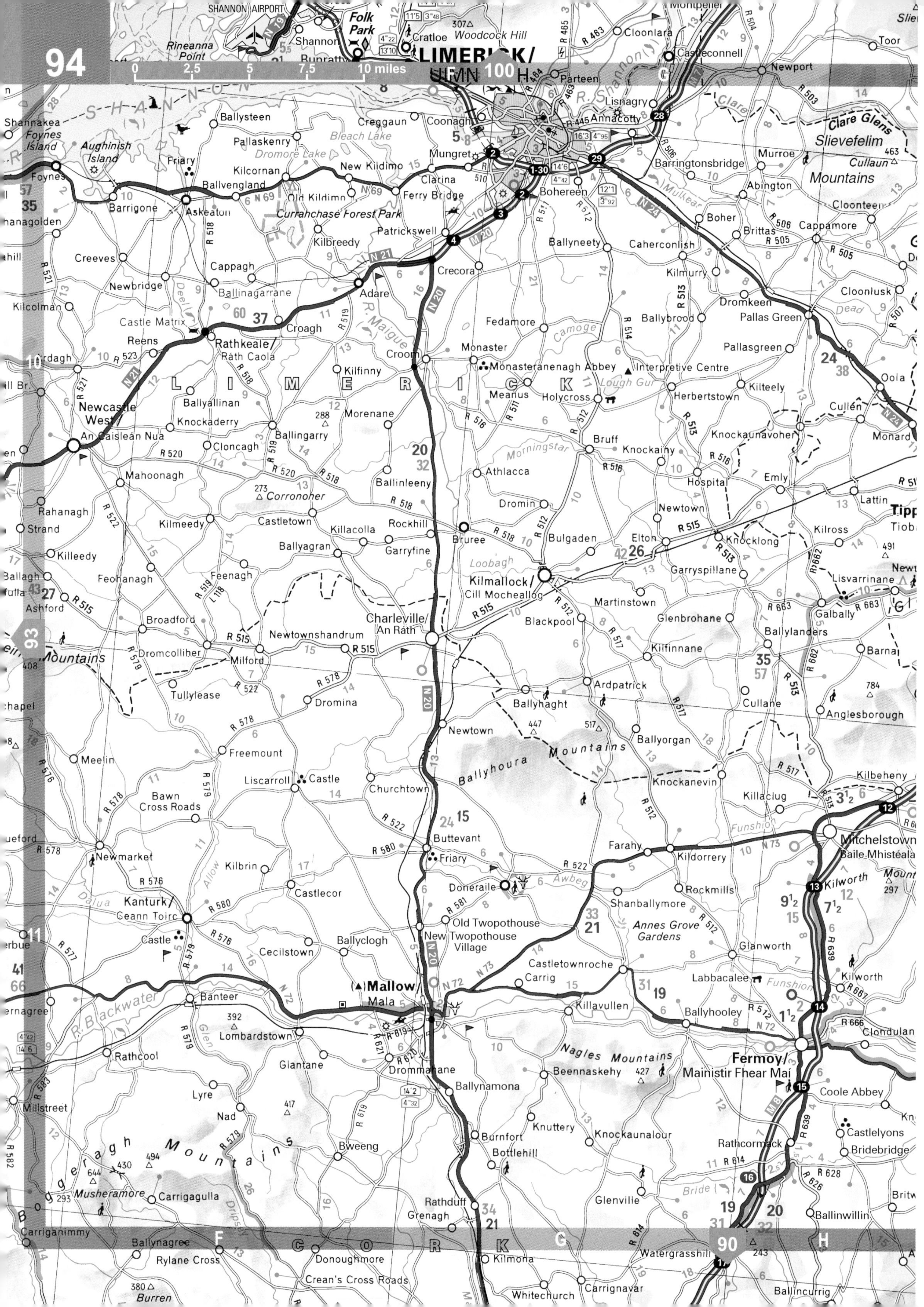

SHANNON AIRPORT
Folk Park
Rineanna Point
Shannon
Bunratty
Cratloe
Woodcock Hill
LIMERICK/
Montpelier
Cloonlara
Castleconnell
Toor
Newport
Parteen
Lisnagry
Annacotty
Clare Glens
Slievefelim
Cullaun
Mountains
0 2.5 5 7.5 10 miles
100
Shannakea
Foynes Island
Aughinish Island
Ballysteen
Pallaskenry
Creggaun
Coonagh
Bleach Lake
Dromore Lake
Friary
Foynes
Kilcornan
New Kildimo
Mungret
Ballvengland
Old Kildimo
Clarina
Ferry Bridge
Barrigone
Askeaton
Currahchase Forest Park
Bohereen
Barringtonsbridge
Murroe
Abington
Clonteen
Boher
Brittas
Cappamore
Shanagolden
Kilbreedy
Patrickswell
Ballyneety
Caherconlish
Creeves
Cappagh
Crecora
Kilmurry
Newbridge
Ballinagarrane
Adare
Dromkeen
Cloonlusk
Kilcolman
Castle Matrix
Croagh
Fedamore
Ballybrood
Pallas Green
Reens
Rathkeale/ Ráth Caola
Monaster
Camoge
Pallasgreen
Ardagh
Croom
Monasteranenagh Abbey
Interpretive Centre
Oola
Kilfinny
Lough Gur
Kilteely
Newcastle West/ An Caisleán Nua
LIMERICK
Ballyallinan
Meanus
Holycross
Herbertstown
Cullen
Knockaderry
Morenane
Monard
Ballingarry
Bruff
Knockaunavoher
Cloncagh
Morningstar
Knockainy
Mahoonagh
Athlacca
Hospital
Emly
Ballinleeny
Lattin
Corronoher
Rahanagh
Dromin
Newtown
Strand
Kilmeedy
Castletown
Killacolla
Rockhill
Bruree
Bulgaden
Elton
Knocklong
Kilross
Tipp
Tiob
Ballyagran
Garryfine
Killeedy
Loobagh
Garryspillane
Ballagh
Feohanagh
Feenagh
Kilmallock/ Cill Mocheallóg
Lisvarrinane
Tulla
Ashford
Martinstown
Galbally
Broadford
Charleville/ An Ráth
Blackpool
Glenbrohane
Ballylanders
Newtownshandrum
Barna
Mountains
Dromcolliher
Milford
Kilfinnane
Tullylease
Dromina
Ardpatrick
Cullane
Ballyhaght
Anglesborough
Newtown
Ballyorgan
Freemount
Mountains
Meelin
Ballyhoura
Liscarroll
Castle
Churchtown
Knockanevin
Kilbeheny
Bawn Cross Roads
Killaclug
Funshion
Buttevant
Farahy
Mitchelstown/ Baile Mhistéala
Newmarket
Friary
Kildorrery
Kilbrin
Allow
Doneraile
Awbeg
Rockmills
Castlecor
Dalua
Kanturk/ Ceann Toirc
Shanballymore
Kilworth
Old Twopothouse
Annes Grove Gardens
Castle
New Twopothouse Village
Cecilstown
Ballyclogh
Glanworth
Castletownroche
Carrig
Labbacalee
Kilworth
Mallow/ Mala
Banteer
R. Blackwater
Killavullen
Ballyhooley
Lombardstown
Clondulane
Rathcool
Glantane
Drommahane
Nagles Mountains
Fermoy/ Mainistir Fhear Maí
Beennaskehy
Ballynamona
Coole Abbey
Lyre
Millstreet
Nad
Knuttery
Castlelyons
Burnfort
Knockaunalour
Rathcormack
Bridebridge
Bweeng
Boggeragh Mountains
Bottlehill
Musheramore
Carrigagulla
Glenville
Bride
Rathduff
Grenagh
Ballinwillin
Carriganimmy
CORK
Ballynagree
Donoughmore
Kilmona
Watergrasshill
Rylane Cross
Crean's Cross Roads
Burren
Whitechurch
Carrignavar
Ballincurrig
90
93

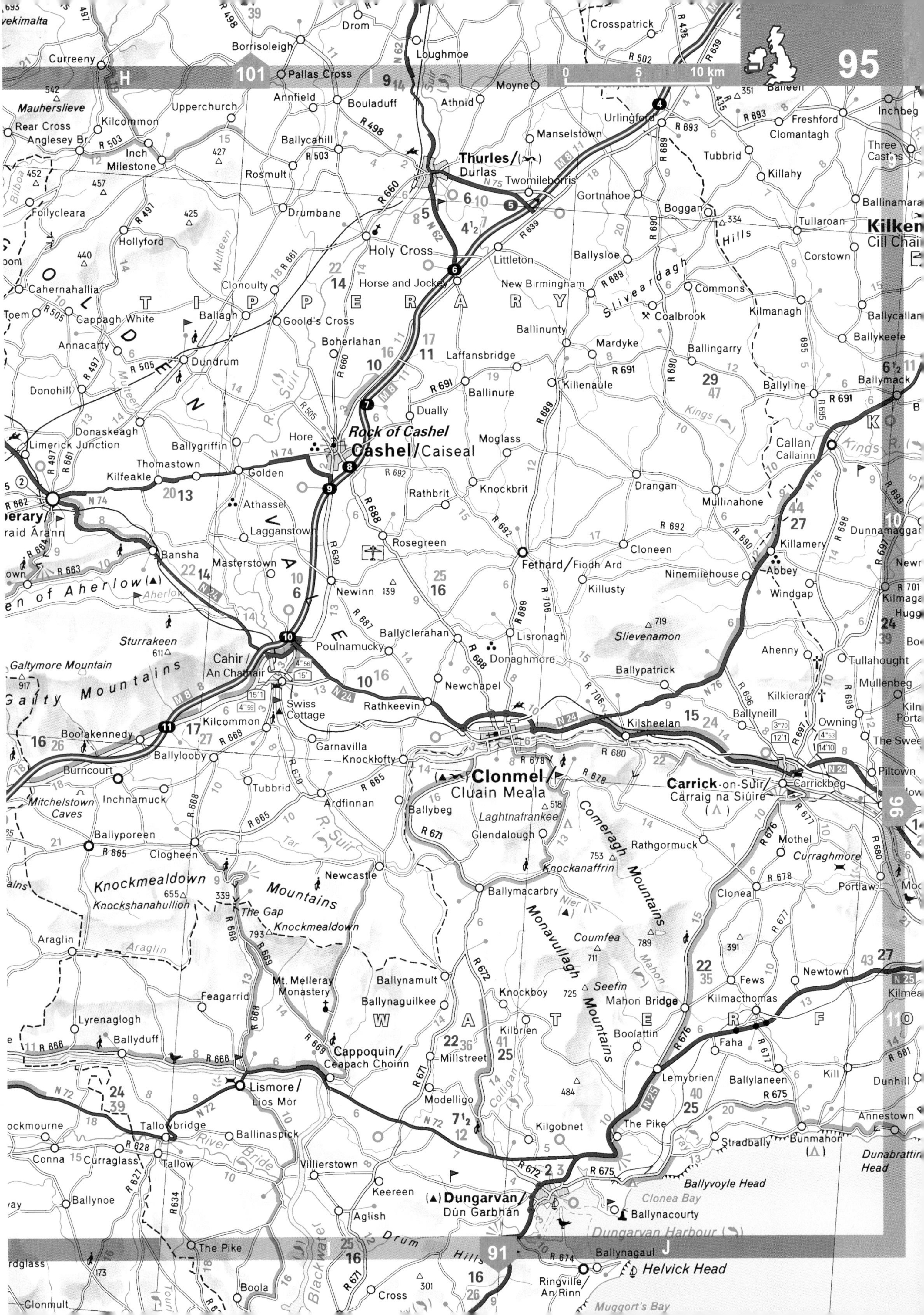

Borrisoleigh
Drom
Crosspatrick
Curreeny
Loughmoe
Pallas Cross
Moyne
Balleen
Inchbeg
Mauherslieve
Annfield
Bouladuff
Athnid
Urlingford
Freshford
Upperchurch
Rear Cross
Kilcommon
Anglesey Br.
Manselstown
Clomantagh
Ballycahill
Inch
Three Castles
Thurles/
Durlas
Tubbrid
Milestone
Rosmult
Twomileborris
Killahy
Gortnahoe
Foilycleara
Drumbane
Boggan
Ballinamara
Tullaroan
Kilkenny
Cill Chainnigh
Hollyford
Holy Cross
Ballysloe
Hills
Corstown
Littleton
Slieveardagh
Cahernahallia
Clonoulty
Horse and Jockey
New Birmingham
Commons
Toem
Cappagh White
Ballagh
Goold's Cross
Coalbrook
Kilmanagh
Ballycallan
Ballinunty
Ballykeefe
Annacarty
Boherlahan
Mardyke
Ballingarry
Dundrum
Laffansbridge
Donohill
Killenaule
Ballinure
Ballyline
Ballymack
Dually
Kings R.
Donaskeagh
Hore
Rock of Cashel
Moglass
Callan/
Callainn
Limerick Junction
Ballygriffin
Cashel/Caiseal
Thomastown
Kilfeakle
Golden
Knockbrit
Drangan
Rathbrit
Mullinahone
Tipperary/
Tiobraid Árann
Athassel
Lagganstown
Killamery
Dunnamaggan
Rosegreen
Cloneen
Bansha
Fethard/Fiodh Ard
Abbey
Masterstown
Ninemilehouse
Glen of Aherlow
Newinn
Killusty
Windgap
Kilmaganny
Aherlow
Slievenamon
Lisronagh
Ballyclerahan
Sturrakeen
Poulnamucky
Ahenny
Cahir/
An Cathair
Donaghmore
Galtymore Mountain
Galty Mountains
Tullahought
Ballypatrick
Newchapel
Mullenbeg
Swiss Cottage
Rathkeevin
Kilkieran
Kilsheelan
Ballyneill
Owning
Kilcommon
Boolakennedy
Ballylooby
Garnavilla
The Sweep
Knocklofty
Burncourt
Clonmel/
Cluain Meala
Carrick-on-Suir/
Carraig na Siúire
Carrickbeg
Piltown
Tubbrid
Inchnamuck
Ardfinnan
Mitchelstown Caves
Laghtnafrankee
Ballybeg
Glendalough
Mothel
Ballyporeen
Rathgormuck
Curraghmore
Clogheen
Tar
R. Suir
Comeragh Mountains
Knockanaffrin
Knockmealdown Mountains
Newcastle
Portlaw
Knockshanahullion
Ballymacarbry
Clonea
The Gap
Knockmealdown
Nier
Araglin
Coumfea
Monavullagh Mountains
Mt. Melleray Monastery
Ballynamult
Newtown
Fews
Feagarrid
Seefin
Ballynaguilkee
Knockboy
Mahon Bridge
Kilmacthomas
Kilmeaden
Lyrenaglogh
Kilbrien
Ballyduff
Cappoquin/
Ceapach Choinn
Boolattin
Millstreet
Faha
Lismore/
Lios Mór
Lemybrien
Ballylaneen
Kill
Dunhill
Modelligo
Tallowbridge
Colligan
The Pike
Annestown
Ballinaspick
Kilgobnet
Stradbally
Bunmahon
Conna
Curraglass
Tallow
River Bride
Villierstown
Dunabrattin Head
Ballyvoyle Head
Keereen
Dungarvan/
Dún Garbhán
Clonea Bay
Ballynoe
Aglish
Ballynacourty
Dungarvan Harbour
Drum Hills
The Pike
Ballynagaul
Helvick Head
Ringville/
An Rinn
Boola
Blackwater
Cross
Glonmult
Mugggort's Bay
Tipperary
Waterford

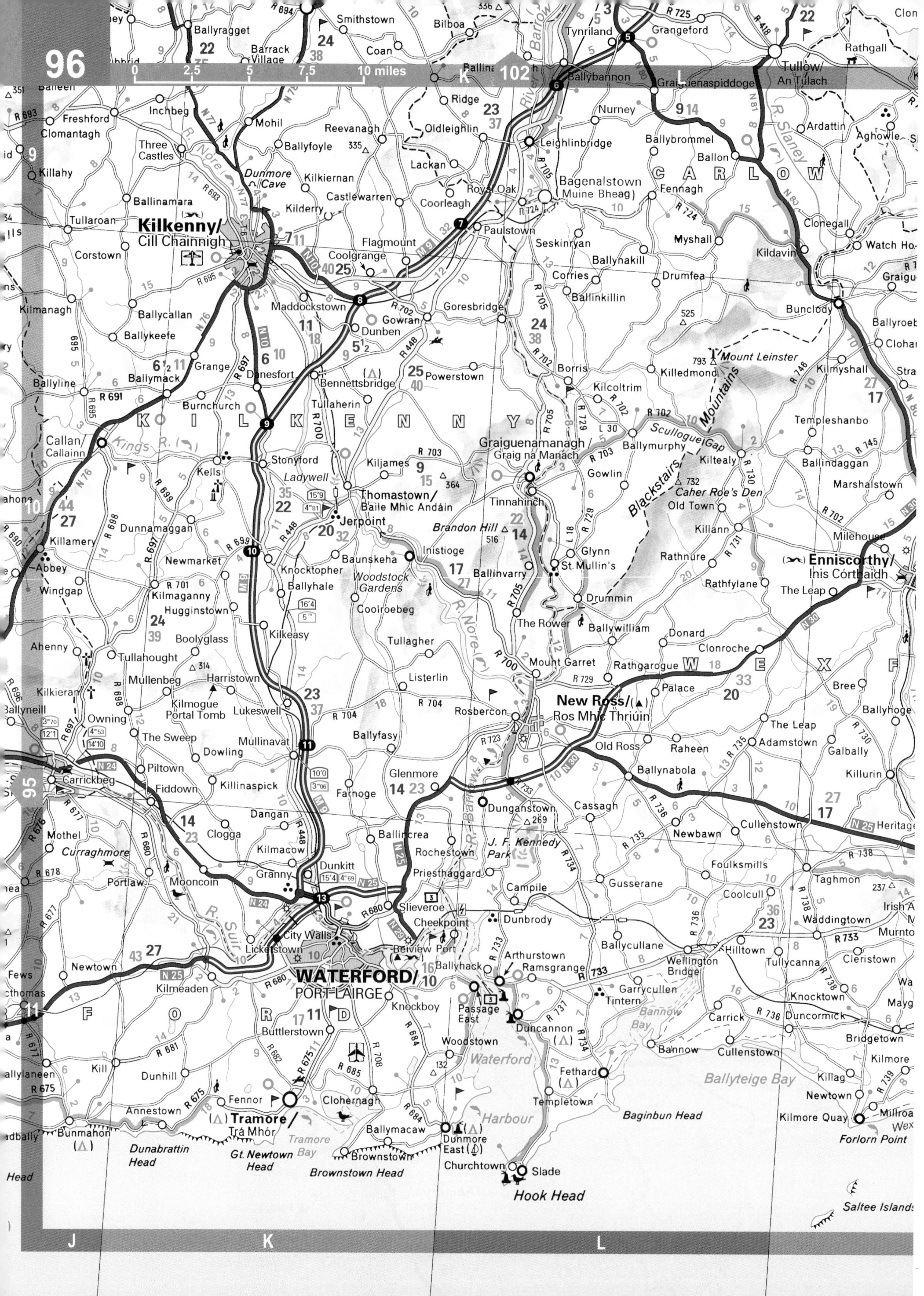

0 2,5 5 7,5 10 miles
102
95
J
K
L
Ballyragget
Barrack Village
Smithstown
Coan
Bilboa
Tynriland
Grangeford
Tullow/
An Tulach
Rathgall
Ballybannon
Graiguenaspiddoge
Ballina
River Barrow
Inchbeg
Freshford
Clomantagh
Mohil
Ridge
Reevanagh
Oldleighlin
Nurney
Ardattin
Aghowle
Three Castles
Killahy
Ballyfoyle
Leighlinbridge
Ballybrommel
Ballon
R. Nore
Dunmore Cave
Kilkiernan
Lackan
Bagenalstown
Muine Bheag)
Fennagh
CARLOW
R. Slaney
Ballinamara
Castlewarren
Royal Oak
Coorleagh
Kilderry
Tullaroan
Kilkenny/
Cill Chainnigh
Paulstown
Seskinryan
Myshall
Clonegall
Flagmount
Kildavin
Watch House
Corstown
Coolgrange
Ballynakill
Corries
Drumfea
Ballinkillin
Maddockstown
Goresbridge
Gowran
Dunben
Bunclody
Kilmanagh
Ballycallan
Ballykeefe
Mount Leinster
Killedmond
Kilmyshall
Borris
Grange
Ballymack
Danesfort
Bennettsbridge
Powerstown
Ballyline
Burnchurch
Tullaherin
Kilcoltrim
KILKENNY
Templeshanbo
Scullogue Gap
Mountains
Graiguenamanagh/
Graig na Manach
Ballymurphy
Callan/
Callainn
Kings R.
Stonyford
Kiljames
Kiltealy
Ballindaggan
Kells
Ladywell
Gowlin
Blackstairs
Caher Roe's Den
Marshalstown
Thomastown/
Baile Mhic Andáin
Tinnahinch
Old Town
Jerpoint
Brandon Hill
Killann
Dunnamaggan
Milehouse
Killamery
Abbey
Newmarket
Knocktopher
Baunskeha
Inistioge
Glynn
St. Mullin's
Rathnure
Enniscorthy/
Inis Córthaidh
Woodstock Gardens
Ballinvarry
Windgap
Kilmaganny
Ballyhale
Rathfylane
The Leap
Coolroebeg
Drummin
Hugginstown
Kilkeasy
The Rower
Ballywilliam
Boolyglass
Tullagher
Donard
Ahenny
Tullahought
Clonroche
Mount Garret
Rathgarogue
WEXFORD
Mullenbeg
Harristown
Listerlin
Kilkieran
Kilmogue Portal Tomb
Palace
Bree
Ballyneill
Lukeswell
New Ross/
Ros Mhic Thriúin
Rosbercon
Ballyhoge
Owning
The Sweep
Ballyfasy
The Leap
Adamstown
Dowling
Mullinavat
Old Ross
Raheen
Galbally
Piltown
Carrickbeg
Ballynabola
Killurin
Killinaspick
Glenmore
Fiddown
Farnoge
Dunganstown
Cassagh
Dangan
Cullenstown
Heritage
Mothel
Clogga
Ballincrea
Newbawn
Curraghmore
Kilmacow
Rochestown
J. F. Kennedy Park
Portlaw
Mooncoin
Dunkitt
Priesthaggard
Foulksmills
Granny
Campile
Gusserane
Taghmon
Slieveroe
Coolcull
R. Suir
Cheekpoint
Dunbrody
Waddingtown
City Walls
Belview Port
Ballycullane
Lickestown
Hilltown
Murntown
Arthurstown
Fews
Newtown
Ballyhack
Ramsgrange
Wellington Bridge
Tullycanna
Cleristown
WATERFORD/
PORT LAIRGE
Garrycullen
Kilmeaden
Tintern
Passage East
Knockboy
Knocktown
FORD
Duncannon
Bannow Bay
Carrick
Duncormick
Buttlerstown
Woodstown
Bannow
Cullenstown
Bridgetown
Waterford
Fethard
Kilmore
Kill
Dunhill
Ballyteige Bay
Killag
Ballylaneen
Clohernagh
Fennor
Tramore/
Trá Mhór
Templetown
Newtown
Annestown
Harbour
Baginbun Head
Kilmore Quay
Bunmahon
Ballymacaw
Dunmore East
Forlorn Point
Tramore Bay
Dunabrattin Head
Gt. Newtown Head
Brownstown
Brownstown Head
Churchtown
Slade
Hook Head
Saltee Islands

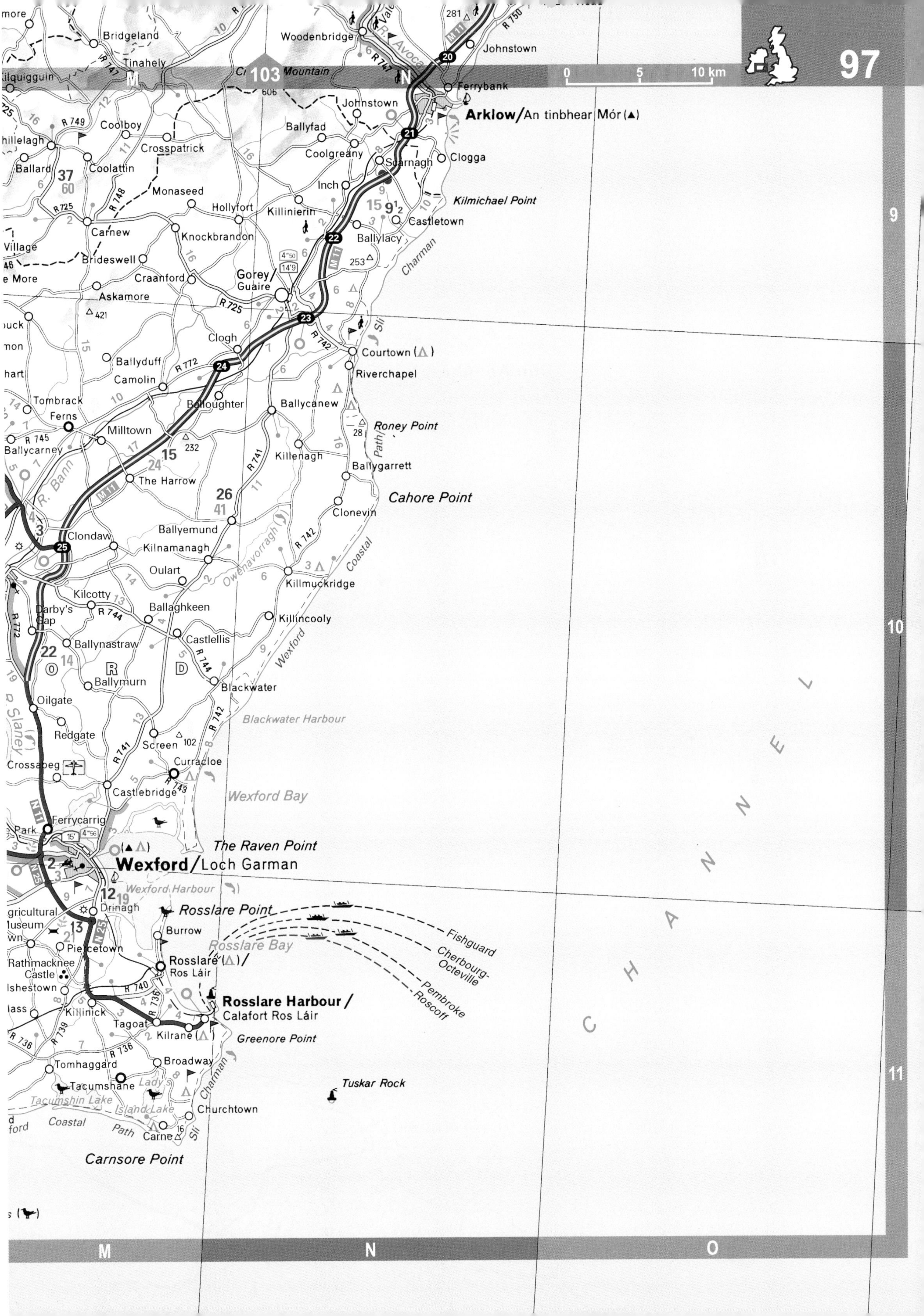
Arklow/An tinbhear Mór
Ferrybank
Johnstown
Woodenbridge
Bridgeland
Tinahely
Kilquiggin
Coolboy
Crosspatrick
Shillelagh
Ballard
Coolattin
Monaseed
Hollyfort
Killinierin
Carnew
Knockbrandon
Brideswell
Craanford
Gorey/Guaire
Askamore
Ballyfad
Coolgreany
Inch
Scarnagh
Clogga
Kilmichael Point
Castletown
Ballylacy
Clogh
Courtown
Riverchapel
Ballyduff
Camolin
Tombrack
Ferns
Milltown
Balloughter
Ballycanew
Roney Point
Ballycarney
Killenagh
Ballygarrett
The Harrow
Cahore Point
Clonevin
Ballyemund
Clondaw
Kilnamanagh
Oulart
Killmuckridge
Kilcotty
Darby's Gap
Ballaghkeen
Killincooly
Castlellis
Ballynastraw
Ballymurn
Blackwater
Oilgate
Blackwater Harbour
Redgate
Screen
Curracloe
Crossabeg
Castlebridge
Wexford Bay
Ferrycarrig
The Raven Point
Wexford/Loch Garman
Wexford Harbour
Drinagh
Rosslare Point
Burrow
Rosslare Bay
Piercetown
Rosslare/Ros Láir
Rathmacknee Castle
Rosslare Harbour/Calafort Ros Láir
Killinick
Tagoat
Kilrane
Greenore Point
Tomhaggard
Broadway
Tacumshane
Tacumshin Lake
Lady's Island Lake
Churchtown
Carne
Coastal Path
Carnsore Point
Tuskar Rock
Fishguard
Cherbourg-Octeville
Pembroke
Roscoff
CHANNEL
M
N
O
9
10
11
103
0 5 10 km

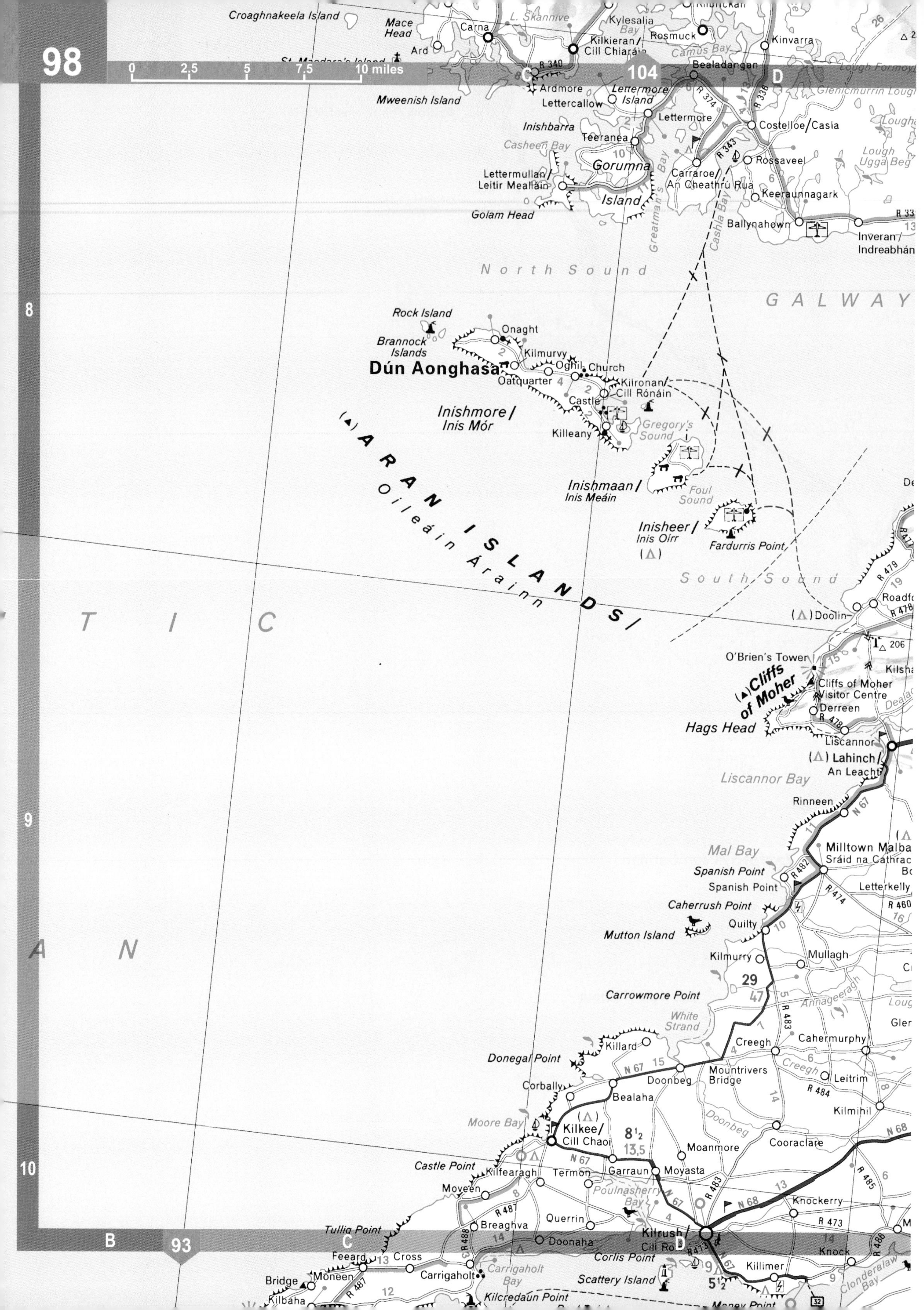
Croaghnakeela Island
Mace Head
Carna
L. Skannive
Kylesalia Bay
Rosmuck
Kinvarra
Ard
Kilkieran / Cill Chiaráin
Camus Bay
0 2,5 5 7,5 10 miles
C
104
Bealadangan
D
Lough Formoyle
Ardmore
Lettermore Island
Glenicmurrin Lough
Mweenish Island
Lettercallow
R 374
R 336
Inishbarra
Lettermore
Costelloe / Casla
Lough
Teeranea
R 343
Casheen Bay
Rossaveel
Lough Ugga Beg
Gorumna
Lettermullan / Leitir Mealláin
Carraroe / An Cheathrú Rua
Island
Keeraunnagark
Golam Head
Greatman's Bay
Cashla Bay
Ballynahown
Inveran / Indreabhán
North Sound
GALWAY
8
Rock Island
Onaght
Brannock Islands
Kilmurvy
Oghil
Church
Dún Aonghasa
Oatquarter
Kilronan / Cill Rónáin
Castle
Inishmore / Inis Mór
Gregory's Sound
Killeany
ARAN ISLANDS / Oileáin Árainn
Inishmaan / Inis Meáin
Foul Sound
Inisheer / Inis Oírr
Fardurris Point
South Sound
R 479
Roadford
R 478
Doolin
T I C
206
O'Brien's Tower
Kilshanny
Cliffs of Moher
Cliffs of Moher Visitor Centre
Derreen
Hags Head
R 478
Liscannor
Lahinch / An Leacht
Liscannor Bay
9
Rinneen
N 67
Milltown Malbay
Sráid na Cathrach
Mal Bay
Spanish Point
Spanish Point
R 482
R 474
Letterkelly
R 460
Caherrush Point
Quilty
Mutton Island
A N
Kilmurry
Mullagh
29
47
Carrowmore Point
Annageeragh
R 483
White Strand
Creegh
Cahermurphy
Killard
Donegal Point
N 67
Creegh
Mountrivers Bridge
Leitrim
Doonbeg
Corbally
R 484
Bealaha
Kilmihil
Doonbeg
Moore Bay
Kilkee / Cill Chaoi
8½
13,5
Moanmore
Cooraclare
N 68
10
N 67
Castle Point
Kilfearagh
Termon
Garraun
Moyasta
R 485
R 483
Moveen
Poulnasherry Bay
N 67
N 68
Knockerry
R 487
Breaghva
Querrin
R 473
Tullig Point
Kilrush / Cill Rois
B
93
C
D
Doonaha
R 488
Feeard
Cross
Corlis Point
Knock
R 486
Carrigaholt Bay
R 473
N 67
Killimer
Clonderalaw Bay
Bridge
Moneen
Carrigaholt
Scattery Island
R 487
Kilbaha
Kilcredaun Point
Money Point

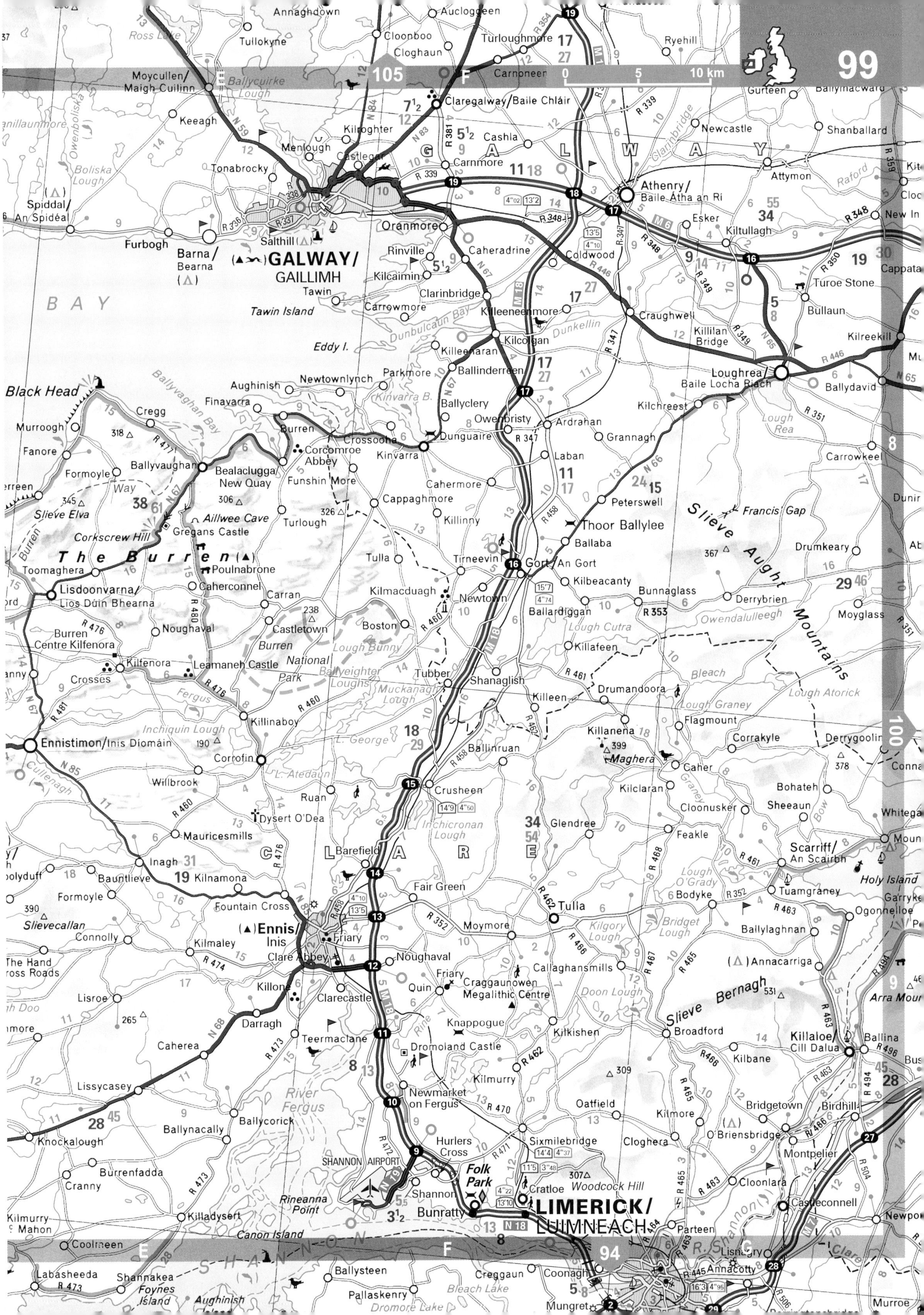

Annaghdown
Auclogeen
Ross Lake
Tullokyne
Cloonboo
Cloghaun
Turloughmore
Ryehill
Moycullen/
Maigh Cuilinn
Ballycuirke Lough
Carnoneen
0 5 10 km
Gurteen
Ballymacward
Claregalway/Baile Chláir
Keeagh
Kilroghter
Cashla
Newcastle
Shanballard
Menlough
Castlegar
G A L W A Y
Boliska Lough
Tonabrocky
Carnmore
Attymon
Raford
Athenry/
Baile Átha an Rí
Spiddal/
An Spidéal
Oranmore
Esker
Kiltullagh
New Inn
Furbogh
Barna/
Bearna
Salthill
GALWAY/
GAILLIMH
Rinville
Caheradrine
Coldwood
Cappataggle
Kilcaimin
Turoe Stone
Tawin
BAY
Tawin Island
Clarinbridge
Carrowmore
Killeeneenmore
Craughwell
Bullaun
Dunbulcaun Bay
Kilcolgan
Dunkellin
Eddy I.
Killeenaran
Killilan Bridge
Kilreekill
Ballinderreen
Loughrea/
Baile Locha Riach
Ballydavid
Black Head
Aughinish
Newtownlynch
Parkmore
Finavarra
Kinvarra B.
Ballyclery
Kilchreest
Cregg
Murroogh
Ballyvaghan Bay
Owenbristy
Ardrahan
Lough Rea
Burren
Crossooha
Dunguaire
Grannagh
Fanore
Corcomroe Abbey
Kinvarra
Laban
Carrowkeel
Ballyvaughan
Bealaclugga/
New Quay
Formoyle
Funshin More
Cahermore
Burren Way
Cappaghmore
Peterswell
Slieve Elva
Aillwee Cave
Turlough
Killinny
Thoor Ballylee
Francis Gap
Gregans Castle
Corkscrew Hill
Ballaba
Slieve Aught Mountains
The Burren
Tulla
Tirneevin
Gort/An Gort
Drumkeary
Toomaghera
Poulnabrone
Lisdoonvarna/
Lios Dúin Bhearna
Caherconnel
Kilmacduagh
Kilbeacanty
Carran
Newtown
Bunnaglass
Derrybrien
Ballardiggan
Moyglass
Noughaval
Castletown
Boston
Lough Cutra
Owendalulleegh
Burren Centre Kilfenora
Burren National Park
Lough Bunny
Killafeen
Kilfenora
Leamaneh Castle
Ballyeighter Loughs
Tubber
Shanaglish
Bleach
Crosses
Muckanagh Lough
Killeen
Drumandoora
Lough Atorick
Lough Graney
Fergus
Killinaboy
Flagmount
Inchiquin Lough
Killanena
Corrakyle
Derrygoolin
Ennistimon/Inis Díomáin
L. George
Ballinruan
Maghera
Corrofin
Caher
Connaught
Cullenagh
L. Atedaun
Crusheen
Kilclaran
Bohateh
Willbrook
Ruan
Cloonusker
Sheeaun
Whitegate
Inchicronan Lough
Dysert O'Dea
Glendree
Feakle
Mauricesmills
Scarriff/
An Scairbh
Mountshannon
Barefield
C L A R E
Holy Island
Inagh
Bauntlieve
Kilnamona
Lough O'Grady
Fair Green
Tuamgraney
Bodyke
Formoyle
Fountain Cross
Tulla
Ogonnelloe
Slievecallan
Ennis/
Inis
Moymore
Kilgory Lough
Bridget Lough
Ballylaghnan
Connolly
Friary
Kilmaley
The Hand Cross Roads
Clare Abbey
Noughaval
Callaghansmills
Annacarriga
Killone
Friary
Craggaunowen Megalithic Centre
Doon Lough
Lisroe
Clarecastle
Quin
Slieve Bernagh
Arra Mountains
Darragh
Knappogue
Broadford
Teermaclane
Dromoland Castle
Kilkishen
Killaloe/
Cill Dalua
Ballina
Caherea
Kilbane
Kilmurry
River Fergus
Lissycasey
Newmarket on Fergus
Oatfield
Bridgetown
Birdhill
Ballycorick
Kilmore
Ballynacally
Knockalough
Hurlers Cross
Sixmilebridge
Cloghera
O'Briensbridge
Shannon Airport
Montpelier
Burrenfadda
Folk Park
Cratloe
Woodcock Hill
Cloonlara
Cranny
Shannon
Bunratty
Rineanna Point
LIMERICK/
LUIMNEACH
Castleconnell
Killadysert
Kilmurry Mahon
Newport
Canon Island
Parteen
Coolmeen
SHANNON
Lisnagry
Annacotty
Labasheeda
Shannakea
Foynes Island
Ballysteen
Creggaun
Coonagh
Aughinish
Pallaskenry
Bleach Lake
Dromore Lake
Mungret
Murroe

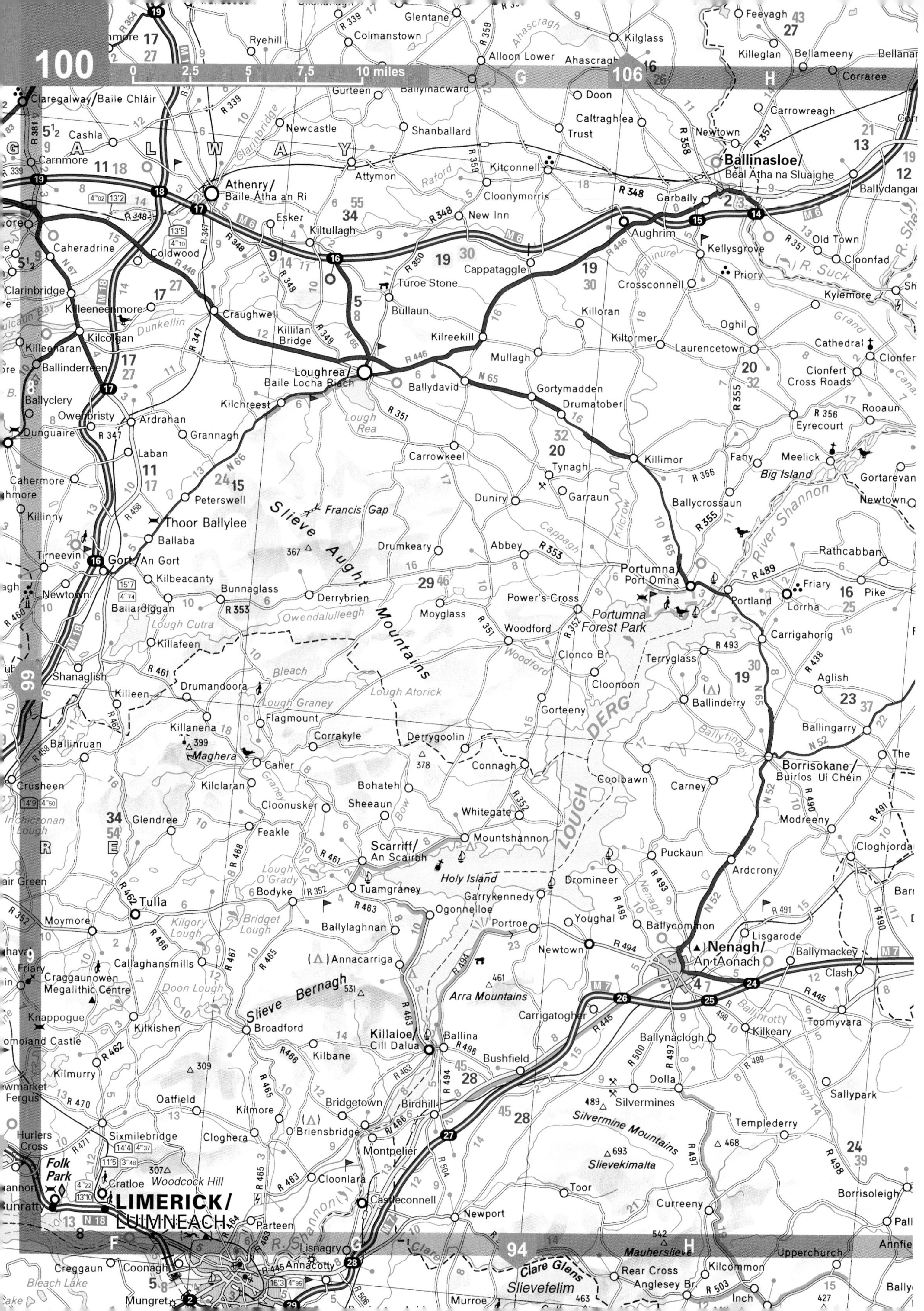
0 2,5 5 7,5 10 miles
G
106
H
GALWAY
Claregalway/Baile Chláir
Cashla
Carnmore
Athenry/ Baile Átha an Rí
Ryehill
Colmanstown
Glentane
Kilglass
Feevagh
Killeglan
Bellameeny
Corraree
Alloon Lower
Ahascragh
Doon
Gurteen
Newcastle
Shanballard
Caltraghlea
Trust
Newtown
Carrowreagh
Ballinasloe/ Béal Átha na Sluaighe
Attymon
Kitconnell
Cloonymorris
Carbally
Ballydangan
Esker
Kiltullagh
New Inn
Aughrim
Old Town
Kellysgrove
Cloonfad
Caheradrine
Coldwood
Turoe Stone
Cappataggle
Priory
Crossconnell
R. Suck
Clarinbridge
Kilyemore
Killeeneenmore
Craughwell
Bullaun
Killilan Bridge
Killoran
Kilcolgan
Dunkellin
Kilreekill
Kiltormer
Oghil
Laurencetown
Cathedral
Killeenaran
Ballinderreen
Loughrea/ Baile Locha Riach
Mullagh
Clonfert
Clonfert Cross Roads
Ballyclery
Ballydavid
Gortymadden
Drumatober
Rooaun
Owenbristy
Kilchreest
Ardrahan
Lough Rea
Eyrecourt
Dunguaire
Grannagh
Laban
Carrowkeel
Killimor
Fahy
Meelick
Big Island
Gortarevan
Cahermore
Peterswell
Tynagh
Garraun
Duniry
Ballycrossaun
Newtown
River Shannon
Killinny
Francis' Gap
Slieve Aught Mountains
Thoor Ballylee
Ballaba
Tirneevin
Drumkeary
Abbey
Cappagh
Kilcrow
Rathcabban
Gort/An Gort
Kilbeacanty
Portumna/ Port Omna
Friary
Pike
Newtown
Bunnaglass
Derrybrien
Power's Cross
Portland
Lorrha
Ballardiggan
Owendalulleegh
Moyglass
Woodford
Portumna Forest Park
Carrigahorig
Lough Cutra
Killafeen
Clonco Br
Terryglass
Aglish
Shanaglish
Bleach
Cloonoon
Ballinderry
Killeen
Drumandoora
Lough Graney
Lough Atorick
Gorteeny
Ballingarry
Flagmount
Killanena
Corrakyle
Derrygoolin
LOUGH DERG
Ballyfinboy
Ballinruan
Maghera
Caher
Connagh
Borrisokane/ Buirios Uí Chéin
Crusheen
Kilclaran
Bohateh
Coolbawn
Carney
Inchicronan Lough
Cloonusker
Sheeaun
Glendree
Whitegate
Modreeny
Feakle
Mountshannon
Cloghjordan
Scarriff/ An Scairbh
Puckaun
Holy Island
Dromineer
Ardcrony
Lough O'Grady
Bodyke
Tuamgraney
Garrykennedy
Tulla
Ogonnelloe
Youghal
Moymore
Ballylaghnan
Portroe
Ballycommon
Kilgory Lough
Bridget Lough
Lisgarode
Newtown
Nenagh/ An tAonach
Ballymackey
Friary
Annacarriga
Callaghansmills
Clash
Craggaunowen Megalithic Centre
Doon Lough
Arra Mountains
Slieve Bernagh
Toomyvara
Knappogue
Carrigatogher
Ballintotty
Kilkishen
Broadford
Kilkeary
Killaloe/ Cill Dalua
Ballina
Ballynaclogh
Kilbane
Bushfield
Kilmurry
Dolla
Silvermines
Sallypark
Oatfield
Kilmore
Bridgetown
Birdhill
Silvermine Mountains
Templederry
Hurlers Cross
Sixmilebridge
Cloghera
O'Briensbridge
Montpelier
Slievekimalta
Folk Park
Woodcock Hill
Cratloe
Cloonlara
Borrisoleigh
Bunratty
LIMERICK/ LUIMNEACH
Castleconnell
Toor
Curreeny
Newport
Parteen
Pallas
F
94
Mauherslieve
Upperchurch
Annfield
Creggaun
Coonagh
Lisnagry
Annacotty
Rear Cross
Kilcommon
Bleach Lake
Mungret
Clare Glens
Slievefelim
Anglesey Br.
Murroe
Inch
99

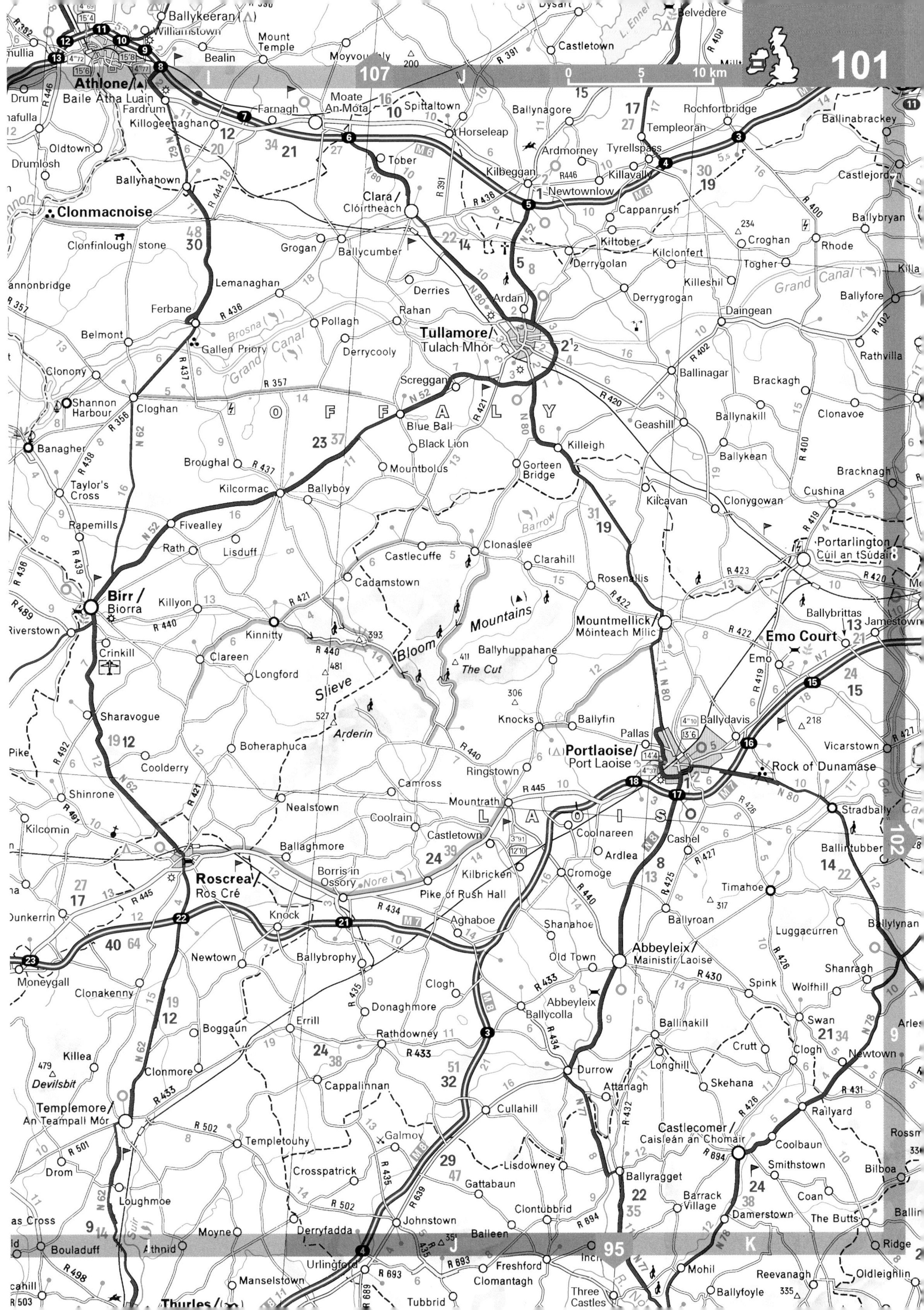
Athlone / Baile Átha Luain
Clonmacnoise
Tullamore / Tulach Mhór
Clara / Clóirtheach
Kilbeggan
Tyrellspass
Rochfortbridge
Birr / Biorra
Portarlington / Cúil an tSúdaire
Mountmellick / Móinteach Mílic
Portlaoise / Port Laoise
Roscrea / Ros Cré
Abbeyleix / Mainistir Laoise
Templemore / An Teampall Mór
Castlecomer / Caisleán an Chomair
Slieve Bloom Mountains
Arderin
The Cut
Emo Court
Rock of Dunamase
O F F A L Y
L A O I S
Grand Canal
Brosna
Barrow
Nore
Banagher
Ferbane
Cloghan
Kinnitty
Durrow
Borris in Ossory
Mountrath
Stradbally
Ballyragget
Urlingford
Thurles
Devilsbit
Moate / An Móta
Horseleap
Daingean
Ballinagar
Clonaslee
Rosenallis
Ballybrittas
Vicarstown
Timahoe
Ballinakill
0 5 10 km
107
95
102

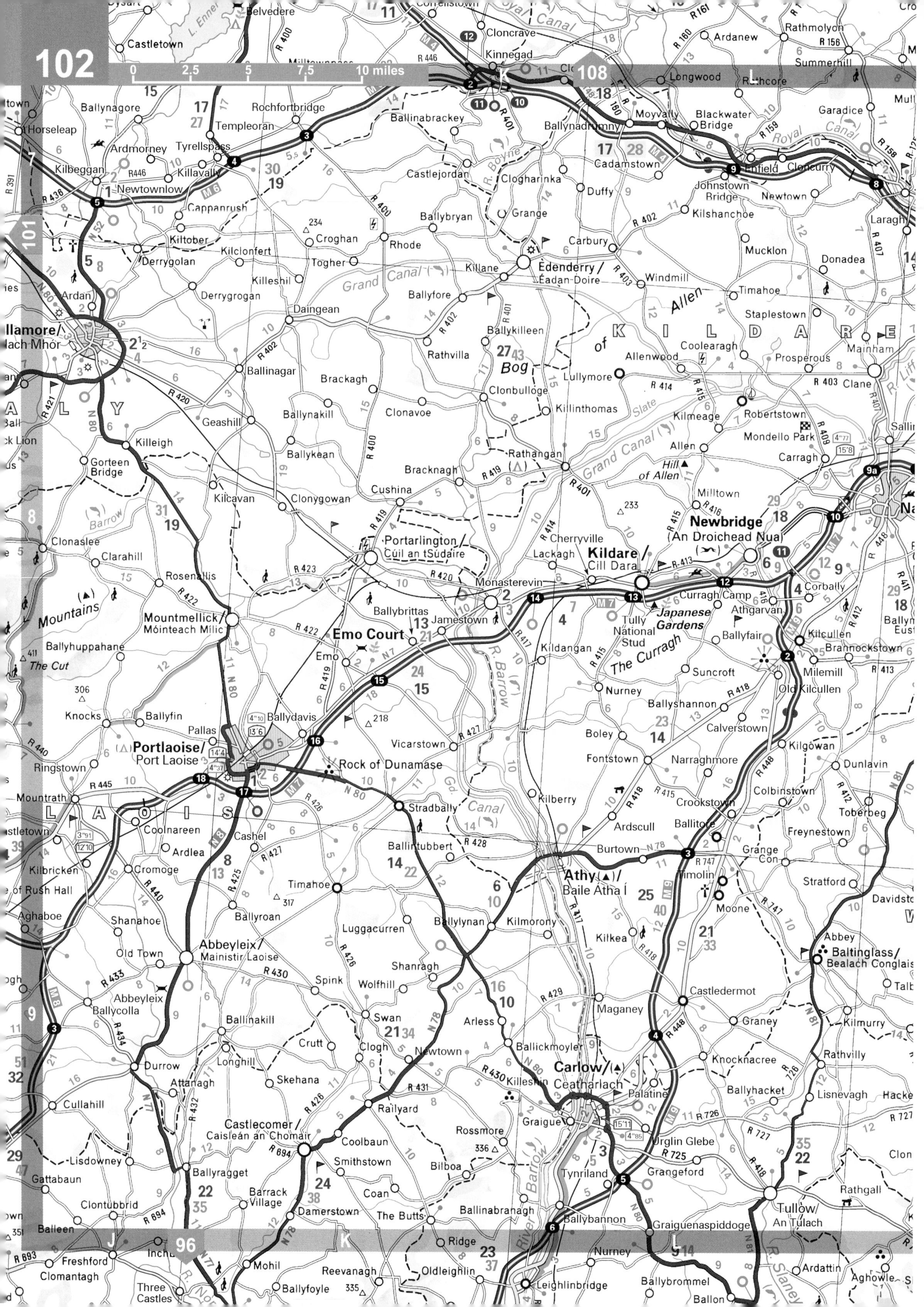
0 2.5 5 7.5 10 miles
108
101
96
Belvedere
Castletown
L. Ennel
Cloncrave
Royal Canal
Kinnegad
Ardanew
Rathmolyon
Summerhill
Longwood
Rathcore
Horseleap
Ballynagore
Rochfortbridge
Templeoran
Ballinabrackey
Ballynadrumny
Moyvally
Blackwater Bridge
Garadice
Ardmorney
Tyrellspass
Kilbeggan
Killavally
Newtownlow
Castlejordan
Clogharinka
Cadamstown
Enfield
Cloncurry
Johnstown Bridge
Newtown
Cappanrush
Kiltober
Kilclonfert
Derrygolan
Croghan
Rhode
Togher
Ballybryan
Grange
Duffy
Kilshanchoe
Laragh
Carbury
Mucklon
Donadea
Killeshil
Killane
Edenderry / Éadan Doire
Windmill
Timahoe
Ardan
Grand Canal
Ballyfore
Derrygrogan
Daingean
Staplestown
Bog of Allen
KILDARE
Tullamore / Tulach Mhór
Ballykilleen
Rathvilla
Coolearagh
Allenwood
Prosperous
Mainham
Clane
Ballinagar
Brackagh
Clonbullogue
Lullymore
Kilmeage
Robertstown
Killinthomas
Ballynakill
Clonavoe
Mondello Park
Sallins
LAOIS
OFFALY
Killeigh
Geashill
Ballykean
Rathangan
Allen
Carragh
Hill of Allen
Gorteen Bridge
Bracknagh
Cushina
Kilcavan
Clonygowan
Milltown
Naas
Newbridge (An Droichead Nua)
Clonaslee
Clarahill
Portarlington / Cúil an tSúdaire
Cherryville
Lackagh
Kildare / Cill Dara
Rosenallis
Monasterevin
Curragh Camp
Corbally
Mountains
Mountmellick / Móinteach Mílic
Ballybrittas
Jamestown
Tully National Stud
Japanese Gardens
Athgarvan
Emo Court
Kilcullen
Ballyfair
Brannockstown
Ballyhuppahane
The Cut
Emo
Kildangan
The Curragh
Milemill
Suncroft
Old Kilcullen
Nurney
Knocks
Ballyfin
Ballydavis
Ballyshannon
Pallas
Portlaoise / Port Laoise
Boley
Calverstown
Vicarstown
Kilgowan
Ringstown
Rock of Dunamase
Fontstown
Narraghmore
Dunlavin
R. Barrow
Mountrath
Stradbally
Kilberry
Crookstown
Colbinstown
Toberbeg
Coolnareen
Ardscull
Ballitore
Freynestown
Castletown
Cashel
Ballintubbert
Burtown
Grange Con
Ardlea
Athy / Baile Átha Í
Timolin
Kilbricken
Cromoge
Stratford
Moone
Davidstown
Timahoe
Rush Hall
Ballyroan
Aghaboe
Shanahoe
Ballylynan
Kilmorony
Luggacurren
Kilkea
Abbey
Baltinglass / Bealach Conglais
Old Town
Abbeyleix / Mainistir Laoise
Shanragh
Spink
Wolfhill
Talbotstown
Castledermot
Abbeyleix
Ballycolla
Ballinakill
Maganey
Arless
Swan
Graney
Kilmurry
Crutt
Clogh
Newtown
Ballickmoyler
Durrow
Longhill
Knocknacree
Rathvilly
Attanagh
Skehana
Carlow / Ceatharlach
Killeshin
Palatine
Ballyhacket
Lisnevagh
Hacketstown
Cullahill
Railyard
Castlecomer / Caisleán an Chomair
Graigue
Urglin Glebe
Coolbaun
Rossmore
Lisdowney
Smithstown
Bilboa
Tynriland
Grangeford
Clonmore
Gattabaun
Ballyragget
Barrack Village
Coan
Rathgall
Tullow / An Tulach
Clontubbrid
Damerstown
The Butts
Ballinabranagh
Ballybannon
Graiguenaspiddoge
Balleen
Ridge
Freshford
Inch
Clomantagh
Mohil
Reevanagh
Oldleighlin
Nurney
Ardattin
Aghowle
Three Castles
Ballyfoyle
Leighlinbridge
Ballybrommel
Ballon
R. Slaney
River Barrow

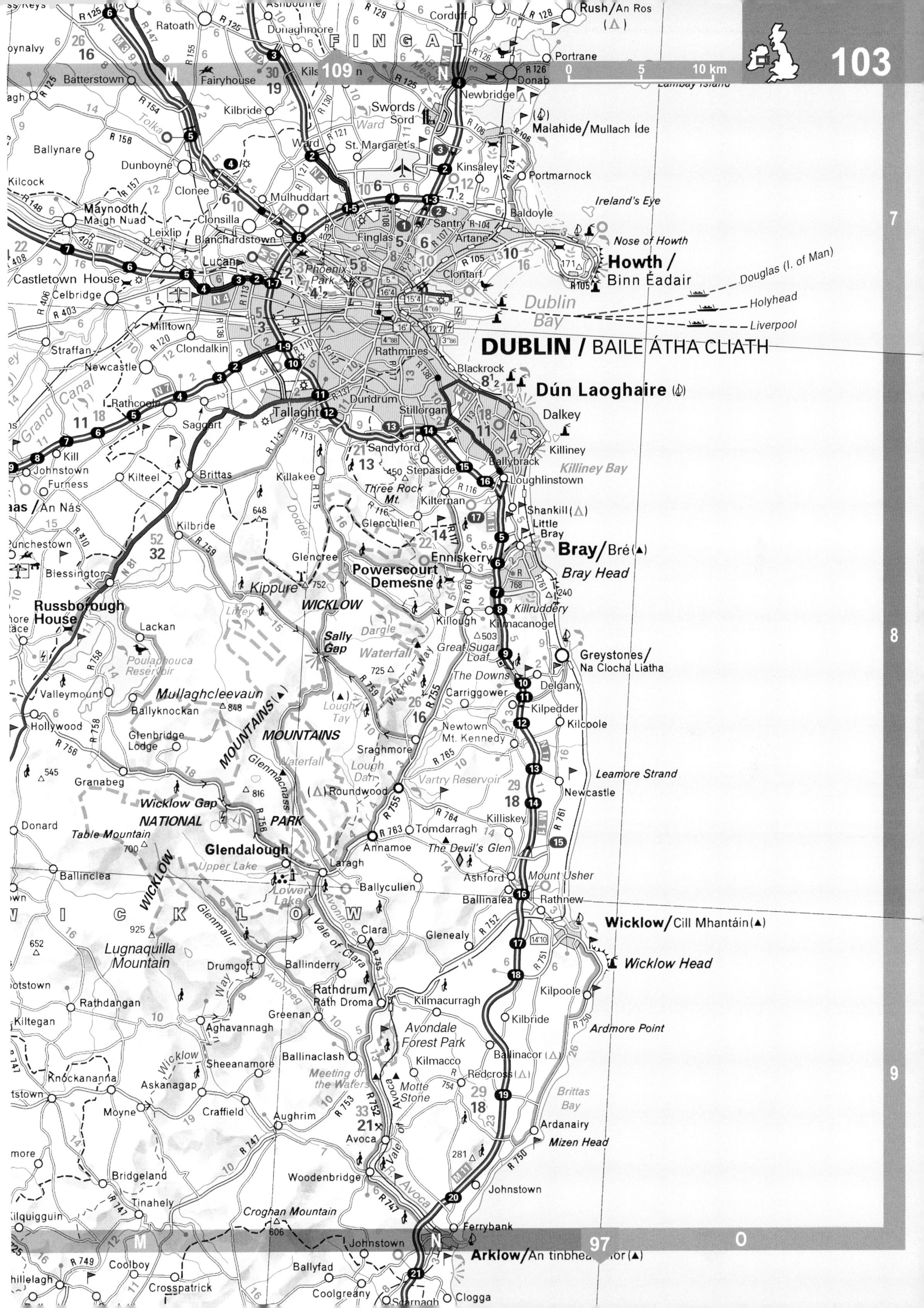
FINGAL
Rush/An Ros
Portrane
Donabate
Swords/Sord
Malahide/Mullach Íde
Portmarnock
Kinsaley
Ratoath
Donaghmore
Batterstown
Fairyhouse
Kilbride
Ballynare
Dunboyne
Clonee
Kilcock
Maynooth/Maigh Nuad
Leixlip
Clonsilla
Blanchardstown
Mulhuddart
St. Margaret's
Ward
Finglas
Santry
Artane
Baldoyle
Ireland's Eye
Nose of Howth
Howth/Binn Éadair
Douglas (I. of Man)
Holyhead
Liverpool
Dublin Bay
Clontarf
Phoenix Park
Lucan
Castletown House
Celbridge
Milltown
Straffan
Clondalkin
Newcastle
Grand Canal
Rathcoole
Saggart
Tallaght
Rathmines
DUBLIN / BAILE ÁTHA CLIATH
Blackrock
Dún Laoghaire
Dalkey
Killiney
Killiney Bay
Dundrum
Stillorgan
Sandyford
Stepaside
Ballybrack
Loughlinstown
Kill
Johnstown
Furness
Kilteel
Brittas
Killakee
Three Rock Mt.
Kilternan
Shankill
Little Bray
Naas/An Nás
Punchestown
Kilbride
Glencullen
Glencree
Enniskerry
Bray/Bré
Bray Head
Blessington
Russborough House
Kippure
Powerscourt Demesne
WICKLOW
Killough
Kilmacanoge
Killruddery
Lackan
Poulaphouca Reservoir
Liffey
Sally Gap
Dargle
Waterfall
Great Sugar Loaf
Greystones/Na Clocha Liatha
Delgany
The Downs
Carriggower
Kilpedder
Kilcoole
Valleymount
Mullaghcleevaun
Ballyknockan
Lough Tay
Wicklow Way
Hollywood
Glenbridge Lodge
MOUNTAINS
Newtown Mt. Kennedy
Sraghmore
Glenmacnass
Lough Dan
Vartry Reservoir
Leamore Strand
Newcastle
Granabeg
Roundwood
Killiskey
Wicklow Gap
NATIONAL
PARK
Donard
Table Mountain
Glendalough
Annamoe
Tomdarragh
The Devil's Glen
Mount Usher
Ashford
Upper Lake
Lower Lake
Laragh
Ballycullen
Ballinclea
Ballinalea
Rathnew
Wicklow/Cill Mhantáin
Wicklow Head
Glenmalur
Avonmore
Vale of Clara
Clara
Glenealy
Lugnaquilla Mountain
Drumgoff
Ballinderry
Rathdrum/Ráth Droma
Kilmacurragh
Kilpoole
Rathdangan
Greenan
Aghavannagh
Kilbride
Ardmore Point
Kiltegan
Avondale Forest Park
Ballinaclash
Kilmacco
Ballinacor
Sheeanamore
Knockananna
Askanagap
Meeting of the Waters
Motte Stone
Redcross
Brittas Bay
Moyne
Craffield
Aughrim
Avoca
Ardanairy
Mizen Head
Bridgeland
Woodenbridge
Johnstown
Tinahely
Croghan Mountain
Ferrybank
Johnstown
Arklow/An tInbhear Mór
Coolboy
Ballyfad
Crosspatrick
Coolgreany
Clogga
Kilquiggin
10 km

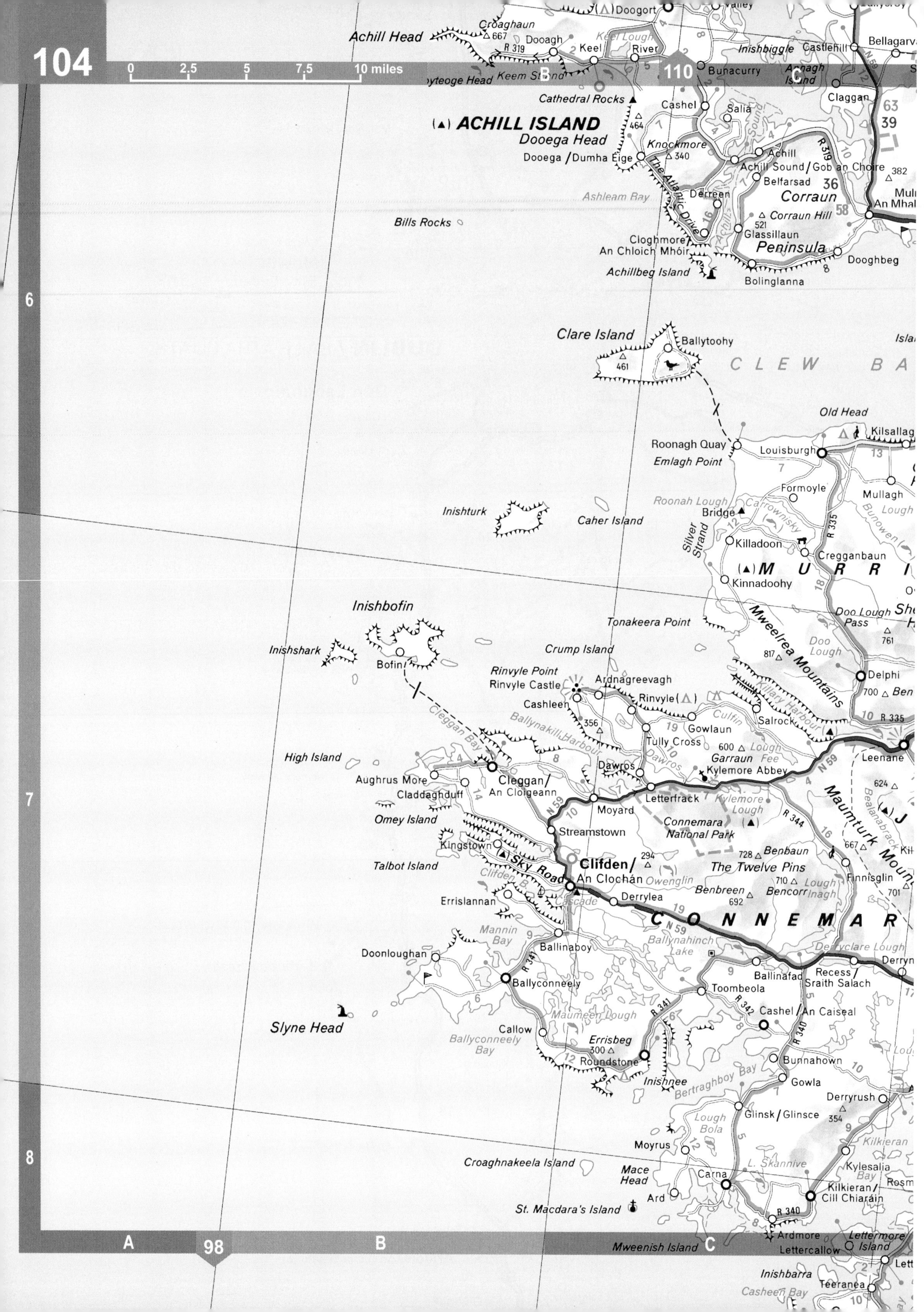
0 2.5 5 7.5 10 miles
110
98
A
B
C
6
7
8
ACHILL ISLAND
Achill Head
Croaghaun
667
Dooagh
Keel
Keel Lough
Doogort
River
Inishbiggle
Castlehill
Bellagarv
Bunacurry
Annagh Island
Keem Strand
Cathedral Rocks
Cashel
Salia
Claggan
Dooega Head
Dooega / Dumha Éige
Knockmore
340
464
Achill
Achill Sound / Gob an Choire
Belfarsad
Corraun
Corraun Hill
521
Glassillaun
Peninsula
The Atlantic Drive
Ashleam Bay
Derreen
Bills Rocks
Cloghmore / An Chloich Mhóir
Achillbeg Island
Bolinglanna
Dooghbeg
382
Mulr
An Mhal
Clare Island
461
Ballytoohy
CLEW BA
Old Head
Kilsallag
Roonagh Quay
Emlagh Point
Louisburgh
Formoyle
Mullagh
Roonah Lough
Bridge
Carrownisky
Silver Strand
Killadoon
Cregganbaun
R 335
Inishturk
Caher Island
MURRI
Kinnadoohy
Mweelrea Mountains
Doo Lough Pass
Doo Lough
761
817
Delphi
700
Ben
Inishbofin
Inishshark
Bofin
Tonakeera Point
Crump Island
Rinvyle Point
Rinvyle Castle
Ardnagreevagh
Rinvyle
Cashleen
Killary Harbour
Salrock
Culfin
Gowlaun
356
Ballynakill Harbour
Tully Cross
600
Lough Fee
Garraun
Kylemore Abbey
Leenane
R 335
N 59
Cleggan Bay
High Island
Dawros
Aughrus More
Claddaghduff
Cleggan / An Cloigeann
Omey Island
Moyard
Letterfrack
Kylemore Lough
R 344
Connemara National Park
Maumturk Mountains
Bealanabrack
624
667
Streamstown
Kingstown
Talbot Island
Sky Road
Clifden Bay
Clifden / An Clochán
294
Owenglin
728
Benbaun
The Twelve Pins
710
Bencorr
Benbreen
692
Lough Inagh
Finnisglin
701
Errislannan
Cascade
Derrylea
CONNEMAR
Mannin Bay
Ballinaboy
Ballynahinch Lake
Derryclare Lough
Derryn
Doonloughan
R 341
Ballyconneely
Ballinafad
Recess / Sraith Salach
Toombeola
R 342
Cashel / An Caiseal
R 340
Slyne Head
Callow
Maumeen Lough
R 341
Ballyconneely Bay
Errisbeg
300
Roundstone
Inishnee
Bertraghboy Bay
Bunnahown
Gowla
Derryrush
354
Glinsk / Glinsce
Lough Bola
Kilkieran
Moyrus
Croaghnakeela Island
L. Skannive
Kylesalia Bay
Mace Head
Carna
Rosm
Ard
Kilkieran / Cill Chiaráin
St. Macdara's Island
R 340
Ardmore
Lettermore Island
Mweenish Island
Lettercallow
Inishbarra
Casheen Bay
Teeranea

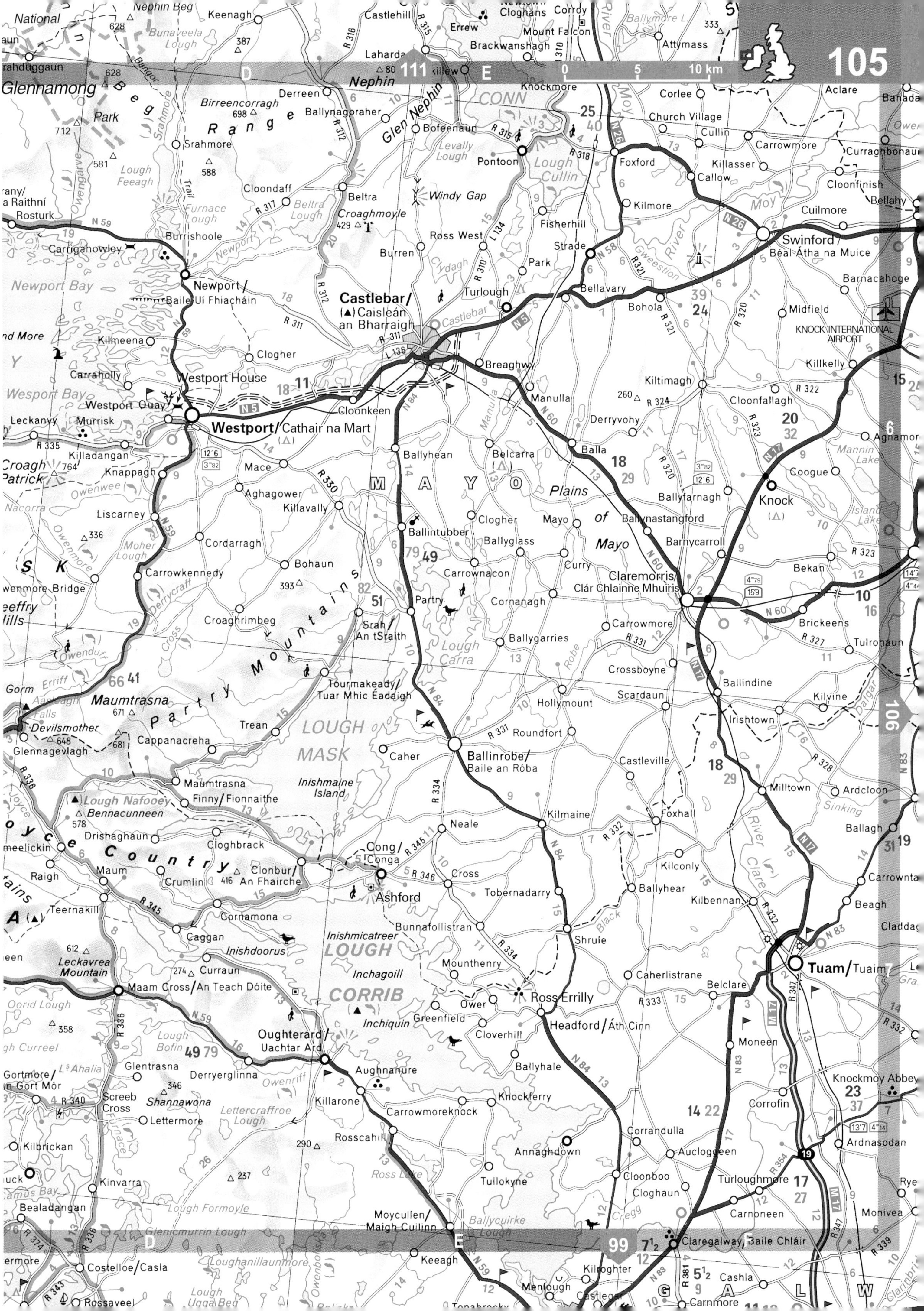
111
0 5 10 km
D
E
F
CONN
Nephin Beg
National
Glennamong
Beg Range
Park
Keenagh
Castlehill
Erew
Cloghans
Corroy
Mount Falcon
Brackwanshagh
Attymass
Laharda
Nephin
Knockmore
Corlee
Aclare
Banada
Derreen
Birreencorragh
Ballynagoraher
Glen Nephin
Bofeenaun
Church Village
Cullin
Carrowmore
Curraghbonaun
Srahmore
Levally Lough
Pontoon
Lough Cullin
Foxford
Killasser
Callow
Cloonfinish
Lough Feeagh
Cloondaff
Beltra
Beltra Lough
Windy Gap
Kilmore
Moy
Bellahy
Cuilmore
Furnace Lough
Croaghmoyle
Fisherhill
Rosturk
Burrishoole
Ross West
Strade
Swinford / Béal Átha na Muice
Carrigahowley
Burren
Park
Gweestion River
Barnacahoge
Newport Bay
Newport / Baile Uí Fhiacháin
Castlebar / Caisleán an Bharraigh
Turlough
Bellavary
Bohola
Midfield
KNOCK INTERNATIONAL AIRPORT
Kilmeena
Clogher
Breaghwy
Killkelly
Carraholly
Westport House
Manulla
Kiltimagh
Cloonfallagh
Wesport Bay
Westport Quay
Cloonkeen
Leckanvy
Murrisk
Westport / Cathair na Mart
Derryvohy
Agnamore
Croagh Patrick
Killadangan
Balla
Mannin Lake
Knappagh
Mace
Ballyhean
Belcarra
Coogue
Aghagower
MAYO
Plains of Mayo
Knock
Nacorra
Killavally
Ballyfarnagh
Liscarney
Ballintubber
Clogher
Mayo
Ballynastangford
Island Lake
Cordarragh
Ballyglass
Barnycarroll
Moher Lough
Bekan
Bohaun
Carrowkennedy
Carrownacon
Curry
Claremorris / Clár Chlainne Mhuiris
Owenmore Bridge
Partry
Cornanagh
Sheeffry Hills
Srah / An tSraith
Brickeens
Croaghrimbeg
Carrowmore
Partry Mountains
Ballygarries
Tulrohaun
Owenduff
Lough Carra
Crossboyne
Ballindine
Gorm
Erriff
Tourmakeady / Tuar Mhic Éadaigh
Hollymount
Scardaun
Kilvine
Maumtrasna
Aasleagh Falls
Irishtown
Devilsmother
Trean
LOUGH MASK
Roundfort
Glennagevlagh
Cappanacreha
Caher
Ballinrobe / Baile an Róba
Castleville
Maumtrasna
Inishmaine Island
Milltown
Ardcloon
Lough Nafooey
Finny / Fionnaithe
Bennacunneen
Kilmaine
Foxhall
Sinking
Drishaghaun
Neale
River Clare
Ballagh
Joyce Country
Cloghbrack
Cong / Conga
Carrowntan
Maum
Clonbur / An Fhairche
Crumlin
Ashford
Cross
Kilconly
Raigh
Tobernadarry
Ballyhear
Kilbennan
Beagh
Teernakill
Cornamona
Bunnafollistran
Caggan
Inishmicatreer
Black
Shrule
Claddagh
Leckavrea Mountain
Inishdoorus
LOUGH CORRIB
Tuam / Tuaim
Curraun
Mounthenry
Caherlistrane
Maam Cross / An Teach Dóite
Inchagoill
Ross Errilly
Belclare
Oorid Lough
Inchiquin
Greenfield
Ower
Headford / Áth Cinn
Lough Bofin
Oughterard / Uachtar Ard
Cloverhill
Moneen
Gh Curreel
Glentrasna
Aughnanure
Ballyhale
Knockmoy Abbey
Gortmore / An Gort Mór
Derryerglinna
Owenriff
Screeb Cross
Shannawona
Killarone
Knockferry
Corrofin
Lettermore
Lettercraffroe Lough
Carrowmoreknock
Corrandulla
Ardnasodan
Kilbrickan
Rosscahill
Annaghdown
Auclogeen
Ross Lake
Turloughmore
Kinvarra
Tullokyne
Cloonboo
Rye
Cloghaun
Carnoneen
Monivea
Bealadangan
Lough Formoyle
Glenicmurrin Lough
Moycullen / Maigh Cuilinn
Ballycuirke Lough
99
Claregalway / Baile Chláir
Costelloe / Casla
Loughanillaunmore
Keeagh
Kilroghter
Cashla
Owenboliska
Lough Ugga Beg
Menlough
Castlegar
Rossaveel
Carnmore
G
A
L
W
106
N 5
N 17
N 26
N 58
N 59
N 60
N 83
N 84
M 17

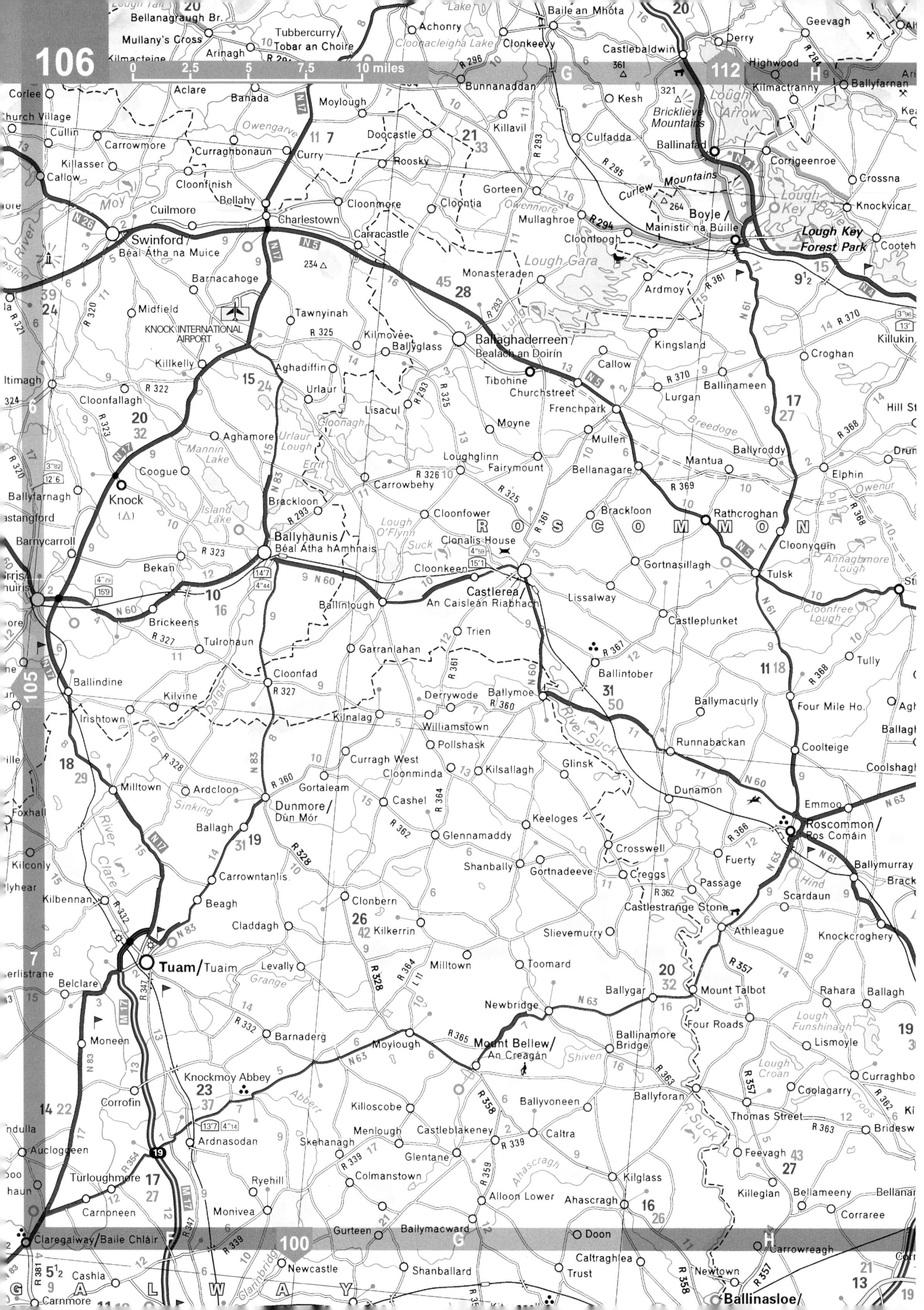
0 2,5 5 7,5 10 miles
112
105
100
Bellanagraugh Br.
Mullany's Cross
Arinagh
Tubbercurry/
Tobar an Choire
Achonry
Cloonacleigha Lake
Baile an Mhóta
Clonkeevy
Castlebaldwin
Derry
Geevagh
Highwood
Kilmactranny
Ballyfarnan
Kilmacteige
Corlee
Aclare
Banada
Moylough
Bunnanaddan
Kesh
Bricklieve Mountains
Lough Arrow
Church Village
Cullin
Owengarve
Doocastle
Killavil
Culfadda
Ballinafad
Carrowmore
Curraghbonaun
Curry
Roosky
Corrigeenroe
Crossna
Killasser
Callow
Cloonfinish
Curlew Mountains
Gorteen
Lough Key
Knockvicar
Moy
Bellahy
Cloonmore
Cloontia
Owenmore
Boyle/
Mainistir na Búille
Lough Key Forest Park
Cooteh
River Moy
Cuilmore
Charlestown
Mullaghroe
Cloonloogh
Swinford/
Béal Átha na Muice
Carracastle
Lough Gara
Barnacahoge
Monasteraden
Ardmoy
Midfield
Tawnyinah
KNOCK INTERNATIONAL AIRPORT
Kilmovee
Ballyglass
Ballaghaderreen/
Bealach an Doirín
Kingsland
Killukin
Croghan
Killkelly
Aghadiffin
Callow
Tibohine
Churchstreet
Lurgan
Ballinameen
Cloonfallagh
Urlaur
Lisacul
Frenchpark
Hill St
Urlaur Lough
Cloonagh L.
Moyne
Mullen
Breedoge
Aghamore
Mannin Lake
Errit L.
Loughglinn
Fairymount
Bellanagare
Mantua
Ballyroddy
Elphin
Coogue
Carrowbehy
Owenur
Knock
Brackloon
Brackloon
Rathcroghan
Ballyfarnagh
Island Lake
Lough O'Flynn
Cloonfower
ROSCOMMON
Barnycarroll
Ballyhaunis/
Béal Átha hAmhnais
Suck
Clonalis House
Cloonyquin
Annaghmore Lough
Bekan
Cloonkeen
Castlerea/
An Caisleán Riabhach
Gortnasillagh
Tulsk
Lissalway
Ballinlough
Brickeens
Cloonfree Lough
Castleplunket
Tulrohaun
Trien
Garranlahan
Ballintober
Tully
Ballindine
Cloonfad
Kilvine
Dalgan
Ballymoe
Derrywode
Ballymacurly
Four Mile Ho.
Irishtown
Kilnalag
Williamstown
River Suck
Pollshask
Runnabackan
Coolteige
Curragh West
Cloonminda
Kilsallagh
Glinsk
Coolshagh
Milltown
Ardcloon
Gortaleam
Cashel
Dunamon
Emmoo
Sinking
Dunmore/
Dún Mór
Keeloges
Roscommon/
Ros Comáin
Foxhall
Ballagh
Glennamaddy
Fuerty
Ballymurray
River Clare
Crosswell
Hind
Kilconly
Shanbally
Gortnadeeve
Creggs
Passage
Carrowntanlis
Scardaun
Kilbennan
Beagh
Clonbern
Castlestrange Stone
Claddagh
Kilkerrin
Athleague
Knockcroghery
Slievemurry
Tuam/Tuaim
Levally
Grange
Milltown
Toomard
Mount Talbot
Rahara
Ballagh
Belclare
Newbridge
Ballygar
Lough Funshinagh
Four Roads
Moneen
Barnaderg
Moylough
Mount Bellew/
An Creagán
Shiven
Ballinamore Bridge
Lismoyle
Lough Croan
Curraghbo
Knockmoy Abbey
Abbert
Ballyvoneen
Ballyforan
Coolagarry
Corrofin
Killoscobe
Thomas Street
Brideswell
Menlough
Castleblakeney
Caltra
Ardnasodan
Skehanagh
Ahascragh
R. Suck
Aucloggeen
Glentane
Feevagh
Colmanstown
Kilglass
Turloughmore
Ryehill
Alloon Lower
Ahascragh
Killeglan
Bellameeny
Carnoneen
Monivea
Corraree
Claregalway/Baile Chláir
Gurteen
Ballymacward
Doon
Carrowreagh
Cashla
Newcastle
Shanballard
Caltraghlea
Trust
Newtown
Ballinasloe/
Carnmore
GALWAY
Clarinbridge
Lough Gall
Lake
N 17
N 5
N 4
N 26
N 61
N 60
N 83
N 63
M 17
R 293
R 294
R 295
R 296
R 320
R 321
R 322
R 323
R 324
R 325
R 326
R 327
R 328
R 332
R 339
R 347
R 354
R 357
R 358
R 359
R 360
R 361
R 362
R 363
R 364
R 365
R 366
R 367
R 368
R 369
R 370
R 381
L 11
361
321
264
234
F
G
H

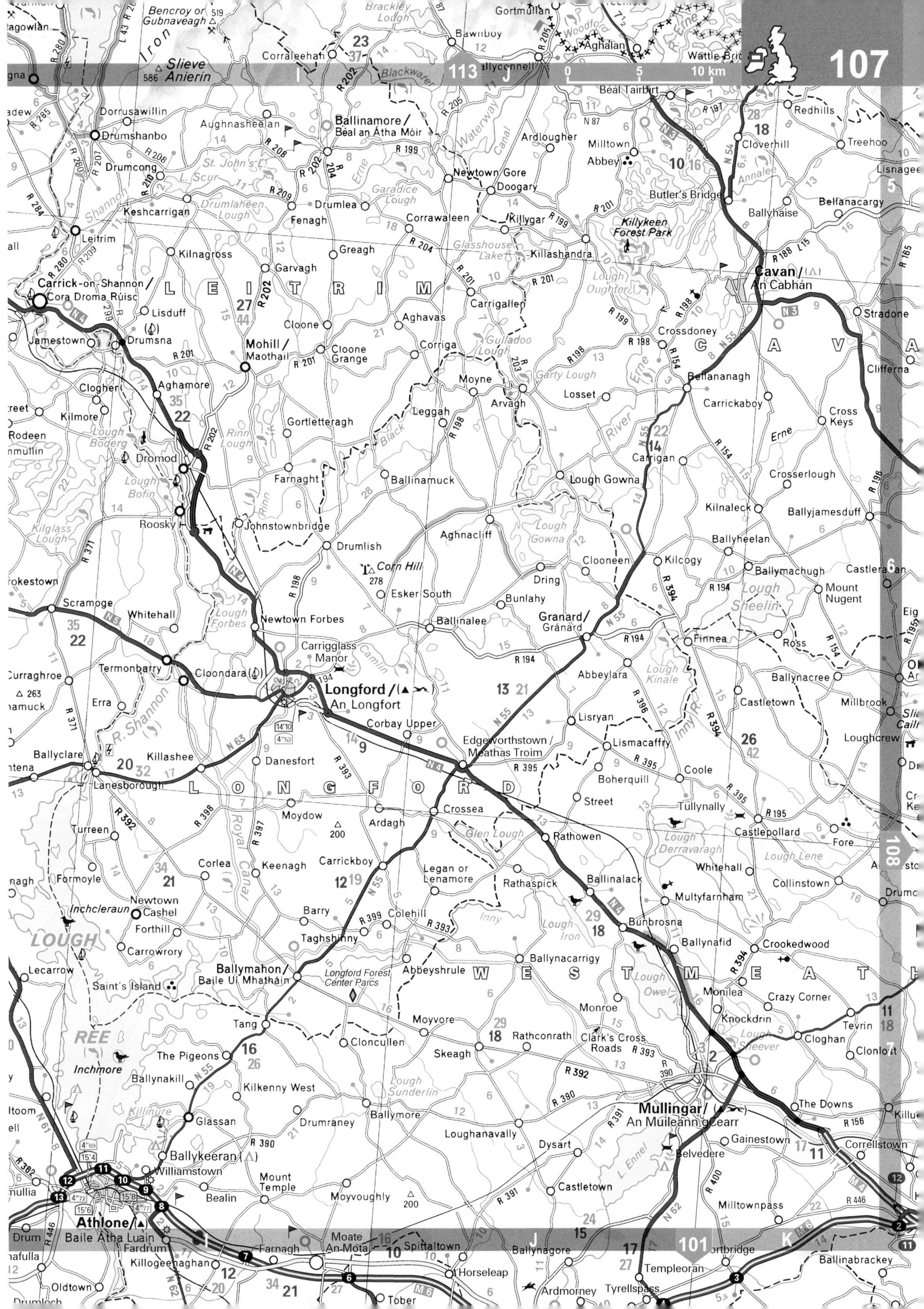
0 5 10 km
113
101
108
LEITRIM
LONGFORD
CAVAN
WESTMEATH
Bencroy or Gubnaveagh
Slieve Anierin
Brackley Lough
Gortmullan
Bawnboy
Corraleehan
Ballyconnell
Aghalan
Wattle Bridge
Béal Tairbirt
Redhills
Cloverhill
Treehoo
Lisnagee
Drumshanbo
Dorrusawillin
Aughnasheelan
Ballinamore / Béal an Átha Móir
Ardlougher
Milltown
Abbey
Drumcong
St. John's L.
Newtown Gore
Doogary
Butler's Bridge
Bellanacargy
Ballyhaise
Keshcarrigan
Drumlaheen Lough
Fenagh
Drumlea
Garadice Lough
Corrawaleen
Killygar
Killykeen Forest Park
Leitrim
Kilnagross
Greagh
Glasshouse Lake
Killashandra
Garvagh
Lough Oughter
Cavan / An Cabhán
Carrick-on-Shannon / Cora Droma Rúisc
Lisduff
Cloone
Carrigallen
Aghavas
Crossdoney
Stradone
Jamestown
Drumsna
Mohill / Maothail
Cloone Grange
Corriga
Gulladoo Lough
Garty Lough
Clifferna
Clogher
Aghamore
Moyne
Arvagh
Losset
Bellananagh
Carrickaboy
Kilmore
Rodeen
Leggah
Cross Keys
Gortletteragh
Rinn Lough
Lough Boderg
Dromod
Erne
Carrigan
Farnaght
Ballinamuck
Lough Gowna
Crosserlough
Lough Bofin
Kilnaleck
Ballyjamesduff
Roosky
Johnstownbridge
Kilglass Lough
Aghnacliff
Lough Gowna
Drumlish
Corn Hill
Ballyheelan
Kilcogy
Clooneen
Ballymachugh
Castlerahan
Esker South
Dring
Lough Sheelin
Mount Nugent
Scramoge
Whitehall
Lough Forbes
Newtown Forbes
Bunlahy
Granard / Gránard
Ballinalee
Finnea
Ross
Carrigglass Manor
Camlin
Abbeylara
Lough Kinale
Ballynacree
Curraghroe
Termonbarry
Cloondara
Longford / An Longfort
Castletown
Millbrook
Erra
Corbay Upper
Lisryan
R. Shannon
Edgeworthstown / Meathas Troim
Lismacaffry
Inny R.
Loughcrew
Ballyclare
Killashee
Danesfort
Coole
Lanesborough
Boherquill
Street
Tullynally
Castlepollard
Turreen
Moydow
Ardagh
Crossea
Royal Canal
Glen Lough
Fore
Rathowen
Lough Derravaragh
Lough Lene
Corlea
Keenagh
Carrickboy
Legan or Lenamore
Whitehall
Collinstown
Formoyle
Rathaspick
Ballinalack
Multyfarnham
Newtown Cashel
Inchcleraun
Barry
Colehill
Bunbrosna
Forthill
Taghshinny
Lough Iron
Ballynafid
Crookedwood
Carrowrory
LOUGH REE
Ballymahon / Baile Uí Mhatháin
Abbeyshrule
Ballynacarrigy
Lough Owel
Lecarrow
Longford Forest Center Parcs
Saint's Island
Monilea
Crazy Corner
Monroe
Knockdrin
Tang
Moyvore
Clark's Cross Roads
Tevrin
Rathconrath
Lough Sheever
Cloghan
Clonlost
The Pigeons
Cloncullen
Skeagh
Inchmore
Ballynakill
Kilkenny West
Lough Sunderlin
Mullingar / An Muileann gCearr
The Downs
Killinure L.
Glassan
Drumraney
Ballymore
Loughanavally
Ballykeeran
Dysart
Gainestown
Correllstown
Williamstown
Mount Temple
L. Ennel
Belvedere
Bealin
Moyvoughly
Castletown
Milltownpass
Athlone / Baile Átha Luain
Drum
Fardrum
Moate / An Móta
Farnagh
Spittaltown
Ballynagore
Tyrrellspass
Templeoran
Rochfortbridge
Ballinabrackey
Killogeenaghan
Horseleap
Oldtown
Tober
Ardmorney

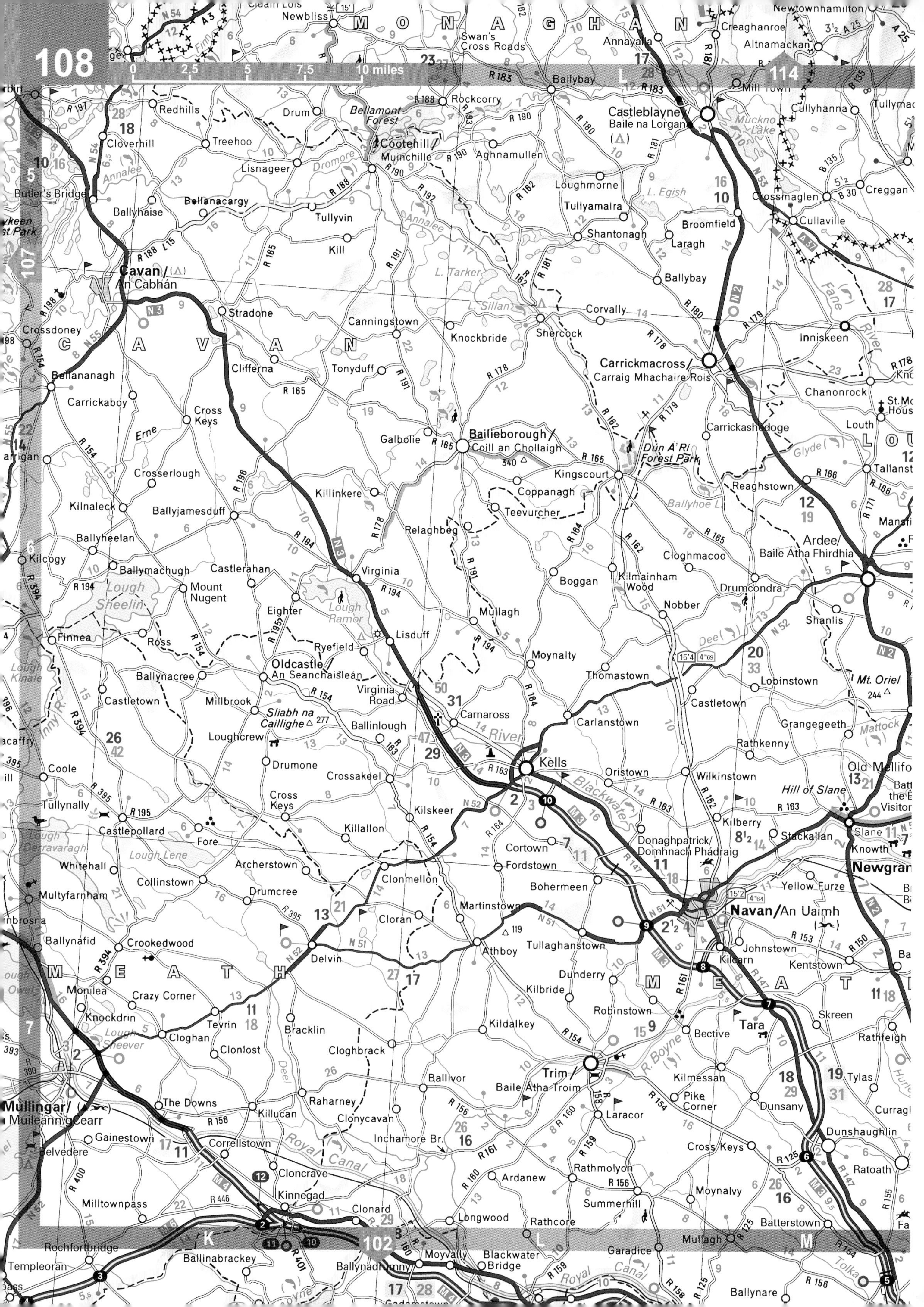

0 2,5 5 7,5 10 miles
MONAGHAN
CAVAN
LOUTH
MEATH
114
107
102
Newbliss
Swan's Cross Roads
Annayalla
Creaghanroe
Newtownhamilton
Altnamackan
Ballybay
Mill Town
Redhills
Drum
Rockcorry
Bellamont Forest
Castleblayney/
Baile na Lorgan
Muckno Lake
Cullyhanna
Tullymac
Cloverhill
Treehoo
Cootehill/
Muinchille
Aghnamullen
Lisnageer
Dromore
Annalee
Butler's Bridge
Bellanacargy
Ballyhaise
Tullyvin
Loughmorne
L. Egish
Crossmaglen
Creggan
Cullaville
Tullyamalra
Shantonagh
Broomfield
Laragh
Kill
Cavan/
An Cabhán
L. Tarker
Ballybay
Stradone
L. Sillan
Corvally
Shercock
Knockbride
Canningstown
Inniskeen
Fane River
Crossdoney
Carrickmacross/
Carraig Mhachaire Rois
Chanonrock
Clifferna
Tonyduff
Bellananagh
Carrickaboy
Cross Keys
Erne
St. Mochta's House
Louth
Carrickashedoge
Galbolie
Bailieborough/
Coill an Chollaigh
Dún A'Rí Forest Park
Glyde
Kingscourt
Coppanagh
Tallanstown
Crosserlough
Reaghstown
Killinkere
Teevurcher
Ballyhoe L.
Kilnaleck
Ballyjamesduff
Relaghbeg
Ardee/
Baile Átha Fhirdhia
Ballyheelan
Cloghmacoo
Kilcogy
Ballymachugh
Castlerahan
Virginia
Boggan
Kilmainham Wood
Lough Sheelin
Mount Nugent
Drumcondra
Eighter
Lough Ramor
Mullagh
Nobber
Shanlis
Finnea
Ross
Lisduff
Ryefield
Oldcastle/
An Seanchaisleán
Moynalty
Thomastown
Lough Kinale
Ballynacree
Mt. Oriel
Lobinstown
Virginia Road
Castletown
Millbrook
Sliabh na Cailligh
Carnaross
Carlanstown
Ballinlough
River
Grangegeeth
Mattock
Loughcrew
Rathkenny
Drumone
Kells
Oristown
Wilkinstown
Old Mellifont
Coole
Crossakeel
Blackwater
Hill of Slane
Tullynally
Cross Keys
Kilskeer
Kilberry
Stackallan
Slane
Knowth
Castlepollard
Fore
Killallon
Cortown
Donaghpatrick/
Domhnach Phádraig
Lough Derravaragh
Lough Lene
Whitehall
Archerstown
Fordstown
Newgrange
Multyfarnham
Collinstown
Clonmellon
Bohermeen
Yellow Furze
Drumcree
Martinstown
Navan/An Uaimh
Cloran
Ballynafid
Crookedwood
Delvin
Athboy
Tullaghanstown
Johnstown
Kilcarn
Kentstown
Dunderry
Monilea
Crazy Corner
Kilbride
Robinstown
Skreen
Knockdrin
Tevrin
Bracklin
Kildalkey
Tara
Bective
Rathfeigh
Lough Owel
Lough Sheever
Cloghan
Clonlost
Cloghbrack
Trim/
Baile Átha Troim
R. Boyne
Kilmessan
Tylas
Ballivor
Deel
Mullingar/
An Muileann gCearr
The Downs
Raharney
Killucan
Pike Corner
Dunsany
Curragh
Clonycavan
Laracor
Gainestown
Correllstown
Royal Canal
Inchamore Br.
Dunshaughlin
Cross Keys
Belvedere
Cloncrave
Ardanew
Rathmolyon
Ratoath
Milltownpass
Kinnegad
Summerhill
Moynalvy
Clonard
Longwood
Rathcore
Batterstown
Rochfortbridge
Mullagh
Ballinabrackey
Garadice
Templeoran
Moyvally
Blackwater Bridge
Ballynadrumny
Royal Canal
Tolka
Ballynare

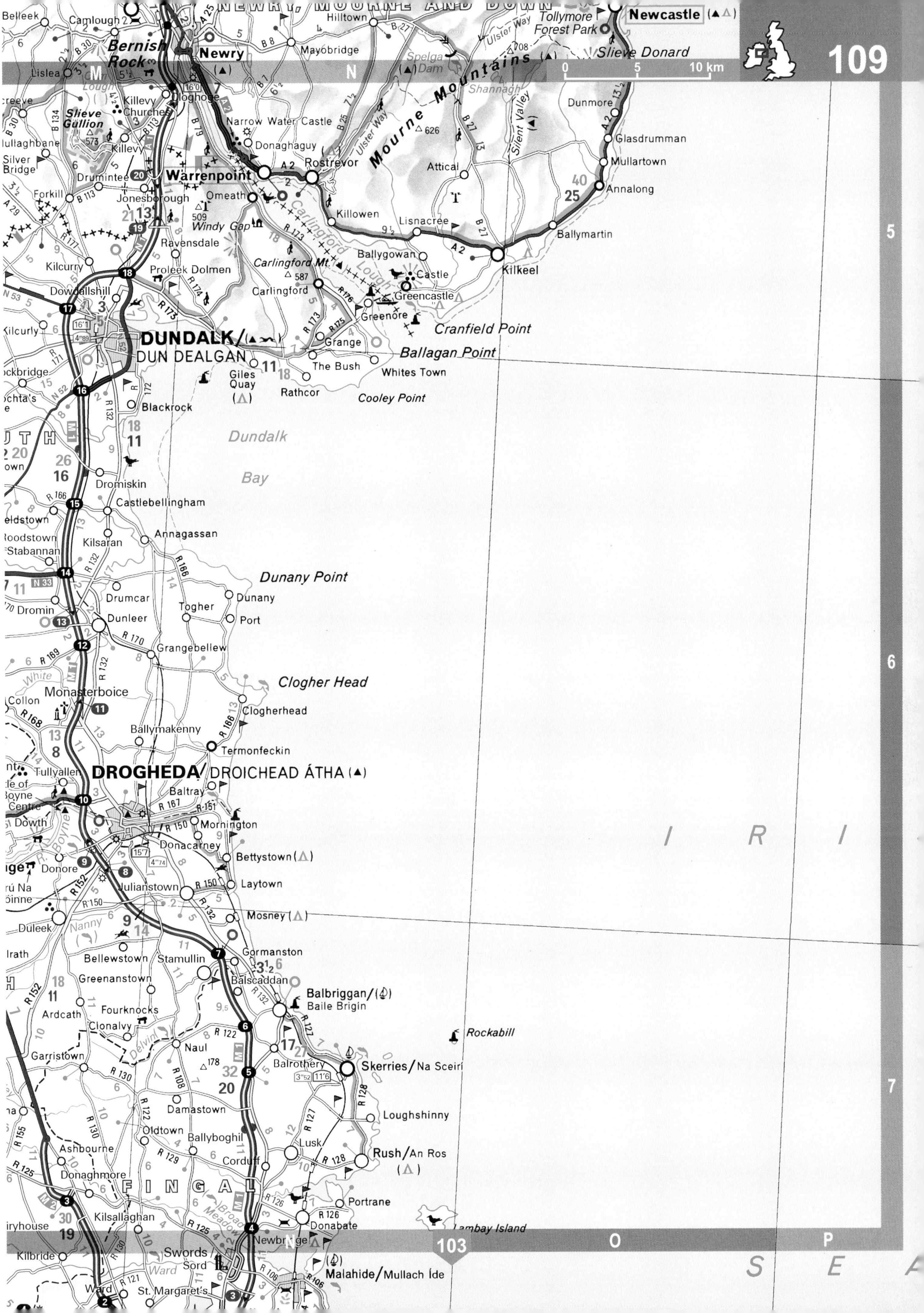
NEWRY, MOURNE AND DOWN
Belleek
Camlough
Bernish Rock
Newry
Hilltown
Mayobridge
Tollymore Forest Park
Newcastle
Slieve Donard
Spelga Dam
Mourne Mountains
Shannagh
Silent Valley
Dunmore
Glasdrumman
Mullartown
Annalong
Ballymartin
Kilkeel
Lisnacree
Attical
Killowen
Rostrevor
Warrenpoint
Narrow Water Castle
Donaghaguy
Omeath
Windy Gap
Carlingford Lough
Carlingford Mt.
Carlingford
Ballygowan
Castle
Greencastle
Greenore
Cranfield Point
Ballagan Point
Grange
The Bush
Whites Town
Cooley Point
Rathcor
Giles Quay
Lislea
Slieve Gullion
Killevy Churches
Killevy
Meigh
Drumintee
Jonesborough
Forkill
Silver Bridge
Ravensdale
Proleek Dolmen
Kilcurry
Dowdallshill
DUNDALK/DUN DEALGAN
Blackrock
Dundalk Bay
Dromiskin
Castlebellingham
Annagassan
Kilsaran
Stabannan
Dunany Point
Dunany
Port
Drumcar
Togher
Dunleer
Dromin
Grangebellew
Clogher Head
Clogherhead
Monasterboice
Collon
Ballymakenny
Termonfeckin
Tullyallen
DROGHEDA/DROICHEAD ÁTHA
Baltray
Mornington
Donacarney
Bettystown
Laytown
Mosney
Donore
Julianstown
Duleek
Nanny
Bellewstown
Stamullin
Gormanston
Balscaddan
Balbriggan/Baile Brigín
Greenanstown
Fourknocks
Ardcath
Clonalvy
Rockabill
Naul
Balrothery
Skerries/Na Sceirí
Garristown
Loughshinny
Damastown
Oldtown
Ballyboghil
Lusk
Rush/An Ros
Ashbourne
Corduff
Donaghmore
FINGAL
Portrane
Lambay Island
Donabate
Kilsallaghan
Newbridge
Swords/Sord
Kilbride
Ward
St. Margaret's
Malahide/Mullach Íde
IRISH SEA
0 5 10 km

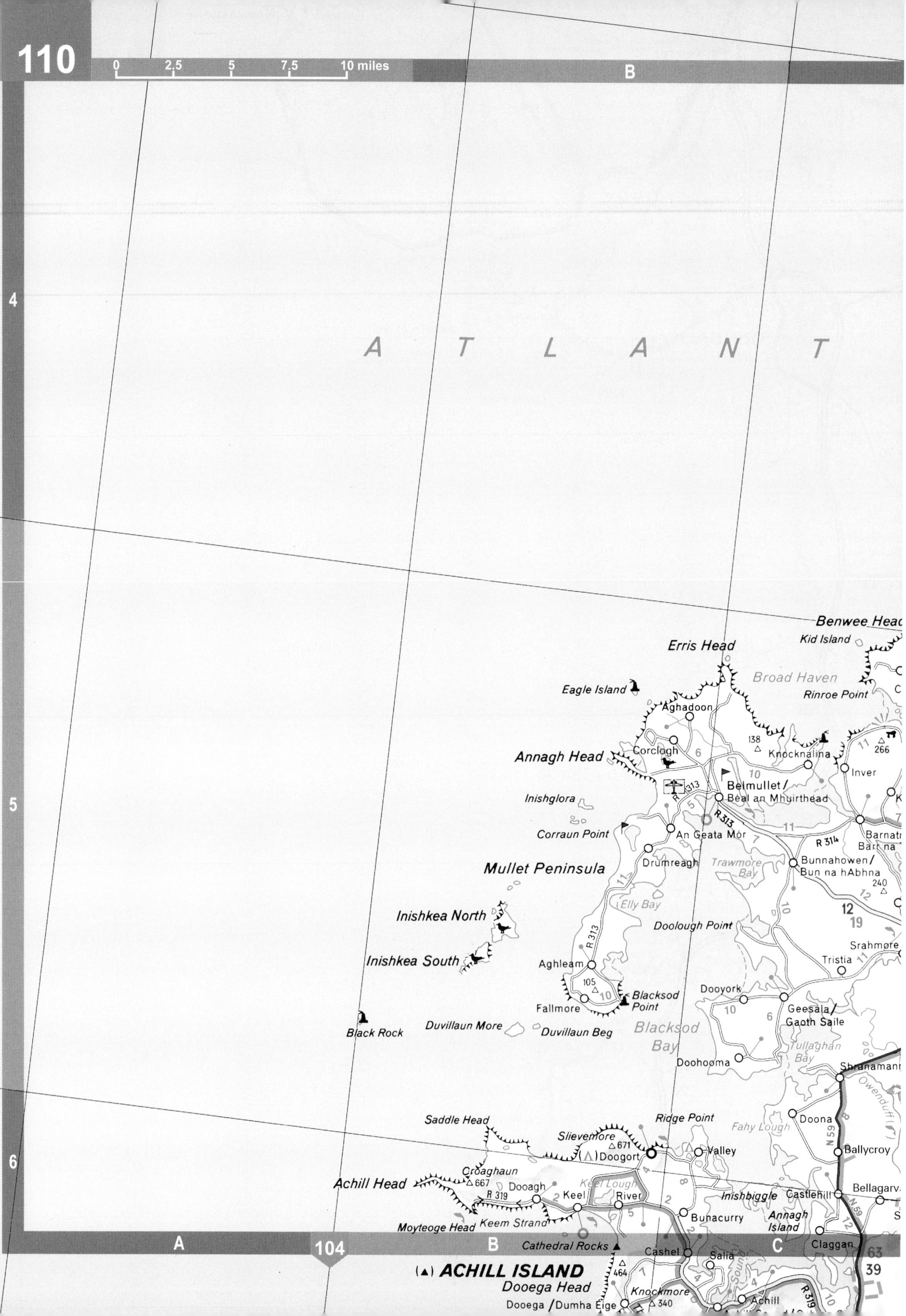
0 2.5 5 7.5 10 miles
B
4
5
6
A
B
C
104
63
39
A T L A N T
Benwee Head
Kid Island
Erris Head
Broad Haven
Rinroe Point
Eagle Island
Aghadoon
Corclogh
138
Knocknalina
266
Annagh Head
Inver
R 313
Belmullet / Béal an Mhuirthead
Inishglora
Corraun Point
An Geata Mór
R 314
Barnatra
Barr na
Drumreagh
Trawmore Bay
Bunnahowen / Bun na hAbhna
240
Mullet Peninsula
Elly Bay
12
19
Doolough Point
Inishkea North
R 313
Srahmore
Tristia
Inishkea South
Aghleam
105
Blacksod Point
Dooyork
Fallmore
Geesala / Gaoth Saile
Duvillaun More
Duvillaun Beg
Black Rock
Blacksod Bay
Tullaghan Bay
Doohooma
Shranamanr
Owenduff
Doona
Saddle Head
Ridge Point
Fahy Lough
Slievemore
671
(Δ) Doogort
Valley
N 59
Ballycroy
Croaghaun
667
Achill Head
Dooagh
Keel Lough
R 319
Keel
River
Inishbiggle
Castlehill
Bellagarv
N 59
Bunacurry
Annagh Island
Moyteoge Head
Keem Strand
Cathedral Rocks
Claggan
Cashel
Salia
(▲) ACHILL ISLAND
464
Dooega Head
Knockmore
Dooega / Dumha Éige
340
Achill
R 319

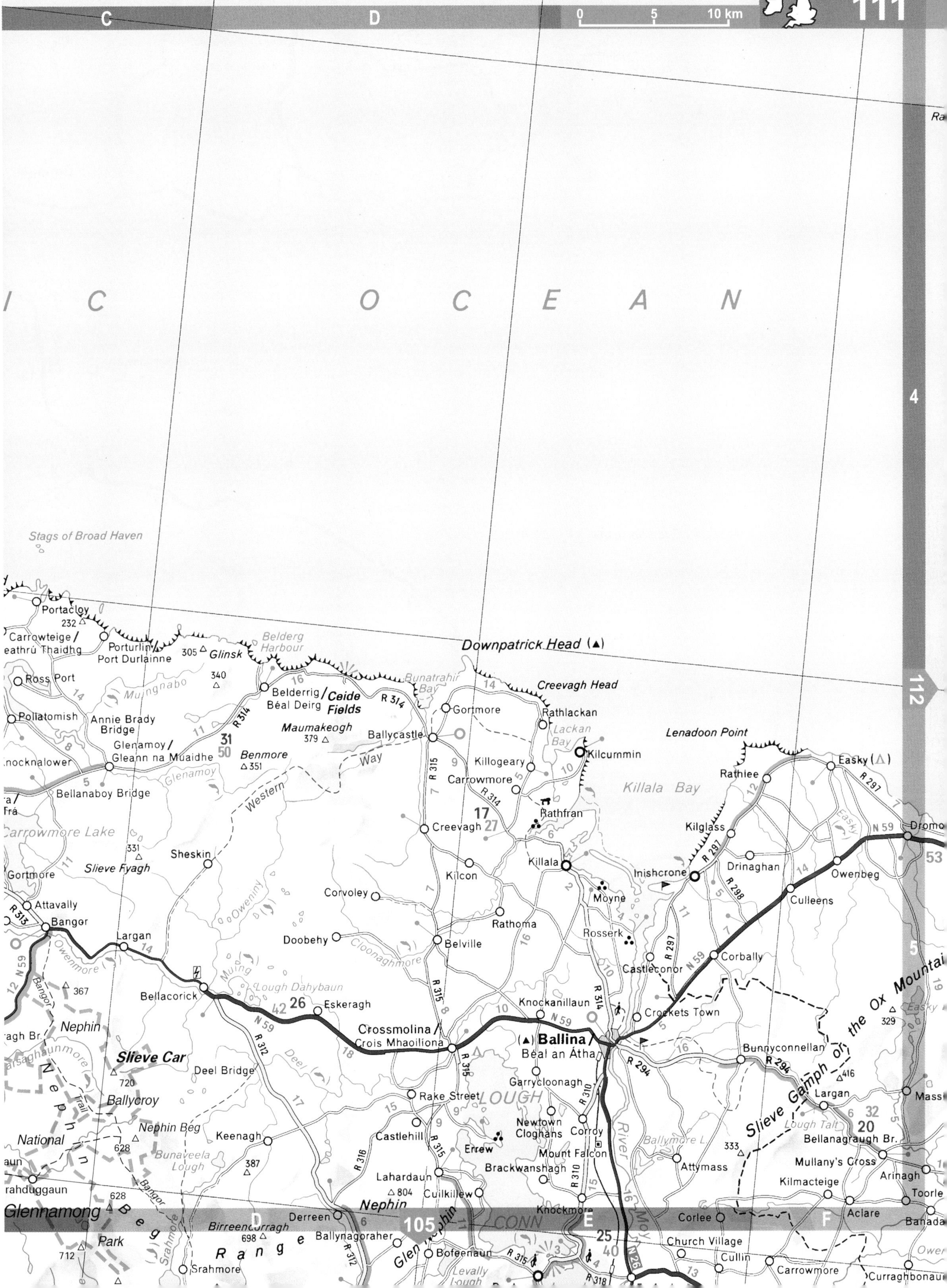

C
D
E
F
0 5 10 km
4
5
112
105
O C E A N
Stags of Broad Haven
Portacloy
232
Carrowteige /
Porturlin
Port Durlainne
305
Glinsk
Belderg Harbour
Downpatrick Head
Creevagh Head
Ross Port
Muingnabo
340
Belderrig / Béal Deirg
Ceide Fields
R 314
Bunatrahir Bay
Gortmore
Rathlackan
Lackan Bay
Pollatomish
Annie Brady Bridge
Maumakeogh
379
Ballycastle
Lenadoon Point
Kilcummin
Glenamoy / Gleann na Muaidhe
31
50
Benmore
351
Way
Killogeary
Carrowmore
R 315
Easky
Rathlee
Bellanaboy Bridge
Glenamoy
Western
Killala Bay
Carrowmore Lake
17
27
Rathfran
Creevagh
Kilglass
Dromore
Sheskin
331
Slieve Fyagh
Gortmore
Kilcon
Killala
Inishcrone
Drinaghan
Owenbeg
N 59
53
Attavally
Corvoley
Moyne
Culleens
R 298
R 297
R 313
Bangor
Largan
Oweniny
Rathoma
Doobehy
Belville
Cloonaghmore
Rosserk
Castleconor
Corbally
Owenmore
367
Bellacorick
Muing
Lough Dahybaun
42
26
Eskeragh
Knockanillaun
R 314
Crockets Town
the Ox Mountains
329
Nephin
Slieve Car
720
Crossmolina / Crois Mhaoiliona
R 312
Deel
Ballina / Béal an Átha
R 294
Bunnyconnellan
Slieve Gamph or
416
Deel Bridge
Garrycloonagh
Largan
Massbrook
Ballycroy
Rake Street
LOUGH
R 310
Lough Talt
32
20
National
Nephin Beg
628
Keenagh
Castlehill
Newtown Cloghans
Corroy
Ballymore L.
Bellanagraugh Br.
Bunaveela Lough
Errew
Mount Falcon
River Moy
333
Attymass
Mullany's Cross
Arinagh
387
R 316
Brackwanshagh
Kilmacteige
Lahardaun
804
Cuilkillew
Toorlestraun
Glennamong
628
Nephin
Knockmore
Corlee
Aclare
Banada
Derreen
Birreencorragh
698
CONN
25
40
Ballynagoraher
Church Village
Park
712
Range
Glen Nephin
Bofeenaun
R 315
N 26
Cullin
Carrowmore
Curraghbonaun
Srahmore
Levally Lough
R 318
13

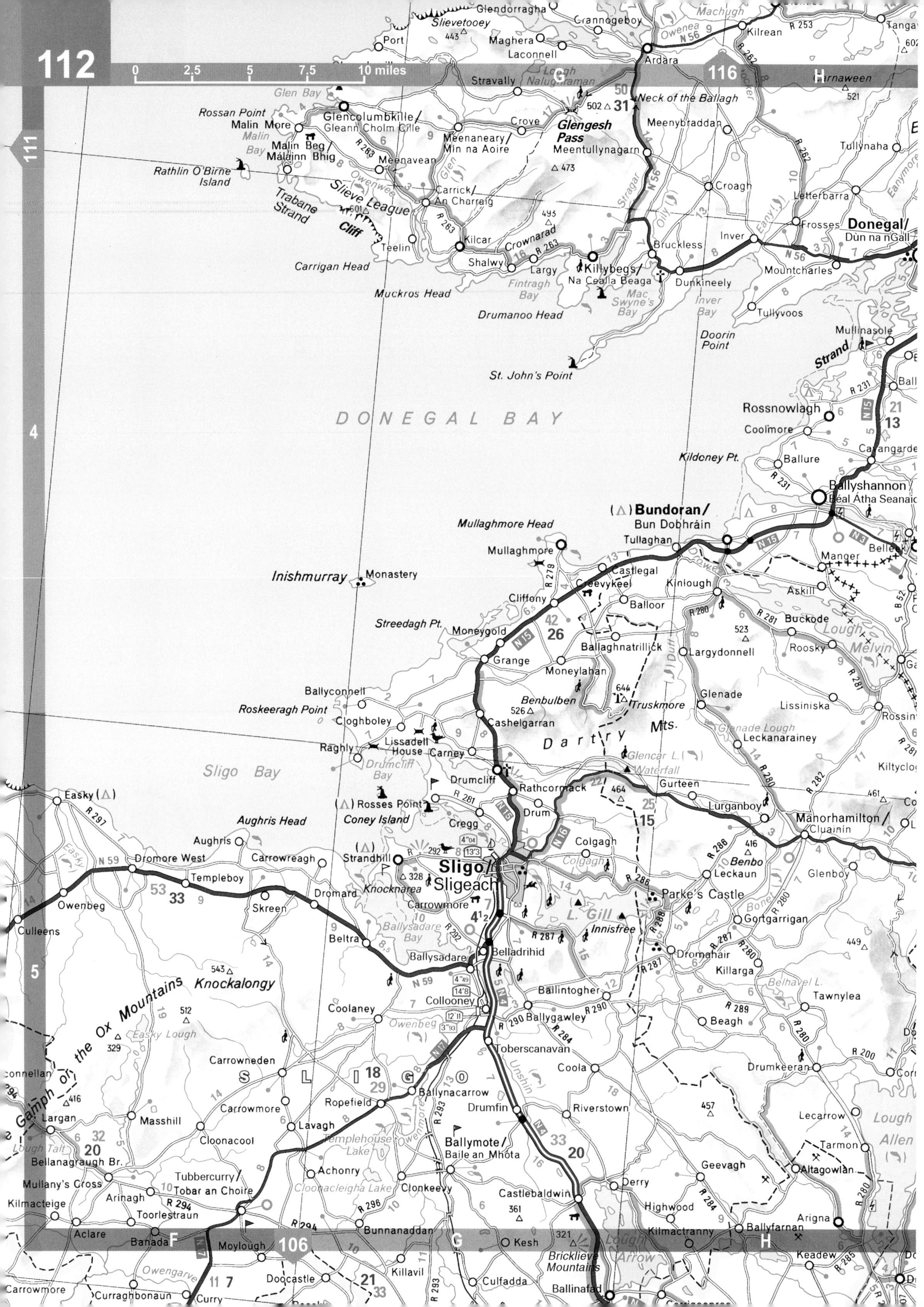
0 2,5 5 7,5 10 miles
111
116
106
G
H
F
4
5
Glendorragha
Slievetooey
Port
Grannogeboy
Maghera
Laconnell
Machugh
Owenea
Kilrean
Ardara
R 253
Tangaveane
Stravally
Lough Nalughraman
Glen Bay
Rossan Point
Malin More
Malin Bay
Glencolumbkille / Gleann Cholm Cille
Malin Beg / Málainn Bhig
Rathlin O'Birne Island
Meenaneary / Mín na Aoire
Meenavean
Crove
Glengesh Pass
Meentullynagarn
Neck of the Ballagh
Meenybraddan
Carnaween
Tullynaha
Croagh
Letterbarra
Frosses
Donegal / Dún na nGall
Trabane Strand
Slieve League
Cliff
Carrick / An Charraig
Teelin
Kilcar
Crownarad
Shalwy
Largy
Killybegs / Na Ceala Beaga
Bruckless
Dunkineely
Inver
Mountcharles
Carrigan Head
Muckros Head
Fintragh Bay
Mac Swyne's Bay
Inver Bay
Drumanoo Head
Tullyvoos
Doorin Point
Mullinasole
Strand
St. John's Point
DONEGAL BAY
Rossnowlagh
Coolmore
Kildoney Pt.
Ballure
Cavangarden
Ballyshannon / Béal Átha Seanaidh
Bundoran / Bun Dobhráin
Mullaghmore Head
Mullaghmore
Tullaghan
Belleek
Manger
Inishmurray
Monastery
Castlegal
Creevykeel
Kinlough
Askill
Cliffony
Balloor
Streedagh Pt.
Moneygold
Buckode
Lough Melvin
Ballaghnatrillick
Largydonnell
Roosky
Grange
Moneylahan
Benbulben
Truskmore
Glenade
Lissiniska
Ballyconnell
Roskeeragh Point
Cloghboley
Cashelgarran
Dartry Mts.
Glenade Lough
Leckanarainey
Raghly
Lissadell House
Carney
Drumcliff Bay
Sligo Bay
Drumcliff
Glencar L.
Waterfall
Easky
Rathcormack
Gurteen
Kiltyclogher
Rosses Point
Coney Island
Drum
Lurganboy
Manorhamilton / Cluainín
Aughris Head
Cregg
Aughris
Colgagh
Strandhill
Dromore West
Carrowreagh
Templeboy
Sligo / Sligeach
Benbo
Leckaun
Glenboy
Owenbeg
Knocknarea
Skreen
Dromard
Carrowmore
Parke's Castle
Culleens
L. Gill
Innisfree
Gortgarrigan
Ballysadare Bay
Beltra
Belladrihid
Dromahair
Ballysadare
Killarga
Knockalongy
Ox Mountains
Ballintogher
Belhavel L.
Tawnylea
Coolaney
Collooney
Ballygawley
Easky Lough
Owenbeg
Beagh
Toberscanavan
Carrowneden
Coola
Drumkeeran
SLIGO
Ballynacarrow
Unshin
Gamph or the Ox Mountains
Largan
Masshill
Carrowmore
Ropefield
Lavagh
Drumfin
Riverstown
Lecarrow
Lough Allen
Lough Talt
Cloonacool
Templehouse Lake
Owenmore
Ballymote / Baile an Mhóta
Tarmon
Bellanagraugh Br.
Tubbercurry / Tobar an Choire
Achonry
Geevagh
Altagowlan
Mullany's Cross
Arinagh
Cloonacleigha Lake
Clonkeevy
Castlebaldwin
Derry
Kilmacteige
Toorlestraun
Highwood
Arigna
Bunnanaddan
Aclare
Banada
Moylough
Kesh
Lough Arrow
Kilmactranny
Ballyfarnan
Keadew
Owengarve
Killavil
Bricklieve Mountains
Carrowmore
Doocastle
Culfadda
Ballinafad
Curraghbonaun
Curry
N 56
N 15
N 16
N 59
N 17
N 4
N 3
R 262
R 263
R 231
R 279
R 280
R 281
R 282
R 286
R 287
R 288
R 289
R 290
R 284
R 292
R 293
R 294
R 296
R 297
R 200
R 285

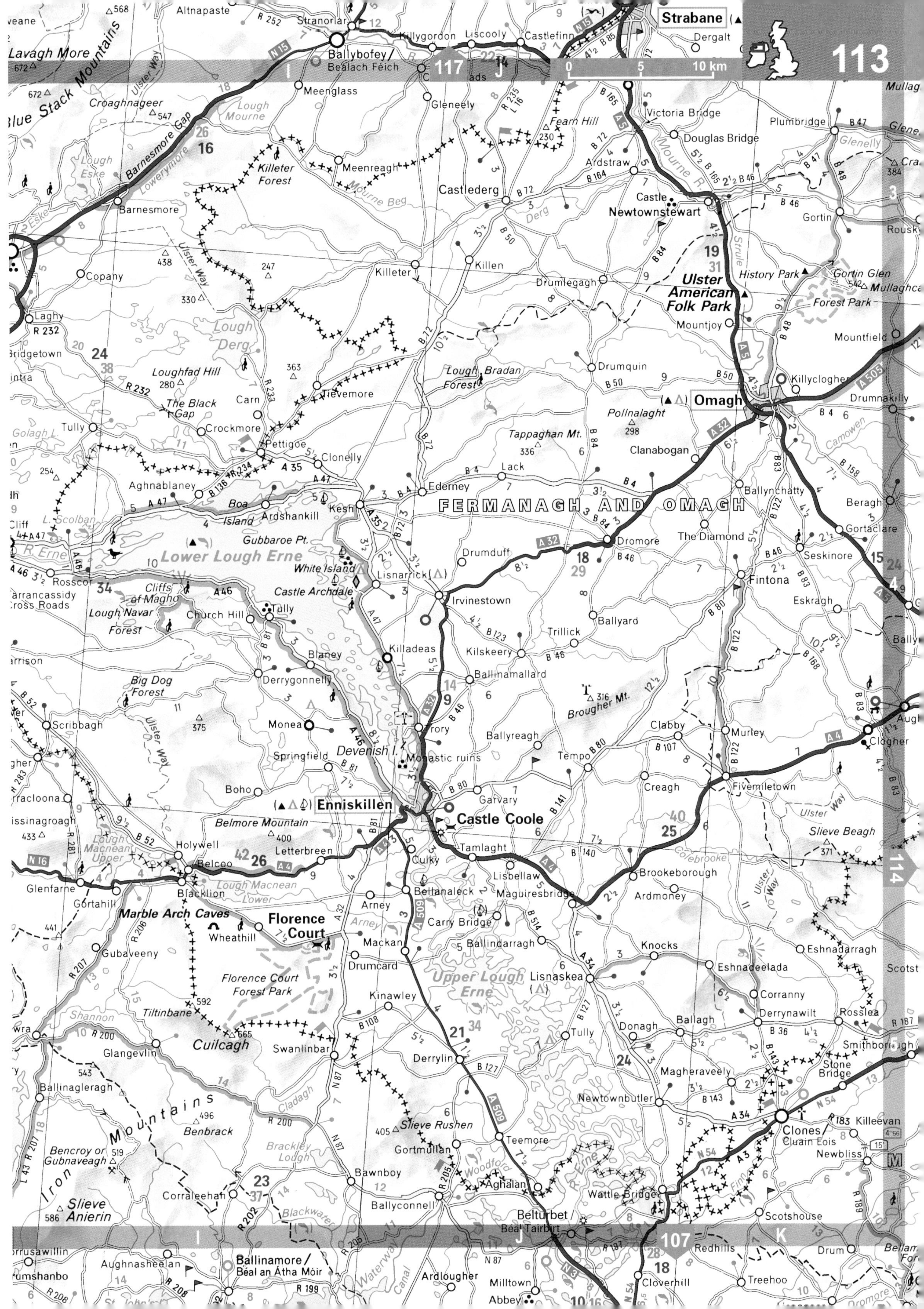
Strabane
Altnapaste
Stranorlar
Ballybofey / Bealach Féich
Killygordon
Liscooly
Castlefinn
Dergalt
117
114
107
0 5 10 km
Lavagh More
Blue Stack Mountains
Ulster Way
Meenglass
Gleneely
Croaghnageer
Lough Mourne
Fearn Hill
Victoria Bridge
Plumbridge
Glenelly
Douglas Bridge
Barnesmore Gap
Lough Eske
Killeter Forest
Meenreagh
Mourne Beg
Ardstraw
Mourne R.
Castlederg
Castle
Newtownstewart
Gortin
Rousky
Barnesmore
Derg
Killeter
Killen
Drumlegagh
Ulster American Folk Park
History Park
Gortin Glen
Forest Park
Mullaghcarn
Copany
Laghy
Lough Derg
Mountjoy
Mountfield
Bridgetown
Loughfad Hill
Lough Bradan Forest
Drumquin
Killyclogher
Omagh
Drumnakilly
The Black Gap
Carn
Tievemore
Pollnalaght
Tully
Crockmore
Tappaghan Mt.
Clanabogan
Camowen
Pettigoe
Clonelly
Lack
Aghnablaney
Ederney
Ballynchatty
Beragh
Boa Island
Ardshankill
Kesh
FERMANAGH AND OMAGH
L. Scolban
Gubbaroe Pt.
Dromore
The Diamond
Gortaclare
R. Erne
Lower Lough Erne
Drumduff
White Island
Seskinore
Rosscor
Lisnarrick
Fintona
Cliffs of Magho
Castle Archdale
Irvinestown
Eskragh
Arrancassidy Cross Roads
Lough Navar Forest
Church Hill
Tully
Ballyard
Trillick
Killadeas
Kilskeery
Blaney
Derrygonnelly
Ballinamallard
Big Dog Forest
Brougher Mt.
Monea
Trory
Scribbagh
Ballyreagh
Clabby
Murley
Augher
Clogher
Devenish I.
Monastic ruins
Springfield
Tempo
Fivemiletown
Creagh
Boho
Enniskillen
Garvary
Castle Coole
Ulster Way
Slieve Beagh
Belmore Mountain
Lough Macnean Upper
Holywell
Letterbreen
Tamlaght
Colebrooke
Belcoo
Culky
Lisbellaw
Brookeborough
Glenfarne
Blacklion
Lough Macnean Lower
Bellanaleck
Maguiresbridge
Ardmoney
Gortahill
Marble Arch Caves
Florence Court
Arney
Carry Bridge
Wheathill
Mackan
Ballindarragh
Knocks
Eshnadarragh
Gubaveeny
Drumcard
Eshnadeelada
Scotstown
Florence Court Forest Park
Upper Lough Erne
Lisnaskea
Kinawley
Corranny
Tiltinbane
Shannon
Derrynawilt
Rosslea
Cuilcagh
Swanlinbar
Tully
Donagh
Ballagh
Smithborough
Glangevlin
Derrylin
Stone Bridge
Magheraveely
Ballinagleragh
Newtownbutler
Clones / Cluain Eois
Killeevan
Iron Mountains
Benbrack
Slieve Rushen
Teemore
Brackley Lough
Bencroy or Gubnaveagh
Gortmullan
Newbliss
Woodford
Bawnboy
Aghalan
Wattle Bridge
Corraleehan
Slieve Anierin
Blackwater
Ballyconnell
Scotshouse
Belturbet / Béal Tairbirt
Redhills
Drum
Aughnasheelan
Ballinamore / Béal an Átha Móir
Ardlougher
Milltown
Cloverhill
Treehoo
Abbey
Waterway
Canal

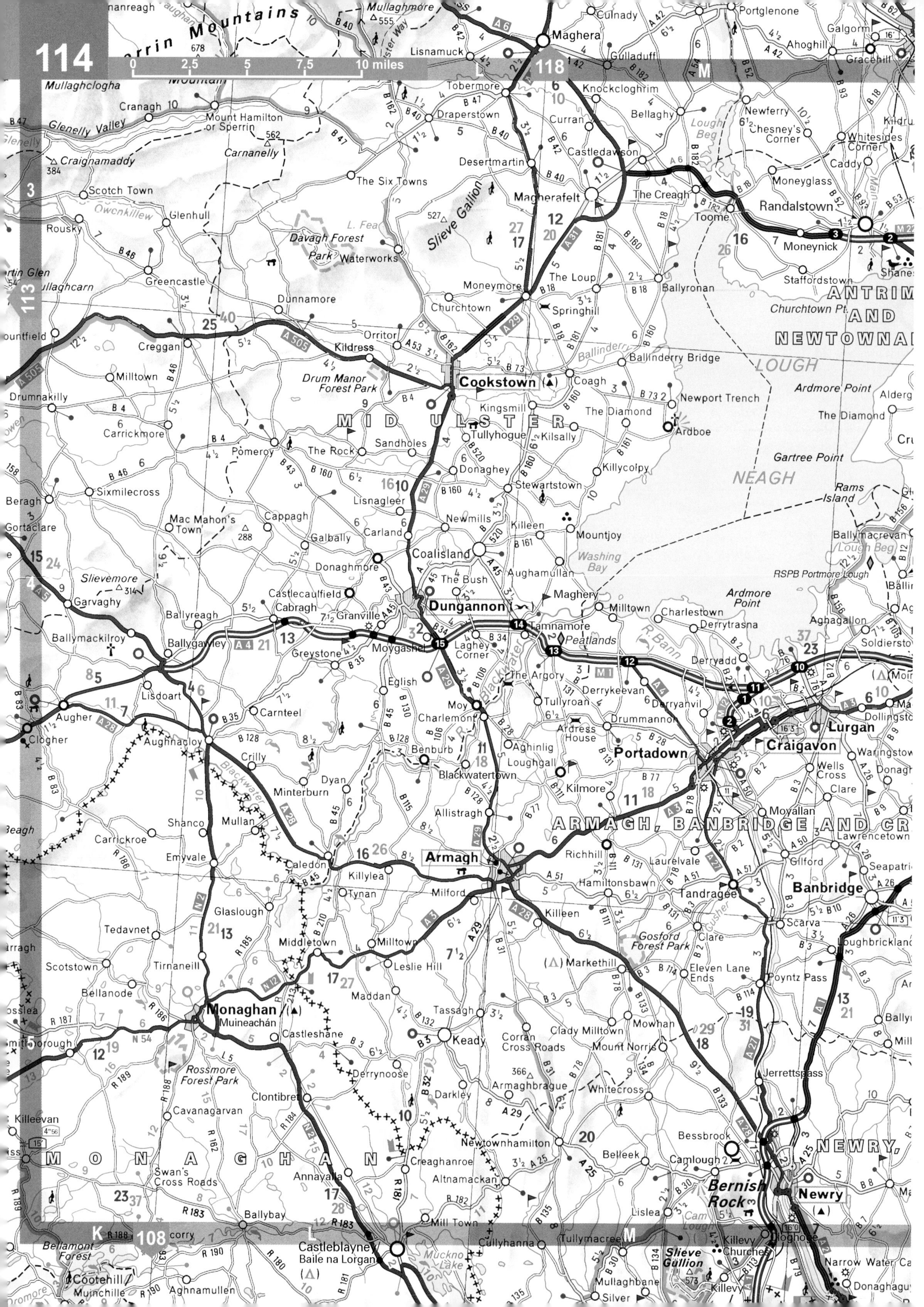
0 2.5 5 7.5 10 miles
118
113
108
Sperrin Mountains
Mullaghclogha
Cranagh
Mount Hamilton or Sperrin
Glenelly Valley
Carnanelly
Craignamaddy
Scotch Town
Owenkillew
Glenhull
Rousky
Greencastle
Davagh Forest Park
Waterworks
Dunnamore
Creggan
Milltown
Drumnakilly
Carrickmore
Pomeroy
Sixmilecross
Beragh
Gortaclare
Mac Mahon's Town
Cappagh
Galbally
Slievemore
Garvaghy
Ballyreagh
Ballymackilroy
Ballygawley
Augher
Clogher
Lisdoart
Aughnacloy
Carnteel
Crilly
Minterburn
Dyan
Caledon
Shanco
Mullan
Carrickroe
Emyvale
Glaslough
Tedavnet
Scotstown
Tirnaneill
Bellanode
Monaghan
Muineachán
Smithborough
Rossmore Forest Park
Castleshane
Clontibret
Cavanagarvan
Killeevan
Swan's Cross Roads
Annayalla
Ballybay
Castleblayney
Baile na Lorgan
Bellamont Forest
Cootehill
Muinchille
Aghnamullen
Muckno Lake
MONAGHAN
Maghera
Culnady
Portglenone
Galgorm
Ahoghill
Gracehill
Gulladuff
Lisnamuck
Mullaghmore
Tobermore
Draperstown
Knockcloghrim
Bellaghy
Newferry
Chesney's Corner
Whitesides Corner
Lough Beg
Curran
Castledawson
Desertmartin
The Six Towns
Magherafelt
The Creagh
Toome
Randalstown
Moneyglass
Caddy
Moneynick
Staffordstown
Shanes
Slieve Gallion
L. Fea
The Loup
Ballyronan
Moneymore
Churchtown
Springhill
Churchtown Pt.
ANTRIM AND NEWTOWNABBEY
Orritor
Kildress
Drum Manor Forest Park
Ballinderry Bridge
Cookstown
Coagh
LOUGH NEAGH
Ardmore Point
Newport Trench
The Diamond
Kingsmill
MID ULSTER
Tullyhogue
Kilsally
Ardboe
The Rock
Sandholes
Donaghey
Killycolpy
Gartree Point
Stewartstown
Lisnagleer
Newmills
Killeen
Mountjoy
Rams Island
Carland
Coalisland
Washing Bay
Donaghmore
The Bush
Aughamullan
Ballymacrevan
RSPB Portmore Lough
Castlecaulfield
Cabragh
Granville
Dungannon
Maghery
Milltown
Charlestown
Derrytrasna
Aghagallon
Tamnamore
Peatlands
Greystone
Moygashel
Laghey Corner
The Argory
Derrykeevan
Derryadd
Soldierstown
Eglish
Moy
Charlemont
Tullyroan
Derryanvil
Drummannon
Ardress House
Aghinlig
Benburb
Loughgall
Blackwatertown
Portadown
Kilmore
Lurgan
Craigavon
Dollingstown
Waringstown
Wells Cross
Clare
Moyallan
Allistragh
Armagh
Richhill
Laurelvale
Lawrencetown
Gilford
Seapatrick
Banbridge
ARMAGH, BANBRIDGE AND CRAIGAVON
Killylea
Tynan
Milford
Hamiltonsbawn
Tandragee
Scarva
Killeen
Gosford Forest Park
Clare
Loughbrickland
Middletown
Milltown
Leslie Hill
Markethill
Eleven Lane Ends
Poyntz Pass
Maddan
Tassagh
Keady
Corran Cross Roads
Clady Milltown
Mowhan
Mount Norris
Derrynoose
Darkley
Armaghbrague
Whitecross
Jerrettspass
Newtownhamilton
Belleek
Bessbrook
Camlough
Creaghanroe
Altnamackan
Bernish Rock
NEWRY
Newry
Mill Town
Lislea
Cullyhanna
Tullymacreeve
Slieve Gullion
Killevy Churches
Meigh
Mullaghbane
Silver Bridge
Narrow Water
Donaghaguy

Ballymena
MID AND EAST ANTRIM
Larne
Isle of Muck
Portmuck
Islandmagee
The Gobbins
Black Head
Whitehead
Carrickfergus
Liverpool
Douglas (I. of Man)
Belfast Lough
Bangor
Groomsport
Copeland Island
Mew Island
Light House Island
Donaghadee
Antrim
Ballyclare
Newtownabbey
Holywood
BELFAST
Newtownards
Lisburn
Comber
Mount Stewart Gardens
ARDS AND NORTH DOWN
Ards Peninsula
Ballywalter
Portavogie
LISBURN AND CASTLEREAGH
Strangford Lough
Killyleagh
Portaferry
Strangford
Ballynahinch
Downpatrick
Ballyquintin Point
Lecale Peninsula
Ardglass
Dundrum Bay
St. John's Point
Castlewellan
Newcastle
MOURNE AND DOWN
Slieve Donard
Mourne Mountains
Rathfriland
CRAIGAVON
Dromore
Saintfield
Carryduff
BELFAST AIRPORT

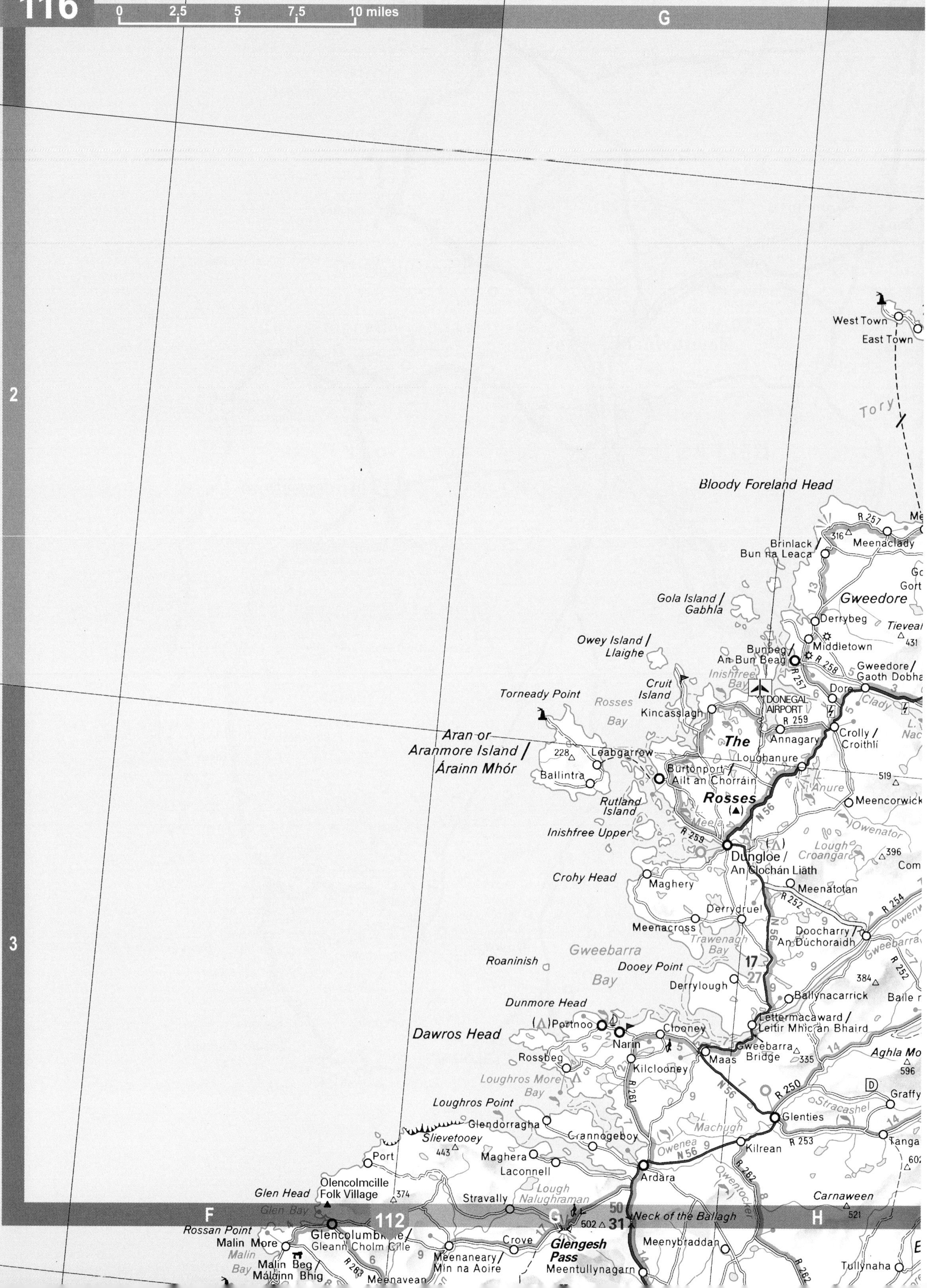

0
2.5
5
7.5
10 miles
G
F
H
2
3
112
West Town
East Town
Tory
Bloody Foreland Head
R 257
Brinlack / Bun na Leaca
316
Meenaclady
Gortahork
Gweedore
Gola Island / Gabhla
Derrybeg
Tievealehid
431
Middletown
Owey Island / Llaighe
Bunbeg / An Bun Beag
R 258
R 257
Gweedore / Gaoth Dobhair
Inishfree Bay
Cruit Island
DONEGAL AIRPORT
Dore
Clady
Torneady Point
Rosses Bay
Kincasslagh
R 259
Crolly / Croithlí
Aran or Aranmore Island / Árainn Mhór
Annagary
The Rosses
228
Leabgarrow
Loughanure
Ballintra
Burtonport / Ailt an Chorráin
519
Anure
Meencorwick
Rutland Island
N 56
Meela
Inishfree Upper
R 259
Owenator
Lough Croangar
396
Dungloe / An Clochán Liath
Crohy Head
Maghery
Meenatotan
R 252
R 254
Derrydruel
Meenacross
Doocharry / An Dúchoraidh
Trawenagh Bay
Gweebarra Bay
Owenwee
Gweebarra
Roaninish
Dooey Point
17
27
Derrylough
384
R 252
Ballynacarrick
Baile na Carraige
Dunmore Head
Portnoo
Lettermacaward / Leitir Mhic an Bhaird
Dawros Head
Narin
Clooney
Gweebarra Bridge
335
Aghla More
596
Rossbeg
Maas
Kilclooney
R 261
N 56
Loughros More Bay
R 250
Graffy
Stracashel
Loughros Point
Glenties
Glendorragha
L. Machugh
Slievetooey
443
Crannogeboy
Kilrean
R 253
Tanga
Owenea
N 56
Port
Maghera
Laconnell
Ardara
R 262
Owentocker
Olencolmcille Folk Village
374
Lough Nalughraman
Glen Head
Stravally
Carnaween
521
Glen Bay
50
31
502
Neck of the Ballagh
Rossan Point
Glencolumbkille / Gleann Cholm Cille
Malin More
Crove
Glengesh Pass
Meenybraddan
Malin Bay
Meenaneary / Mín na Aoire
Malin Beg / Málainn Bhig
R 263
Meentullynagarn
Tullynaha
Meenavean
R 262

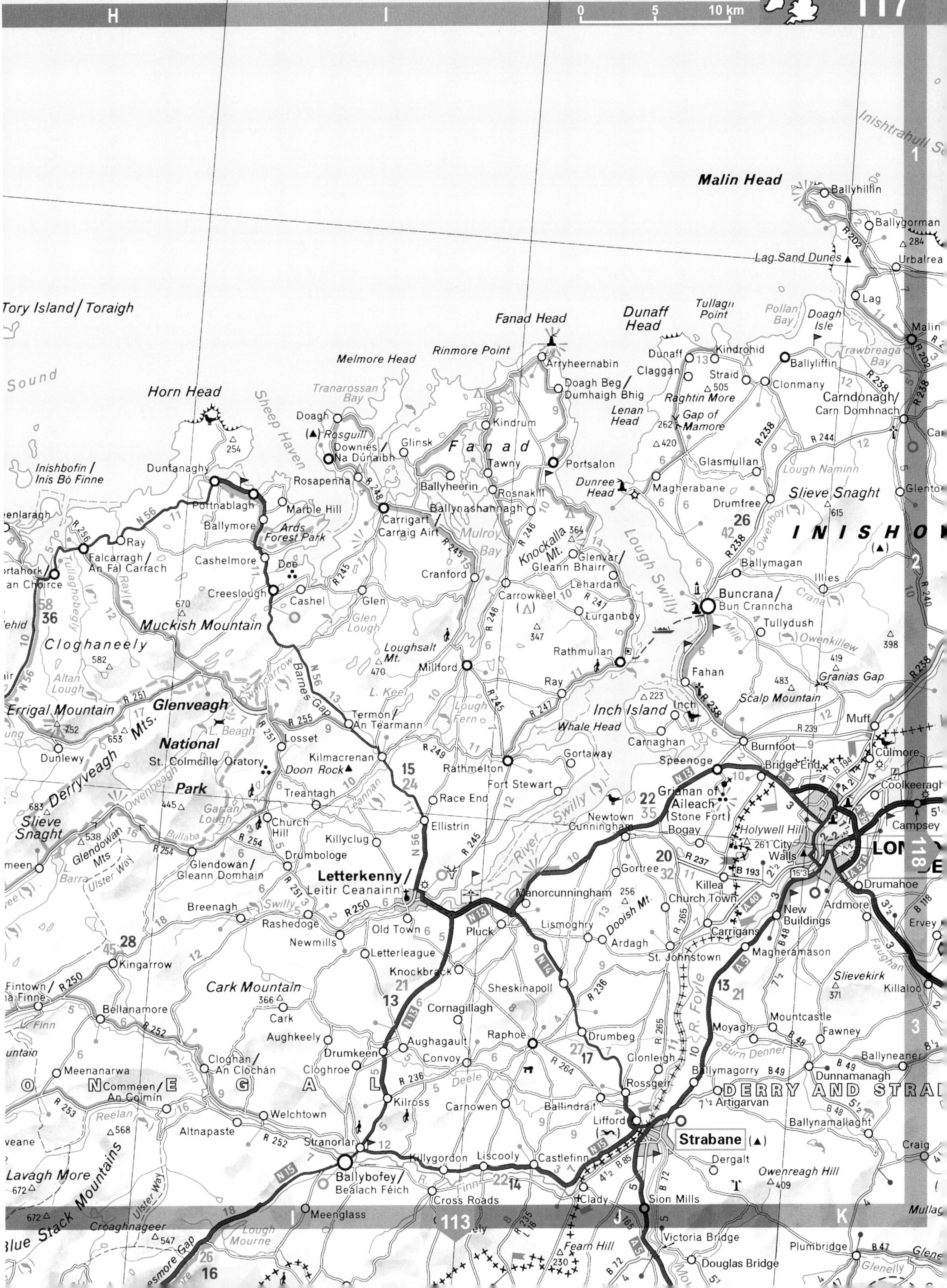

H
I
J
K
0 5 10 km
1
2
3
118
113
Inishtrahull Sound
Malin Head
Ballyhillin
Ballygorman
Lag Sand Dunes
Urbalreagh
Lag
Malin
Tory Island / Toraigh
Fanad Head
Dunaff Head
Tullagh Point
Pollan Bay
Doagh Isle
Trawbreaga Bay
Rinmore Point
Melmore Head
Arryheernabin
Dunaff
Kindrohid
Ballyliffin
Claggan
Straid
Clonmany
Doagh Beg / Dumhaigh Bhig
Raghtin More
Carndonagh / Carn Domhnach
Sound
Horn Head
Sheep Haven
Tranarossan Bay
Lenan Head
Gap of Mamore
Doagh
Kindrum
Rosguill
Downies / Na Dúnaibh
Glinsk
Fanad
Tawny
Portsalon
Glasmullan
Inishbofin / Inis Bó Finne
Dunfanaghy
Rosapenna
Ballyheerin
Rosnakill
Dunree Head
Magherabane
Lough Naminn
Slieve Snaght
Glentogher
Portnablagh
Marble Hill
Carrigart / Carraig Airt
Ballynashannagh
Drumfree
Ballymore
Ards Forest Park
Mulroy Bay
Knockalla Mt.
INISHOWEN
Falcarragh / An Fál Carrach
Ray
Glenvar / Gleann Bhairr
Ballymagan
Gortahork / Gort an Choirce
Cashelmore
Doe
Cranford
Lough Swilly
Illies
Creeslough
Lehardan
Cashel
Glen
Carrowkeel
Buncrana / Bun Cranncha
Crana
Tullaghobegly
Muckish Mountain
Glen Lough
Lurganboy
Tullydush
Owenkillew
Cloghaneely
Loughsalt Mt.
Rathmullan
Granias Gap
Altan Lough
Millford
Fahan
Scalp Mountain
Errigal Mountain
Glenveagh
Barnes Gap
L. Keel
Ray
Inch Island
Inch
Owencarrow
Lough Fern
Whale Head
Muff
Termon / An Tearmann
Carnaghan
Burnfoot
Culmore
National
L. Beagh
Dunlewy
Derryveagh Mts.
Losset
Kilmacrenan
Speenoge
Bridge End
St. Colmcille Oratory
Doon Rock
Rathmelton
Grianan of Aileach (Stone Fort)
Coolkeeragh
Park
Fort Stewart
Slieve Snaght
Gartan Lough
Owenbeagh
Treantagh
Race End
Newtown Cunningham
Holywell Hill
Campsey
Glendowan Mts
Church Hill
River Swilly
Bogay
City Walls
LONDONDERRY
Bullaba
Killyclug
Ellistrin
Glendowan / Gleann Domhain
Drumbologe
Gortree
Drumahoe
Ulster Way
Letterkenny / Leitir Ceanainn
Manorcunningham
Killea
Dooish Mt.
Church Town
Ardmore
Breenagh
Swilly
Rashedoge
Lismoghry
Carrigans
New Buildings
Erveyarn
Old Town
Pluck
Ardagh
Newmills
St. Johnstown
Magheramason
Faughan
Kingarrow
Letterleague
Knockbrack
Slievekirk
Fintown / Baile na Finne
Cark Mountain
Sheskinapoll
R. Foyle
Killaloo
Bellanamore
Cark
Cornagillagh
Mountcastle
Finn
Aughkeely
Raphoe
Drumbeg
Moyagh
Fawney
Cloghan / An Clochán
Drumkeen
Aughagault
Convoy
Clonleigh
Burn Dennet
Ballyneaner
Meenanarwa
Cloghroe
Ballymagorry
Dunnamanagh
Commeen / An Coimín
DONEGAL
Deele
Rossgeir
DERRY AND STRABANE
Reelan
Kilross
Carnowen
Ballindrait
Artigarvan
Welchtown
Lifford
Strabane
Ballynamallaght
Altnapaste
Stranorlar
Killygordon
Liscooly
Castlefinn
Dergalt
Owenreagh Hill
Craig
Lavagh More
Ballybofey / Bealach Féich
Clady
Cross Roads
Sion Mills
Mullaghcarn
Blue Stack Mountains
Meenglass
Croaghnageer
Lough Mourne
Fearn Hill
Victoria Bridge
Plumbridge
Glenelly
Douglas Bridge
Barnesmore Gap

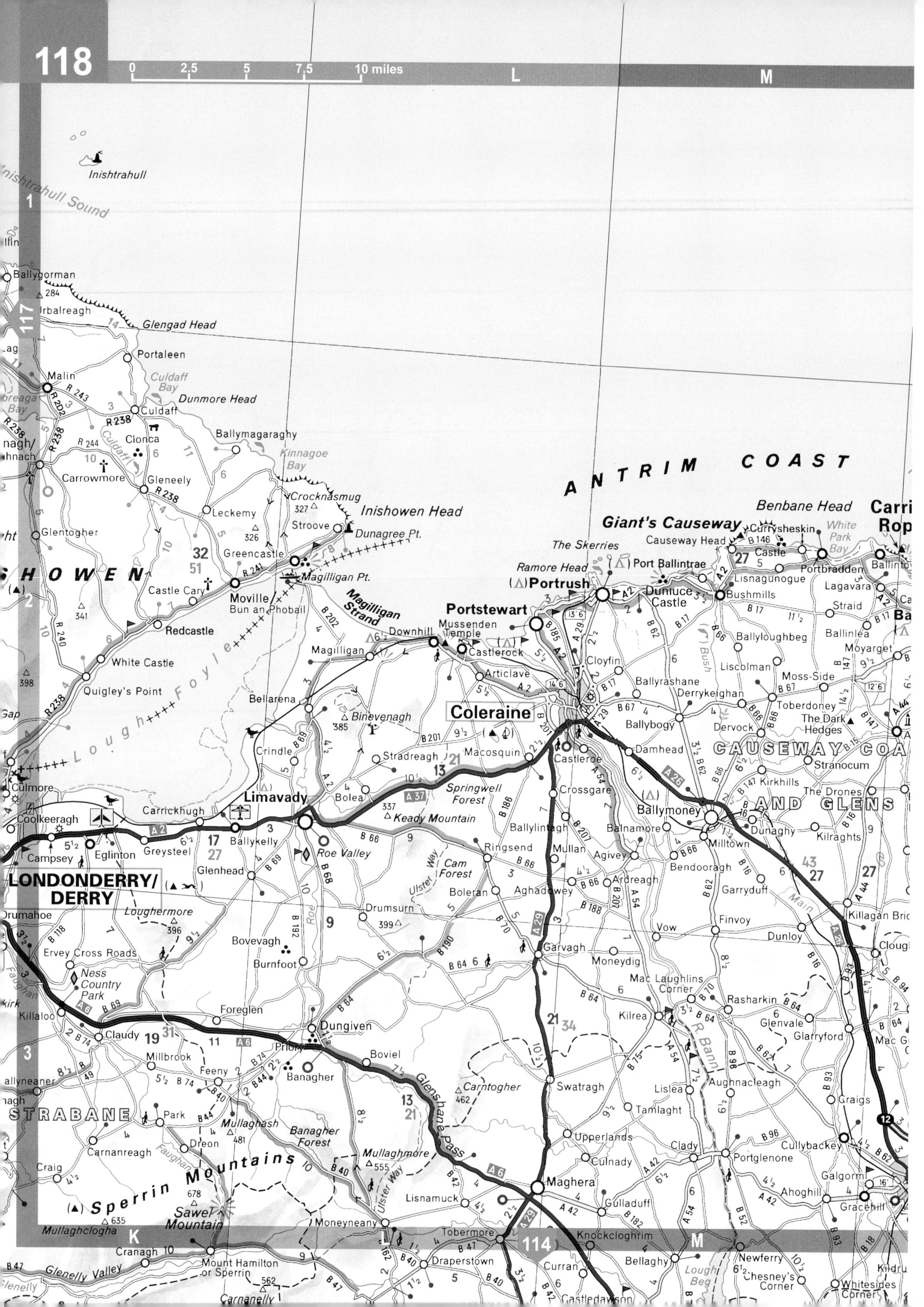
0 2,5 5 7,5 10 miles
L
M
Inishtrahull
Inishtrahull Sound
Ballygorman
Glengad Head
Portaleen
Malin
Culdaff Bay
Dunmore Head
Culdaff
Clonca
Ballymagaraghy
Kinnagoe Bay
Carrowmore
Gleneely
Crocknasmug
Inishowen Head
Leckemy
Stroove
Dunagree Pt.
Glentogher
Greencastle
Magilligan Pt.
INISHOWEN
Castle Cary
Moville/ Bun an Phobail
Magilligan Strand
Redcastle
White Castle
Quigley's Point
Lough Foyle
Downhill
Mussenden Temple
Castlerock
Magilligan
Bellarena
Binevenagh
Crindle
Stradreagh
Culmore
Coolkeeragh
Campsey
Eglinton
Greysteel
Carrickhugh
Limavady
Ballykelly
Bolea
Keady Mountain
Springwell Forest
Roe Valley
LONDONDERRY/ DERRY
Glenhead
Drumahoe
Loughermore
Bovevagh
Burnfoot
Drumsurn
Ervey Cross Roads
Ness Country Park
Killaloo
Foreglen
Claudy
Dungiven
Priory
Banagher
Boviel
Glenshane Pass
Millbrook
Feeny
STRABANE
Park
Mullaghash
Banagher Forest
Dreon
Carnanreagh
Craig
Sperrin Mountains
Sawel Mountain
Mullaghclogha
Mullaghmore
Lisnamuck
Moneyneany
Tobermore
Draperstown
Cranagh
Glenelly Valley
Mount Hamilton or Sperrin
Carnanelly
ANTRIM COAST
Giant's Causeway
Benbane Head
Causeway Head
Currysheskin
White Park Bay
The Skerries
Ramore Head
Portrush
Port Ballintrae
Dunluce Castle
Bushmills
Portballintrae
Portbradden
Lisnagunogue
Lagavara
Straid
Portstewart
Ballyloughbeg
Ballinlea
Moyarget
Cloyfin
Articlave
Liscolman
Moss-Side
Ballyrashane
Derrykeighan
Toberdoney
The Dark Hedges
Coleraine
Ballybogy
Dervock
Macosquin
Castleroe
Damhead
CAUSEWAY COAST AND GLENS
Stranocum
Kirkhills
The Drones
Crossgare
Ballymoney
Ballylintagh
Balnamore
Milltown
Dunaghy
Kilraghts
Ringsend
Mullan
Agivey
Bendooragh
Cam Forest
Ulster Way
Ardreagh
Boleran
Aghadowey
Garryduff
Finvoy
Killagan Bridge
Vow
Dunloy
Garvagh
Moneydig
Mac Laughlins Corner
Rasharkin
Kilrea
Glenvale
Glarryford
R. Bann
Swatragh
Carntogher
Aughnacleagh
Lislea
Tamlaght
Craigs
Upperlands
Culnady
Clady
Portglenone
Cullybackey
Maghera
Galgorm
Ahoghill
Gracehill
Gulladuff
Knockcloghrim
Curran
Bellaghy
Lough Beg
Newferry
Chesney's Corner
Whitesides Corner
Castledawson
114

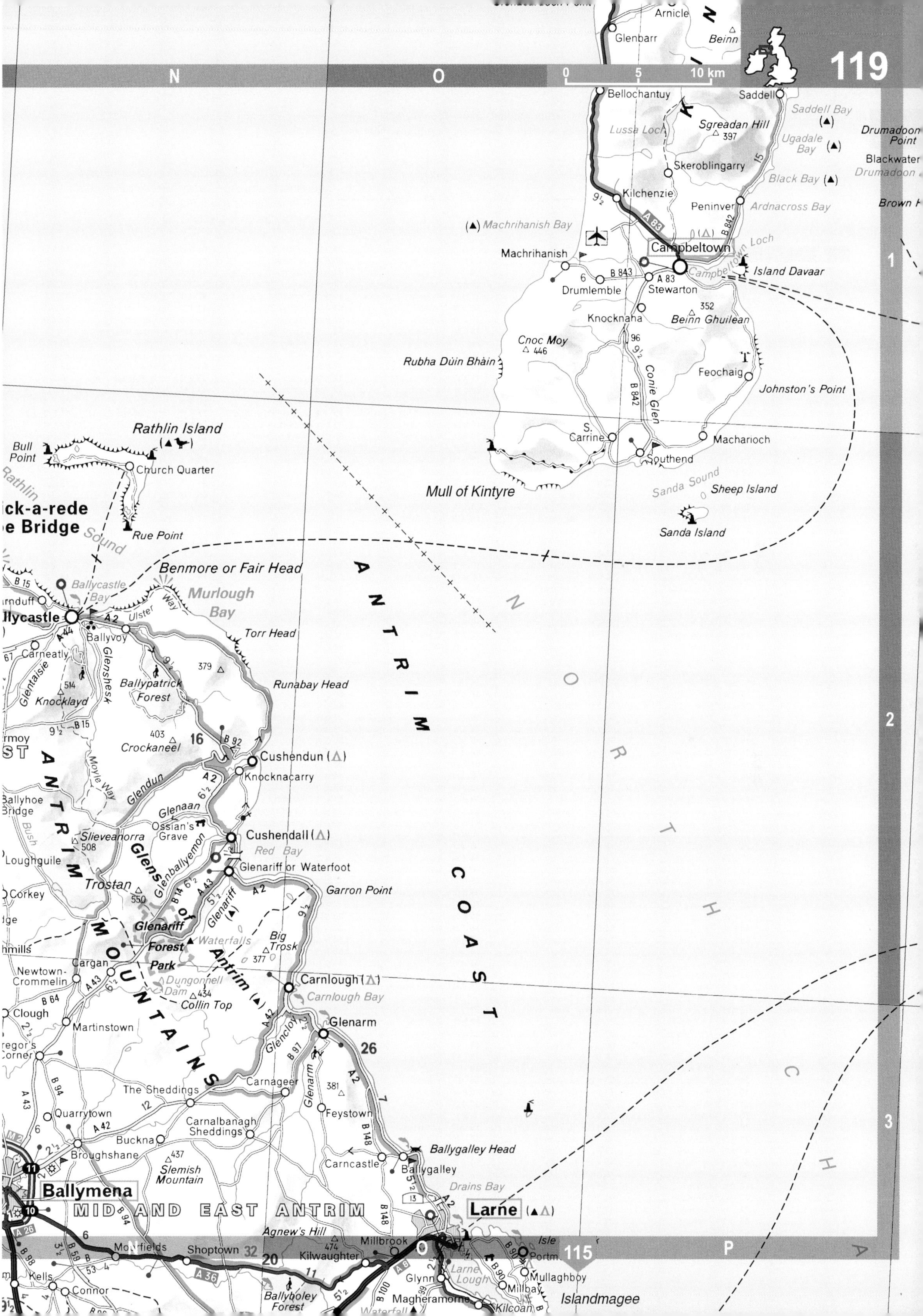

N
O
P
1
2
3
0 5 10 km
Glenbarr
Arnicle
Bellochantuy
Saddell
Saddell Bay
Sgreadan Hill
397
Lussa Loch
Ugadale Bay
Drumadoon Point
Blackwater
Drumadoon
Skeroblingarry
Black Bay
Brown H
Kilchenzie
Peninver
Ardnacross Bay
Machrihanish Bay
A 83
B 842
Campbeltown
Campbeltown Loch
Machrihanish
B 843
Drumlemble
Stewarton
Island Davaar
Knocknaha
352
Beinn Ghuilean
Cnoc Moy
446
Rubha Dùin Bhàin
Conie Glen
Feochaig
Johnston's Point
S. Carrine
Macharioch
Southend
Mull of Kintyre
Sanda Sound
Sheep Island
Sanda Island
Rathlin Island
Bull Point
Church Quarter
Rathlin Sound
Rue Point
ick-a-rede
e Bridge
Benmore or Fair Head
Murlough Bay
Ballycastle Bay
B 15
Ballycastle
A 2
Ulster Way
Ballyvoy
Torr Head
Carneatly
Glenshesk
379
Glentaisie
514
Knocklayd
Ballypatrick Forest
Runabay Head
NORTH CHANNEL
ANTRIM COAST
403
Crockaneel
16
B 92
Cushendun
Knocknacarry
Moyle Way
Glendun
Ballyhoe Bridge
Glenaan
Ossian's Grave
Cushendall
Red Bay
Slieveanorra
508
Loughguile
Glenballyemon
Glenariff or Waterfoot
Garron Point
Trostan
550
Corkey
Glens of Antrim
Glenariff
Glenariff Forest Park
Waterfalls
Big Trosk
377
Cargan
Newtown-Crommelin
A 43
Dungonnell Dam
434
Collin Top
Carnlough
Carnlough Bay
Clough
B 64
Martinstown
ANTRIM MOUNTAINS
Glencloy
Glenarm
26
B 97
The Sheddings
Carnageer
381
B 94
Quarrytown
A 42
12
Feystown
Carnalbanagh Sheddings
B 148
Buckna
437
Broughshane
Slemish Mountain
Ballygalley Head
Carncastle
Ballygalley
Drains Bay
Ballymena
MID AND EAST ANTRIM
Larne
Agnew's Hill
474
Millbrook
Isle
Portm
Moorfields
Shoptown
32
20
Kilwaughter
A 36
B 98
Kells
Connor
A 26
Glynn
Larne Lough
B 90
Mullaghboy
Millbay
Islandmagee
Ballyboley Forest
Magheramorne
B 100
A 8
Waterfall
Kilcoan
115

Page number / Numéro de page / Seitenzahl
Paginanummer / Numero di pagina / Número de Página

Place / Localité / Ort
Plaatsen / Località / Localidad

Achmelvich ....84 E 9

Grid coordinates / Coordonnées de carroyage
Koordinatenangabe / Verwijstekens ruitsysteem
Coordinate riferite alla quadrettatura
Coordenadas en los mapas

A

C

D

F

G

H

I

J

K

L

A B C D E F G H I J K L M N O P Q R S T U V W X Y Z

Lydney 18 M 28
Lydstep 15 F 29
Lyme Bay 5 L 32
Lyme Park 43 N 23
Lyme Regis 5 L 31
Lyminge 13 X 30
Lymington 10 P 31
Lymm 42 M 23
Lympne 13 X 30
Lympstone 4 J 32
Lyndhurst 10 P 31
Lyne 61 K 17
Lyneham *North Wiltshire* 19 O 29
Lyneham *West Oxfordshire* 27 P 28
Lynemouth 56 P 18
Lyness 86 K 7
Lynmouth 17 I 30
Lynton 17 I 30
Lyon (Glen) 73 H 14
Lyonshall 26 L 27
Lytchett Matravers 9 N 31
Lytchett Minster 9 N 31
Lytes Cary 8 L 30
Lyth 86 K 8
Lytham 42 L 22
Lytham St. Anne's 42 K 22
Lythe 51 R 20

M

Maaruig 82 Z 10
Mabie 53 J 18
Mablethorpe 45 U 23
Macaskin (Island) 65 D 15
Macclesfield 43 N 24
Macduff 81 M 10
Machars (The) 52 G 19
Machen 18 K 29
Machir Bay 58 A 16
Machrihanish 58 C 17
Machrihanish Bay 58 C 17
Machynlleth 33 I 26
Madderty 67 I 14
Maddiston 67 I 16
Maddy (Loch) 76 Y 11
Madeley *Staffs* 35 M 24
Madeley *Telford and Wrekin* 35 M 26
Madingley 29 U 27
Madron 2 D 33
Maenclochog 15 F 28
Maentwrog 33 I 25
Maerdy *Conwy* 33 J 25
Maerdy *Rhondda, Cynon, Taf* 17 J 28
Maes Howe 86 K 7
Maesbrook 34 K 25
Maesteg 17 J 29
Maghull 42 L 23
Magor 18 L 29
Maiden Bradley 9 N 30
Maiden Castle 8 M 31
Maiden Newton 8 M 31
Maidenhead 20 R 29
Maidens 59 F 17
Maidford 28 Q 27
Maids Morelon 28 R 27
Maidstone 22 V 30
Maidwell 28 R 26
Mainland *Orkney Islands* 86 J 6
Mainland *Shetland Islands* 87 R 3
Mainstone 26 K 26
Maisemore 27 N 28
Malborough 4 I 33
Maldon 22 W 28
Malham 49 N 21
Mallaig 71 C 12
Mallory Park Circuit 36 P 26
Mallwyd 33 I 25
Malmesbury 19 N 29
Malpas 34 L 24
Maltby 44 Q 23
Maltby-le-Marsh 45 U 24
Malton 50 R 21
Malvern Wells 27 N 27
Mamble 26 M 26
Mamore Forest 72 F 13
Man (Isle of) 46 G 21
Manaccan 2 E 33
Manaton 4 I 32
Manchester 43 N 23
Manderston 62 N 16
Manea 29 U 26
Mangersta 82 Y 9
Mangotsfield 18 M 29
Manish 76 Z 10
Manningford Bruce 19 O 30
Mannings Heath 11 T 30
Manningtree 31 X 28
Manorbier 15 F 29
Mansfield 36 Q 24
Mansfield Woodhouse 36 Q 24
Manstone 9 N 31
Manton 36 R 26
Manuden 30 U 28
Maplebeck 36 R 24
Mapledurham 20 Q 29
Mappleton 45 T 22
Mappowder 9 M 31
Mar (Forest of) 74 J 12
Marazion 2 D 33
March 37 U 26
Marcham 20 P 29
Marchington 35 O 25
Marchwood 10 P 31
Marden 22 V 30
Maree (Loch) 78 D 10
Mareham-le-Fen 37 T 24
Maresfield 11 U 31
Margam 17 I 29
Margaretting 22 V 28
Margate 23 Y 29
Margnaheglish 59 E 17
Marham 38 V 26
Marhamchurch 6 G 31
Marholm 37 T 26
Marian-Glas 40 H 22
Marishader 77 B 11
Mark *Sedgemoor* 18 L 30
Mark *South Ayrshire* 52 E 18
Market Bosworth 36 P 26
Market Deeping 37 T 25
Market Drayton 34 M 25
Market Harborough 28 R 26
Market Lavington 19 O 30
Market Overton 36 R 25
Market Rasen 45 T 23
Market Weighton 44 S 22
Markfield 36 Q 25
Markinch 68 K 15
Marks Tey 30 W 28
Marksbury 18 M 29
Markyate 21 S 28
Marlborough 19 O 29
Marldon 4 J 32
Marlesford 31 Y 27
Marloes 14 E 28
Marlow 20 R 29
Marnhull 9 N 31
Marple 43 N 23
Marros 15 G 28
Marsden 43 O 23
Marsett 49 N 21
Marsh Gibbon 28 Q 28
Marsham 39 X 25
Marshaw 48 M 22
Marshchapel 45 U 23
Marshfield *Casnewydd / Newport* 18 K 29
Marshfield *South Gloucestershire* 19 N 29
Marshwood 8 L 31
Marske 49 O 20
Marske-by-the-Sea 57 Q 20
Marstch 20 Q 28
Marston 37 R 25
Marston Magna 8 M 31
Marston Moretaine 29 S 27
Martham 39 Y 25
Martin *New Forest* 9 O 31
Martin *North Kesteven* 37 T 24
Martin (Isle) 84 E 10
Martin Mill 23 Y 30
Martindale 48 L 20
Martinstown 5 M 31
Martlesham 31 X 27
Martletwy 15 F 28
Martley 27 M 27
Martock 8 L 31
Marton *Harrogate* 50 P 21
Marton *Macclesfield* 35 N 24
Marvig 82 A 9
Marwell Zoological Park 10 Q 31
Mary Arden's House 27 O 27
Mary Tavy 4 H 32
Marybank 79 G 11
Maryburgh 79 G 11
Maryculter 75 N 12
Maryfield 87 Q 3
Marykirk 75 M 13
Marypark 80 J 11
Maryport *Allerdale* 53 J 19
Maryport *Dumfries and Galloway* 52 F 19
Marywell *Aberdeenshire* 75 L 12
Marywell *Angus* 69 M 14
Masham 49 P 21
Matching Green 22 U 28
Mathry 14 E 28
Matlock 36 P 24
Matlock Bath 35 P 24
Mattersey 44 R 23
Mattingley 20 R 30
Mattishall 38 X 26
Mauchline 60 G 17
Maud 81 N 11
Maughold 46 H 21
Maughold Head 46 H 21
Mawbray 54 J 19
Mawnan 2 E 33
Maxstoke 27 P 26
Maxton 62 M 17
Maybole 60 F 17
Mayfield *East Sussex* 12 U 30
Mayfield *Staffs* 35 O 24
Mc Arthur's Head 58 B 16
Meadie (Loch) 84 G 9
Meal Bank 48 L 20
Mealsgate 54 K 19
Meare 8 L 30
Measach (Falls of) 78 E 10
Measham 36 P 25
Meavaig 82 Z 10
Meavy 4 H 32
Medbourne 28 R 26
Medmenham 20 R 29
Medstead 10 Q 30
Medway (River) 22 W 29
Meidrim 15 G 28
Meifod 34 K 25
Meigle 68 K 14
Meikleour 68 J 14
Melbost 83 B 9
Melbourn 29 U 27
Melbourne *East Riding of Yorkshire* 44 R 22
Melbourne *South Derbyshire* 36 P 25
Melbury Osmond 8 M 31
Meldon 56 O 18
Melfort 65 D 15
Melgarve 73 G 12
Melksham 19 N 29
Melldalloch 65 E 16
Mellerstain 62 M 17
Melling 48 M 21
Mellon Charles 78 D 10
Mellon Udrigle 78 D 10
Mells 19 M 30
Melmerby *Eden* 55 M 19
Melmerby *Harrogate* 50 P 21
Melrose 62 L 17
Meltham 43 O 23
Melton 31 X 27
Melton Mowbray 36 R 25
Melvaig 77 C 10
Melvich 85 I 8
Memsie 81 N 11
Menai Bridge / Porthaethwy 40 H 23
Menai Strait 33 H 24
Mendip Hills 18 L 30
Mendlesham 31 X 27
Menheniot 3 G 32
Mennock 61 I 17
Menston 43 O 22
Menstrie 67 I 15
Menteith Hills 67 H 15
Mentmore 29 R 28
Meonstoke 10 Q 31
Meopham 22 V 29
Mepal 29 U 26
Mere *Cheshire* 42 M 24
Mere *Wilts* 9 N 30
Mereworth 22 V 30
Meriden 27 P 26
Merkland Lodge 84 F 9
Mermaid Inn 32 H 24
Merrick 52 G 18
Merriott 8 L 31
Merrylaw 62 K 18
Mersey (River) 42 M 23
Merthyr Cynog 25 J 27
Merthyr Tydfil 17 J 28
Merton *Cherwell* 20 Q 28
Merton *Devon* 7 H 31
Merton *London Borough* 21 T 29
Meshaw 7 I 31
Messing 30 W 28
Messingham 44 S 23
Metfield 31 Y 26
Metheringham 37 S 24
Methil 69 K 15
Methlick 81 N 11
Methven 68 J 14
Methwold 38 V 26
Mevagissey 3 F 33
Mexborough 44 Q 23
Mhòr (Loch) 73 G 12
Miavaig 82 Z 9
Michaelchurch Escley 26 L 27
Michaelstow 3 F 32
Micheldever 10 Q 30
Michelham Priory 12 U 31
Micklefield 44 Q 22
Mickleover 36 P 25
Mickleton *Cotswold* 27 O 27
Mickleton *Teesdale* 55 N 20
Mid Ardlaw 81 N 10
Mid Calder 61 J 16
Mid Lavant 10 R 31
Mid Sannox 59 E 17
Mid Yell 87 Q 2
Midbea 86 L 6
Middle Barton 28 P 28
Middle Rasen 45 S 23
Middle Tysoe 28 P 27
Middle Wallop 9 P 30
Middle Woodford 9 O 30
Middlebie 54 K 18
Middleham 49 O 21
Middlesbrough 57 Q 20
Middlestown 43 P 23
Middleton *Argyll and Bute* 64 Z 14
Middleton *Berwick-upon-Tweed* 63 O 17
Middleton *Bradford* 49 O 22
Middleton *Gtr. Mches* 43 N 23
Middleton Cheney 28 Q 27
Middleton-in-Teesdale 55 N 20
Middleton-on-Sea 11 S 31
Middleton on the Wolds 51 S 22
Middleton St. George 50 P 20
Middleton Tyas 49 P 20
Middletown *Powys* 34 K 25
Middlewich 35 M 24
Midgeholme 55 M 19
Midhurst 10 R 31
Midlem 62 L 17
Midsomer Norton 18 M 30
Midtown 78 C 10
Miefield 53 H 19
Migdale (Loch) 79 H 10
Milborne Port 8 M 31
Milborne St. Andrew 9 N 31
Milbourne 56 O 18
Milburn 55 M 20
Mildenhall *Forest Heath* 30 V 26
Mildenhall *Kennet* 19 O 29
Mile End 30 W 28
Milfield 63 N 17
Milford 11 S 30
Milford Haven / Aberdaugleddau 14 E 28
Milford-on-Sea 9 P 31
Milland 10 R 30
Millbrook 3 H 32
Millhouse 59 E 16
Millmeece 35 N 25
Millom 47 K 21
Millport 59 F 16
Milltown *Dumfries and Galloway* 54 K 18
Milltown *Highland* 78 F 11
Milltown *Moray* 80 L 11
Milnathort 68 J 15
Milngavie 67 H 16
Milnrow 43 N 23
Milnthorpe 48 L 21
Milovaig 76 Z 11
Milton 79 H 10
Milton *Cambs* 29 U 27
Milton *Carlisle* 55 L 19
Milton *Dumfries* 53 I 18
Milton *Highland* 79 G 11
Milton *Stranraer* 52 F 19
Milton Abbas 9 N 31
Milton Abbot 3 H 32
Milton Bryan 29 S 28
Milton Ernest 29 S 27
Milton Keynes 28 R 27
Milton Libourne 19 O 29
Milton of Campsie 67 H 16
Milton of Cushnie 75 L 12
Milton-on-Stour 9 N 30
Miltonduff 80 J 11
Miltown of Edinvillie 80 K 11
Milverton 8 K 30
Milwich 35 N 25
Minard 65 E 15
Minch (The) 83 C 9
Minehead 17 J 30
Minety 19 O 29
Mingary 76 X 12
Minginish 77 B 12
Mingulay 70 X 13
Minnigaff 52 G 19
Minster *near Sheerness* 22 W 29
Minster *near Ramsgate* 23 X 29
Minsterley 34 L 26
Minsterworth 19 N 28
Minterne Magna 8 M 31
Minting 45 T 24
Mintlaw 81 O 11
Minto 62 L 17
Mirfield 43 O 22
Miserden 19 N 28
Misson 44 R 23
Misterton *Notts* 44 R 23
Misterton *Somerset* 8 L 31
Mistley 31 X 28
Mitcheldean 26 M 28
Mitchell 2 E 32
Mitford 56 O 18
Mithcham 21 T 29
Mithian 2 E 33
Moaness 86 K 7
Mochdre 41 I 23
Mochrum 52 G 19
Modbury 4 I 32
Moelfre 40 H 22
Moffat 61 J 17
Moidart 72 C 13
Moira 36 P 25
Mol-Chlach 71 B 12
Mold / Yr Wyddgrug 34 K 24
Molland 7 I 30
Monach Islands 76 W 11
Monadhliath Mountains 73 H 12
Monar (Loch) 78 E 11
Monar Lodge 78 F 11
Monaughty Forest 80 J 11
Moneydie 68 J 14
Moniaive 53 I 18
Monifieth 69 L 14
Monikie 69 L 14
Monk Fryston 44 Q 22
Monkland 26 L 27
Monkokehampton 7 H 31
Monks Eleigh 30 W 27
Monksilver 7 K 30
Monkton 60 G 17
Monmouth / Trefynwy 18 L 28
Monreith 52 G 19
Montacute 8 L 31
Montgarrie 75 L 12
Montgomery / Trefaldwyn 34 K 26
Montrose 75 M 13
Monyash 35 O 24
Monymusk 75 M 12
Monzie 67 I 14
Moonen Bay 76 Z 11
Moor Monkton 50 Q 21
Moorends 44 R 23
Moorfoot Hills 61 K 16
Moors (The) 52 F 19
Moortown 45 S 23
Morar 71 C 13
Moray Firth 79 H 11
Morchard Bishop 7 I 31
Morcott 37 S 26
Morden 9 N 31
Mordiford 26 M 27
More (Glen) 65 C 14
More (Loch) *near Kinloch* 84 F 9
More (Loch) *near Westerdale* 85 J 8
Morebath 7 J 30
Morebattle 62 M 17
Morecambe 48 L 21
Morecambe Bay 48 L 21
Moresby 53 J 20
Moreton *Epping Forest* 22 U 28
Moreton *Purbeck* 9 N 31
Moreton-in-Marsh 27 O 28
Moreton-on-lugg 26 L 27
Moreton Say 34 M 25
Moretonhampstead 4 I 32
Morfa Nefyn 32 G 25
Moricambe Bay 54 K 19
Morie (Loch) 79 G 10
Moriston (Glen) 72 F 12
Morland 55 M 20
Morley 43 P 22
Morlich (Loch) 74 I 12
Morpeth 56 O 18
Morriston 17 I 29
Morte Bay 6 H 30
Mortehoe 16 H 30
Mortimer 20 Q 29
Morton *near Bourne* 37 S 25
Morton *near Gainsborough* 44 R 23
Morton *North East Derbyshire* 36 P 24
Morton on Swale 50 P 21
Morval 3 G 32
Morven 85 I 9
Morvern 71 C 14
Morvich 72 D 12
Morville 34 M 26
Morwelham 3 H 32
Morwenstow 6 G 31
Mosborough 43 P 24
Moss Bank 42 L 23
Mossdale 53 H 18
Mossend 60 H 16
Mossley 43 N 23
Mosstodloch 80 K 11
Mostyn 41 K 23
Motherwell 61 I 16
Moulin 74 I 13
Moulton *Forest Heath* 30 V 27
Moulton *Lincs* 37 T 25
Moulton *Northants* 28 R 27
Moulton Chapel 37 T 25
Mount Pleasant 9 P 31
Mountain Ash / Aberpennar 17 J 28
Mount's Bay 2 D 33
Mountsorrel 36 Q 25
Mousa 87 Q 4
Mousehole 2 D 33
Mouswald 54 J 18
Mow Cop 35 N 24
Mowtie 75 N 13
Moy 79 H 11
Muasdale 59 C 17
Much Dewchurch 26 L 28
Much Hadham 29 U 28
Much Hoole 42 L 22
Much Marcle 26 M 28
Much Wenlock 34 M 26
Muchalls 75 N 12
Muchelney 8 L 30
Muchrachd 78 F 11
Muck 71 B 13
Muckle Roe 87 P 2
Mucklestone 35 M 25
Muddiford 7 H 30
Mudford 8 M 31
Mugeary 77 B 11
Muick (Loch) 74 K 13
Muie 85 H 9
Muir of Fowlis 75 L 12
Muir of Ord 79 G 11
Muirdrum 69 L 14
Muirhead 60 H 16
Muirkirk 60 H 17
Muirshearlich 72 E 13
Muker 49 N 20
Mulbarton 39 X 26
Mulben 80 K 11
Muldoanich 70 X 13
Mull (Isle of) 64 B 14
Mull (Sound of) 71 C 14
Mull of Galloway 52 F 20
Mull of Oa 58 A 17
Mullardoch (Loch) 78 E 12
Mullardoch House 78 F 11
Mullion 2 E 33
Mumbles (The) 15 H 29
Mumby 45 U 24
Mundesley 39 Y 25
Mundford 30 V 26
Mundham 10 R 31
Munlochy 79 H 11
Munlochy Bay 79 H 11
Munslow 26 L 26
Murlaggan 72 E 13
Murrayfield 68 K 16
Mursley 28 R 28
Murton *Easington* 57 P 19
Murton *Eden* 55 M 20
Musbury 5 K 31
Musselburgh 68 K 16
Muston 51 T 21
Muthill 67 I 15
Mwnt 15 G 27
Mybster 85 J 8
Myddfai 25 I 28
Myddle 34 L 25

Q

R

S

Sherborne *Cotswold* 19 O 28
Sherborne *West Dorset* 8 M 31
Sherborne St. John 20 Q 30
Sherburn *Durham* 56 P 19
Sherburn *Ryedale* 51 S 21
Sherburn-in-Elmet 44 Q 22
Shere 21 S 30
Sherfield English 9 P 31
Sheriff Hutton 50 Q 21
Sheriffhales 35 M 25
Sheringham 39 X 25
Sherington 28 R 27
Shernborne 38 V 25
Sherston 19 N 29
Sherwood Forest 36 Q 24
Shetland Islands 87
Shevington 42 L 23
Shiant (Sound of) 82 A 10
Shiant Island 82 A 10
Shiel (Glen) 72 D 12
Shiel (Loch) 72 D 13
Shieldaig *Loch Gairloch* 78 C 10
Shieldaig *Loch Torridon* 78 D 11
Shieldaig (Loch) 78 C 11
Shieldhill 67 I 16
Shifnal 35 M 25
Shilbottle 63 O 17
Shildon 56 P 20
Shillay 76 W 11
Shillingford 7 J 30
Shillingstone 9 N 31
Shillington 29 S 28
Shilton *Rugby* 28 P 26
Shilton *West Oxfordshire* 19 P 28
Shimpling 31 X 26
Shin (Loch) 84 G 9
Shiney Row 56 P 19
Shinfield 20 R 29
Shipdham 38 W 26
Shiplake 20 R 29
Shipley *Salop* 35 N 26
Shipley *West Yorks.* 43 O 22
Shipston-on-Stour 27 P 27
Shipton *Bridgnorth* 26 M 26
Shipton *Cotswold* 27 O 28
Shipton *Hambleton* 50 Q 21
Shipton Moyne 19 N 29
Shipton-under-Wychwood 19 P 28
Shiptonthorpe 44 R 22
Shira (Lochan) 66 F 14
Shirebrook 36 Q 24
Shiremoor 56 P 18
Shirenewton 18 L 29
Shirley *Derbyshire* 35 O 25
Shirley *Solihull* 27 O 26
Shoadoxhurst 12 W 30
Shobdon 26 L 27
Shoeburyness 22 W 29
Shoreham 11 T 31
Shorne 22 V 29
Shotesham 39 X 26
Shotley Bridge 56 O 19
Shotley Gate 31 X 28
Shottenden 22 W 30
Shottermill 10 R 30
Shotton Colliery 57 P 19
Shotts 61 I 16
Shouldham 38 V 26
Shrewsbury 34 L 25
Shrewton 19 O 30
Shrivenham 19 P 29
Shuna Sound 65 D 15
Shurdington 27 N 28
Shurrery 85 J 8
Sibbertoft 28 Q 26
Sibford Ferris 28 P 27
Sible Hedingham 30 V 28
Sibsey 37 U 24
Sidbury 5 K 31
Siddington 19 O 28
Siddlington 43 N 24
Sidford 5 K 31
Sidinish 76 Y 11
Sidlaw Hills 68 K 14
Sidlesham 10 R 31
Sidmouth 5 K 31
Sighthill 68 K 16
Sileby 36 Q 25
Silecroft 47 K 21
Silkstone 43 P 23
Silloth 54 J 19
Silsden 49 O 22
Silver End 30 V 28
Silverdale *Lancaster* 48 L 21
Silverdale
Newcastle-under-Lyme 35 N 24
Silverstone 28 Q 27
Silverstone Circuit 28 Q 27
Silverton 7 J 31
Simonburn 55 N 18
Simonsbath 7 I 30
Sinclair's Bay 86 K 8
Sinclairston 60 G 17
Singleton *Chichester* 10 R 31
Singleton *Fylde* 42 L 22
Sionascaig (Loch) 84 E 9
Sissinghurst 12 V 30
Sithney 2 E 33
Sittingbourne 22 W 29
Sixpenny Handley 9 N 31
Skara Brae 86 J 6
Skares 60 H 17
Skeabost 77 B 11
Skegness 38 V 24
Skellingthorpe 44 S 24
Skelmanthorpe 43 P 23
Skelmersdale 42 L 23
Skelmorlie 59 F 16
Skelpick 85 H 8
Skelton *Cleveland* 50 R 20
Skelton *Cumbria* 55 L 19
Skelwith Bridge 48 K 20
Skene 75 M 12
Skene (Loch of) 75 M 12
Skenfrith 26 L 28
Skeroblingarry 59 D 17
Skerray 85 H 8
Skervuile Lighthouse 65 C 16
Skidby 44 S 22
Skiddaw 54 K 20
Skigersta 83 B 8
Skilgate 7 J 30
Skillington 37 S 25
Skinburness 54 J 19
Skipness 59 D 16
Skipport (Loch) 76 Y 12
Skipsea 51 T 22
Skipton 49 N 22
Skipton-on-Swale 50 P 21
Skipwith 44 R 22
Skirlaugh 45 T 22
Skirling 61 J 17
Skirwith 55 M 19
Skirza 86 K 8
Skokholm Island 14 E 28
Skomer Island 14 E 28
Skye (Isle of) 77 B 12
Slaggyford 55 M 19
Slaidburn 49 M 22
Slaithwaite 43 O 23
Slamannan 67 I 16
Slapin (Loch) 71 B 12
Slapton 4 J 33
Sleaford 37 S 25
Sleagill 48 M 20
Sleat (Sound of) 71 C 12
Sledmere 51 S 21
Sleekburn 56 P 18
Sleights 51 S 20
Slickly 86 K 8
Sligachan 77 B 12
Sligachan (Loch) 77 B 12
Slimbridge 19 M 28
Slindon 11 S 31
Slingsby 50 R 21
Slochd 79 I 12
Slockavullin 65 D 15
Slough 21 S 29
Sloy (Loch) 66 F 15
Slumbay 78 D 11
Slyne 48 L 21
Smailholm 62 M 17
Smailholm Tower 62 M 17
Small Dole 11 T 31
Small Hythe 12 W 30
Smallfield 11 T 30
Smarden 12 W 30
Smart'Hill 12 U 30
Smedmore 9 N 32
Smithfield 55 L 19
Snaefell 46 G 21
Snainton 51 S 21
Snaith 44 Q 22
Snape 31 Y 27
Snetterton Circuit 30 W 26
Snettisham 38 V 25
Snitterfield 27 O 27
Snizort (Loch) 77 A 11
Snodland 22 V 30
Snowdon / Yr Wyddfa 33 H 24
Snowdonia National Park 33 I 24
Snowshill 27 O 27
Soa 70 Z 14
Soa Island 64 A 15
Soar (River) 36 Q 25
Soay 71 B 12
Soay Sound 71 B 12
Soham 30 V 26
Solent (The) 10 Q 31
Solihull 27 O 26
Sollas 76 X 11
Solva 14 E 28
Solway Firth 53 J 19
Somerby 36 R 25
Somercotes 36 P 24
Somerford Keynes 19 O 29
Somersham
Huntingdonshire 29 U 26
Somersham *Mid Suffolk* 31 X 27
Somerton *Norfolk* 39 Y 25
Somerton *Oxon.* 28 Q 28
Somerton *Somerset* 8 L 30
Sompting 11 S 31
Sonning Common 20 R 29
Sopley 9 O 31
Sorbie 52 G 19
Sorisdale 71 A 13
Sorn 60 H 17
Sortat 86 K 8
Soulby 49 M 20
Sound (The) 4 H 32
Sourhope 63 N 17
South-Alloa 67 I 15
South Balloch 60 G 18
South Brent 4 I 32
South Cairn 52 E 19
South Carrine 59 C 18
South Cave 44 S 22
South Cerney 19 O 28
South Charlton 63 O 17
South Croxton 36 R 25
South Downs 11 R 31
South Elmsall 44 Q 23
South Esk (River) 75 L 13
South Ferriby 44 S 22
South Foreland 23 Y 30
South Glendale 70 Y 12
South Hanningfield 22 V 29
South Harris 76 Z 10
South Harris Forest 82 Z 10
South Hayling 10 R 31
South-Heighton 11 U 31
South Hetton 56 P 19
South Kelsey 45 S 23
South Killingholme 45 T 23
South Kirkby 44 Q 23
South Kyme 37 T 24
South Lancing 11 T 31
South Leverton 44 R 24
South Lopham 30 X 26
South-Marston 19 O 29
South Mary Bourne 20 P 30
South Mimms 21 T 28
South Molton 7 I 30
South Morar 72 C 13
South Moreton 20 Q 29
South Newington 28 P 28
South-Newton 9 O 30
South Normanton 36 P 24
South Ockendon 22 U 29
South Otterington 50 P 21
South Oxhey 21 S 29
South Petherton 8 L 31
South Petherwin 3 G 32
South Queensferry 68 J 16
South Rauceby 37 S 25
South Raynham 38 W 25
South Ronaldsay 87 L 7
South Shields 56 P 19
South Shore 42 K 22
South Stack 40 F 23
South Stainley 50 P 21
South Tawton 4 I 31
South Thoresby 45 U 24
South Uist 70 X 12
South Walls 86 K 7
South Warnborough 20 R 30
South Witham 37 S 25
South Woodham Ferrers 22 V 29
South Wootton 38 V 25
South Wraxall 19 N 29
South Zeal 4 I 31
Southam
Stratford-on-Avon 28 P 27
Southam *Tewkesbury* 27 N 28
Southampton 10 P 31
Southborough 12 U 30
Southbourne *Dorset* 9 O 31
Southbourne *West Sussex* 10 R 31
Southend 59 D 18
Southend-on-Sea 22 W 29
Southerness 53 J 19
Southery 38 V 26
Southill 29 T 27
Southminster 22 W 29
Southport 42 K 23
Southrop 19 O 28
Southsea 10 Q 31
Southwaite 55 L 19
Southwater 11 S 30
Southwell 36 R 24
Southwick
East Northamptonshire 29 S 26
Southwick *Sunderland* 56 P 19
Southwick *West Sussex* 11 T 31
Southwick *Wilts.* 19 N 30
Southwick Widley 10 Q 31
Southwold 31 Z 27
Sowerby Bridge 43 O 22
Spalding 37 T 25
Spaldwick 29 S 26
Spanish Head 46 F 21
Sparkford 8 M 30
Spaxton 8 K 30
Spean (Glen) 73 F 13
Spean Bridge 72 F 13
Speeton 51 T 21
Speldhurst 12 U 30
Spelsbury 28 P 28
Spelve (Loch) 65 C 14
Spennymoor 56 P 19
Spey (River) 73 G 12
Spey Bay 80 K 10
Speymouth Forest 80 K 11
Spilsby 37 U 24
Spinningdale 79 H 10
Spithead 10 Q 31
Spittal *Dumfries*
and Galloway 52 G 19
Spittal *Highland* 85 J 8
Spittal *Northumb.* 63 O 16
Spittal *Pembrokeshire /*
Sir Benfro 24 F 28
Spittal of Glenshee 74 J 13
Spixworth 39 X 25
Spofforth 50 P 22
Spondon 36 P 25
Spooner Row 39 X 26
Spott 69 M 16
Spreyton 7 I 31
Spridlington 44 S 23
Springfield 68 K 15
Springholm 53 I 18
Sproatley 45 T 22
Sprotbrough 44 Q 23
Sproughton 31 X 27
Sprouston 62 M 17
Sprowston 39 X 26
Spurn Head 45 U 23
Sronlairig Lodge 73 G 12
Sronphadruig Lodge 73 H 13
Stack (Loch) 84 F 8
Stack Island 70 Y 12
Stack Rocks 16 E 29
Staffa 64 A 14
Staffin Bay 77 B 11
Stafford 35 N 25
Stagsden 29 S 27
Staincross 43 P 23
Staindrop 56 O 20
Staines-upon-Thames 21 S 29
Stainforth *North Yorks.* 49 N 21
Stainforth *South Yorks.* 44 Q 23
Stainton 55 L 20
Stainton-le-Vale 45 T 23
Staintondale 51 S 20
Stair *Allerdale* 54 K 20
Stair *South Ayrshire* 60 G 17
Staithes 50 R 20
Stakeford 56 P 18
Stalbridge 9 M 31
Stalham 39 Y 25
Stalisfield 22 W 30
Stalling Busk 49 N 21
Stallingborough 45 T 23
Stalmine 48 L 22
Stalybridge 43 N 23
Stamford 37 S 26
Stamford Bridge 50 R 22
Stamfordham 56 O 18
Stanbridge 29 S 28
Standford-in-the-Vale 20 P 29
Standing Stones 82 Z 9
Standish 42 M 23
Standlake 20 P 28
Standon 29 U 28
Stane 61 I 16
Stanford 13 X 30
Stanford-le-Hope 22 V 29
Stanford-on-Avon 28 Q 26
Stanghow 50 R 20
Stanhoe 38 W 25
Stanhope 55 N 19
Stanion 29 S 26
Stanley *Durham* 56 O 19
Stanley
Perthshire and Kinross 68 J 14
Stanley *Wakefield.* 43 P 22
Stanmer Park 11 T 31
Stannington 43 P 23
Stanstead Abbotts 21 U 28
Stansted Mountfitchet 30 U 28
Stanton 30 W 27
Stanton Harcourt 20 P 28
Stanton Long 26 M 26
Stanton-upon-Hine-Heath 34 M 25
Stanway 27 O 28
Stanwell 21 S 29
Stanwick 29 S 27
Staple Fitzpaine 8 K 31
Stapleford *Melton* 36 R 25
Stapleford *Notts.* 36 Q 25
Stapleford *Wilts.* 9 O 30
Staplehurst 22 V 30
Starcross 4 J 32
Start Point 4 J 33
Startforth 49 O 20
Stathern 36 R 25
Staughton Highway 29 S 27
Staunton *Forest of Dean* 27 N 28
Staunton *Monmouthshire /*
Sir Fynwy 18 M 28
Staveley *Cumbria* 48 L 20
Staveley *Derbs.* 43 P 24
Staxigoe 86 K 8
Staxton 51 S 21
Staylittle 25 J 26
Steart 18 K 30
Stebbing 30 V 28
Stedham 10 R 31
Steep 10 R 30
Steeple 22 W 28
Steeple Ashton 19 N 30
Steeple Aston 28 Q 28
Steeple Barton 28 P 28
Steeple Bumpstead 30 V 27
Steeple Claydon 28 R 28
Steeple Langford 9 O 30
Steeple Morden 29 T 27
Steeton 49 O 22
Stelling Minnis 23 X 30
Stenhousemuir 67 I 15
Stenness *Orkney Islands* 86 K 7
Stenness *Shetland Islands* 87 P 2
Stenton 69 M 16
Steppingley 29 S 27
Stevenage 29 T 28
Stevenston 60 F 17
Steventon 20 Q 29
Stewartby 29 S 27
Stewarton 60 G 16
Stewkley 28 R 28
Steyning 11 T 31
Steynton 16 E 28
Stichill 62 M 17
Sticker 3 F 33
Sticklepath 4 I 31
Stickney 37 U 24
Stiffkey 38 W 25
Stilligarry 76 X 12
Stillingfleet 44 Q 22
Stillington *Hambleton* 50 Q 21
Stillington
Stockton-on-Tees 56 P 20
Stilton 29 T 26
Stirling 67 I 15
Stithians 2 E 33
Stob Choire Claurigh 72 F 13
Stobo 61 K 17
Stobs Castle 62 L 17
Stock 22 V 29
Stockbridge 10 P 30
Stocke Talmage 20 Q 28
Stockland 8 K 31
Stockland Bristol 18 K 30
Stockport 43 N 23
Stocksbridge 43 P 23
Stocksfield 56 O 19
Stockton Heath 42 M 23
Stockton-on-Tees 50 P 20
Stockton-on-Teme 27 M 27
Stockton on the Forest 50 R 22
Stoer 83 D 9
Stogumber 7 K 30
Stogursey 18 K 30
Stoke 22 V 29
Stoke Albany 28 R 26
Stoke Ash 31 X 27
Stoke-by-Nayland 30 W 28
Stoke Climsland 3 H 32
Stoke Fleming 4 J 33
Stoke Gabriel 4 J 32
Stoke Goldington 28 R 27
Stoke Hammond 28 R 28
Stoke Lacy 26 M 27
Stoke Lyne 28 Q 28
Stoke Mandeville 20 R 28
Stoke-on-Trent 35 N 24
Stoke Orchard 27 N 28
Stoke Poges 21 S 29
Stoke-St. Mary 8 K 31
Stoke-St. Michael 18 M 30
Stoke St. Milborough 26 M 26
Stoke sub Hamdon 8 L 31
Stokeham 44 R 24
Stokenchurch 20 R 29
Stokenham 4 I 33
Stokesay 26 L 26
Stokesley 50 Q 20
Stone *Bucks.* 20 R 28
Stone *Staffs.* 35 N 25
Stone Edge 36 P 24
Stonehaugh 55 N 18
Stonehaven 75 N 13
Stonehenge 9 O 30
Stonehouse *Glos.* 19 N 28
Stonehouse
South Lanarkshire 61 I 16
Stoneleigh 28 P 26
Stonesfield 20 P 28
Stoney Cross 9 P 31
Stoney Stanton 36 Q 26
Stoneybridge 76 X 12
Stoneykirk 52 F 19
Stoneywood 75 N 12
Stony Stratford 28 R 27
Stornoway 82 A 9
Storr (The) 77 B 11
Storrington 11 S 31
Stort (River) 29 U 28
Stotfold 29 T 27
Stottesdon 26 M 26
Stoughton 10 R 31
Stoul 72 C 13
Stoulton 27 N 27
Stour (River)
English Channel 9 N 31
Stour (River) *North Sea* 30 V 27
Stour (River) *R. Severn* 27 N 26
Stourbridge 27 N 26
Stourhead House 9 N 30
Stourport-on Severn 27 N 26
Stourton Caundle 9 M 31
Stow 62 L 16
Stow-on-the-Wold 27 O 28
Stowbridge 38 V 26
Stowe-by-Chartley 35 O 25
Stowe School 28 Q 27
Stowmarket 30 W 27
Stowupland 30 X 27
Straad 59 E 16
Strachan 75 M 12
Strachur 66 E 15
Stradbroke 31 X 27
Stradishall 30 V 27
Stradsett 38 V 26
Straiton 60 G 18
Straloch 74 J 13
Stranraer 52 E 19
Strata Florida Abbey 25 I 27
Stratfield Saye 20 Q 29
Stratford St. Mary 30 W 28
Stratford-upon-Avon 27 O 27
Strath Brora 85 H 9
Strath Dearn 79 I 11
Strath Halladale 85 I 8
Strath Isla 80 K 11
Strath More 78 E 10
Strath Mulzie 78 F 10
Strath of Kildonan 85 I 9
Strath Oykel 84 F 10
Strath Skinsdale 85 H 9
Strath Tay 68 J 14
Strathallan 67 I 15
Strathan 72 E 13
Strathardle 74 J 13
Strathaven 60 H 16
Strathbeg (Loch of) 81 O 11
Strathblane 67 H 16
Strathbogie 80 L 11
Strathbraan 67 I 14
Strathcanaird 84 E 10

T

Y

Z

A

B

C

L

M

N

O

Town plans

Sights
Place of interest - Tower
Interesting place of worship

Roads
Motorway - Dual carriageway
Numbered junctions: complete, limited
Major thoroughfare
Tunnel
Pedestrian street
Tramway
Car park - Park and Ride
Station and railway
Funicular
Cable-car

Various signs
Place of worship
Tower - Ruins
Windmill
Garden, park, wood
Cemetery
Stadium
Golf course - Racecourse
Outdoor or indoor swimming pool
View - Panorama
Monument - Fountain
Beach - Zoo
Pleasure boat harbour - Lighthouse
Tourist Information Centre
Airport
Underground station - Coach station
Ferry services:
passengers and cars - passengers only
Main post office with poste restante - Hospital
Covered market
Police - Town Hall
Suggested stroll

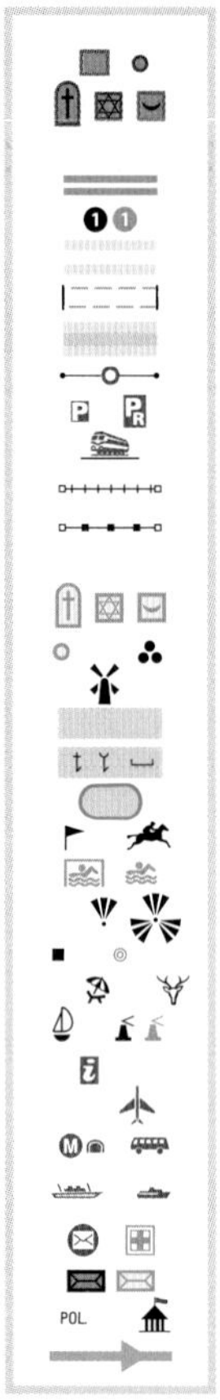

Plans

Curiosités
Bâtiment intéressant - Tour
Édifice religieux intéressant

Voirie
Autoroute - Double chaussée de type autoroutier
Échangeurs numérotés : complet - partiels
Grande voie de circulation
Tunnel
Rue piétonne
Tramway
Parking - Parking Relais
Gare et voie ferrée
Funiculaire, voie à crémailère
Téléphérique, télécabine

Signes divers
Édifice religieux
Tour - Ruines
Moulin à vent
Jardin, parc, bois
Cimetière
Stade
Golf - Hippodrome
Piscine de plein air, couverte
Vue - Panorama
Monument - Fontaine
Plage - Zoo
Port de plaisance - Phare
Information touristique
Aéroport
Station de métro - Gare routière
Transport par bateau :
passagers et voitures, passagers seulement
Bureau principal de poste restante - Hôpital
Marché couvert
Police - Hôtel de ville
Suggestion de promenade

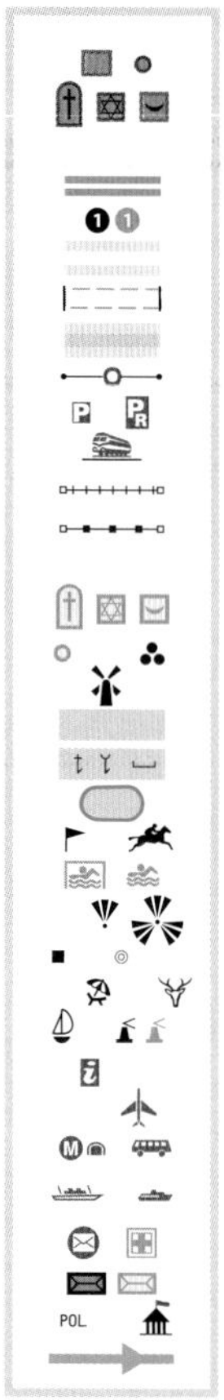

Stadtpläne

Sehenswürdigkeiten
Sehenswertes Gebäude - Turm
Sehenswerter Sakralbau

Straßen
Autobahn - Schnellstraße
Nummerierte Voll - bzw. Teilanschlussstellen
Hauptverkehrsstraße
Tunnel
Fußgängerzone
Straßenbahn
Parkplatz - Park-and-Ride-Plätze
Bahnhof und Bahnlinie
Standseilbahn
Seilschwebebahn

Sonstige Zeichen
Sakralbau
Turm - Ruine
Windmühle
Garten, Park, Wäldchen
Friedhof
Stadion
Golfplatz - Pferderennbahn
Freibad - Hallenbad
Aussicht - Rundblick
Denkmal - Brunnen
Badestrand/ Strand - Zoo
Yachthafen- Leuchtturm
Informationsstelle
Flughafen
U-Bahnstation - Autobusbahnhof
Schiffsverbindungen:
Autofähre, Personenfähre
Hauptpostamt (postlagernde Sendungen) - Krankenhaus
Markthalle
Polizei - Rathaus
Vorschlag für einen Spaziergang

Plattegronden

Bezienswaardigheden
Interessant gebouw - Toren
Interessant kerkelijk gebouw

Wegen
Autosnelweg - Weg met gescheiden rijbanen
Knooppunt / aansluiting: volledig, gedeeltelijk
Hoofdverkeersweg
Tunnel
Voetgangersgebied
Tramlijn
Parkeerplaats - P & R
Station, spoorweg
Kabelspoor
Tandradbaan

Overige tekens
Kerkelijk gebouw
Toren - Ruïne
Windmolen
Tuin, park, bos
Begraafplaats
Stadion
Golfterrein - Renbaan
Zwembad: openlucht, overdekt
Uitzicht - Panorama
Gedenkteken, standbeeld - Fontein
Strand - Zoo
Jachthaven - Vuurtoren
Informatie voor toeristen
Luchthaven
Metrostation - Busstation
Vervoer per boot:
Passagiers en auto's - uitsluitend passagiers
Hoofdkantoor voor poste-restante - Ziekenhuis
Overdekte markt
Politie - Stadhuis
Aanbevolen wandeling

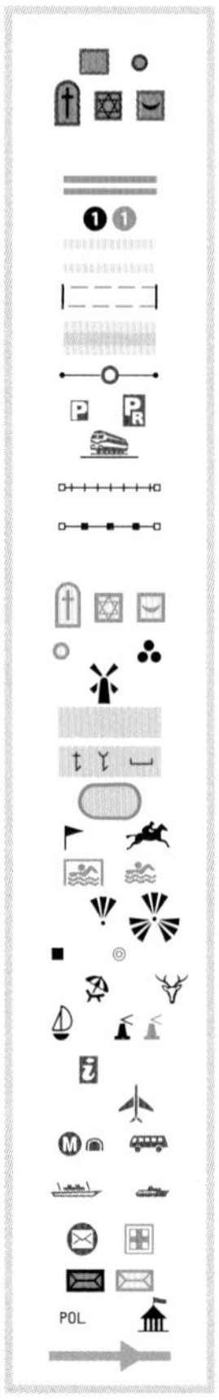

Piante

Curiosità
Edificio interessante - Torre
Costruzione religiosa interessante

Viabilità
Autostrada - Doppia carreggiata tipo autostrada
Svincoli numerati: completo, parziale
Grande via di circolazione
Galleria
Via pedonale
Tranvia
Parcheggio - Parcheggio Ristoro
Stazione e ferrovia
Funicolare
Funivia, cabinovia

Simboli vari
Costruzione religiosa
Torre - Ruderi
Mulino a vento
Giardino, parco, bosco
Cimitero
Stadio
Golf - Ippodromo
Piscina: all'aperto, coperta
Vista - Panorama
Monumento - Fontana
Spiaggia- Zoo
Porto turistico - Faro
Ufficio informazioni turistiche
Aeroporto
Stazione della metropolitana - Autostazione
Trasporto con traghetto:
passeggeri ed autovetture - solo passeggeri
Ufficio centrale di fermo posta - Ospedale
Mercato coperto
Polizia - Municipio
Passeggiata consigliata

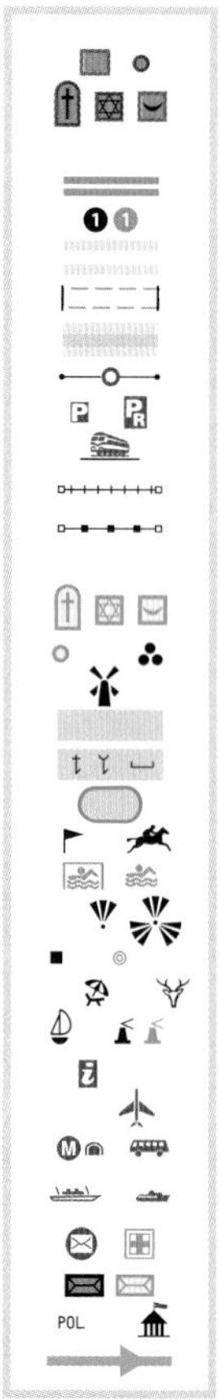

Planos

Curiosidades
Edificio interesante - Torre
Edificio religioso interesante

Vías de circulación
Autopista - Autovía
Enlaces numerados: completo, parciales
Via importante de circulacíon
Túnel
Calle peatonal
Tranvía
Aparcamiento - Aparcamientos «P+R»
Estación y línea férrea
Funicular, línea de cremallera
Teleférico, telecabina

Signos diversos
Edificio religioso
Torre - Ruinas
Molino de viento
Jardín, parque, madera
Cementerio
Estadio
Golf - Hipódromo
Piscina al aire libre, cubierta
Vista parcial - Vista panorámica
Monumento - Fuente
Playa - Zoo
Puerto deportivo - Faro
Oficina de Información de Turismo
Aeropuerto
Estación de metro - Estación de autobuses
Transporte por barco:
pasajeros y vehículos, pasajeros solamente
Oficina de correos - Hospital
Mercado cubierto
Policía - Ayuntamiento
Propuesta de paseo

Plans de ville
Town plans / Stadtpläne / Stadsplattegronden
Piante di città / Planos de ciudades

GREAT BRITAIN

IRELAND

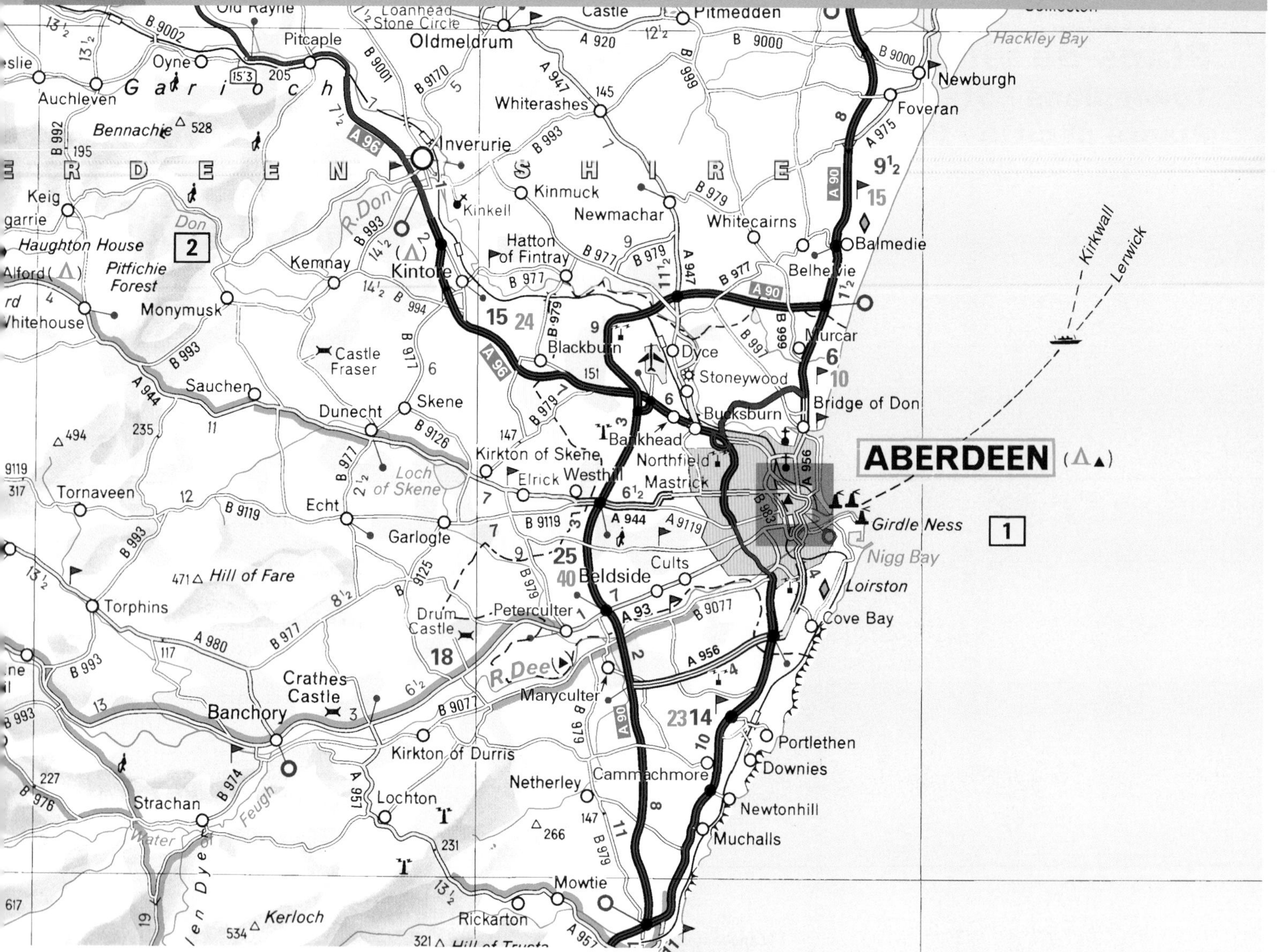
Tarves
Ellon
Slains Castle
Kirkton of Rayne
Old Rayne
Loanhead Stone Circle
Castle
Pitmedden
Hackley Bay
Pitcaple
Oldmeldrum
Oyne
Auchleven
Garioch
Newburgh
Whiterashes
Foveran
Bennachie 528
Inverurie
ABERDEENSHIRE
Keig
Kinmuck
Kinkell
Newmachar
Whitecairns
R. Don
Haughton House
Hatton of Fintray
Balmedie
Alford
Pitfichie Forest
Kemnay
Kintore
Belhelvie
Whitehouse
Monymusk
Castle Fraser
Blackburn
Dyce
Murcar
Stoneywood
Kirkwall
Lerwick
Sauchen
Skene
Dunecht
Bucksburn
Bridge of Don
Bankhead
Northfield
Kirkton of Skene
ABERDEEN
Tornaveen
Loch of Skene
Elrick
Westhill
Mastrick
Echt
Garlogie
Girdle Ness
Nigg Bay
Hill of Fare
Cults
Beldside
Loirston
Torphins
Drum Castle
Peterculter
Cove Bay
R. Dee
Crathes Castle
Maryculter
Banchory
Portlethen
Kirkton of Durris
Downies
Netherley
Cammachmore
Strachan
Lochton
Newtonhill
Water of Feugh
Muchalls
Mowtie
Kerloch
Rickarton
Hill of Trusta
Stonehaven
Dunnottar Castle
Thornyhive Bay
Farnell
Ferryden

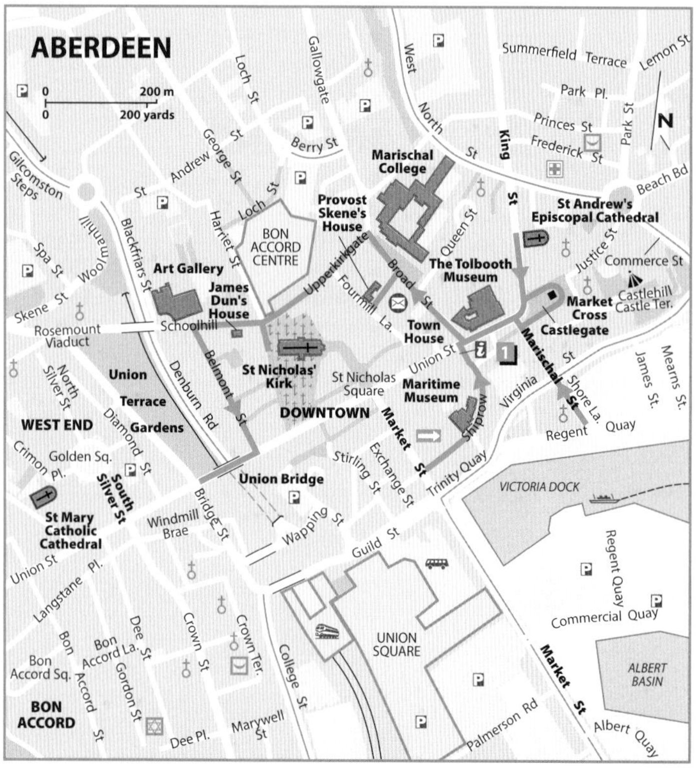
ABERDEEN
0 200 m
0 200 yards
Loch St
Gallowgate
West North St
Summerfield Terrace
Lemon St
Park Pl.
Park St
Princes St
Frederick St
King St
Berry St
Marischal College
George St
Andrew St
Gilcomston Steps
Provost Skene's House
St Andrew's Episcopal Cathedral
Beach Bd
BON ACCORD CENTRE
Queen St
Upperkirkgate
Justice St
Commerce St
Art Gallery
The Tolbooth Museum
Castlehill
Castle Ter.
Skene St
James Dun's House
Broad St
Market Cross
Castlegate
Rosemount Viaduct
Schoolhill
Town House
Union St
Union Terrace Gardens
St Nicholas' Kirk
St Nicholas Square
Maritime Museum
Marischal St
WEST END
DOWNTOWN
Market St
Shiprow
Virginia St
Shore La.
James St
Mearns St
Regent Quay
Golden Sq.
Diamond St
Union Bridge
Stirling St
Exchange St
Trinity Quay
VICTORIA DOCK
St Mary Catholic Cathedral
South Silver St
Windmill Brae
Bridge St
Wapping St
Guild St
Union St
Langstane Pl.
UNION SQUARE
Commercial Quay
Crown St
Crown Ter.
College St
ALBERT BASIN
BON ACCORD
Dee Pl.
Marywell St
Palmerson Rd
Albert Quay

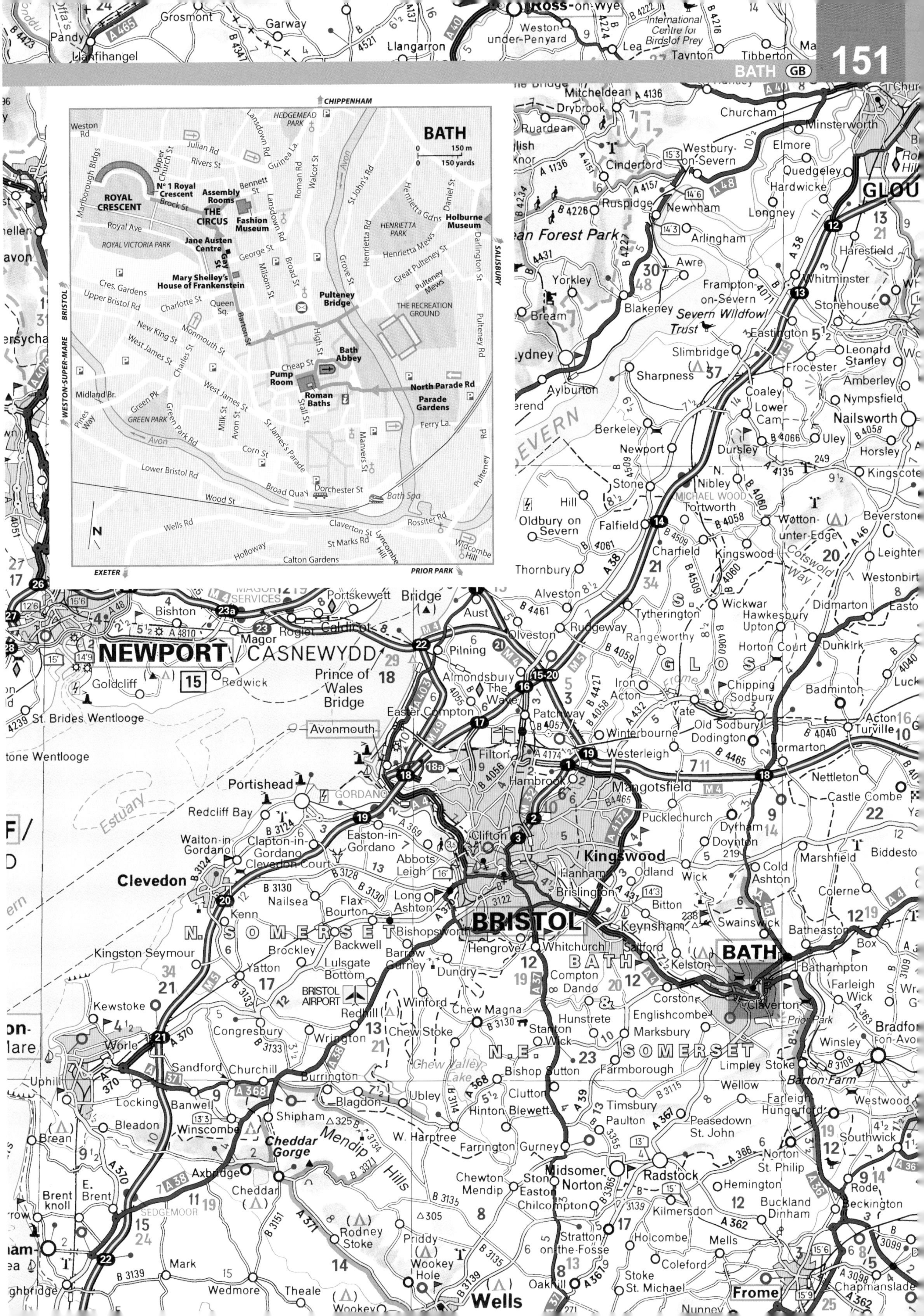
BATH
0 150 m
0 150 yards
CHIPPENHAM
SALISBURY
BRISTOL
WESTON-SUPER-MARE
EXETER
PRIOR PARK
Weston Rd
Julian Rd
Rivers St
HEDGEMEAD PARK
Lansdown Rd
Guinea La.
Roman Rd
Walcot St
Avon
St John's Rd
Marlborough Bldgs
Upper Church St
ROYAL CRESCENT
N° 1 Royal Crescent
Brock St
Assembly Rooms
Bennett St
THE CIRCUS
Fashion Museum
Henrietta Gdns
Daniel St
Holburne Museum
HENRIETTA PARK
Henrietta Rd
Henrietta Mews
Great Pulteney St
Pulteney Mews
Darlington St
Royal Ave
ROYAL VICTORIA PARK
Jane Austen Centre
Gay St
George St
Milsom St
Broad St
Grove St
Mary Shelley's House of Frankenstein
Cres. Gardens
Upper Bristol Rd
Charlotte St
Queen Sq.
Barton St
Pulteney Bridge
THE RECREATION GROUND
Pulteney Rd
New King St
Monmouth St
High St
West James St
Charles St
Cheap St
Bath Abbey
Pump Room
Roman Baths
North Parade Rd
Parade Gardens
Midland Br.
Green Pk
GREEN PARK
Green Park Rd
Pines Way
Milk St
Avon St
St James's Parade
Stall St
Manvers St
Ferry La.
Corn St
Lower Bristol Rd
Broad Quay
Dorchester St
Bath Spa
Wood St
Wells Rd
Claverton St
Lyncombe Hill
Rossiter Rd
St Marks Rd
Widcombe Hill
Holloway
Calton Gardens
N
Grosmont
Garway
Pandy
Llanfihangel
Llangarron
Ross-on-Wye
Weston-under-Penyard
International Centre for Birds of Prey
Lea
Taynton
Tibberton
Mitcheldean
Drybrook
Ruardean
Cinderford
Westbury-on-Severn
Churcham
Minsterworth
Elmore
Quedgeley
Hardwicke
GLOU
Ruspidge
Newnham
Longney
Dean Forest Park
Arlingham
Yorkley
Awre
Frampton-on-Severn
Haresfield
Whitminster
Stonehouse
Bream
Blakeney
Severn Wildfowl Trust
Eastington
Lydney
Slimbridge
Sharpness
Frocester
Leonard Stanley
Amberley
Aylburton
Coaley
Lower Cam
Nympsfield
Nailsworth
SEVERN
Berkeley
Dursley
Uley
Horsley
Newport
Stone
N. Nibley
MICHAEL WOOD
Kingscote
Hill
Tortworth
Oldbury on Severn
Falfield
Wotton-under-Edge
Beverstone
Charfield
Kingswood
Cotswold Way
Leighterton
Westonbirt
Thornbury
Alveston
Wickwar
Didmarton
Tytherington
Hawkesbury Upton
Rudgeway
Rangeworthy
Olveston
Aust
Portskewett
Caldicot
Magor
Rogiet
MAGOR SERVICES
Bishton
NEWPORT / CASNEWYDD
Goldcliff
Redwick
Prince of Wales Bridge
Pilning
Almondsbury
The Wave
Horton Court
Dunkirk
G L O S.
Iron Acton
Chipping Sodbury
Badminton
Luckington
St. Brides Wentlooge
Easter Compton
Patchway
Yate
Acton Turville
Avonmouth
Winterbourne
Old Sodbury
Dodington
Filton
Westerleigh
Tormarton
Peterstone Wentlooge
Portishead
GORDANO
Hambrook
Mangotsfield
Nettleton
Castle Combe
Redcliff Bay
Estuary
Pucklechurch
Dyrham
Doynton
Walton-in-Gordano
Clapton-in-Gordano
Clevedon Court
Easton-in-Gordano
Clifton
Kingswood
Marshfield
Biddestone
Clevedon
Abbots Leigh
Hanham
Odland
Wick
Cold Ashton
Nailsea
Flax Bourton
Long Ashton
Brislington
Bitton
Colerne
Kenn
BRISTOL
Keynsham
Swainswick
Batheaston
N. SOMERSET
Bishopsworth
Backwell
Hengrove
Whitchurch
Saltford
Box
Kingston Seymour
Brockley
Barrow Gurney
BATH
Kelston
Bathampton
Yatton
Lulsgate Bottom
Dundry
Compton Dando
Farleigh Wick
BRISTOL AIRPORT
Corston
Claverton
Kewstoke
Winford
Chew Magna
Englishcombe
Prior Park
Bradford-on-Avon
Redhill
Hunstrete
Stanton Wick
Marksbury
Winsley
Congresbury
Wrington
Chew Stoke
Weston-super-Mare
Worle
Chew Valley Lake
N.E. SOMERSET
Farmborough
Limpley Stoke
Sandford
Churchill
Burrington
Bishop Sutton
Barton Farm
Uphill
Blagdon
Ubley
Clutton
Timsbury
Wellow
Farleigh Hungerford
Westwood
Locking
Banwell
Hinton Blewett
Paulton
Peasedown St. John
Bleadon
Winscombe
Shipham
Brean
Cheddar Gorge
Mendip Hills
W. Harptree
Farrington Gurney
Southwick
Norton St. Philip
Axbridge
Midsomer Norton
Radstock
Cheddar
Chewton Mendip
Ston Easton
Hemington
Rode
Brent Knoll
E. Brent
SEDGEMOOR
Chilcompton
Kilmersdon
Buckland Dinham
Beckington
Rodney Stoke
Priddy
Stratton-on-the-Fosse
Holcombe
Mells
Highbridge
Burnham-on-Sea
Mark
Wookey Hole
Coleford
Wedmore
Theale
Wookey
Wells
Oakhill
Stoke St. Michael
Frome
Chapmanslade
Nunney

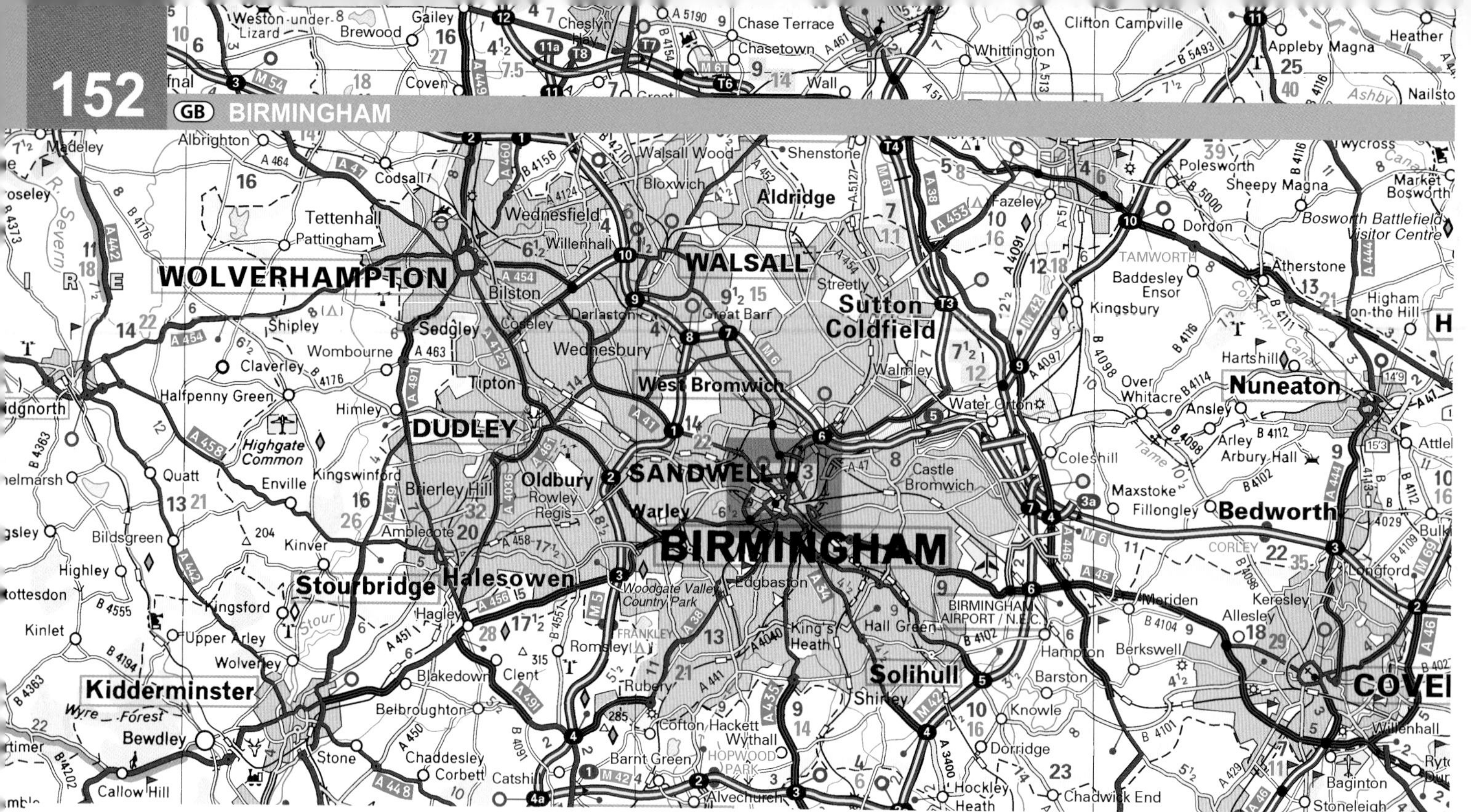

WOLVERHAMPTON
WALSALL
Sutton Coldfield
DUDLEY
SANDWELL
BIRMINGHAM
Stourbridge
Halesowen
Kidderminster
Solihull
Nuneaton
Bedworth
West Bromwich
Oldbury
Wednesbury
Bilston
Sedgley
Tipton
Aldridge
Brierley Hill
Amblecote
Rowley Regis
Warley
Castle Bromwich
Coleshill
Edgbaston
Kings Heath
Hall Green
Shirley
Knowle
Dorridge
Bewdley
Wyre Forest
Highgate Common
Halfpenny Green
Codsall
Tettenhall
Pattingham
Wombourne
Kinver
Hagley
Clent
Rubery
Cofton Hackett
Wythall
Barnt Green
Alvechurch
Meriden
Hampton
Berkswell
Balsall Common
Kenilworth
Tamworth
Polesworth
Atherstone
Kingsbury
BIRMINGHAM AIRPORT / N.E.C.
Woodgate Valley Country Park
Lickey Hills Country Park

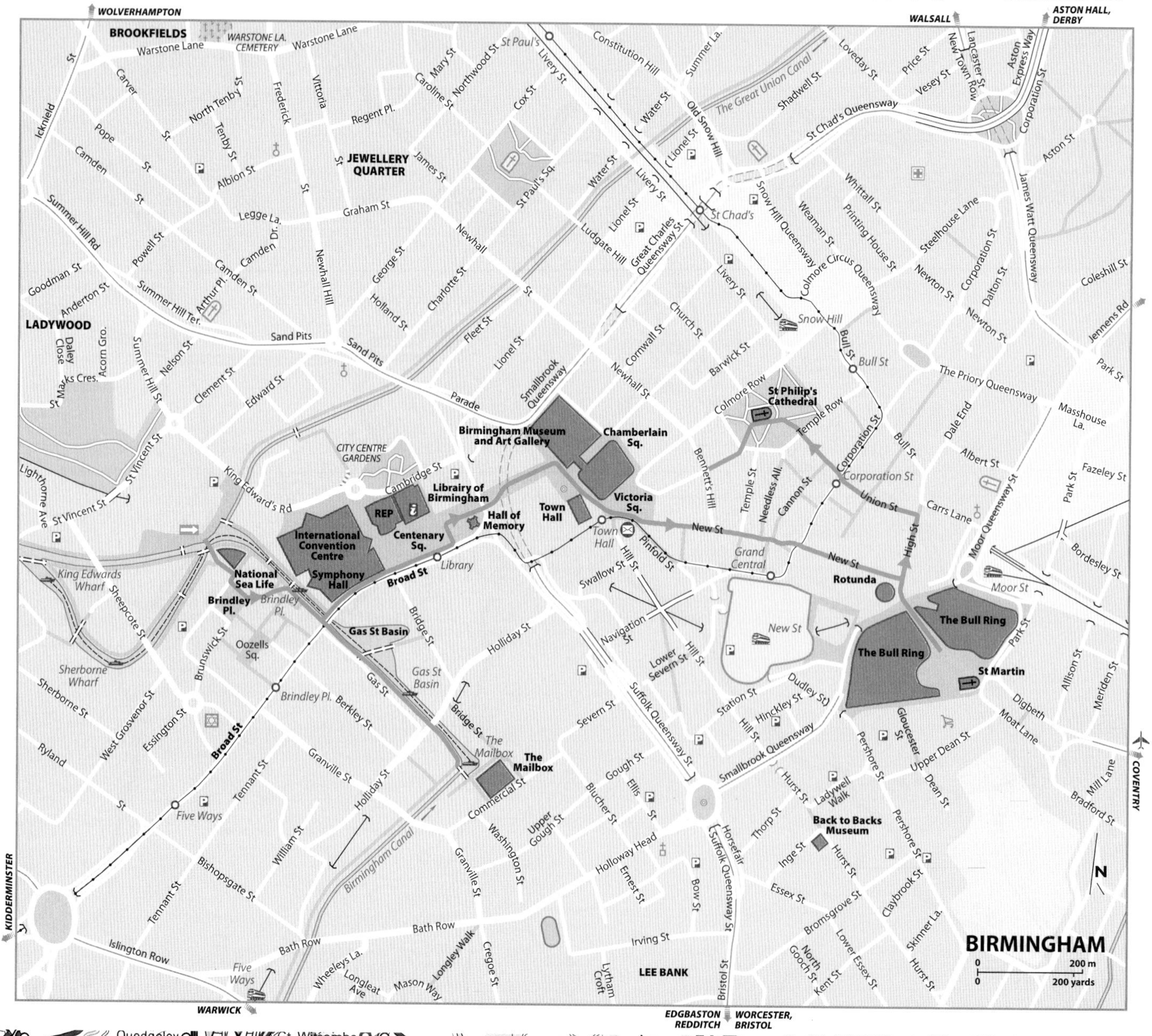

WOLVERHAMPTON
WALSALL
ASTON HALL, DERBY
BROOKFIELDS
WARSTONE LA. CEMETERY
JEWELLERY QUARTER
LADYWOOD
St Paul's
The Great Union Canal
St Chad's Queensway
St Chad's
Snow Hill
Bull St
St Philip's Cathedral
Birmingham Museum and Art Gallery
Chamberlain Sq.
Victoria Sq.
Town Hall
Hall of Memory
Library of Birmingham
REP
Centenary Sq.
International Convention Centre
Symphony Hall
National Sea Life
Brindley Pl.
Gas St Basin
King Edwards Wharf
Sherborne Wharf
Oozells Sq.
CITY CENTRE GARDENS
Corporation St
New St
Grand Central
Rotunda
The Bull Ring
St Martin
Digbeth
Moor St
The Mailbox
Back to Backs Museum
Five Ways
Birmingham Canal
Broad St
Smallbrook Queensway
Suffolk Queensway St
Moor Queensway
James Watt Queensway
The Priory Queensway
Colmore Circus Queensway
Snow Hill Queensway
Great Charles Queensway
LEE BANK
KIDDERMINSTER
COVENTRY
WARWICK
EDGBASTON REDDITCH
WORCESTER, BRISTOL
BIRMINGHAM
0 200 m
0 200 yards
N

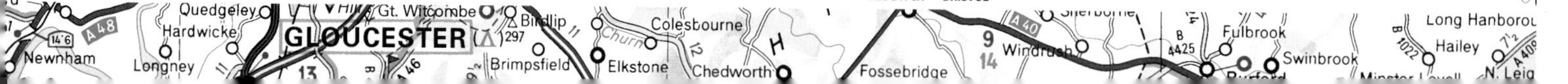

GLOUCESTER
Quedgeley
Hardwicke
Longney
Newnham
Birdlip
Brimpsfield
Colesbourne
Elkstone
Chedworth
Withington
Fossebridge
Fulbrook
Swinbrook
Long Hanborough
Hailey

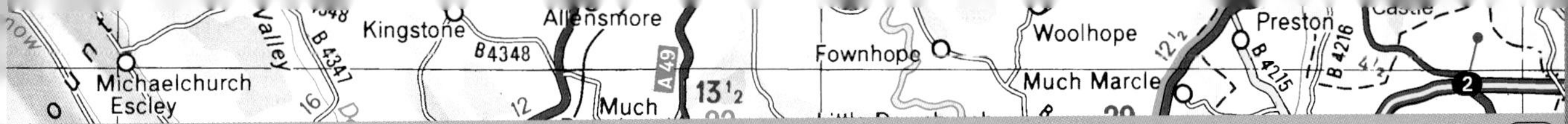

Kingstone
Allensmore
Fownhope
Woolhope
Preston
Much Marcle
Michaelchurch Escley
Much

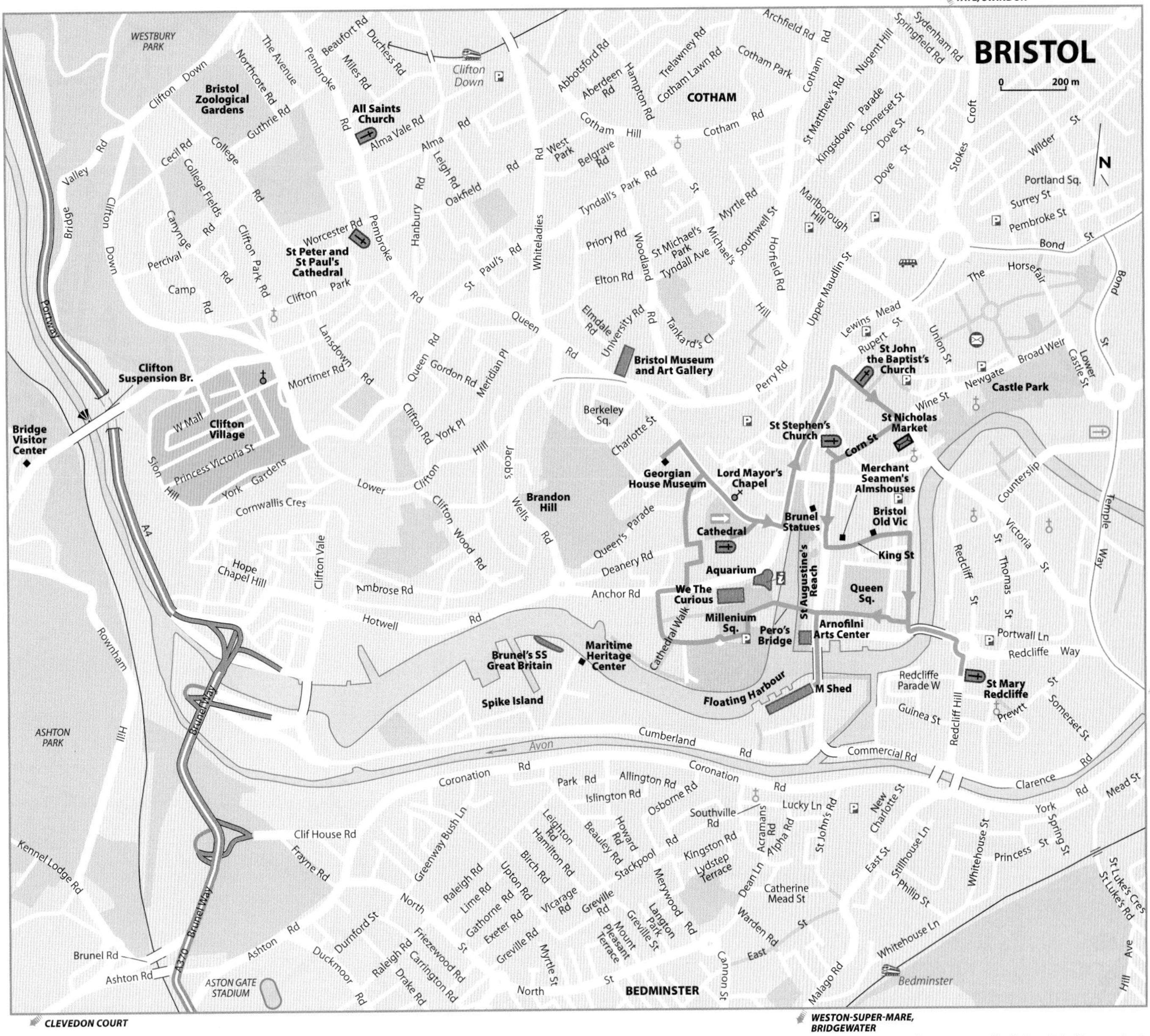

BRISTOL
0 200 m
AEROSPACE BRISTOL, YATE, SWINDON
NEWPORT, GLOUCESTER
KEYNSHAM, BATH
CLEVEDON COURT
WESTON-SUPER-MARE, BRIDGEWATER
WESTBURY PARK
COTHAM
Bristol Zoological Gardens
All Saints Church
Clifton Down
St Peter and St Paul's Cathedral
Clifton Suspension Br.
Bridge Visitor Center
Clifton Village
Bristol Museum and Art Gallery
St John the Baptist's Church
Castle Park
St Nicholas Market
St Stephen's Church
Corn St
Georgian House Museum
Lord Mayor's Chapel
Merchant Seamen's Almshouses
Bristol Old Vic
Brunel Statues
Brandon Hill
Cathedral
Aquarium
We The Curious
Millenium Sq.
Pero's Bridge
Arnofilni Arts Center
Queen Sq.
King St
St Augustine's Reach
Maritime Heritage Center
Brunel's SS Great Britain
Spike Island
Floating Harbour
M Shed
St Mary Redcliffe
Avon
Cumberland Rd
Coronation Rd
Commercial Rd
ASHTON PARK
ASTON GATE STADIUM
BEDMINSTER
Bedminster
Portway
Hotwell Rd
Brunel Way
A4
A370

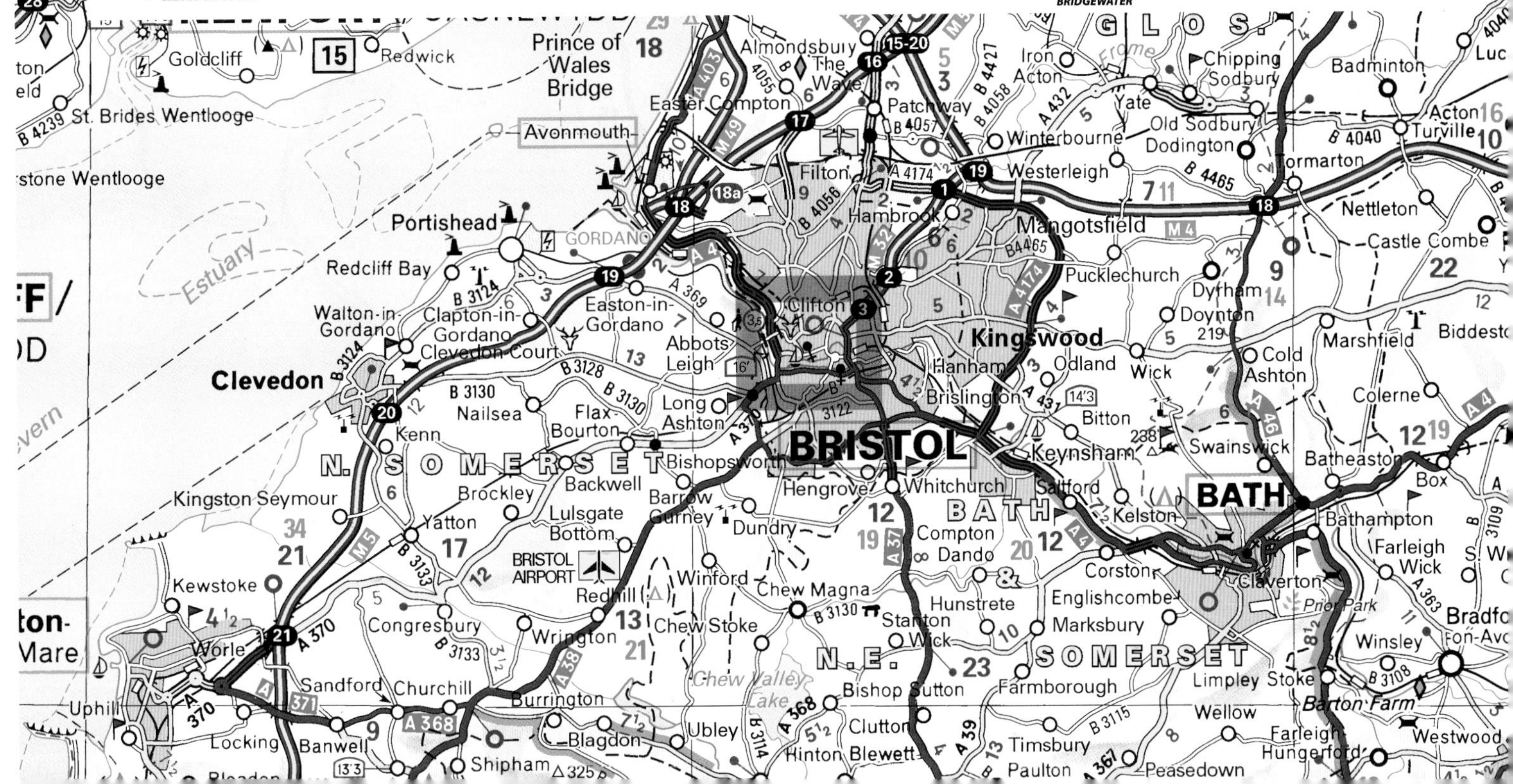

Prince of Wales Bridge
Avonmouth
Portishead
Redcliff Bay
Walton-in-Gordano
Clapton-in-Gordano
Easton-in-Gordano
Clevedon
Clevedon Court
Nailsea
Flax Bourton
Long Ashton
Abbots Leigh
Clifton
BRISTOL
Kingswood
Hanham
Brislington
Keynsham
Whitchurch
Hengrove
Bishopsworth
Backwell
Brockley
Kingston Seymour
Yatton
Congresbury
Wrington
BRISTOL AIRPORT
Winford
Chew Magna
Chew Stoke
Chew Valley Lake
Blagdon
Ubley
Burrington
Churchill
Sandford
Banwell
Locking
Worle
Kewstoke
Uphill
Shipham
Bishop Sutton
Clutton
Hinton Blewett
Timsbury
Paulton
Peasedown
Farmborough
Marksbury
Englishcombe
Corston
Compton Dando
Stanton Wick
Hunstrete
Saltford
Kelston
BATH
Bathampton
Batheaston
Claverton
Prior Park
Limpley Stoke
Farleigh Hungerford
Winsley
Bradford-on-Avon
Westwood
Wellow
Swainswick
Bitton
Wick
Cold Ashton
Marshfield
Colerne
Box
Pucklechurch
Mangotsfield
Dyrham
Doynton
Westerleigh
Winterbourne
Yate
Chipping Sodbury
Old Sodbury
Dodington
Tormarton
Acton Turville
Badminton
Nettleton
Castle Combe
Filton
Patchway
Almondsbury
Easter Compton
Iron Acton
Hambrook
Redwick
Goldcliff
St. Brides Wentlooge
Estuary
N. SOMERSET
N.E. SOMERSET
BATH
GLOS.
GORDANO

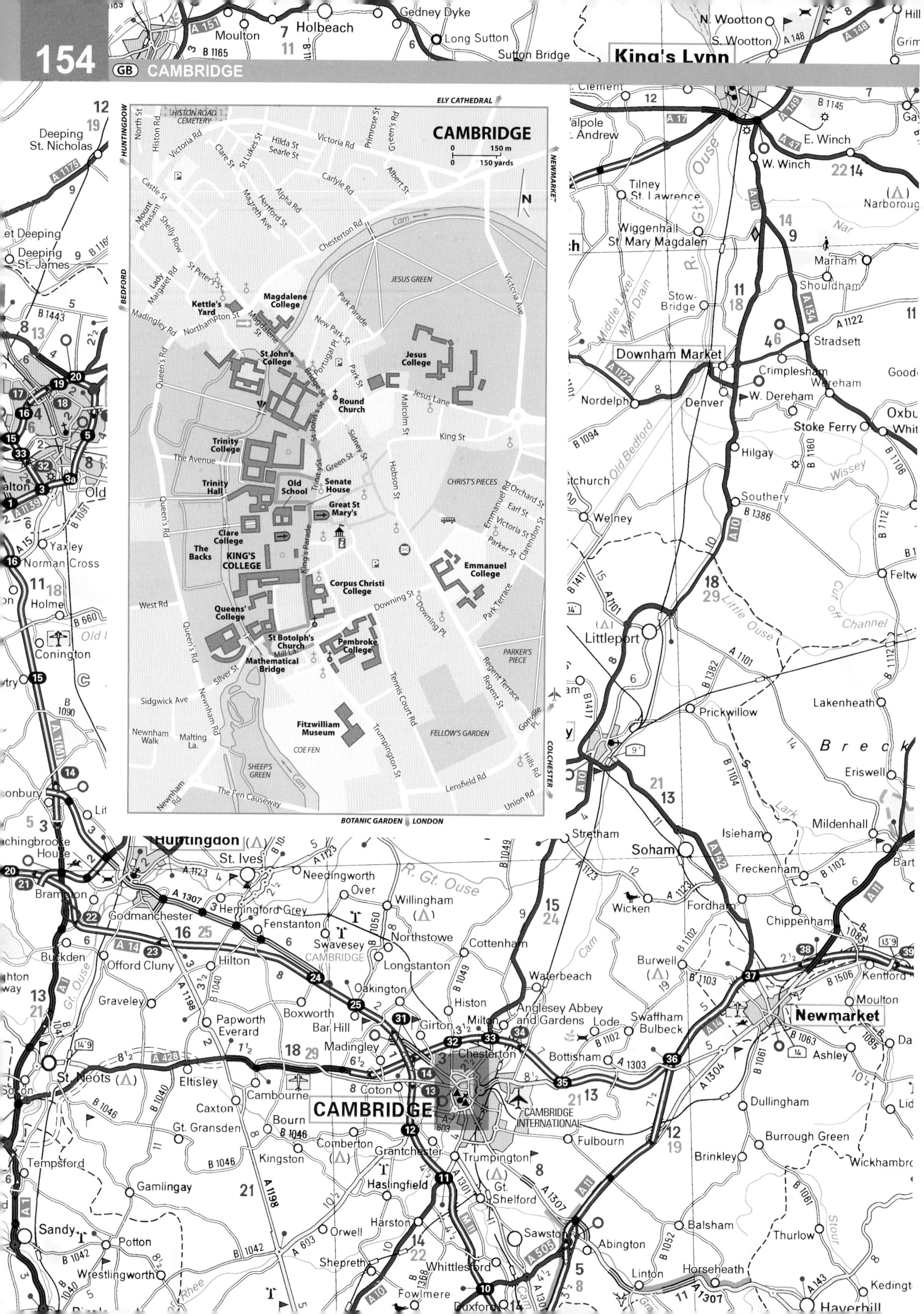

Holbeach
Moulton
Gedney Dyke
Long Sutton
Sutton Bridge
N. Wootton
S. Wootton
King's Lynn
Deeping St. Nicholas
Deeping St. James
Walpole St. Andrew
Tilney St. Lawrence
Wiggenhall St. Mary Magdalen
E. Winch
W. Winch
Narborough
Marham
Shouldham
Stow Bridge
Stradsett
Downham Market
Crimplesham
Wereham
Nordelph
Denver
W. Dereham
Stoke Ferry
Hilgay
Southery
Welney
Littleport
Prickwillow
Lakenheath
Eriswell
Mildenhall
Isleham
Soham
Stretham
Freckenham
Wicken
Fordham
Chippenham
Burwell
Kentford
Moulton
Newmarket
Ashley
Swaffham Bulbeck
Lode
Anglesey Abbey and Gardens
Bottisham
Dullingham
Burrough Green
Brinkley
Wickhambrook
Balsham
Thurlow
Linton
Horseheath
Haverhill
Yaxley
Norman Cross
Holme
Conington
Huntingdon
Hinchingbrooke House
St. Ives
Brampton
Godmanchester
Buckden
Offord Cluny
Graveley
Needingworth
Over
Hemingford Grey
Fenstanton
Hilton
Swavesey
Willingham
Northstowe
Cottenham
Longstanton
Oakington
Waterbeach
Histon
Milton
Girton
Boxworth
Bar Hill
Papworth Everard
Madingley
Chesterton
St. Neots
Eltisley
Caxton
Cambourne
Bourn
Coton
CAMBRIDGE
CAMBRIDGE INTERNATIONAL
Fulbourn
Gt. Gransden
Kingston
Comberton
Grantchester
Trumpington
Tempsford
Gamlingay
Haslingfield
Gt. Shelford
Sawston
Abington
Harston
Orwell
Sandy
Potton
Shepreth
Whittlesford
Wrestlingworth
Fowlmere
Duxford
R. Gt. Ouse
Old Bedford
Little Ouse
Cut off Channel
Wissey
Lark
Cam
Breck
CAMBRIDGE
150 m
150 yards
ELY CATHEDRAL
HUNTINGDON
NEWMARKET
BEDFORD
COLCHESTER
BOTANIC GARDEN
LONDON
HISTON ROAD CEMETERY
North St
Histon Rd
Victoria Rd
Clare St
St Lukes St
Hilda St
Searle St
Victoria Rd
Primrose St
Green's Rd
Albert St
Carlyle Rd
Castle St
Mount Pleasant
Shelly Row
Magrath Ave
Hertford St
Alpha Rd
Chesterton Rd
Cam
JESUS GREEN
Victoria Ave
Lady Margaret Rd
St Peter's St
Madingley Rd
Northampton St
Kettle's Yard
Magdalene College
Magdalene St
Park Parade
New Park St
Portugal Pl.
Park St
Jesus College
St John's College
Bridge St
Round Church
Jesus Lane
Malcolm St
Queen's Rd
Trinity College
St John's St
Sidney St
King St
The Avenue
Green St
Trinity St
Trinity Hall
Old School
Senate House
Great St Mary's
Hobson St
CHRIST'S PIECES
Emmanuel Rd
Orchard St
Earl St
Victoria St
Parker St
Clarendon St
Clare College
The Backs
KING'S COLLEGE
King's Parade
Emmanuel College
Corpus Christi College
West Rd
Queens' College
Downing St
Downing Pl.
Park Terrace
St Botolph's Church
Mill La.
Mathematical Bridge
Pembroke College
PARKER'S PIECE
Regent Terrace
Regent St
Silver St
Sidgwick Ave
Newnham Rd
Tennis Court Rd
Gonville Pl.
Fitzwilliam Museum
Newnham Walk
Malting La.
COE FEN
Trumpington St
FELLOW'S GARDEN
SHEEP'S GREEN
Hills Rd
Lensfield Rd
Newnham Rd
The Fen Causeway
Union Rd

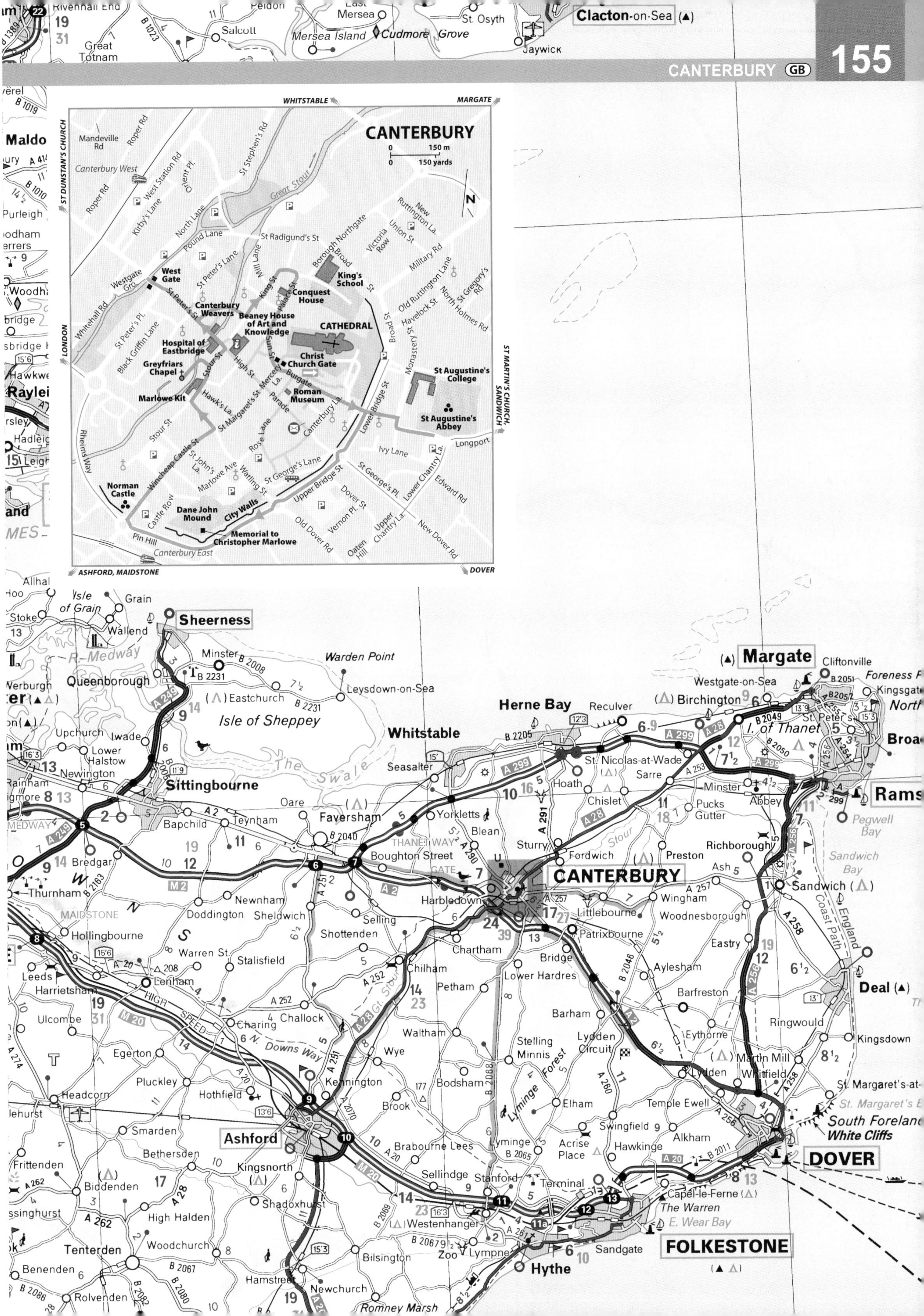
Clacton-on-Sea
Jaywick
St. Osyth
Mersea Island
Cudmore Grove
Salcott
Great Totnam
CANTERBURY
150 m
150 yards
WHITSTABLE
MARGATE
ST DUNSTAN'S CHURCH
ST MARTIN'S CHURCH, SANDWICH
LONDON
ASHFORD, MAIDSTONE
DOVER
Canterbury West
Canterbury East
Great Stour
West Gate
Westgate Gro.
Canterbury Weavers
Hospital of Eastbridge
Greyfriars Chapel
Marlowe Kit
Beaney House of Art and Knowledge
Conquest House
King's School
CATHEDRAL
Christ Church Gate
Roman Museum
St Augustine's College
St Augustine's Abbey
Norman Castle
Dane John Mound
City Walls
Memorial to Christopher Marlowe
Mandeville Rd
Roper Rd
West Station Rd
Orient Pl.
St Stephen's Rd
North Lane
Kirby's Lane
Pound Lane
St Radigund's St
Mill Lane
St Peter's Lane
St Peter's St
Whitehall Rd
St Peter's Pl.
Black Griffin Lane
Stour St
High St
King St
Palace St
Sun St
Mercery La.
Burgate
Borough Northgate
Broad St
Victoria Row
Union St
New Ruttington La.
Military Rd
Old Ruttington Lane
Havelock St
North Holmes Rd
St Gregory's Rd
Monastery St
Lower Bridge St
Longport
Ivy Lane
Lower Chantry La.
Edward Rd
New Dover Rd
St George's Pl.
Dover St
Upper Chantry La.
Oaten Hill
Vernon Pl.
Old Dover Rd
Upper Bridge St
St George's Lane
Watling St
Marlowe Ave
Rose Lane
Parade
St Margaret's St
Hawk's La.
St John's La.
Wincheap Castle St
Castle Row
Pin Hill
Rheims Way
Canterbury La.
Sheerness
Isle of Grain
Grain
Wallend
Stoke
Hoo
R. Medway
Queenborough
Minster
Warden Point
Eastchurch
Leysdown-on-Sea
Isle of Sheppey
The Swale
Whitstable
Seasalter
Herne Bay
Reculver
Birchington
Westgate-on-Sea
Margate
Cliftonville
Foreness P.
Kingsgate
I. of Thanet
St. Peter's
Broa
Rams
Pegwell Bay
Sandwich Bay
Upchurch
Iwade
Lower Halstow
Newington
Rainham
Sittingbourne
Bapchild
Teynham
Oare
Faversham
Yorkletts
Blean
THANET WAY
Hoath
St. Nicolas-at-Wade
Sarre
Chislet
Minster
Abbey
Pucks Gutter
Sturry
Fordwich
Stour
Preston
Richborough
Ash
Sandwich
CANTERBURY
Boughton Street
Harbledown
Bredgar
Thurnham
MAIDSTONE
Newnham
Doddington
Sheldwich
Selling
Shottenden
Chartham
Littlebourne
Wingham
Woodnesborough
Patrixbourne
Bridge
Lower Hardres
Eastry
Coast Path
England
Hollingbourne
Warren St.
Stalisfield
Chilham
Petham
Aylesham
Barfreston
Deal
Leeds
Harrietsham
Lenham
HIGH SPEED
Charing
Challock
Waltham
Barham
Stelling Minnis
Lydden Circuit
Eythorne
Ringwould
Kingsdown
Martin Mill
Whitfield
Lydden
St. Margaret's-at-
St. Margaret's B.
South Foreland
White Cliffs
Ulcombe
Egerton
N. Downs Way
Wye
Pluckley
Hothfield
Kennington
Brook
Bodsham
Lyminge Forest
Elham
Temple Ewell
Swingfield
Alkham
Headcorn
Smarden
Ashford
Bethersden
Kingsnorth
Brabourne Lees
Lyminge
Acrise Place
Hawkinge
DOVER
Frittenden
Biddenden
Shadoxhurst
Sellindge
Stanford
Terminal
Capel-le-Ferne
The Warren
E. Wear Bay
High Halden
Westenhanger
Woodchurch
Tenterden
Bilsington
Zoo
Lympne
Hythe
Sandgate
FOLKESTONE
Benenden
Rolvenden
Hamstreet
Newchurch
Romney Marsh
Maldo
Purleigh
Rayleigh
Hadleigh
Leigh
Allhal
Thames

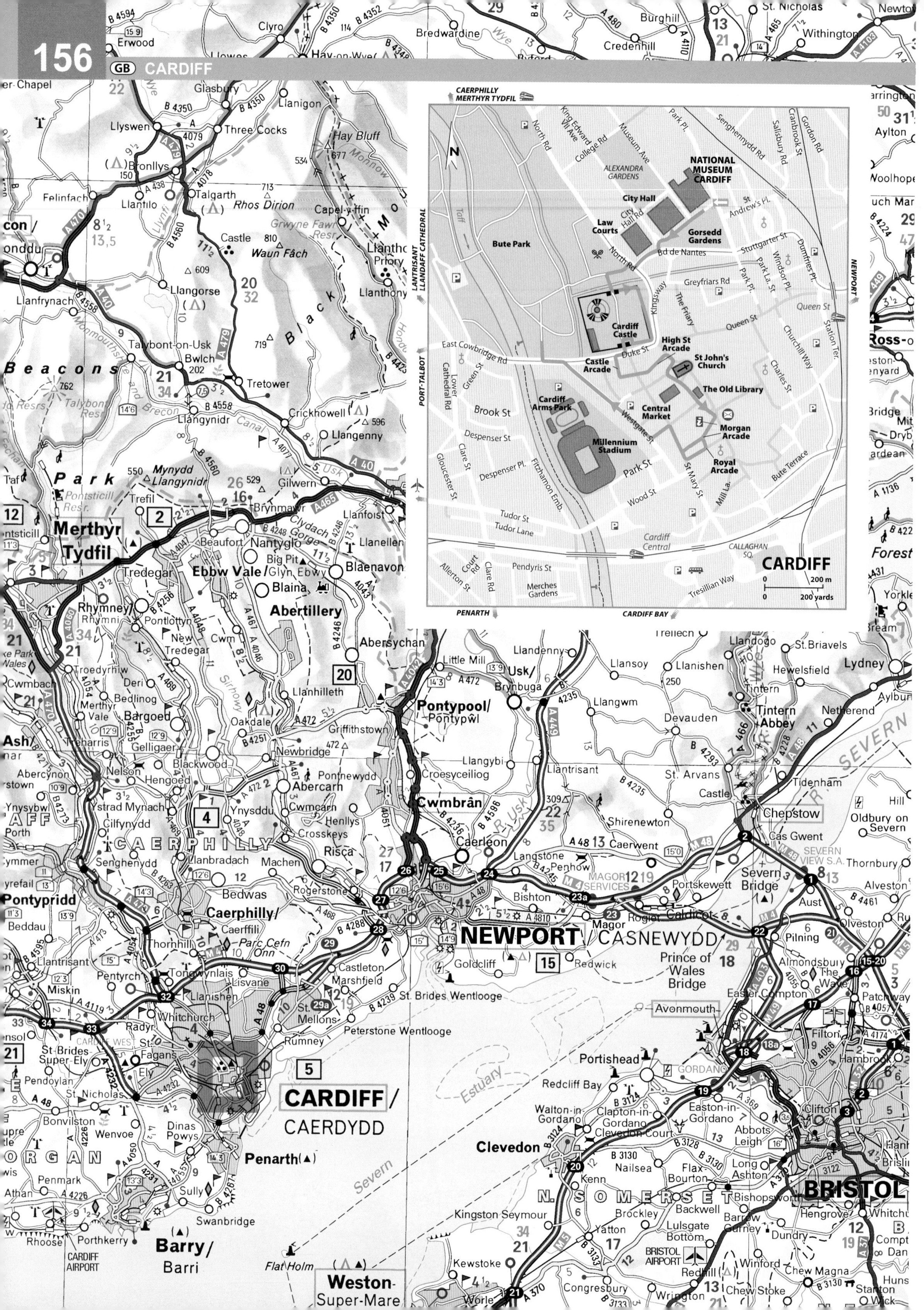
CARDIFF
CAERPHILLY
MERTHYR TYDFIL
NORTH
NATIONAL MUSEUM CARDIFF
ALEXANDRA GARDENS
City Hall
Law Courts
Gorsedd Gardens
Bute Park
Cardiff Castle
Castle Arcade
High St Arcade
St John's Church
The Old Library
Cardiff Arms Park
Central Market
Morgan Arcade
Millennium Stadium
Royal Arcade
Cardiff Central
CALLAGHAN SQ.
LANTRISANT LLANDAFF CATHEDRAL
PORT-TALBOT
NEWPORT
PENARTH
CARDIFF BAY
North Rd
King Edward VII Ave
College Rd
Museum Ave
Park Pl.
Senghennydd Rd
Salisbury Rd
Cranbrook St
Gordon Rd
St Andrew's Pl.
Stuttgarter St
Bd de Nantes
Greyfriars Rd
Kingsway
The Friary
Park Pl.
Park La. St
Windsor Pl.
Dumfries Pl.
Queen St
Station Ter.
Churchill Way
Charles St
East Cowbridge Rd
Duke St
Green St
Lower Cathedral Rd
Brook St
Dispenser St
Despenser Pl.
Clare St
Gloucester St
Fitzhamon Emb.
Westgate St
St Mary St
Mill La.
Park St
Wood St
Bute Terrace
Tudor St
Tudor Lane
Court Rd
Clare Rd
Allerton St
Pendyris St
Merches Gardens
Tresillian Way
Taff
200 m
200 yards
Merthyr Tydfil
Ebbw Vale / Glyn Ebwy
Abertillery
Blaenavon
Pontypool / Pontypŵl
Cwmbrân
Usk / Brynbuga
Caerleon
NEWPORT / CASNEWYDD
Caerphilly / Caerffili
Pontypridd
CARDIFF / CAERDYDD
Penarth
Barry / Barri
CARDIFF AIRPORT
Weston-Super-Mare
Clevedon
Portishead
BRISTOL
BRISTOL AIRPORT
Chepstow
Tintern Abbey
Severn Bridge
Prince of Wales Bridge
Avonmouth
Severn
Estuary
Flat Holm
Brecon Beacons Park
Black Mountains
Crickhowell
Talgarth
Tredegar
Rhymney / Rhymni
Blackwood
Risca
Magor
Caldicot
N. SOMERSET
GLAMORGAN

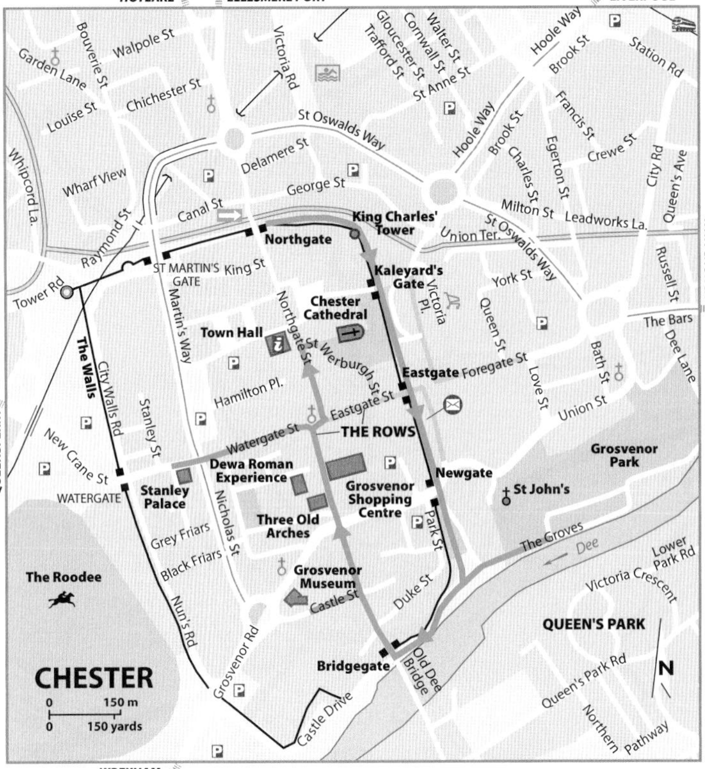
HOYLAKE
ELLESMERE PORT
MANCHESTER, LIVERPOOL
NANTWICH, WHITCHURCH
QUEENSFERRY
WREXHAM, CONWY
Northgate
King Charles' Tower
ST MARTIN'S GATE
Kaleyard's Gate
Chester Cathedral
Town Hall
Eastgate
THE ROWS
Dewa Roman Experience
Stanley Palace
WATERGATE
Newgate
St John's
Grosvenor Park
Grosvenor Shopping Centre
Three Old Arches
Grosvenor Museum
The Roodee
Bridgegate
Old Dee Bridge
QUEEN'S PARK
The Walls
CHESTER
150 m
150 yards
N

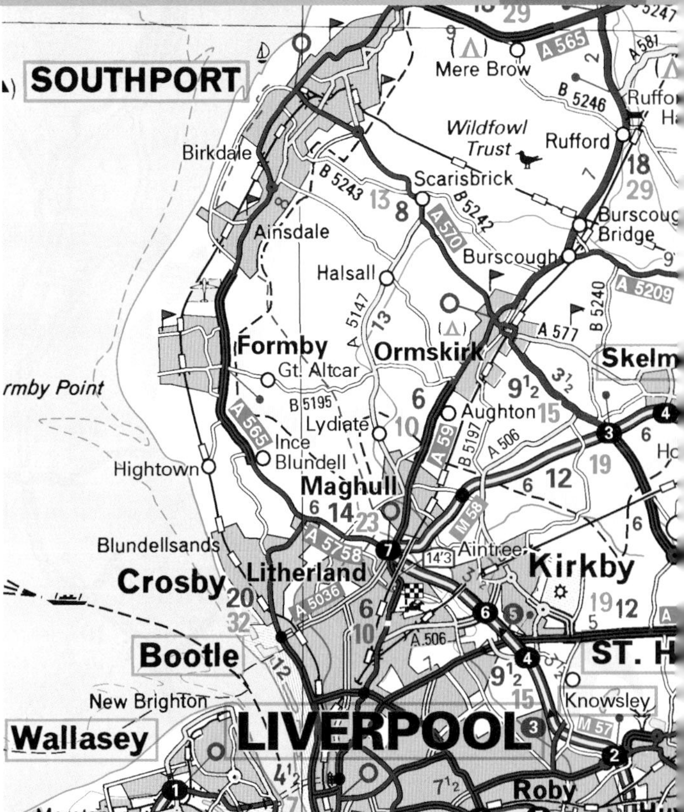

SOUTHPORT
Birkdale
Ainsdale
Formby
Ormskirk
Maghull
Crosby
Litherland
Bootle
Kirkby
New Brighton
Wallasey
LIVERPOOL
Moreton
BIRKENHEAD
West Kirby
Bebington
Heswall
Neston
Ellesmere Port
CHESTER
Rhyl
Prestatyn
Abergele
Holywell / Treffynnon
Flint / Fflint
Connah's Quay
Denbigh / Dinbych
Mold / Yr Wyddgrug
Ruthin / Rhuthun
Wrexham / Wrecsam
DENBIGHSHIRE
FLINTS
CHESHIRE AND CHESTER
Clocaenog Forest
Welsh Channel
River Dee
River Mersey
LIVERPOOL JOHN LENNON AIRPORT

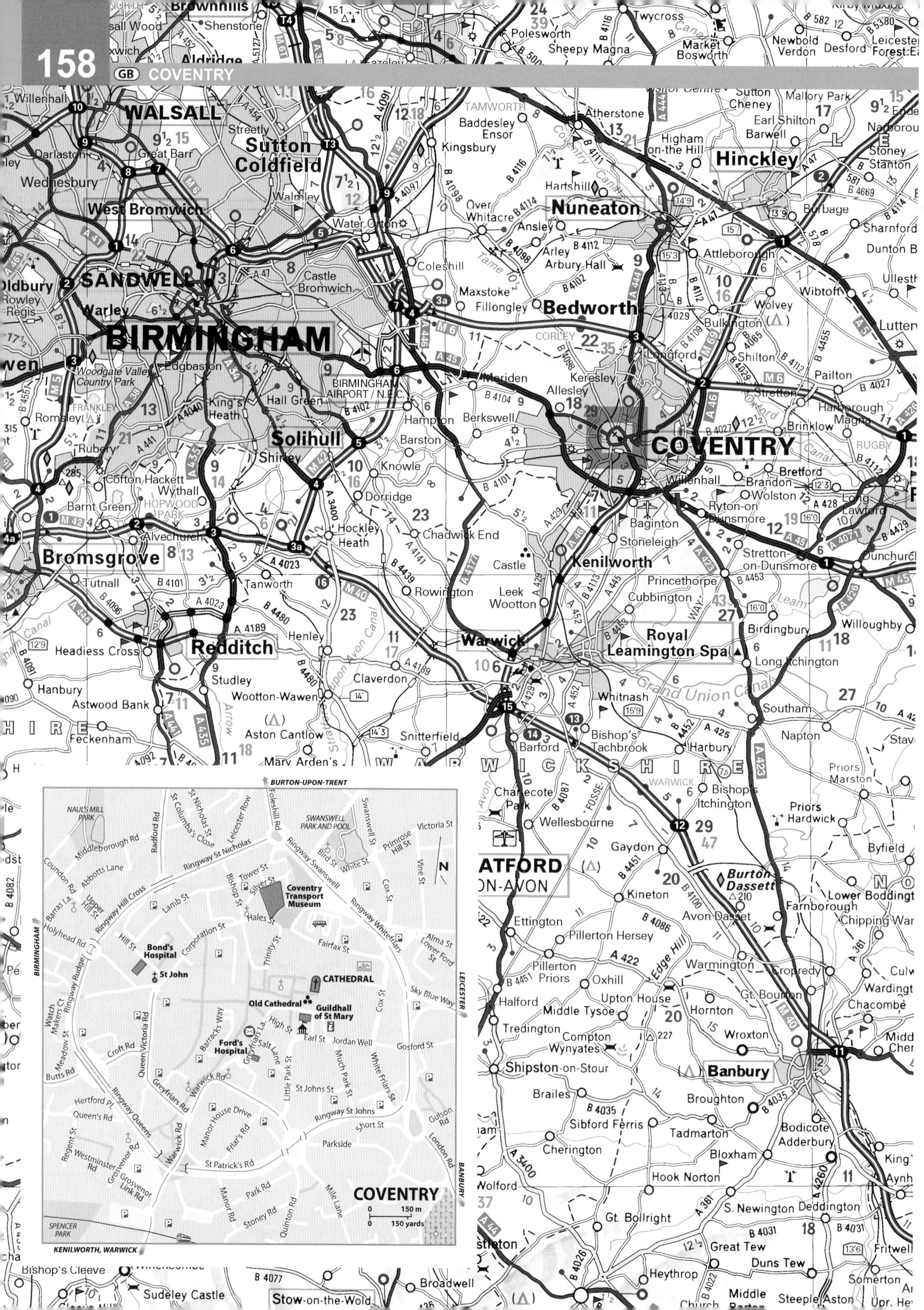

WALSALL
Sutton Coldfield
West Bromwich
SANDWELL
Oldbury
Rowley Regis
Warley
BIRMINGHAM
Woodgate Valley Country Park
Edgbaston
King's Heath
Hall Green
Solihull
Shirley
BIRMINGHAM AIRPORT / N.E.C.
Castle Bromwich
Water Orton
Coleshill
Maxstoke
Fillongley
Bedworth
Nuneaton
Atherstone
Hinckley
Burbage
Attleborough
Bulkington
Wolvey
Shilton
Longford
Keresley
Allesley
Meriden
Berkswell
Hampton
Barston
Knowle
Dorridge
Hockley Heath
Chadwick End
COVENTRY
Willenhall
Brandon
Wolston
Bretford
Ryton-on-Dunsmore
Baginton
Stoneleigh
Kenilworth
Castle
Leek Wootton
Warwick
Royal Leamington Spa
Whitnash
Bishop's Tachbrook
Barford
Cubbington
Princethorpe
Stretton-on-Dunsmore
Dunchurch
Long Itchington
Birdingbury
Southam
Napton
Harbury
Bishop's Itchington
Charlecote Park
Wellesbourne
Kineton
Gaydon
Burton Dassett
Avon Dassett
Farnborough
Warmington
Cropredy
Banbury
Wroxton
Hornton
Upton House
Middle Tysoe
Oxhill
Pillerton Priors
Pillerton Hersey
Ettington
Halford
Tredington
Shipston-on-Stour
Compton Wynyates
Brailes
Sibford Ferris
Cherington
Tadmarton
Broughton
Bloxham
Bodicote
Adderbury
Hook Norton
Gt. Bollright
S. Newington
Deddington
Great Tew
Duns Tew
Heythrop
Middle Barton
Steeple Aston
Somerton
Fritwell
Wolford
Stow-on-the-Wold
Broadwell
Sudeley Castle
Bishop's Cleeve
Bromsgrove
Redditch
Alvechurch
Barnt Green
Cofton Hackett
Wythall
Rubery
Romsley
Tutnall
Headless Cross
Hanbury
Astwood Bank
Feckenham
Studley
Henley
Wootton Wawen
Aston Cantlow
Claverdon
Snitterfield
Mary Arden's
Tanworth
Rowington
Stratford-upon-Avon Canal
Grand Union Canal
Coventry Canal
Ashby Canal
ATFORD
ON-AVON
WARWICKSHIRE
Twycross
Polesworth
Sheepy Magna
Market Bosworth
Newbold Verdon
Desford
Shenstone
Aldridge
Brownhills
Streetly
Great Barr
Darlaston
Wednesbury
Walmley
Kingsbury
Baddesley Ensor
Over Whitacre
Ansley
Arley
Arbury Hall
Hartshill
Higham on-the Hill
Sutton Cheney
Mallory Park
Earl Shilton
Barwell
Stoney Stanton
Sharnford
Wibtoft
Pailton
Stretton
Harborough Magna
Brinklow
Long Lawford
Willoughby
Priors Marston
Priors Hardwick
Byfield
Lower Boddington
Chipping Warden
Wardington
Chacombe
Fenny Compton

COVENTRY
BURTON-UPON-TRENT
LEICESTER
BANBURY
KENILWORTH, WARWICK
BIRMINGHAM
NAUL'S MILL PARK
SWANSWELL PARK AND POOL
Coventry Transport Museum
CATHEDRAL
Old Cathedral
Guildhall of St Mary
Bond's Hospital
St John
Ford's Hospital
SPENCER PARK
Ringway St Nicholas
Ringway Swanswell
Ringway Whitefriars
Ringway Hill Cross
Ringway Rudge
Ringway Queens
Ringway St Johns
Foleshill Rd
Radford Rd
Middleborough Rd
Abbotts Lane
Coundon Rd
Holyhead Rd
Corporation St
Trinity St
High St
Jordan Well
Gosford St
Sky Blue Way
Warwick Rd
Greyfriars Rd
Queen Victoria Rd
Manor House Drive
Parkside
St Patrick's Rd
London Rd
Quinton Rd
Mile Lane
150 m
150 yards

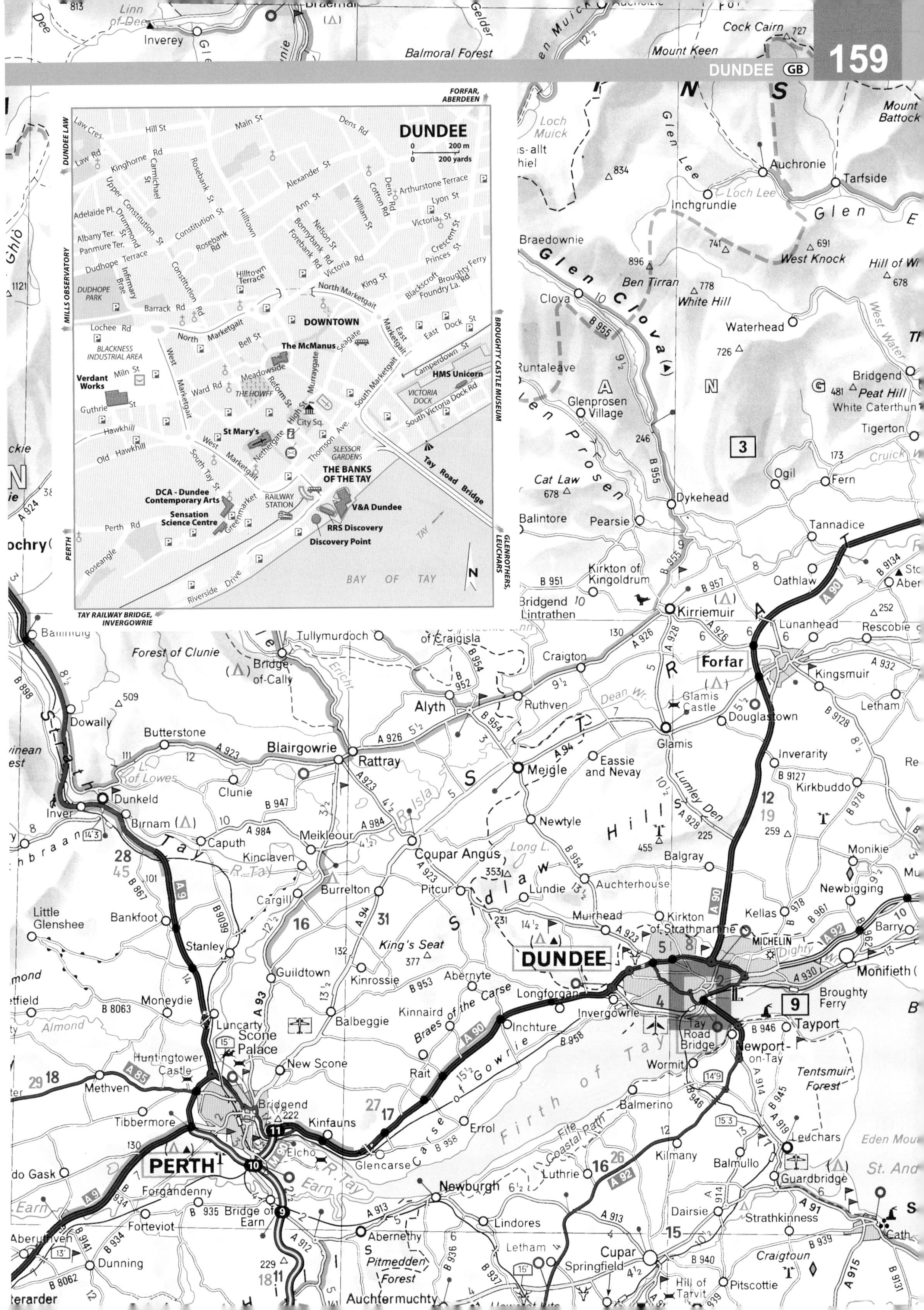
DUNDEE
0 200 m
0 200 yards
FORFAR, ABERDEEN
DUNDEE LAW
MILLS OBSERVATORY
BROUGHTY CASTLE MUSEUM
GLENROTHERS, LEUCHARS
PERTH
TAY RAILWAY BRIDGE, INVERGOWRIE
DOWNTOWN
The McManus
HMS Unicorn
VICTORIA DOCK
Verdant Works
BLACKNESS INDUSTRIAL AREA
DUDHOPE PARK
THE HOWFF
St Mary's
City Sq.
SLESSOR GARDENS
THE BANKS OF THE TAY
DCA - Dundee Contemporary Arts
Sensation Science Centre
RAILWAY STATION
V&A Dundee
RRS Discovery
Discovery Point
Tay Road Bridge
BAY OF TAY
Law Cres.
Hill St
Main St
Dens Rd
Law Rd
Kinghorne Rd
Alexander St
Arthurstone Terrace
Lyon St
Victoria St
Adelaide Pl.
Albany Ter.
Panmure Ter.
Dudhope Terrace
Constitution St
Rosebank Rd
Hilltown
Victoria Rd
Princes St
Crescent St
Broughty Ferry Rd
Blackscroft
Foundry La. Rd
Hilltown Terrace
North Marketgait
King St
Barrack Rd
Lochee Rd
Bell St
Seagate
East Dock St
East Marketgait
Camperdown St
Milns St
Ward Rd
Meadowside
Reform St
Murraygate
South Marketgait
South Victoria Dock Rd
Guthrie St
Hawkhill
Old Hawkhill
West Marketgait
Nethergate
High St
Thomson Ave.
South Tay St
Greenmarket
Perth Rd
Roseangle
Riverside Drive
Braemar
Inverey
Balmoral Forest
Cock Cairn
Mount Keen
Mount Battock
Loch Muick
Auchronie
Tarfside
Inchgrundle
Loch Lee
Glen Lee
Braedownie
Glen Clova
Ben Tirran
White Hill
West Knock
Hill of Wirren
Clova
Waterhead
Runtaleave
Glenprosen Village
Glen Prosen
Bridgend
Peat Hill
White Caterthun
Tigerton
Cat Law
Dykehead
Ogil
Fern
Balintore
Pearsie
Tannadice
Kirkton of Kingoldrum
Oathlaw
Bridgend of Lintrathen
Kirriemuir
Lunanhead
Rescobie
Tullymurdoch
Forest of Clunie
Bridge of Cally
Craigton
Forfar
Kingsmuir
Letham
Alyth
Ruthven
Glamis Castle
Douglastown
Dowally
Butterstone
Blairgowrie
Rattray
Glamis
Meigle
Eassie and Nevay
Inverarity
Kirkbuddo
Loch of Lowes
Clunie
Dunkeld
Inver
Birnam
Caputh
Meikleour
Coupar Angus
Newtyle
Sidlaw Hills
Lumley Den
Kinclaven
Balgray
Monikie
Burrelton
Pitcur
Lundie
Auchterhouse
Newbigging
Little Glenshee
Bankfoot
Cargill
Muirhead
Kirkton of Strathmartine
Kellas
Barry
Stanley
Guildtown
King's Seat
DUNDEE
Monifieth
Kinrossie
Abernyte
Longforgan
Broughty Ferry
Moneydie
Luncarty
Balbeggie
Kinnaird
Braes of the Carse
Invergowrie
Tayport
Scone Palace
Inchture
Tay Road Bridge
Newport-on-Tay
Huntingtower Castle
New Scone
Rait
Wormit
Tentsmuir Forest
Methven
Firth of Tay
Carse of Gowrie
Balmerino
Tibbermore
Bridgend
Kinfauns
Errol
Leuchars
Eden Mouth
PERTH
Elcho
Glencarse
Fife Coastal Path
Kilmany
Balmullo
St. Andrews
Forgandenny
Newburgh
Luthrie
Guardbridge
Bridge of Earn
Forteviot
Lindores
Dairsie
Strathkinness
Aberuthven
Abernethy
Pitmedden Forest
Letham
Cupar
Springfield
Craigtoun
Dunning
Hill of Tarvit
Pitscottie
Auchtermuchty
Auchterarder
MICHELIN

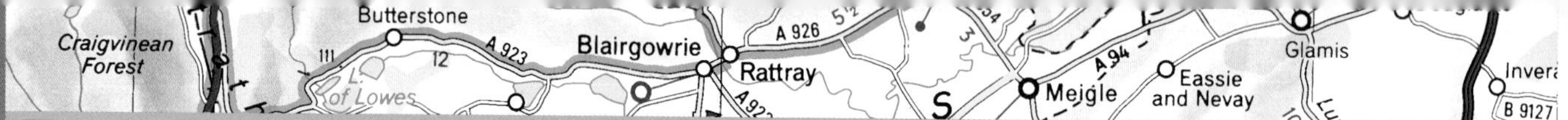
Craigvinean Forest
Butterstone
Blairgowrie
Rattray
A 923
A 926
A 94
Meigle
Eassie and Nevay
Glamis
Loch of Lowes
B 9127

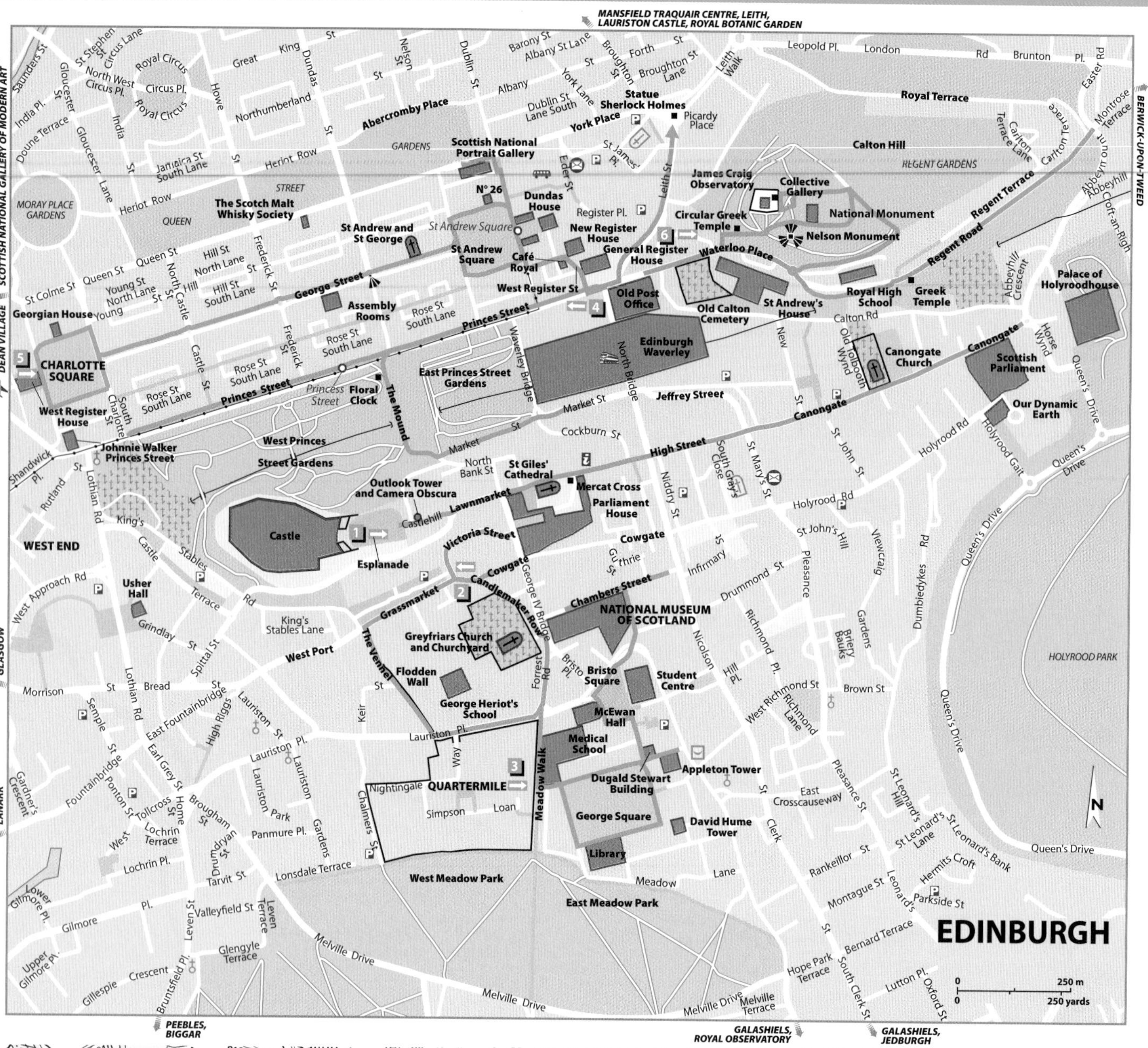
EDINBURGH
MANSFIELD TRAQUAIR CENTRE, LEITH, LAURISTON CASTLE, ROYAL BOTANIC GARDEN
FORTH BRIDGE, EDINBURGH ZOO, STOCKBRIDGE, SCOTTISH NATIONAL GALLERY OF MODERN ART
BERWICK-UPON-TWEED
DEAN VILLAGE
GLASGOW
LANARK
PEEBLES, BIGGAR
GALASHIELS, ROYAL OBSERVATORY
GALASHIELS, JEDBURGH
CHARLOTTE SQUARE
Georgian House
West Register House
Johnnie Walker Princes Street
WEST END
Usher Hall
Castle
Esplanade
Outlook Tower and Camera Obscura
St Giles' Cathedral
Mercat Cross
Parliament House
Floral Clock
West Princes Street Gardens
East Princes Street Gardens
The Mound
Assembly Rooms
St Andrew and St George
St Andrew Square
Café Royal
Dundas House
Scottish National Portrait Gallery
Nº 26
The Scotch Malt Whisky Society
MORAY PLACE GARDENS
QUEEN STREET GARDENS
New Register House
General Register House
West Register St
Old Post Office
Edinburgh Waverley
Statue Sherlock Holmes
Picardy Place
York Place
James Craig Observatory
Collective Gallery
Circular Greek Temple
National Monument
Nelson Monument
Calton Hill
REGENT GARDENS
Royal Terrace
Regent Terrace
Regent Road
Waterloo Place
Old Calton Cemetery
St Andrew's House
Royal High School
Greek Temple
Palace of Holyroodhouse
Canongate Church
Scottish Parliament
Our Dynamic Earth
HOLYROOD PARK
High Street
Canongate
Lawnmarket
Castlehill
Victoria Street
Cowgate
Grassmarket
Candlemaker Row
Greyfriars Church and Churchyard
The Vennel
Flodden Wall
George Heriot's School
NATIONAL MUSEUM OF SCOTLAND
Chambers Street
Bristo Square
Student Centre
McEwan Hall
Medical School
Appleton Tower
Dugald Stewart Building
George Square
David Hume Tower
Library
QUARTERMILE
West Meadow Park
East Meadow Park
Meadow Walk
Melville Drive
West Port
Lauriston Pl.
Princes Street
George Street
Rose Street
Jeffrey Street
Market St
Cockburn St
North Bridge
Waverley Bridge
Leith Walk
Leith St
Abercromby Place
Heriot Row
Northumberland
Great King St
Dundas St
Queen's Drive
Holyrood Rd
St Leonard's St
Pleasance
Nicolson St
Clerk St
0 250 m
0 250 yards
N

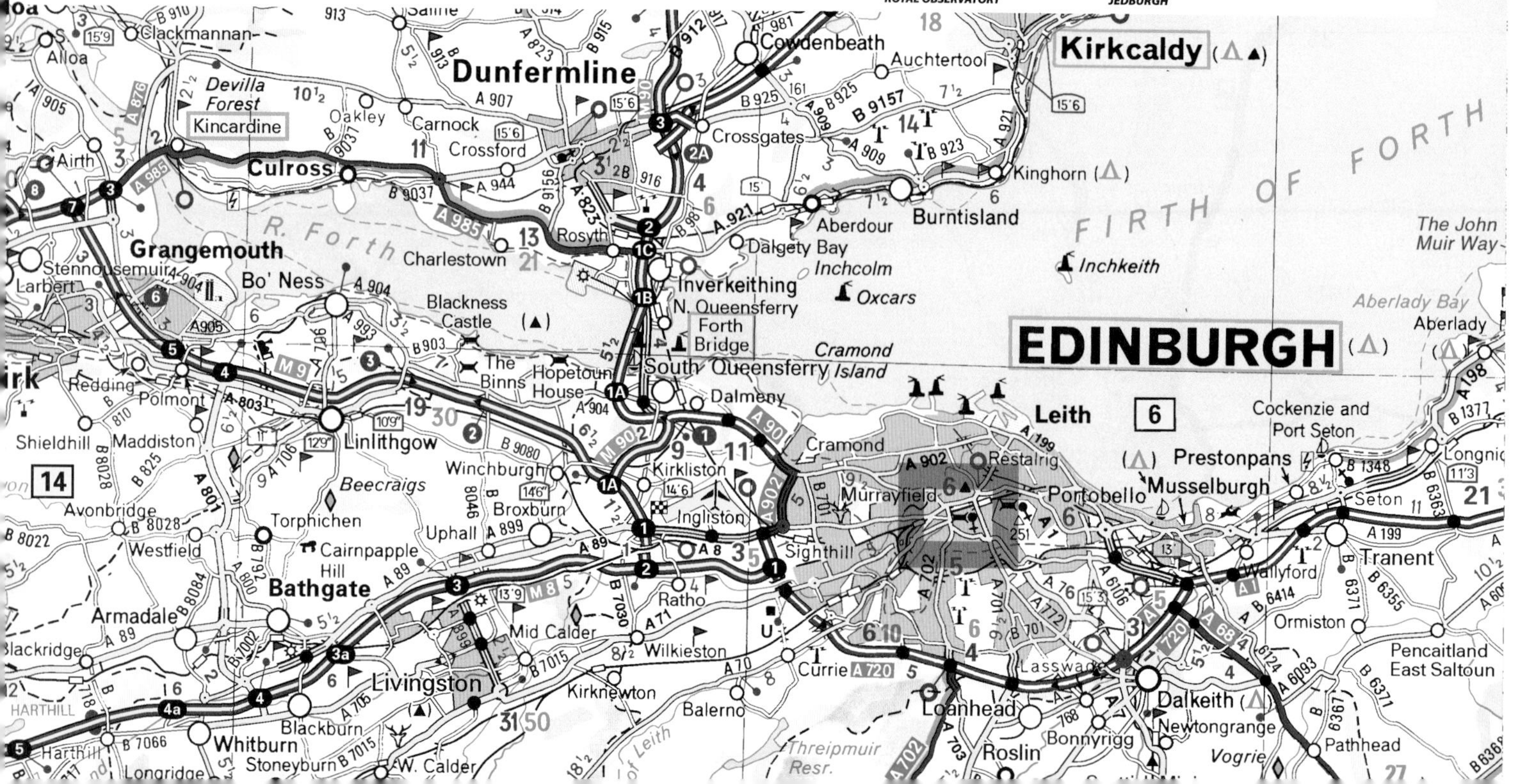
Alloa
Clackmannan
Kincardine
Devilla Forest
Culross
Dunfermline
Cowdenbeath
Auchtertool
Kirkcaldy
Crossgates
Kinghorn
Burntisland
Aberdour
Dalgety Bay
Inchcolm
Inchkeith
Oxcars
FIRTH OF FORTH
Rosyth
Charlestown
Inverkeithing
N. Queensferry
Forth Bridge
Grangemouth
Bo' Ness
Blackness Castle
Stenhousemuir
Larbert
Polmont
Redding
Linlithgow
The Binns
Hopetoun House
South Queensferry
Dalmeny
Cramond Island
EDINBURGH
Leith
Cramond
Restalrig
Murrayfield
Portobello
Musselburgh
Prestonpans
Cockenzie and Port Seton
Aberlady Bay
Aberlady
The John Muir Way
Tranent
Wallyford
Ormiston
Pencaitland
East Saltoun
Dalkeith
Lasswade
Loanhead
Bonnyrigg
Newtongrange
Pathhead
Roslin
Vogrie
Kirkliston
Ingliston
Sighthill
Currie
Balerno
Ratho
Wilkieston
Kirknewton
Mid Calder
Livingston
Broxburn
Uphall
Winchburgh
Torphichen
Cairnpapple Hill
Beecraigs
Bathgate
Armadale
Westfield
Avonbridge
Maddiston
Shieldhill
Whitburn
Blackburn
Stoneyburn
Harthill
Longridge
Blackridge
W. Calder
Threipmuir Resr.

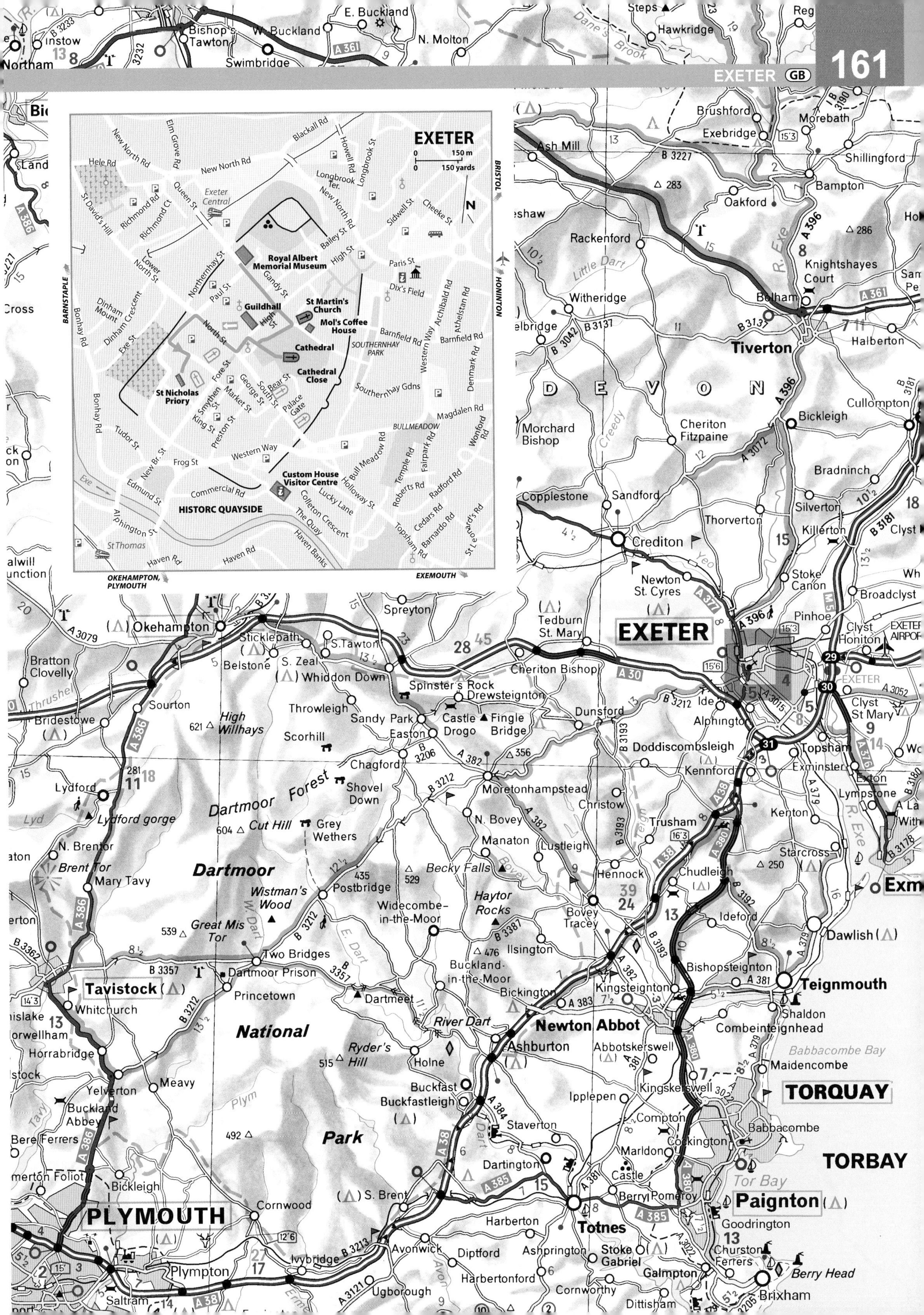
EXETER
150 m
150 yards
New North Rd
Elm Grove Rd
Blackall Rd
Howell Rd
Longbrook St
Hele Rd
Queen St
Exeter Central
Longbrook Ter.
St David's Hill
Richmond Rd
Richmond Ct
Sidwell St
Cheeke St
Bailey St
High St
Lower North St
Northernhay St
Royal Albert Memorial Museum
Gandy St
Paris St
Dix's Field
Paul St
Guildhall
St Martin's Church
Mol's Coffee House
Cathedral
Cathedral Close
Southernhay Park
Barnfield Rd
Western Way
Archibald Rd
Athelstan Rd
Denmark Rd
Dinham Mount
Dinham Crescent
Exe St
North St
St Nicholas Priory
Fore St
George St
South St
Bear St
Smythen St
Market St
King St
Preston St
Palace Gate
Southernhay Gdns
Magdalen Rd
Bullmeadow
Wonford Rd
Bonhay Rd
Tudor St
New Br. St
Frog St
Western Way
Bull Meadow Rd
Temple Rd
Fairpark Rd
Custom House Visitor Centre
Commercial Rd
Historc Quayside
Edmund St
Holloway St
Lucky Lane
Roberts Rd
Radford Rd
Colleton Crescent
The Quay
Alphington St
St Thomas
Haven Rd
Haven Banks
Cedars Rd
Barnardo Rd
Topsham Rd
St Leonard's Rd
Barnstaple
Bristol
Honiton
Okehampton, Plymouth
Exemouth
Exe
Northam
Instow
Bishop's Tawton
W. Buckland
E. Buckland
Swimbridge
N. Molton
Steps
Hawkridge
Dane's Brook
Brushford
Exebridge
Morebath
Ash Mill
Shillingford
Bampton
Oakford
Rackenford
Knightshayes Court
Little Dart
Witheridge
Bolham
Tiverton
Halberton
DEVON
Cullompton
Bickleigh
Morchard Bishop
Cheriton Fitzpaine
Creedy
Bradninch
Copplestone
Sandford
Silverton
Thorverton
Killerton
Crediton
Yeo
Newton St. Cyres
Stoke Canon
Broadclyst
Pinhoe
Tedburn St. Mary
EXETER
Clyst Honiton
Exeter Airport
Okehampton
Sticklepath
S. Tawton
Spreyton
Bratton Clovelly
Belstone
S. Zeal
Whiddon Down
Cheriton Bishop
Thrushel
Bridestowe
Sourton
Spinster's Rock
Drewsteignton
Dunsford
Ide
Alphington
Clyst St Mary
High Willhays
Throwleigh
Sandy Park
Castle Drogo
Fingle Bridge
Easton
Scorhill
Doddiscombsleigh
Topsham
Chagford
Kennford
Exminster
Exton
Lydford
Shovel Down
Moretonhampstead
Christow
Lympstone
Lydford gorge
Dartmoor Forest
Cut Hill
Grey Wethers
N. Bovey
Trusham
Kenton
Lyd
N. Brentor
Manaton
Lustleigh
Starcross
Brent Tor
Mary Tavy
Dartmoor
Postbridge
Becky Falls
Hennock
Chudleigh
Exmouth
Wistman's Wood
Haytor Rocks
Widecombe-in-the-Moor
Bovey Tracey
Ideford
Dawlish
Great Mis Tor
Ilsington
Two Bridges
Buckland-in-the-Moor
Bishopsteignton
Teignmouth
B 3357
Tavistock
Dartmoor Prison
Princetown
Dartmeet
Bickington
Kingsteignton
Whitchurch
Shaldon
Combeinteignhead
Newton Abbot
National
River Dart
Horrabridge
Ashburton
Abbotskerswell
Babbacombe Bay
Ryder's Hill
Holne
Maidencombe
Yelverton
Meavy
Buckfast
Buckfastleigh
Ipplepen
Kingskerswell
TORQUAY
Buckland Abbey
Plym
Staverton
Compton
Babbacombe
Bere Ferrers
Park
Cockington
Dartington
Marldon
TORBAY
Bickleigh
Castle
Tor Bay
S. Brent
Berry Pomeroy
Paignton
PLYMOUTH
Cornwood
Harberton
Totnes
Goodrington
Plympton
Ivybridge
Avonwick
Diptford
Ashprington
Stoke Gabriel
Churston Ferrers
Berry Head
Galmpton
Saltram
Erme
Ugborough
Harbertonford
Cornworthy
Dittisham
Brixham
A 30
A 38
A 386
A 396
A 361
A 377
A 382
A 385
A 380
A 381
A 379
A 3072
A 3079
M 5

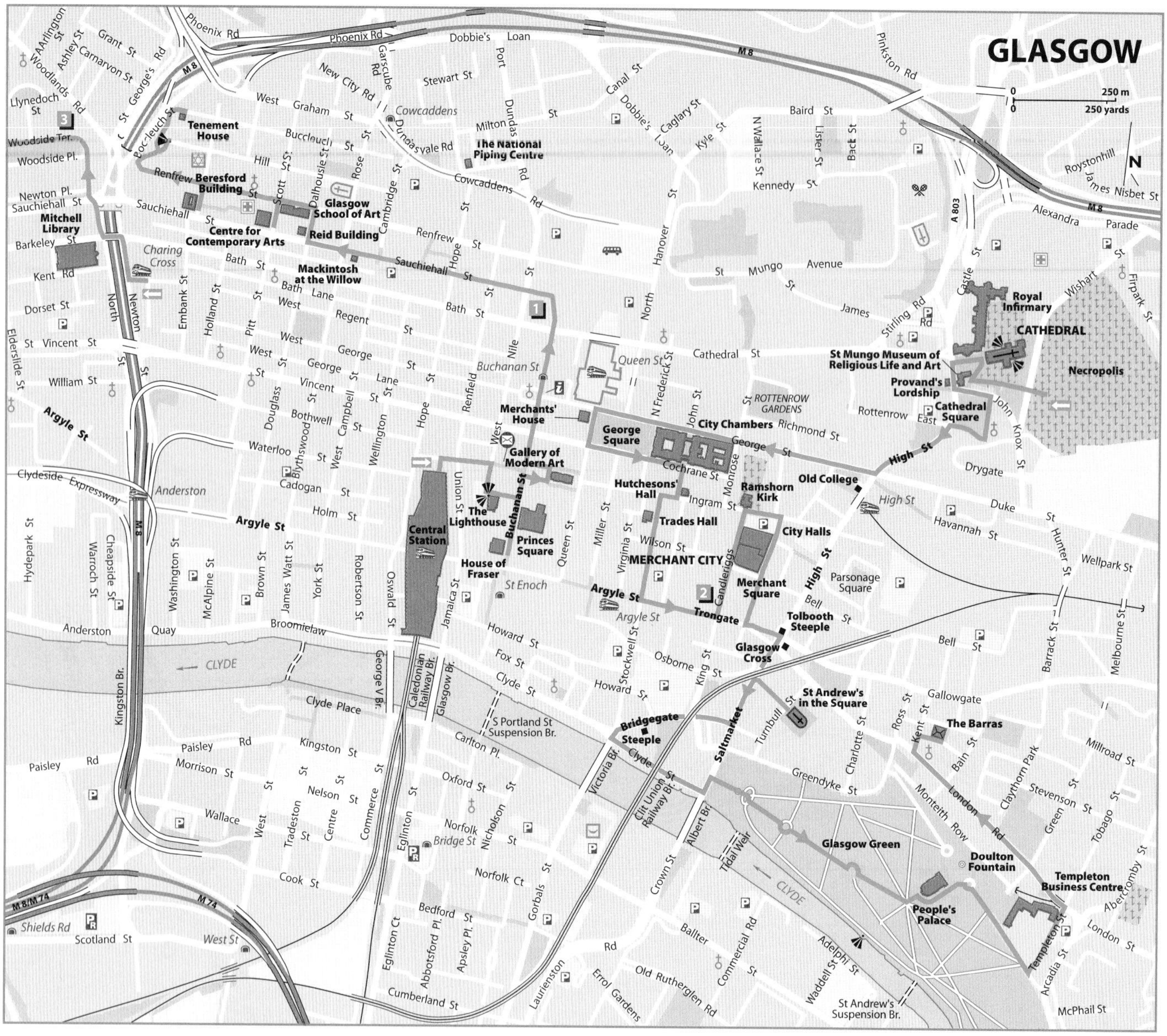
GLASGOW
250 m
250 yards
N
Phoenix Rd
M8
New City Rd
Cowcaddens
The National Piping Centre
Tenement House
Beresford Building
Glasgow School of Art
Centre for Contemporary Arts
Reid Building
Mackintosh at the Willow
Mitchell Library
Charing Cross
Sauchiehall St
Bath St
West Regent St
West George St
St Vincent St
Argyle St
Anderston
Clydeside Expressway
Merchants' House
Gallery of Modern Art
George Square
City Chambers
Hutchesons' Hall
Trades Hall
Ramshorn Kirk
Old College
City Halls
MERCHANT CITY
The Lighthouse
Central Station
Princes Square
House of Fraser
St Enoch
Merchant Square
Trongate
Tolbooth Steeple
Glasgow Cross
Royal Infirmary
CATHEDRAL
St Mungo Museum of Religious Life and Art
Provand's Lordship
Cathedral Square
Necropolis
High St
Broomielaw
CLYDE
Bridgegate Steeple
St Andrew's in the Square
The Barras
Glasgow Green
Doulton Fountain
People's Palace
Templeton Business Centre
Saltmarket
S Portland St Suspension Br.
St Andrew's Suspension Br.
Kingston Br.
George V Br.
Caledonian Railway Br.
Glasgow Br.
Victoria Br.
Albert Br.
Tidal Weir
Gorbals St
Crown St
Eglinton St
Norfolk St
Cumberland St
M74
M8/M74
Shields Rd
Scotland St
Paisley Rd
London Rd
Gallowgate
Duke St
Alexandra Parade
Castle St
Cathedral St
Rottenrow

Port Glasgow
Dumbarton
Kilpatrick Hills
Erskine Bridge
Milngavie
Bearsden
Kirkintilloch
Cumbernauld
Clydebank
Renfrew
Paisley
Johnstone
GLASGOW
Coatbridge
Airdrie
Rutherglen
Barrhead
Bothwell
Motherwell
Hamilton
Wishaw
East Kilbride
Carluke
Larkhall
Eaglesham
Newton Mearns
Cambuslang
Uddingston
Bellshill
Stepps
Lenzie
Lennoxtown
Campsie
Kilmacolm
Houston
Bridge of Weir
Kilbarchan
Lochwinnoch
Beith
Lugton
Dunlop
Neilston
Busby
Carmunnock
Blantyre
Holytown
Newmains
Shotts
Salsburgh
Chapelhall
Slamannan
Caldercruix
Riggend
Torrance
Condorrat
Linwood
Howwood
Langbank
Bishopton
Uplawmoor
Barrmill
Auldhouse
Ballageich Hill
Law
Overtown
Cleland
Allanton

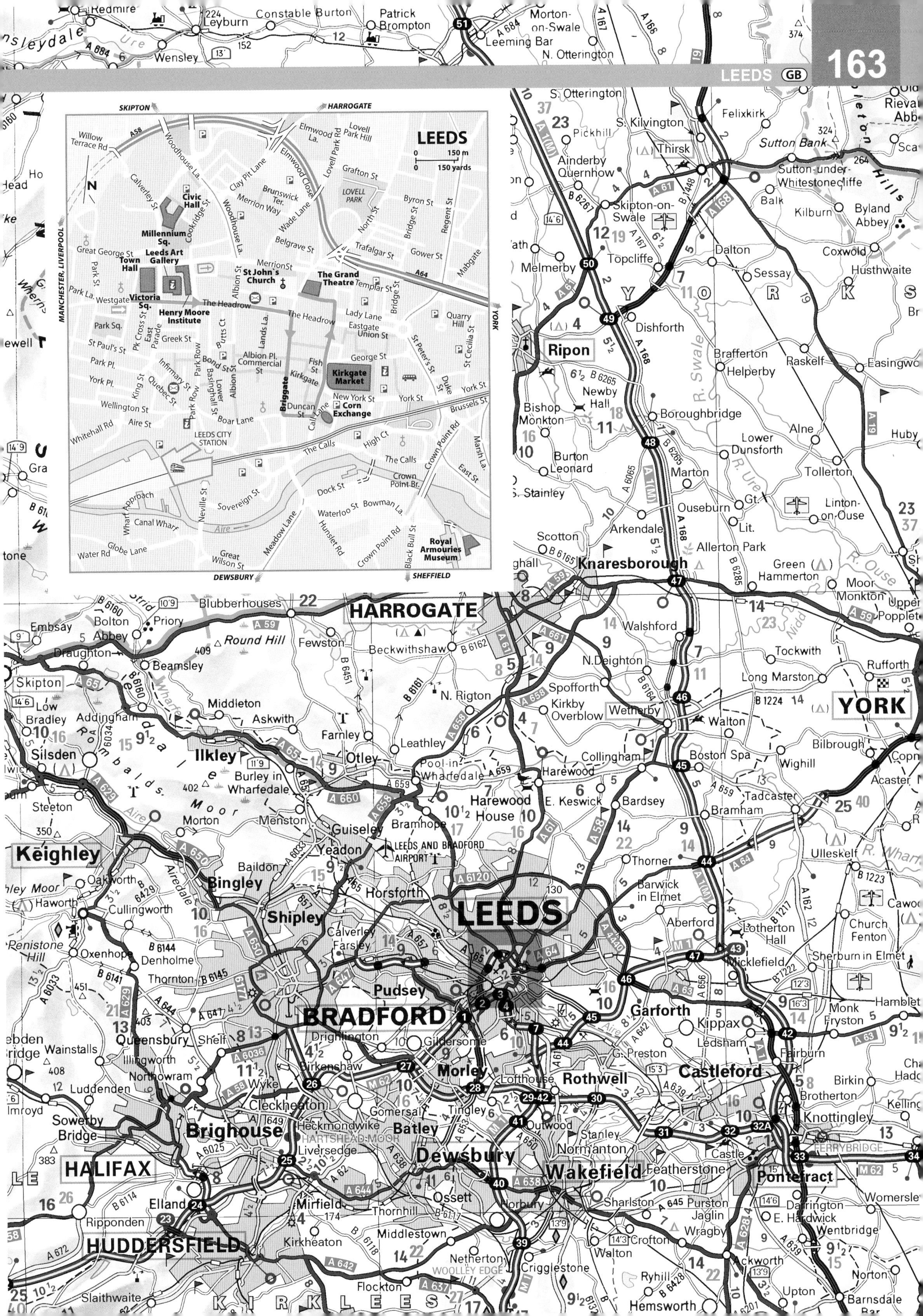

LEEDS
150 m
150 yards
SKIPTON
HARROGATE
YORK
DEWSBURY
SHEFFIELD
MANCHESTER, LIVERPOOL
Civic Hall
Millennium Sq.
Leeds Art Gallery
Town Hall
Victoria Sq.
Henry Moore Institute
St John's Church
The Grand Theatre
Kirkgate Market
Corn Exchange
LEEDS CITY STATION
Royal Armouries Museum
LOVELL PARK
The Headrow
Briggate
Park Row
Boar Lane
Wellington St
Whitehall Rd
The Calls
Dock St
Aire
HARROGATE
Knaresborough
Ripon
Thirsk
Boroughbridge
Wetherby
YORK
Tadcaster
Ilkley
Otley
Keighley
Bingley
Shipley
LEEDS
BRADFORD
Pudsey
Horsforth
Guiseley
Yeadon
LEEDS AND BRADFORD AIRPORT
Harewood House
Garforth
Rothwell
Morley
Castleford
Pontefract
Knottingley
Brighouse
HALIFAX
HUDDERSFIELD
Dewsbury
Batley
Wakefield
Featherstone
Ossett
Elland
Skipton
Silsden
Rombalds Moor
Leeming Bar
Leyburn
Wensley
Sutton Bank
KIRKLEES

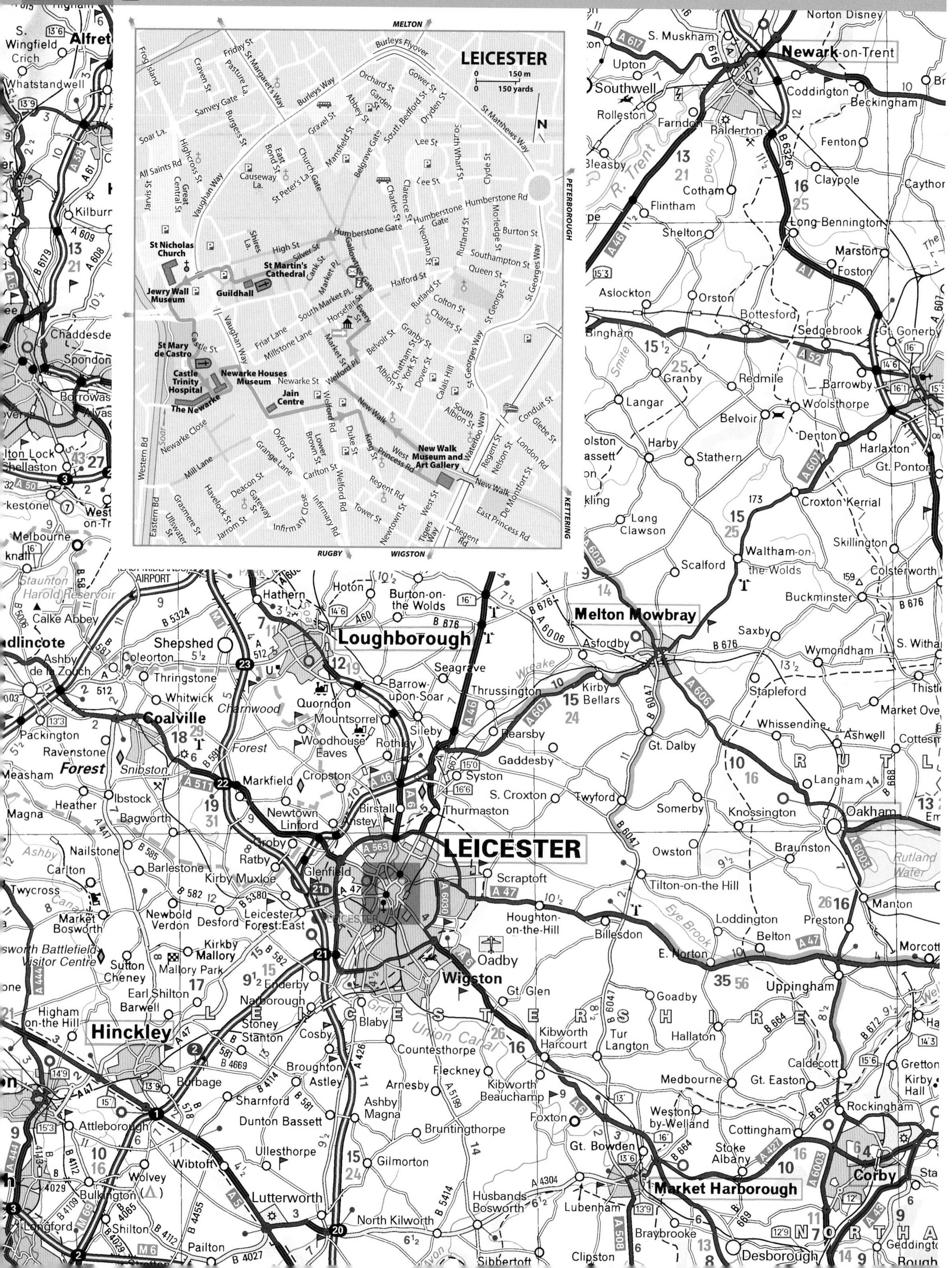
LEICESTER
150 m
150 yards
N
MELTON
PETERBOROUGH
KETTERING
RUGBY
WIGSTON
Burleys Flyover
St Matthews Way
Humberstone Gate
Humberstone Rd
High St
St Nicholas Church
St Martin's Cathedral
Guildhall
Jewry Wall Museum
St Mary de Castro
Castle Trinity Hospital
The Newarke
Newarke Houses Museum
Jain Centre
New Walk Museum and Art Gallery
New Walk
London Rd
Welford Rd
Vaughan Way
St Georges Way
Charles St
Granby St
Belgrave Gate
Church Gate
Mansfield St
Gallowtree Gate
Halford St
Rutland St
Western Bd
Mill Lane
Oxford St
Regent Rd
East Princess Rd
Mansfield
Eakring
Bilsthorpe
Maplebeck
Caunton
Collingham
Swinderby
Tibshelf
Huthwaite
Alfreton
S. Wingfield
Crich
Whatstandwell
Kilburn
Chaddesden
Spondon
Borrowash
Elvaston
Chellaston
Melbourne
Calke Abbey
Staunton Harold Reservoir
East Midlands Airport
Swadlincote
Ashby de la Zouch
Shepshed
Coleorton
Thringstone
Whitwick
Coalville
Charnwood Forest
Packington
Ravenstone
Measham
Snibston
Heather
Ibstock
Bagworth
Markfield
Nailstone
Barlestone
Carlton
Twycross
Market Bosworth
Newbold Verdon
Desford
Kirby Muxloe
Ratby
Groby
Glenfield
Leicester Forest East
Kirkby Mallory
Mallory Park
Bosworth Battlefield Visitor Centre
Sutton Cheney
Earl Shilton
Barwell
Higham on the Hill
Hinckley
Burbage
Sharnford
Attleborough
Wolvey
Bulkington
Shilton
Longford
Pailton
Wibtoft
Lutterworth
Ullesthorpe
Dunton Bassett
Gilmorton
Ashby Magna
Arnesby
Bruntingthorpe
Broughton Astley
Countesthorpe
Blaby
Cosby
Stoney Stanton
Narborough
Enderby
Fleckney
Kibworth Beauchamp
Kibworth Harcourt
Foxton
Husbands Bosworth
North Kilworth
Lubenham
Market Harborough
Gt. Bowden
Weston by-Welland
Medbourne
Gt. Easton
Caldecott
Cottingham
Rockingham
Corby
Stoke Albany
Braybrooke
Desborough
Clipston
Sibbertoft
Union Canal
Tur Langton
Hallaton
Goadby
Gt. Glen
Oadby
Wigston
Houghton-on-the-Hill
Scraptoft
Billesdon
Loddington
Tilton-on-the Hill
Owston
E. Norton
Belton
Uppingham
Preston
Manton
Braunston
Oakham
Rutland Water
Langham
Knossington
Somerby
Twyford
S. Croxton
Gaddesby
Thurmaston
Syston
Birstall
Anstey
Newtown Linford
Cropston
Woodhouse Eaves
Rothley
Mountsorrel
Quorndon
Sileby
Barrow-upon-Soar
Seagrave
Thrussington
Rearsby
Loughborough
Hathern
Hoton
Burton-on-the Wolds
Melton Mowbray
Asfordby
Kirby Bellars
Gt. Dalby
Saxby
Wymondham
Stapleford
Whissendine
Ashwell
Cottesmore
Market Overton
Buckminster
Colsterworth
Skillington
Waltham-on-the Wolds
Scalford
Long Clawson
Croxton Kerrial
Harlaxton
Gt. Ponton
Denton
Stathern
Harby
Belvoir
Woolsthorpe
Barrowby
Redmile
Granby
Langar
Bingham
Sedgebrook
Gt. Gonerby
Bottesford
Orston
Aslockton
Foston
Marston
Long Bennington
Shelton
Flintham
Cotham
Claypole
Fenton
Balderton
Farndon
Rolleston
Southwell
Upton
S. Muskham
Newark-on-Trent
Coddington
Beckingham
Norton Disney
Fleasby
R. Trent
LEICESTERSHIRE
RUTLAND
NORTHAMPTONSHIRE

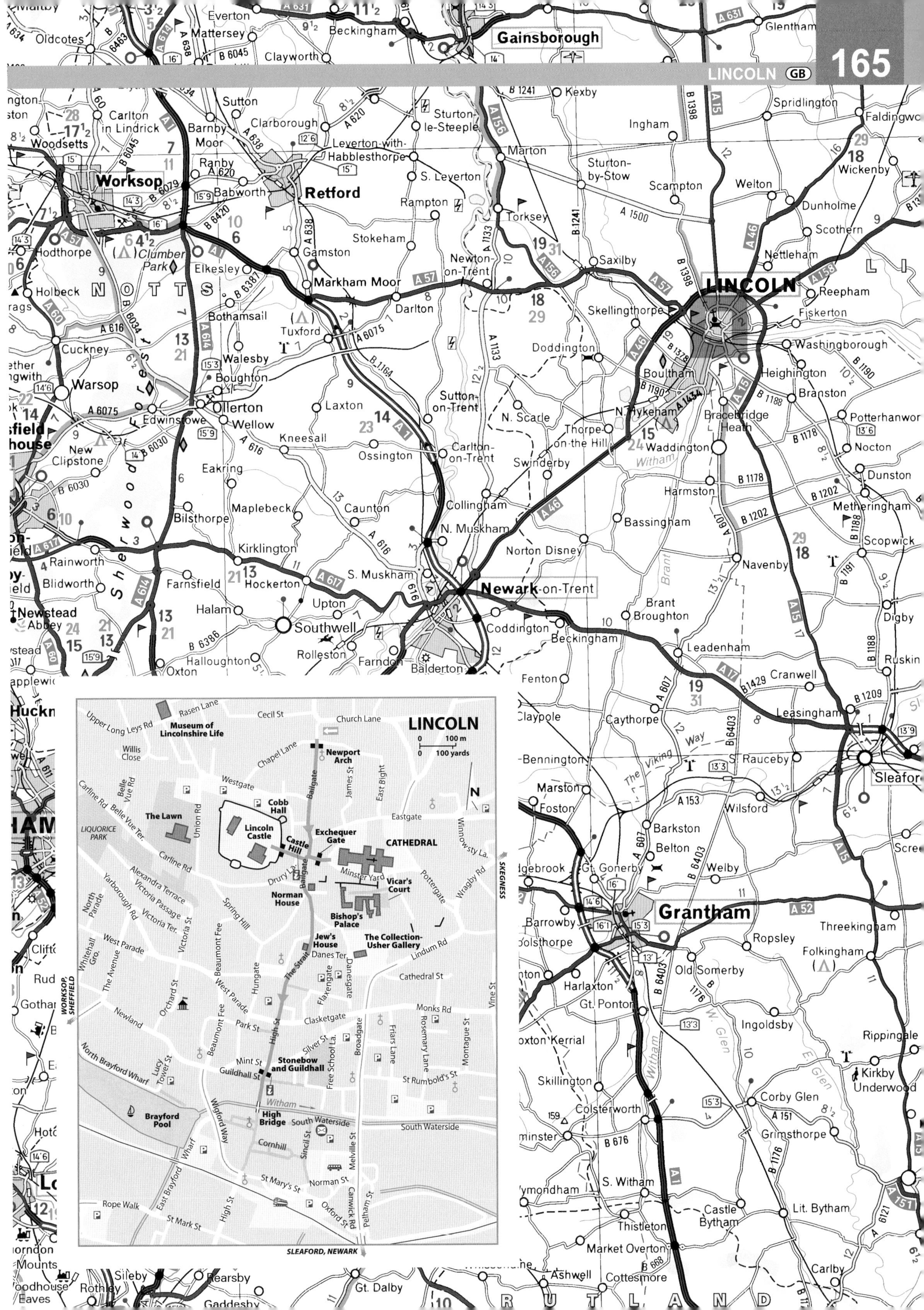
Oldcotes
Everton
Mattersey
Beckingham
Clayworth
Gainsborough
Glentham
Kexby
Spridlington
Faldingworth
Carlton in Lindrick
Woodsetts
Sutton
Barnby Moor
Clarborough
Sturton-le-Steeple
Ingham
Leverton-with-Habblesthorpe
Marton
Sturton-by-Stow
Scampton
Welton
Wickenby
Worksop
Ranby
Babworth
Retford
S. Leverton
Rampton
Torksey
Dunholme
Scothern
Hodthorpe
Clumber Park
Gamston
Stokeham
Newton-on-Trent
Saxilby
Nettleham
Elkesley
Markham Moor
Darlton
Holbeck
NOTTS
LINCOLN
Reepham
Bothamsall
Tuxford
Skellingthorpe
Fiskerton
Cuckney
Walesby
Doddington
Washingborough
Boughton
Boulthan
Heighington
Warsop
Branston
Laxton
Sutton-on-Trent
Ollerton
Edwinstowe
Wellow
N. Scarle
N. Hykeham
Bracebridge Heath
Potterhanworth
Kneesall
Thorpe-on-the Hill
New Clipstone
Ossington
Carlton-on-Trent
Waddington
Nocton
Swinderby
Witham
Eakring
Harmston
Dunston
Maplebeck
Caunton
Collingham
Metheringham
Bilsthorpe
Bassingham
Sherwood Forest
N. Muskham
Norton Disney
Scopwick
Rainworth
Kirklington
Navenby
Blidworth
Farnsfield
Hockerton
S. Muskham
Newark-on-Trent
Brant
Newstead Abbey
Halam
Upton
Brant Broughton
Digby
Southwell
Coddington
Beckingham
Rolleston
Leadenham
Farndon
Halloughton
Balderton
Ruskin
Oxton
Fenton
Cranwell
Claypole
Caythorpe
Leasingham
The Viking Way
Bennington
S. Rauceby
Sleaford
Marston
Foston
Wilsford
Barkston
Belton
Welby
Gt. Gonerby
Barrowby
Grantham
Threekingham
Ropsley
Folkingham
Harlaxton
Old Somerby
Gt. Ponton
Ingoldsby
Rippingale
W. Glen
E. Glen
Skillington
Kirkby Underwood
Colsterworth
Corby Glen
Grimsthorpe
S. Witham
Castle Bytham
Lit. Bytham
Thistleton
Market Overton
Ashwell
Cottesmore
Carlby
RUTLAND
Sileby
Rearsby
Rothley
Gt. Dalby
Gaddesby
LINCOLN
100 m
100 yards
Rasen Lane
Cecil St
Church Lane
Upper Long Leys Rd
Museum of Lincolnshire Life
Willis Close
Chapel Lane
Newport Arch
Westgate
Bailgate
James St
East Bight
Belle Vue Rd
Carline Rd
Belle Vue Ter.
Union Rd
Cobb Hall
The Lawn
Lincoln Castle
LIQUORICE PARK
Castle Hill
Exchequer Gate
Eastgate
CATHEDRAL
Wragby Rd
Winnowsty La.
Minster Yard
Vicar's Court
Pottergate
Alexandra Terrace
Victoria Passage
Yarborough Rd
Victoria Ter.
Drury La.
Norman House
Bishop's Palace
Spring Hill
North Parade
West Parade
Jew's House
Danes Ter.
The Collection-Usher Gallery
Lindum Rd
Whitehall Gro.
Victoria St
Beaumont Fee
Hungate
The Strait
Danesgate
Flaxengate
Cathedral St
The Avenue
Orchard St
Newland
Park St
Clasketgate
Monks Rd
Rosemary Lane
Montague St
Vine St
High St
Silver St
Broadgate
Friars Lane
North Brayford Wharf
Lucy Tower St
Mint St
Guildhall St
Stonebow and Guildhall
Free School La.
St Rumbold's St
Brayford Pool
Wigford Way
High Bridge
South Waterside
Cornhill
Sincil St
Melville St
St Mary's St
Norman St
Oxford St
Canwick Rd
Pelham St
Rope Walk
East Brayford
St Mark St
WORKSOP, SHEFFIELD
SKEGNESS
SLEAFORD, NEWARK

LIVERPOOL
CROSBY
PRESTON
MANCHESTER
WARRINGTON
WIDNES
LARK LANE, PALM HOUSE
ISLE OF MAN
SEACOMBE
BIRKENHEAD
WOODSIDE
MERSEY
World Museum
Walker Art Gallery
Central Library
St George's Hall
ST JOHN'S GARDEN
Western Approaches Museum
Statue of Eleanor Rigby
Royal Liver Building
British Music Experience
Cunard Building
PIER HEAD
Port of Liverpool Building
Open Eye Gallery
Museum of Liverpool
Merseyside Maritime Museum
ROYAL ALBERT DOCK
Tate Liverpool
Beatles Story
Liverpool One
Bluecoat Art Centre
CHAVASSE PARK
Metropolitan Cathedral of Christ the King
The Hardman's House
Chinese Arch
CHINATOWN
Liverpool Anglican Cathedral
BALTIC TRIANGLE QUARTER
Moorfields
Lime St
Central
James St
Waterloo Rd
Paisley St
Roberts St
Leeds St
Eaton St
Gascoyne St
Vauxhall Rd
Oriel St
Naylor St
Scotland Rd
Pall Mall
Midghall St
Marlborough St
Addison St
Byrom St
Byrom Way
Christian St
St Josephs Cres.
St Anne St
Soho St
Bidder St
John St
Canterbury St
Shaw St
Langsdale St
Salisbury St
North College St
South College St
Brunswick Rd
Walker St
Low Hill
Phythian St
New Islington
Devon St
Kempston St
Moss St
Epworth St
Prescot St
Hunter St
Lace St
Great Crosshall St
Highfield St
Old Leeds St
East St
Gibraltar Row
King Edward St
William Jessop Way
Bath St
Princes Parade
Brook St
Old Hall St
Bixteth St
Cheapside
Cunliffe St
Vernon St
Hatton Garden
Trueman St
North St
Fontenoy St
Fraser St
Norton St
Craven St
Stafford St
London Rd
Bridport St
Lord Nelson St
Seymour St
Hart St
Pembroke Pl.
Great Newton St
Gill St
Dansie St
Trowbridge St
Brownlow St
Dover St
Ashton St
Crown St
West Derby St
Minshull St
Smithdown La.
New Quay
Fazakerley St
Dale St
Crosshall St
Whitechapel
Victoria St
Stanley St
Temple St
Princes St
Rumford St
Lower Castle St
Fenwick St
Castle St
Cook St
North John St
Lord St
Williamson St
Tarleton St
Basnett St
Church St
School La.
Parker St
Copperas Hill
Lime St
Bolton St
Hawke St
Ranelagh Pl.
Ranelagh St
Brownlow Hill
Russell St
Pleasant St
Mount Pleasant
Peach St
Grove St
Red Cross St
Strand St
Queensway Tunnel
Paradise St
Hanover St
Wood St
Bold St
Renshaw St
Oldham St
Rodney St
Hope St
Arrad St
Mulberry St
Cambridge St
Oxford St
Melville Pl.
Canning Pl.
Duke St
Argyle St
Campbell Henry St
Slater St
Back Seel St
Parr St
Colquitt St
Seel St
Berry St
Hardman St
Myrtle St
Caledonia St
Chatham St
Salthouse Quay
Gower St
Wapping
Park Lane
Shaws All St
Gilbert St
Kent St
Upper Frederick St
Falkner St
Back Canning St
Little St
South Bedford St
Canning St
Little Canning St
Tabley St
Kings Dock St
Blundell St
Jamaica St
Kitchen St
Bridgewater St
Watkinson St
Norfolk St
Keel Wharf
Upper Pitt St
St James St
Great George St
Percy St
Huskisson St
Egerton St
Lowther St
Upper Parliament St
Upper Hampton St
Selborne St
Kings Parade
Queens Wharf
Chaloner St
Brick St
Jordan St
New Bird St
Greenland St
Flint St
Parliament St
St James Rd
Hampton St
Upper Stanhope St
Princes Rd
Windsor St
Bluefields St
Emerson St
Carter St
Gibson Rd
Princes Ave
Rosebery St
Mulgrave St
Halftide Wharf
0 300 m
0 300 yards

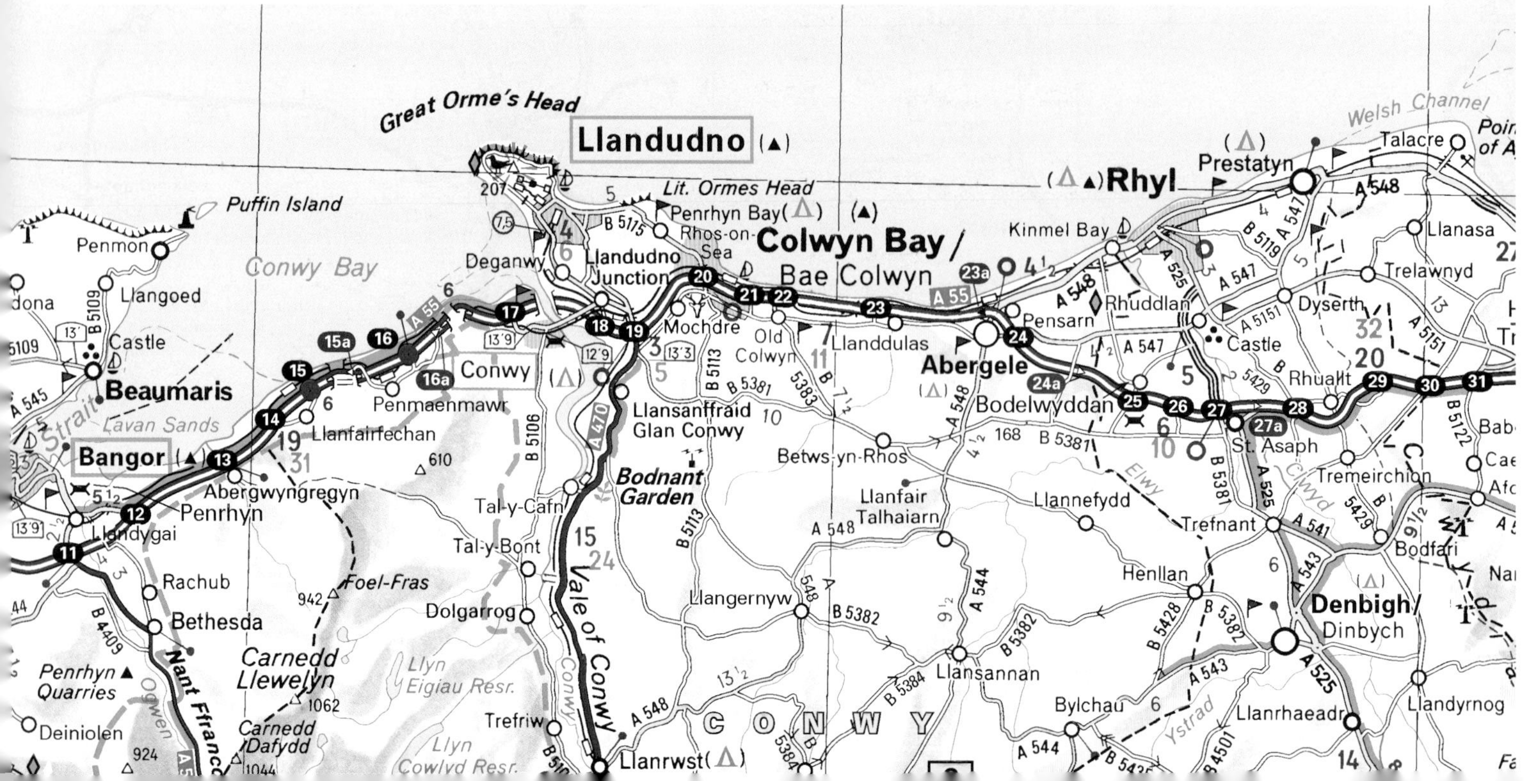
Great Orme's Head
Llandudno
Lit. Ormes Head
Welsh Channel
Talacre
Point of Ayr
Puffin Island
Penmon
Conwy Bay
Llangoed
Beaumaris
Castle
Lavan Sands
Bangor
Penrhyn
Llandygai
Rachub
Bethesda
Penrhyn Quarries
Deiniolen
Nant Ffrancon
Ogwen
Foel-Fras
Carnedd Llewelyn
Carnedd Dafydd
Llyn Eigiau Resr.
Llyn Cowlyd Resr.
Abergwyngregyn
Llanfairfechan
Penmaenmawr
Conwy
Deganwy
Llandudno Junction
Penrhyn Bay
Rhos-on-Sea
Colwyn Bay / Bae Colwyn
Mochdre
Old Colwyn
Llanddulas
Abergele
Pensarn
Kinmel Bay
Rhyl
Prestatyn
Rhuddlan
Dyserth
Llanasa
Trelawnyd
Castle
Rhuallt
Bodelwyddan
St. Asaph
Tremeirchion
Bodfari
Denbigh / Dinbych
Trefnant
Henllan
Llannefydd
Betws-yn-Rhos
Llanfair Talhaiarn
Llangernyw
Llansannan
Bylchau
Llanrhaeadr
Llandyrnog
Llansanffraid Glan Conwy
Bodnant Garden
Tal-y-Cafn
Tal-y-Bont
Dolgarrog
Vale of Conwy
Trefriw
Llanrwst
CONWY
Elwy
Clwyd
Ystrad
A 55
A 470
A 548
A 547
A 525
A 543
A 544
A 541
A 5151
A 545
B 5109
B 5106
B 5113
B 5115
B 5381
B 5383
B 5382
B 5384
B 5428
B 5429
B 5119
B 5122
B 4409
Foel-Fras 942
1062
1044
924
610

BLACKPOOL
PRESTON
BLACKBURN
Lytham St. Anne's
SOUTHPORT
Chorley
BOLTON
WIGAN
Skelmersdale
Ormskirk
Formby
Crosby
Bootle
Kirkby
ST. HELENS
LIVERPOOL
Wallasey
BIRKENHEAD
Bebington
Widnes
Runcorn
WARRINGTON
Ellesmere Port
CHESTER
Leigh
Hindley
Atherton
Golborne
Ashton-in-Makerfield
Leyland
Huyton
Roby
Hoylake
West Kirby
Heswall
Neston
Flint/Fflint
Connah's Quay
Queensferry
Mold
Frodsham
Northwich
Winsford
Kirkham
Fulwood
Maghull
Litherland
Halton
Lymm
Prescot
Newton-le-Willows
LIVERPOOL JOHN LENNON AIRPORT
Formby Point
Liverpool Bay
Dublin
Douglas (Isle of Man)
Belfast
R. Ribble
River Mersey
River Dee
Delamere Forest
FLINTS

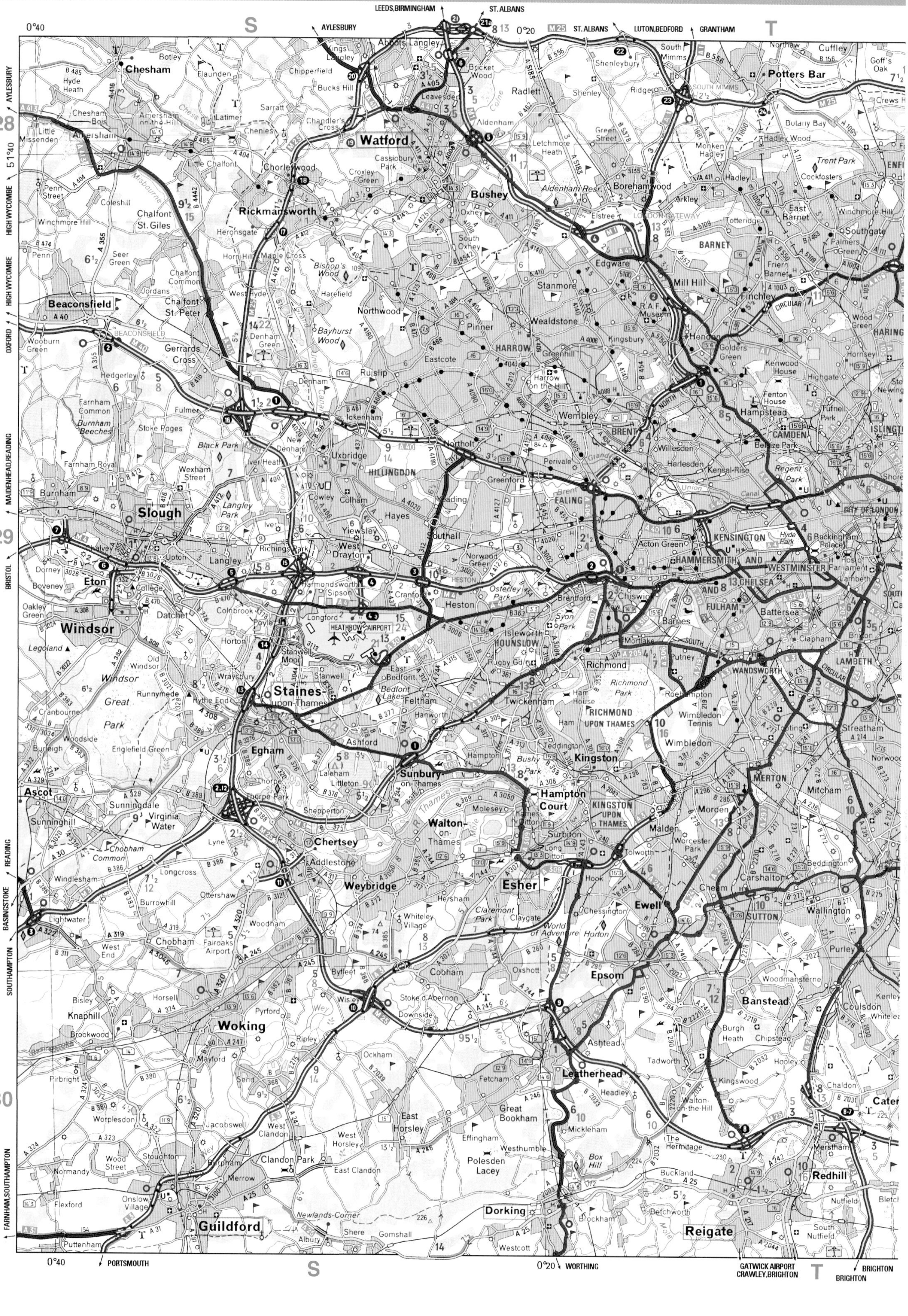
LEEDS, BIRMINGHAM
ST. ALBANS
AYLESBURY
LUTON, BEDFORD
GRANTHAM
S
T
28
29
30
Chesham
Amersham
Watford
Rickmansworth
Bushey
Radlett
Borehamwood
Potters Bar
Barnet
Edgware
Beaconsfield
Gerrards Cross
Harrow
Wembley
Hendon
Hampstead
Camden
Islington
Uxbridge
Hillingdon
Ealing
Slough
Eton
Windsor
Kensington
Hammersmith
Westminster
City of London
Chelsea
Fulham
Battersea
Lambeth
Wandsworth
Heathrow Airport
Hounslow
Richmond
Twickenham
Staines
Egham
Sunbury
Kingston
Wimbledon
Merton
Ascot
Chertsey
Walton-on-Thames
Esher
Weybridge
Epsom
Ewell
Sutton
Woking
Leatherhead
Banstead
Guildford
Dorking
Reigate
Redhill
PORTSMOUTH
WORTHING
GATWICK AIRPORT
CRAWLEY, BRIGHTON
BRIGHTON
0°40
0°20
51°40
AYLESBURY
HIGH WYCOMBE
OXFORD
MAIDENHEAD, READING
BRISTOL
READING
BASINGSTOKE
SOUTHAMPTON
FARNHAM, SOUTHAMPTON

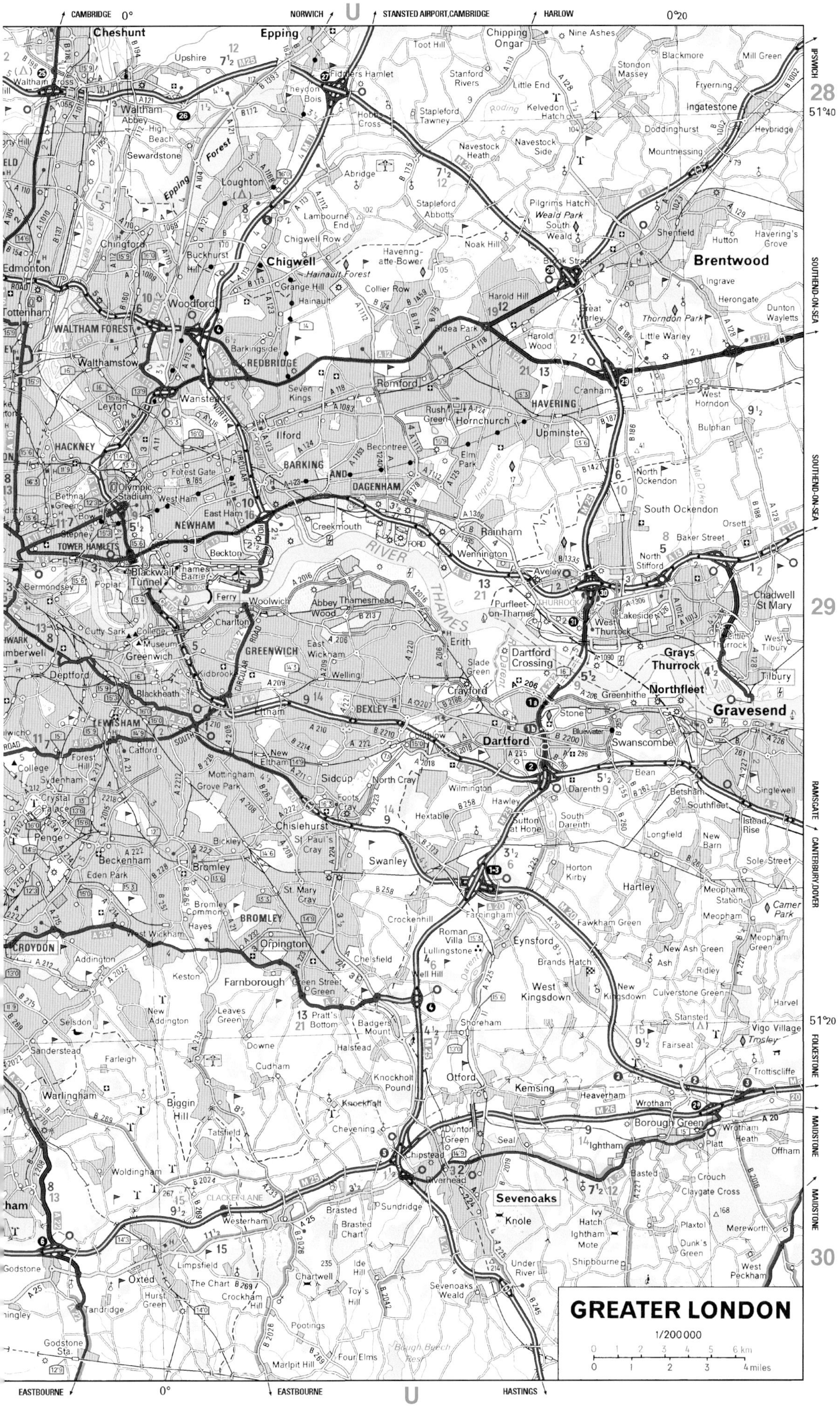

LAMBETH Borough

Underground station

Greater London Boroughs

Barking and Dagenham	105	U 29
Barnet	104	T 29
Bexley	105	U 29
Brent	104	T 29
Bromley	105	U 29
Camden	104	T 29
City of London	104	T 29
Croydon	104	T 29
Ealing	104	T 29
Enfield	104	T 29
Greenwich	105	U 29
Hackney	105	T 29
Hammersmith and Fulham	104	T 29
Haringey	104	T 29
Harrow	104	S 29
Havering	105	U 29
Hillingdon	104	S 29
Hounslow	104	S 29
Islington	104	T 29
Kensington and Chelsea	104	T29
Kingston-upon-Thames	104	T 29
Lambeth	104	T 29
Lewisham	105	T 29
Merton	104	T 29
Newham	105	U 29
Redbridge	105	U 29
Richmond-upon-Thames	104	T 29
Southwark	104	T 29
Sutton	104	T 29
Tower Hamlets	105	T 29
Waltham Forest	105	T 29
Wandsworth	104	T 29
Westminster	104	T 29

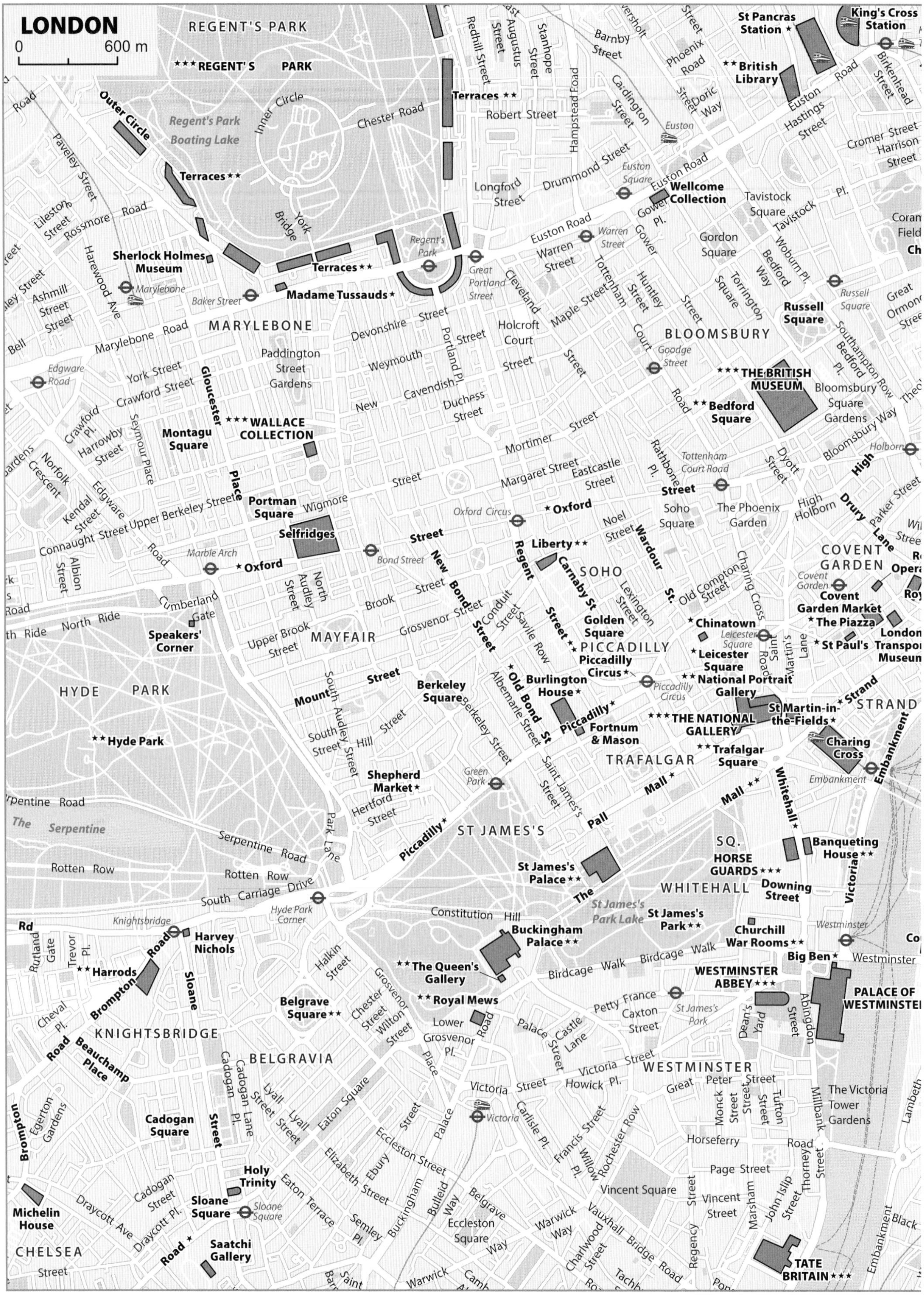
LONDON
0 600 m
REGENT'S PARK
*** REGENT'S PARK
Regent's Park Boating Lake
Outer Circle
Inner Circle
Chester Road
York Bridge
Terraces **
Terraces **
Terraces **
Sherlock Holmes Museum
Madame Tussauds *
Marylebone
Baker Street
Regent's Park
Great Portland Street
MARYLEBONE
*** WALLACE COLLECTION
Montagu Square
Portman Square
Selfridges
Marble Arch
* Oxford
Bond Street
Oxford Circus
* Oxford
Street
Liberty **
Carnaby St
SOHO
Golden Square
** PICCADILLY
Piccadilly Circus *
Burlington House *
Fortnum & Mason
Piccadilly *
Speakers' Corner
HYDE PARK
** Hyde Park
The Serpentine
Serpentine Road
Rotten Row
South Carriage Drive
Hyde Park Corner
Knightsbridge
Harvey Nichols
** Harrods
KNIGHTSBRIDGE
BELGRAVIA
Belgrave Square **
** Royal Mews
** The Queen's Gallery
Buckingham Palace **
St James's Palace **
ST JAMES'S
St James's Park Lake
St James's Park **
Green Park
Shepherd Market *
MAYFAIR
Berkeley Square
BLOOMSBURY
*** THE BRITISH MUSEUM
** Bedford Square
Russell Square
** British Library
St Pancras Station *
King's Cross Station
Euston
Euston Square
Wellcome Collection
Warren Street
Goodge Street
Tottenham Court Road
Soho Square
The Phoenix Garden
Holborn
COVENT GARDEN
Covent Garden
Covent Garden Market
* The Piazza
London Transport Museum
* St Paul's
* Chinatown
* Leicester Square
Leicester Square
** National Portrait Gallery
*** THE NATIONAL GALLERY
St Martin-in-the-Fields *
* Strand
STRAND
Charing Cross
Embankment
TRAFALGAR
** Trafalgar Square
Mall **
The Mall *
Pall Mall
Whitehall *
Banqueting House **
HORSE GUARDS SQ. ***
WHITEHALL
Downing Street
Churchill War Rooms **
Westminster
Big Ben *
WESTMINSTER ABBEY ***
PALACE OF WESTMINSTER
St James's Park
WESTMINSTER
The Victoria Tower Gardens
Victoria
Vincent Square
TATE BRITAIN ***
Saatchi Gallery
Holy Trinity
Sloane Square
Cadogan Square
Michelin House
CHELSEA
Euston Road
Marylebone Road
Baker Street
Gloucester Place
Wigmore Street
Oxford Street
New Bond Street
Old Bond St
Regent Street
Park Lane
Piccadilly
Constitution Hill
Birdcage Walk
Brompton Road
Sloane Street
Victoria Street
Tottenham Court Road
Gower Street
Charing Cross Road
Wardour St.
Shaftesbury Avenue
Drury Lane
High Holborn
Southampton Row
Kingsway
Millbank
Horseferry Road
Vauxhall Bridge Road
Eccleston Street
Ebury Street
Grosvenor Place
Belgrave Road

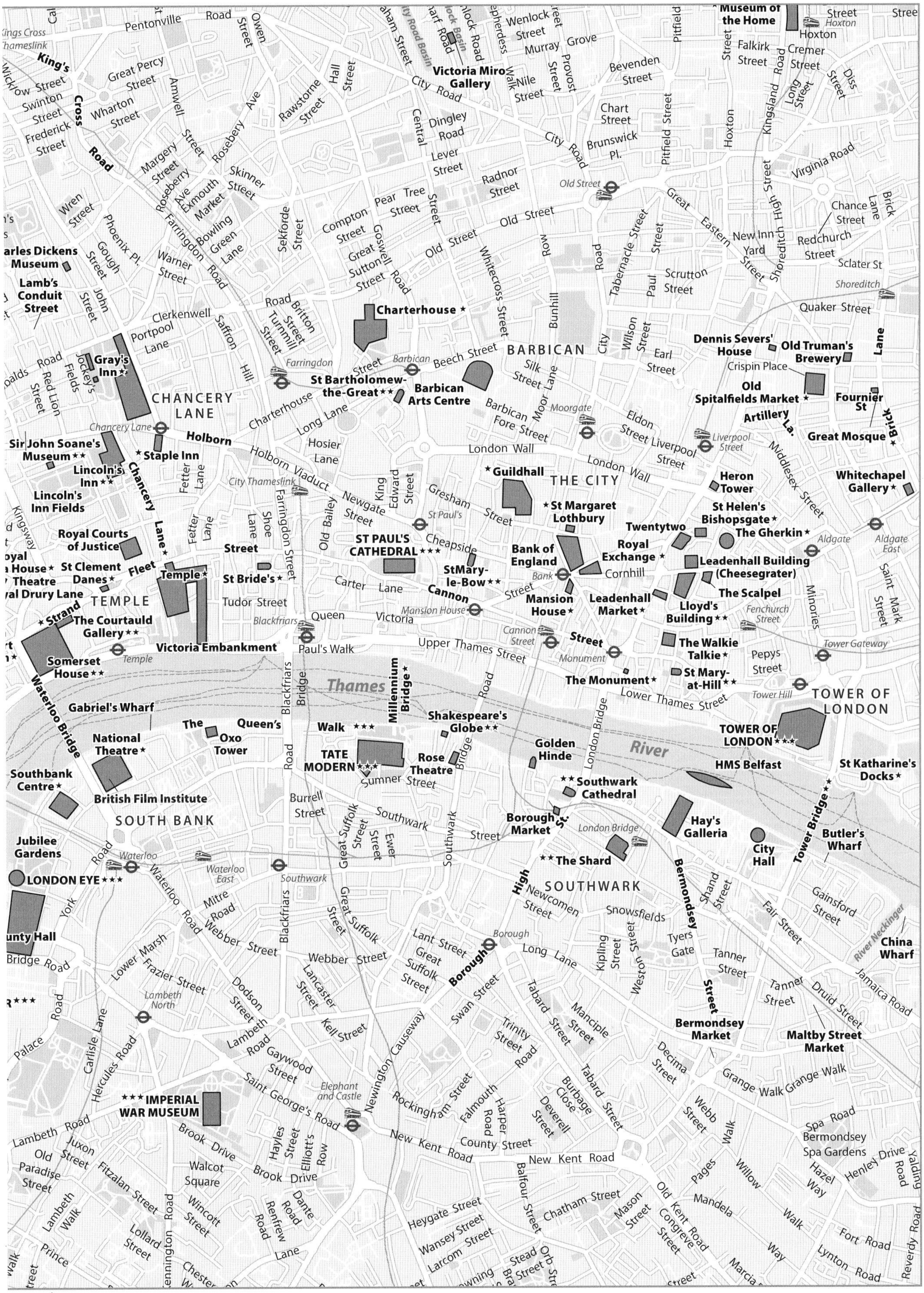

King's Cross Thameslink
King's Cross
Pentonville Road
Museum of the Home
Hoxton
Victoria Miro Gallery
City Road
Old Street
Charles Dickens Museum
Lamb's Conduit Street
Charterhouse
BARBICAN
Farringdon
Barbican
Gray's Inn
CHANCERY LANE
St Bartholomew-the-Great
Barbican Arts Centre
Dennis Severs' House
Old Truman's Brewery
Old Spitalfields Market
Fournier St
Great Mosque
Sir John Soane's Museum
Staple Inn
Lincoln's Inn
Lincoln's Inn Fields
Holborn
Chancery Lane
Moorgate
Liverpool Street
Guildhall
THE CITY
St Margaret Lothbury
Heron Tower
Whitechapel Gallery
St Helen's Bishopsgate
Twentytwo
The Gherkin
Royal Courts of Justice
ST PAUL'S CATHEDRAL
Bank of England
Royal Exchange
Leadenhall Building (Cheesegrater)
Aldgate
Aldgate East
St Clement Danes
Temple
St Bride's
StMary-le-Bow
Mansion House
Leadenhall Market
Lloyd's Building
The Scalpel
TEMPLE
Strand
The Courtauld Gallery
Blackfriars
Cannon Street
Monument
The Walkie Talkie
Somerset House
Victoria Embankment
Upper Thames Street
The Monument
St Mary-at-Hill
Tower Gateway
Tower Hill
TOWER OF LONDON
Thames
River
Millennium Bridge
Waterloo Bridge
Gabriel's Wharf
The Oxo Tower
Queen's Walk
Shakespeare's Globe
National Theatre
TATE MODERN
Rose Theatre
Golden Hinde
HMS Belfast
St Katharine's Docks
Southbank Centre
British Film Institute
Southwark Cathedral
SOUTH BANK
Borough Market
London Bridge
Hay's Galleria
City Hall
Tower Bridge
Butler's Wharf
Jubilee Gardens
LONDON EYE
Waterloo
Waterloo East
Southwark
The Shard
SOUTHWARK
County Hall
Borough
China Wharf
River Neckinger
Lambeth North
Bermondsey Market
Maltby Street Market
Elephant and Castle
IMPERIAL WAR MUSEUM
Spa Road
Bermondsey Spa Gardens
New Kent Road
Old Kent Road

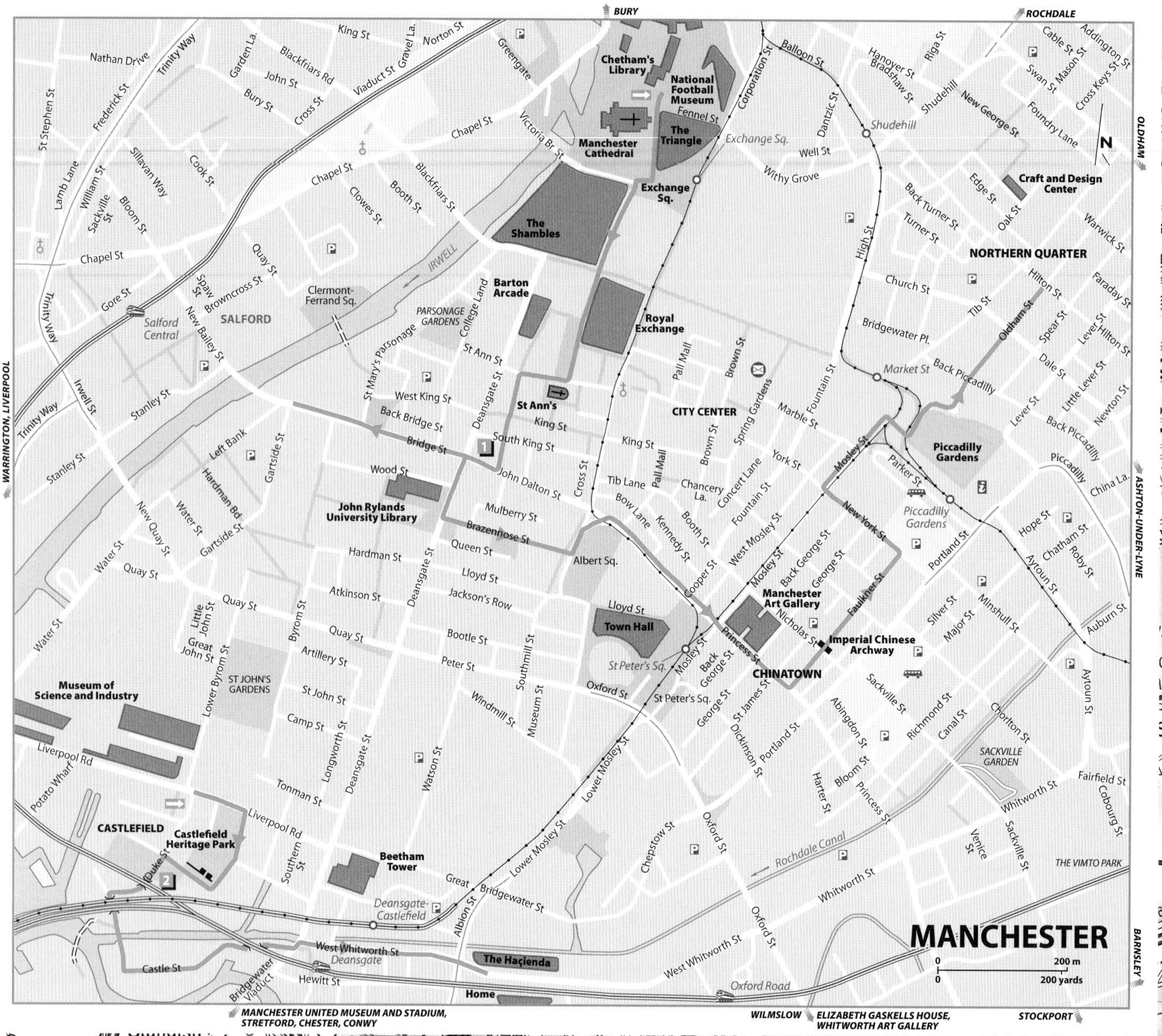
MANCHESTER
BURY
ROCHDALE
OLDHAM
ASHTON-UNDER-LYNE
BARNSLEY
STOCKPORT
WILMSLOW
ELIZABETH GASKELLS HOUSE, WHITWORTH ART GALLERY
MANCHESTER UNITED MUSEUM AND STADIUM, STRETFORD, CHESTER, CONWY
WARRINGTON, LIVERPOOL
Chetham's Library
National Football Museum
Manchester Cathedral
The Triangle
Exchange Sq.
The Shambles
Barton Arcade
Royal Exchange
St Ann's
John Rylands University Library
Town Hall
Manchester Art Gallery
Imperial Chinese Archway
Craft and Design Center
NORTHERN QUARTER
CITY CENTER
CHINATOWN
SALFORD
CASTLEFIELD
Piccadilly Gardens
Museum of Science and Industry
Castlefield Heritage Park
Beetham Tower
The Haçienda
Home
ST JOHN'S GARDENS
PARSONAGE GARDENS
SACKVILLE GARDEN
THE VIMTO PARK
Salford Central
Deansgate-Castlefield
Deansgate
Oxford Road
Piccadilly
Market St
Shudehill
St Peter's Sq.
IRWELL
Rochdale Canal
Clermont-Ferrand Sq.
Albert Sq.
Deansgate
Oxford St
Oxford Road
Portland St
Princess St
Mosley St
Whitworth St
Great Bridgewater St
Liverpool Rd
Quay St
Peter St
King St
Market St
Corporation St
High St
Oldham St
Chapel St
Bridge St
Hanging Ditch
0 200 m
0 200 yards

BOLTON
WIGAN
Skelmersdale
Westhoughton
Farnworth
Heywood
Middleton
OLDHAM
Radcliffe
Whitefield
Prestwich
Chadderton
Failsworth
Ashton-under-Lyne
Mossley
Stalybridge
Hindley
Atherton
Leigh
Ince-in-Makerfield
Ashton-in-Makerfield
Tyldesley
Worsley
Eccles
SALFORD
MANCHESTER
Golborne
Urmston
Stretford
Audenshaw
Denton
Dukinfield
Hyde
Newton-le-Willows
Haydock
Culcheth
Irlam
Cadishead
Partington
Sale
Altrincham
Hale
Gatley
Cheadle
STOCKPORT
Bredbury
Romiley
Marple
Hazel Grove
Bramhall
Disley
New Mills
Hayfield
WARRINGTON
Woolston
Grappenhall
Lymm
High Legh
Penketh
Great Sankey
Prescot
Rainford
Billinge
Winwick
Burtonwood
Fearnhead
Walkden
Kearsley
Pendlebury
Little Lever
Shevington
Aspull
Blackrod
Newburgh
Up Holland
Orrell
Abram
Withington
Heald Green
Handforth
Poynton
Shaw
Royton
Delph
Uppermill
Greenfield
Lees
Tintwistle
Hollingworth
Hadfield
Denshaw
M 60
M 62
M 6
M 61
M 56
A 580
A 6
A 34
A 62

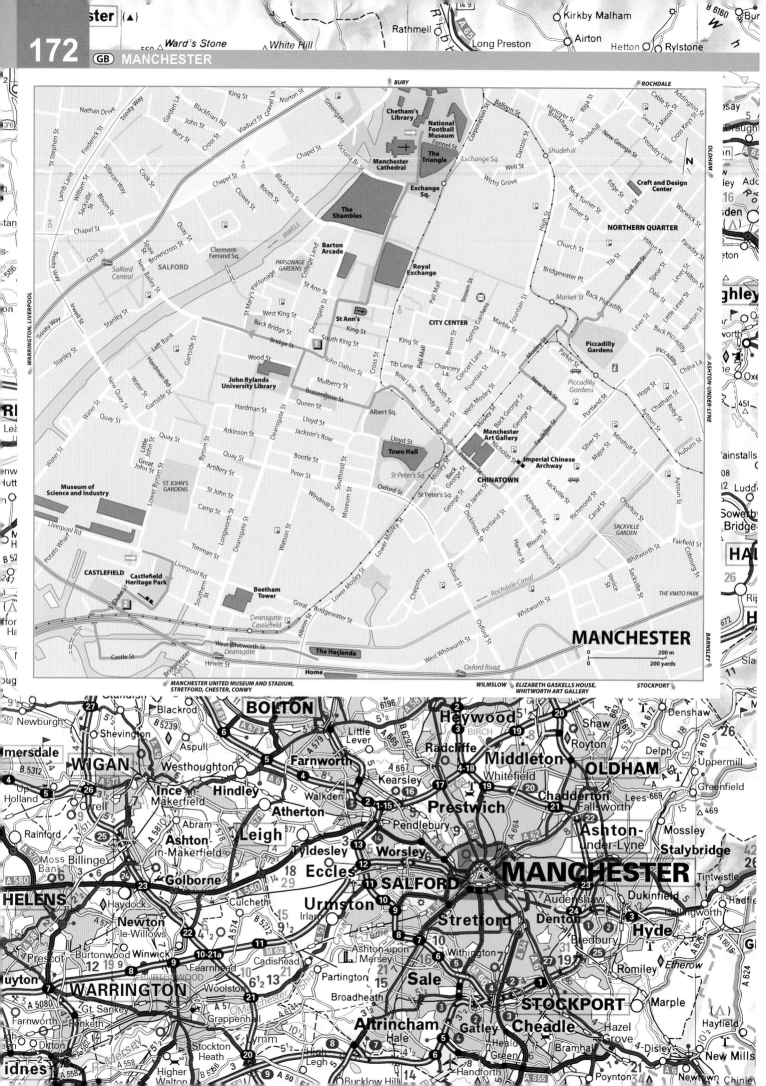

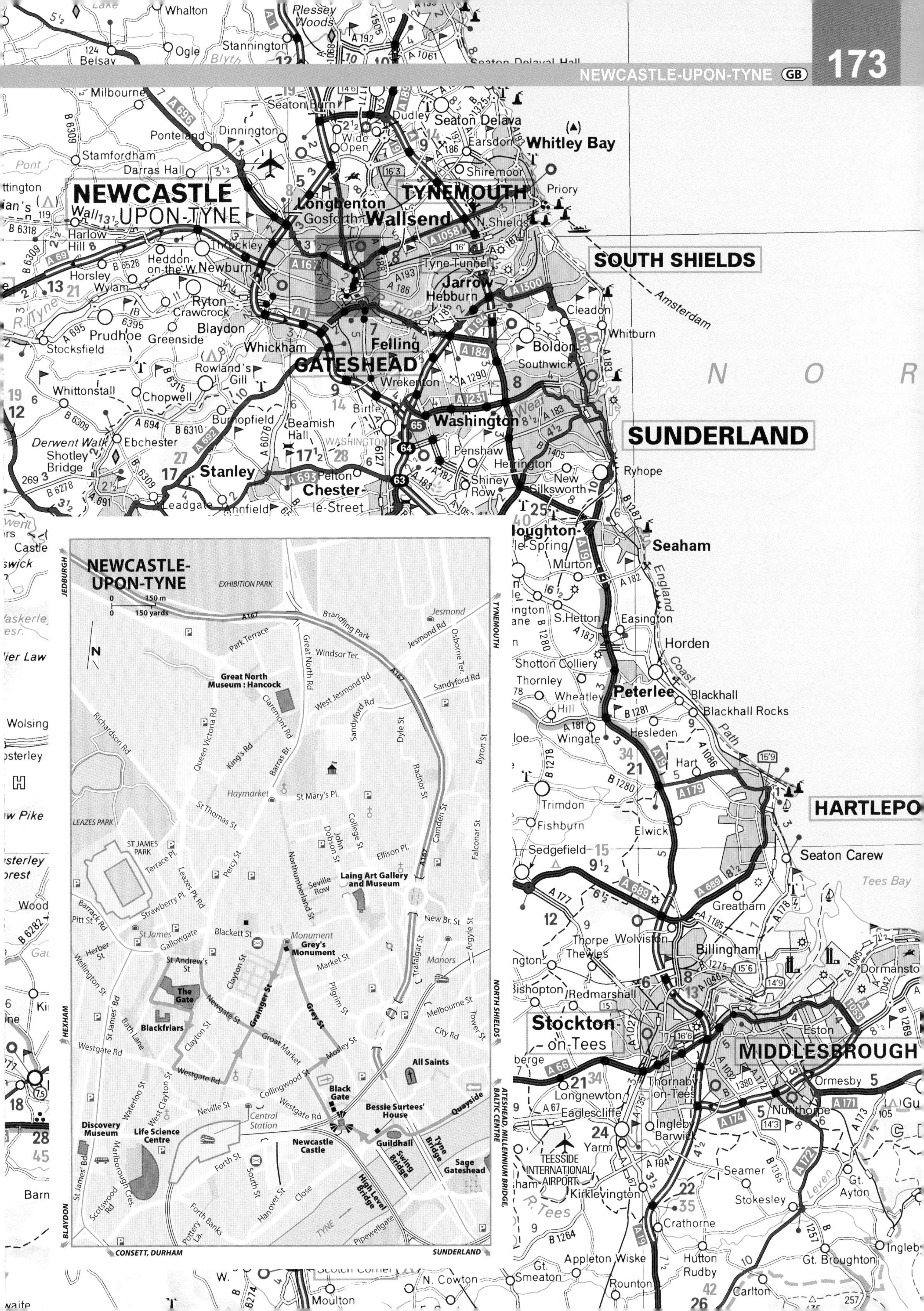
NEWCASTLE UPON TYNE
TYNEMOUTH
Whitley Bay
SOUTH SHIELDS
GATESHEAD
SUNDERLAND
HARTLEPO
Stockton-on-Tees
MIDDLESBROUGH
Longbenton
Gosforth
Wallsend
Jarrow
Hebburn
Felling
Washington
Chester-le-Street
Stanley
Houghton-le-Spring
Seaham
Peterlee
Billingham
Whalton
Stannington
Ogle
Belsay
Plessey Woods
Seaton Delaval Hall
Milbourne
Seaton Burn
Dudley
Seaton Delava
Earsdon
Ponteland
Dinnington
Wide Open
Shiremoor
Stamfordham
Darras Hall
Priory
N. Shields
Harlow Hill
Throckley
Heddon-on-the-W.
Newburn
Horsley
Wylam
Tyne Tunnel
Ryton
Crawcrook
Blaydon
Whickham
Prudhoe
Greenside
Stocksfield
Cleadon
Whitburn
Boldon
Southwick
Amsterdam
Rowland's Gill
Wrekenton
Whittonstall
Chopwell
Birtley
Burnopfield
Beamish Hall
Derwent Walk
Ebchester
Shotley Bridge
Penshaw
Herrington
Ryhope
New Silksworth
Shiney Row
Pelton
Leadgate
Annfield
Murton
S.Hetton
Easington
Horden
Shotton Colliery
Thornley
Wheatley Hill
Blackhall
Blackhall Rocks
Hesleden
Wingate
Hart
Trimdon
Fishburn
Elwick
Sedgefield
Seaton Carew
Tees Bay
Greatham
Wolviston
Thorpe Thewles
Redmarshall
Bishopton
Dormanston
Eston
Ormesby
Thornaby-on-Tees
Longnewton
Eaglescliffe
Ingleby Barwick
Nunthorpe
Yarm
TEESSIDE INTERNATIONAL AIRPORT
Kirklevington
Seamer
Stokesley
Gt. Ayton
Crathorne
Appleton Wiske
Hutton Rudby
Gt. Broughton
Gt. Smeaton
Rounton
Carlton
N. Cowton
Moulton
Wolsing
Castle
NEWCASTLE-UPON-TYNE
EXHIBITION PARK
JEDBURGH
TYNEMOUTH
NORTH SHIELDS
GATESHEAD, MILLENNIUM BRIDGE, BALTIC CENTRE
HEXHAM
BLAYDON
CONSETT, DURHAM
SUNDERLAND
150 m
150 yards
Brandling Park
Jesmond
Jesmond Rd
Osborne Ter.
Park Terrace
Windsor Ter.
Great North Rd
Sandyford Rd
West Jesmond Rd
Great North Museum : Hancock
Claremont Rd
Richardson Rd
Queen Victoria Rd
King's Rd
Barras Br.
Dyle St
Byron St
Radnor St
Haymarket
St Mary's Pl.
St Thomas St
LEAZES PARK
ST JAMES PARK
Terrace Pl.
Percy St
John Dobson St
College St
Ellison Pl.
Camden St
Falconar St
Leazes Pk Rd
Northumberland St
Seville Row
Laing Art Gallery and Museum
Strawberry Pl.
Barrack Rd
Pitt St
St James
Gallowgate
Blackett St
Monument
Grey's Monument
Market St
New Br. St
Argyle St
Herber St
Wellington St
St Andrew's St
Clayton St
Grainger St
Manors
Trafalgar St
Pilgrim St
Melbourne St
The Gate
Blackfriars
Newgate St
Grey St
City Rd
Tower St
St James' Bd
Bath Lane
Groat Market
Mosley St
Westgate Rd
All Saints
Waterloo St
West Clayton St
Collingwood St
Neville St
Central Station
Black Gate
Bessie Surtees' House
Quayside
Discovery Museum
Life Science Centre
Newcastle Castle
Guildhall
Tyne Bridge
Swing Bridge
Sage Gateshead
Forth St
South St
Hanover St
Close
High Level Bridge
Marlborough Cres.
Scotswood Rd
Forth Banks
Pottery La.
TYNE
Pipewellgate

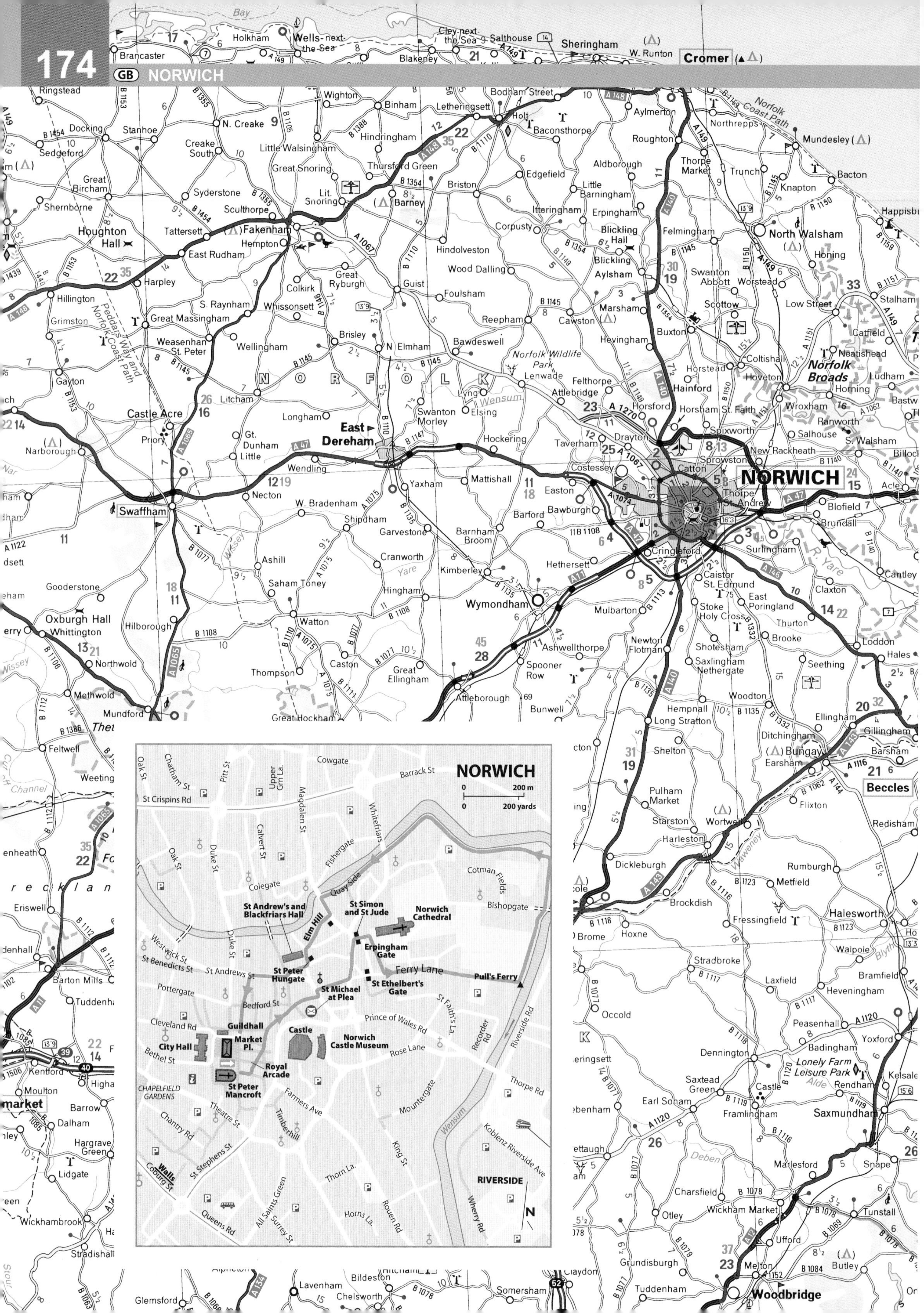
NORWICH
0 200 m
0 200 yards
St Andrew's and Blackfriars Hall
St Simon and St Jude
Norwich Cathedral
Erpingham Gate
Ferry Lane
Pull's Ferry
St Peter Hungate
St Ethelbert's Gate
St Michael at Plea
Guildhall
Market Pl.
City Hall
Castle
Norwich Castle Museum
Royal Arcade
St Peter Mancroft
CHAPELFIELD GARDENS
RIVERSIDE
Walls
Elm Hill
Quay Side
Cowgate
Barrack St
Whitefriars
Magdalen St
Fishergate
Colegate
Cotman Fields
Bishopgate
Riverside Rd
Recorder Rd
Rose Lane
Prince of Wales Rd
St Faith's La.
Thorpe Rd
Koblenz Riverside Ave
Wherry Rd
Rouen Rd
King St
Mountergate
Timberhill
Farmers Ave
Theatre St
Chantry Rd
St Stephens St
Queens Rd
All Saints Green
Surrey St
Thorn La.
Horns La.
Bethel St
Cleveland Rd
Pottergate
Bedford St
St Andrews St
St Benedicts St
Westwick St
Duke St
Calvert St
Oak St
Chatham St
Pitt St
St Crispins Rd
Upper Grn La.
Coburg St
Wensum
N
NORWICH
Cromer
Sheringham
Wells-next-the-Sea
Fakenham
East Dereham
Swaffham
Wymondham
Aylsham
North Walsham
Norfolk Broads
Beccles
Bungay
Halesworth
Saxmundham
Woodbridge
Framlingham
Attleborough
Castle Acre
Houghton Hall
Oxburgh Hall
N O R F O L K

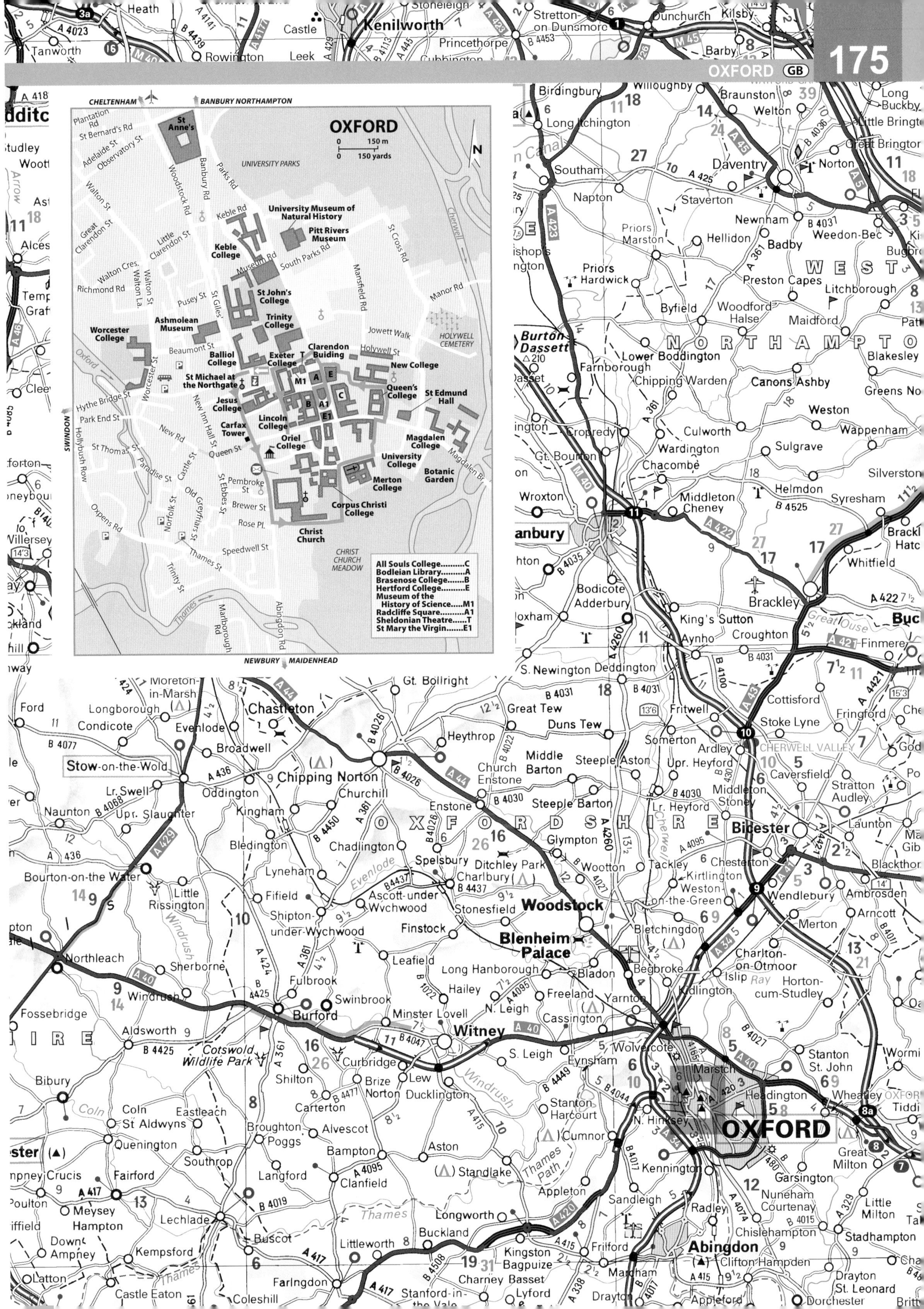
OXFORD
0 150 m
0 150 yards
N
CHELTENHAM
BANBURY NORTHAMPTON
SWINDON
NEWBURY MAIDENHEAD
St Anne's
UNIVERSITY PARKS
University Museum of Natural History
Pitt Rivers Museum
Keble College
St John's College
Trinity College
Ashmolean Museum
Worcester College
Balliol College
Exeter College
Clarendon Buiding
New College
St Michael at the Northgate
Queen's College
St Edmund Hall
Jesus College
Lincoln College
Carfax Tower
Oriel College
Magdalen College
University College
Botanic Garden
Merton College
Corpus Christi College
Christ Church
CHRIST CHURCH MEADOW
HOLYWELL CEMETERY
Pembroke St
All Souls College..........C
Bodleian Library..........A
Brasenose College.......B
Hertford College..........E
Museum of the History of Science.....M1
Radcliffe Square..........A1
Sheldonian Theatre......T
St Mary the Virgin.......E1
Kenilworth
Daventry
Banbury
Brackley
Bicester
Chipping Norton
Stow-on-the-Wold
Woodstock
Blenheim Palace
Witney
Burford
OXFORD
Abingdon
NORTHAMPTON
OXFORDSHIRE
Chastleton
Northleach
Bourton-on-the Water
Kidlington
Headington
Wheatley
Faringdon
Lechlade
Fairford
Bampton
Eynsham
Kennington
Radley
Deddington
Adderbury
Bodicote
Great Tew
Charlbury
Chadlington
Shipton-under-Wychwood
Carterton
Cotswold Wildlife Park
Thames
Cherwell
Windrush
Evenlode
A 40
A 44
A 34
A 361
A 420
A 415
A 417
A 423
A 422
A 43
M 40
M 45

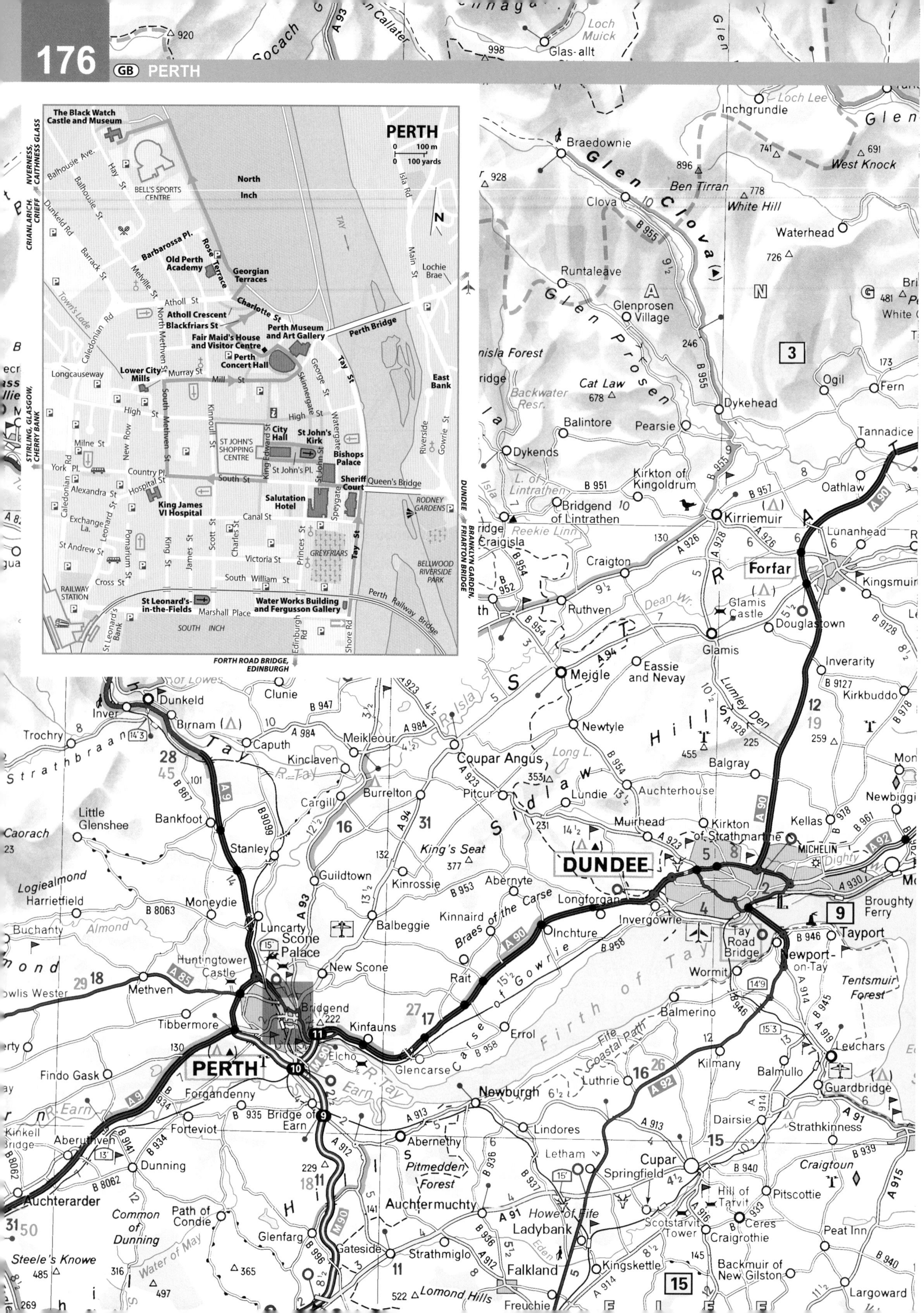
PERTH
0 100 m
0 100 yards
N
The Black Watch Castle and Museum
BELL'S SPORTS CENTRE
North Inch
Balhousie Ave.
Hay St
Balhousie St
Dunkeld Rd
Barrack St
Melville St
Barbarossa Pl.
Rose Terrace
Old Perth Academy
Georgian Terraces
Charlotte St
Atholl St
Atholl Crescent
Blackfriars St
Fair Maid's House and Visitor Centre
Perth Museum and Art Gallery
Perth Bridge
Perth Concert Hall
Town's Lade
Caledonian Rd
North Methven St
Lower City Mills
Murray St
Mill St
Longcauseway
High St
Kinnoull St
George St
Skinnergate
Tay St
City Hall
St John's Kirk
Bishops Palace
ST JOHN'S SHOPPING CENTRE
King Edward St
St John's Pl.
St John St
Watergate
Sheriff Court
Queen's Bridge
South St
South Methven St
New Row
Milne St
York Pl.
Country Pl.
Alexandra St
Hospital St
King James VI Hospital
Salutation Hotel
Speygate
Canal St
Exchange La.
Leonard St
Pomarium St
King St
James St
Scott St
Charles St
Princes St
GREYFRIARS
St Andrew St
Victoria St
South William St
Cross St
RAILWAY STATION
St Leonard's-in-the-Fields
Marshall Place
Water Works Building and Fergusson Gallery
SOUTH INCH
St Leonard's Bank
Edinburgh Rd
Shore Rd
Perth Railway Bridge
Isla Rd
Main St
Lochie Brae
East Bank
Riverside
Gowrie St
RODNEY GARDENS
BELLWOOD RIVERSIDE PARK
TAY
INVERNESS, CAITHNESS GLASS
CRIANLARICH, CRIEFF
STIRLING, GLASGOW, CHERRY BANK
DUNDEE
BRANKLYN GARDEN, FRIARTON BRIDGE
FORTH ROAD BRIDGE, EDINBURGH
Loch Muick
Glas-allt
Inchgrundle
Loch Lee
Glen Clova
Braedownie
Ben Tirran
White Hill
West Knock
Clova
Waterhead
Runtaleave
Glen Prosen
Glenprosen Village
3
Cat Law
Backwater Resr.
Dykehead
Ogil
Fern
Balintore
Pearsie
Tannadice
Dykends
Kirkton of Kingoldrum
Oathlaw
Bridgend of Lintrathen
Kirriemuir
Lunanhead
Reekie Linn
Craigisla
Craigton
Forfar
Kingsmuir
Ruthven
Glamis Castle
Douglastown
Glamis
Inverarity
Meigle
Eassie and Nevay
Kirkbuddo
Dunkeld
Clunie
Inver
Birnam
Trochry
Caputh
Meikleour
Kinclaven
Coupar Angus
Newtyle
Sidlaw Hills
Balgray
Lumley Den
Little Glenshee
Bankfoot
Cargill
Burrelton
Pitcur
Lundie
Auchterhouse
Newbigging
Kellas
Muirhead
Kirkton of Strathmartine
DUNDEE
MICHELIN
Stanley
King's Seat
Guildtown
Kinrossie
Abernyte
Logiealmond
Harrietfield
Moneydie
Braes of the Carse
Longforgan
Broughty Ferry
Invergowrie
Kinnaird
Luncarty
Scone Palace
Balbeggie
Inchture
Tay Road Bridge
Tayport
Buchanty
Huntingtower Castle
New Scone
Rait
Newport-on-Tay
Wormit
Tentsmuir Forest
Methven
Carse of Gowrie
Firth of Tay
Bridgend
Kinfauns
Balmerino
Tibbermore
Errol
Leuchars
PERTH
Elcho
Fife Coastal Path
Kilmany
Findo Gask
Glencarse
Luthrie
Balmullo
Guardbridge
Forgandenny
Newburgh
Bridge of Earn
Forteviot
Aberuthven
Abernethy
Lindores
Dairsie
Strathkinness
Dunning
Pitmedden Forest
Letham
Springfield
Cupar
Craigtoun
Auchterarder
Auchtermuchty
Hill of Tarvit
Pitscottie
Common of Dunning
Path of Condie
Howe of Fife
Ladybank
Scotstarvit Tower
Ceres
Craigrothie
Peat Inn
Glenfarg
Water of May
Steele's Knowe
Gateside
Strathmiglo
Falkland
Kingskettle
Backmuir of New Gilston
Lomond Hills
Freuchie
Largoward
15

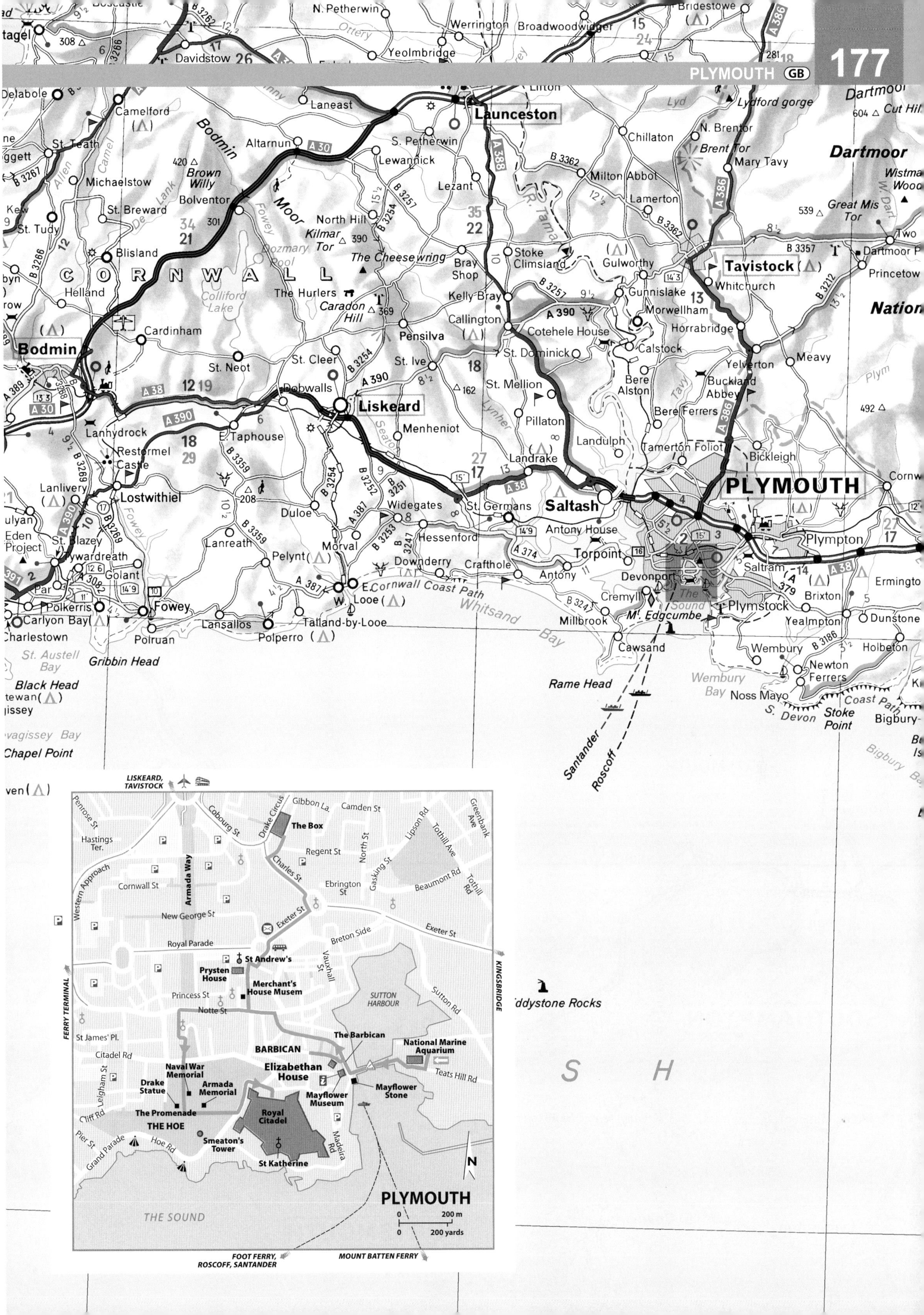
N. Petherwin
Bridestowe
Werrington
Broadwoodwidger
Yeolmbridge
Davidstow
Delabole
Camelford
Laneast
Launceston
Lydford gorge
Dartmoor
Cut Hill
N. Brentor
Chillaton
Brent Tor
Mary Tavy
Bodmin
Altarnun
S. Petherwin
Lewannick
Brown Willy
Michaelstow
St. Teath
Lezant
Milton Abbot
Bolventor
Moor
Lamerton
Great Mis Tor
St. Breward
North Hill
Kilmar Tor
St. Tudy
Dozmary Pool
Blisland
The Cheesewring
Stoke Climsland
Gulworthy
Tavistock
Dartmoor P
Princetown
Bray Shop
CORNWALL
Helland
The Hurlers
Colliford Lake
Caradon Hill
Kelly Bray
Gunnislake
Whitchurch
Morwellham
Callington
Cotehele House
Horrabridge
Cardinham
Pensilva
Bodmin
St. Cleer
St. Neot
St. Ive
St. Dominick
Calstock
Yelverton
Meavy
Dobwalls
Liskeard
St. Mellion
Bere Alston
Buckland Abbey
Lanhydrock
E. Taphouse
Menheniot
Pillaton
Bere Ferrers
Restormel Castle
Landulph
Tamerton Foliot
Bickleigh
Landrake
Lanlivery
Lostwithiel
PLYMOUTH
Saltash
St. Germans
Widegates
Duloe
Eden Project
St. Blazey
Tywardreath
Lanreath
Hessenford
Antony House
Plympton
Pelynt
Morval
Torpoint
Golant
Downderry
Crafthole
Antony
Saltram
Ermington
Devonport
Cornwall Coast Path
Fowey
Polkerris
Carlyon Bay
E. Looe
W. Looe
Whitsand Bay
Cremyll
The Sound
Plymstock
Brixton
Charlestown
Lansallos
Talland-by-Looe
Millbrook
Mt. Edgcumbe
Yealmpton
Dunstone
Polruan
Polperro
Cawsand
Wembury
Holbeton
St. Austell Bay
Gribbin Head
Newton Ferrers
Black Head
Rame Head
Wembury Bay
Noss Mayo
Coast Path
S. Devon
Stoke Point
Bigbury
Mevagissey Bay
Chapel Point
Santander
Roscoff
Eddystone Rocks
Bigbury Bay
LISKEARD, TAVISTOCK
Penrose St
Gibbon La.
Camden St
Cobourg St
Drake Circus
The Box
Lipson Rd
Tothill Ave
Greenbank Ave
Hastings Ter.
Armada Way
Regent St
North St
Charles St
Cornwall St
Western Approach
Ebrington St
Gasking St
Beaumont Rd
Tothill Rd
New George St
Exeter St
Exeter St
Royal Parade
Breton Side
St Andrew's
Prysten House
Vauxhall St
Merchant's House Musem
Princess St
Notte St
SUTTON HARBOUR
Sutton Rd
FERRY TERMINAL
KINGSBRIDGE
St James' Pl.
The Barbican
National Marine Aquarium
Citadel Rd
BARBICAN
Naval War Memorial
Elizabethan House
Teats Hill Rd
Drake Statue
Armada Memorial
Mayflower Stone
Leigham St
Mayflower Museum
The Promenade
Royal Citadel
Cliff Rd
THE HOE
Smeaton's Tower
Madeira Rd
Pier St
Hoe Rd
Grand Parade
St Katherine
PLYMOUTH
THE SOUND
200 m
200 yards
FOOT FERRY, ROSCOFF, SANTANDER
MOUNT BATTEN FERRY

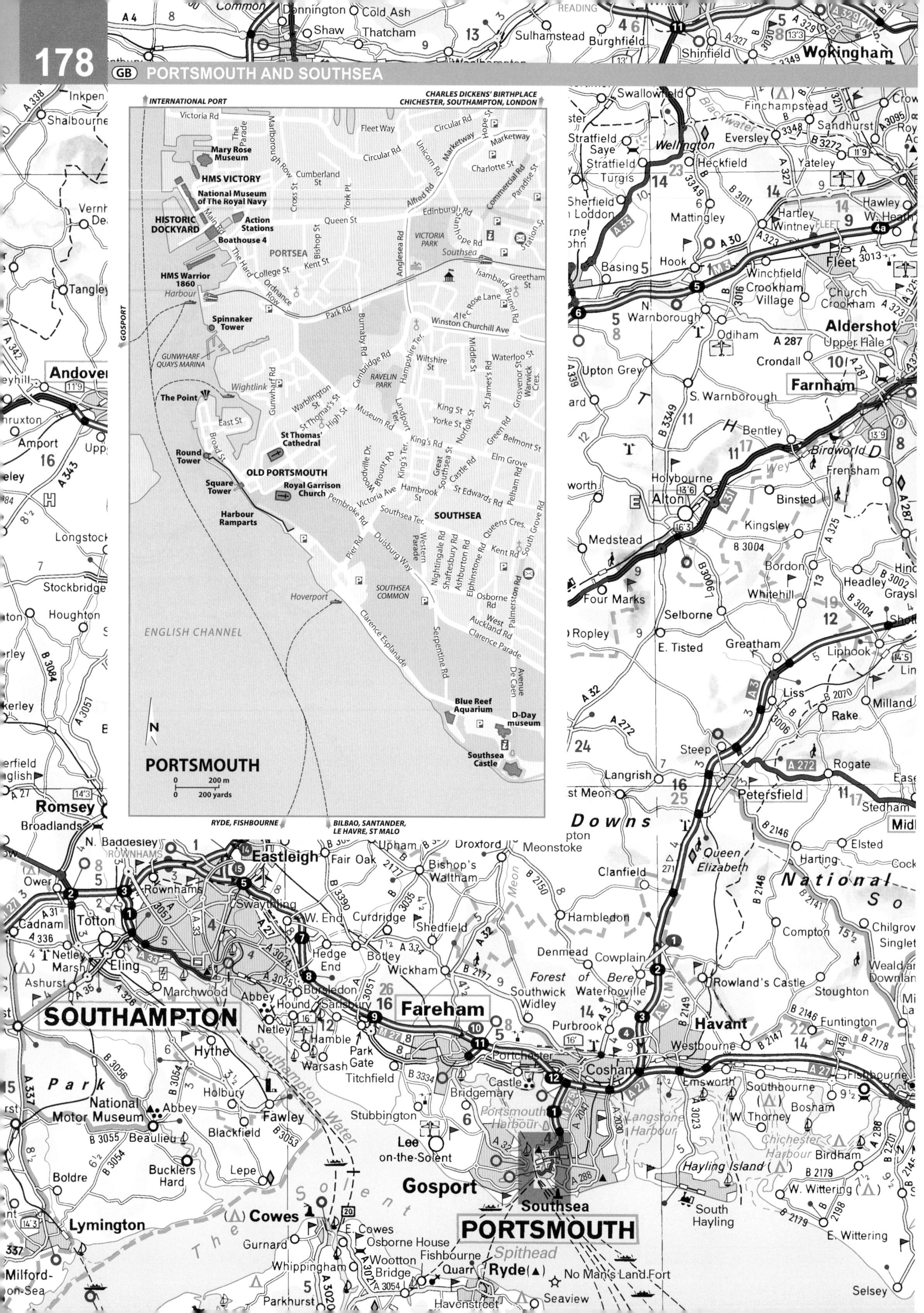
INTERNATIONAL PORT
CHARLES DICKENS' BIRTHPLACE
CHICHESTER, SOUTHAMPTON, LONDON
Victoria Rd
The Parade
Marlborough Row
Fleet Way
Circular Rd
Hope St
Marketway
Mary Rose Museum
HMS VICTORY
National Museum of The Royal Navy
HISTORIC DOCKYARD
Main Rd
Action Stations
Boathouse 4
Cumberland St
Cross St
York Pl.
Alfred Rd
Unicorn Rd
Charlotte St
Commercial Rd
Paradise St
Queen St
Edinburgh Rd
Stanhope Rd
VICTORIA PARK
Station St
Bishop St
Kent St
PORTSEA
The Hard
College St
Ordnance Row
Anglesea Rd
Southsea
Greetham St
Isambard Brunel Rd
HMS Warrior 1860
Harbour
Park Rd
Alec Rose Lane
Winston Churchill Ave
GOSPORT
Spinnaker Tower
GUNWHARF QUAYS MARINA
Burnaby Rd
Cambridge Rd
Hampshire Ter.
Wiltshire St
Middle St
Waterloo St
Grosvenor St
Warwick Cres.
St James's Rd
Gunwharf Rd
RAVELIN PARK
Wightlink
The Point
Warblington St
St Thomas's St
High St
Museum Rd
Landport Ter.
King St
Yorke St
Norfolk St
Green Rd
Belmont St
East St
Broad St
Round Tower
St Thomas' Cathedral
King's Rd
Elm Grove
Square Tower
OLD PORTSMOUTH
Royal Garrison Church
Woodville Dr.
Blount Rd
King's Ter.
Great Southsea St
Castle Rd
Pelham Rd
Hambrook St
St Edwards Rd
Victoria Ave
Pembroke Rd
Southsea Ter.
SOUTHSEA
Harbour Ramparts
Queens Cres.
South Grove Rd
Pier Rd
Duisburg Way
Western Parade
Nightingale Rd
Shaftesbury Rd
Ashburton Rd
Elphinstone Rd
Kent Rd
SOUTHSEA COMMON
Hoverport
Osborne Rd
Palmerston Rd
ENGLISH CHANNEL
West Auckland Rd
Clarence Parade
Clarence Esplanade
Serpentine Rd
Avenue De Caen
Blue Reef Aquarium
D-Day museum
N
Southsea Castle
PORTSMOUTH
0 200 m
0 200 yards
RYDE, FISHBOURNE
BILBAO, SANTANDER, LE HAVRE, ST MALO
Donnington
Cold Ash
Shaw
Thatcham
Sulhamstead
Burghfield
READING
Shinfield
Wokingham
Inkpen
Shalbourne
Andover
Amport
Tangley
Longstock
Stockbridge
Houghton
Romsey
Broadlands
Swallowfield
Finchampstead
Sandhurst
Stratfield Saye
Wellington
Eversley
Heckfield
Yateley
Stratfield Turgis
Sherfield
Mattingley
Hartley Wintney
Hawley
Basing
Hook
Winchfield
Fleet
Crookham Village
Church Crookham
N. Warnborough
Odiham
Aldershot
Upper Hale
Upton Grey
Crondall
Farnham
S. Warnborough
Bentley
Birdworld
Holybourne
Frensham
Alton
Binsted
Kingsley
Medstead
Four Marks
Bordon
Whitehill
Headley
Selborne
Ropley
E. Tisted
Greatham
Liphook
Liss
Milland
Rake
Steep
Rogate
Langrish
Petersfield
Stedham
Downs
Meonstoke
Queen Elizabeth
Elsted
Harting
National
Clanfield
N. Baddesley
Eastleigh
Fair Oak
Upham
Droxford
Bishop's Waltham
Rownhams
Swaythling
Ower
Totton
Cadnam
W. End
Curdridge
Shedfield
Hambledon
Compton
Chilgrove
Netley Marsh
Eling
Hedge End
Botley
Denmead
Cowplain
Wickham
Forest of Bere
Waterlooville
Rowland's Castle
Stoughton
Ashurst
Marchwood
Bursledon
Southwick
Widley
Fareham
Havant
Funtington
SOUTHAMPTON
Abbey
Hound
Sarisbury
Netley
Hamble
Purbrook
Westbourne
Hythe
Warsash
Park Gate
Titchfield
Portchester
Cosham
Emsworth
Southbourne
Fishbourne
Park
National Motor Museum
Holbury
Southampton Water
Bridgemary
Castle
Abbey
Fawley
Stubbington
Portsmouth Harbour
Langstone Harbour
Thorney
Bosham
Beaulieu
Blackfield
Lee on-the-Solent
Chichester Harbour
Birdham
Bucklers Hard
Lepe
Hayling Island
Boldre
Gosport
W. Wittering
Lymington
Cowes
South Hayling
The Solent
Southsea
PORTSMOUTH
E. Wittering
E. Cowes
Osborne House
Gurnard
Spithead
Whippingham
Wootton Bridge
Fishbourne
Quarr
Ryde
No Man's Land Fort
Milford-on-Sea
Parkhurst
Havenstreet
Seaview
Selsey

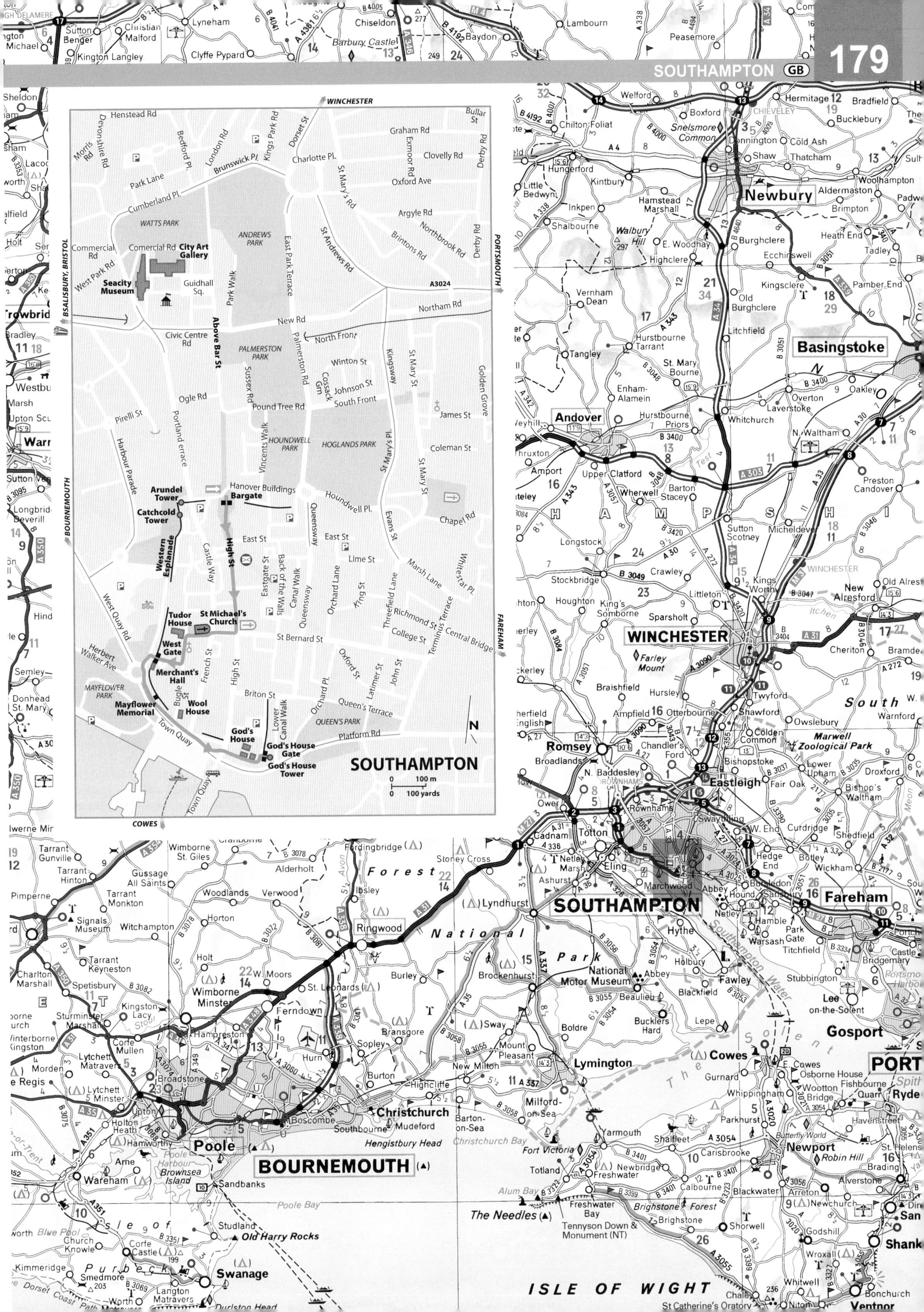
SOUTHAMPTON
0 100 m
0 100 yards
WINCHESTER
BASINGSTOKE, BRISTOL
PORTSMOUTH
BOURNEMOUTH
FAREHAM
COWES
WATTS PARK
ANDREWS PARK
PALMERSTON PARK
HOUNDWELL PARK
HOGLANDS PARK
MAYFLOWER PARK
QUEEN'S PARK
City Art Gallery
Seacity Museum
Guildhall Sq.
Above Bar St
Bargate
Arundel Tower
Catchcold Tower
Western Esplanade
Tudor House
St Michael's Church
West Gate
Merchant's Hall
Wool House
Mayflower Memorial
God's House
God's House Gate
God's House Tower
Town Quay
High St
New Rd
Northam Rd
Civic Centre Rd
Portland Terrace
Commercial Rd
Cumberland Pl.
London Rd
Dorset St
Palmerston Rd
East Park Terrace
St Mary's Rd
Kingsway
St Mary St
Houndwell Pl.
Chapel Rd
Marsh Lane
Central Bridge
Platform Rd
Queen's Terrace
Briton St
St Bernard St
East St
Bugle St
French St
Castle Way
West Quay Rd
Herbert Walker Ave
Harbour Parade
Pirelli St
Ogle Rd
Pound Tree Rd
Winton St
Johnson St
South Front
North Front
James St
Coleman St
Golden Grove
Derby Rd
Northbrook Rd
Brintons Rd
Argyle Rd
Oxford Ave
Clovelly Rd
Graham Rd
Charlotte Pl.
Brunswick Pl.
Park Lane
Henstead Rd
Bullar St
A3024
Newbury
Basingstoke
Andover
WINCHESTER
Romsey
Eastleigh
SOUTHAMPTON
Fareham
Gosport
Lymington
Christchurch
Poole
BOURNEMOUTH
Swanage
Wareham
Ringwood
Wimborne Minster
Cowes
Newport
Ryde
Yarmouth
ISLE OF WIGHT
The Needles
Forest National Park
The Solent
Southampton Water
Isle of Purbeck
Hungerford
Kingsclere
Whitchurch
Stockbridge
Totton
Hythe
Fawley
Brockenhurst
Lyndhurst
Beaulieu
New Milton
Milford-on-Sea
Marwell Zoological Park
Old Harry Rocks
Hengistbury Head
Brownsea Island
Sandbanks
Ventnor
Shanklin

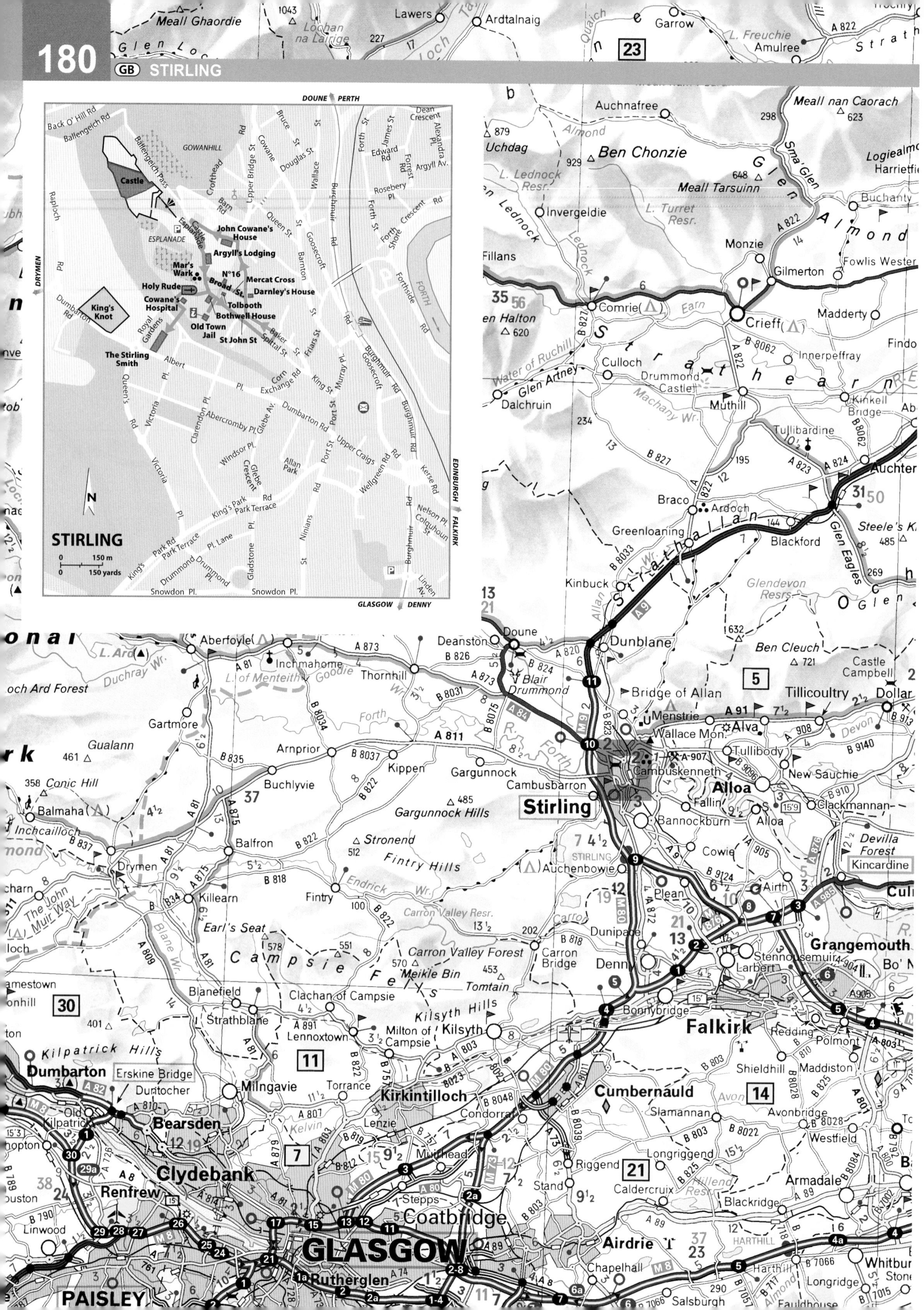
STIRLING
Doune Perth
Drymen
Edinburgh Falkirk
Glasgow Denny
Castle
Gowanhill
Esplanade
John Cowane's House
Argyll's Lodging
Mar's Wark
N°16
Mercat Cross
Darnley's House
Holy Rude
Cowane's Hospital
Tolbooth
Bothwell House
Old Town Jail
St John St
King's Knot
Royal Gardens
The Stirling Smith
Back O' Hill Rd
Ballengeich Rd
Ballengeich Pass
Raploch Rd
Dumbarton Rd
Broad St
Baker St
Spittal St
Albert Pl.
Queen's Rd
Victoria Pl.
Clarendon Pl.
Abercromby Pl.
Glebe Av.
Windsor Pl.
Glebe Crescent
Allan Park
Corn Exchange Rd
King St
Murray Pl.
Port St
Upper Craigs
Wellgreen Rd
Goosecroft Rd
Burghmuir Rd
Kerse Rd
Nelson Pl.
Colquhoun St
Linden Av.
King's Park Rd
Park Terrace
Drummond Pl.
Drummond Pl. Lane
Gladstone Pl.
Snowdon Pl.
St Ninians Rd
Forth St
Forthside
Forth Crescent
Shore Rd
Rosebery Pl.
Edward Rd
Forrest Rd
Argyll Av.
Alexandra Pl.
James St
Dean Crescent
Douglas St
Wallace St
Cowane St
Upper Bridge St
Crofthead Rd
Barn Rd
Queen St
Barnton St
Friars St
Forth
0 150 m
0 150 yards
N
Meall Ghaordie
Glen Lochay
Lochan na Lairige
Lawers
Ardtalnaig
Garrow
L. Freuchie
Amulree
Strath Braan
Auchnafree
Meall nan Caorach
Almond
Uchdag
Ben Chonzie
L. Lednock Resr.
Invergeldie
L. Turret Resr.
Meall Tarsuinn
Sma'Glen
Glen Almond
Logiealmond
Harrietfield
Buchanty
Monzie
Gilmerton
Fowlis Wester
Fillans
Comrie
Crieff
Madderty
Earn
Strathearn
Culloch
Drummond Castle
Innerpeffray
Water of Ruchill
Glen Artney
Dalchruin
Muthill
Machany Wr.
Kinkell Bridge
Tullibardine
Braco
Ardoch
Greenloaning
Blackford
Strathallan
Glen Eagles
Steele's Knowe
Kinbuck
Glendevon Resrs.
Ochil Hills
Doune
Dunblane
Ben Cleuch
Castle Campbell
Dollar
Tillicoultry
Aberfoyle
L. Ard
Loch Ard Forest
Inchmahome
L. of Menteith
Goodie Wr.
Deanston
Thornhill
Blair Drummond
Bridge of Allan
Menstrie
Alva
Wallace Mon.
Tullibody
Devon
Gartmore
Gualann
Arnprior
Kippen
Forth
R. Forth
Gargunnock
Cambusbarron
Cambuskenneth
New Sauchie
Alloa
Fallin
Clackmannan
Conic Hill
Buchlyvie
Balmaha
Gargunnock Hills
Stirling
Bannockburn
Inchcailloch
Balfron
Stronend
Fintry Hills
Auchenbowie
Cowie
Devilla Forest
Kincardine
Drymen
Killearn
Fintry
Endrick Wr.
Plean
Airth
The John Muir Way
Earl's Seat
Carron Valley Resr.
Dunipace
Carron
Grangemouth
Campsie Fells
Carron Valley Forest
Carron Bridge
Denny
Stenhousemuir
Larbert
Meikle Bin
Tomtain
Blanefield
Clachan of Campsie
Strathblane
Kilsyth Hills
Bonnybridge
Lennoxtown
Milton of Campsie
Kilsyth
Falkirk
Redding
Polmont
Kilpatrick Hills
Dumbarton
Erskine Bridge
Dumtocher
Milngavie
Torrance
Kirkintilloch
Cumbernauld
Shieldhill
Maddiston
Old Kilpatrick
Bearsden
Condorrat
Lenzie
Kelvin
Slamannan
Avonbridge
Westfield
Clydebank
Muirhead
Riggend
Longriggend
Armadale
Renfrew
Stepps
Stand
Caldercruix
Hillend Resr.
Blackridge
Coatbridge
Linwood
GLASGOW
Airdrie
Harthill
Whitburn
Rutherglen
Chapelhall
Longridge
Salsburgh
Fauldhouse
PAISLEY

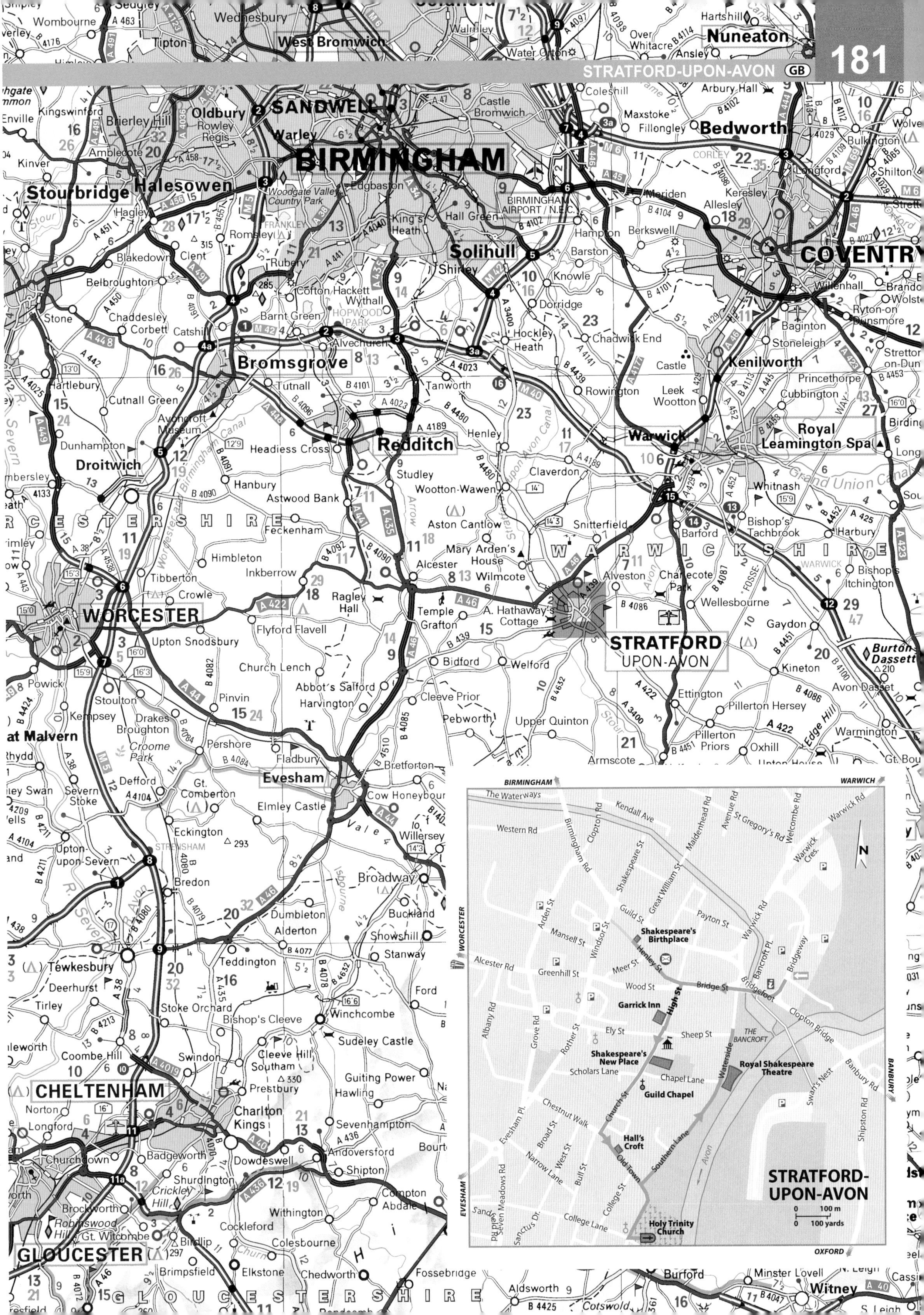
BIRMINGHAM
SANDWELL
West Bromwich
Wednesbury
Walsall
Nuneaton
Bedworth
COVENTRY
Solihull
BIRMINGHAM AIRPORT / N.E.C.
Stourbridge
Halesowen
Oldbury
Warley
Bromsgrove
Redditch
Droitwich
WORCESTER
Kenilworth
Warwick
Royal Leamington Spa
STRATFORD UPON-AVON
Evesham
Tewkesbury
CHELTENHAM
GLOUCESTER
W A R W I C K S H I R E
G L O U C E S T E R S H I R E
Alcester
Henley
Studley
Feckenham
Pershore
Broadway
Winchcombe
Sudeley Castle
Ragley Hall
A. Hathaway's Cottage
Mary Arden's House
Charlecote Park
Wellesbourne
Kineton
Ettington
Shipston
Burford
Witney
BIRMINGHAM
WARWICK
WORCESTER
EVESHAM
BANBURY
OXFORD
N
The Waterways
Kendall Ave
Western Rd
Birmingham Rd
Clopton Rd
Maidenhead Rd
Avenue Rd
St Gregory's Rd
Welcombe Rd
Warwick Rd
Warwick Cres.
Shakespeare St
Great William St
Payton St
Guild St
Arden St
Mansell St
Windsor St
Shakespeare's Birthplace
Henley St
Meer St
Alcester Rd
Greenhill St
Wood St
Bridge St
Bancroft Pl.
Bridgeway
Bridgefoot
Clopton Bridge
Garrick Inn
High St
Albany Rd
Grove Rd
Rother St
Ely St
Sheep St
THE BANCROFT
Shakespeare's New Place
Scholars Lane
Chapel Lane
Waterside
Royal Shakespeare Theatre
Guild Chapel
Swan's Nest
Banbury Rd
Chestnut Walk
Church St
Evesham Pl.
Broad St
Hall's Croft
Southern Lane
Avon
Shipston Rd
Narrow Lane
West St
Bull St
Old Town
Seven Meadows Rd
Sanctus Dr.
College St
College Lane
Holy Trinity Church
STRATFORD-UPON-AVON
0 100 m
0 100 yards

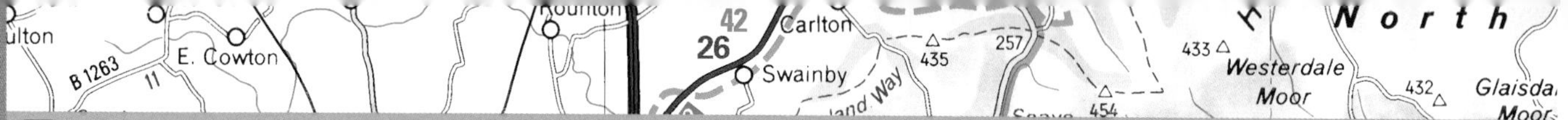
E. Cowton
Carlton
Swainby
Westerdale Moor
North
Glaisdale Moor
B 1263
435
433
454
432

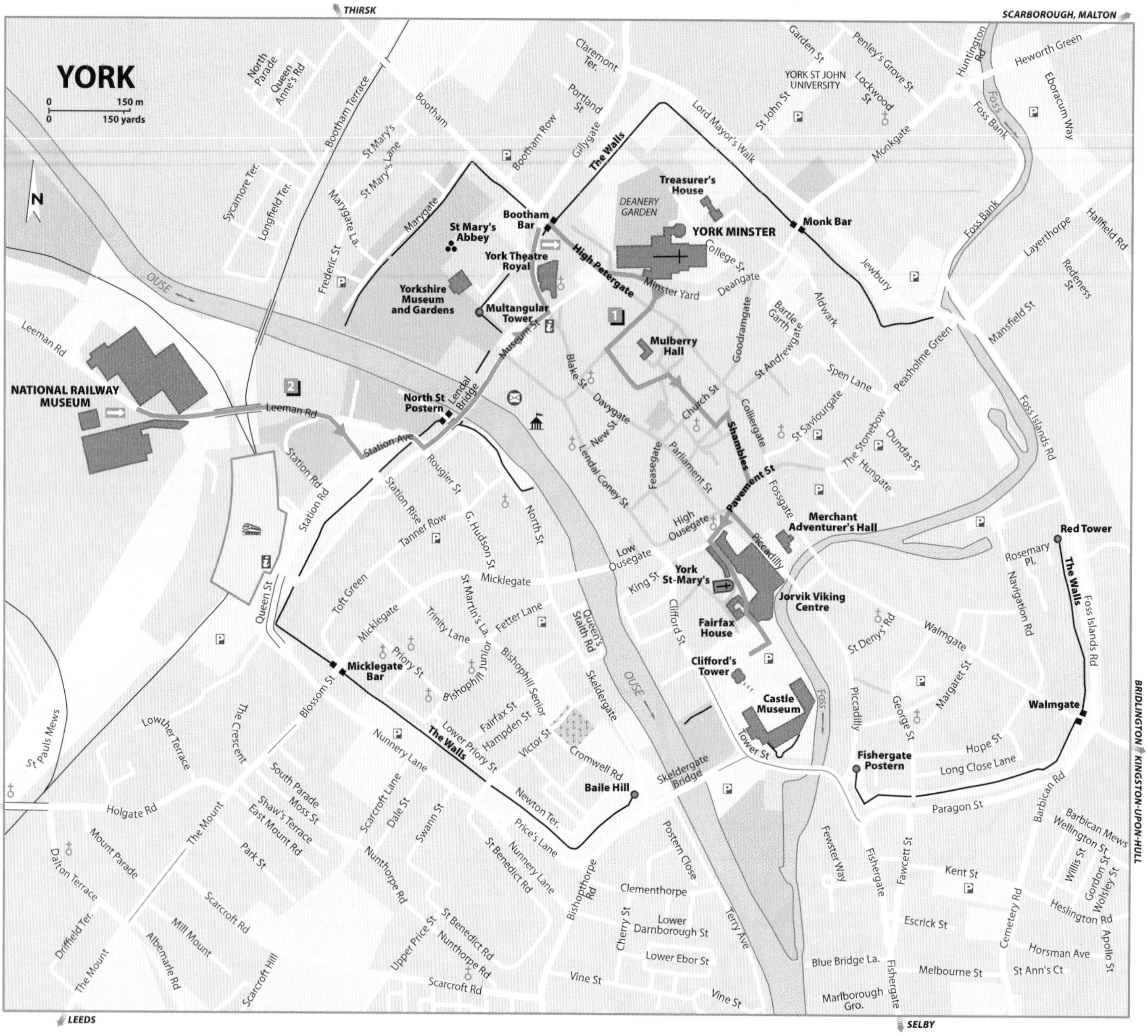
YORK
150 m
150 yards
THIRSK
SCARBOROUGH, MALTON
LEEDS
SELBY
WETHERBY HARROGATE
BRIDLINGTON KINGSTON-UPON-HULL
NATIONAL RAILWAY MUSEUM
York St John University
Treasurer's House
Deanery Garden
YORK MINSTER
Bootham Bar
St Mary's Abbey
York Theatre Royal
Yorkshire Museum and Gardens
Multangular Tower
Monk Bar
Mulberry Hall
North St Postern
Merchant Adventurer's Hall
Red Tower
York St-Mary's
Jorvik Viking Centre
Fairfax House
Clifford's Tower
Castle Museum
Micklegate Bar
Walmgate
Fishergate Postern
Baile Hill
The Walls
Shambles
Pavement St
High Petergate
Lendal Bridge
Skeldergate Bridge
Ouse
Foss
Leeman Rd
Station Ave
Station Rd
Station Rise
Queen St
Blossom St
Holgate Rd
Micklegate
Bootham
Gillygate
Lord Mayor's Walk
Monkgate
Goodramgate
Stonebow
Piccadilly
Walmgate
Paragon St
Fishergate
Tower St
Clifford St
Coney St
Davygate
Parliament St
Church St
Colliergate
Fossgate
Low Ousegate
High Ousegate
Nunnery Lane
Bishophill Senior
Bishophill Junior
Skeldergate
Cromwell Rd
Victor St
Newton Ter.
Price's Lane
Clementhorpe
Terry Ave
Vine St
Scarcroft Rd
The Mount
Mount Parade
Dalton Terrace
Heworth Green
Huntington Rd
Foss Bank
Foss Islands Rd
Lawrence St
Barbican Rd
Heslington Rd
Kent St
Melbourne St
Cemetery Rd
Hope St
Long Close Lane
Margaret St
George St
St Denys Rd
Navigation Rd
Rosemary Pl.
Hallfield Rd
Layerthorpe
Mansfield St
Peasholme Green
Jewbury
Aldwark
St Andrewgate
Spen Lane
St Saviourgate
Hungate
Dundas St
Marygate
Bootham Row
Portland St
Claremont Ter.
Gilly gate
Garden St
Penley's Grove St
Lockwood St
St John St
Sycamore Ter.
Longfield Ter.
Frederic St
Bootham Terrace
St Mary's
Queen Anne's Rd
North Parade
Museum St
Blake St
New St
Feasegate
Rougier St
Tanner Row
G. Hudson St
North St
Toft Green
Trinity Lane
Priory St
Fetter Lane
Queen's Staith Rd
Lower Priory St
Fairfax St
Hampden St
Lowther Terrace
The Crescent
St Pauls Mews
South Parade
Moss St
Shaw's Terrace
East Mount Rd
Park St
Dale St
Swann St
Nunthorpe Rd
St Benedict Rd
Upper Price St
Mill Mount
Albemarle Rd
Driffield Ter.
Scarcroft Hill
Scarcroft Lane
Bishopthorpe Rd
Cherry St
Lower Darnborough St
Lower Ebor St
Postern Close
Fewster Way
Fawcett St
Escrick St
Blue Bridge La.
Marlborough Gro.
Horsman Ave
St Ann's Ct
Apollo St
Wellington St
Barbican Mews
Willis St
Gordon St
Wolsley St
Minster Yard
College St
Deangate
Bartle Garth
King St
Eboracum Way
Redeness St

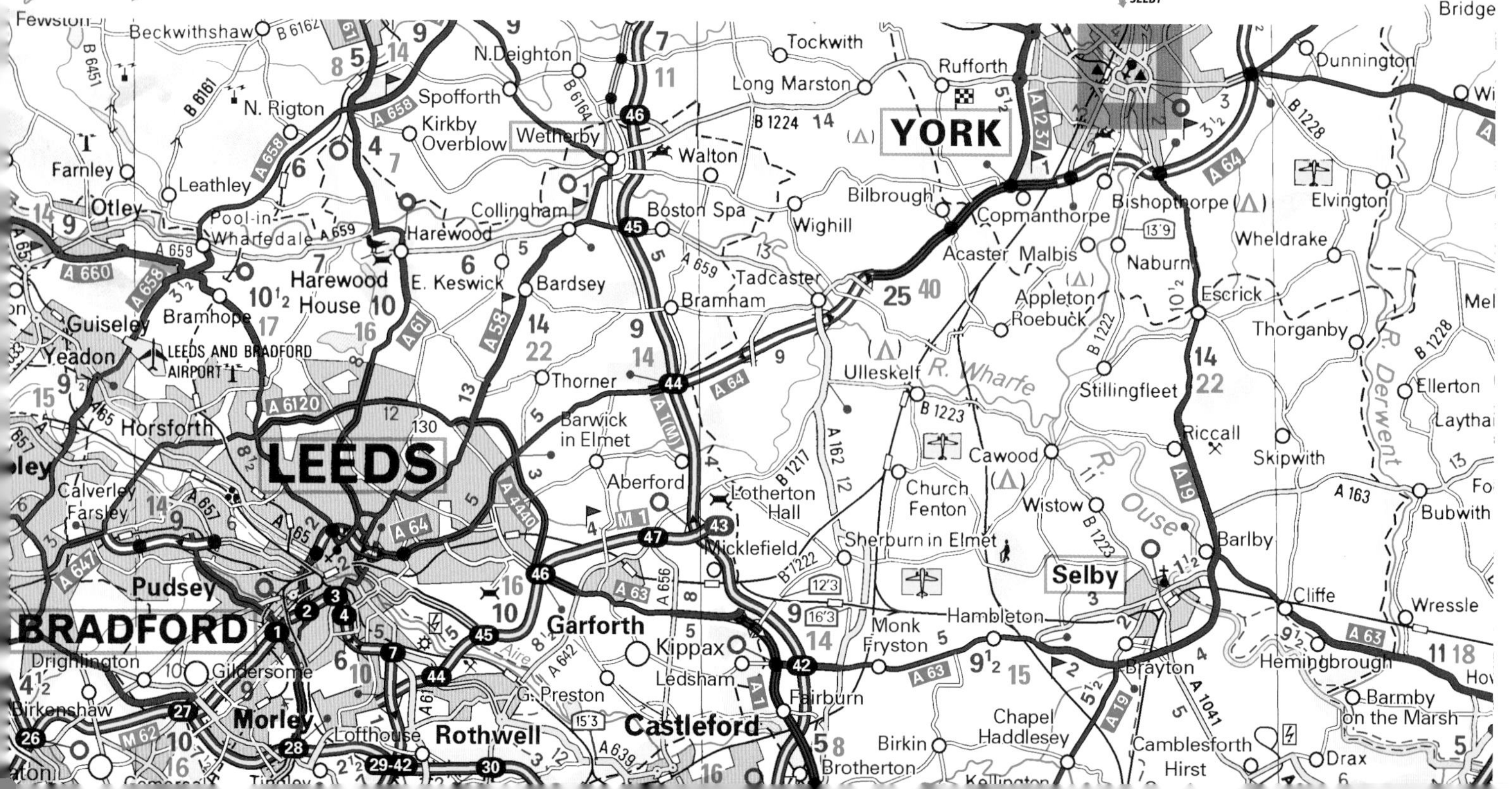
Beckwithshaw
N. Deighton
Tockwith
Rufforth
Dunnington
Spofforth
Kirkby Overblow
Wetherby
Long Marston
YORK
N. Rigton
Farnley
Leathley
Otley
Pool-in-Wharfedale
Collingham
Walton
Boston Spa
Wighill
Bilbrough
Copmanthorpe
Bishopthorpe
Elvington
Harewood
Harewood House
E. Keswick
Bardsey
Bramham
Tadcaster
Acaster Malbis
Naburn
Wheldrake
Guiseley
Bramhope
Appleton Roebuck
Escrick
Thorganby
Yeadon
LEEDS AND BRADFORD AIRPORT
Thorner
Ulleskelf
R. Wharfe
Stillingfleet
Horsforth
Barwick in Elmet
Riccall
Skipwith
Ellerton
LEEDS
Aberford
Lotherton Hall
Church Fenton
Cawood
Wistow
R. Ouse
Calverley
Farsley
Micklefield
Sherburn in Elmet
Barlby
Bubwith
Pudsey
Selby
Cliffe
Wressle
BRADFORD
Garforth
Kippax
Monk Fryston
Hambleton
Hemingbrough
Drighlington
Gildersome
Ledsham
Brayton
Barmby on the Marsh
Birkenshaw
Morley
G. Preston
Fairburn
Lofthouse
Rothwell
Castleford
Birkin
Chapel Haddlesey
Camblesforth
Hirst
Drax
Brotherton
R. Derwent
R. Aire
A 64
A 1(M)
A 19
A 63
M 1
M 62
A 1237
A 659
A 61
A 58
A 6120
A 162
A 1041
B 1223
B 1222
B 1228
B 1217
B 1224
B 6164
B 6161
B 6451
A 163

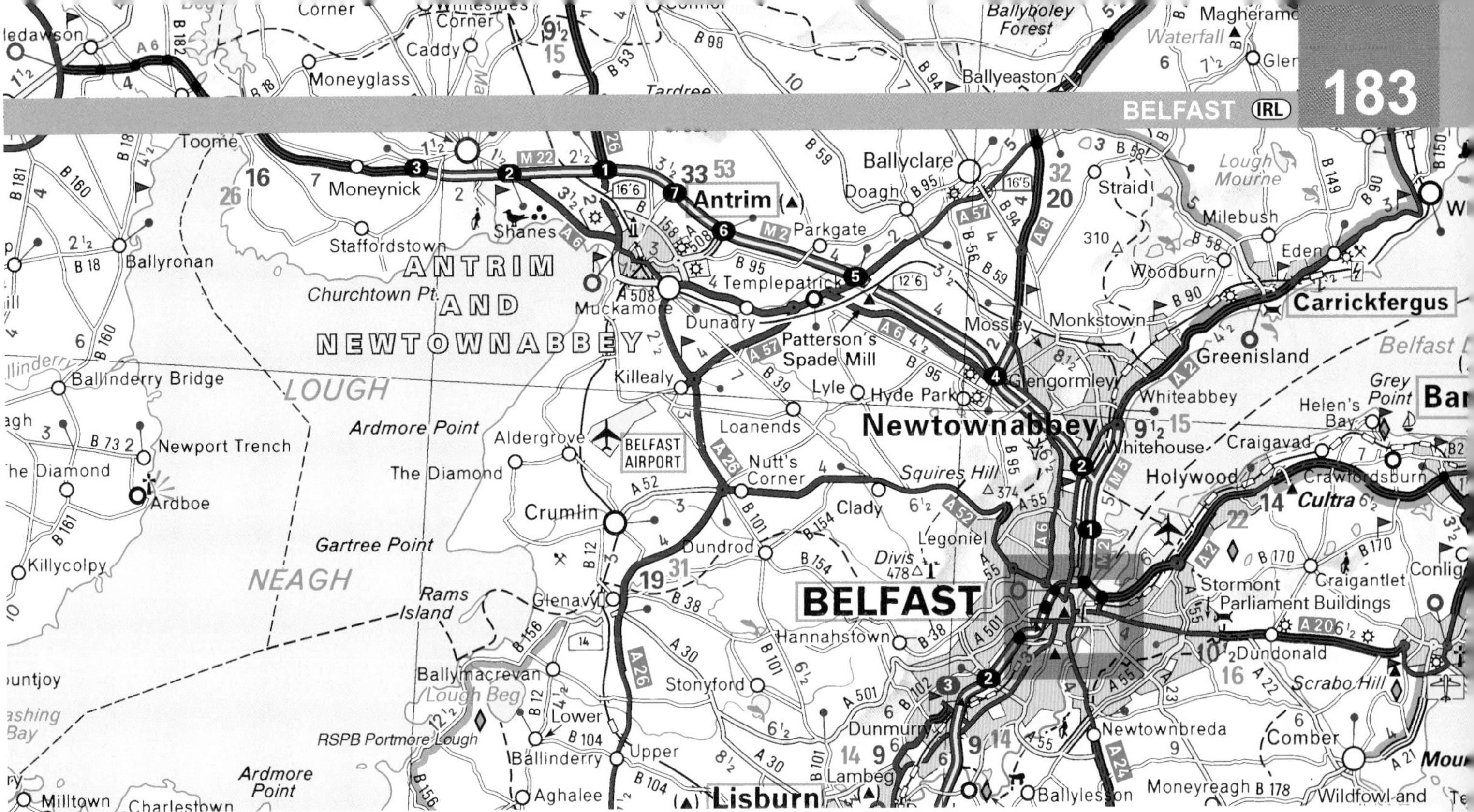
Antrim
Toome
Moneynick
Staffordstown
Ballyronan
Shanes
Muckamore
Templepatrick
Parkgate
Ballyclare
Doagh
Straid
Lough Mourne
Milebush
Eden
Woodburn
Carrickfergus
Greenisland
Monkstown
Mossley
Glengormley
Whiteabbey
Newtownabbey
Whitehouse
Holywood
Cultra
Crawfordsburn
Craigavad
Helen's Bay
Grey Point
ANTRIM AND NEWTOWNABBEY
Churchtown Pt.
LOUGH NEAGH
Ballinderry Bridge
Newport Trench
The Diamond
Ardboe
Killycolpy
Ardmore Point
Aldergrove
BELFAST AIRPORT
Killealy
Dunadry
Patterson's Spade Mill
Lyle
Hyde Park
Loanends
Nutt's Corner
Squires Hill
Crumlin
Clady
Legoniel
Gartree Point
Dundrod
Divis
BELFAST
Stormont Parliament Buildings
Craigantlet
Conlig
Rams Island
Glenavy
Hannahstown
Dundonald
Scrabo Hill
Ballymacrevan
Lough Beg
Lower Ballinderry
Upper Ballinderry
RSPB Portmore Lough
Stonyford
Dunmurry
Newtownbreda
Comber
Lambeg
Ballylesson
Moneyreagh
Wildfowl and
Aghalee
Lisburn
Ardmore Point
Milltown
Charlestown
Moneyglass
Caddy
Ballyboley Forest
Ballyeaston
Magheramorne
Waterfall
Glenoe
Tardree
Jonesborough
Windy Gap
Killowen
Lisnacree
Ballymartin

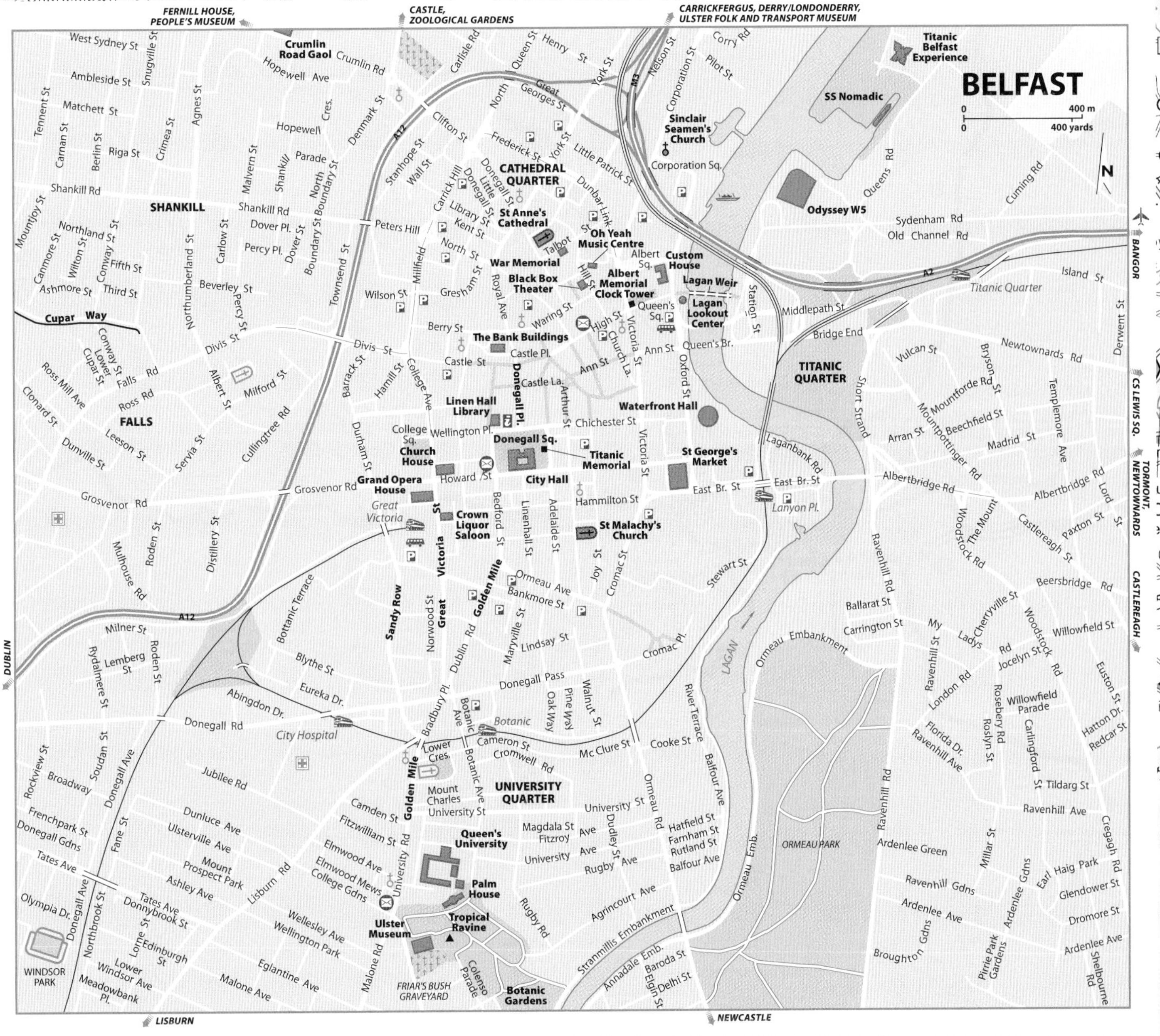
BELFAST
FERNILL HOUSE, PEOPLE'S MUSEUM
CASTLE, ZOOLOGICAL GARDENS
CARRICKFERGUS, DERRY/LONDONDERRY, ULSTER FOLK AND TRANSPORT MUSEUM
Titanic Belfast Experience
SS Nomadic
Crumlin Road Gaol
Sinclair Seamen's Church
Corporation Sq.
Odyssey W5
CATHEDRAL QUARTER
St Anne's Cathedral
Oh Yeah Music Centre
War Memorial
Black Box Theater
Albert Memorial Clock Tower
Custom House
Lagan Weir
Lagan Lookout Center
SHANKILL
Cupar Way
The Bank Buildings
Linen Hall Library
Waterfront Hall
TITANIC QUARTER
Titanic Quarter
Donegall Sq.
Titanic Memorial
City Hall
Church House
Grand Opera House
Crown Liquor Saloon
Great Victoria
St George's Market
St Malachy's Church
FALLS
Lanyon Pl.
Bridge End
City Hospital
Botanic
UNIVERSITY QUARTER
Mount Charles
Queen's University
Palm House
Tropical Ravine
Ulster Museum
Botanic Gardens
FRIAR'S BUSH GRAVEYARD
WINDSOR PARK
ORMEAU PARK
LAGAN
DUBLIN
LISBURN
NEWCASTLE
BANGOR
CS LEWIS SQ.
TORMONT, NEWTOWNARDS
CASTLEREAGH
400 m
400 yards
N

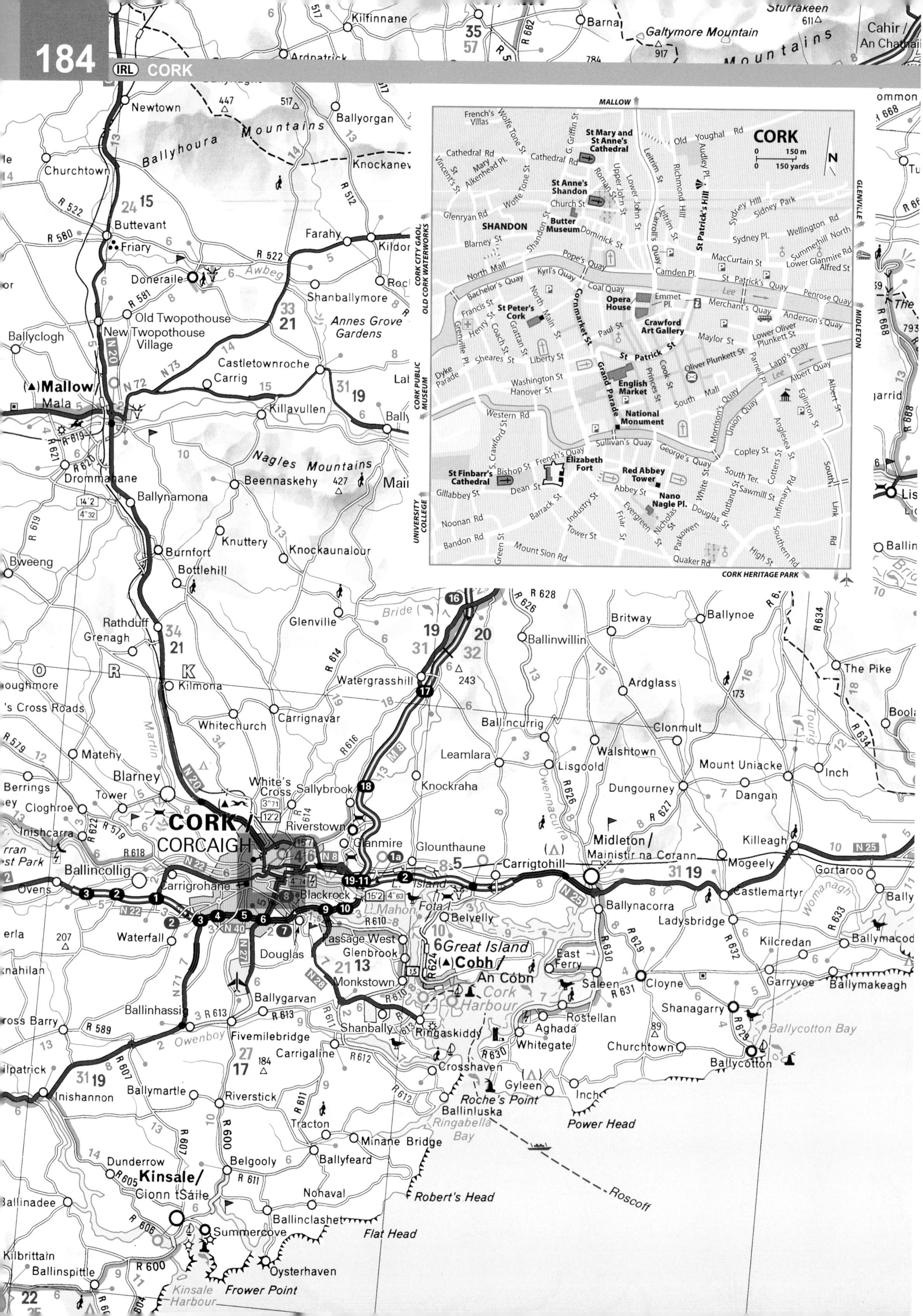
CORK
0 150 m
0 150 yards
MALLOW
GLENVILLE
MIDLETON
CORK HERITAGE PARK
UNIVERSITY COLLEGE
CORK PUBLIC MUSEUM
OLD CORK WATERWORKS
CORK CITY GAOL
St Mary and St Anne's Cathedral
St Anne's Shandon
SHANDON
Butter Museum
Opera House
Crawford Art Gallery
St Peter's Cork
English Market
National Monument
Elizabeth Fort
St Finbarr's Cathedral
Red Abbey Tower
Nano Nagle Pl.
St Patrick St
Grand Parade
Cornmarket St
North Main St
Lee
Kilfinnane
Barna
Galtymore Mountain
Mountains
Cahir / An Cathair
Ardpatrick
Newtown
Ballyhoura Mountains
Ballyorgan
Knockanevin
Churchtown
Buttevant
Friary
Farahy
Kildorrery
Doneraile
Awbeg
Shanballymore
Annes Grove Gardens
Old Twopothouse
New Twopothouse Village
Ballyclogh
Castletownroche
Carrig
(▲)Mallow / Mala
Killavullen
Nagles Mountains
Beennaskehy
Drommahane
Ballynamona
Knuttery
Burnfort
Knockaunalour
Bottlehill
Bweeng
Glenville
Rathduff
Grenagh
Watergrasshill
Kilmona
Whitechurch
Carrignavar
Matehy
Blarney
Tower
White's Cross
Sallybrook
Riverstown
Glanmire
Knockraha
Leamlara
Ballincurrig
Britway
Ballynoe
Ballinwillin
Ardglass
The Pike
Clonmult
Walshtown
Lisgoold
Mount Uniacke
Inch
Dungourney
Dangan
Killeagh
Midleton / Mainistir na Corann
Mogeely
Gortaroo
Castlemartyr
Ballynacorra
Ladysbridge
Kilcredan
Ballymacoda
Garryvoe
Ballymakeagh
Cloghroe
Inishcarra
CORK / CORCAIGH
Ballincollig
Ovens
Carrigrohane
Blackrock
Glounthaune
Carrigtohill
Little Island
Fota I.
Belvelly
Great Island
(▲)Cobh / An Cóbh
Cork Harbour
East Ferry
Saleen
Cloyne
Shanagarry
Rostellan
Aghada
Whitegate
Churchtown
Ballycotton
Ballycotton Bay
Waterfall
Douglas
Passage West
Glenbrook
Monkstown
Ballygarvan
Ballinhassig
Fivemilebridge
Owenboy
Carrigaline
Shanbally
Ringaskiddy
Crosshaven
Gyleen
Inch
Roche's Point
Ballinluska
Ringabella Bay
Power Head
Roscoff
Inishannon
Ballymartle
Riverstick
Tracton
Minane Bridge
Ballyfeard
Belgooly
Dunderrow
Kinsale / Cionn tSáile
Nohaval
Ballinclashet
Robert's Head
Flat Head
Summercove
Oysterhaven
Ballinadee
Kilbrittain
Ballinspittle
Kinsale Harbour
Frower Point

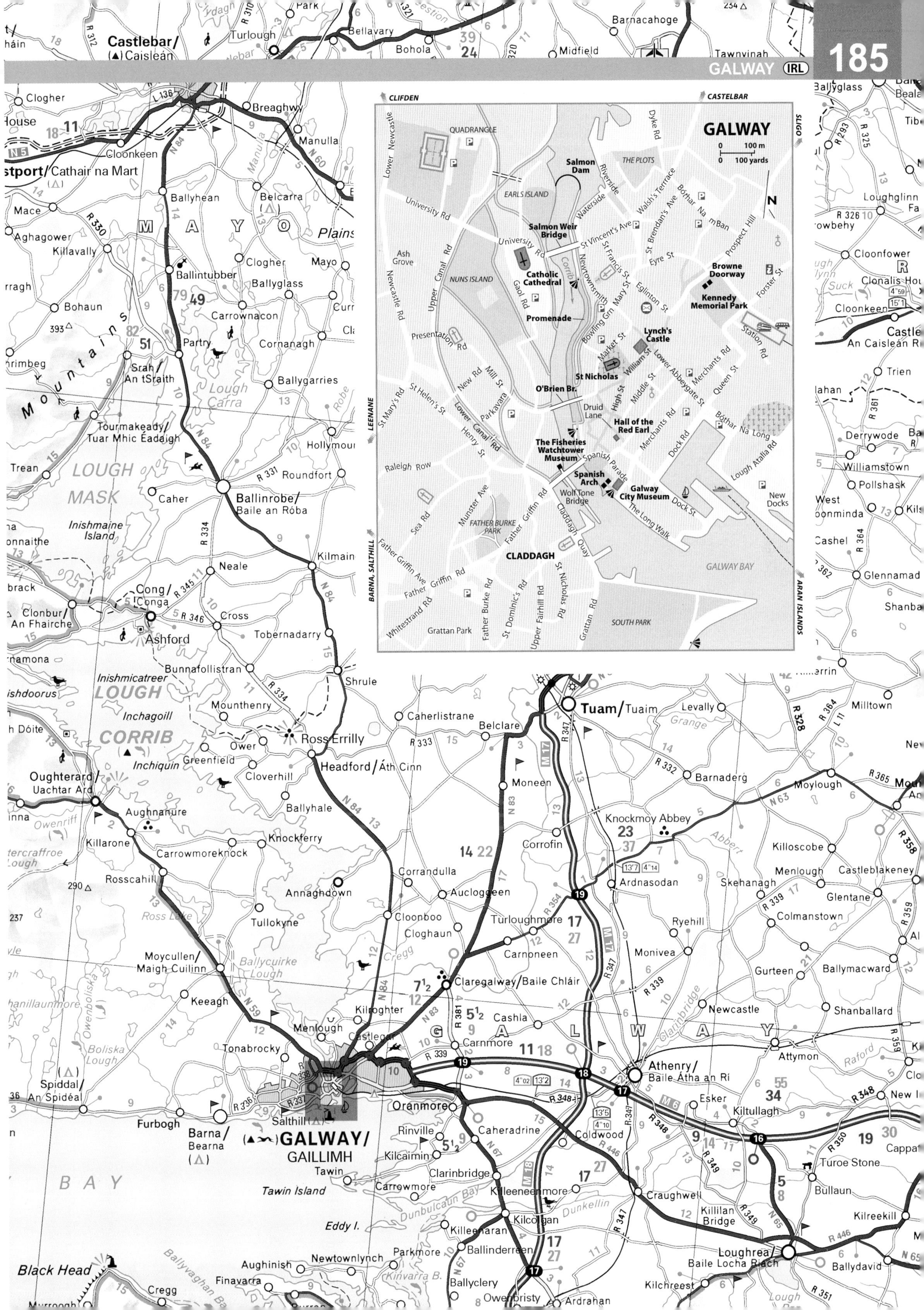
GALWAY
CLIFDEN
CASTLEBAR
SLIGO
LEENANE
BARNA, SALTHILL
ARAN ISLANDS
QUADRANGLE
Lower Newcastle
University Rd
Ash Grove
Newcastle Rd
Upper Canal Rd
EARLS ISLAND
Salmon Dam
Salmon Weir Bridge
Catholic Cathedral
NUNS ISLAND
Gaol Rd
Promenade
THE PLOTS
Dyke Rd
Riverside
Waterside
Walsh's Terrace
Bóthar Na mBan
St Brendan's Ave
St Vincent's Ave
Newtownsmith
St Francis St
Eyre St
Prospect Hill
Browne Doorway
Kennedy Memorial Park
Forster St
Station Rd
Eglinton St
Mary St
Bowling Grn
Lynch's Castle
Market St
St Nicholas
William St
Lower Abbeygate St
Merchants Rd
Queen St
Middle St
High St
O'Brien Br.
Druid Lane
Hall of the Red Earl
Presentation Rd
New Rd
Mill St
Parkavara
Lower Canal Rd
Henry St
St Mary's Rd
St Helen's St
The Fisheries Watchtower Museum
Spanish Parade
Spanish Arch
Wolf Tone Bridge
Galway City Museum
Dock Rd
Bóthar Na Long
Lough Atalia Rd
New Docks
Dock St
The Long Walk
Raleigh Row
Sea Rd
Munster Ave
FATHER BURKE PARK
Father Griffin Rd
Claddagh Quay
CLADDAGH
GALWAY BAY
Father Griffin Ave
Whitestrand Rd
Grattan Park
Father Burke Rd
St Dominic's Rd
Upper Fairhill Rd
St Nicholas Rd
Grattan Rd
SOUTH PARK
0 100 m
0 100 yards
Castlebar/ Caisleán
Turlough
Bellavary
Bohola
Midfield
Barnacahoge
Tawnyinah
Westport/Cathair na Mart
Clogher
Breaghwy
Manulla
Cloonkeen
Ballyhean
Belcarra
Mace
Aghagower
Killavally
MAYO
Plains
Ballintubber
Clogher
Mayo
Ballyglass
Bohaun
Carrownacon
Partry
Cornanagh
Srah/ An tSraith
Mountains
Lough Carra
Ballygarries
Tourmakeady/ Tuar Mhic Éadaigh
Hollymount
Trean
LOUGH MASK
Roundfort
Caher
Ballinrobe/ Baile an Róba
Inishmaine Island
Kilmain
Neale
Cong/ Conga
Clonbur/ An Fhairche
Cross
Ashford
Tobernadarry
Bunnafollistran
Inishmicatreer
LOUGH CORRIB
Shrule
Mounthenry
Inchagoill
Caherlistrane
Belclare
Tuam/Tuaim
Levally
Ross Errilly
Owér
Greenfield
Inchiquin
Headford/Áth Cinn
Cloverhill
Oughterard/ Uachtar Ard
Moneen
Barnaderg
Moylough
Aughnanure
Ballyhale
Knockmoy Abbey
Killarone
Knockferry
Carrowmoreknock
Corrofin
Killoscobe
Rosscahill
Corrandulla
Ardnasodan
Skehanagh
Menlough
Castleblakeney
Annaghdown
Auclogeen
Glentane
Tullokyne
Cloonboo
Turloughmore
Ryehill
Colmanstown
Cloghaun
Carnoneen
Monivea
Moycullen/ Maigh Cuilinn
Ballycuirke Lough
Gurteen
Ballymacward
Claregalway/Baile Chláir
Keeagh
Kiltoghter
Newcastle
Shanballard
Cashla
Menlough
GALWAY
Castlegar
Carnmore
Tonabrocky
Athenry/ Baile Átha an Rí
Attymon
Boliska Lough
Spiddal/ An Spidéal
Oranmore
Esker
Kiltullagh
Furbogh
Barna/ Bearna
Salthill
GALWAY/ GAILLIMH
Rinville
Caheradrine
Coldwood
Turoe Stone
Kilcaimin
Tawin
Clarinbridge
Tawin Island
Carrowmore
Killeeneenmore
Craughwell
Bullaun
BAY
Dunbulcaun Bay
Killilan Bridge
Kilreekill
Eddy I.
Killeenaran
Kilcolgan
Black Head
Aughinish
Newtownlynch
Parkmore
Ballinderreen
Loughrea/ Baile Locha Riach
Ballydavid
Finavarra
Ballyclery
Kilchreest
Cregg
Owenbristy
Ardrahan

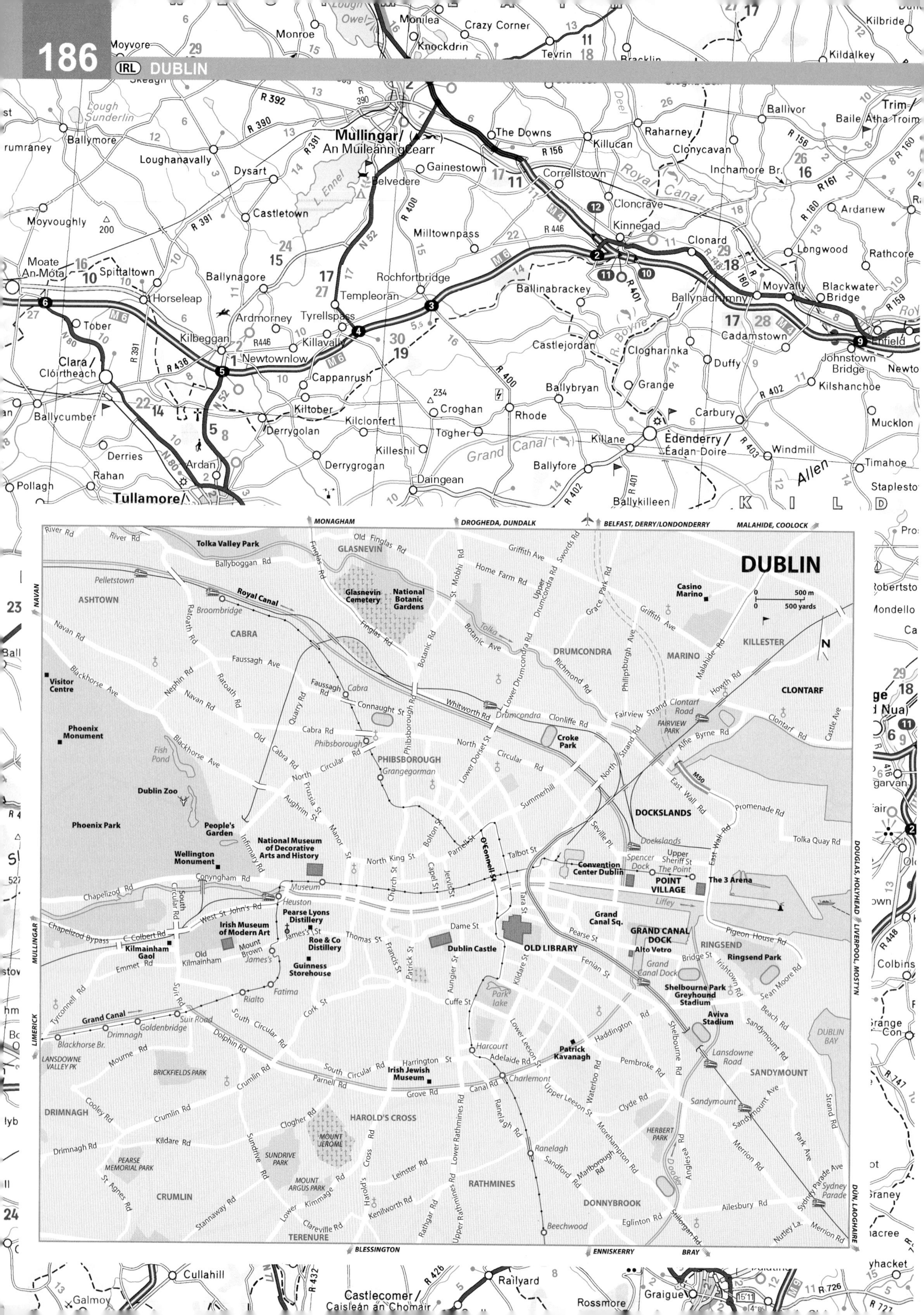
Mullingar / An Muileann gCearr
Monilea
Crazy Corner
Monroe
Moyvore
Knockdrin
Tevrin
Kilbride
Kildalkey
Lough Owel
Lough Sunderlin
Ballymore
Loughanavally
Dysart
Belvedere
Gainestown
The Downs
Killucan
Raharney
Clonycavan
Ballivor
Trim / Baile Átha Troim
Inchamore Br.
Correllstown
Royal Canal
Cloncrave
Kinnegad
Clonard
Longwood
Rathcore
Ardanew
Moyvoughly
Castletown
Milltownpass
Moate / An Móta
Spittaltown
Ballynagore
Rochfortbridge
Templeoran
Horseleap
Ballinabrackey
Ballynadrummy
Moyvally
Blackwater Bridge
Enfield
Tober
Ardmorney
Tyrrellspass
Kilbeggan
Killavally
Newtownlow
Castlejordan
Clogharinka
Cadamstown
Johnstown Bridge
Clara / Clóirtheach
Cappanrush
Duffy
Grange
Ballybryan
Kilshanchoe
Ballycumber
Kiltober
Croghan
Rhode
Carbury
Mucklon
Derrygolan
Kilclonfert
Togher
Killane
Edenderry / Éadan Doire
Windmill
Derries
Killeshil
Grand Canal
Ballyfore
Timahoe
Rahan
Ardan
Derrygrogan
Daingean
Allen
Pollagh
Tullamore
Ballykilleen
Staplestown
DUBLIN
MONAGHAM
DROGHEDA, DUNDALK
BELFAST, DERRY/LONDONDERRY
MALAHIDE, COOLOCK
NAVAN
MULLINGAR
LIMERICK
BLESSINGTON
ENNISKERRY
BRAY
DUN LAOGHAIRE
DOUGLAS, HOLYHEAD, LIVERPOOL, MOSTYN
500 m
500 yards
Tolka Valley Park
Glasnevin
Glasnevin Cemetery
National Botanic Gardens
Pelletstown
Ashtown
Royal Canal
Broombridge
Cabra
Casino Marino
Drumcondra
Marino
Killester
Clontarf
Visitor Centre
Phoenix Monument
Fish Pond
Croke Park
Fairview Park
Phibsborough
Grangegorman
Dublin Zoo
Phoenix Park
People's Garden
National Museum of Decorative Arts and History
Wellington Monument
Docklands
Convention Center Dublin
Point Village
The 3 Arena
Heuston
Museum
Liffey
Pearse Lyons Distillery
Irish Museum of Modern Art
Roe & Co Distillery
Guinness Storehouse
Kilmainham Gaol
Dublin Castle
Old Library
Grand Canal Sq.
Grand Canal Dock
Ringsend
Ringsend Park
Alto Vetro
Shelbourne Park Greyhound Stadium
Aviva Stadium
Dublin Bay
Fatima
Rialto
Suir Road
Goldenbridge
Drimnagh
Blackhorse Br.
Lansdowne Valley Pk
Brickfields Park
Patrick Kavanagh
Harcourt
Charlemont
Irish Jewish Museum
Lansdowne Road
Sandymount
Drimnagh
Harold's Cross
Mount Jerome
Herbert Park
Ranelagh
Pearse Memorial Park
Sundrive Park
Mount Argus Park
Rathmines
Donnybrook
Crumlin
Beechwood
Sydney Parade
Terenure
Cullahill
Galmoy
Castlecomer / Caisleán an Chomair
Railyard
Rossmore
Graigue

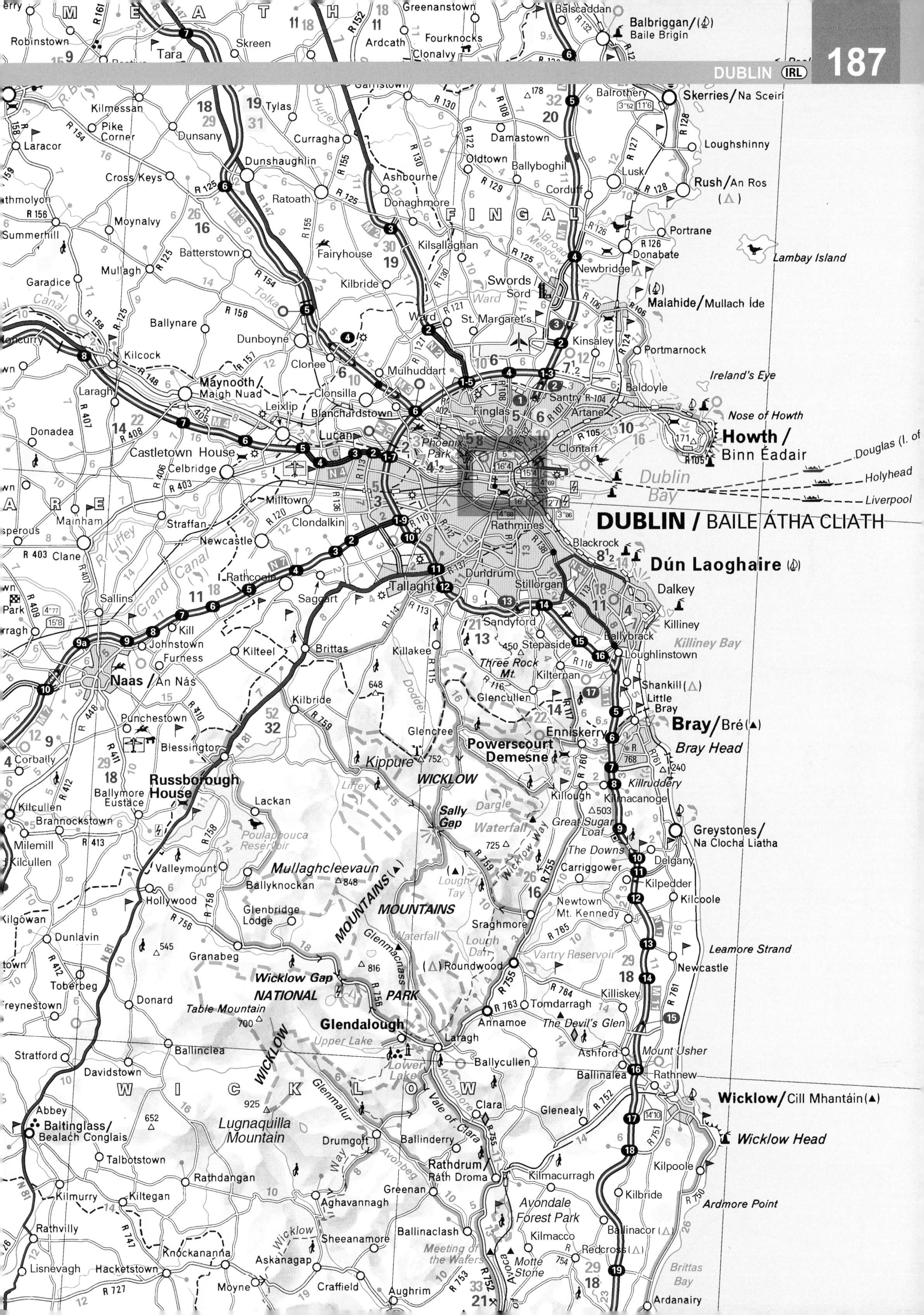
DUBLIN / BAILE ÁTHA CLIATH
Balbriggan/Baile Brigín
Skerries/Na Sceirí
Loughshinny
Rush/An Ros
Lusk
Portrane
Donabate
Lambay Island
Malahide/Mullach Íde
Portmarnock
Ireland's Eye
Baldoyle
Nose of Howth
Howth / Binn Éadair
Dublin Bay
Douglas (I. of
Holyhead
Liverpool
Blackrock
Dún Laoghaire
Dalkey
Killiney
Killiney Bay
Loughlinstown
Shankill
Little Bray
Bray/Bré
Bray Head
Killruddery
Kilmacanoge
Greystones/Na Clocha Liatha
Delgany
Kilpedder
Kilcoole
Leamore Strand
Newcastle
Wicklow/Cill Mhantáin
Wicklow Head
Kilpoole
Ardmore Point
Brittas Bay
Ardanairy
Redcross
Ballinacor
Kilmacurragh
Avondale Forest Park
Kilmacoo
Motte Stone
Rathdrum/Ráth Droma
Ballinderry
Clara
Vale of Clara
Glenealy
Ballinalea
Rathnew
Ashford
Mount Usher
The Devil's Glen
Killiskey
Tomdarragh
Annamoe
Roundwood
Vartry Reservoir
Newtown Mt. Kennedy
Sraghmore
Lough Dan
Lough Tay
The Downs
Carriggower
Great Sugar Loaf
Kilough
Powerscourt Demesne
Enniskerry
Dargle
Waterfall
Sally Gap
Kippure
Glencree
Glencullen
Kilternan
Three Rock Mt.
Stepaside
Sandyford
Stillorgan
Dundrum
Rathmines
Ballybrack
Tallaght
Saggart
Brittas
Killakee
Kilbride
Clondalkin
Milltown
Newcastle
Rathcoole
Straffan
Celbridge
Castletown House
Lucan
Leixlip
Phoenix Park
Finglas
Santry
Artane
Clontarf
Blanchardstown
Clonsilla
Mulhuddart
Clonee
Maynooth/Maigh Nuad
Kilcock
Dunboyne
Ballynare
Ward
St. Margaret's
Kinsaley
Swords/Sord
Newbridge
Kilsallaghan
Fairyhouse
Kilbride
Donaghmore
Ashbourne
Ratoath
Oldtown
Ballyboghil
Corduff
Damastown
Balrothery
Garristown
Curragha
Dunshaughlin
Dunsany
Tylas
Kilmessan
Pike Corner
Laracor
Cross Keys
Moynalvy
Summerhill
Batterstown
Mullagh
Garadice
Laragh
Donadea
Mainham
Clane
Sallins
Kill
Johnstown
Furness
Kilteel
Naas/An Nás
Punchestown
Blessington
Russborough House
Ballymore Eustace
Corbally
Kilcullen
Brannockstown
Milemill
Poulaphouca Reservoir
Lackan
Valleymount
Hollywood
Ballyknockan
Mullaghcleevaun
Glenbridge Lodge
WICKLOW MOUNTAINS
Glenmacnass Waterfall
Granabeg
Dunlavin
Toberbeg
Donard
Wicklow Gap
WICKLOW MOUNTAINS NATIONAL PARK
Table Mountain
Glendalough
Upper Lake
Lower Lake
Laragh
Ballycullen
Ballinclea
Stratford
Davidstown
Lugnaquilla Mountain
Glenmalur
Drumgoff
Baltinglass/Bealach Conglais
Talbotstown
Rathdangan
Kilmurry
Kiltegan
Aghavannagh
Greenan
Ballinaclash
Meeting of the Waters
Rathvilly
Knockananna
Sheeanamore
Askanagap
Lisnevagh
Hacketstown
Moyne
Craffield
Aughrim
Greenanstown
Balscaddan
Fourknocks
Clonalvy
Ardcath
Skreen
Tara
Robinstown
M E A T H
F I N G A L
K I L D A R E
W I C K L O W

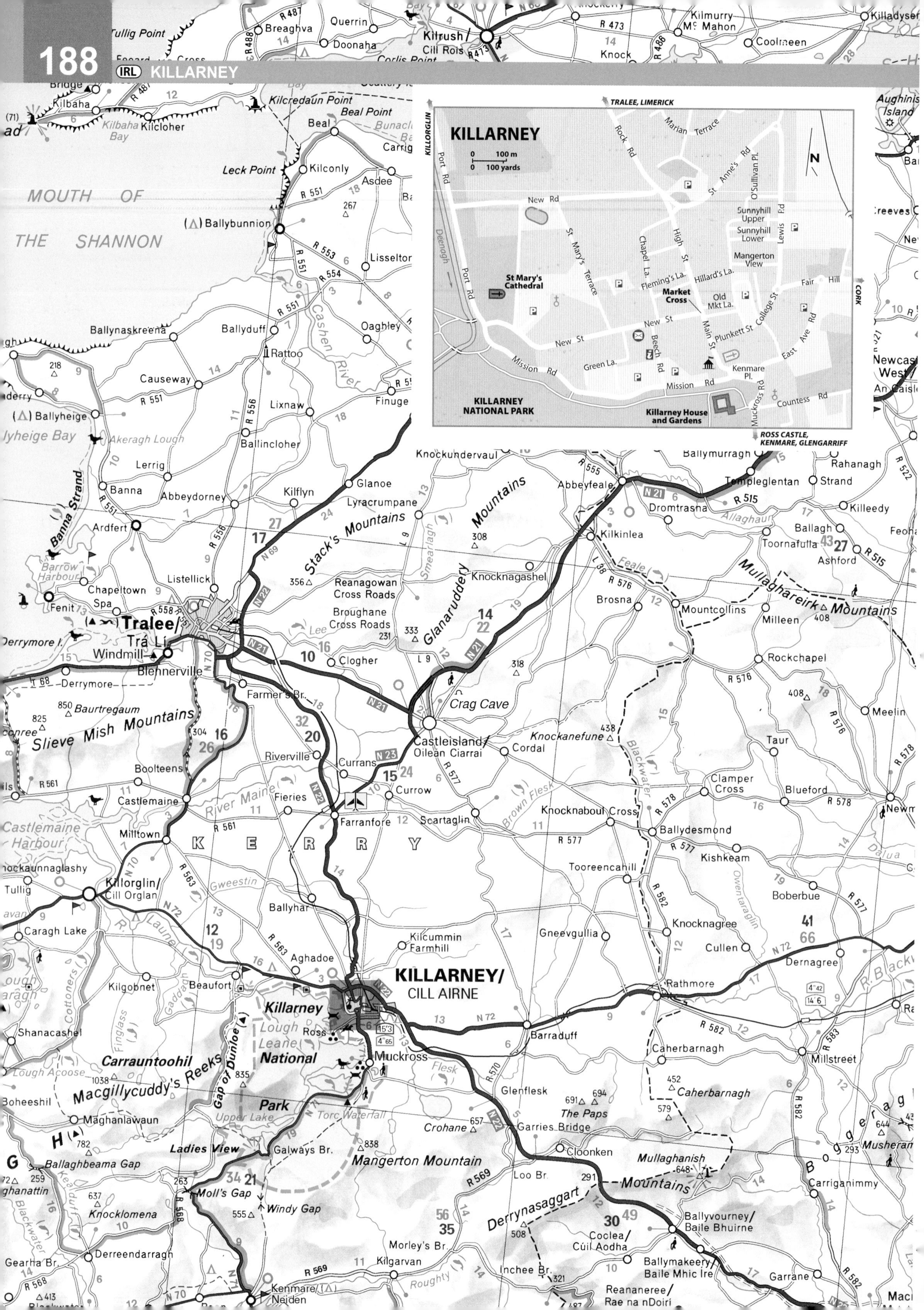
KILLARNEY
TRALEE, LIMERICK
KILLORGLIN
CORK
ROSS CASTLE, KENMARE, GLENGARRIFF
0 100 m
0 100 yards
N
Port Rd
Rock Rd
Marian Terrace
St Anne's Rd
O'Sullivan Pl.
Sunnyhill Upper
Sunnyhill Lower
Lewis Rd
New Rd
St Mary's Terrace
Chapel La.
High St
Mangerton View
Deenagh
St Mary's Cathedral
Fleming's La.
Hillard's La.
Fair Hill
Market Cross
Old Mkt La.
College St
New St
Main St
Plunkett St
East Ave Rd
Beech Rd
Green La.
Mission Rd
Kenmare Pl.
KILLARNEY NATIONAL PARK
Killarney House and Gardens
Muckross Rd
Countess Rd
MOUTH OF THE SHANNON
Tullig Point
Breaghva
Querrin
Doonaha
Kilrush/ Cill Rois
Kilmurry Mc Mahon
Killadysert
Coolmeen
Knock
Kilbaha
Kilcloher
Kilbaha Bay
Kilcredaun Point
Beal Point
Beal
Leck Point
Kilconly
Asdee
Ballybunnion
Lisselton
Ballynaskreena
Ballyduff
Rattoo
Oaghley
Cashen River
Causeway
Lixnaw
Finuge
Ballyheige
Ballyheige Bay
Akeragh Lough
Ballincloher
Lerrig
Banna
Banna Strand
Abbeydorney
Kilflyn
Glanoe
Knockundervaul
Ardfert
Lyracrumpane
Stack's Mountains
Barrow Harbour
Chapeltown
Listellick
Fenit
Spa
Tralee/ Trá Lí
Windmill
Blennerville
Derrymore
Reanagowan Cross Roads
Broughane Cross Roads
Clogher
Glanaruddery Mountains
Mountains
Abbeyfeale
Kilkinlea
Knocknagashel
Brosna
Mountcollins
Dromtrasna
Templeglentan
Ballymurragh
Rahanagh
Strand
Killeedy
Ballagh
Toornafulla
Ashford
Mullaghareirk Mountains
Milleen
Rockchapel
Meelin
Crag Cave
Castleisland/ Oileán Ciarraí
Cordal
Knockanefune
Blackwater
Taur
Baurtregaum
Slieve Mish Mountains
Farmer's Br.
Riverville
Currans
Boolteens
Castlemaine
Castlemaine Harbour
River Maine
Fieries
Farranfore
Currow
Scartaglin
Brown Flesk
Knocknaboul Cross
Ballydesmond
Clamper Cross
Blueford
Milltown
KERRY
Tooreencahill
Kishkeam
Owentaraglin
Boberbue
Killorglin/ Cill Orglan
Tullig
Gweestin
Ballyhar
Knocknagree
Gneevgullia
Cullen
Dernagree
Caragh Lake
R. Laune
Kilcummin Farmhill
Aghadoe
KILLARNEY/ CILL AIRNE
Rathmore
Kilgobnet
Beaufort
Killarney
Lough Leane
National Park
Ross
Muckross
Barraduff
Caherbarnagh
Millstreet
Shanacashel
Cottoners
Gaddagh
Finglass
Carrauntoohil
Lough Acoose
Macgillycuddy's Reeks
Gap of Dunloe
Flesk
Glenflesk
The Paps
Boheeshil
Maghanlawaun
Upper Lake
Torc Waterfall
Crohane
Garries Bridge
Musheran
Boggeragh
Ladies View
Galways Br.
Mangerton Mountain
Cloonken
Mullaghanish
Ballaghbeama Gap
Moll's Gap
Loo Br.
Mountains
Carriganimmy
Knocklomena
Windy Gap
Derrynasaggart
Ballyvourney/ Baile Bhuirne
Coolea/ Cúil Aodha
Morley's Br.
Kilgarvan
Derreendarragh
Gearha Br.
Roughty
Inchee Br.
Ballymakeery/ Baile Mhic Íre
Garrane
Kenmare/ Neiden
Reananeree/ Rae na nDoirí
N 21
N 22
N 69
N 70
N 72
N 23

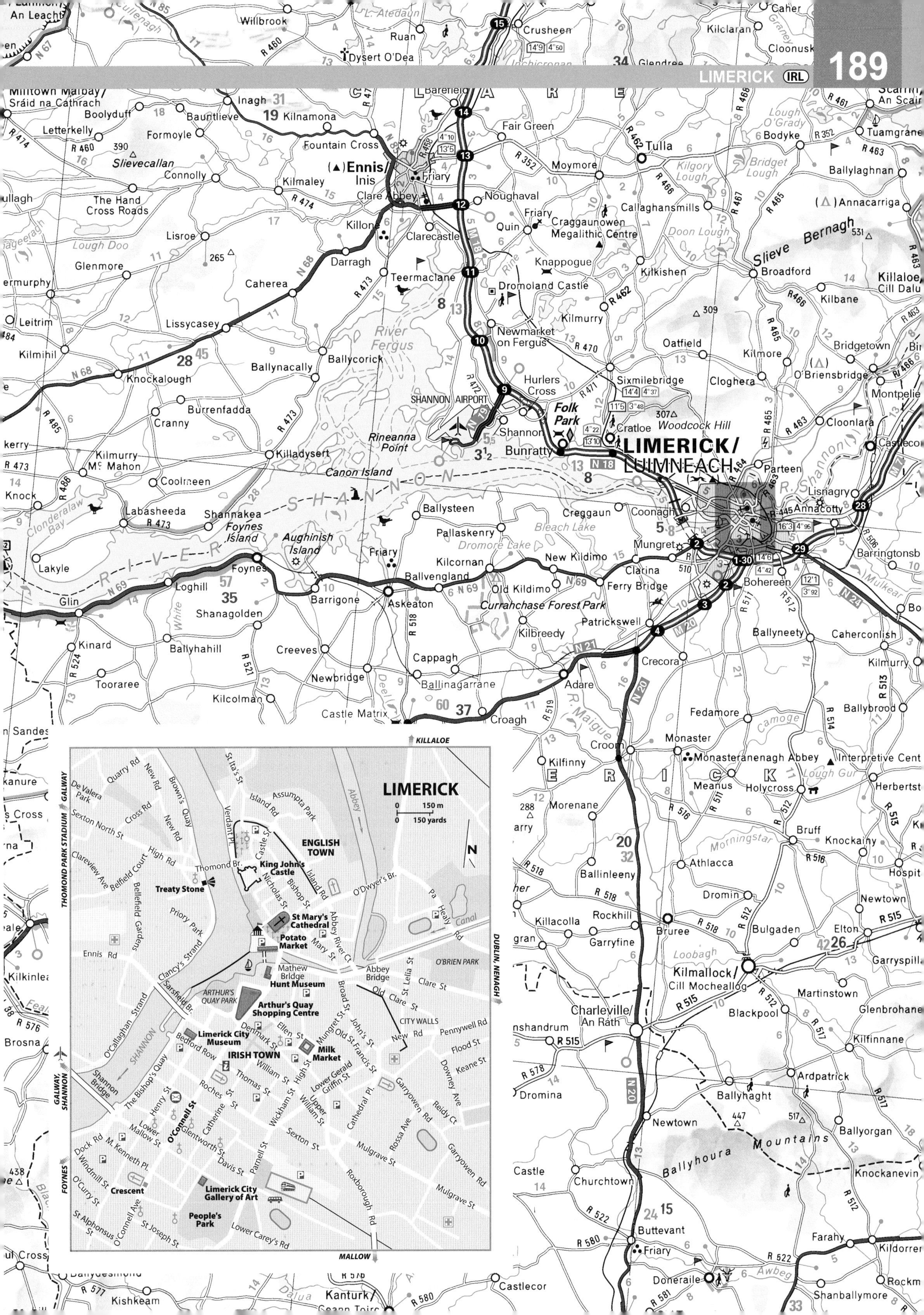
Ennis/ Inis
Tulla
Kilnamona
Inagh
Fountain Cross
Clare Abbey
Quin
Craggaunowen Megalithic Centre
Clarecastle
Dromoland Castle
Newmarket on Fergus
River Fergus
Shannon Airport
Shannon
Bunratty
Folk Park
Sixmilebridge
Cratloe
Woodcock Hill
LIMERICK/ LUIMNEACH
Broadford
Slieve Bernagh
Killaloe/ Cill Dalua
O'Briensbridge
Castleconnell
Annacotty
Parteen
Mungret
Patrickswell
Adare
Croom
Bruff
Kilmallock/ Cill Mocheallóg
Charleville/ An Ráth
Buttevant
Doneraile
Kanturk
Ballyhoura Mountains
Lough Gur
Monasteranenagh Abbey
Askeaton
Foynes
Foynes Island
Glin
Shanagolden
Labasheeda
Kildysart
Killadysert
Canon Island
Aughinish Island
Rineanna Point
River Shannon
Currahchase Forest Park
Castle Matrix
Newcastle West
LIMERICK
ENGLISH TOWN
King John's Castle
Treaty Stone
St Mary's Cathedral
Potato Market
Hunt Museum
Arthur's Quay Shopping Centre
ARTHUR'S QUAY PARK
Limerick City Museum
IRISH TOWN
Milk Market
CITY WALLS
Limerick City Gallery of Art
People's Park
Crescent
O'Connell St
O'BRIEN PARK
THOMOND PARK STADIUM GALWAY
DUBLIN, NENAGH
GALWAY, SHANNON
FOYNES
KILLALOE
MALLOW
150 m
150 yards

Eochair

Bóithre
Mótarbhealach - Limistéar seirbhíse
Carrbhealach dúbailte le saintréithe mótarbhealaigh
Acomhail mótarbhealaigh: iomlán - teoranta
Vlmhreacha ceangall
Líonra idirnáisiúnta agus náisiúnta bóithre
Bóthar idir-réigiúnach nach bhfuil chomh plódaithe
Bóthar nuadheisithe - gan réitiú
Cosán - Conair mharcáilte / Cosán marcaíochta
Mótarbhealach, bóthar á dhéanamh (an dáta oscailte sceidealta, mas eol)

Leithead bóithre
Carrshlí dhéach
4 lána - 2 leathanlána
2 lána - 2 chunglána

Fad bóthar
(iomlán agus meánfhad)
Bhóithre dola ar an mótarbhealach
Saor ó dhola ar an mótarbhealach
i mílte - i gciliméadair
ar an mbóthar

Aicmiú oifigiúil bóithre
Mótarshl - GB: Príomhbhealach (Primary route)
IRL: Bóithre eile , (National primary and secondary route)
Príomhbóithre agus fobhóithre náisiúnta
Ceann scríbe ar ghréasán bóithre príomha

Constaicí
Timpeall - Bearnas agus a airde os cionn leibhéal na mara (i méadair)
Fána ghéar (suas treo an gha)
IRL: Bealach deacair nó baolach
Bóthar cúng le hionaid phasála (in Albain)
Crosaire comhréidh: iarnród ag dul, faoi bhóthar, os cionn bóthair
Bóthar toirmeasctha - Bóthar faoi theorannú
Bacainn dola - Bóthar aonsli
Teorainneacha airde (faoi 15'6" IRL, faoi 16'6" GB)
Teorann Mheáchain (faoi 16t)

Iompar
Leithead caighdeánach - Stáisiún paisinéirí
Aerfort - Aerpháirc
Longsheirbhísí : (Seirbhísí séasúracha: dearg)
Bád
Fartha (uas - ulach : tonnaí méadracha)
Coisithe agus lucht rothar

Lóistín - Riarachán
Teorainneacha riaracháin
Teorainn na hAlban agus teorainn na Breataine Bige
Teorainn idirnáisiúnta - Custam

Áiseanna Spóirt agus Súgartha
Machaire Gailf - Ráschúrsa
Timpeall rásaíochta - Cuan bád aeraíochta
Láthair champa , láthair charbhán
Conair mharcáilte - Páirc thuaithe
Zú - Tearmannéan mara
IRL: Lascaireacht - Ráschúrsa con Larnród thraein ghaile
Traein cábla
Carr cábla , cathaoir cábla

Amhairc
Príomhradharcanna: féach AN EOLAÍ UAINE
Bailte nó áiteanna inspéise, baill lóistín
Foirgneamh Eaglasta - Caisleán
Fothrach - Leacht meigiliteach - Pluais
Páirc, Gáirdíní - Ionaid eile spéisiúla
IRL: Dunfort - Cros Cheilteach - Cloigtheach
Lánléargas - Cothrom Radhairc
Bealach Aoibhinn

Comharthaí Eile
Cáblashlí thionsclaíoch
Crann teileachumarsáide - Teach solais
Stáisiún Giniúna - Cairéal
Mianach - Tionsclaíocht
Scaglann - Aill
Páirc Fhoraoise Naisiúnta - Páirc Naisiúnta

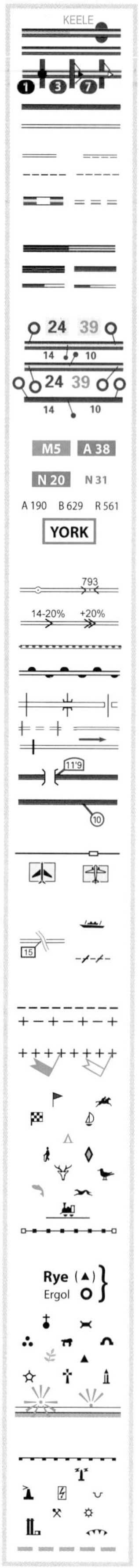

Allwedd

Ffyrdd
Traffordd - Mannau gwasanaeth
Ffordd ddeuol â nodweddion traffordd
Cyfnewidfeyd: wedi'i chwblhau - cyfyngedig
Rhifau'r cyffyrdd
Ffordd ar rwydwaith rhyngwladol a chenedlaethol
Ffordd rhyngranbarthol a llai prysur
Ffordd ac wyneb iddi - heb wyneb
Llwybr troed - Llwybr troed ag arwyddion / Llwybr ceffyl
Traffordd - ffordd yn cael ei hadeiladu (Os cyfodl yr achos: dyddiad agor disgwyliedig)

Ffyrdd
ffordd ddeuol
4 lôn - 2 lôn lydan
2 lôn - 2 lôn gul

Pellter
(cyfanswm a'r rhyng-bellter)
Tollffyrdd ar y drafford
Rhan di-doll ar y drafford
mewn miltiroedd - mewn kilometrau
ar y ffordd

Dosbarthiad ffyrdd swyddogol
Traffordd - GB : Prif ffordd (Primary route)
IRL: Prif ffordd genedlaethol a ffordd eilradd (National primary and secondary route)
Ffyrdd eraill
Cylchfan ar rwydwaith y prif ffrydd

Rhwystrau
Cylchfan - Bwlch a'i uchder uwchlaw lefel y môr (mewn metrau)
Rhiw serth (esgyn gyda'r saeth)
IRL: Darn anodd neu beryglus o ffordd
Yn yr Alban : ffordd gul â mannau pasio
Croesfan rheilffordd: croesfan rheilffordd, o dan y ffordd, dros y ffordd
Ffordd waharddedig - Ffordd a chyfyngiadau arni
Rhwystr Toll - Unffordd
Terfyn uchder (llai na 15'6" IRL, 16'6" GB)
Terfyn pwysau (llai na 16t)

Cludiant
Lled safonol - Gorsaf deithwyr
Maes awyr - Maes glanio
Llongau ceir: (Gwasanaethau tymhorol: mewn coch)
llong
Fferi (llwyth uchaf: mewn tunelli metrig)
Teithwyr ar droed neu feic yn unig

Llety - Gweinyddiaeth
Ffiniau gweinyddol
Ffin Cymru, ffin yr Alban
Ffin ryngwladol - Tollau

Cyfleusterau Chwaraeon a Hamdden
Cwrs golf - Rasio Ceffylau
Rasio Cerbydau - Harbwr cychod pleser
Leoedd i wersylla
Llwybr troed ag arwyddion - Parc gwlad
Parc saffari, sw - Gwarchodfa natur
IRL: Pysgota - Maes rasio milgwn
Trên twristiaid
Rhaffordd, car cêbl, cadair esgyn

Golygfeydd
Gweler Llyfr Michelin
Trefi new fannau o ddiddordeb, mannau i aros
Adeilag eglwysig - Castell
Adfeilion - Heneb fegalithig - Ogof
Gerddi, parc - Mannau eraill o ddiddordeb
IRL: Caer - Croes Geltaidd - twr crwn
Panorama - Golygfan
Ffordd dygfeydd

Symbolau eraill
Lein gêbl ddiwydiannol
Mast telathrebu - Goleudy
Gorsaf bwer - Chwarel
Mwyngloddio - Gweithgarwch diwydiannol
Purfa - Clogwyn
Parc Coedwig Cenedlaethol - Parc Cenedlaethol

Comnarthaí ar phleanna bailte

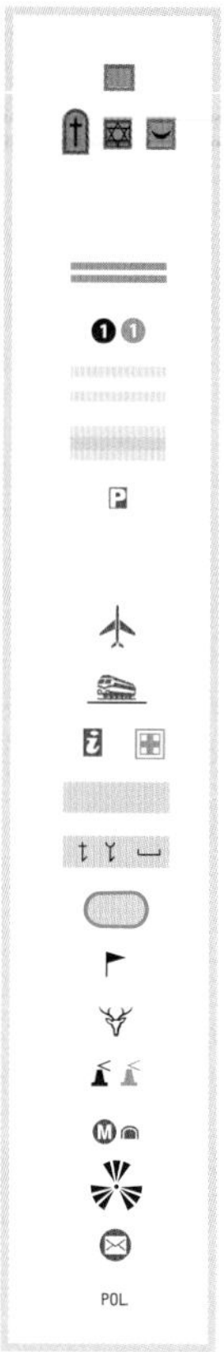

Ionad inspéise
Ionad inspéise agus
Ionad inspéise adhartha

Bóithre
Mótarbhealach, carrbhealach dúbailte le saintréithe mótai
Acomhail mótarbhealaigh : iomlán - teoranta
Priomh-thrébhealach
Sráid: coisithe
Carrchlós

Comharthaí Éagsúla
Aerfort
Leithead caighdeánach - Stáisiún paisinéirí
Ionad eolais turasóireachta - Ospidéal
Gairdín, páirc, coill
Reilig
Staidiam
Galfchúrsa
Zú
Teach Solais
Stáisiún traenach faoi thalamh
Lánléargas
Príomhoifi g phoist le poste restante
Póitíní (ceanncheathrú)

Symbolau ar gynlluniau'r trefi

Golygfeydd
Man diddorol
Lle diddorol o addoliad

Ffyrdd
Traffordd, ffordd ddeuol
Cyfnewidfeyd : wedi'i chwblhau - cyfyngedig
Prif ffordd drwodd
Stryd: Cerddwr
Parc ceir

Arwyddion amrywiol
Maes awyr
Lled safonol - Gorsaf deithwyr
Canolfan croeso - Ysbyty
Gardd, parc, coedwig
Mynwent
Stadiwm
Cwrs golff
Sŵ
Goleudy
Gorsaf danddaearol
Panorama
Prif swyddfa bost gyda poste restante
Yr Heddlu (pencadlys)

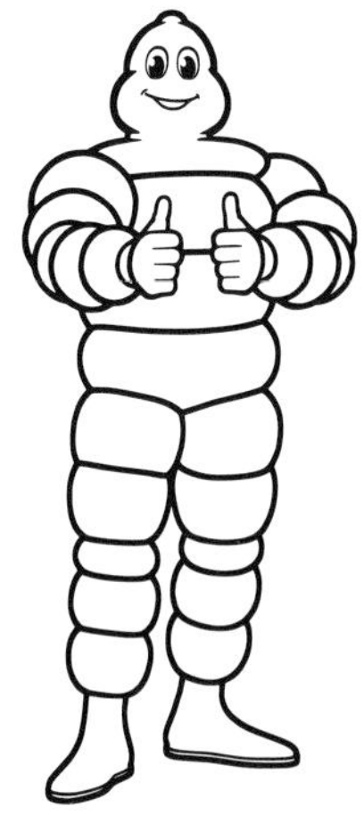

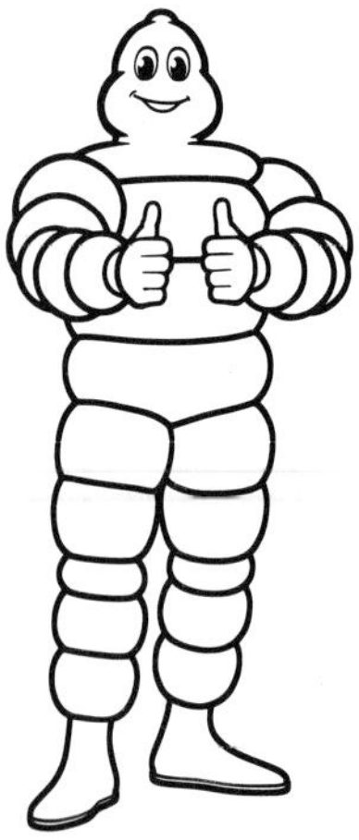